L_YONS INQUIRY

into Local Government

Place-shaping: a shared ambition for the
future of local government

Final Report

Sir Michael Lyons

March 2007   London: The Stationery Office   £50.00

Lyons Inquiry contacts

This document can be found on the Lyons Inquiry website at:

www.lyonsinquiry.org.uk

The Lyons Inquiry website will be transferred at a later date to the
National Archives website at:

www.nationalarchives.gov.uk

Printed on at least 75% recycled paper.
When you have finished with it please recycle it again.

ISBN: 978-0-11-989854-5
PU041
Printed by The Stationery Office   03/07   361408

Thanks go to Chelmsford Borough Council, Nottingham City
Council, Southampton City Council, the London Borough of
Tower Hamlets and Trafford Council for supplying some of the
images used on the cover of this document.

Preface

From the beginning of this Inquiry in the autumn of 2004, I have taken the view that questions about local government taxation and the funding of local services are not simply matters for technical analysis, but need instead to be considered in a wider context. They must be part of a broader debate about the type of country we want to live in: the balance we strike between citizen, community and government in terms of both power and voice, and how we manage the inevitable tensions between diversity, choice and a desire for common standards. In this respect, I follow firmly in the footsteps of Sir Frank Layfield, who reached similar conclusions in the 1976 report of the Committee of Inquiry into Local Government Finance.

Sir Michael Lyons

The extension of my remit in 2005, when ministers asked me to consider the future role and function of local government in this country, as well as its funding, reflects this concern to consider the wider context. I have interpreted even that remit generously, looking to describe how we can develop a new, stronger relationship between central and local government, founded on a shared interest in the prosperity and well-being of this country and its citizens. I have sought to explore whether a strong, national framework, together with greater local flexibility and choice, and improved engagement with the individual, might better enable us to tackle the complex challenges that we face as a nation. These 'wicked issues' include: the need to build a cohesive society in which everyone feels they have a stake; to improve our own competitiveness and meet the growing challenge of the emerging economies; to respond to climate change; and to strike a balance between immediate improvements to public services and the longer-term investments in infrastructure, skills and research that will underpin our future prosperity.

In order to strengthen the connections between the individual and government, and contribute to our wider national objectives, I believe that we must rebalance the relationship between centre and locality. My second interim report *National prosperity, local choice and civic engagement,* published in May 2006, outlined the steps that need to be taken to create the space for local government to take on its full 'place-shaping' role, as well as the measures that councils would themselves have to adopt to be ready for that challenge. I warmly welcome the Government's subsequent White Paper, *Strong and Prosperous Communities,* published in October 2006, and the promise it holds for greater devolution.

No one should underestimate the sustained effort which will be required to achieve a real shift in the balance of influence between centre and locality. The history of the last 30 years is marked by a series of well-intentioned devolution initiatives, which have often evolved into subtle instruments of control. But it is an effort worth making.

This report seeks to develop my arguments further and includes my recommendations on how the future funding of local government could contribute to this rebalancing. However, I am clear that neither funding, nor powers, nor structures, are by themselves the key to the revitalisation of local government, and the improved self-confidence of local communities. I stress instead the importance of changed behaviours in all tiers of government, of local flexibility, and the pressing need to inspire a sense of powerfulness in local government. This is not a simple argument in favour of the local, and I stress throughout the importance of improving our 'single system of government' through clarity of responsibility, alignment of purpose, and lean and efficient working practices.

We now have a real opportunity – with clear evidence of improvement in local authorities across the country, resurgent and self-assured cities, and an acceptance across the political spectrum of the need once again to empower our communities – to foster a new public confidence in local government, and perhaps in representative government at all levels. To meet this opportunity, central government needs to provide the space, the framework and the incentives that will release the energies of local councils – but they must in turn embrace the wider place-shaping role, further strengthen their engagement with those they serve, and establish themselves as unequivocal champions of value for money.

Just as our present situation is the product of many years, so we must approach this task with the intention, above all, of setting the right direction for the future, building the constructive relationships that will enable better decisions in the future. My proposals for the future funding of local government and the taxation to support it are therefore explicitly developmental. I lay out recommendations for early changes and others that can follow in due course. These should properly be seen as a mosaic of related changes, rather than a menu for separate choice. Together they could improve the fairness and flexibility of current arrangements; introduce greater incentives for local effort; and provide wider choices to future governments.

Many readers will be preoccupied with my conclusions on the future of council tax (the impatient should turn to Chapter 7). I conclude that it has a continuing part to play in the future funding of local government either on its own or alongside other taxes. However, early steps must be taken to reduce the pressures upon it. I also recommend measures to change the definition of, and eligibility for, council tax benefit, and believe these must be addressed as soon as possible in order to improve the perceived fairness of the tax. Concern for fairness has inevitably been raised with me on many occasions. There is no doubt that the perception of fairness in questions of both taxation and public expenditure is essential to the sustainability of the system, but there will always be different views about just what is fair; often dependant on the personal circumstances of the individual, including their income, wealth and age. I have tried to expose those tensions in my report. There remain concerns, however, about the lack of buoyancy of council tax and its continued unpopularity which may mean future governments need and want to consider more radical change in the longer-term.

I have also explored issues of business taxation in some detail. I offer recommendations which are again intended to be evolutionary in nature, but do respond to the strong messages I heard about the need for a closer working relationship between local government and the business community, and the importance of facilitating substantial new investment in infrastructure improvements and related measures to foster local economic prosperity.

We elect governments to make difficult choices on our behalf, but I am clear that ministers can only make changes where they can be confident of public support, or at least tolerance. So my message, the tensions I expose, and my conclusions, are as much a matter for the people of this country as for its current Government. I have become increasingly concerned that our expectations of what government can do for us grow faster than our willingness to meet the costs of those expectations through taxation, and possibly even beyond what can actually be delivered. Helping citizens to engage in honest debate about our choices, both as a nation and as individual communities, is the big challenge for this and for future governments.

Local government could play a more active part in the management of these pressures, but it needs to have both the space, and the willingness, to work with residents and other parts of the local community to establish clear local priorities, to shape public services to local needs and preferences, and to strike the right balance between what is done for us and what we do for ourselves. We should, I believe, be as interested in how we might develop the distinctiveness of different places and how we leave space for different local choices which improve people's satisfaction, as we are about how we seek to achieve potentially expensive, and frequently elusive, 'consistent' standards.

I, for one, would hope to see debate about postcode lotteries being replaced, over time, by discussion of 'managed difference' – recognising the right and the ability of local communities to make their own choices, confident in their own competence, and in the knowledge of their own preferences.

In closing let me thank, most of all, Sally Burlington and the team that has supported me in this work. Their talent, enthusiasm and unfailing good spirits (even through several extensions to both remit and timetable) have been an inspiration to me. I also want to thank the many people and organisations that have contributed to my research and the wider discussion around it. Special thanks go to the 'critical friends' who have served on my reference group. Finally, let me express my gratitude to the thousands of people who responded to our extensive efforts to engage the public in these knotty questions about taxation and local expenditure. The balance and good humour of the many respondents I met, and their willingness to engage in genuine debate, gives me confidence that we can find a way forward on these highly contested issues. The views expressed in this report, together with its conclusions, are of course my responsibility alone.

List of Contents

Annexes

The following annexes and supplementary tables and charts are available for download at www.lyonsinquiry.org.uk:

Annex A   Understanding the current grant distribution system

Annex B   Introduction to the modelling used in the report

Annex C   Background to support Chapter 7

Annex D   Background to support Chapter 8

Annex E   Background to support Chapter 9

Annex F   Summary of submissions

Annex G   Stakeholder views on Barker, Eddington and Leitch

Annex H   Research and stakeholder engagement

Supplementary tables and charts

The Lyons Inquiry website will be accessible until June 2007. After this date, the website will be held by The National Archive, for historic and reference purposes and will be accessible at: http://www.nationalarchives.gov.uk. All key reports will also be available from the main department of Communities and Local Government and HM Treasury websites.

Executive summary

LOCAL GOVERNMENT: A CONTINUING DEBATE

1   I was asked to undertake this Inquiry into Local Government by the Chancellor and the Deputy Prime Minister in July 2004 at a time of considerable public and political interest in and concern about the funding of local government, and council tax in particular. My initial terms of reference asked me to make recommendations on the reform of council tax, to consider the case for shifting the balance of funding, and to conduct analysis of other options for local taxation, including local income tax, non-domestic (business) rates and other local taxes and charges.

2   During the course of my work on funding, I came to the conclusion that changes to the finance system could not proceed effectively without the role of local government being more clearly established. In September 2005 ministers asked me to extend my work to consider the strategic role of local government, devolution and decentralisation, and how pressures on local services could better be managed. The full terms of reference are set out at the end of the report.

3   The final stage of my work has been the consideration of the Barker Review of Land Use Planning, the Eddington Transport Study and the Leitch Review of Skills, three independent reviews with significant implications for local government.

4   Much has changed since the beginning of my work, including:

- the transfer of schools funding from unhypothecated local government grant to the ring-fenced Dedicated Schools Grant;

- the Government's decision to postpone the planned revaluation of domestic properties for council tax purposes; and

- the publication of various important contributions to the debate including the Local Government Association's (LGA) *Closer to people and places – a new vision for local government*, and the Government's proposals for the future of local government and local public services in *Strong and Prosperous Communities – the Local Government White Paper* in October 2006.

5   During the Inquiry I have periodically set out my thinking on both funding and function issues. My *Interim Report and Consultation Paper*, published in December 2005, set out some early thinking on both, including the results of extensive analysis on options for revaluation and reform of council tax. My May 2006 report, *National prosperity, local choice and civic engagement: a new partnership between central and local government for the 21st century*, set out my conclusions on the role of local government, emphasising the advantages to be secured from an enhanced level of choice and flexibility at the local level for communities to make their own decisions. I also discussed my views on the strategic role of local government for the future, a role I call 'place-shaping', discussed further in this report. I want to emphasise that in our discussions about the role of local government, we must not become fixated on the service delivery role that has become so important over the last century. There are three, inter-related but identifiable, sets of roles that local government has played in the past, and continues to play: as service provider; as a vehicle for investment in public infrastructure; and as an institution of government – a place for debate,

discussion and collective decision-making. An analysis of the modern role of local government needs to take into account all three of those roles, recognising that the appetite for self-determination is as much a part of local government's background as its role as a service provider.

6 Following my May report, the Government set out its proposals for the future direction of local government in *Strong and Prosperous Communities – the Local Government White Paper*, published in October 2006. The White Paper is intended to devolve more power to the local level and reduce the level of central prescription, while strengthening leadership and expanding the opportunities for local people to influence local decision-making.

7 I welcome the direction set out by the White Paper and subsequent Bill. However, it is clear that it is only the beginning of a process and, as this report will demonstrate, much will depend on how it is implemented, and how both central and local government respond to it. My recommendations are intended to lay out a 'developmental' approach in which steps that should be taken quickly to improve the current situation can provide greater space for local action, helping to build trust and effective behaviours in the future and paving the way for possible further reform.

LOCAL GOVERNMENT IN THE 21ST CENTURY – WHAT IS IT FOR?

8 Government is a device that allows us to frame and enforce rules and laws for behaviour, manage the provision of public services, redistribute resources and manage frameworks for long-term economic, social and environmental sustainability. Local government has an important contribution to make as part of a single system of government, allowing different communities to make choices for themselves, and relating and shaping the actions of government and the public sector to the needs of the locality.

Pursuing the well-being of citizens
9 There are strong and compelling arguments for it as a device for allocating public resources and effort efficiently and effectively to secure the well-being of citizens. While individual and quasi-market approaches are important, there remains a set of issues which are resolutely collective. This includes decisions about the best use of public money and the management of public good and other publicly subsidised services in particular places. That does not necessarily mean that those services need to be publicly owned and directly provided, but it does mean that there must be the capacity for collective action and choices about the use of public revenues.

Place remains relevant
10 Though some economic and sociological analyses have challenged the importance of place and the importance of the local in modern society and economics, place remains relevant. As our understanding of the multi-faceted nature of social and economic problems grows, and as our aspirations to solve them and to govern uncertainty and diversity increase, the arguments for a local role in determining the actions of government and the provision of public services are becoming stronger. In addition, economic analysis continues to identify local factors and institutions as important influences on economic change and growth.

Necessity of local choice
11 Accepting these arguments means accepting some degree of variation and difference between different parts of the country in their decisions and their use of resources. Some would not agree with that view, but it is a point of fundamental importance. The argument that this will lead to an unfair 'postcode lottery' over-simplifies some complex issues. If the people of one area collectively choose to use the public resources at their disposal in a different way to the people of another area, it is hard to argue that is unfair.

12 There are therefore strong arguments in favour of a degree of local choice. In practice there is a desire to see both national standards and local variation. The research I commissioned suggests that people want an assurance that key services will be delivered to similar (generally minimum) standards across the country, but also that they want the ability to influence the shape and delivery

of services and take decisions locally. There is clearly a balance to be struck between an appropriate set of national or minimum service standards, and the variety of choices that different communities can make, and which in my view are a positive part of a healthy and sophisticated system of governance. My conception of the modern role for local government is therefore of a system which can deliver this 'managed difference'.

Importance of engagement 13 However, all of these advantages of local government as a way of pursuing the well-being of communities depend on it being able to understand and respond to the needs and concerns of its citizens. This is an area in which it has been criticised, but one where I believe it has a great deal to offer. Ensuring that local government is fully and transparently accountable to local people for the decisions it takes in the pursuit of their interests and the use of their resources is critical to an effective system of local government.

Place-shaping 14 Throughout my work, I have promoted a wider, strategic role for local government, which I have termed 'place-shaping' – the creative use of powers and influence to promote the general well-being of a community and its citizens. It includes the following components:

- building and shaping local identity;

- representing the community;

- regulating harmful and disruptive behaviours;

- maintaining the cohesiveness of the community and supporting debate within it, ensuring smaller voices are heard;

- helping to resolve disagreements;

- working to make the local economy more successful while being sensitive to pressures on the environment;

- understanding local needs and preferences and making sure that the right services are provided to local people; and

- working with other bodies to response to complex challenges such as natural disasters and other emergencies.

Services 15 Local authorities are responsible for a wide range of services. However, debate too often focuses on which services local government is responsible for, as if this is the true measure of the importance and worth of local representative government. A new conception of the role for local government needs to go further, to reflect the well-being and place-shaping agenda. Whatever the legal and constitutional arrangements for the provision of a service or function, if it has impacts on local people, then the local authority should have a role in representing the community interest and influencing that service. That requires not just the joining-up of resources and activities, but also a leadership and influencing role to ensure that the efforts of all agencies are focused on the outcomes of greatest importance to local people. Local government is well-placed to play this convening role.

16 Local authorities also have the potential to use their purchasing power and long-term perspective to shape markets, and to use their ability to engage with citizens and service users in the design and delivery of services. This would allow them to take advantage of the potential of co-production to deliver better outcomes and greater efficiency.

Key challenges for local government

17   There are four areas where I think local government has a significant role to play in delivering important outcomes that arise from the manifold opportunities and challenges we face. Those are first, in providing safe and secure places to live, where communities are cohesive and integrated; second, in helping to foster the greater prosperity which benefits individuals and allows us to fund public services, including engaging with the challenges and opportunities posed by globalisation; and third, in addressing the impact we are having on the environment by taking steps to make our lifestyles more sustainable through engagement with citizens and through the performance of its statutory functions.

Satisfaction and trust in government

18   The final challenge that I believe exists for government, as a whole, is to address levels of trust and satisfaction among the public. Trust in government and elected representatives in the UK is low, and so is participation in political activity through the most obvious route – voting in elections. This seems to be a long-term problem, rather than an immediate crisis.

19   Local government also has a particular problem with fairness, linked both to concerns about 'postcode lotteries', and to concerns about the council tax. But fairness can often be an ill-defined and highly contested concept, meaning different things to different people at different times, and consensus on what is fair is almost certainly impossible.

20   Addressing these problems will be a complex and lengthy task in which local and central government have a joint interest, as I believe that what undermines trust in one part of government is likely to colour people's opinions of the wider system of government. Improving trust is also essential if other reform is to succeed. When concerns about council tax dominate discussions about local government to the extent that they do now, it can become very difficult to take a wider view of what sort of governance we want in this country, and what reforms might take us there.

21   Local government can help to strengthen the relationship between the individual citizen and the state through measures to build trust, honest taxation and a recognition that people do want to be able to influence government and public choice decisions. There is a risk that if local government has too little flexibility then this can result in a more passive, less connected citizenry.

WHAT IS LIMITING MODERN LOCAL GOVERNMENT?

22   Local government's ability fully to perform its place-shaping role, and respond fully to local needs and preferences is currently limited, and it also has limited flexibility to manage pressures on local budgets and spread the burden of local taxation. There are many different reasons for this – some are systemic, some are behavioural, and some are based on assumptions about public attitudes to choice and difference.

High degree of central control

23   Over the 1980s and 1990s there has been increasing centralisation across a range of local public services, driven by concerns to control public sector expenditure and to improve public services. In recent years this has been driven through new systems of performance management and targets, greater emphasis on delivery and central government's willingness to take greater responsibility for specific issues. This has helped to improve performance, but it has also inhibited the ability of local government to respond to local needs and preferences, and to manage financial pressures.

24   While the extent and impact of formal controls has been recognised in the recent Local Government White Paper, there has been less attention to informal, 'soft' controls, which include guidance, central encouragements and conditions on grant. These soft controls are more indirect and more difficult to assess than direct targets and indicators, but their impact can be profound.

25   The weight of central controls – both formal and informal – can lead to local choices being crowded out. That can mean that resources are not focused on the top local priorities, potentially reducing levels of satisfaction, and limiting the ability of authorities to manage pressures effectively. It can also crowd out place-shaping, reducing the role of local government to a set of of silo-based service activities. Finally, it can stifle innovation and experiment, both of which are promoted by decentralisation.

Lack of flexibility over existing resources

26   A large proportion of local government funds come from specific grants, which are often tightly tied to government requirements and expectations either formally through ring-fencing, or informally through expectations over what resources will be used for, and the monitoring of expenditure.

27   The introduction of Dedicated Schools Grant, reflecting the importance of education to the Government, has radically changed how local government receives its resources, substantially increasing the proportion of resources provided through hypothecated grants, and in the process greatly reducing the scope of local authorities to prioritise and manage pressures between services.

Limited flexibility to raise additional resources

28   English local government is highly dependent on central funding and relies on a single locally variable tax. In other western countries such as the United States, France and Germany, local authorities have significantly greater access to locally raised taxes. This means that the local tax burden can be spread across a range of taxpayers and that marginal increases in local authority budgets are not affected by the 'gearing' effect which magnifies the impact on council tax increases.

29   Capping is the other main restriction within our system of local government finance. Capping cuts across local accountability and carries simplistic connotations about local inefficiency. At an individual authority level it can also produce perverse results. It does not allow the underlying pressures on local government to be understood and better managed, and fails to recognise the Government's own role in creating pressures. There is also evidence that such central controls run counter to public attitudes, with survey work showing that the public support local authorities – rather than central government – bearing the responsibility for the setting of council tax levels.

Pressures on services

30   There is considerable debate about the causes of these pressures at the national level and at individual authority level, and a wide range of predictions about how significant future pressures on local budgets will be. The importance of managing pressures effectively is likely to increase in the next few years, as the money available for public spending will grow less quickly than over the past decade. Analysis of pressures raises important questions about the adequacy of national funding, and the degree to which local government can achieve efficiency savings.

Confused accountability

31   Clear lines of accountability are a precondition for an effective relationship between central and local government and are essential to allow people and communities to engage with, understand and challenge the decisions which affect their lives. Without such clarity local communities cannot know who to hold responsible for taxation and spending decisions.

32   A lack of public understanding of how the system works contributes to this confused accountability, and enables both local and central government to blame the other for problems. There is also a very poor understanding of the costs of services that can only lead the public to be dissatisfied with both local and central government, as they have unrealistic expectations of what can be delivered for the level of tax they pay.

Improved governance needed for economic prosperity

33   Recent work comparing the UK with the USA and Europe has concluded that the lack of devolution and local discretion in the UK is a constraint on economic performance, particularly in the cities. There are important questions about what is the best level of governance to drive economic prosperity, but the fact that functional economic boundaries are not precisely defined, are different for different kinds of activity, and change over time, means that we should avoid simplistic solutions to what are complex problems.

Attitudes to local government and choice

34   My research suggests that public views about local government are more nuanced than is generally suggested and that there would be support for 'managed difference' between areas as long as there was sufficient influence and voice for local people. There is the scope to move away from a simplistic division between total standardisation and total local flexibility, towards the idea of minimum national standards, with communities able to make different choices about the level of service they receive beyond that, based on their own preferences and priorities.

Lack of trust in the system of government

35   Building trust is a complex activity, as trust is based on both rational and emotional responses. However, it is a necessary aspect of dealing with the complex problems that face local government. Confused accountability is, I believe, one of the major factors limiting trust at present.

36   Public concern about council tax rises and its fairness and associated media coverage also affects attitudes to local government. Central government has a duty, alongside its responsibility for the overall national finance and taxation framework, to maintain a viable tax for local government. The problems with council tax are not solely local problems – many of the pressures and unfairnesses associated with the tax are likely to require national action. Another factor that affects public trust is the fall-out from the adversarial relationship between central and local government, which creates a climate of criticism and a competition for legitimacy, rather than a shared agenda for meeting the needs of citizens.

37   It may also be that one of the reasons people do not engage with local government as much as they might, is because local councillors are perceived as having only limited powers. There is some evidence that the local government sector has become disempowered, with a lack of confidence in its ability to make change happen.

Need for effective engagement

38   Local government needs to engage with local communities to understand their preferences for services and other aspects of local government activities. However, at present this is limited by central and local government frameworks which focus solely on service improvement against formal targets at the expense of overall satisfaction and a wider understanding of community needs and preferences. It is also undermined by too great a focus on the centre, not the local community, in terms of performance reporting and target setting.

Poor incentives in the distribution of national resources

39   Even accounting for some specific initiatives, local authorities have a limited share in the general growth of housing or business tax bases. Neither growth in council tax, nor business rates in England results in any systematic increase in local resources because the grant system automatically takes into account any growth in tax base. Housing growth does have some benefit for the local community in that it allows council tax increases to be spread across a larger tax base, but the new residents' use of services imposes costs as well. On business rates, local authorities only see a very long run benefit from growth in business tax base in the form of more resources for central government to allocate at the national level.

40   This question of incentives is particularly important when considering the role of local authorities in fostering economic prosperity and housing supply in their area, and the views of local communities. These are important aspects of their place-shaping role and so a link between the

health of the economy and the size of local tax base would be a key motivation for local communities to take growth seriously.

Conclusions 41   I have concluded from this analysis that what is required is:

- **clearer accountability** over who is responsible for what;

- **greater flexibility**, both over finances and to enable local government to manage local services in response to local needs;

- **better incentives** on local government to own and grow their tax bases and on both central and local government to develop a more productive relationship over time;

- **tackling perceived unfairness**, in order to improve satisfaction and trust in the system of local government as a whole; and

- **continued improvements in efficiency** to help relieve pressures on council tax under the current system. In doing so, it is also essential that public expenditure is allocated to best meet the needs and preferences of the community – delivering the right priorities rather than just doing them as cheaply as possible. Both of these objectives require greater scope for local choice.

CENTRAL GOVERNMENT'S CONTRIBUTION TO REFORM

42   Central government has a responsibility for the overall framework within which local government operates, and can enable local government to take on its place-shaping role more fully by making changes to that framework. The proposals in the Local Government White Paper, and the subsequent Local Government and Public Involvement in Health Bill, represent a significant step forward, though there are some risks and challenges which will need to be addressed if the potential benefits of the White Paper are to be realised.

Improving accountability

43   A key priority is to improve accountability throughout our system of local government, so that each tier of government has every reason to improve their own contribution to the well-being of citizens and communities, and to support others in doing so. This requires improvements across a range of issues:

- greater clarity about the respective roles of central and local government. This means being clearer about where central and local government can each add most value, and delivering on the commitment to pursue a much smaller number of nationally set central priorities, in order to leave real space for local choice;

- ensuring the new regulatory regime for local government is focused on the right issues, and allows enough space for local choice and priorities to be taken forward, while minimising burdens across the sector;

- improving the framework for local governance to promote effective local leadership and engagement, to better inform local choices which help manage public expectations and service pressures; and

- seeking to clarify how local services are funded to provide greater transparency over what local services cost, and how decisions on spending and resources have been made.

Clarifying
responsibility

44   The most obvious way to clarify accountability would be to make a definite distinction between which services are national and which are local responsibilities, but such a formal separation is not possible. Modern public services are complex, both in terms of what they do, and how they aim to do it. Most services have some elements which are appropriately centrally determined, and some which should be locally determined, and some have regional or sub-regional aspects, which suggests decision-making should take place at different levels. In some areas central government will want to set standards which it wants to see everywhere, or to define a 'national promise' for citizens across the country.

45   In order to clarify the responsibilities of local and central government a number of changes are therefore necessary. First, both central and local government need to acknowledge the contribution that the other can make to their shared agenda for improving the well-being of our communities. This means recognising that central government should not expect to do the things which local government is better equipped to do, and vice versa. For example, local government by virtue of its closer connection with citizens, is better placed to engage with them about what they want, to manage expectations about what is possible, and to work with service users to improve the effectiveness of local public services.

46   Second, central government should be much clearer about those areas in which responsibility should be firmly local, and resist calls to intervene in those areas. This requires an acceptance that variability between areas is not only inevitable, but also desirable if pressures are to be managed.

47   Third, central government needs to take a more consistent and corporate approach so that local government is clear about what is expected of it, particularly in negotiations on Local Area Agreements. Government departments may need to change their behaviours and approach, and there may also be room for Government Offices to play a part in helping to develop a stronger corporate style in central government by reflecting back to departments the challenges that their own behaviours (however well-intentioned) can create at the local level.

Streamlining the
performance
framework

48   I welcome the objectives set out in the White Paper to streamline the performance framework. If implemented fully they will mark a real step-change, providing a much more streamlined system of regulation which will provide greater space for local flexibility and choice.[1]

49   In particular, I strongly support the principle that local people should be the ultimate judges of the performance of their local authorities in place-shaping, delivering services and convening the work of other public services. The performance framework should support this, but it should not prescribe arrangements. Local authorities should have the primary responsibility for their own performance, and for designing transparent and effective mechanisms for engaging with their citizens.

50   Given the challenges in implementing the ambitions for the new performance framework, it will be important to monitor how well the new system is achieving its objectives, to check whether it, as well as the performance frameworks of partner bodies, is supporting joint working adequately, and whether it leaves sufficient space for place-shaping. An independent assessment should be published two years after the introduction of the new arrangements.

---

[1] By this I mean the wide range of activities undertaken by central government and inspectorates to regulate the behaviour and performance of local authorities. The performance framework incorporates regulation but also a much wider range of activities such as peer review and support, and other mechanisms included in the Local Government White Paper.

Improving the framework for local governance

51   Improving local accountability and governance rely to a large degree on local government changing its behaviours. Central government needs to design a framework which encourages and enables local authorities to take responsibility for how their communities are governed, and to design, and demonstrate the value of governance structures which work for their locality. No single model will work everywhere and too much central prescription could result in inappropriate local solutions and reduced innovation.

52   The Government has emphasised the role of strong and clear local leadership in providing accountability, in particular by placing an emphasis on elected mayors and the role of the council leader. I agree that leadership is important, but in setting the national frameworks we must acknowledge that effective leadership is not a simple concept and should not be reduced to a simple prescription.

53   Too strong a focus on the leadership of one individual for every area risks losing some of the strengths of the current system in terms of collective leadership and being able to represent diverse interests. Communities are complex and need broadly-based leadership, based on a number of people across a number of institutions. It is therefore important that, if local areas opt for a directly elected mayor or executive under the new governance arrangements provided for in the current Bill, this should not be fixed in stone. Central government should ensure that local communities retain the flexibility to choose models of leadership that best suit their circumstances, and to adapt them as and when they judge appropriate.

54   I also argue that central government should not seek to define any further lead councillor and officer roles and structures and existing prescriptive models should be kept under review.

Funding an accountable system

55   The complexity of the current finance system and its lack of transparency is a barrier to clear accountability. It is, I believe, virtually impossible to come to a definitive view about whether funding is 'adequate' even to fund central government commitments under the current system. This is in part a reflection of the intrinsic difficulty of assessing the spending pressures on such a large and complex system, but it is also a design feature of the current funding system. The move to a new system of distribution in 2006-07, commonly known as the Four Block Model (described in Annex A), ensures that annual changes to grant are now explicitly determined by relative need and resources, rather than by absolute figures.

56   However, while the grant system appears to recognise the practical impossibility and policy costs of central determination of 'correct' levels of spending in individual areas, government announcements and statements still often tend to imply that the public should be able to expect the same high standards of services everywhere – across a wide range of services. The raising of such unrealistic expectations makes it difficult to manage pressures effectively at the local level, and it raises questions about whose 'fault' council tax increases are, which are impossible to answer.

57   It may never be possible to create a system in which anyone can determine precisely whether the total funding available to local authorities is enough to enable them to achieve all of central government's ambitions. I would certainly not wish to promote a relationship between central and local government which simply focuses on inputs and costs rather than outcomes. Nevertheless, it is crucial that if central government makes promises about what local government will deliver, the funding system should provide some certainty that sufficient money will be available to do that, and in a way that helps local people to hold local and central government to account for their respective actions much more clearly.

58   In the short term, the most straightforward way to move towards this goal is to reduce the extent and ambition of the national promises made by central government which have to be met by local government funding.

59   In the medium term, there is a need to improve the transparency of the funding system, its objectives and how well it is achieving them, in a way that improves understanding and the quality of debate. I recommend that central and local government should agree, and formalise in a written agreement, what central government requires of local government, how it should be funded, and the ways in which central government should influence and control other aspects of local government activity (and the limits to that control).

60   In addition, an independent and authoritative voice is needed to provide better information on funding to inform the public and Parliament about the impact of new burdens on local government and the evidence of future pressures. This could build on the Audit Commission's existing role but other options considered should include an independent commission.

61   In order to achieve a more accountable system of local government, the Government should end the use of its capping powers, and then abolish those powers, as part of a wider package of measures to re-establish clear local accountability for local tax and spending decisions. Capping is a sign that central and local government have together failed to make the system work, and represents a short-term response to tax increases which are a symptom of problems elsewhere in the system – namely the pressure on local budgets and hence council tax, combined with a lack of local flexibility and unclear accountability. While it is born out of understandable motives, capping confuses accountability and can have perverse effects.

Protecting flexibility

62   The Local Government White Paper sets a welcome path towards a system with the potential for greater local flexibility, particularly by reducing central targets, with a focus on outcomes rather than outputs and processes and a recognition of the convening role. This responds directly to concerns that I outlined in my May report.

63   The challenge will be to deliver this through the Comprehensive Spending Review, and to maintain this approach over time. It is a substantial change in mindset, not only for central government departments and ministers, but also for citizens, the media and Parliament. It requires a shift towards a situation where ministers respond to issues of local discretion by referring them to the local council, and where central government resists encouragements to meet the particular objectives of lobby groups, professional organisations and representative bodies through central action, and instead encourages such groups to work with local government. In a country so preoccupied by fears of a 'postcode lottery' we should not underestimate the challenge that this poses – though it is one worth taking on.

Soft controls   64   The scale of this challenge means that there is a risk that some of the central controls that have been eliminated will instead 'leak' into either separate mechanisms such as ring-fenced grants, or soft controls which are less transparent and easy to measure. There are measures that can be taken to ensure that soft controls do not take the place of formal targets. I recommend that central government should:

- with the inspectorates, reduce the levels of guidance, reporting requirements and central pronouncements on areas which are of local concern and responsibility;

- develop a code of practice for government departments and agencies which clarifies the limited circumstances under which it is appropriate to place conditions on funding streams for local government, drawing on the work of the Lifting the Burdens task force; and

- set a target to reduce the extent of prescriptive guidance, process and reporting requirements. Progress against the target should be monitored transparently by an independent body such as the Audit Commission.

65   Local Area Agreements (LAA) should be developed in a way which leaves enough space for local priorities. New central government priorities which emerge between negotiations over the LAA should be incorporated into the framework on a strictly 'one in, one out' basis in order to avoid gradual re-growth of central control.

More flexible finance system

66   The inflexibility of the current funding system inhibits local responsiveness. In addition to my detailed analysis and recommendations on local government finance I make recommendations on other ways of improving financial flexibility, by enabling resources to better reflect local priorities and to support partnership working.

67   Central government has been able to influence local government behaviour through ring-fenced or specific grants, which come with specific targets or other conditions attached. These still make up a high proportion of local government spending and reduce the flexibility to respond to local priorities, work closely with partners on joint priorities and place-shape.

68   I therefore recommend that central government should commit to significant further reductions in the amount of conditional, ring fenced and specific grants – to local government and its partner agencies – and set a clear targets and a timetable for doing so. An independent body should report on progress annually. Where conditional and hypothecated funding remains there should be consideration of ways in which reporting arrangements for pooled budgets could be more flexible to support joint working, and a focus on outcomes to enable resources to be used to meet local priorities and circumstances.

69   Greater flexibility in the funding system should also help local partners to work more effectively together on crucial issues such as preventative work, which have tended to be crowded out by short term priorities. Enabling longer term planning through three-year settlements should also help – as preventative work is often the activity which gets squeezed out by short-term budget cuts.

Reorganisation

70   It is argued that reorganising local government, particularly in two-tier shire areas, can provide greater efficiency, and improve accountability. Although it did not form part of my remit, I do want to offer some comment on this debate. The past experience of reorganisation in this country provides a warning about the risks of poorly developed or executed change, and shows that it is by no means a panacea. I therefore put a much stronger emphasis on the responsibility of authorities to develop effective and flexible coalitions which transcend boundaries, and to seek joint solutions to problems where those offer potential advantages.

71   I agree with the Government that improved joint working is also needed in two tier areas, and that authorities in these areas need to aspire to operate as 'virtual' unitaries with greater efficiency through shared back office functions and integrated service delivery mechanisms. Some authorities have already made great progress towards this. There is a need in taking forward such relationships to recognise the roles which each partner is best placed to fulfil – as I have argued with respect to the relationship between central and local government. I include a series of tests for efficient joint working in Chapter 5.

Strengthening the convening role

72   The Local Government White Paper acknowledges the convening role of local authorities in taking responsibility for outcomes across an area even when those outcomes are most directly affected by other agencies. It notes that Local Strategic Partnerships should be co-ordinated by local authorities who should prepare the Sustainable Community Strategy in consultation with others.

The Government's intention is to ensure elected members are fully involved in the Local Strategic Partnership processes, that named partners are under a duty to cooperate with the local authority to agree and have regard to targets in the Local Area Agreement, and local government has enhanced scrutiny and overview arrangements.

73   In taking forward these intentions, I recommend that central government should:

- seek to ensure the suite of targets and national indicators for local government is internally consistent and outcome-focused. Negotiation of Local Area Agreements should make it a priority to allow the local alignment of targets across all local public services;

- acknowledge the role of local authorities in having lead accountability for local outcomes across all local agencies;

- support the convening role in their approach to Local Area Agreements and other activities – particularly in relation to services not provided by local government; and

- ensure that there is sufficient stability in the system to enable local government and its partnership agencies to develop strategies and actions to meet local needs and preferences.

74   Full recognition of the convening role of local government should take account of the complex relationship which local government has with other sectors, including particularly the third sector which is a key partner in service design and delivery.

Efficiency and choice
75   Local authorities need to establish themselves as champions of efficiency and value for money. I distinguish between two different types of efficiency. First, public services need to be delivered in the most cost-effective way possible – which I define as managerial efficiency. Second, the system should enable what economists call allocative efficiency, allowing public expenditure to be allocated in the way that best meets the needs and preferences of each community. There may sometimes be a tension between improving cost effectiveness to find financial savings and prioritising the right activities in each area, but ensuring value for money in the broadest sense is likely to become an even greater necessity as public finances become more constrained in the future.

76   There has been significant improvement by local government, with the support of central government, in driving cost effectiveness in the delivery of local services. This has been achieved through a variety of means including greater service collaboration, exploiting technology, and better procurement and commissioning. Figures released in December 2006 suggest that local authorities will deliver £1.3 billion of efficiencies in 2006–07, in excess of the £1 billion target set by the Government and building on performance in previous years.

77   However, the current level of centralised control still restricts scope to improve cost effectiveness, especially by hindering innovation. Over-emphasis on setting frameworks which have to work in every area can mean that the whole country is forced to go at the pace of the slowest. But, equally, over-experimentation runs the risk that many areas spend time reinventing new approaches and wasting time and resources. The challenge here is to strike the right balance, allowing those communities which are ready to innovate to do so, and ensuring that appropriate support and guidance based on best practice and evaluation evidence is available to support others. This does not mean central government should routinely issue guidance on innovation – rather the family of local government should take more of the responsibility for this, building on work already

ongoing, with organisations such as IDeA and LGA leading on providing information and good practice.

78   The submissions I have received from local authorities and others reflect a sense that managerial efficiency or cost effectiveness is too frequently emphasised in the public sector at the expense of allocative efficiency or broader value for money – we tend to care more about doing things cheaply rather than delivering the right priorities locally; which should be those that have the greatest impact on well-being.

79   I have therefore recommended that the Audit Commission should develop the Use of Resources judgement in the new performance assessment framework to include delivering the 'right' priorities to meet the needs and wishes of the local community, as well as doing them more cheaply. Central and local government should together challenge the presumption that difference between areas – the 'postcode lottery' – is always a bad thing. And central government should explicitly recognise that for a range of local services the best way to improve well-being is to enable greater local collective choice.

80   In order to enable local government to make the choices which are best for local well-being, the framework also needs to encourage effective public engagement, and provide the flexibility for authorities and particularly local councillors to respond to concerns raised with them.

Powers and powerfulness
81   One of the questions which has arisen persistently in my Inquiry is whether local authorities have sufficient powers to undertake their place-shaping role already. The strong message I received from authorities was that they key problem was not necessarily a lack of powers, but a lack of flexibility to do what was needed locally, as a result of the burden of central controls and performance management described earlier.

82   Local authorities already have wide legal powers, extended significantly by the introduction of the power of well-being in section 2 of the Local Government Act 2000 which enables authorities to do anything which promotes or improves the economic, social and environmental well-being of their area. Moreover, there is still some way to go to ensure that all local authorities are aware of and able to use their existing powers fully.

83   The report discusses a range of areas where local authorities are constrained by the way in which existing powers are drafted or used, and where powers and resources are potentially located at an inappropriate level of government. But it is important to recognise an equally important point, often missed in these discussions. Local government has become dependent on central government not only financially, but in many cases also for guidance, encouragement, and permission to innovate, across a wide range of fields. Confidence and capability must be driven from within the local government community itself, though central government can help to encourage a sense of powerfulness by expecting decisions to be taken locally and by devolving powers.

Economic prosperity
84   The concept of place-shaping underlines the importance of communities taking responsibility for their own economic fortunes, and for striking the right balance between economic, environmental and social objectives and concerns. Patterns of economic activity do not match the administrative boundaries of local authorities, and sub-regional working by groups of local authorities is therefore needed if they are to effectively address economic issues. However, resolving this issue in a way which undermines or cuts across the place-shaping role risks disengaging local government from the economic prosperity agenda.

85   The Government is rightly, in my view, not pursuing a structural reorganisation to address this issue. Nevertheless, it understandably wants to be confident that robust and effective

approaches are in place. I propose that it should establish a framework in which proposals for sub-regional working are determined locally, but tested against a clear set of expectations and tests to ensure that the partnerships have clear objectives, can take a long-term view and are sufficiently strong to support the greater responsibilities that would then be provided. Chapter 4 sets out the tests that I think Government might expect local arrangements to meet.

86   This would be a developmental solution to the challenge, with the capacity for improvement and change as relationships developed. The development of Multi Area Agreements, as signalled in the White Paper, provides a possible model for such an approach. The creation of new institutional structures where these do not currently exist should be avoided unless a consensus exists at local level, or local authorities fail to put in place adequate arrangements through robust collaboration.

What this means for services

87   The analysis for my Inquiry used a range of techniques to assess the problems facing local government and possible solutions. Although my work was never intended to provide an exhaustive analysis of all the services which local government provides or influences, I did examine a range of specific services in order to inform my work using case studies, public engagement and a series of expert seminars. They were selected to cover a range of different issues in terms of pressures, degree of central control and contribution to place-shaping.

Planning 88   Land use planning is an important aspect of place-shaping, perhaps the most immediate tool which authorities can use to influence the physical shape of localities. The Government should pursue devolution and clarification in the planning system as set out by Kate Barker in her Review of Land Use Planning, by reducing the complexity and detail of central control and setting out clearer criteria for the use of call-in powers. In taking forward reforms to the planning process for major infrastructure projects it should ensure that the new arrangements apply only to issues of unambiguously national importance, that local communities have an opportunity to make their views known, and that a clear process for reporting back to local communities is established.

Transport 89   The recommendations I have made for enhanced sub-regional working will be particularly important for transport. There is also one particular area where both local and central government currently have limited capacity to influence activity and provision. That is, as identified in the Eddington Transport Study, bus services, which were deregulated in all areas outside London in 1986. The Government has recently announced plans to enhance and extend the powers and options at the disposal of local authorities and these should be implemented as soon as practicable.

Skills 90   The UK's competitive position is now, and will increasingly in the future be dependent on the level of skills of its workforce, and the Leitch Review of Skills sets out powerful arguments for further investment in skills. The vital contribution that skills can make to economic development makes it essential that local authorities in their place-shaping role, engage with these issues. In taking forward reforms the Government should ensure that provision is appropriately tailored at the local level, that local authorities can play an appropriate role in any future Employment and Skills Boards, and seek to build on existing arrangements between employers and local authorities where possible.

Housing 91   Patterns of housing development and mobility, the availability and condition of housing and the willingness of individuals and developers to invest in it are all important influences on, and reflections of, the health of our communities. That applies to social housing as it does to privately rented and owner-occupied housing. Looking at housing issues in a strategic context is an essential part of the place-shaping role of local authorities. The Government should ensure that local authorities have appropriate influence over housing issues in that role, including by considering whether to extend the duty to cooperate to housing associations and other social landlords.

Adult social care   92   In relation to social care for older people there is a clear need for reform to enable the system to cope more effectively with future pressures, which raises some profound questions that need to be debated and resolved nationally. Reforming the system of social care to align incentives for efficiency – balancing costs against outcomes and satisfaction – with the ability to control eligibility and pressures as effectively as possible is a huge challenge. In my view it can only be solved by a well-informed and honest debate about the challenges the system faces and the difficult questions they raise.

93   There needs to be a clear, shared agenda between central and local government about how we care for older people. An important outcome from the 2007 Comprehensive Spending Review should therefore be to ensure that the solutions for managing the future of social care effectively are properly debated by central and local government, service users, carers and private and third sector providers.

94   If Government makes a 'national promise' about future adult social care, local government must be adequately funded to enable it to deliver that part of the promise for which it is asked to be responsible. As part of this it is important that responsibility for managing pressures lies with those who are able to do so most effectively.

Domestic waste   95   Waste is the other area of significant cost pressures which I examined in my case studies. Rising costs in waste management are a widespread problem, as our dependence on cheap landfill must be reduced in line with European legislation.

96   The Government recently announced its intention to legislate for Joint Waste Authorities in those areas where local councils wished to establish such formal partnership structures. This is a positive step in a context where joint working may make it easier for authorities to procure alternatives to landfill and streamline their dealings with private sector firms. It will, however, be important that there is room for structures to be tailored to, and driven by, local partnerships and not imposed according to a central template.

97   There may also be a case for examining the tools local authorities have to influence not just how waste is disposed of, but the volumes emerging in the first place. Later sections of the report consider the case for giving local authorities greater powers to influence the behaviour of local people through variable charges for the collection and disposal of domestic waste.

Community safety   98   Community safety offers a very good example of a set of concerns and activities which can only be delivered effectively where there is a strong local element – particularly to influence behaviour, working very closely with local communities. It is key to supporting social cohesion, which is one of the most important roles for local government in modern society.

99   One of the clearest messages to emerge from my case studies relates to the need for more stable funding for community safety to enable strategic planning and to encourage partnerships to grow. This problem may have emerged in relation to community safety more strongly than other services, because of the strong reliance on focused, time-limited grants provided through a range of channels. A key role for Local Area Agreements should be to allow the funding and flexibility for those sources of funding to become more streamlined and stable over time.

Health and well-being   100   The protection and improvement of public health is a role which clearly benefits from local determination, arguably to an even greater degree than social care – since the benefits of enhancing health and well-being are likely to accrue to the local community as a whole, and the health needs of each community (and therefore what needs to be done) vary dramatically.

101   Some of the targets which have proved most intractable for the Government relate to health and well-being – particularly in terms of tackling inequalities in health outcomes, for example childhood obesity and life expectancy. It is clear that there are great difficulties in improving the health of some groups, with poor health being strongly linked to deprivation, and determined very strongly by cultures, behaviours and wider environments.

102   Given the importance of health for every other aspect of people's well-being, and its impact on overall public expenditure, I would expect this emphasis on public health to grow over time. In particular, councils need to exploit their advantages in working with communities and individuals to improve outcomes – as they are given greater flexibility to carry out their place-shaping role. I therefore recommend a stronger and more explicit role for local government as convenor in the realm of health and well-being.

Children's services   103   Children's services have been an area of dramatic reform in recent years. The Children Act 2004 introduced a significant reorganisation of children's services, bringing services and partners together with the aim of promoting better outcomes for all children and improving the child protection system. By 2008 every council is expected to lead the creation of a Children's Trust, bringing together strategic oversight of all services for children and young people in an area.

104   Schools provide a national service directly to the community, and therefore provide a potentially vital link between local communities and the local authority, crucial to any place-shaping agenda which focuses on improving the well-being of families. No other service providers, except perhaps GPs, play such a vital role.

105   Schools are excluded from the duty to cooperate which applies to other partners in relation to the Local Area Agreement. They are, however, required to have regard to the Children and Young People's Plan, which informs and is informed by the Sustainable Community Strategy. Nevertheless, I am concerned that this link may be too weak to ensure a high degree of cooperation, and the Government should consider more formal mechanisms to ensure greater collaboration on place-shaping issues.

LOCAL GOVERNMENT'S CONTRIBUTION TO REFORM

106   I have argued that the centralisation of governmental and public service functions has confused accountability and generated a relationship that 'crowds out' local government's role in responding to local needs and priorities. I have made significant recommendations to central government to try to tackle these issues. But responsibility for changing the dynamic of local–central relationships and re-energising the relationship between the citizen and their locality primarily rests with local government itself. I do not want to downplay the progress that many local authorities have made already but, while there is no comprehensive blueprint for success, I am convinced that major changes of approach are needed if councils are to embrace the place-shaping role in all our communities and rise to the challenge that ambition presents. My recommendations concentrate on those changes which are most urgent.

Focusing on the future

107   Place-shaping requires local government to be more consistent in raising its sights beyond the immediate delivery of services, the short-term electoral cycle and the timetables of funding and performance management – and to do this with greater ambition. It needs to focus on developing a vision for an area and its communities, including local businesses.

108   The best authorities are already taking this longer term strategic approach to securing sustainable strategies that address the issues facing their communities. However, despite many strong examples of long-term planning, I have detected a sense that some local authorities have developed a tendency to 'wait and see' where central government will go next, rather than setting out their own long-term strategic plans. In some cases this reflects political instability or other obstacles to making difficult decisions, but also insufficient confidence about the long-term budgetary position of the authority. Sometimes this is linked to too narrow a focus on service delivery rather than a wider strategic view of service provision within the locality.

109   In their forward planning, local authorities should look further ahead than even the ten-year time frame of the community strategy; making best use of intelligence and evidence of future trends; engaging local partners, businesses and residents in a debate about the long-term aspirations for the area; and focussing their performance management on outcomes.

Leading communities and places

Political and managerial leadership

110   Visibility of leadership is very important and a key component of accountability. Where people know who is in charge, they know whom to call to account. This is important in terms of public recognition, but also in building the personal networks and relationships with key local partners. If leading councillors, whatever the leadership model being used, adopt an outward-looking approach, communicate and engage local people with energy and enthusiasm and also develop credibility with their partners, they can be excellent place-shapers, even where leadership is not focused on a single individual. A summary of these place-shaping behaviours, which apply as much to small localities as major cities, is set out in Chapter 5.

111   Managerial leadership also remains important but the recent emphasis on this has not always been thought through with the danger of overlapping roles and confused expectations, particularly when there are changes of political leadership. One of the key roles of managerial leadership is to develop the organisation in terms of competencies, behaviours and understanding, including the ability to build coalitions outside the organisation. I am convinced by Jim Collins's argument that the 'flywheel' of public sector achievement is the development of "brand reputation – built upon tangible results and emotional share of heart – so that potential supporters believe not only in your mission, but in your capacity to deliver on that mission." Again, I feel strongly that facilitating this role of local government is not a matter of legislation or formal frameworks, it is primarily a question of behaviours. Chapter 5 sets out the managerial behaviours which I think best support councils' place-shaping role.

Convening

112   Local government – at political and managerial levels – also needs to exercise leadership of the whole community, creating a shared agenda that recognises the roles that different partners can play in bringing it to life. Convening requires local government to be able to identify a direction of travel, articulate a sense of the future and enthuse others to be part of a common mission. Significant progress has been made but there is still a long way to go. Local authorities need to ensure that local partnership structures are fit for purpose and have a genuine focus on the needs of the local community. More broadly, local authorities need to adopt a leadership style that engages local partners, builds alliances and secures support for joint priorities. It should facilitate, advocate, arbitrate and influence rather than dominate.

Two-tier working

113   There are many who believe that we should move to a unitary structure of local government across the country. However, two-tier government does have advantages; indeed many urban areas are trying to find ways of getting the balance right between locality and city-wide governance, forming voluntary two-tier arrangements. A key aspect of the convening role is the challenge for those tiers to work productively together. Chapter 5 sets out a range of characteristics of effective two-tier working.

Local government's national voice

114   The leadership challenge in local government is primarily about councils gaining the confidence and sense of power to speak for their local communities, but there is also a need for the local government community to be represented and led nationally. The development of the LGA in 1997 significantly strengthened local government's national voice and there has been important progress in recent years through approaches such as the central–local partnership, to generate a more equal relationship between local and central government. Nonetheless, local government still finds it difficult – particularly in the public's view – to be regarded as having sufficient stature in many debates with central government.

115   I therefore welcome the LGA's review of its role and relationships through the Best Commission. The LGA is likely to have a critical role in reshaping the role of local government and developing the relationship between local and central government. This will particularly depend on its work with partners to provide leadership to the sector and challenge to underperforming councils. Local government will also need to strengthen its performance in contributing to debate on major policy issues of the day, and its key role of communicating with the public about local government's value, its challenges and its successes.

The role of political parties

116   There is also an important role for political parties. In order to improve the calibre and performance of councillors, parties need to refresh their approach to recruiting local councillors, actively seeking out talent and reaching out beyond their traditional activist base. This needs to be accompanied by greater clarity about expectations and time commitment involved in being a councillor. Political parties, mainly at the local level but supported by national parties, should also place stronger performance management pressures on councillors, including provision of information to the public about their activities.

117   Political groups need to reflect on how they are organised and should consider how to achieve the right balance between enforcing the party whip and allowing councillors to represent local issues. Automatic adherence to a party line can undermine councillor credibility with ward constituents. Such a change needs to be accompanied with a focus on developing skills at cross-party working.

Frontline councillors

118   The frontline role of all councillors – both non-executive and executive in their ward role – is one of the keys to effective engagement with the local community and one which receives insufficient attention and support. The White Paper proposals provide an opportunity for all councils to reflect on how members can be more outward facing and how the balance can be shifted towards engagement with their communities. There is a role for the local government family, including IDeA and the LGA to develop new models for frontline councillor working and local government itself should experiment to get the best out of this role.

119   More generally, there is a need for more effective support for local councillors in their frontline role. For example, they should have timely access to the information they need to do their job effectively, and should be clear about how they can influence the council's policy decisions. They should have clear job descriptions and training specifically for their ward member role, and councils should consider the use of individual ward budgets.

Improving local accountability

120   Councils need to go beyond elections to ensure an ongoing mandate to act in the interests of the whole community. Changing expectations about the accountability of government mean that councils need to earn the confidence of local people, to ensure that they are responsive to their views and that they understand their needs and priorities. The White Paper makes clear that central government expects that a shift in powers and flexibility to local authorities must be accompanied by greater local accountability and I support this 'deal'. Local government can go a long way towards improving its accountability to local people even within the current framework and has no need to await further legislation.

Improving public engagement

121   Local government's ability to engage local people lies at the heart of its place shaping role. If local government is to act in the interests of its community, influence its partners and ensure it tailors its work to the most important local priorities, it needs to make a step-change in the quality of its engagement work. Councils need to be selective with their resources with a focus on what matters, avoid allowing statutory requirements for consultation to dictate their approach and to accord higher status to the skills needed by officers and councillors to engage effectively with the public.

Developing scrutiny

122   Scrutiny by non-executive councillors of the executive's decisions, policies and strategies is increasingly playing an important role in the accountability of local government; strengthening public engagement and improving council performance. Scrutiny has a core role to play in place-shaping. Done well, it can provide a focus for community and stakeholder engagement, harness local expertise, challenge current performance and service priorities and secure changes that mean services better meet local needs. There are many examples of effective scrutiny but there is also evidence that in practice the use of scrutiny as a tool for local accountability is mixed. There are also major differences in the extent to which councils prioritise and resource the scrutiny role. There is a need for councils and other participants to resource scrutiny appropriately and to link it to local partnership work.

Innovative, local solutions to public service challenges

123   Councils may be able to provide adequate and even good services without fully embracing their place-shaping role, but real achievements can not be made without local authorities focusing on the sense of place, to enable services to be tailored to the needs of a local area. For services to be provided in this way, innovative local solutions may be necessary which sometimes involve taking carefully judged risks.

Creative use of powers

124   In order to act effectively and innovatively in its place-shaping role, local government needs to make fuller use of the powers at its disposal. It needs to demonstrate that it is ambitious and innovative in the use of existing powers if local government is to be given new ones. The limited use of the well-being power set out in the Local Government Act 2000 is a powerful example of local government not making full use of its powers, with research suggesting that this has been due largely to the need for a more entrepreneurial approach to problem solving.

Local Area Agreements

125   There is a key challenge for local government in making best use of LAAs for the local community as intended in the White Paper. This means negotiating the 'right' 35 targets with central government and partners, and selecting an appropriate set of local targets. These should reflect a proper strategic discussion of priorities for the whole local community with partners, resisting any temptation to rely on a standard list.

Commissioning role 126 The need for innovation also requires local authorities to assess whether they are the optimum provider of services or whether they should adopt a commissioning role, working in partnership with other public service providers, the third sector or the private sector. Such commissioning can have a number of benefits in bringing skills and experience from other sectors, a greater focus on user involvement and users as co-producers. It can also change the dynamic of local government away from being a provider of service, to one of a stronger community advocate taking a strategic view on the needs of the community at times – seeking to help develop community and market responses which reduce the pressure on the public purse.

Improving efficiency 127 Improving efficiency will continue to be a major driver for local government, not least because of the imperative for councils to manage pressures on public expenditure and to secure the trust and confidence of both their local population and central government. Councils role in effective place-shaping will depend on them establishing themselves more clearly as champions for efficiency.

128 Public engagement can help councils to develop innovative solutions which can deliver more effective outcomes. Councils, should consistently involve users in the design and delivery of services, to find ways to enhance user choice and harness the benefits of co-production.

129 Pursuing the broader definition of allocative efficiency – delivering the right local priorities – requires, however, a really clear understanding of local needs and aspirations, together with good levels of engagement to both inform and explain hard choices. Chapter 5 provides examples of approaches which can improve efficiency.

Performing for the community 130 The new performance framework offers opportunities for local government to retain its focus on performance but re-orient its performance management towards greater community and public accountability so that the whole organisation – managerially and politically – knows exactly how it is working for the good of the local community, whether it is achieving its goals and what more it needs to do to meet its own targets.

FUNDING REFORM – INTRODUCTION

131 Reform of the local government finance system should not be seen in isolation, but must be part of the process of empowering the kind of local government that we want. My recommendations on finance are guided by a set of broad objectives for reform, in the context of the wider vision of place-shaping described in this report. These objectives are:

- greater local flexibility and choice;

- stronger national and local accountability based on clearer responsibilities;

- better incentives for local government;

- efficiency in local tax and spending;

- better management of pressures; and

- improved fairness, and perceived fairness in the tax system.

132 Taken together, these objectives shape a package of reforms to ensure the sustainability of the local government finance system, in the immediate term and into the future.

Balances and trade-offs 133 Some commentators have argued that a key objective for reform should be changing the so-called 'balance of funding', making local authorities more reliant on locally raised revenues and less dependent on funding from Whitehall. It is suggested that this would help to ensure that local government is more self-reliant and democratically accountable to the local community.

134   I agree that accountability for local decisions, including decisions about tax, is an essential part of meaningful local government. However, it is not obvious that a new or larger local revenue stream would by itself create greater independence from central government. Indeed, greater responsibility for painfully accountable revenue-raising – if it came without greater discretion about the services and outcomes being pursued – might be the worst of all worlds.

135   Equally, it is important that the finance settlement does not put local authorities in a position where local choices about tax rates are continually overridden by external pressures. However, I have some doubts about whether changing the balance of funding or 'gearing ratio' would, of itself, solve these problems. Recent changes to schools funding show that altering the headline balance of funding may have little impact on local authorities' freedom to set locally-appropriate spending plans. In some circumstances it may even reduce their ability to do so.

136   I have not made it an explicit objective of this Inquiry to change the balance of funding. Instead I have aimed to focus on the underlying causes of pressures on local budgets, and to ensure flexibility and accountability in both tax and spending at the local level.

Balances and trade-offs   137   It will be important, in arriving at a series of reforms, to consider how different objectives for reform may pull in different directions. Important judgements include: balancing the interests of different groups of taxpayers, for whom 'fairness' may mean different things; judging the appropriate role within the finance system of both taxes and user-charges for services; the appropriate role for equalisation between areas while retaining the scope to introduce financial incentives for authorities; and the trade-off between stability and buoyancy in local revenues.

Principles for good local taxes   138   Tax policy should have regard to a set of general principles for good taxation, and should consider the elements that contribute to a good local tax. These are set out in Chapter 6. Taxes on property (and land) have particular advantages as local sources of revenue, not least in providing a strong connection between the tax people pay and their residence in an area. Taxes on property value reflect residents' (and owners') financial stake in a community and its prosperity, and their interest in local services and investment, which themselves impact on the desirability of property in a given area.

Framing a package of reform   139   There is, I believe, a strong and growing case that change is necessary. The 'no change' option is itself a painful one: the pressure on local services, on council tax as the only local tax, and hence on council tax payers, will not disappear and may indeed sharpen in some areas as growth in public spending, including central government funding for local services, slows down in the coming years. I believe there is enough evidence to justify action to make the finance system more sustainable into the future.

140   However, although it is true that the status quo is problematic, it is very clear that there are no easy options for change, and no simple 'golden key' that will unlock the problems of the finance system. Any change in taxation creates 'winners' and 'losers', with those who pay more tending to react much more strongly to change than those who benefit. A package of complementary measures will be crucial if we are to balance the impact of change on different groups in an acceptable way.

141   My central proposition is that a mosaic of changes, implemented over time, through a 'developmental approach' to reform, is the best way to move forward. I have aimed to shape a package of reforms which both deal with the immediate challenges facing the finance system and pave the way for wider choices in the future. In the report I also consider the implications of my recommendations for Scotland, Wales and Northern Ireland.

HOUSEHOLD TAXATION AND LOCAL CHARGES

Council tax

142   Council tax is a hybrid tax: partly a charge for local services and partly a property tax. Since its inception in 1991, council tax has been the only locally levied tax on households, and the only tax whose rate is decided by local authorities. With a total yield of over £22 billion in 2006–07, council tax makes a significant contribution to the funding of local public services. It is also the most visible and well-known tax in the country, with public awareness of the tax at 99 per cent.

143   Property taxes have a number of things to recommend them, and since council tax incorporates a property tax element, it shares many of these advantages. Council tax is relatively easy to collect and difficult to evade. Since properties do not move, tax bases are stable and revenues relatively predictable, allowing local authorities a degree of certainty in their financial planning. Property taxes are widely used around the world as a source of finance for local government, reflecting the crucial link between residents of an area and the services that are provided there.

144   These factors lead me to the view that council tax remains broadly sound and should be retained as a local tax. It does, however, have some important shortcomings some of which can be mitigated through reform in the short term, and others which may require more radical or longer-term reforms.

145   Concerns about council tax have several dimensions, all of which are exacerbated by the highly visible nature of the tax. A solution to the council tax problem must address:

- the perceived fairness of the way council tax distributes the tax burden, particularly in relation to people on low and fixed incomes, and especially older people;

- the burden of expectation and spending pressures that have been placed on council tax, with consequences for the rate of increase in bills; and

- concerns about the continued reliance on a single local tax which is not naturally buoyant.

Better management of pressures to contain council tax increases

146   Council tax tends to bear the strain of pressures in the whole local government finance system. Making council tax sustainable for the future will depend not just on the design of the tax itself, but on whether service expectations can be managed and met in a way that stops council tax from coming under unsustainable pressure. Local authorities need real flexibility to set spending plans in a way that reflects local choice about service provision and tax rates, even where this means doing less in areas which are not a high priority for local people.

Fairness and reform of council tax

147   During the course of my Inquiry I have been struck by the strength of feeling that property taxes provoke, including resistance to the idea that tax bills should reflect property values. Many people view ability to pay, generally measured by income, as a key criteria for a 'fair' tax. However, fairness is a complex question: other submissions to the Inquiry have also discussed the fairness of council tax in relation to the benefits different households receive from local services. Another definition of fairness would suggest that bills should reflect property values, with the most expensive homes facing the highest bills and vice versa.

148   Nonetheless, the fact that council tax bills may not reflect ability to pay, or income, is the most commonly cited reason for council tax's perceived unfairness. Concerns about people on low or fixed incomes who struggle to pay their council tax bill are widespread and valid, and I have looked at the options to protect these groups.

Options for reform

149   In the short term, reforms should target the most commonly cited source of council tax 'unfairness': that related to ability to pay, particularly for the poorest. It is the nature of property markets in England that there is no simple correlation between a household's income and the value of their home; reforms of council tax as a property-based tax will therefore have only a limited impact on its overall progressiveness to income. The key to adjusting the tax burden on the poorest is therefore likely to be council tax benefit.

150   However, if a short-term solution to income fairness can be found, this might make space for reform in the medium term to the structure of council tax, with a view to strengthening its progressiveness to property value. Doing so could have a number of advantages, including:

- greater fairness as a property tax by ensuring that the most valuable homes are not taxed more lightly than less valuable ones;

- through this, potentially ensuring that council tax could act as a more effective stabiliser of the property market, or at least correct the relatively favourable tax treatment of valuable homes at present; and

- introducing some greater progressiveness to income overall, both to make council tax 'fairer' in terms of ability to pay, and to generate potentially significant savings in the council tax benefit bill.

151   The Inquiry has examined a range of options for reform of council tax as a property tax, both in the context of my original remit to consider reform alongside the planned revaluation of properties, and since then as part of a wider look at the scope for council tax reform. Chapter 7 discusses the advantages and disadvantages of those options.

Council tax revaluation

152   The revaluation of domestic properties was postponed in September 2005. While I understand the Government's reasons for postponing the revaluation exercise, it is my view that there are advantages to revaluing the property base that have not been adequately explained so far. It is worth noting that postponement itself created 'winners' and 'losers' – 3.7 million households (or 17 per cent of all households in England) that would have been moved down the bands by revaluation are arguably paying too much council tax, subsidising those who would be paying more because their properties had grown in value more quickly.

153   History has shown that it is possible, though not ideal, to keep levying property taxes based on out-of-date valuations. Revaluation would, however, have two significant benefits: it would underpin the credibility of a property tax by maintaining a meaningful relationship between relative property values and bills; and would create an opportunity to make structural changes to council tax. The technology now exists to go ahead with a revaluation relatively cost effectively should the Government choose to do so.

154   There is no doubt that a first revaluation of properties would be a challenging exercise, especially given the long period of time since the original valuations were carried out in 1993. Some form of transitional arrangements might well be appropriate to ensure that any significant changes in liability for individual households – for example upward movements of more than one band – can be implemented in stages.

155   Nonetheless, it is my view that the Government has a responsibility for maintaining the foundations of such an important revenue stream, since an out-of-date tax base will mean that the credibility of council tax as a property tax will gradually be eroded. There is a real risk that failure to revalue only makes it more difficult ever to do so, whereas an expectation of regular revaluations

(as is already the norm in business rates) would contribute to the long-term sustainability of a property tax. While not the most urgent priority, I recommend that the Government should conduct a revaluation of all domestic properties for council tax and regularly thereafter.

Reform of the council tax bands

156   At the point of revaluation the Government should reform council tax by adding new bands at the top and bottom of the current band structure. This would help to improve the progressiveness of council tax in relation to values, recognising that the effective floor and ceiling on current eligibility are a product of judgements made in 1993, not of natural law. Reducing the burden for many band A households by creating a new lower band would benefit many low-income households, while new top bands would affect those in the most valuable properties, where the correlation between income and house price is strongest. The Government should also consider introducing separate bands for Inner London, to reflect the unique shape of the property market in that region and to reduce the turbulence caused by revaluation there.

Council tax as a service charge

157   While income or ability to pay is often the focus of discussions around council tax fairness, for others, 'fairness' means paying according to the benefits received from services. It appears that popular emphasis on the service-charge element of the council tax may have contributed to the strong, and sometime unrealistic expectations people have of a very direct return on their payment for local services. In practice, the balance between tax paid and services consumed will vary between individuals and households, and indeed over time.

158   I believe it is right that council tax should continue in the short to medium term to incorporate elements of both a property tax and a service charge. The service charge element of council tax is well understood by the public and reflects an important link between residence in an area, and a household's interest in local services and local prosperity. Retaining a hybrid tax, which operates as a service charge but which also incorporates some of the advantages of a property tax, appears to be the right model in the present system. There is, however, room for a wider and more transparent debate about the balance between taxes and user-charges in paying for local public services, as discussed below.

Council tax discounts and exemptions

159   I have also looked at scope for reform of the discounts and exemptions currently available against council tax. In particular, I recommend that the Government ensures that grant to areas with large student populations is based on realistic data about the numbers of exempt households in the area, in order to be fair to other council taxpayers. The Government should also consult local authorities on the scope for greater flexibility in tax on second homes, including the possibility of levying a local supplement on council tax for second homes, particularly where these represent a significant proportion of local housing.

Council tax benefit

160   Council tax benefit (CTB) was designed to protect those on low incomes who may not be able to afford to pay their council tax bill. I believe that reform and more effective delivery of council tax benefit are the key to dealing with perceptions of unfairness associated with council tax.

161   If current entitlement to council tax benefit were fully taken up, council tax would be progressive to income overall for the poorest households. However, CTB is not yet fully achieving that aim in practice, primarily because not all entitlement is being taken up – only 62–68 per cent of households entitled to CTB actually receive it. For the poorest ten per cent of households council tax therefore remains a large average burden relative to income.

162   Making council tax benefit work better is particularly important to ensure that older people are not paying an unacceptable share of their income in council tax. Take-up of entitlements by

older people is lower than average at just 53 to 58 per cent, and the great majority of unclaimed benefit is owed to pensioner households.

Rebate, not benefit

163　The term benefit has a particular resonance, which may prevent some people from taking up their entitlements. It is also something of a misnomer: council tax benefit's primary purpose is not to provide income support as such, but to adjust households' liability for council tax according to their ability to pay. CTB should therefore be recognised as a rebate and be renamed 'council tax rebate'.

164　I believe that renaming CTB is justified in its own right. However, I am clear that this is not purely a question of presentation, but implies a wider recognition that steps should be taken to ensure rebates reach those households that are entitled to them. Ideally, CTB would therefore be renamed alongside the announcement of measures to improve take-up and delivery of entitlements.

Improving take-up

165　Local authorities will always have an important role to play in reaching their citizens and connecting them with services and other entitlements and there is scope for more effective action in many areas, learning from the efforts of the best performers. But they cannot be solely responsible for the successful delivery of CTB; central government has a prior responsibility for getting the framework right. It is clear to me that with up to £1.8 billion per year in CTB entitlement going unclaimed, much of it by older people, low take-up is a systemic rather than just a local problem, and as such requires a structural change in the way rebates are administered.

166　Many of the barriers to claiming are administrative in nature, putting a premium on joined-up action by public bodies to help make claiming easier for taxpayers. In the short term, the Government should take steps within the current system to ensure that rebate entitlements are delivered as effectively and as fully as possible. These steps should build on recent efforts to streamline delivery of CTB through the Pension Service, including by enabling them to help those people who are eligible for CTB but not Pension Credit. The barrier to the Pension Service liaising directly with local authorities in processing claims should be removed.

167　However, given the particularly low take-up of CTB compared with other benefits, and the fact that there appear to be significant barriers to take-up, I believe there is also a need to look at a more radical overhaul of the way council tax rebates are delivered in the medium term.

168　The government should therefore consider the scope for data sharing between agencies to proactively deliver council tax rebates to those who are entitled, with a view to achieving a step-change in take-up. The ultimate extension of this approach would be that, in theory, households could be billed for council tax net of any rebate entitlement, but with a responsibility to inform the government if the details on which it was calculated were incorrect.

169　Increasing take-up in this way would involve significant costs; the amounts currently unclaimed are large (up to £1.8 billion in 2004–05) and additional money spent on increased CTB take-up would clearly reduce the amount of money available to spend elsewhere. Nonetheless, I am clear that the success of the system of council tax rebates – and particularly its success in reaching entitled pensioners – is critical if council tax is to continue to play such a major role in the local government finance system, and should be considered a priority.

Eligibility criteria

170　Achieving high levels of take-up would be a real step forward; however, even with full take-up of current entitlements some households would still face a relatively high council tax burden as a proportion of income. There is a strong case for more generous eligibility criteria for council tax rebates to some groups.

171   My primary focus in considering changes to eligibility criteria has been on pensioners, as the group most likely to be on fixed incomes, and about whom I have received by far the greatest number of submissions expressing concern. Evidence from survey and public deliberation work carried out for the Inquiry also supports a focus on older people as the group around whom concerns about council tax fairness are strongest.

172   The Government should increase savings limits on council tax eligibility for pensioners, which act as a disincentive to save for retirement and are currently set at a modest £16,000. The upper capital threshold should be increased to £50,000 and could over time be abolished altogether, in line with capital thresholds for pension credits.

173   I have also considered the impact of council tax and benefit eligibility criteria on working-age households, and particularly the income thresholds at which council tax liability begins. It would be possible to make adjustments to the income thresholds that would benefit large numbers of households, though the amounts gained would be relatively small. It may be better that hardship for working-age households is considered in the context of wider welfare policy.

174   I have also considered wider options for helping to ensure that no household pays an unacceptably high burden of council tax in relation to their income. For instance, some US states use a circuit breaker rebate to ensure no household pays more than a set proportion of their income in property tax. Other countries operate schemes which allow pensioner homeowners to defer payment of taxes against equity in their homes. If the costs of council tax benefit reform proved a barrier to its implementation, these other options might deserve serious consideration.

Local income tax

175   While the immediate focus should be on council tax benefit and management of pressures to stabilise council tax, it may be that in future, a developmental approach to reform could allow a wider look at the balance of local taxation. It is part of my remit to consider both alternatives to council tax and possible sources of supplementary revenue for local government. In that context, local income tax (LIT) has been a prominent feature of the debate on local government finance.

176   Survey evidence suggests that, in principle, many people like the idea that council tax should be replaced with a local income tax, with nearly half of all respondents to an Inquiry-commissioned survey saying that council tax should be partly or fully replaced by a LIT. Many saw income as a fairer basis for taxation than property, since it would be seen to reflect 'ability to pay'. A local income tax would indeed be more progressive to income than council tax, even with full take-up of council tax benefit.

177   However, it may be that support for the idea of the local income tax is not based on a true understanding of what it would mean for respondents' own bills. While people recognise that pensioners would probably do well from a move to income-based taxation, relatively few think that they would pay more themselves.

178   Income tax, unlike council tax, is naturally 'buoyant', in that revenues grow as earnings or employment levels increase. By the same token, revenues could fall during bad times, so local authorities would need to be equipped to manage this risk if they were to depend on income taxes for part of their revenues. It is important also not to overstate the extent to which a local income tax would be buoyant. My research indicates that while the natural buoyancy of an income-based tax would be an advantage, it would not make a local income tax immune to the pressures that are felt in relation to council tax.

179   Modelling for the Inquiry suggests that for income tax to be levied locally, it would probably have to apply to the basic rate of tax, since the higher rate of income tax provides a much less even tax base for local authorities. If levied on the basic rate, a local income tax of, on average, 7.7 pence in the pound would raise the same amount as council tax does now. I have also explored the possibility of introducing a LIT as a supplement to sit beside a reduced council tax and to relieve some of the pressure on it. A supplement of one pence in the pound on the basic rate would raise approximately £2.9 billion in 2006–07, though survey evidence suggested a lack of public appetite for LIT as a supplement to council tax, because of a concern among respondents that they might be paying twice for the same services.

180   The implementation of a new local income tax would be complex, and would be likely to require a long lead time of around six to seven years from the point at which the Government decided to work towards it, to the point at which the new tax went into operation. Particular attention would need to be given to the likely impact on employers of operating locally-variable tax rates through their payroll system.

181   While I am not recommending a local income tax at this time, my work indicates it would be feasible to implement one in England. It remains therefore a choice for future governments.

Local service charges

182   Income from charges already represents a significant part of local authorities' revenue comprising about 8.5 per cent of total income. Over a quarter of all councils raised more income from sales fees and charges than from council tax.

183   There is significant variation between areas in their use of charging powers, and it seems likely that while some of that variation reflects local choice or circumstances, it also partly reflects councils' willingness to engage with charging and take a strategic approach to its use.

184   I am convinced that there is room for a much fuller conversation with local service users and taxpayers about the best way to fund local services. Given the pressures on council tax, a move towards services users meeting some costs directly might be a valid local choice, and one which councils could legitimately open up for public debate. I would encourage all local authorities to take a strategic approach to the use of charges, including as part of the range of levers available for managing pressures on budgets and on council tax.

185   I am not recommending changes to the general framework of charging powers, though the powers to trade and charge conferred on 'best value' authorities in the Local Government Act 2003 should be extended to all local authorities.

186   As discussed above, there are specific and growing pressures on waste services as the UK aims to reduce its dependence on cheap landfill, in the face of growing waste volumes. In that context, the Government should create permissive powers for local authorities to charge for domestic waste collection, as a means by which incentives can be created to reduce household waste and manage costs – and to help ensure that the remaining costs may be shared in a way that is perceived as fair.

187   Road pricing is likely to play a larger role in the future. Under the Transport Act 2000, local authorities outside London may operate congestion charging schemes in line with their Local Transport Plan. As such, it is likely that the difficult engagement necessary to get a road pricing scheme off the ground would be delivered locally. It is therefore right that locally accountable bodies should also have the freedom to invest revenues according to the 'deal' communicated to and agreed with local citizens. The Government should consider removing restrictions on the use

of road pricing revenues, and as a minimum should ensure that any hypothecation operates at a strategic level that allows local authorities to take a broad view of their investment priorities and the views of their communities.

BUSINESS TAXATION

Business rates

188   Business rates are an important part of the local government finance system, providing around £18.4billion in 2006-07 to support public services delivered by local government. Until 1990, business rates and domestic rates were aspects of the same tax. It is not, therefore, true to say, as some continue to believe, that local authorities were able to choose to place a greater weight of taxation on businesses rather than residents. Since 1990, the tax rate has been set centrally and levied at a national rate, with the revenues redistributed by the government. However, local authorities still collect the tax and this contributes to some confusion about the purpose of business rates – they are still perceived by many businesses as a local tax linked to the provision of local services, but are actually used to fund at least in part the provision of services according to national expectations and requirements (something which has been intensified by the introduction of the Dedicated Schools Grant).

Rate of tax   189   Businesses as a whole have been protected from real term increases in rates. As local government grants and council tax revenues have both risen significantly faster than inflation, business rates have provided a falling proportion of local government spending over time. In 1990, when the national business rates system was introduced, business rates raised £9.6billion and provided 29 per cent of local government revenues. In 2006–07 business rates are expected to provide around £17.5 billion, 20 per cent of local government spending. Some of those who made submissions to my Inquiry felt that this was unfair, particularly given the significant real term increases in council tax since 1993, and argued that the contribution made by businesses should be increased.

190   However, I have concluded that for the present, the national business rate is not an appropriate way to raise additional resources to fund general local government spending. The most pressing need is to develop much more constructive relationships between local authorities and businesses, focused on joint interests in promoting economic prosperity and investment in local infrastructure. A general national tax rise to support local government funding could put the development of those relationships in jeopardy.

191   Nonetheless, I believe that communities need more power to choose to raise new local revenues to invest in themselves. In my discussions with businesses I have also found an appetite for greater engagement with local authorities on economic development issues. Businesses have identified a need to invest more in the infrastructure required to support future growth – a concern that can perhaps most easily be exemplified by reference to the debate in London on Crossrail, but of which examples exist across the country. Combined with effective incentives on local communities, greater flexibility over raising revenues to invest at the local level should allow communities to strengthen their own economies and tax bases over time.

Business   192   Business Improvement Districts (BIDs) do already provide some additional flexibility and
Improvement   have been welcomed by businesses. However, BIDs have a number of limitations and they are not
Districts   the answer to all problems, first, their purpose is specific and limited, focused on particular projects in tightly defined geographical areas. Second, concerns have been raised that the costs of developing and administering BIDs can be a barrier. Third, there is a concern that their priorities can be skewed towards short-term issues rather than longer term investments.

Localisation 193   Transferring business rates revenues and decisions over tax rates to local control would give local authorities a substantial new local revenue source and considerable flexibility over revenue raising. The business community has concerns that localisation would lead to increases in taxation without a greater say over local priorities and spending, and that the number of different local rates would increase complexity. There are also wider concerns about the impact of localisation on the ability to equalise resources between authorities. To maintain current levels of equity under a localised business rates system, around 70 authorities would need to pay some of their local tax revenues to central government to support other authorities.

194   It is technically possible to do this and other countries adopt such an approach. However, I am not attracted to it. I do not believe that it would help to create the direct and accountable relationship between local authorities and businesses needed. In many areas businesses would be paying taxes to their local authority that would then be reallocated elsewhere in the country. In addition, I think that local authorities and the business community still have to work on developing trust and shared objectives, and I am therefore concerned to avoid changes which could put the developing shared agenda at risk.

Supplement 195   An alternative option for reforming the business rates to provide additional flexibility would be to introduce a power for local authorities to levy a supplement on the national business rate within their area. This would provide authorities with a more limited flexibility to raise revenues, but it would also be more transparent and have a more limited impact on businesses. Chapter 8 examines the possible impacts of a supplementary rate.

196   Local supplementary powers should be designed in a way which can gain credibility with business and the wider community. The key issues to be considered are:

- the appropriate scale of the supplement. At the upper end, some Business Improvement Districts have levied supplements as high as four pence. A lower limit would provide less revenue and less flexibility, but might enable confidence in new arrangements to develop more gradually. In that situation, there might be a case for allowing a higher limit in some cases subject to more stringent approval mechanisms;

- retention of revenue, where I believe all revenues should be retained locally;

- the right form of accountability to business taxpayers. The most obvious options are some form of voted approval or a statutory consultation process. On balance, I propose that there should be a requirement to consult local businesses, and the wider community, before introducing a supplement with a clear proposal and timetable. Revenues from a supplement should be hypothecated to the purposes agreed through consultation;

- how to ensure that supplements contribute to, rather than detract from, the local economy. I propose that authorities should be required to make an assessment of the impact of a supplement on the local economy, and the potential economic benefits of the spending they propose to finance from the revenues generated;

- the authority by which supplements should be levied. I recommend that supplements should be levied by unitary authorities and metropolitan districts, and in London and areas with two-tier local government, a single rate should be set through agreement between the relevant authorities, with a joint plan for the use of revenues. Where arrangements develop for collaborative working between authorities elsewhere in the country this could usefully include cooperating around supplements. Powers to introduce Business Improvement Districts should remain with shire districts and the London boroughs;

- whether authorities should have a degree of flexibility over which sizes of business pay the levy, which I would support; and

- whether there should be a threshold below which small businesses do not pay the supplement.

Reliefs and exemptions

197   The existence of reliefs and exemptions can create distortions, or weaken incentives to make the best use of land and propety. In addition, they represent a cost in terms of revenue foregone – money which could otherwise be used to cut the overall rate of tax or fund service enhancements.

198   Empty property relief provides a substantial relief from taxation for all empty property and full relief for some types. Although in the main, the prospect of commercial returns from the property should ensure full use of properties, the risk of not earning a return does not just result from external factors but is also determined by the actions of the owner. It is also clear that given concerns to protect the environment and support urban regeneration we need to ensure that all previously developed land is used most effectively. I recommend that the empty property relief be reformed to provide better incentives for this.

199   These arguments also apply to derelict property and previously developed land and suggest that a tax on such land (which is currently exempt) would provide a way of improving incentives to use this land. It would also provide a way of closing a potential loophole which allows property owners to avoid taxation by deliberating making their property derelict. These proposals are not yet fully developed, and further work will be needed to test whether this is a feasible proposition and how implementation and administration could be undertaken. I recommend that the Government consults further on this proposal.

200   There are myriad other reliefs and exemptions in the business rates system. The most substantial in terms of revenue foregone are the reliefs for charities (£700million), and the exemption for agricultural land and buildings (£450million). Some of those who made submissions to my Inquiry also called for new reliefs to support the environmental agenda. I recommend that the Government should undertake its own review of the reliefs and exemptions in the system in order to consider whether current reliefs and exemptions remain justified, and to consider the case for environmentally motivated reliefs.

Options for future governments

201   My recommendation for the introduction of a local supplementary power is a limited new power for local authorities. In the longer term, the re-localisation of the business rate, including the option to set a lower tax rate, could be considered. Businesses have made clear their concerns about such a radical step in the short term, although they are supportive of greater local choice and flexibility. It is a question future governments may wish to consider as new arrangements evolve.

Section 106 and Planning-gain Supplement

202   Both Section 106 contributions and the proposed Planning-gain Supplement (PGS) have been extensively reviewed by Kate Barker in her work on housing supply and land use planning.

203   If the Planning-gain Supplement is introduced, it should be designed primarily as a local revenue source, with a regional share of an appropriate scale, not as a national source which may or may not be allocated to authorities. It is imperative that a transparent and predictable link between local development and local resourcing exists if development is to take place or incentive effects are to be realised. Therefore, I think that in two-tier areas there is considerable merit in

pursuing a joint option for the management of the revenues, in which county and district councils would be jointly responsible for developing and implementing a plan for the use of the revenues from the Planning-gain Supplement in the area.

Taxes on tourism pressures

204   Some local authorities have supported the proposal for some form of tax on tourist pressures. Over the past year, this proposal has generated significant debate within the tourism industry and beyond. Accommodation taxes have been deployed in a number of places around the world, with varying degrees of success. It is clearly important to weigh the contribution that tourists make to the local economy against the costs they impose and the likely impact on the tourist industry of any taxation proposal.

205   I do not support the introduction of any new taxation powers carelessly, and proposals for these sorts of taxes are likely to be relevant only in some areas. In my view, a local accommodation tax is only likely to be acceptable if a local authority can demonstrate that there is a robust evidence base, local support for the tax, and has a proposal developed in partnership with local businesses and residents, who will continue to have a voice in the evolution and review of the scheme.

206   With that in mind, I think that the Government should consult on the costs and benefits of providing a permissive power for local authorities to levy taxes on tourism, including a possible tax on accommodation, and on whether local authorities would use such a power. It should use the results of that consultation to examine the case for extension of such powers to local authorities.

GRANT AND THE USE OF NATIONAL TAXATION TO SUPPORT LOCAL SERVICES

207   Reforms are needed to produce a more productive and transparent settlement between central and local government. This should aim to re-balance the current grant system to improve incentives for local areas to grow their tax bases. There should also be consideration of ways of improving the transparency of the funding system by seeking ways to reflect more explicitly the shared nature of revenues (from central and local taxation) which support local services.

Grant and incentives   208   Grant is at the centre of the relationship between central and local government and the equalisation process which, while having aims that I support, acts to insulate local authorities from the effects of differences in local tax bases and growth. The impact of this is that, while local authorities see it as a core part of their concern to pay attention to local prosperity and to the needs and future prospects of their citizens and their local areas, there are no coherent or systematic financial incentives that encourage growth either for them or, more importantly, for their communities.

209   There is a strong case for equity and stability to remain key objectives of the grant system. However, in order for local authorities to be able and encouraged to perform their place-shaping role to the full, I believe that a further objective needs to be considered for the funding system – providing financial incentives for local authorities and communities to promote economic prosperity and residential growth.

210   My proposals are not intended to dramatically reduce equalisation or to impact on local government's ability to plan by increasing instability. Rather, I want to find a way to provide space – at the margins, but with enough weight to change local government behaviours – to incentivise local authorities to grow their tax bases and, crucially, to enable local communities to receive some reward for allowing their areas to develop and grow.

211   Providing incentives to grow local tax bases could serve three purposes:

- it could aid a more balanced decision-making process, because financial benefits for the community could be used to compensate those affected through either improved services or reductions in tax bills. In this sense they will help to rebalance the costs and benefits of economic or housing growth by providing clearer local benefits to offset the costs of this growth – such as additional congestion and pressure on services – to the current residents;

- it could help to influence local authority behaviour in general by providing a more direct relationship between local authority finances and the health of the local economy encouraging investment to make the area attractive to businesses and to strengthen the local skills base;

- it could provide a potential source of revenue which could be used for local investment in measures to promote growth, such as infrastructure improvement, which may need long term-planning and greater certainty over funding mechanisms.

Incentives within the system   212   While limited incentive schemes do exist, I believe that incentives rooted in the wider system of local government finance could have the potential to be a more constant feature of local-central relations and could, over time, embed a different relationship between authorities and their tax base, creating better incentives to support growth and prosperity.

213   The complexity and short-term nature of the Local Authority Business Growth Incentives (LABGI) scheme are felt to reduce its incentive effects. A significant part of the scheme's complexity can be ascribed to the objectives the Government set when designing it, as LABGI attempts to redistribute resources for policy reasons at the same time as providing a growth incentive based on increases in the size of the tax base. In the short term, reform of LABGI seems likely to be the most effective way to continue to provide business growth incentives to local authorities. That reform needs to deliver a more transparent and long-term scheme.

214   There is potential, however, to introduce incentives into the grant system to ensure better reward for growing both residential and business tax bases. The current design of the grant distribution system through the four-block model, based as it is on relative measures of tax raising capacity, means that it is difficult to implement such schemes for residential or business growth. A fuller explanation of the current grant regime is provided at Annex A. This means, therefore, that changes to the grant system should be considered to accommodate incentives on council and business rates.

Shared revenues   215   There are some services which are clearly driven by a national promise, and there is a case, in principle at least, for arguing that these should be funded from national taxation in order that it is clear that central government is, in some sense, responsible for these services. Conversely, there are issues that are rightly local, and again there could, in principle, be a case for funding these from local resources.

216   However, there are many service areas where it is not possible to distinguish clearly between national and local responsibilities. Such services can be considered a shared responsibility and, given this, there is benefit, in terms of accountability, in such services being funded more explicitly from a shared source of revenue.

217   Better information about the degree to which both national and local taxation support local services should improve public understanding of the cost of services and how they are funded. This could make it easier to manage expectations, and pressures, and to have a more informed discussion about the priorities for local services.

A shared revenue to support shared services

218   In the short term, I am interested in there being a clear annual statement of the proportion of national taxation that is used for local services. Local authorities should be able to use council tax bills and accompanying leaflets to communicate this information if they choose. This would require a relaxation in the regulations that prescribe the information that can go onto these documents and the form they take.

Assigning taxes

219   There are more radical options that can be envisaged in relation to shared revenues, such as dedicating part of income tax to support local authorities expenditure – this is formally known as assignment.

220   These options could also give local government access to a buoyant form of tax whose yield would grow and fall back in line with the general economy, without the rate having to be increased as is the case in council tax. Income from this buoyancy could be used to relieve the pressure on council tax or services. It is important to recognise that this is not 'free' money but would represent a transfer – in the form of buoyancy – from central to local government.

221   Such changes would be a radical departure for the way in which national taxation is currently used to support local services and could only be seriously considered as part of a 'new deal' between local and central government. If local government had access to a buoyant tax source central government could properly expect it to act with more self-reliance and be less concerned about the detail of the grant settlement.

222   I examine a range of options for assignment in the report. These are in the main illustrative with the aim to stimulate thinking and debate on whether assignment could be a viable and positive way of funding local government in England. I conclude there would be merit in central government considering introducing a form of national assignment.

A DEVELOPMENTAL APPROACH

223   I have sought to describe a vision of local authorities as part of a single system of government, playing a place-shaping role, engaging with citizens to build an understanding of their needs and preferences, working with central government and contributing to greater satisfaction and the more efficient use of resources. To go back to the question that the Layfield Committee posed, I do believe that many of the decisions of government can and should be taken in different places, by people of diverse experience, associations, background and political persuasion.

224   Achieving this vision will take time. It requires not just the development of new relationships between local and central government, but also a strengthening of public understanding of, trust in and support for local government (and indeed, to a significant extent, government in general). For some of the more radical possibilities discussed during the report to be feasible, a much greater level of public confidence in local government will be needed. Reflecting this, I seek to set out an approach that is explicitly developmental – that acknowledges that trust and relationships need to be built, and seeks to use a wide-ranging but reasonably modest set of short-term changes to create the space and the mutual understanding needed for wider reforms in the future.

Changing behaviours

225   One of the conclusions that I have drawn from my work is that legal obstacles are not, in the main, the major hindrance to local government performing its place-shaping role. While I have

made a number of recommendations for substantive legal and policy changes for the Government to implement, more important is that local authorities develop a sense of powerfulness and capability to perform their place-shaping role and change their behaviours to pursue that goal.

226 Changes in behaviours will be important for both central and local government, including:

- for local government, the recognition of the place-shaping role and a greater focus on engagement with citizens and being recognised as a champion of efficiency; and

- for central government, providing greater flexibility for local authorities and the space for local decisions on priorities, with a reduction in centrally determined and monitored targets and the pressures these can create. The Comprehensive Spending Review later this year offers a key opportunity to implement changes, and particularly to ensure a corporate approach across government to the necessary prioritisation and resourcing.

Legislative and policy changes 227 The Government also needs to take action in the short term to ensure a sustainable finance system, including:

- making council tax fairer through changes to council tax benefit, including increased take-up, and increasing local flexibility to manage pressures on council tax;

- a package of measures on business rates to promote economic prosperity, provide local flexibility and capacity to invest, and support improved relationships between local authorities and businesses;

- building incentives into the system to enable communities to receive some of the financial benefits of growth and development;

- enabling local authorities to show clearly on council tax bills what proportion of national taxation is being used to support local services;

- other measures to support the place-shaping role, particularly with regard to local government's role in fostering economic prosperity.

228 Council tax should be retained as a local tax. In order to underpin its sustainablity, the Government should conduct a revaluation of properties in the near future – with appropriate transitional protection – and introduce a process of regular revaluation for the future.

Options for future governments 229 However, even a reformed council tax would still have problems such as lack of buoyancy. Over time, more radical reforms could be considered to take further pressure off council tax, to improve the fairness of the local taxation system and to further increase flexibility and choice.

230 Successful implementation of my recommendations, combined with behavioural change by central government and local authorities, should allow future governments greater space to consider options which are at present not technically or politically practical, including;

- more substantial changes such as a more radical reform of council tax or the introduction of a local income tax as a partial or full replacement for council tax, or the assignment of a fixed proportion of national taxation to local government; and

- reforms to business rates, such as re-localisation, together with the power to reduce the tax rate.

Constitutional settlement	231 In order to reinforce and support this process of change, central and local government should negotiate a contractual agreement which sets out what central government requires of local government, how it should be funded, and the ways in which central government should appropriately influence and control other aspects of local government activity. That agreement should be open to external and parliamentary scrutiny.

CONCLUSION

232   My definition of place-shaping as the modern role of local government within a single system of government is intended to reflect the ambitions which are shared by both local and central government for the country we live in. What I have set out is not an agenda for technical and administrative changes, but a basis for the improvement of public trust and satisfaction through closer engagement, honest debate and transparent decision-making. That is something that all involved in government, at whatever level, should care about. It is about strong, self-confident communities shaping their destinies and making choices for themselves.

233   There is no simple solution to the problems affecting the system of local government and local government funding. These are profoundly complex and difficult issues which have their roots not only in legislation, but also in behaviours and deeply ingrained expectations on the part of local government, central government and the public they serve. Any reform will involve political trade-offs and is likely to have widespread impacts, and will therefore require a strong case for change. I have sought throughout my work, and throughout this report, to recognise the complexity and diversity of the country we live in and the relationships we share, while focusing on the genuine choices we have to make in developing and empowering government to act in the best interests of all our communities.

Part I

Background to the Inquiry

Chapter 1   **Local government: a continuing debate**

A short history of the recent events and political perspectives that have shaped local government, and a brief review of the Inquiry's progress.

Chapter 2   **Local government in the 21st century: what is it for?**

The modern role of local government, and the key challenges facing society in the 21st century to which local government can contribute.

1

Local government: a continuing debate

Summary

This chapter argues that neither council tax nor the wider debates on the role and funding of local government can be understood without an appreciation of the events and the politics of the past 30 years.

The Layfield Committee, which reported in 1976, felt that perhaps the most important issue was one of principle: whether all important governmental decisions should be taken by national government, or whether they could be made differently in different places. That dilemma has never been resolved.

The role of the state and the efficiency and responsiveness of publicly provided services, including local government, were challenged by the Conservative governments of the 1980s. Changes – the legacy of which remain with us today – included the introduction of the community charge (more popularly known as the poll tax), the nationalisation of business rates and the creation of central government's capping powers.

Since 1997, the Government has delivered devolution to Scotland, Wales and Northern Ireland, and re-established city-wide government in London. It has also provided additional resources, and introduced reforms, which have contributed to significant improvements in public services. However, its approach has also involved more detailed oversight of local policy decisions and a reduction in local flexibility.

The 2006 Local Government White Paper, *Strong and Prosperous Communities*, is a welcome step towards greater flexibility and local choice, though much will depend on how the Government implements its measures. In turn, there is a stretching challenge for local government to respond to this opportunity and new direction.

Looking back over a longer perspective, it is possible to discern three different roles for local government: it has been a way for communities to organise and represent themselves; it has been a vehicle for them to raise resources for investment in infrastructure and local improvement; and more recently it has become an important element of the welfare state, managing the delivery of key public services. In order to fully appreciate the potential role for local government in the future, we need to consider all three of these functions.

INTRODUCTION

1.1   Concern about the level of council tax, and continuing debates, particularly around local government's dependence on central funding, form the immediate background to my Inquiry into Local Government. However, neither the council tax itself nor the wider debates on the role and funding of local government can properly be understood without an appreciation of the events, and the political perspectives of the past 30 years, since a similar period of large increases in local taxation in the early 1970s and the establishment of the Layfield Committee on Local Government Finance in 1974. It is also important to consider some of the events that have taken place during my work, in particular the recent Local Government White Paper, *Strong and Prosperous*

Communities. This chapter therefore gives a brief history of the past three decades, and of the progress of the Inquiry to provide the necessary context.

1.2   In addition, it includes a longer history of local government. The purpose of this is to show that while local government has an important role in delivering major public services such as education and social services, that role is a development of, and in addition to, its initial purpose and origins in the need and desire of communities to govern themselves, to regulate behaviour, and to deal with conflicts. That longer backdrop is an important context for the views I develop in this report on the modern role for local government.

CONTEXT FOR THE INQUIRY

The past 30 years

Rates rises in the 1970s and the Layfield Committee 1.3   The economic difficulties of the early 1970s associated with the oil price hikes of 1973, which brought to an end the period of post-war economic growth and stability, caused problems for central and local government alike. Growing central resources were no longer available to support rising local spending – Tony Crosland, then Secretary of State for the Environment, famously told local authorities in 1975 that "the party's over" – and price inflation contributed to large increases in local rates bills, creating substantial public concern and opposition. It was in this context that in 1974, Sir Frank Layfield and his committee were asked to make recommendations for improving the system of local government finance.

1.4   When the Layfield Committee reported in 1976, it identified confusion in accountability as the major weakness in the system of local government finance. It argued that a fundamental political choice was needed as to where accountability lay for local government finance. It offered two alternative approaches, one based on central accountability and one on local accountability. The Committee felt that arguably the most important issue was:

> *whether all important governmental decisions affecting people's lives and livelihood should be taken in one place on the basis of national policies; or whether many of the decisions could not as well, or better, be taken in different places, by people of diverse experience, associations, background and political persuasion.*[1]

1.5   The government of the day rejected Layfield's view that an explicit choice was needed, and in any case, decisions were overtaken; first by further economic difficulties in the form of the International Monetary Fund crisis of 1976, and then by the advent of a new political philosophy with the victory of the Conservative Party in 1979. However, one could argue that the dilemma Layfield identified has never been resolved, and continues to affect the way we approach the role of local government today.

Changes in the 1980s 1.6   The role of the state, and the efficiency and responsiveness of publicly provided services, were both radically challenged by the Conservative governments of the 1980s. This challenge had far-reaching implications for national services (for example in the privatisation of state-owned assets and companies) but the government also implemented a substantial programme of change in local government. A key part of this was the attempt to tackle what was perceived as excessive spending by local authorities and weak accountability for that spending. The government used changes to the grant system and the introduction of budget capping powers to pursue its agenda, and the community charge (which replaced domestic rates in 1990) was also intended to provide better accountability by sharpening the local impact of 'over-spending' and extending local taxation to people who had not previously paid domestic rates.

---

[1] HMSO, *Local Government Finance: Report of the Committee of Inquiry*, 1976.

1.7   The community charge sparked considerable opposition, and its unpopularity was a factor in Margaret Thatcher's resignation as Prime Minister. Although it was replaced in 1993 by the council tax, the legacy of the community charge and the other changes of the 1980s continue to influence the present. The structure of the council tax, with its elements of both personal and property taxation, the nationalisation of business rates, the continued interest of central government in controlling local budgets, and – I would argue – some of the current distrust of local government and local taxation, can all be traced back to the events and decisions of the late 1980s.

1.8   Another important theme during the 1980s and early 1990s was the need to improve the responsiveness and efficiency of public services. The government was concerned that public services were too often run in the interests of producers, and that they needed to be held in check by stronger market pressures. It therefore took a number of steps, including: moving responsibilities to newly appointed bodies such as Training and Enterprise Councils; creating more market incentives and rules (for example, through the introduction of compulsory competitive tendering) and increasing and formalising the inspection and regulation of public services.[2]

Reform since 1997   1.9   The present Government was elected in 1997, promising (and subsequently delivering) new investment and improvements in public services, as well as action to tackle inequality and disadvantage. It also devolved power to devolved governments in Scotland, Wales and Northern Ireland, and re-established city-wide government in London. In later years it also proposed to devolve powers to elected regional assemblies in England, though these proposals were not implemented due to their rejection in a referendum in the North East in 2004.

1.10   The Government's devolution agenda recognises that different communities should be enabled to make their own choices and take their own decisions, but there has been a tension between that recognition and some of the ways in which the improvement and reform of public services have been delivered, as the Government's approach has involved taking a number of directive and interventionist steps towards local government. There has been more detailed engagement in local policy decisions, a rapid growth in ring-fenced and specific grants, and increased control over education spending. The use of inspections and targets has been expanded substantially, focused not just on outputs and outcomes for individuals and communities, but also on the capacity of local government as an institution.

1.11   Enhancing individual choice in public services that were previously managed through collective choices has also become more important as a way of seeking to make services more responsive to service users' preferences, for example in the health service, in school autonomy and choice, and through the extension of direct payments in social care (though as I noted in my May 2006 report, *National prosperity, local choice and civic engagement*, this policy in particular built on the innovation of pioneering local authorities in the 1980s).

1.12   It is important to acknowledge that, in many policy areas, the additional resources made available by the Government, and the strong focus on improvement, partly reflected in the challenging targets set for departments, agencies and local authorities, have led to significant improvements in performance. The Government has also taken action to expand the power and flexibility of local authorities, through the recognition of their community leadership role in local decision-making, and through specific measures such as the introduction of the well-being power and prudential borrowing. Innovations such as Local Public Service Agreements and Local Area Agreements, developed with contributions from local government, have also been welcomed.

---

[2] Stoker, G., *Transforming Local Governance: From Thatcherism to New Labour*, 2004.

Recent developments

The context and progress of the Inquiry

1.13 While recent debates on the role of local government and the reform of public services are an important background, it was a set of financial issues that led to my Inquiry being established in summer 2004.

1.14 First, a series of substantial increases in council tax, including a record average increase of 12.9 per cent in 2003, had sparked considerable and continuing public concern and opposition, and the reintroduction of capping by the Government. Second, the Government had, along with local authorities, experts and partners, been considering the future of local government funding, and in particular the dependence of local government on central government grants. The Balance of Funding Review (chaired by Nick Raynsford MP, then Minister for Local Government), which ran from 2003 to 2004, considered the various means by which the balance of funding between local and central sources could be changed, particularly through the reform of council tax, the localisation of business rates and/or the introduction of a local income tax or other new local taxes. Finally, at the same time (indeed, in substantial part because of work commissioned by the Review) it was becoming increasingly clear that the revaluation of domestic properties for council tax in England would be a significant event, with financial implications (both positive and negative) for many people.

1.15 It was in the context of these events – and therefore of significant public and political interest in the future of local government finance – that I was asked, in July 2004, by the Chancellor and the Deputy Prime Minister to investigate and make recommendations on local government funding (the full terms of reference are set out at the end of this report). During my work on the funding remit, I came to the conclusion that changes to the finance system could not proceed effectively without the role of local government being more clearly established. Following discussions with ministers, they asked me, in September 2005, to extend my remit to look at the role and function of local government (at which point they also made the decision to delay the council tax revaluation). The final stage of my work has been the consideration of the Barker Review of Land Use Planning, the Eddington Transport Study and the Leitch Review of Skills, three independent reviews with significant implications for local government.

1.16 Over the course of the Inquiry I have taken pains to consult widely with experts, stakeholders and the public, and to visit a host of towns, cities and rural areas across the country. Details of those activities have been published in previous reports, in a number of stand-alone documents, and in the annexes to this report. Chart 1.1 shows the places that I and members of my team visited, and where we held events.

Chart 1.1: Events and visits during the Lyons Inquiry

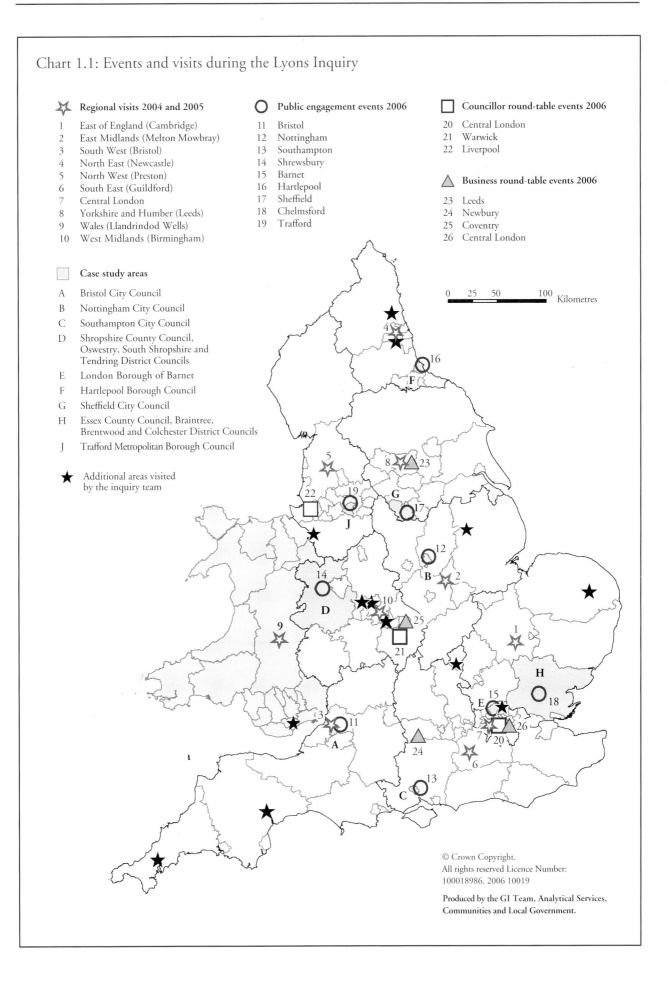

☆ **Regional visits 2004 and 2005**

1 East of England (Cambridge)
2 East Midlands (Melton Mowbray)
3 South West (Bristol)
4 North East (Newcastle)
5 North West (Preston)
6 South East (Guildford)
7 Central London
8 Yorkshire and Humber (Leeds)
9 Wales (Llandrindod Wells)
10 West Midlands (Birmingham)

○ **Public engagement events 2006**

11 Bristol
12 Nottingham
13 Southampton
14 Shrewsbury
15 Barnet
16 Hartlepool
17 Sheffield
18 Chelmsford
19 Trafford

□ **Councillor round-table events 2006**

20 Central London
21 Warwick
22 Liverpool

△ **Business round-table events 2006**

23 Leeds
24 Newbury
25 Coventry
26 Central London

▢ **Case study areas**

A Bristol City Council
B Nottingham City Council
C Southampton City Council
D Shropshire County Council, Oswestry, South Shropshire and Tendring District Councils
E London Borough of Barnet
F Hartlepool Borough Council
G Sheffield City Council
H Essex County Council, Braintree, Brentwood and Colchester District Councils
J Trafford Metropolitan Borough Council

★ Additional areas visited by the inquiry team

0   25   50   100
                                    Kilometres

Produced by the GI Team, Analytical Services,
Communities and Local Government.

1.17   During the Inquiry I have periodically set out my thinking on both funding and function issues. My *Interim Report and Consultation Paper*, published in December 2005, set out some early views on both. My May 2006 report, *National prosperity, local choice and civic engagement*, set out my conclusions on the role of local government, emphasising the advantages to be secured from appropriate choice and flexibility at the local level, in order for communities to make their own decisions. I also presented my views on the strategic role of local government for the future, a role I call 'place-shaping', which I discuss in more detail later in this report.

The Local Government White Paper

1.18   The Government has, following my May 2006 report and other contributions such as the Local Government Association's *Closer to People and Places – A New Vision for Local Government*, set out its agenda for the future direction of local government in *Strong and Prosperous Communities – the Local Government White Paper*, published in October 2006. The White Paper is intended to devolve more power to the local level and reduce the level of central prescription, while strengthening leadership and expanding the opportunities for local people to influence local decision-making.

1.19   I welcome the direction set out by the White Paper. It builds on the analysis and argument I presented in my May 2006 report and acknowledges local government's strategic role in place-shaping. The commitments to greater devolution of choices to local communities and local government and to a reduction in central requirements, in order to give greater space for local priorities to be pursued are positive developments, as is the key role for local authorities in convening the work of the wider public sector at local level.

1.20   However, it is clear that the White Paper itself is only the beginning of a process, and much will depend on how it is implemented, and on how both central and local government respond to it. The development of a more constructive and healthier relationship between central and local government, with greater space for local communities to make their own decisions, will require continued effort and changes. Those changes will be at least as much about behaviours and expectations as they are about legislation and powers. The Government as a whole, and individual ministers within it, will need to ensure that their decisions provide local communities with the space to make their own choices. The Government will need to accept that allowing local communities to choose services better tailored to their needs and desires will mean variation across the country (though of course we by no means have uniformity at the present), and that this is a positive development because of the potential it offers for meeting different local preferences about the use of limited resources. Less emphasis should be placed on national targets and standards, along with a much lighter touch from the centre: less inspection; less centrally accountable performance management; and a reduced emphasis on national guidance. Much will also depend upon the development of a funding regime – both in terms of taxation and grant funding – that supports local flexibility and responsiveness.

1.21   In turn, there is a stretching challenge for local government to respond to this opportunity and new direction. With a reduced set of national targets and expectations, local authorities will need to engage more effectively with citizens and communities, and to seek to respond properly to local challenge and scrutiny. They will also need to become the acknowledged champions of value for money and the effective use of taxpayers resources. To fulfil their place-shaping role, authorities will need to develop a new confidence and a new sense of powerfulness, and they must take greater responsibility for their own performance and improvement. While there may be a larger role than in the past for the Local Government Association and the Improvement and Development Agency in providing advice and support – reflecting a greater sense of collective responsibility within local government – the ultimate objective must be for councils to become more self-reliant and to recognise when they need to seek external support and guidance. This report sets out how I think local and central government can both work to develop their relationship and their own behaviours to build a new role for local government in the 21st century.

THE HISTORY OF LOCAL GOVERNMENT

1.22   The history of local government shows how communities have made collective decisions in the past, and how the context for those decisions has changed over time. I deliberately begin this summary in the middle ages, not because our system of local government's roots in the distant past give it a special legitimacy in the modern world, but because it illustrates that the necessity for, and the challenges of, collective action and choice have existed for many centuries.

The origins of local government

1.23   Local government in England has a long and complex history, with its origins lying as far back as the various independent kingdoms of the early middle ages, which in some cases form the basis of our modern units of local government.

1.24   The assertion of royal power, and royal desire to levy taxes and to maintain law and order throughout the country, has been a significant influence on the development of local institutions, seen for example in the introduction of a system of counties and hundreds in the 10th and 11th centuries, and in the appointment of Justices of the Peace from the 14th century. However, we should not neglect the long history of the assertion of local identity, and the desire of communities to protect and extend their powers and privileges, which is as much responsible for the development of successful local institutions. Providing arrangements for building consensus, for dealing with conflicts and for regulating behaviours, was essential if local communities were to act effectively. In the towns in particular, but also elsewhere, it is possible to trace the development of local identities and assertions of local interest against external forces. Parish and county meetings, town assemblies and councils offered the opportunity for local debate, decision-making and the development of collective views.[3] One historian, writing of the pre-Norman period, suggests that:

> *Local government ... was a collaborative venture involving royal officials, local notables, and the entire free (male) population of the shire, hundred or borough acting in accordance with royal directives and legislation as well as the "folk law" preserved in the collective memory of the area.*[4]

1.25   Indeed, it would be anachronistic to think that royal power could be easily asserted without the consent of powerful local figures. To secure its objectives, royal power had to work with locally appointed officials and the influence of local elites, and indeed this remained the case even as the state became more powerful in the 16th and 17th centuries.[5] Royal appointments were often chosen from the important men of the area, and a Crown-appointed official who was unacceptable to the political community of an area might well have difficulty in successfully carrying out his responsibilities.

1.26   Local institutions also provided the context for the expression of the political views and the political influence of communities. Numerous royal charters, including King John's explicit acceptance in Magna Carta that "the city of London shall enjoy all its ancient liberties and free customs, both by land and by water" provide evidence of the ability of economically powerful and organised communities such as London to pursue their own interests. Boroughs and counties began to return members to Parliament to represent their interests in the 13th century, during the early stages of the development of that institution. They remained important players in national politics and conflicts through to the Civil War, the Restoration and well beyond.[6] Indeed, some historians see the role of local representatives, who were not beholden to the Crown and were able

---

[3] Reynolds, S., *Kingdoms and Communities in Western Europe 900-1300*, 1984.
[4] Ertmann, T., *Birth of the Leviathan: Building States and Regimes in Medieval and Early Modern Europe*, 1997.
[5] Archer, I., in Clark, P. (ed.), *Cambridge Urban History of Britain*, vol. 2, 2000.
[6] Archer, in Clark, *Cambridge Urban History of Britain*.

to scrutinise and challenge it through Parliament, as a crucial contribution to England's growing success and power in the 17th century.[7]

1.27   In terms of their specific responsibilities in this early period, the most important activity in the counties was the administration of justice and the maintenance of law and order, though they also dealt with a number of other matters including the building and maintenance of bridges. In the towns, the problems associated with managing collective interests and providing public goods were even more clearly evident. Medieval and early modern towns – through town councils, and sometimes through associations of craftsmen – had a role not just in the administration of justice, but also in regulating weights and measures, and in providing necessary public infrastructure such as marketplaces, walls, harbours, courts and refuse disposal sites. Such investments were vital to their continued economic success.

1.28   It is important to acknowledge the complexity of local institutional arrangements in this period. There was no pre-eminent locally representative body, nor a system of multi-purpose local government as we think of it today. The term 'local government' was not used until 1835, and even then it was not used in a sense that implied any general system as we would understand it.[8] Aside from the counties and the boroughs, where magistrates or elected or appointed councils ran the various administrative and legal functions, there was a host of other arrangements for dealing with different aspects of governance and the needs of different localities. Sources of legitimacy and power were often functionally focused and spread across different organisations. For example, the parishes dealt with poor relief, and there were usually various boards of appointed commissioners responsible for activities such as lighting and paving.

Improvement and industrialisation

1.29   While making improvements to localities was an element of the activities of some local authorities in earlier centuries, Liverpool's Improvement Act of 1748 is seen by historians as a milestone in the popularity of such legislation. 'Improvement' often included investment in street lighting, paving and security, but it might also include spending on social and cultural activities to attract people to places. For example, in 1733 the Corporation of York encouraged the building of a theatre and sponsored the local races.[9] Behaviour and development were also sometimes subject to local regulation – for example, a Private Act for Dover in 1810 prevented new houses from having overhanging balconies because of concerns about the look of the streets, and seaside towns sometimes regulated the activities of sea bathers.[10]

1.30   This expansion of activity led to the further multiplication of boards and commissioners responsible for different aspects of local public activity and infrastructure. These included the turnpike trusts, which maintained the roads and levied tolls, and improvement boards responsible for lighting, paving and the watch. These bodies were generally promoted by members of the locality through the parish vestry, the county or borough, and sometimes through commissioners, but, they had to be established through a private act of Parliament (since local government in the UK has no formal constitutional status or protection, and no inherent powers of its own, unlike in many other countries).[11] Such acts increased substantially in number during the 18th century.

[7] Ertmann, *Birth of the Leviathan*.

[8] Keith-Lucas, B., *The Unreformed Local Government System*, 1980.

[9] Innes, J. and Rogers, N. in Clark, *Cambridge Urban History of Britain*.

[10] Keith-Lucas, *The Unreformed Local Government System*.

[11] Scottish Office Central Research Unit, *The Constitutional Status of Local Government in Other Countries*, 1998.

1.31   As the power of Parliament grew, it replaced the Crown as the institution responsible for the central framework of laws within which local government functioned. The Municipal Corporations Act of 1835 is often seen as the beginning of modern local government, as it substantially reformed the old boroughs and corporations, many of which had degenerated into closed arrangements centred on the power to elect a Member of Parliament (the so-called 'rotten boroughs') and instituted elected town councils. However, it did not give these councils particularly substantial powers in their own right and the system of governance remained fragmented. Some significant towns did not set up such councils for a number of years afterwards, and in the meantime continued to be governed through traditional arrangements such as parish vestries. Even new institutions, such as the locally elected school boards created in 1870, might remain separate from the council. Significant changes to the governance of non-urban areas did not take place until the introduction of county councils in 1888, with districts (urban and rural) created in 1894.

1.32   However, it was in the urban areas that the new challenges of the 19th century, caused by industrialisation and increasingly dense populations, required a substantial response. During this period, local communities, working through the various kinds of authority, engaged in investment and the regulation of private activity to address problems with water supply, sewerage and sanitation, the quality of housing, and the provision of other utilities and services. In many cases, the initiative came from the local community, empowered through local or private acts of Parliament, making the relationship with Parliament at least as important as that with the executive part of central government. In other cases, local bodies were enabled and sometimes prompted by central government.

1.33   The motivation for action was a mixture of enlightened self-interest – disease epidemics affected the rich too, and their economic success often depended on an adequate municipal infrastructure – and moral concern for those living in appalling conditions. There were also many ratepayers who resisted spending to tackle these problems. Indeed, the Public Health Act of 1848 was deliberately designed to circumvent the resistance of many local ratepayers (who, at a time when voters had to own property, dominated political decisions) by providing for local boards of health to be established on petition from just one-fiftieth of local ratepayers. However, the 'civic gospel' of the mid 19th century prompted influential and important citizens to take a lead in developing and improving the infrastructure and the conditions of their towns and cities through the institutions of local government. Local communities made substantial investments in public health services, particularly in the later 19th century, and these improvements made an important contribution (alongside rising standards of living) to the rapid fall in mortality during that period.[12] Local authorities in many areas also developed gas and electricity supplies (which as natural monopolies were not always effectively delivered by private activity, and might also provide surpluses for investment elsewhere) and built schools and hospitals to provide better facilities for local people.

1.34   These expenditures were financed, as local expenditures had been from the early days of local government, through a variety of property taxes known as the rates. There were many different rates levied by different authorities, ranging from the traditional poor rate levied by parishes, to rates for improving paving, drainage and lighting in urban areas. In this period, particularly in the later 19th century, while rates continued to provide the vast majority of revenues, central government began to contribute to local spending through grants to local authorities to support and encourage expenditure on specific services, particularly policing and education. A system of assigned national revenues also played a part in the funding of local authorities between 1888 and 1929 (although it declined in importance after 1912).

---

[12] Millward, in Morris and Trainor (eds.), *Urban Governance: Britain and Beyond since 1750*, 2000; Dawson, in Loughlin et al. (eds.), *Half a Century of Municipal Decline*, 1985.

The growth of the welfare state

1.35   Measures to improve the physical condition of places and to provide the infrastructure necessary for decent health and living standards in urban areas remained important well into the 20th century (for example in the slum clearances of the 1960s and 1970s), although arguments about administrative efficiency and the need for sustained large-scale investment led to the creation of central boards to manage electricity and gas after the Second World War, and the removal of water from local authority control in 1974. Land use planning and the regulation of development also became an important part of local authority responsibilities through measures such as the Town Planning Act of 1909, and even more significantly the Town and Country Planning Act of 1947, which established the basis of the modern system.

1.36   However, the main growth in the activity of government at all levels from the early decades of the 20th century was the development of the welfare state, funded by the country's increasing wealth and motivated by the growing political power of the poor and the working classes. The welfare state was intended to provide a national system of entitlement and support, and it cemented the role of government, particularly central government, in managing a national response to the social and economic challenges of the time. The growth of the welfare state thus had profound implications for the role of local government and its relationship to central government, particularly in the areas of poor relief, housing, health and social care services, and education.

1.37   Since its origins in the 16th century, poor relief had been administered by parishes. However, that structure had never been very satisfactory as it created incentives for the poor to move to places with the most generous support and for administrators to minimise their liability (for example, by making sure pregnant women did not give birth in their parish). The financial responsibility for the poor and those unable to work was taken on by central government in the early decades of the 20th century, culminating in the National Assistance Act of 1948 which formally repealed the Poor Law of 1601.

1.38   Although local authorities took a role in the provision of new housing for working people and the poor, and the clearing of slums, from the late 19th century, it was after the First World War that the large scale construction of council housing began with government subsidies to authorities to build houses. This role continued after the Second World War, with housing seen as an important part of the welfare state.

1.39   The establishment of the National Health Service (NHS) in 1948 was perhaps the most prominent mark of the continuing moves to create a universal national system of support after the Second World War. There were debates at the time over whether the service could or should be administered by local government (as with schools), but the concern for direct ministerial accountability and control led to the establishment of a new, centrally managed, system. (Interestingly, its architect, Aneurin Bevan, later altered his views somewhat, writing in the *Municipal Journal* in the 1950s that subject to radical reorganisation, he supported local authorities managing local health services in an agency capacity).

1.40   While these changes moved some responsibilities from local to national government, local authorities also took on an important role in the welfare state, which quickly became the mainstay of their spending. Personal social services, including the protection and care of children and the elderly, were not included in the NHS, but have over the years become key welfare services. So too has education, now the biggest local authority service. In both, central government was heavily involved, and has become more so, through the growing provision of grants, and also through legislative powers – for example, the 1944 Education Act provided that local education authorities would function under the 'control and direction' of the minister.

1.41 Government grants became increasingly important as a way of funding such services. In addition to grants for specific services, new types of grant were introduced, designed to take account of different levels of needs and resources, and thus to enable the delivery of a more equitable level of services across the country. Sidney and Beatrice Webb had written in 1897 of the need for government intervention to reduce inequalities within the country, and equalising grants had been suggested by Lord Balfour and others in the minority report of the 1901 Royal Commission on Local Taxation. Some equalisation was introduced within London in 1921, following the famous refusal of Poplar Council to collect the precepts for pan-London authorities, such as the London County Council, in protest at the lack of support being provided to the East End by the wealthier parts of London. The block grant introduced in 1929 took some account of both needs and resources, and explicit equalisation was introduced through the Exchequer Equalisation Grant in 1948.[13] Though these grants were essential if authorities everywhere were to deliver expected standards and entitlements, by the early 1970s contemporaries were concerned at the implications of an increasing dependence on grants for local government's flexibility and autonomy. One noted that he could "foresee with alarm the time when local authorities will draw by far the greater part of their funds from the centre".[14]

CONCLUSION

1.42 This takes our history up to the 1970s, with a recognisably modern set of responsibilities for local government, many of them part of a national welfare state. While it does not demonstrate that local government should have any special importance in the modern world, it does show that there are three inter-related but identifiable sets of roles that local government has played and continues to play: as service provider; as a vehicle for investment in public infrastructure; and as an institution of government, a place for debate, discussion and collective decision-making. An analysis of the modern role of local government needs to take into account all three of those roles, and this report seeks to do just that.

[13] Foster, C., Jackman, R. and Perlman, M., *Local Government Finance in a Unitary State*, 1980.
[14] Marshall, *New Revenues for Local Government*, Fabian Research Series 295, 1971.

2 Local government in the 21st century: what is it for?

Summary

This chapter argues that local government enables communities to make necessary collective choices, and has an important role in responding to diversity and distinctiveness, and to modern economic challenges.

While critics question local government's relevance in a modern age and suggest that it can be unresponsive and inefficient, it remains a necessary and important part of our system of government. Our communities are more complex than in the past, which increases the need for local knowledge and understanding, and globalisation is arguably making place more, not less, relevant to economic success. But to be effective, local authorities must engage with citizens and communities to understand their needs, preferences and priorities.

The modern role of local government can be described as 'place-shaping' – the creative use of powers and influence to promote the general well-being of a community and its citizens.

Local government's role in the management and provision of services should include convening the work of other local agencies to pursue the well-being of citizens; providing services, or commissioning them from private and voluntary providers as appropriate; and making full use of the potential of co-production.

Local government thus has an important part to play in contributing to our response as a society to key challenges including building social cohesion in our communities, fostering economic prosperity, and contributing to greater environmental sustainability. It can also help to improve the trust and satisfaction of citizens in government as a whole, and there is a risk that if local government has too little flexibility and scope to respond to views, this can contribute to a more passive, less connected citizenry.

INTRODUCTION

2.1   "Great part of that order which reigns among mankind is not the effect of government. It has its origin in the principles of society and the natural constitution of man. It existed prior to government, and would exist if the formality of government was abolished."[1] So wrote Thomas Paine in 1792. There is much truth in that statement – our ability to create and sustain social bonds, and to form communities of common interest, does not depend on the formal institution of a government, but on our need for help and society, and our ability to join together voluntarily to pursue collective interests.

2.2   But I would argue that there is value in government, as a device which allows us to frame and enforce rules and laws for behaviour, manage the provision of public services, redistribute resources, and manage frameworks for long-term economic, social and environmental sustainability. All of these things require collective action and collective choices, often choices which have to be binding on a whole community or the whole nation if they are to be effective.

---

[1] Paine, T., *The Rights of Man*, 1792.

2.3   Local government is potentially an important part of that system of government – and I believe that it is important we consider it as a component of a single system of government, not as something separate. Local government is an important element of the system of governance around the world, and as Chapter 1 showed, has provided an important contribution to governance in the UK in different ways across the centuries. While today's circumstances and the challenges we face in the future are not the same as they were in the past, they too require collective decisions and collective choices, some of which are best made by smaller communities acting for themselves, rather than by national government.

2.4   This chapter draws on the main political theories about the value of local government, and my own work, to set out what I think the role of local government in the future should be. It then discusses how local government can, through place-shaping and its approach to the delivery and management of services, contribute to the overall well-being of citizens, and sets out what I see as the key challenges and opportunities for local government in the future.

THEORIES OF LOCAL GOVERNMENT

2.5   There are many different arguments about the role and value of local government within a political and constitutional system. While a complete review of them is beyond the scope of this report, a brief consideration of some of the main theories will help to set the scene for my description of the modern role for local government.

Economic efficiency

2.6   Perhaps the most prominent arguments in the whole debate come from an economic efficiency perspective. Such arguments were first set out by utilitarian political thinkers such as John Stuart Mill, but have been developed by many writers since then and underlie many modern theories of local government. I drew heavily on these arguments in setting out the arguments in favour of local government in my May 2006 report, *National prosperity, local choice and civic engagement*.

2.7   This approach seeks to deliver the greatest overall 'welfare' for society from the resources available. A local level of government has a set of potential advantages from this perspective. First, by being close to local circumstances and having local knowledge, local government can undertake or influence activity more effectively and efficiently than a national institution, which must always be somewhat separate from the front line. Second, since local bodies should be more accessible than a national government, and are directly concerned only with one local area, local government can be more engaged with the local community, and hence more responsive. Finally, and most importantly, local government enables different communities to choose to have different sorts of services, different levels of taxation and to define acceptable behaviour in different ways in order to respond to their own needs, preferences and opinions. An economist would say that this helps to increase 'allocative efficiency' – targeting resources at the things that most matter in different places increases the overall level of satisfaction and welfare that can be produced from the limited resources available.

Participation and education

2.8   Local government should be the tier of government in which citizens can most easily get involved, because it is physically closer to them and because there are more opportunities for engagement or participation. For these reasons, local government has been seen as offering an opportunity for citizens to engage with the activities of government and political decision-making more easily than they could at a national level, and thus to learn about the operation of government and society. This was a particular concern in the 19th century as successive extensions of the electoral franchise gave political power to new sections of society. Indeed, it has been argued that "the central justification for local government discretion in the British liberal tradition is ... the problem of developing a society which could sustain and nurture a rational morally educated society".[2]

[2] Chandler, J., 'Liberal Justifications for Local Government in Britain: The Triumph of Expediency over Ethics' in *Political Studies*, forthcoming.

Constraints on government

2.9   Writers with a range of views have argued that the existence of a number of autonomous local governments leads to a number of potential benefits through the fact that they put constraints, either explicit or implicit, on the power of other parts of government.

2.10   From the perspective of the maintenance of liberal democracy, some have argued that the separate political legitimacy of local government, gained through democratic election, guards against national government wielding absolute power. Jones and Stewart, for example, argue that local government is "a guardian of fundamental values" and that it helps to protect liberal democracy through the "diffusion of power in a society which cannot afford concentrating power in one central location".[3]

2.11   From a libertarian standpoint, others, including the famous economist and political philosopher Friedrich Hayek, see competition between local governments for mobile citizens as a constraint on the freedom of action of government (both national and local), and thus as a way of tempering the tendency of governments to expand their power and revenues.[4] A version of this argument suggests that this division of powers can help to preserve the power and operation of markets and private enterprise against the actions of government, and credits such divisions of power with the economic success of the UK and USA in the 18th and 19th centuries respectively.[5]

Liberty and self-government

2.12   The arguments discussed above emphasise the contribution that local government can make to a successful overall system of effective and efficient government, rather than necessarily as something valuable or legitimate in itself. However, other writers have emphasised a greater inherent worth for local government, based on their views on individual liberty. This is not an argument that has tended to have a great deal of support in British political discussions, but it formed the basis for the anti-centralisation arguments of Joshua Toulmin Smith in the 1850s. He argued that:

> *Every man knows best how to manage his affairs; and it is his right and duty to manage them; – points which apply to associated groups of men, in reference to all the affairs which concern them as individual groups.*[6]

2.13   Looking more widely, one can see a related argument in de Tocqueville's writings, for example in his *Democracy in America*. His support for democracy was based on the principle that communities should be sovereign in decisions that affected only those within the community and did not impinge on the freedom of others. He saw municipal independence as "a natural consequence of the principle of the sovereignty of the people".[7] Woodrow Wilson's distinction between structures that have been invited to exist by central government, "like plants in a tended garden", and "self-originated, self-constituted, self-confident, self-sustaining, veritable communities" also reflects something of this approach.[8] In modern political debate, concepts like subsidiarity, and the support for local self-government seen in documents such as the European Charter of Local Self-Government, owe much to these arguments.

---

[3] Jones, G. and Stewart, J., *The Case for Local Government*, 1985.

[4] Hayek, F.A., *The Constitution of Liberty*, 1960; Brennan, G. and Buchanan J.M., *The Power to Tax: Analytical Foundations of a Fiscal Constitution*, 1980.

[5] Weingast, B., 'The Economic Role of Political Institutions: Market-Preserving Federalism and Economic Development', in *Journal of Law, Economics & Organisation*, vol. 11, 1995.

[6] Smith, J.T., *Local Self Government*, quoted in Chandler, 'Liberal Justifications for Local Government'.

[7] De Tocqueville, A., *Democracy in America*, 1835.

[8] Woodrow Wilson, *Constitutional Government in the United States*, New York: Columbia University Press, 1908, pp.182–3, quoted at Martha Derthick (ed.), *Dilemmas of Scale in America's Federal Democracy*, Cambridge University Press, 1999, p.8. According to Derthick, Wilson appears to have been referring to the states rather than localities.

2.14   This line of thinking has some similarities with wider theories about the basis of government, such as those of Hobbes, Locke, Rousseau and Paine. These arguments concentrate on the rationale for, and moral basis of, national governments, but I would argue that the underlying issue – the idea that people have to band together to achieve and protect the benefits of society – applies in certain circumstances to the role of smaller communities and their rights to govern their own affairs.

2.15   It is worth recognising explicitly that the economic efficiency argument described earlier depends in large part on views about individual and collective liberty. The economic efficiency argument is based on a recognition that different communities will have different wishes and preferences and make different collective choices, and argues that allowing communities to make their own choices will lead to the greatest overall welfare. One can see that argument emerging in analyses from a range of different perspectives, including that of Beatrice and Sidney Webb, founders of the Fabian Society and influential figures in the development of local government in the early 20th century. They argued that:

> *The case for a local administration of industries and services rests primarily on the consciousness among inhabitants of a given area, of neighbourhood and of common needs, differing from those of other localities; and of the facility with which neighbours can take counsel together in order to determine for themselves what shall be their mental and physical environment and how it can be best maintained and improved.*[9]

2.16   A combination of these arguments underpinned widespread views on the role of local government in 19th century Britain. The existence of powerful local self-government was seen as something that separated Britain from the rest of Europe, particularly France. For example, in 1855 *The Times* argued that "local self-government is the most distinctive peculiarity of our race and has mainly made England what she is, while the nations of continental Europe are still held in tutelage by their rulers".[10]

Criticisms of local government

2.17   While political and economic theory sets out a potentially powerful and important role for a local tier of government, the institution of local government in this country has come in for significant criticism, particularly in the past three decades. It is worth considering those challenges, for there is much in them that is valid and needs to be acknowledged in setting out the role of local government for the future.

Government is inefficient and unresponsive

2.18   Local government has been criticised for being inefficient and unresponsive, often as one part of a wider critique of government or state action in general. Its critics have argued that, lacking the pressure that comes from operating in a competitive market, and able to take money from citizens by compulsion through taxation, it has little incentive to provide services efficiently, or to take pains to ensure that it provides the services that people want and in the manner they want. These critics fear that governmental bureaucracies, lacking external challenge, are more likely to pursue their own interests and those of provider and professional groups, rather than the interests of the citizen. These sorts of arguments formed part of the justification for a number of reforms of government and the public sector, including local government, during the 1980s and 1990s, which sought to expose services to greater competition and stronger accountability.

---

[9] Quoted in Chandler, 'Liberal Justifications for Local Government'.
[10] *The Times*, 15 November 1855, quoted in Hunt, *Building Jerusalem*, 2004.

2.19   In a related vein, public choice theories have also argued that some of the services provided on the basis of collective choices by local government can and should be made subject to individual choices. Such an approach gets closer to a market situation by allowing each person to choose what best meets their needs, and creating incentives for providers to be responsive to users' choices, and thus should improve satisfaction and efficiency.[11] These theories have supported a number of reforms introduced by the current Government, including several in health, education and housing.

Local choice creates and perpetuates unfairness

2.20   There is a long history of support for the equalisation of resources between communities to tackle deprivation and poverty, often associated with a recognition of the limits of local government as a vehicle for securing those ends, because of its reliance on unequally distributed local tax resources.[12] There are also those who would go further, and argue that the discretion to make different local choices in itself creates undesirable differences within different parts of the nation. The so-called 'postcode lottery' – the idea that it is unfair if access to services, and service standards, differ between areas – is frequently raised by the media and in public debate on public service provision, and it also appeared in the opinion research conducted for the Inquiry. We can perhaps link the concern about this to a sense of national entitlement created by the development of a national welfare state over the past century. Council tax has also been heavily criticised as contributing to unfairness because of its design, a subject to which I will return later.

Place and locality are no longer relevant

2.21   A final challenge to the institution of local government concerns the power and importance of place in modern society. Increasingly rapid communications and cheaper transport, and a growing concern about global, rather than local, issues potentially reduce the importance of place and the relevance of locality in both the social and economic spheres.

2.22   From a social perspective, some would argue that the greater speed and lower cost of travel and communication, both within one country and across the world, are reducing the importance of place as a way of organising our lives and framing our identities. We construct our identities in a more complex way, and we may not have the social and family relationships at a local level that we once did, because we can now maintain social connections across a much wider area and with a larger group of people. As one academic puts it, "individuals are free to build relations and communities across space, throwing into disarray the old hierarchical order of local communities."[13] That potentially means that people are less interested in, and feel less connected with, their immediate community, and that decisions made on the basis of communities defined by geography risk being arbitrary, rather than responsive to the needs of differentiated communities. For example, a study of community identity in shire areas of England in the mid-1990s found that "the largest group [of people] have no sense of attachment to any of their neighbourhood/village, their district or their county. Nearly one in three fall into this category."[14]

2.23   Related arguments about the impact of changes in information and communications technology and transportation suggest that places will become less important for understanding patterns of economic activity and pursuing economic prosperity. For example, while suggesting that the notion that 'geography is dead' is only half true, Kevin Kelly argues that "the new economy operates in a 'space' rather than a place, and over time more and more economic transactions will migrate to this new space".[15] The importance of government action, and particularly that of local action, is much less important in the pursuit of economic prosperity in such an analysis, and will become less so in the future.

---

[11] Le Grand, J., *Motivation, Agency and Public Policy: Of Knights and Knaves, Pawns and Queens*, 2003.

[12] See, for example, Walker, D., *In Praise Of Centralism*, Catalyst, 2002.

[13] Strassoldo, R., 'Globalism and localism: Theoretical reflections and some evidence' in Zdravko Mlinar (ed.), *Globalization and Territorial Identities*, 1992.

[14] Young, K., Gosschalk, B. and Hatter, W., *In Search of Community Identity*, Joseph Rowntree Foundation, 1996.

[15] Kelly, K., 'New Roles for the New Economy', 1998.

2.24   These criticisms of the legitimacy and value of local government all have some validity. However, I do not believe that they tell the whole story, nor, where they seek to provide solutions to the problems they identify, that those solutions deal with all of the issues involved in collective decision-making, and the management of public services. Informed by this discussion, I now go on to set out my conception of the modern role for local government.

THE MODERN ROLE FOR LOCAL GOVERNMENT

2.25   We need a new vision for local government's role, which combines its role as a place for discussion, representation and decision-making with its role as deliverer of the welfare state and public services, and a desire to achieve efficient and responsive services and government. As I will shortly discuss, my concept of place-shaping aims to encompass all these elements. In considering this issue, it is important to see local government as part of a single system of government, focused on meeting the needs of citizens.

Pursuing the well-being of citizens

2.26   The arguments in favour of local government as a device for allocating public resources and effort efficiently and effectively to secure the well-being of citizens remain strong and compelling. While competitive markets, in which individuals make free choices about where and how they spend their money, are the most efficient approach to the allocation of resources in many situations, and while quasi-market approaches can be used in some public services to enhance the quality and responsiveness of provision, some issues remain resolutely collective. This includes the provision of what an economist would call 'public goods', but also decisions about the best use of public money and the management of other publicly subsidised services in particular places.[16] That does not necessarily mean that those services need to be publicly owned and directly provided, but it does mean that there must be the capacity for collective action and choices about the use of public revenues. Local government has a unique role in that it can not only exploit its local basis and knowledge, but it is also the sole body in the locality which has a responsibility for stewardship of that place, and accountability to all the citizens in the area and a responsibility to enhance their well-being.

2.27   The need for local government to have space and flexibility to act on local preferences and choices is strengthened by the fact that, while people have sought to define measures of well-being, there is no single definition or blueprint for how governments should act to improve it. Indeed, there are significant risks in any one person, or central government, or an inspectorate, defining and measuring well-being as an indicator of success, because all individuals, and all communities, are different. What a community most values and would benefit from at a particular point in time will not necessarily be the same at a different time or in a different area. Economists and philosophers have long grappled with this dilemma. The best practical solution is to allow people to make their own choices – in the language of economists, to show their 'revealed preferences'.[17] In considering how best to improve the well-being of local communities, similar questions arise – while it may not be possible or desirable for people to make individual choices, we can and should give people the choice to make decisions as communities when individual choices are not possible.

---

[16]   The economic definition of a public good is one which is non-excludable (once provided, no-one can be prevented from benefiting from it) and non-rival (one person's consumption does not diminish the amount another person can consume). Local government services which are to some extent public goods include street-lighting and parks and open spaces.

[17]   See, among many others, Dowding, K., *A Defence of Revealed Preference Analysis*, London School of Economics, 2002.

2.28   For this reason I am in principle attracted to giving satisfaction greater weight as a measure of well-being, because it can reflect the opinions of local people themselves – in fact explicitly because it is a subjective measure, rather than being defined on behalf of local communities by distant bureaucrats or experts. I recognise this raises significant challenges, since satisfaction is often not a consistent measure of service quality or well-being over time or between areas, but nevertheless I want to recognise the value of people's own conception of what is important to them, rather than designing systems which assume that one definition of well-being can capture what is important for all communities or all individuals.

Place remains relevant

2.29   For this analysis to have weight, we need to be confident that geographically defined communities are still relevant, that needs and preferences do vary between places, and that some issues will affect some communities in different ways than they will affect others. Changes in communications and individual mobility are undoubtedly changing the way people look at the world, and their ability to sustain contact, and feelings of community well beyond the boundaries imposed by geographically defined communities.

2.30   However, the fact that our communities are now more complex than in the past, because of social changes and greater mobility and cultural and ethnic diversity, can in some cases accentuate the need for local knowledge and understanding. The arguments for a local role in determining the actions of government and the provision of public services are, in fact, becoming stronger as our understanding of the multi-faceted nature of social and economic problems grows, and as our aspirations to solve them and to govern uncertainty and diversity increase. A recent study by the Tavistock Institute concluded that the need for distinctive responses will become stronger in the future as our society becomes more complex and more diverse:

> *in 2015 many of the pressures on government will manifest most dramatically at a local level. More flexibility and responsiveness at a local level would significantly enhance government's capacity to meet those challenges successfully: to enhance life chances; improve the responsiveness of the economy; regulate and change behaviour; and address social tensions and conflicts.*[18]

2.31   There are also a number of arguments which show that locality and place are still relevant as a focus for collective decisions. Analysis in my May report showed that the people of different local authority areas do have different views, both on what it is that makes somewhere a good place to live, and on what they would prioritise for improvement in their area. Other academic studies confirm this, demonstrating that the people of different local areas would choose to spend additional resources in different ways.[19] Research shows that many people continue to feel a strong sense of attachment to the local level – though this attachment is often at a lower level than that represented by our present administrative boundaries, something which poses a challenge to local authorities.[20]

2.32   In addition, a host of issues remain fundamentally local issues because of the scope of their impact. That is particularly the case for matters concerned with land use planning – the location of new housing, the accessibility of public services, shops and businesses, and the impact on the environment and local public space of new development, for example, are never likely to be issues that fail to spark local interest, support and opposition.

---

[18] Tavistock Institute, *All Our Futures*, ODPM, 2006.

[19] Dowding, K. and Mergoupis, T., *Local government and its discontents: citizen preferences for local services*, Economic and Social Research Council, 2005.

[20] Young, K. et al., *In search of community identity*; see also research conducted for the Boundary Committee for England for the local government reviews in the North East at www.boundarycommittee.org.uk

2.33 It is also clear that place still matters a great deal from an economic perspective – indeed some would argue that globalisation and the increasing mobility of highly skilled people and firms makes place more important as a competitive asset, and thus puts more of a premium on the management of that asset. Different theories give different explanations about why some places succeed and others do not – but all identify local characteristics as important to outcomes, whether that is about local physical and human capital assets, local market failures and the way in which those are addressed, or local conditions and amenities which make some places more attractive to talented and creative people than others.[21]

2.34 Modern economic theories also emphasise the importance of sub-national economies being able to respond to the challenges of both growth and decline through the utilisation of local assets and local comparative advantages. The Organization for Economic Cooperation and Development (OECD) has argued that national policies which simply seek to redistribute investment between places, for example by providing simple fiscal incentives to relocation by firms, "do little to stimulate growth and employment ... and may even be costly blind alleys".[22] That puts a greater premium on the ability of local economies to adopt an evidence-based approach to using their comparative advantages, and to adopt different approaches in different places in order to tackle local market failures.

Necessity of local choice

2.35 Accepting these arguments means accepting some degree of variation and difference between different parts of the country in their governments and their use of resources. Some would not agree with that view, as I noted above, but it is a point of fundamental importance. As the Layfield Committee recognised, I believe that we face choices in the way in which we are governed. At one extreme, we can be governed in a way that places a high value on people receiving similar standards of service, regardless of where they live. On the other hand we can be governed in a way where it is accepted that standards of service may vary from place to place, where this is a consequence of local choice. Local government can engage with the local community and work with local partners to design and deliver services that meet the community's priorities – a plural system which values diversity and delivers greater overall well-being. In a world of constrained resources, where we cannot all have everything that we want, the need for local choice in order to respond to pressures on resources through prioritisation is also critically important.

2.36 The argument that this will lead to an unfair 'postcode lottery' thus over-simplifies some complex issues. As I said in my May report, if the people of one area collectively choose to use the public resources at their disposal in a different way to the people of another area, it is hard to argue that this is unfair. Some commentators have in fact argued that local choice and variation, backed by national minimum standards, can be a way of pursuing greater social justice by addressing inequality.[23] We should also acknowledge that proponents of 'universal' provision tend to underestimate or ignore the level of prevailing variation.

---

[21] See, for example, Florida, R., *The Rise of the Creative Class*, 2002.
[22] OECD, *Devolution and Globalisation: Implications for Local Decision-Makers*, 2001.
[23] Pearce, N. and Paxton, W., *Social Justice – Building a Fairer Britain*, ippr, 2005.

2.37   There are therefore strong arguments in favour of a degree of local choice. In practice, the public desires both national standards and local variation, with opinions varying between different services. The research I commissioned suggests that people want an assurance that key services will be delivered to similar (generally minimum) standards across the country, but also that they want the ability to influence the shape and delivery of services and to take decisions locally – and where they have that opportunity they are much less concerned about difference between places. There is a balance to be struck between an appropriate set of national or minimum service standards, and the variety and community choice which, in my view, is a positive part of a healthy and sophisticated system of governance. My conception of the modern role for local government is therefore of a system which delivers the right degree of 'managed difference' through meaningful local choice over public services, and through place-shaping more broadly.

Importance of engagement

2.38   However, all of these advantages of local government as a way of pursuing the well-being of communities depend on it being able to understand and respond to the needs and concerns of its citizens – and on the well-being of citizens, rather than the interests of the organisation or producer groups, being the objective and motivating principle of its actions. As noted above, this is an area in which it has been criticised – with low levels of turnout, a lack of diversity within the councillor body and a generally poor opinion of local authorities, who are seen as separating local government from local people. While this is an area to which local government undoubtedly needs to devote more attention, it is one where I do believe it has a great deal to offer. Ensuring that local government is fully and transparently accountable to local people, for the decisions it takes in the pursuit of their interests and the use of their resources, is critical to an effective system of local government.

2.39   The local democratic process of debate, scrutiny and, ultimately, election is a means by which local citizens can hold local authorities to account, and make choices about how they want to be governed, what they want for their communities and what they want from local public services. However, election alone does not confer knowledge and legitimacy on local government, and closer engagement with the public is needed to develop a more finely grained understanding of what local people want – as citizens, service users, and as taxpayers. It is only through ongoing engagement and dialogue with the community that local choices can be informed by a strong understanding of people's needs, expectations and aspirations, balanced by a grasp of what they are willing to pay for through charges and local taxes. Results from recent surveys suggest there is a relationship between satisfaction with the authority as a whole, and opportunities for participation and the degree to which respondents think they can influence local decisions.[24] Creating robust and effective arrangements for engagement and influence at the community and neighbourhood level, beyond the council offices, is also likely to be important as part of this process of engagement.

2.40   Many elements of this will be inherently political, and part of the process of local government for which only elected councillors can take responsibility. We should emphasise the role of the elected as 'representatives', not as managers. This includes making judgements where difficult choices and trade-offs need to be made for which there is no 'right' administrative answer, and where there may well be tensions concerning the different priorities of taxpayers and service consumers. Those judgements – and their acceptance by local people – rely on the council's ability to make well-informed decisions which are based on a clear understanding of local priorities and views on the necessary trade-offs. The local authority has a part to play as arbitrator, as different parts of the community will have different experiences, needs and aspirations.

---

[24] Communities and Local Government, *Best Value User Satisfaction Surveys 2006–07*, 2007.

Single system of
government

2.41   This description of the role and value of local government in the 21st century is not intended to imply that local institutions are always the best way to deal with the governmental needs of our society, nor that local choices are necessary or appropriate on all topics or for all situations. There are decisions we may wish to make as a society – for example on many aspects of taxation, healthcare and law and order – at a national level, and there are governmental activities which benefit from a consistent national approach or national coordination. In some cases, for example on climate change, a global approach may be needed. My concern is rather to ensure that the unique value of local government is recognised as part of a single system of government.

2.42   Despite all of this, in discussing the role of government, at any level, we should take care not to give it too great a share of the story. As I noted at the beginning of this chapter, government exists to serve and support society, but it is not the same thing as society, nor is government inherently necessary for collective activity and the benefits of such activity to exist. Even the architect of the welfare state, William Beveridge, was clear on that. His third report, *Voluntary Action*, published in 1948, argued strongly that self-help and voluntary action were a key contribution to a successful society, and that government should be wary of eroding the potential for such action. That remains an important lesson for us today.

Place-shaping

2.43   The modern role of local government can be described as 'place-shaping' – the creative use of powers and influence to promote the general well-being of a community and its citizens. It includes the following components:

- building and shaping local identity;

- representing the community, including in discussions and debates with organisations and parts of government at local, regional and national level;

- regulating harmful and disruptive behaviours;

- maintaining the cohesiveness of the community and supporting debate within it, ensuring smaller voices are heard;

- helping to resolve disagreements, such as over how to prioritise resources between services and areas, or where new housing and development should be located;

- working to make the local economy more successful, to support the creation of new businesses and jobs in the area, including through making the area attractive to new investment and skilled workers, and helping to manage economic change;

- understanding local needs and preferences, and making sure that the right services are provided to local people through a variety of arrangements including collective purchasing, commissioning from suppliers in the public, private and voluntary sectors, contracts or partnerships, and direct delivery; and

- working with other bodies to respond to complex challenges such as natural disasters and other emergencies.

2.44 Some have seen the place-shaping role as being in the main about physical development and regeneration, but it is actually a much wider role. Fundamentally, I see place-shaping as a way of describing my view that the ultimate purpose of local government should not be solely to manage a collection of public services, but rather to pursue the well-being of a place and the people who live there by whatever means are necessary and available. This does not mean that I advocate that the improvement of public services should become a lower priority than it has been in recent years. Rather, I think that wider local outcomes will be improved by a broader view of the locality's interests now and in the future, with local government's role in delivering and influencing services providing many of the tools necessary for place-shaping to happen.

Services

2.45 Total local government current and capital expenditure in England in 2005–06 was over £140 billion, funded from government grants, redistributed business rates, council tax, and various other forms of income including rents, sales, fees and charges. Local government spending makes up around 27 per cent of total government expenditure and supports a wide range of services. My *Interim Report and Consultation Document* provided a breakdown of local authority spending on services, and I do not propose to repeat that here, but detailed information can be found in *Local Government Financial Statistics England*, produced by Communities and Local Government. Table 2.1, below, provides a slightly simplified summary of local authority service responsibilities.

Table 2.1: Local authority responsibilities

	Met. areas		Shire areas			London		
	Single purpose	MD	SC/UA	SD/UA	Single purpose	City	LB	GLA
Education		X	X			X	X	
Highways		X	X			X	X	X
Transport planning		X	X			X	X	X
Passenger transport	X		X			X		X
Social services		X	X			X	X	
Housing		X		X		X	X	
Libraries		X	X			X	X	
Leisure and recreation		X		X		X	X	
Environmental health		X		X		X	X	
Waste collection		X		X		X	X	
Waste disposal	X	X	X			X	X	
Planning application		X		X		X	X	
Strategic planning		X	X			X	X	X
Police	X				X	X		X
Fire	X		X		X			X

MD=metropolitan district; SC=shire county; SD=shire district; UA=unitary authority; LB=London borough; GLA=Greater London Authority.

Source: Local Government Financial Statistics, England, CLG.

2.46   While this is useful context, debate too often focuses on which services local authorities are directly responsible for, as if this is the true measure of the importance and worth of local representative government. This is perhaps a reflection of the changes that took place during the 20th century, as particular responsibilities or powers were moved in and out of local government, and new welfare services developed inside and outside the formal scope of its responsibilities. It also reflects, particularly in more recent times, arguments about whether local authorities should own and provide services in-house or whether services should be privatised or commissioned from private and voluntary sector providers, which should really be a separate discussion.

Well-being and convening   2.47   A new conception of the role for local government needs to go beyond these debates to reflect the well-being and place-shaping agenda. The issues that affect communities and the lives of individual citizens are not confined to the organisational limits and boundaries of different service agencies. The work of these different agencies therefore needs to be brought together. That requires not just the joining-up of resources and activities, but also a leadership and influencing role to ensure that the efforts of all agencies are focused on the outcomes of greatest importance to local people. Local government is well-placed to play this convening role.

2.48   The local authority should have a role in representing the community interest and influencing any service that has an impact on local people, whatever the formal arrangements for the management of that service. That is especially important where those impacts fall on the community as a whole, or in a way which means that they are unlikely to be dealt with through the actions of individuals alone. Local authorities should be recognised as the body in the locality with the responsibility of bringing together the efforts of the public sector, and also of relevant parts of the private and voluntary sectors, to secure local well-being through a convening role. That is at the heart of what place-shaping is about.

2.49   Concentrating on the promotion of well-being also helps to cut through some of the difficulties involved in the debate on the role of private and voluntary sector provision. The focus should be on the objectives and outcomes from the service, and who sets and manages those, not about whether the service is ultimately delivered by the private, public or voluntary sectors.

Market-shaping   2.50   Local authorities also have the potential to use their power, particularly their purchasing power, and their long-term perspective to shape markets so that independent provision can meet the needs of individuals and communities, where the market may not immediately be able to do so unaided. Appropriate regulation and effective commissioning enable the reliable and trusted independent provision of services that might once have been seen as the prerogative of the public sector, for example in childcare and domestic care for the elderly.

Co-production   2.51   Many of the key governmental and public service challenges we face – from reducing obesity, to improving community safety or tackling climate change – require the active participation of citizens, communities and service users if efficient and effective outcomes are to be secured. Local government's ability to engage with individuals and communities in a direct way should make it well-placed to enable the 'co-production' of services and outcomes from public services – what has been described as "the missing factor – labour from the consumer – that is needed in every sphere of social endeavour".[25]

---

[25]   Boyle, D., Clark, S. and Burns, S., *Hidden Work: Co-production by people outside paid employment*, Joseph Rowntree Foundation, 2006.

2.52   This will be a critical role for local government in the future, working with individuals and voluntary sector institutions, as we seek to address complex and seemingly intractable problems that cannot be resolved through straightforward service delivery approaches. This is not just about providing services at lower cost, but, more importantly, about delivering services better suited to the needs of individuals, and thus helping to enhance satisfaction. In some cases – our impact on the environment and use of natural resources, for example – it will involve changing behaviours as well as engaging people more closely in provision.

Role in service delivery   2.53   There remains an important discussion to have about which services are best determined by local authorities, and which by other agencies, and the role which local and central government should have in determining the approach, standards and financing of those services. I do not propose in this report to come to detailed conclusions on all of the many services in which local government has a role, and how responsibilities and powers should be allocated between the different tiers of government. The detailed analysis and investigation required would be beyond my remit and my resources. More importantly, such conclusions involve a strong element of political choice – views of national entitlements and acceptable standards are inherently political decisions – and I do not wish to prescribe the job of the elected or of governments by implying there is a single right answer. Across the world, one can see that almost all services are delivered by a state, regional or local government somewhere in the world, even including services which have a strongly national tone in this country such as defence and social security. There are genuine choices here for governments and societies to make.

2.54   However, I do want to offer some observations in this report on specific issues that have come out of my work. In my May report, I set out the following principles which can help to inform decisions on which aspects of services are most appropriately determined locally:

- local variation in needs, preferences and costs of provision: if these factors vary, then the most efficient way to use resources will also vary between areas. Under this heading we should also consider the extent to which a service is seen as one to which people should have an entitlement as a citizen of England or the UK;

- local benefit: if the benefits of a service are felt by local people, then decisions taken locally will reflect the value people put on the service. This is particularly significant where the benefits fall on people as a group, rather than on specific individuals;

- local costs: if the costs of the service, both in financial terms and also in terms of environmental and other impacts, are felt by local people, and there are few spillovers onto other areas, then decisions should be made locally, again because they will better match the value local people put on the service;

- strongly influenced by the behaviour of the individual and with potential value from co-production: engagement with citizens and consumers can be easier and more effective if undertaken in a locally responsive and tailored fashion. This also suggests that if there are benefits in value for money or outcomes to be found by engaging users in the co-production of a service, then such services will benefit from local discretion;

- synergies and economies of scope with other local services which mean there are benefits from joining-up at the local level. If the quality of a service or the way in which it is delivered has an impact on the outcomes achieved by other local services, those should be taken into account when making decisions;

- limited economies of scale: if the savings to be made by managing or procuring more of a service are small, there is less of an efficiency argument for not managing it as locally as possible (taking into account the costs and difficulties of achieving economies of scale in practice); and

- potential advantages from innovation or experimentation to test and develop new approaches: we do not always know the most effective way to solve complex problems and the possibility of testing out different approaches in a smaller area, without risk to the whole of the country, offers potential benefits.

2.55   Later chapters of this report return to these points when discussing specific services on which I undertook more detailed work or commissioned research.

WHAT DO WE WANT FROM LOCAL GOVERNMENT?

2.56   There are many different ways in which we can summarise and analyse the opportunities and challenges that we face as a country and as a society. In my May report I highlighted five in particular:

- a rapidly changing global economy;

- demographic and socio-economic change;

- growing expectations of the responsiveness and customisation of goods and services;

- environmental pressures and climate change; and

- the changing nature of political engagement.

2.57   The Government has also recently published its own detailed analysis of the key long-term challenges and opportunities for the UK in preparation for the 2007 Comprehensive Spending Review.[26]

2.58   In this report, I want to take a slightly different approach, building on this prior analysis, to identify four areas where I think local government has a significant role to play in delivering important outcomes that arise from the manifold opportunities and challenges we face:

- first, in providing safe and secure places to live in, where communities are cohesive and integrated;

- second, in helping to foster the greater prosperity which benefits individuals and allows us to fund public services, including engaging with the challenges and opportunities posed by globalisation;

- third, addressing the impact we are having on the environment by taking steps to make our lifestyles more sustainable through engagement with citizens and through the performance of its statutory functions; and

- fourth – and this needs to underpin all of our work if the overall system of government is to be sustainable – improving the level of engagement with, and trust in, our system of government, at both local and national levels.

---

[26] HM Treasury, *Long-term opportunities and challenges for the UK: analysis for the 2007 Comprehensive Spending Review*, 2006.

2.59   I consider each of these issues in further detail below.

Building social
cohesion

2.60   Social cohesion – the existence of mutual trust and relationships between individuals and communities of different backgrounds and characteristics – is an important quality for communities. The basic values of trust, respect and tolerance on which it is built are fundamental to life and economic activity in a modern democratic society. Social cohesion also contributes to quality of life and the attractiveness of communities, and its absence can create significant challenges for the maintenance of law and order, and detract from the sense of safety and security which can be so important to individual well-being. Indeed, the term 'co-production' was originally coined to explain why neighbourhood crime rates went up in Chicago when police stopped walking the beat and lost their vital connections with local community members.[27]

2.61   Building and maintaining social cohesion is becoming more challenging and more important as our society becomes more diverse and more open to information, comparison and influence from elsewhere in the world, and as the ethnic and religious backgrounds of the population of the country become more varied. However, social cohesion is not just about ethnicity and religion. As the Commission on Integration and Cohesion has argued, "differences and tensions can arise between people from different age or income groups, different political groups, and within the boundaries of single ethnic groups".[28] The nature of relationships between different age groups can be important; debates on anti-social behaviour, for example, show the importance of understanding and trust between people of different age groups. There is also a live debate among sociologists about the ways in which relationships between individuals in general are changing over time, with a general concern, perhaps most clearly set out by Robert Puttnam in his work, that the links and trust between individuals are being eroded by modern lifestyles and attitudes.[29]

2.62   Such connections are often referred to as social capital. Definitions of social capital vary, but the key elements include 'neighbourliness', belonging to social groups and networks, and taking part in local activities. Social capital may be seen in networks which bond individuals together through shared race, faith, social class or locality. But it is also needed to form bridges between communities, creating a wider and more inclusive identity leading to mutual understanding between people with different backgrounds. Building social capital can support a range of policy objectives. Research has shown that higher levels of social capital are associated with better health, higher educational achievement, better employment outcomes and lower crime rates.[30]

2.63   The influences on social cohesion and social capital come from a variety of sources. Some are the reflection of wider trends in society and lifestyles, and many others are the result of national and international events and policies, including foreign and immigration policies. However, the characteristics of individual places and the relationships between people within them are also of great importance and, whatever the causes, any attempt to address deficiencies or develop greater cohesion must reflect the complexity of those places and people.

---

[27] Boyle, D., Clark, S. and Burns, S., *Hidden Work: Co-production by people outside paid employment,* Joseph Rowntree Foundation, 2006.

[28] Commission on Integration and Cohesion, *Our Interim Statement,* 2007.

[29] Puttnam, R., *Bowling Alone: The Collapse and Revival of American Community,* 2001.

[30] Woolcock, M., 'The place of social capital in understanding social and economic outcomes', in *ISUMA* 2 (1), 2001.

2.64   Given the importance of local characteristics and relationships, and the need for locally relevant and sensitive solutions, local authorities, with their detailed local knowledge and ability to engage, should have a central role to play in building cohesion and helping to develop social capital. Engagement and action by authorities can provide the connections for integration and cohesion by developing trust and mutual respect within the wider community, building community identity and pride in place, and developing relationships between citizens within a locality. The Commission for Integration and Cohesion argues that the need to develop shared civic values is an opportunity for local government, and Ted Cantle, who chaired the independent review into the disturbances in Burnley, Bradford and Oldham in 2001, has argued strongly that the local authority has to lead on social cohesion issues – and is particularly well-placed to support this by involving local people in building a compelling vision for the area, which everyone can understand and feel able to accept.[31] It has not been something that local authorities have always seen as part of their role.

2.65   The principles for improving cohesion set out by Sir Robert Kerslake are a useful illustration of what local government can contribute in addressing challenges to social cohesion.[32] They all require the detailed local knowledge and engaged and sympathetic approach from government that local government should be able to demonstrate:

- understand the changing mix of local communities and the challenges they face;

- recognise that there is a positive leadership role for councils to create a sense of belonging, standards and values for a community;

- create a level-playing field. Iron out issues of myths and perception by communicating why specific actions are taken for one neighbourhood over another;

- create a feeling of being part of the community by ensuring equal representation of all residential groups in local decision making; and

- prevent groups becoming isolated by helping new communities interact with those that are more settled.

2.66   The work on social capital conducted by the London Borough of Camden and the Institute for Public Policy Research since 2002, and Camden's response to the London bombings, shows how local authorities can engage in these issues.

---

[31] IDeA, 'A diverse agenda: local authorities and local identity', 2006.
[32] As cited in *Local Government Chronicle*, 11 January 2007.

Community cohesion in Camden

Camden is one of the most ethnically diverse parts of London, with a large Muslim population. The council sees promoting community cohesion through building and supporting mutual understanding and respect as one of its core roles.

It has taken a number of steps to reinforce cohesion through mainstream services, specific projects and partnerships with community and faith groups. These include a statement of common public values produced by the faith communities partnership, and the publication of a 'myth-busting' booklet about refugees and asylum seekers to tackle misconceptions and prejudice. In 2005 the Council ran its second large-scale survey on social capital to assess the state of community relations, neighbourliness and people's sense of empowerment, which is helping to inform service developments and cross-cutting strategies.

Community cohesion became especially important in July 2005 when Camden was at the centre of the terrorist attacks on London, with two of the bombsites located in the borough. In addition to working with the police, the community safety partnership and voluntary groups to provide reassurance, the Council took steps to address possible tension. In the days following the attack, it brought together local faith, community and civic leaders to demonstrate unity in defiance of the terrorists and reaffirm a shared commitment to a united Camden. It decided to go ahead with several community festivals, including the Bangladeshi Mela in Regents Park, even though it presented security and other risks, and also brought children from across Camden's schools together to provide a means for them to share their feelings and responses. These and other immediate steps succeeded in avoiding major community tensions.

Promoting economic prosperity

2.67 Government at all levels has a role in enabling individuals to create and benefit from wealth, with due regard to fairness and to environmental sustainability. Greater wealth can provide more choices, greater security and more opportunities for personal realisation for individuals. Greater prosperity can also fund the provision of better public services and support for vulnerable groups, by increasing the revenues that governments can raise through taxation – the 'cake' available to fund our collective ambitions for the country. Indeed, over the years a significant proportion of our growing national wealth has been used for new and expanded services and welfare support – for example, the introduction of pensions, other forms of social protection and also the creation and expansion of the National Health Service, as part of the development of the welfare state. Growth also allows us to invest for the future in the public and private assets like transport infrastructure and education which are necessary for our continued prosperity.

2.68 Our expectations of the potential for improvements and expansions in public services, and for the provision of more generous financial support to those who need it, are substantial – in part encouraged by the ambitions of successive governments. Not all of those expectations can ever be met, but a focus on continuing the growth of the economy offers the potential to meet some of them as tax revenues increase.

2.69 While it is in the main private sector activity and investment that generates economic growth, government and the public sector do have an important role to play in setting frameworks, dealing with collective issues and trade-offs and intervening to address market failures. Fostering economic prosperity and growth needs to be a shared objective for all levels of government. Many critical factors, including basic legal and financial frameworks, monetary and most aspects of fiscal policy, and international trade arrangements, are clearly national responsibilities.

2.70   The performance of the UK economy in recent years has been enviable, with the longest period of unbroken growth on record combined with historically high levels of employment and low levels of unemployment and interest rates. The Government's economic reforms must be given a substantial share of the credit for this, with the OECD stating that "this performance is a testament to the strength of the institutional arrangements for setting monetary and fiscal policy as well as to the flexibility of labour and product markets".[33] However, as noted earlier, recent economic theory and analysis identifies local factors and institutions as important influences on economic change and growth, and emphasises the importance of sub-national economies being able to respond to the challenges of both growth and decline.

2.71   Local government thus has a part to play. It already has many powers and responsibilities relevant to economic development and prosperity, not the least of which are its responsibilities for land use planning. Given the wide range of factors that contribute to a successful economy, and the unique characteristics of each local economy, it is desirable that the agencies which seek to improve economic prosperity should have a wide range of powers, and the capability and legitimacy to influence and guide others. Local government is well placed to do that, and studies have shown the importance of strategic capacity and leadership in local government in achieving economic growth.[34] The case study of Sheffield below shows how local government can respond to changing economic conditions.

Economic Development in Sheffield

For the first half of the 20th century Sheffield prospered as a producer of high quality steels and cutlery. However, during the late 1970s and 1980s, it suffered a severe economic shock from the loss of jobs in steel and manufacturing as its major industry struggled to compete with a range of new producer countries in a world economy where steel capacity was running ahead of demand. Within a decade the city had lost a quarter of its jobs. This heavy reliance on steel production made Sheffield's challenge in modernising its economic base greater than in many cities of comparable size.

Sheffield has recovered impressively over the past ten years from a very low point. Gross Value Added per head has increased at a rate matching the best of the major cities in the UK, business growth has been strong in key industries, investor confidence has returned to the area and unemployment has fallen significantly to converge with the UK rate. Key contributions to this progress have been the pivotal leadership role played by the Council in harnessing the strong sense of partnership in the city, and the use of innovative arm's length arrangements that enabled a clear focus on economic objectives and an unremitting focus on delivery.

In an increasingly competitive environment, the Council's focus is now on targeting new objectives. They want to accelerate the growth of knowledge-based businesses, capitalising on the excellent research facilities of Sheffield's universities and business innovation capacity, and inculcating a far stronger sense of enterprise, particularly in Sheffield's more deprived areas. They would also like to significantly increase educational and skill levels throughout the city. The Council hopes to extend the success of the city centre renaissance into other parts of the city, and to strengthen the overall marketing of the city. This includes capitalising on Sheffield's environmental and cultural assets in order to position the city in the UK and internationally, raising its profile as a competitive location for knowledge economy businesses and promoting it as a key tourism destination.

---

[33] OECD, *Economic Survey of the UK 2005*, 2005.

[34] See, for example, Kauffman, Leautier and Mastruzzi, 'Governance and the City: An Empirical Exploration into Global Determinants of Urban Performance', World Bank Discussion Paper, 2004 and Parkinson et al., *Competitive European Cities: Where Do The Core Cities Stand?*, ODPM, 2004.

Sustainable environmental policy

2.72   As we pursue greater economic prosperity, undeniable scientific evidence is making it increasingly clear that we also need to face up to the threats posed to the sustainability of our planet's environment and natural resources.

2.73   Sir Nicholas Stern's recent report, *The Economics of Climate Change*, has demonstrated that, without concerted action, global warming will have a significant impact on societies and economies across the world. However, it also shows that action is possible, and is more efficient than doing nothing. Taking action to ensure we are using resources in a sustainable way is necessary if we are to maintain our quality of life and economic progress, and to secure them for our future and for future generations.

2.74   There is also a range of other pressures on natural resources and the environment which should not be forgotten. Ensuring that we use finite resources effectively, and that we balance economic development with environmental protection and the protection of biodiversity, are all significant challenges, again with important implications for our quality of life and the sustainability of our lifestyles.

2.75   Tackling environmental problems like these often requires collective solutions as the impacts do not fall solely on those who consume resources or undertake certain forms of activity. Sir Nicholas Stern has described climate change as "the greatest market failure the world has seen", requiring governments and societies across the world to act to reduce carbon emissions. Some of the environmental challenges are less global than climate change – ensuring sustainable and appropriate mixes of land use within a country or a community, for example – but they still require collective solutions and often a greater or lesser level of government intervention in the operation of the free market, whether at national or local level.

2.76   Local approaches and solutions are particularly relevant to the issues with a more local focus. Local authorities are responsible for the development of local plans to regulate land use, for waste management and for other aspects of the natural and built environment. They can make a very substantial contribution to sustainable development through their statutory responsibilities and through their wider place-shaping responsibilities for the well-being of their citizens and communities.

2.77   Local government can also make a significant contribution to even the most global of challenges, such as climate change. While local authorities cannot solve such problems alone, it is clear that the sense of responsibility felt by local people, local politicians and local authorities as institutions to the world and to the future of their places has led to action on this issue. A good example of local authority commitment in this area is the Nottingham Declaration, a voluntary pledge to take action on climate change, described in the box overleaf.

The Nottingham Declaration on climate change

The Nottingham Declaration is a voluntary pledge committing local authorities to take action to address the causes and impacts of climate change. It commits them to:

- work with central government to contribute locally to the delivery of the UK climate change programme;

- prepare a plan with their local community to address the causes and effects of climate change;

- commit, within that plan, to reducing greenhouse gas emissions produced by the Council's own operations;

- work with and encourage all sectors of the local community and key service providers to reduce greenhouse gas emissions and to assess, identify and suggest ways to adapt to the potential effects of climate change; and

- provide opportunities for the development of renewable energy generation in their area.

Advice and support helps councils to reduce their greenhouse gas emissions and help their community adapt to the impacts of climate change through developing a community-wide strategy, and focusing on council estate management, services provision and their role as community leaders.

The pledge was originally launched in 2000, and re-launched in December 2005. Over 200 councils have signed up to date and examples of the work being done include:

- Kirklees Metropolitan Council, whose SunCities project involved installing solar electricity panels and hot water panels on six care homes, two schools and around 500 homes. Kirklees now generates 4.9 per cent of the UK's solar electricity.

- Brighton and Hove City Council, one of the earliest signatories to the declaration, whose all-encompassing approach to sustainable energy extends from in-house green procurement policies, to the design of their public library – the most energy efficient public building in the country.

Further details on the Nottingham Declaration, and the councils who have already signed up, are available from: http://www.nottinghamdeclaration.org.uk

2.78   A number of local authorities, including Woking (which featured as a case study in my May report), Nottinghamshire, Shropshire, Cornwall, Leicester, Nottingham, Lewisham and High Peak have taken this agenda particularly seriously and sought to minimise the carbon impact of the authority and the community. In the future, new frameworks and expectations which may be introduced, such as the emissions trading schemes advocated by bodies such as the Sustainable Development Commission, could further enhance the importance and necessity for local action on this issue.

2.79   Addressing climate change and sustainable development will require individuals, as well as governments, to make different decisions. Here there is another role for local government. While people's 'environmental literacy' is increasing all the time, there is more to do to explain and influence behavioural change. Local government's closeness to the community should enable it to contribute to this as well, for example through work with schools and community groups.

Satisfaction and trust in government

2.80 The final challenge that I believe exists for local government (and, indeed, for central government) is to address levels of trust and satisfaction among the public. Neither of these concepts are necessarily inherently desirable – many would argue that citizens should not trust governments because of the risk that those with power will be tempted to abuse that trust, and the fact that it is very difficult for any individual citizen to know enough about the processes and decisions of government to be sure that they agree with the decisions taken. Nevertheless, if we are to completely ignore criteria such as this, we are left with little means of assessing the health of our democracy. A lack of trust is a problem for today because it makes it more difficult for governments (including local government) to make difficult trade-offs and reconcile conflicting views within the local community while retaining support. It is also a problem for the future because it weakens the breadth of our political culture, and is likely to make it more difficult to build participation in politics from across the community at both political and officer level, and to motivate people to engage in public service, whether in local government or in other local agencies of government such as local health trusts.

2.81 Trust in government and politicians in the UK, and participation in politics through the most obvious route – voting in elections – is low and, while it varies from election to election, appears to be on a downward trend. Analysis, including that of the Power Inquiry, has diagnosed a population less and less willing to engage with formal political processes such as party membership and voting in elections, but more interested in pursuing interests through single-issue campaigns and boycotts.[35] Thus, the problem may not be one of a lack of interest in politics arising from contented apathy, but failure in the systems and institutions of government.

2.82 We should not be alarmist in this analysis. It is true that trust in politicians is low, and in an Ipsos MORI survey in 2006 72 per cent of the public said they did not trust politicians to tell them the truth, compared to 5 per cent not trusting doctors and 56 per cent not trusting business leaders.[36] But that level of distrust has remained fairly constant over the past 25 years – 75 per cent did not trust politicians to tell the truth in the same survey in 1983. That is nothing to be proud of, but it does suggest that we are dealing with a long-term problem, not a new crisis.

2.83 Local government as an institution also suffers from problems with public trust, and the public are less likely to trust their local councils than other local public sector organisations such as local hospitals or the local police force. In 2003, 48 per cent of survey respondents did not trust their local council very much or at all compared to 18 per cent for local NHS hospitals and 24 per cent for the local police force.[37] This is perhaps not entirely surprising, given that local authorities are responsible for less popular activities such as taxation and regulation, not just the provision of widely-supported public services.

2.84 Local government also has a particular problem with public perceptions of fairness, linked both to concerns about 'postcode lotteries' and to concerns about council tax. But fairness can often be an ill-defined and highly contested concept, meaning different things to different people at different times, and consensus on what is fair is almost certainly impossible. For example, in relation to the financing of local public services, many people wrote to the Inquiry to complain at the unfairness of the council tax, but they did not agree on what that unfairness was. Some thought it was unfair that council tax did not take account of someone's ability to pay. Others, on the other hand, thought that it was unfair that it was not a flat rate tax for service use.

---

[35] Power Inquiry, *Power to the People*, 2006.
[36] Ipsos MORI, for the Royal College of Physicians. Base: 2,074 GB residents, aged 15+, in-home face-to-face, October 2006.
[37] MORI, *Trust in Public Institutions*, Audit Commission, 2003.

2.85   Addressing these problems will be a complex and lengthy task, but it is an essential one. It is one in which local and central government have a joint interest, as I believe that what undermines trust in one part of government is likely to colour people's opinions of the wider system of government. A blame game between local and central government, and the lack of transparency in decision-making, damages opinions of government and politics at all levels.

2.86   Addressing the issue of fairness in particular is both important in its own right and essential if other reforms are to succeed. People's worries about council tax and the provision of services in their area are real and deserve careful consideration. But when concerns about council tax dominate discussions about local government to the extent that they do now, it can become very difficult to take a wider view of what sort of governance we want in this country and what reforms might take us there.

2.87   Local government has the potential to contribute to increasing public trust in government as a whole. Trust and involvement are built through responsiveness, choice and voice. Local government can thus help to strengthen the relationship between the individual citizen and the state through measures to build trust, honest taxation and a recognition that people do want to be able to influence government and public choice decisions. There is a risk that if local government – the most immediate level of government and the one with which people are most likely to engage – has too little flexibility and scope to respond to views, this can contribute to a more passive, less connected citizenry. That means engagement is crucial, and given that most people will not want to be directly involved most of the time, it puts a premium on clear lines of responsibility, good information, good feedback and elected representatives who are able to make a difference, be held to account and challenge the authority and expose it to scrutiny.

2.88   Local authorities can also contribute to improving fairness and social justice (and perceptions of fairness) at the local level, through the services they provide and more widely through their responsibility for the well-being of communities. There is inevitably a need for local authorities to make difficult decisions which benefit some people and disappoint others – and therefore a critical need for them to engage with communities to inform and validate those choices, and to explain them so people can understand why they were made. Understanding the difficulties involved in making choices locally can, I believe, help citizens to feel the decisions themselves are fair ones, even if they are not the choices they themselves would prefer.

CONCLUSION

2.89   To address the challenges and opportunities of the future, we need government as a whole to be flexible and responsive, able to react to economic and social change, and engaged with citizens. I believe that local government has a crucial part to play in that overall system. The place-shaping role, which I have set out in this chapter and in earlier work as the strategic role for local government, is intended to be a role that local government can play across a wide range of agendas through responding to local needs and preferences and in shaping and managing difficult social, economic and political issues. It is important to see this as part of a single system of government – it should not be a competition between local and central government for a finite amount of legitimacy, power and resources, but a shared agenda to which each brings particular skills and advantages.

2.90   However, we do not at present have a local government system which is likely to support or enable all local authorities to take on this place-shaping role. The following chapters of the report therefore consider the problems and barriers that currently exist, and then set out a series of recommendations and challenges on function and funding. Both central and local government will need to respond if we are to succeed in developing the confident and responsive local government we need to play its part in our overall system of government.

Part II

Problems and solutions

3

What is limiting modern local government?

Summary

This chapter examines the constraints and inhibitions on modern local government and what this means for the place-shaping role that I advocated in my May report, *National prosperity, local choice and civic engagement*. The constraints on local government are systemic, behavioural and also, in part, based on assumptions about public attitudes to choice and difference. This chapter explores:

- the high degree of central control, both through formal targets and monitoring regimes, and through softer and less direct controls;

- the lack of flexibility that English local authorities have to raise additional revenues and use existing resources to support local priorities;

- the role of needs, expectations, national funding, efficiency and local choice in determining pressures on council tax;

- the confused accountability in the finance system which contributes to a poor understanding of how the system works and unrealistic expectations of how much services cost. It also considers the complex governance arrangements within English local government and how this affects work across authority boundaries to drive economic prosperity;

- public attitudes to local government, which are more complex than generally accepted and supportive of 'managed difference' when based on effective engagement;

- the lack of trust in local government caused by poor accountability, concern about council tax and the impact of the adversarial relationship between central and local government; and

- the incentives in the system that distributes national resources, in particular how they can help to develop a more constructive relationship between central and local government and also to support local authorities in pursuing improvements in economic prosperity and housing supply in their area.

This chapter concludes that the important issues for reform are: greater flexibility, better incentives, clearer accountability, tackling perceived unfairness and continued improvements in efficiency – both in delivering services as cost-effectively as possible and in ensuring that local government is working with local partners to deliver the right priorities.

INTRODUCTION

3.1   The presenting problems which preceded the setting up of the Inquiry were public concerns around council tax and the balance of funding between local and central government. However, it became clear early in the course of work that these issues are driven by larger systemic issues about the role and function of local government. In order to answer questions about how best to fund local government, it was important first to develop a clearer understanding of the appropriate role and function of local government, which I addressed in my May report.

3.2   Chapter 2 explored the modern role for local government based on the fundamental goal of improving the well-being of its citizens, through the exercise of collective local choice based on effective engagement. My May report proposed that this is best achieved through what I have called place-shaping. This encapsulates a wider, strategic role for local government rather than one solely focused on service provision, and it more fully recognises that it has a unique responsibility for its local community and its local area.

3.3   This chapter analyses the reasons why local government is not currently able to fulfil its place-shaping role in every area. It explores this in relation to the actions and behaviours of central and local government and the relationship between them, as well as the incentives and constraints imposed by the tax and finance system. It is based on a wide range of analysis and expert input. Some of this was commissioned for the Inquiry, but I have also drawn on other published work and evidence from the Inquiry's seminar series, submissions and other meetings and events. The content of this chapter is complemented by a more detailed analysis of the issues surrounding local government finance, in Chapters 6 to 9, and by annexes on the research commissioned for my Inquiry and a summary of the submissions that I have received.

3.4   Some of the analysis and research that underpins this assessment is common to the Local Government White Paper, *Strong and Prosperous Communities*. Consideration of the White Paper's proposals and their implications are included in later chapters.

HIGH DEGREE OF CENTRAL CONTROL

The balance between central and local control

3.5   As described in Chapter 1, the 1980s and 1990s saw increasing centralisation across a range of local public services, driven by concerns to control public sector expenditure and efforts to improve public services. In recent years this has been driven through new systems of performance management and Public Service Agreement targets, greater emphasis on delivery and a willingness by central government to take responsibility for specific issues across the country. This has clearly improved performance on a wide range of measures.[1] However, it has inhibited the ability of local government to respond to local needs and preferences and manage pressures on their budgets.

3.6   The 2001 White Paper, *Strong Local Leadership – Quality Public Services*, sought to release local government from some regulatory burdens and provide greater freedom to use powers and resources to meet local needs and aspirations. The recent evaluation of this concluded that there was a mixed picture in relation to how far this agenda had taken hold. Central government departments differed in how far they were prepared to give local authorities more flexibility, particularly in relation to the degree of ring-fencing of grants. The evaluators also recorded limited changes in the overall level of inspection of local authorities and highlighted the need for a more commercial attitude on the part of some local authorities to take advantage of trading and charging

[1] Martin, S., *Implications of Local Devolution for Efficiency and Effectiveness in Service Delivery,* Lyons Inquiry Seminar: Greater Devolution: Evidence in Support, June 2005.

powers. The conclusion was that 'a shift in mindsets [is] still required by elements of both central and local government'.[2]

3.7   This sense of opportunities not taken is reflected in the submission from the National Audit Office, where they set out their estimate that the overall cost of monitoring local government was in the region of £2 billion a year. Recent work which informed the 2006 White Paper and led to the 'Lifting the Burdens Task Force', found that central government and its agencies collectively demand 566 performance items from local authorities, at an average cost of £1.8 million per authority.[3] The most significant burdens were from Department for Education and Skills, Department of Health and Communities and Local Government but other central departments also required substantial performance evidence.[4]

3.8   The Local Government Association argues that the extent of the central control over local government is not proportionate to the local role – it estimates that local government is responsible for 25 per cent of public expenditure but has 81 per cent of central targets.[5] This definition includes all expenditure, including welfare benefits, but none the less suggests that, given the level of central funding, local services are disproportionately controlled by central government.

Soft controls   3.9   The recent Local Government White Paper has recognised the burden of performance management and national target setting. However, I am also concerned about the extent of central government influence exerted through a range of softer and less direct controls such as guidance, central encouragements and conditions on grant. The indirectness of these soft controls, and the subtle forms they take, make them more difficult to assess than direct targets and indicators. Their impact can be profound in terms of the time and attention that are paid to them at the local level and the strength of direction that is inherent in them, as illustrated in the following quotes taken from the research commissioned for the Inquiry:[6]

> *There's been quite a subtle change in the prescription from central government when legislation's drafted. I use licensing as an example, [the legislation states] you have to have regard to statutory guidance, the statutory guidance is 200 pages long.*

> *Some partners faced a lack of flexibility regarding how they could spend their budgets. For example, 80 per cent of youth service funding has to be spent on young people aged 14 and upwards, but in this area the police would like to develop activities for young people aged 10 onwards.*

Causes of central prescription   3.10   I recognise that the drivers of central control over local government are complex and not simply the result of a narrow central control objective. Indeed, central control and prescription is often driven by well-intentioned actions by ministers in the face of strong pressure from the media and lobbying from special interest groups to take action to tackle a problem found in one or a few areas of the country. Our country appears uniquely preoccupied with the 'postcode lottery' in a way which can lead us to value uniformity far above the need to find the right solution for each area.

---

[2] *Evaluation of Freedom and Flexibilities on Local Government: Baseline Study*, Communities and Local Government, 2006.

[3] On performance see: *Mapping the Local Government Performance Reporting Landscape,* Communities and Local Government, 2006; on the task force, see the announcement by Ruth Kelly MP, Secretary of State for Communities and Local Government, to the LGA conference on 5 July, 2006.

[4] It should be noted that the assessment of the department for Communities and Local Government's role includes costs for some frameworks where it acts as a performance management channel for other government departments, for instance, Local Area Agreements.

[5] *Meeting the Challenges Ahead*, Local Government Association, 2006

[6] Entwhistle, T. et al., *Perspectives on Place-shaping and Service Delivery: A Report of Case Study Work*, Lyons Inquiry, 2007.

3.11   In this context public opinion is often used to justify central action. However, as the survey and research work commissioned for the Inquiry shows, public opinion is more sophisticated than is sometimes recognised. My research reinforces the view that people want to ensure that there is an element of national fairness and protection via minimum standards, but it also shows that the public recognise the need for flexibility to provide services in the way that best meets local needs. These issues are discussed in detail later in the chapter.

3.12   There is also evidence that champions of individual services within local government itself often encourage intervention by central government to protect their particular service areas. As my case study research found, among managers working within local government, "service respondents generally … saw considerable benefit in the continued, and in some cases heightened, use of hierarchical policy instruments". Local government officers were themselves in many cases arguing for new central government targets or direction because they were "inclined to see central government as a source of much needed resource and direction" some even calling for more ring-fencing to protect their funding.[7]

3.13   This contrasted with calls from those local government officers who saw their work in a more strategic and corporate way and who were frustrated by such central controls, arguing that they damage the ability of the local authority to meet local needs and priorities in pursuing the more strategic aims of place-shaping. As the research states:

> At the other extreme, strategic interviewees wanted to see less command and control and rather more local autonomy. These interviewees claimed that their work was positively frustrated by excessive central involvement in local decision-making, and they called for a series of reforms which would increase the autonomy of local authorities.

3.14   Many of the service respondents who argued for greater central direction worked with vulnerable people and children, so their concerns are, perhaps, understandable and arguably fall within those service areas that can be rightly considered a mainly national responsibility. However, there is a need for local government to recognise the potential tension between the messages they give central government from within service-based parts of their organisations and the messages emerging from their strategic functions. This has implications for the way in which local authorities are led across the full range of their functions, and I discuss this more fully in Chapter 5.

3.15   Whatever the causes, it is clear to me that too much central control damages the strategic, place-shaping role of local government, which needs to be driven by the needs, preferences and priorities of the local community. As the case study research recognises "this is not just a debate about the appropriateness of different policy instruments to different areas. It is also a debate about the kind of relationship that local authorities should have with their local communities". It is this latter relationship that is underplayed in the current funding system and framework within which local government operates.

Crowding out local choice   3.16   I argued in my May report, in line with the wide literature on fiscal federalism, that central government cannot fully understand or respond to different local needs and wishes, and there is therefore a need for local variation and choice.[8] Public services which are delivered according to a national sense of priority may not best fit every local community's needs and wants. The current breadth and detail of central prescription, outlined above, effectively prevents authorities from

---

[7] Entwhistle, T. et al., *Perspectives on Place-shaping and Service Delivery: A Report of Case Study Work*, Lyons Inquiry, 2007.

[8] See for example, Oates, E., 'An Essay on Fiscal Federalism' *Journal of Economic Literature*, vol. 37, no. 3 (Sept. 1999).

shaping services and taking action on local, rather than national priorities. This runs major risks of restricting local choice and wasting resources on delivering services that are not a local priority, impacting both on citizens' sense of satisfaction and on the ability of local government to manage pressures effectively.

3.17   The case study research and submissions to the Inquiry gave many instances of where national priorities were in conflict with local priorities and could result in perverse outcomes at the local level. The impact of these processes on local priorities is illustrated by this quote:

> *With the Crime and Disorder Act, the original intention was to let local communities decide which were the important things for their areas, which to tackle. We were required to do an audit for that, to determine what the strategy and the action plan would be. We very quickly found that central government said well, yes, you do all that, but in addition you will need this and this in your strategy too … In the last strategy we did, 100 per cent of it was dictated by central government.*[9]

Crowding out place shaping   3.18   As well as affecting individual services, such centralisation has the potential to oversimplify the role of local government, reducing organisations that are managing complex, interlinked processes to delivering a series of activities in silos. As evidenced in submissions, this risks crowding out local authorities' ability to progress their wider place-shaping role: responding to local priorities to enhance well-being, strengthening the sense of cohesion within and between their communities, developing the local environment and driving local prosperity.

3.19   There is a specific concern that the combination of limitations on revenues and the focus on specific service improvements has tended to crowd out councils' role in economic development.[10] All local authorities should be concerned with the economic prosperity of their area and citizens. The desire to improve employment opportunities, address local skills problems or revitalise town and city centres almost always makes some appearance in the community strategy or other local plans and strategies. However, evidence to the Inquiry from the business community and others suggests that councils do not always adequately focus on or prioritise this role, particularly since the nationalisation of the business rate in the early 1990s, and this has become a major concern for business. There may also be a case for reforming the grant system to improve the incentives and rewards for authorities which successfully grow the local economy, which I discuss later in the report.

3.20   If authorities had more freedom to decide on their priorities and spending choices, I believe many would choose to give the local economy greater attention. A sense of frustration can be seen in the following quote:

> *Spending on economic development has to be assessed against other City Council priorities … first priority tends to be given to those departments with high spending requirements, especially those obliged to meet recent Government initiatives around old people and children and young people's services.* (Stoke on Trent City Council)

3.21   Strict central control also risks sub-optimal decisions – for example, grant schemes which require spending on one sort of economic intervention will skew activity in that direction, even if the most serious issue for the local economy is something else. The Eddington Study sets out potential concerns in the area of transport if resources cannot be directed towards the most appropriate modes of transport, looking across the piece.

---

[9] Entwhistle, T. et al., *Perspectives on Place-shaping and Service Delivery: A Report of Case Study Work,* Lyons Inquiry 2007.
[10] Lyons Inquiry Seminar, *Greater Local Devolution: evidence in support,* 22 June 2005.

Stifling innovation 3.22 Innovation and experiment can be stifled by centralising processes. There is evidence that decentralisation promotes innovation across a wide range of activities including economic, development, service design, technology and problem solving.[11]

3.23 The Audit Commission's forthcoming work on innovation in local public services concludes that there were five drivers for change in local authorities: the pressure to make efficiency savings, examples of innovation elsewhere, internal pressure from locally-elected councillors, the demands and expectations of local communities, and top-down pressure from central government. While a focus on efficiency was cited as the strongest driver of innovation, their work also concluded that top-down pressure from central government is a less effective driver than local political pressure or the demands of users and citizens.[12]

3.24 There is a risk that an emphasis on common national standards and central government responsibility means that we, as a society, are missing out on the benefits of local innovation. I believe that the reaction of some local authorities further limits innovation as their perception of the best strategy for success is to 'play it safe':

> *Authorities complain that there are too few incentives for them to experiment with new approaches. The system appears to be weighted to 'playing it safe' (i.e. doing what the inspectors are looking for). As a result the current approach had had the greatest impact in the worst performers. There has been much less impact, it is argued, on the best authorities. It has 'raised the floor', but had far less impact on the 'height of the ceiling.'*[13]

LACK OF FLEXIBILITY

Existing resources

Limited flexibility to manage pressures 3.25 Any grant regime which imposes strict conditions on funding means there is limited scope for local authorities to reduce or 'flex' their activities across all their services in order to manage pressures in the most efficient way possible.

3.26 This is a significant issue for local authorities as large proportions of their funds come from specific grants, which are often tied to government requirements and expectations either formally, through ring-fencing, or informally through expectations over what resources will be used for and the monitoring of expenditure. I am aware that even in highly devolved countries specific grants play an important role in enabling the delivery of national priorities.[14] However, there is an issue about their pervasiveness in England when set against other national controls over services.

---

[11] See Turok, I., *Local and National Competitiveness: Is Decentralisation Good for the Economy?* Lyons Inquiry Seminar: Greater Devolution: Evidence in Support, June 2005; Oates, W.E., 'An Essay on Fiscal Federalism', *Journal of Economic Literature*, vol. 37, no. 3 (Sept. 1999), 1120–1149; Walsh, K., 'Public Services, Efficiency and Local Democracy' in King, D. and Stoker, G., *Rethinking Local Democracy*, 1996; and North, D., *Institutions, Institutional Change and Economic Performance*, 1990.
[12] Taken from a forthcoming Audit Commission report with permission, http://www.audit-commission.gov.
[13] Martin, S., *Implications of Local Devolution for Efficiency and Effectiveness in Service Delivery* Lyons Inquiry Seminar: Greater Devolution: Evidence in Support, June 2005
[14] Loughlin, J. and Martin, S., *Options for Reforming Local Government Funding to Increase Local Streams of Funding: International Comparisons*, Lyons Inquiry 2005.

3.27   Central government has recognised this concern and, in stating in the 2001 Local Government White Paper that ring-fencing would be restricted, it argued that:[15]

> *ring-fencing remains an important means of bringing about change ... However, the growth in ring-fencing is excessive – from 5 per cent of all grants in 1997 to 12 per cent this year and on present trends to 15 per cent in 2003–04. This growth threatens to erode local decision making, limit authorities' ability to tackle important local environmental priorities ... and to increase council tax levels.*

3.28   It was announced in 2002 that progress had been made on reducing ring-fenced grants.[16] However, the proportion of funding that comes from specific grants, in general, has increased: since 1998–99 from 6 per cent of central funding for local government to 23 per cent in 2003/04.[17] While figures remain to be finalised, specific grants are likely to be well above half by 2007–08 with the introduction of the ring-fenced grant for schools – Dedicated Schools Grant – in 2006–07. Many of these grants leave local authorities with little discretion over how they should be spent. For instance, the advice accompanying the Waste Performance and Efficiency Grant specifies the aim of the grant, what it should be used to support and provides a detailed list of options that local authorities should consider.[18] Inspections also reinforce local authorities' impression that even non ring-fenced grants are in essence to be spent on achieving national priorities. An example of this latter point can be found in a social care inspection report where it was reported that expenditure on non ring-fenced grants was in line with national priorities and had been 'appropriately' used.[19]

3.29   This can have a profound impact on local authorities' decision-making. For example, one of our case study councils, as shown in Chart 3.1 below, reported that specific grants – including schools grant – now represent approximately half of their total budget and are governed by around 80 different sets of rules and reporting requirements.

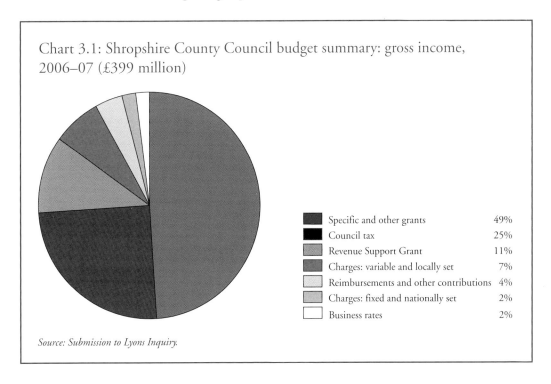

Chart 3.1: Shropshire County Council budget summary: gross income, 2006–07 (£399 million)

Specific and other grants	49%
Council tax	25%
Revenue Support Grant	11%
Charges: variable and locally set	7%
Reimbursements and other contributions	4%
Charges: fixed and nationally set	2%
Business rates	2%

Source: Submission to Lyons Inquiry.

[15] *Strong Local Leadership – Quality Public Services*, DTLR, December 2001.
[16] House of Commons Debate (2002–03) 2 December 2002, col. 1068.
[17] Local Government Finance Statistics, England, various years, Communities and Local Government.
[18] *Waste Performance and Efficiency Grant: Advisory Note to Local Authorities*, DEFRA, December 2005.
[19] *Inspection of Social Care: Warrington Borough Council*, CSCI, May 2006.

3.30   An area of particular concern to me, and one on which I have received representations, is the specific impact of recent decisions on schools funding which, as mentioned above, is now funded through a very large ring-fenced grant – the Dedicated Schools Grant. The decision to have such strict control around school funding is a reflection of the importance of education to the Government. However, it has radically changed how local government receives its resources, decreasing the amount of unhypothecated grants they receive from £44.7 billion to £21 billion and in the process greatly reducing the scope of local authorities to prioritise and manage pressures between services. The submission from the representative group for metropolitan authorities, among others, highlighted this issue:

> *Greater devolution has been compromised with the increase in passporting of funding to local services, reducing the freedom of local councils to decide where their spending priorities should lie. Developments like the Dedicated Schools Grant have made this situation more difficult, giving local councils less room to manoeuvre and invest in local priorities.* (Special Interest Group of Metropolitan Authorities)

3.31   In a similar vein, representations from police authorities have argued that the National Policing Plan and the Crime Fighting Fund, in effect, determine the make-up of police authorities' workforces. They established the numbers of police officers that each force must employ and, if these levels are not met, the result is a loss of central revenues. This narrow focus on police officers created a perverse pressure to undo the previously cost-effective process of employing civilian staff for administrative and routine tasks, leaving skilled police officers to focus on the safety of their communities. The impact of these processes can be seen in the following submission:

> *The Government's obsession with police officer numbers severely restricts the flexibility of local police authorities and chief officers, who would like to be able to consider other configurations for delivering services.* (Association of Police Authorities)

3.32   The impact of this lack of flexibility has recently been recognised by Government with the Home Office agreeing, in December 2006, to suspend the criteria and allow police forces to determine police officer numbers, which is a very welcome move.

Limited flexibility to raise additional resources

Dependence on central funding   3.33   In other western countries such as the USA, France and Germany, local authorities have significantly greater access to locally raised funds. This is demonstrated in Chart 3.2 which sets out the respective roles of local taxation, central grants and other sources of revenue in funding local services. It shows a wide variation in how local services in different countries are supported and that the United Kingdom is firmly at the grant-dependent end of the spectrum.

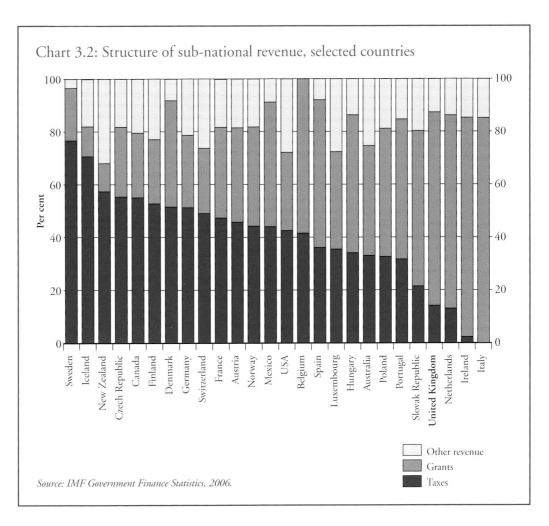

Chart 3.2: Structure of sub-national revenue, selected countries

Source: IMF Government Finance Statistics, 2006.

Other revenue
Grants
Taxes

Sources of revenue   3.34   Local government does, of course, have access to a number of other sources of revenue. The main one is council tax, which is discussed in detail below, and the others include:

- charging for services as defined by specific statutes or within the general power to charge for discretionary services given through the Local Government Act 2003;

- trading, where powers were extended through the Local Government Act 2003 to enable local authorities to trade at a profit with non-public bodies and non-local authorities;

- 'Section 106' contributions from residential and commercial developments whereby developers are expected to make a contribution to a local government's infrastructure costs;

- Business Improvement Districts, which are schemes to raise additional revenue from businesses, where they agree, for limited purposes and on a limited timescale;

- for authorities with housing stock, that is council housing, the Housing Revenue Account which is separate from the general funding of local government (and cannot be cross-subsidised from other services, or indeed used to subsidise other services) is partly or completely supported by rents from their stock; and

- Corporation of London has a special power to raise an additional business rate which is used, for example, to provide security for the area.

3.35   Authorities, to varying degrees, already make significant use of all of these sources of revenue; for example, charging already accounts for more revenue than council tax in a third of local authorities. However, the picture varies widely between services and authorities.

3.36   Controls over the uses to which the revenues may be put differ between the sources. There are direct controls for BIDs and Section 106 funding, and the use of some revenues from charging is restricted. Some charges are hypothecated to different service areas, or limited to recovery of costs; some are set by central government departments and are not locally variable. This range of different restrictions reflects the way that they have evolved separately over time and some submissions to the Inquiry have asked whether the current suite of financial powers are logical and sufficiently flexible at present.

> *Councils should be freer to determine the balance between providing services as a community benefit and charging users ... Moreover councils at the moment have the greatest ability to charge for the most life-supporting services, for the most vulnerable people (social care users), and the least for nice-to-have services (e.g. libraries).* (Surrey County Council)

3.37   Therefore, while these flexibilities deliver significant income in many areas, a point which is discussed further in Chapter 7, they have limitations as sources of general revenue.

Council tax – a single variable tax   3.38   Council tax is the only locally variable tax that local government in this country can use. England is unusual in its reliance on a single variable local tax – few other countries are in a similar position.[20] This is important, as the burden of taxation can be spread between different groups of taxpayers in countries that have more than one form of local taxation.

3.39   Council tax, in addition, is not an inherently buoyant tax. This compares with taxes such as income tax, its yield increasing as jobs are created or wages rise, and VAT, which increases as consumer sales increase. There is, therefore, a contrast between the use of buoyant taxes to support national government and a non-buoyant source of taxation to support local government. This is a key factor in explaining some of the tensions over council tax, where the rate has to be increased year on year simply to keep pace with inflation, and being a very visible tax, coming as it does in the form of an annual bill and receiving widespread media coverage. In contrast, income tax and VAT are buoyant and grow as the overall wealth of the country grows. As already noted, unless there are major pressures on public expenditure or large scale down-turns in growth, central government need not consider increasing tax rates.

Gearing   3.40   Commentators, particularly during the Balance of Funding Review, raised the issue of gearing as contributing to high percentage increases in council tax.

---

[20] Sweden and Ireland also rely on single forms of local taxation. Ireland is similar to England in that it has local property tax and is heavily reliant on central funding. Sweden, however, is quite different. Local government is funded out of a single local income tax but this pays for the majority of their services with central resources in the minority.

Gearing

Gearing is the term used to express the fact that a given percentage increase in local authority spending will require a larger percentage increase in council tax. At the time of the Balance of Funding Review, local authorities' dependence on Government grant meant that for every one per cent increase in spending, they needed on average to increase council tax by four per cent, a gearing ratio of 4:1.[21]

There was, however, a wide variation in gearing across individual authorities which varied from around 2:1 in authorities with the largest council tax base to 9:1 or more in authorities with the smallest tax bases.

Because of the gearing effect, comparatively small spending pressures can lead to some big increases in council tax for individual taxpayers.

Source: Balance of Funding Review – Report, ODPM, 2002.

3.41   This gearing effect was an explicit design feature of the present system introduced at the time of the community charge, intended to sharpen local accountability and act as an incentive on both local authorities and voters to keep spending down. There is no comparable mechanism incorporated into any national tax, but the 1986 Green Paper, *Paying for Local Government*, argued:

> *If local electors have to bear the full cost of marginal increases in their local authority's expenditure, they will have a stronger incentive to take a much keener interest in the levels of such expenditure and may be less inclined to tolerate large increases.*

3.42   During recent years the concern has been more about the impact on the overall level of council tax increases and how this constrains local authorities' ability to raise additional tax revenue. Those concerns led, for instance, to the Local Government Association recommending a 'combination option' for local government funding which would shift the balance of funding towards greater local funding and help mitigate the impact of gearing as well as allowing local authorities "the flexibility to address local priorities and enhance local democracy and accountability".[22]

3.43   The merits of sharpened local accountability inherent in gearing can be debated. However, in a world where central government is in part driving marginal increases in local expenditure, gearing can create a disproportionate burden on local taxation for which local authorities are held to account. We need to find ways to ensure that citizens understand better what and who are driving tax changes rather than just whoever is sending out the bill.

Capping   3.44   Local authorities are also constrained in setting council tax in years where central government 'caps' the rate of increase, further limiting local authorities' ability to raise additional revenues to meet new spending pressures or fund local priorities. Capping has its origins in the 1980s and has been updated by the present Government with the aim of making it a more sophisticated tool in controlling what central government perceives to be excessive increases.

---

[21] The Dedicated Schools Grant has changed the balance of funding between central and local government and the gearing ratio since the Balance of Funding Report. This is discussed in detail in Chapter 6.
[22] LGA, *The Balance of Funding: Implementing the Combination Option*, 2004.

History of capping

Government powers to limit local government spending, known as 'rate capping', were originally introduced in the Rates Act 1984 and remained in place throughout the 1980s with parallel powers contained in the 1988 and 1992 Local Government Finance Acts. Between 1991 and 1997, the Conservative Government used a system known as 'universal capping' under which it published provisional capping criteria before councils set their budgets, thereby enabling councils to be sure that the budgets they set would not be capped. Thirty-five English councils were subject to capping between 1991–92 and 1998–99.

In its 1997 election manifesto Labour promised the removal of 'crude and universal' council tax capping, while retaining 'powers to control excessive spending'. The Local Government Act 1999 introduced new legislation requiring the Secretary of State to determine a set of principles to decide whether an authority's budget requirement is excessive. The new rules allow the Secretary of State to take decisions in the light of budgets which have already been set and provide a choice of actions: capping in year or the following year, or setting a notional budget against which future increases will be measured for capping purposes. There was an indication, confirmed in Parliament in 2003, that Government did not intend to cap councils that received an excellent or good rating under the Comprehensive Performance Assessment. Despite the new legislation, no councils were subject to capping between 1999 and 2003.

However, in 2003–04 council tax increases averaged 12.9 per cent leading to considerable public concern, especially from pensioners, and to pressure from the Government on authorities to reduce their council tax increases in the following year. The Audit Commission report on the 2003–04 council tax increases suggested that spending by councils went up by more than had been allowed for in the grant settlement and the effect of gearing magnified these increases. The Audit Commission found that the causes of increased spending by councils included cost pressures such as pay and price increases, additional demand pressures including the need to provide social services to increasing numbers of elderly people, national priorities such as schools, waste recycling and local priorities, and that the changes in the level of grants to local authorities had also caused some local authorities to raise their council tax. This work concluded that these rises were justifiable but not in all cases unavoidable, and that local authorities had felt under less pressure to keep down spending increases than in previous years.

Following the large increases in 2003–04, the Government made it clear that it considered the trend in council tax rises to be unsustainable and that it was prepared to use its new capping powers, even for those councils previously categorised as excellent or good under the Comprehensive Performance Assessment. In 2004–05 the Secretary of State used the new capping powers for the first time when six councils were capped in year and notional budgets were set for eight nominated authorities. The six authorities capped in year were each required to re-bill householders – bill reductions to council tax payers in band D properties ranged from £15.51 per year in Shepway District Council to £2.48 in Nottingham City Council.

In the two years that have followed, a total of eight local authorities have been capped in year and three have been set notional budgets.

3.45   As this history suggests, capping is the result of successive central government attempts to control increases in an unpopular tax. Central government is responding to popular pressure, often expressed through the media, to protect taxpayers from the impact of high council tax rises. Recent experience, particularly increases in 2003–04, have reinforced their concern about the consequences of removing this pressure and allowing council tax to operate without capping.

However, capping is not without cost. Leaving aside the invidious impact it has on accountability, which is discussed later, I am convinced capping is the wrong response to concerns about council tax increases for the following reasons.

3.46   Capping a local authority carries strong connotations of inefficiency on the part of that authority. Such a simplistic message is counter-productive to creating an understanding of the pressures on budgets which would enable the causes of the pressures, rather than their effect, to be tackled. The Audit Commission work, referred to in the box above, found that the increases in 2003–04 council tax were caused by a variety of factors. Capping cuts across this complexity and, in particular, I consider it counter-productive to constrain local taxes without reference to the adequacy of national funding and the wider system affecting the pressures themselves. It does not support the need for the public to be engaged in, and understand, the complex and difficult trade-offs outlined above.

3.47   Capping also restricts the ability of local authorities to deliver on local needs and preferences. The protection afforded to national priorities through the associated targets and inspection regimes means that they are more protected from cuts than local priorities when an authority is threatened with capping. For example, there is evidence that people value local policing highly and where there are local concerns about community safety and cohesion they may choose to 'buy' more police via a local tax – under capping, such choices are restricted.

3.48   Although council tax remains unpopular, and objections to high council tax rises are widely voiced, local government responsibility for determining the level of council tax is one that is supported by the public. The survey work for the Inquiry found that two-fifths of respondents considered that local councils should have the most say in setting levels of council tax, while under one-quarter thought that central government should fulfil this role. More telling, perhaps, is that only one in ten of the respondents thought that local councils should have the least say, but over half thought that central government should have the least say.

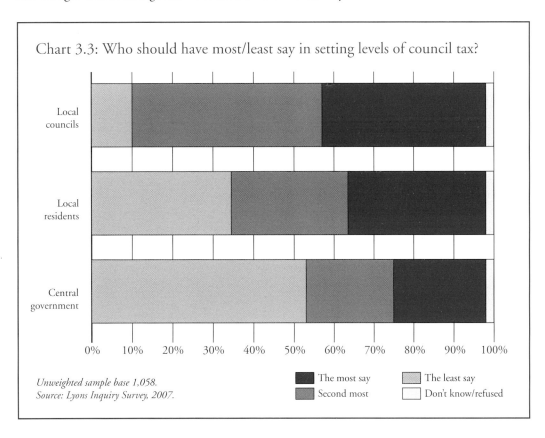

Chart 3.3: Who should have most/least say in setting levels of council tax?

Unweighted sample base 1,058.
Source: Lyons Inquiry Survey, 2007.

■ The most say   ▨ The least say
▨ Second most   ▢ Don't know/refused

3.49   Furthermore, even though there is a more sophisticated capping procedure in operation it is still a relatively blunt tool applied to a small set of diverse local circumstances. This has had perverse consequences in individual cases. For example:

- **Nottingham City Council** was subject to capping in 2004–05. The implications of that year's threshold for them could not have been known before the tax was set. However, the council was capped even though the cost of issuing new council tax bills was larger than the tax savings of £2.48 per band D household.

- **Telford & Wrekin Council** were given a 'notional budget requirement' which meant the starting point for the 2005–06 budget was £31,000 lower than the actual budget for 2004/05 – to reflect the Government's judgement that their 2004–05 budget increase had been too high. This avoided re-billing and other costs estimated to be around £250,000, but is arguably a disproportionate response when the adjustment for each band D household was 64 pence on their annual bill.

3.50   Finally, capping thresholds are set for and within a given year, but have longer-term implications. For example, capping prevents authorities with historically low tax rates from increasing their tax levels towards the average, even if such changes are locally supported, necessary or have a relatively low cash impact. This can be seen in the experience of Mid-Bedfordshire District Council. This council was capped in 2005–06 despite being a historically low-tax authority with the tenth lowest district council tax at the time, having used reserves to hold bills down in the past. The cap called for a reduction in band D bills by £7.04 per household, while re-billing costs were estimated at £85,000.

3.51   This militates against expecting local government to be prudent managers of the local tax base. It could also provide a perverse incentive for local authorities to maintain as high a level of increase as possible within a potential cap in case they require extra resources in future years that may go above the cap. I discuss capping further in Chapter 4.

EXPECTATIONS AND PRESSURES ON SERVICES

The pressure on council tax   3.52   As set out above, one of the most well-rehearsed concerns about council tax relates to the rate at which bills have been increasing, at an average of around 6.4 per cent per year since council tax was introduced in 1993. Despite significant increases in grant at times during the period, average band D bills have risen faster than either Retail Price Index inflation or earnings over the period, which can prove particularly difficult for those on low or fixed incomes. However, solving the council tax 'problem' is not just about tax: it is necessary to understand what drives council tax pressures, what measures can be used to manage them, who (whether central or local government) is best placed to do so, and whether they have the right tools to manage them effectively.

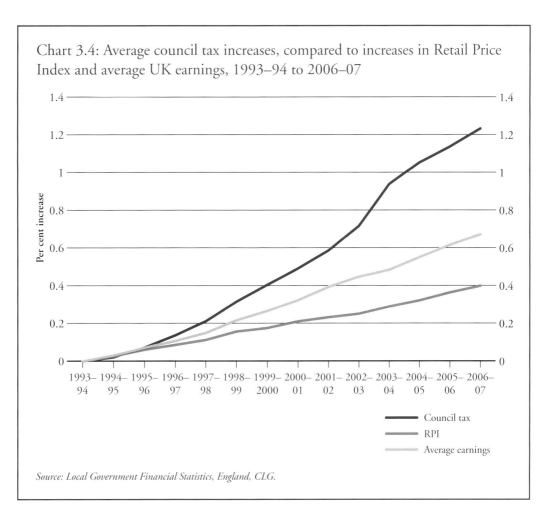

Chart 3.4: Average council tax increases, compared to increases in Retail Price Index and average UK earnings, 1993–94 to 2006–07

Source: Local Government Financial Statistics, England, CLG.

3.53   Chart 3.5 shows, in simplified terms, that council tax tends to operate as the 'balancing item' in local budgets, absorbing any spending requirements that are left after grant, charging, efficiency savings and any local choices about service provision have been taken into account. The impact of rising needs, costs or expectations may be allowed for through central government grant, and can to some extent be managed or responded to through a range of options open to local government, but at a certain point it tends to become concentrated on council tax. If funding and local flexibility are too restricted, council tax can become a 'safety valve' for pressure on local public services.

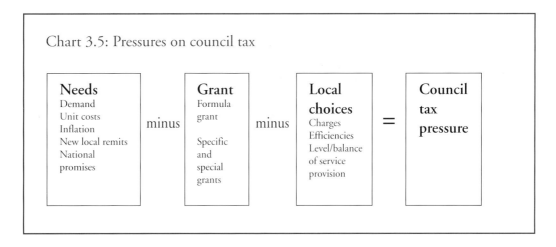

Chart 3.5: Pressures on council tax

| **Needs** Demand Unit costs Inflation New local remits National promises | minus | **Grant** Formula grant Specific and special grants | minus | **Local choices** Charges Efficiencies Level/balance of service provision | = | **Council tax pressure** |

3.54   Many have argued that pressures on local budgets could continue to impact on council tax in the future, potentially driving further above-inflation increases. However, the extent to which this happens will depend on a range of factors including the level of central government's contribution to local funding and, crucially, on local government's ability to influence the level of overall spending growth by having greater flexibility to manage pressures and find efficiency savings across their budget and to deliver services in line with local priorities.

The nature of future pressures

3.55   There is much debate and analysis about the causes of cost pressures at the national level and at individual authority level, and a wide range of predictions of how significant future pressures will be. Whilst always a difficult debate, the importance of managing pressures effectively is likely to increase in the next few years, as the money available for public spending is likely to grow less quickly than over the past decade. The Government has signalled that grant growth is likely to slow over the coming Spending Review period. Through the Comprehensive Spending Review (CSR) the Government is working with local government to identify pressures across the sector until 2010–11.

3.56   The Local Government Association last year identified waste and adult social care as the two areas of greatest pressure in the coming Spending Review period (up to 2010–11).[23] Analysis by other commentators reinforces the argument that these pressures could be significant, both during the CSR period and into the medium term:

- the Wanless Review of Social Care predicted a 53 per cent increase in the number of older people with some social care needs over the next 20 years, and a 54 per cent increase in the numbers of those with a high level of need.[24] For care provision to continue at current levels, this would imply average annual growth in social care budgets for older people of more than six per cent a year. This assumes that the level of voluntary effort provided by carers remains constant, and that we remain able as a society to rely on the care and compassion of friends and family to look after many older people who might otherwise require greater support from the state;[25]

- the Commission for Social Care Inspection (CSCI) suggests that rising demand for, and expectations of, social care, combined with rising wage costs, are already having an impact on the level at which eligibility for care is set, with councils increasingly rationing care to those with the most acute needs;[26] and

- the Department for Environment, Food and Rural Affairs (Defra) has predicted that rising waste volumes, and EU requirements that the UK find alternatives to landfill, could contribute to average growth in waste budgets of just under 6 per cent a year (cash), with steeper increases in the short term.[27]

3.57   There are also indications that social care provision for disabled adults and for children may be subject to many of the same pressures as provision for older people: the Commission for Social Care Inspection reports growing demand for intensive care services across these groups.

3.58   Aside from pressures within particular services, local authorities face other corporate pressures. These include legislative and policy changes such as the move to single status on pay for

---

[23] Local Government Association, *Meeting the Challenges Ahead*, 2006.
[24] Wanless, D., *Securing Good Care for Older People: Taking a long-term view*, King's Fund, 2006.
[25] There are no definitive estimates of the value of voluntary care although the Wanless review estimated the replacement cost of care to over-65s at £3.5 billion a year.
[26] Commission for Social Care Inspection, *The State of Social Care in England 2005–06*, 2006.
[27] Defra, Review of Waste Strategy, 2005.

male and female employees for local authorities that have not already addressed this issue and deficits in the pension funds for retired local government employees.

3.59   There are other sources of pressure, driven by public expectations over what services should be delivered, and to which standard. At times these are the subject of national promises and ministerial commitments which make it difficult for local authorities to modify services in light of local priorities, with little scope to balance national requirements against other needs and preferences. There is a tendency for local budgets, including those funds which are notionally un-hypothecated, to become 'spoken for' by national promises and the expectations they generate, leaving only limited scope for local communities to shape their own spending plans.

> *[Central direction of services] disempowers local councillors and distorts the use of local government finances because these 'national' services have to be resourced to national standards which means that when resources are reduced the locally preferred services are disadvantaged. A recent example of this effect is the decision by government to extend the scheme for concessionary bus fares.* (Eastbourne Borough Council)

3.60   Other pressures include the strong demands, often led by the business sector, for improvements in infrastructure. This is often driven by population increases in growth areas, but also the need to support investment in regeneration, or to provide better transport infrastructure. Local authorities, such as Kent County Council, also argue that investment in maintenance of highways has had to be squeezed over time to pay for more essential services, resulting in a backlog of maintenance needs.

3.61   In addition, there is a wide range of pressures which can affect a small number of local authorities. I have received a range of representations from individual authorities, and groups of authorities, addressing particular circumstances which they argue require special funding, or changes in the national distribution of resources.[28] Such pressures are arguably most appropriately considered in terms of how grant is shared between authorities, rather than in determining the overall total.

3.62   However, these future pressures must be set against savings from services where needs or costs may be reducing over time. Such savings are likely to be captured through overall efficiency processes which can, as local government and others have demonstrated, yield improvements and cost savings year on year. The Chancellor announced in his Pre-Budget report that the Comprehensive Spending Review would include the expectations that three per cent year on year value for money savings will be achieved by central and local government.

Managing pressures in the future

3.63   I have not sought to duplicate the detailed analysis being undertaken in the Comprehensive Spending Review. Modelling likely costs across the whole range of services provided by local government is extremely challenging. Moreover, many of the pressures faced by local government are affected by central government's decisions about priorities and targets (which are decided in Spending Reviews), and the framework it sets for local government, as well as by external factors and local choices. However, in order to understand the impact of possible future changes on council tax the Inquiry has modelled some simplified scenarios for future local spending and revenues over the next 20 years, as set out in Annex B. This modelling examines the possible impact of changes in some of the key variables determining pressure on council tax, and the potential

---

[28] For instance, some commentators have argued that services may be under pressure from population growth associated with internal migration and immigration. The Audit Commission in a recent report *Crossing Borders* argued that while migrants on the whole bring net economic benefits to areas, some local areas were experiencing a degree of 'strain' on public services. A recent report for London Councils (Travers, T. et al., *Population and Mobility and Service Provision*, 2007) also highlights the challenges facing local authorities with highly mobile populations.

implications of a range of possible futures, including different trends in revenues, spending growth and value for money savings.

3.64   The results of that modelling, based as they are on possible scenarios, change to a great degree depending on the assumptions that are made about overall growth in service budgets. Even allowing for known pressures on waste and social care, council tax rises at inflation, or even real terms reductions, could be delivered if overall spending was kept down. This might involve a number of measures – reduced demands from central government, efficiency savings or local choices to reduce the quality or scale of some services at the local level.

3.65   Looking more broadly, long-term trends such as demographic change and the need to manage impacts on the environment create pressures for public services in general and local government in particular. Unless managed effectively by central and local government, these could result in pressures on council tax. However, this is not inevitable, and even then the measures outlined above, perhaps alongside additional national spending, could help to manage them. In local government as elsewhere there has naturally been debate about the role of and scope for efficiency savings, and how they can be achieved in the context of long-term contracting arrangements. More independent analysis could help to build on the work done by central and local government and provide a more secure basis for consensus.

3.66   All of this serves to emphasise the value of allowing local government greater flexibility and local choice – to find ways to improve efficiency and value for money as well as to provide greater local public satisfaction by focusing more closely on local priorities.

3.67   Central and local government share the desire to manage pressures on the finance system to avoid unsustainable increases in council tax and to maximise value for money. They therefore have a shared interest in making it possible for local government to make choices which find the best set of outcomes for local citizens. This means allowing greater space and powers to change behaviour to reduce costs and improve effectiveness, and to make local choices which, where necessary, place less emphasis on those services and outcomes which are not a high priority locally. It also means giving local authorities the power and credibility they need to engage with their communities in setting priorities and taking responsibility for making realistic (and difficult) choices which take account of resources available and the full range of pressures on them.

CONFUSED ACCOUNTABILITY

3.68   Clear lines of accountability are a precondition for an effective relationship between central and local government, and are essential to allow people and communities to engage with, understand and challenge the decisions which affect their lives. Without such clarity local communities cannot know who to hold responsible for taxation and spending decisions, which can then become a major area of friction and public disquiet when spending is tight and pressures on services are high. As research for my Inquiry with the public concluded: "There was a strong and pervasive feeling that those charged with spending public money should be held to account".[29]

3.69   All levels of government need to be accountable for their actions. This drives the requirement for local government to act in the interest of all its citizens. Accountability is determined by the way in which communities can understand and challenge the decisions that local authorities have made on their behalf. This is most easily understood through elections, but also encompasses the more general processes through which local authorities receive 'customer' feedback such as ongoing engagement, complaints and lobbying by special interest groups. The

---

[29] Palmer, A. and Thompson, M., *Qualitative Survey into Public Attitudes to Taxation and Public Services*, Lyons Inquiry, 2005.

current system of local government – both in terms of function and finance – obscures proper accountability due to:

- a lack of public understanding of how the system works, which enables both local and central government to blame the other for problems;

- complexity in both function and funding; and

- a poorly understood link between local businesses and local services.

Lack of understanding of local government finance system

3.70   Research for the Inquiry, which I reported on in depth in my December 2005 Interim Report, showed high levels of confusion and misunderstanding of the current finance system. This led me to conclude at that time that there is "both a weak knowledge of the actual finance regime, and a poor understanding of the cost of public services".[30]

3.71   There was confusion over what council tax paid for – the general view being that it paid for a very large range of services and that most funding for local services came from council tax, yet still only a minority thought it represented value for money. This demonstrates a fundamental misunderstanding of the costs of services which, I believe, can only lead the public to be dissatisfied with both local and central government. There was also only limited awareness that local authorities received grants from central government to support services and, while there was a high awareness of council tax, people did not know which council tax band their property was in.

3.72   This poor understanding both facilitates and is compounded by local and central government blaming each other for increases in costs which lead to tax increases or difficult spending decisions. This obscures any balanced analysis of drivers for tax increases and also contributes to a confrontational approach to issues that are rightly of both local and national concern. It leaves complex societal issues – such as how we should care for the frail elderly – over which there should be a mature public debate, to be resolved at the local level in the context of febrile debates about the rate of local tax.

3.73   It also means that the lack of understanding of the costs of services contributes to unrealistically high expectations of what local government should be able to deliver for an average annual council tax bill of under £1,300.

3.74   The National Audit Office, in their submission to the Inquiry, summarised this lack of understanding of local government:

> *To put all this briefly: local government is to most people a mystery. Few understand how it works; what you can do to influence it; whether it is really local at all, or just a set of covert Whitehall agencies.*

A system with unclear accountability

3.75   The current system of local government finance does not help to clarify which level of government should be held to account for which decisions. This can be most clearly seen in relation to the capping of council tax. In essence, central government controls what is supposed to be a local tax, taking away a key aspect of local accountability, to the detriment of both local and central government. This issue was raised by many contributors to the regional events that I conducted in 2005. The main concerns were about the use of capping cutting across accountability to the local electorate and the impact it had on services that were wanted locally, ranging from more policing to cleaner streets and to free bus passes for needy groups.

---

[30] *Lyons Inquiry into Local Government: Consultation Paper and Interim Report*, Lyons Inquiry, 2005.

Complex
governance

3.76   There is an increasing, and laudable, emphasis on delivering services in a cross-cutting way via partnerships, based on an understanding in recent years of the need to join-up services to improve effectiveness for those who use them. However, if this is not done within a clear framework it also has the potential to complicate governance. Submissions to my Inquiry have indicated that multiple accountabilities can increase the risk of drawing the focus away from local communities and their needs and responsibilities.

> *The complexity of the existing governance and administrative structures can act as a barrier. In terms of the complexity of governance structures, we mean not only the different tiers of local government, but also the numerous agencies which operate at national, regional and sub-regional levels ... [this] can mean that that there is less clarity about who is accountable, more negotiation is needed and decision-making is often slower.* (St. Edmundsbury Borough Council)

3.77   There are also instances of partners having to respond differently to different government departments. In the case study research, councils attempting to tackle employment issues via their Local Strategic Partnership cited problems with Learning and Skills Councils and Job Centre Plus having nationally set targets which did not align, exacerbated by a mismatch in the eligibility criteria each partner was using for skills-related interventions.[31] This also manifests itself in budget and performance management arrangements, which do not align, for example between social services and primary care trusts.

Structural
complexities

3.78   The local government arrangements in England add complexity to our finance system with particular impacts on the public understanding of how the council tax bill is made up. Fire and police authorities operate as major preceptors, parishes operate as minor preceptors and various other bodies levy funds from the council tax bill. In parts of England the two-tier arrangements also add a further layer of complexity with shire counties receiving council tax funds via a precept on district authority bills and the Greater London Authority precepting on London borough bills.

---

[31] Entwhistle, T. et. al., *Perspectives on Place-shaping and Service Delivery: A Report of Case Study Work*, Lyons Inquiry, 2007.

Precepting

Of the 478 principal local authorities in England,

- 354 are billing authorities, that is the primary issuer of the council tax bill to householders – these are all lower tier (district) or unitary authorities;

- 102 are major precepting authorities – major precepting authorities include the GLA, county councils, police authorities and fire authorities; and

- 22 authorities levy a charge on another authority for the services they provide. Levying bodies include waste authorities, national parks authorities and passenger transport authorities.

The main difference between a precept and a levy is that precepts appear as separate elements on the face of the council tax bill and levies form part of either the billing or precepting authority's budget.

There are also over 8,700 parish and town councils and a further 1,500 parish meetings (where there is no council because there are fewer than 150 electors) which are classed as local precepting authorities. Central government does not collect information directly from such councils, although information on the total amount of council tax required for parish councils in each billing authority's area is collected from returns provided by billing authorities.

3.79   During the course of my Inquiry I have received many suggestions about how to improve this situation including: calls to move from two-tier arrangements to unitary government across the country; the possibility of the major revenue user in two-tier areas – the county – becoming the billing authority with the districts precepting; there being separate bills for each preceptor – something that was advocated by some police authorities; and calls for council tax bills to more clearly reflect the fact that they support a range of agencies other than the billing authority.

3.80   There has also been discussion about whether the public is further confused by two-tier government because they do not understand the respective responsibilities of counties and districts. These are issues that I discuss further in Chapters 4 and 5.

A poor link between local business taxes and local services

3.81   I am also concerned about how central and local government are accountable to local businesses. When the business rate was locally variable there was a clear understanding that this tax was used to support services in the locality but the nationalisation of the business rate and the introduction of Dedicated Schools Grant mean that there is some confusion about the purpose of the business rates system. Because of its history and the way it is collected, it is still perceived by many businesses as a local tax, but it is actually used in great part to fund the provision of services according to national expectations and requirements. Since the removal of schools funding from RSG in 2006–07 business rate revenues have become an essential source of the funding required to allow equalisation between authorities for needs and resources.

3.82   This has led to concerns about the status of business rates in the current finance system and the question of whether business rates are a national or a local tax. These are reflected in businesses' concerns about the weakening of the link between their sector and local authorities as reflected in the following quotes:

Government decision makers continue to regard the capital's economy in terms of subsidising 'poorer' regions. Residents and businesses in central London provide billions of pounds annually. (Central London Partnership)

My borough is economically vibrant but residents don't really benefit from this because business rates go directly to central government. We suffer from issues such as congestion and parking in residential areas but receive little benefit.[32] (Councillor Engagement Event).

Economic prosperity

3.83　Recent work comparing the UK economy with those of the USA and Europe has concluded that the lack of devolution and local discretion in the UK is a constraint on economic performance, particularly in the cities. It is argued that too many decisions on issues like transport, planning and skills are still taken at a national or regional level without sufficient flexibility or responsiveness to the situations of local economies. For example, the Centre for Cities has found that it is a "lack of autonomy in the areas of physical regeneration, transport infrastructure and skills development that most constrains cities in their pursuit of growth".[33]

3.84　This disadvantages English cities compared with their counterparts in many European countries and North America. The *State of the English Cities* report states:

Many English cities … are not performing as well as their competitors in Europe and beyond. In this context the framework set by national government matters a great deal. Although there are differences, the trend in continental Europe is to decentralise and regionalise decision-making, placing powers at the lowest level. The evidence suggests that where cities are given more freedom and resources they have responded by being more proactive, entrepreneurial and successful.[34]

3.85　There are a number of economic arguments which suggest that the devolution of powers and responsibilities to a sub-national level can have economic benefits. Identifying whether the level of devolution and decentralised decision-making is optimal is challenging – while theory shows there is a role for some level of devolution it is not easy to judge what that level is. There are benefits and drawbacks to devolution. One study of high-income countries over a 30-year period found that an intermediate level of decentralisation is associated with higher growth than either extreme.[35] Other cross-country studies which attempt to identify whether decentralised countries experience high levels of economic growth have come to a mixture of conclusions. However, given that the UK is recognised as one of the most centralised developed countries, we must give serious consideration to whether there are advantages to be had from greater decentralisation and devolution of decisions in this area of policy.[36]

3.86　Economic theory suggests that decisions on issues relevant to economic activity should ideally be taken at a spatial scale which reflects the pattern of that activity if they are to take into account all of the costs and benefits, and there are widespread concerns that since the current structure of local authority boundaries does not reflect economic geography, local authorities are not appropriate bodies to which to devolve greater powers.

---

[32] *Report on the Councillor Engagement Events*, Lyons Inquiry, 2006.
[33] Centre for Cities, *City Leadership*.
[34] Parkinson, M. et al., *State of the English Cities*, vol. 1, Office of the Deputy Prime Minister, 2006.
[35] Thießen, U., 'Fiscal Decentralisation and Economic Growth in High-Income OECD Countries' in *Fiscal Studies* 2003, vol. 24, no. 3.
[36] Turok, I., 'Local and National Competitiveness: Is Decentralisation Good for the Economy?', Lyons Inquiry 2005.

3.87   Analysis in a host of recent publications including that of the Centre for Cities and various Government documents illustrates this point, though it has been a live issue at least since city-regions were raised in the context of the Redcliffe-Maud report of 1969. To give just one example, the 2001 Census shows that 40 per cent of people crossed at least one local authority boundary when travelling to work, and that number is higher if one looks just at highly skilled individuals.[37] Decisions made solely on the basis of an authority's administrative boundary will not therefore usually reflect the reality of where local people actually work, or where local firms find their employees. Issues like this provide the rationale for making a number of decisions related to economic development at the level of the region or even the nation as a whole.

3.88   However, it is worth reflecting on the fact that while local authority boundaries may be too small a level at which to make these decisions, the regional and the national level may well be too large. The Local Government Association's *Prosperous Communities II* illustrates that point very clearly, showing the variety of different economic patterns and markets that exist within England. It argues that a pattern of sub-regions is more useful in explaining economic and market connections, and that "there is a distinctive sub-regional layer of the real economy, as evidenced in markets for labour, goods and services, in industrial clusters and in relative economic performance".[38] The complexity and variability of these economic relationships is, of course, something that has already been recognised by the Regional Development Agencies and by local authorities, who have in many cases established sub-regional partnerships of various kinds to tailor approaches more effectively. Some, however, have called for new types of local authority to be created, which would better reflect sub-regional economic geography and could have greater powers devolved to them.

3.89   There clearly are issues to be addressed here, though this should not lead us to quickly assume that we can find simple structural solutions to these complex issues by creating a new tier of government. Functional economic boundaries are not precisely defined, are different for different kinds of activity and different types of people and businesses, and they change over time. It is by no means clear, for example, that the old metropolitan counties – which for some seem to be the obvious model for new city regions – do now reflect the reality of economic activity and transport patterns in all of the metropolitan areas. While we can argue about whether nations, regions, sub-regions or localities are the best spatial level on which to consider these issues, the truth is rather more complex and, in fact, as the OECD argues:

> We are not witnessing a shift from nation-state to wholly independent city and region governments, but the emergence of multi-level government that requires coordination between cities and regions, nation-states and international agencies.[39]

3.90   It is also important that the arrangements maintain local knowledge and the trust and engagement of local citizens. This is especially true when dealing with contentious issues like planning, where there is the potential to create real dissatisfaction and disengagement with governmental and political processes if handled poorly or if people do not accept decisions as legitimate.

3.91   We therefore need to recognise the complexity involved in these issues and not seek simplistic solutions to what are complex problems. The debate should focus on the key goals – how to achieve a prosperous, cohesive and sustainable society – and how to enhance behaviours and working relationships to deliver responsive and accountable decision-making arrangements.

---

[37] *Devolving Decision Making: 3 – Meeting the Regional Economic Challenges: The Importance of Cities to Regional Growth*, HMT, DTI and ODPM, 2006.
[38] *Prosperous Communities II: vive la devolution!*, 2007, Local Government Assocation.
[39] *Devolution and Globalisation: Implications for Local Decision Makers*, OECD, 2001.

PUBLIC ATTITUDES

Public attitudes to central control over local government

3.92   Public opinion and, in particular, concern about the 'postcode lottery' – the concern that there should be similar standards of outcomes in services areas in all parts of the country – is sometimes used to justify the need for central action.

3.93   As already noted however, research for my Inquiry shows, that public opinion is more complex than this suggests. Chart 3.6 shows that the majority of respondents believe that central government should have responsibility for controlling standards in health, education, police and fire and rescue services. This was mirrored in the results of focus group work for my Inquiry which concluded that central government should set national standards for 'core' services, including social services, in addition to those listed above. However, even in these core services there was a recognition that they needed to be able to reflect local circumstances.

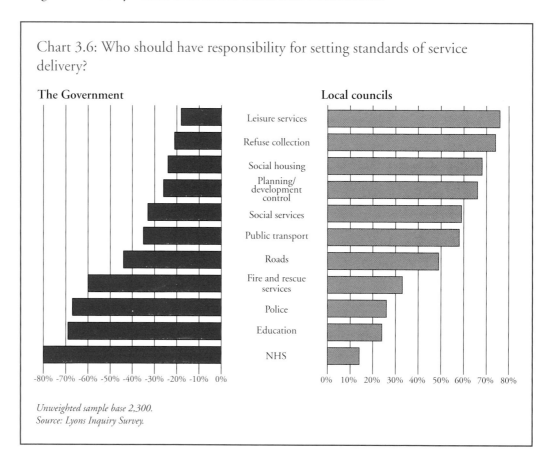

Chart 3.6: Who should have responsibility for setting standards of service delivery?

Unweighted sample base 2,300.
Source: Lyons Inquiry Survey.

3.94   The survey work also found a clear view that, for the majority of services asked about, local government should have a greater role in setting priorities than central government (see Chart 3.7).

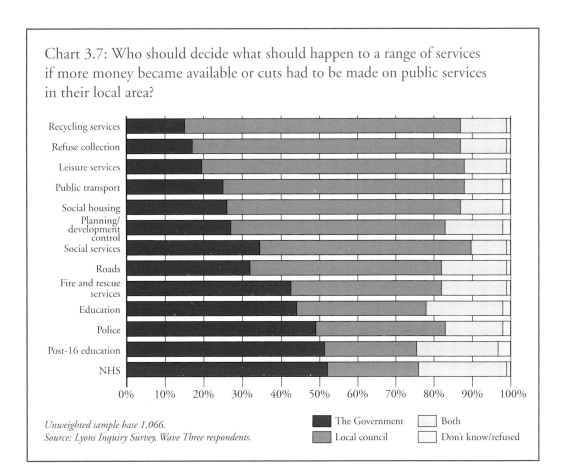

Chart 3.7: Who should decide what should happen to a range of services if more money became available or cuts had to be made on public services in their local area?

Unweighted sample base 1,066.
Source: Lyons Inquiry Survey, Wave Three respondents.

The Government   Both
Local council   Don't know/refused

3.95   In public engagement events, participants firmly supported the idea that there should be neither total standardisation, nor total local flexibility, but rather minimum national standards above which councils could provide a better level of service where it was wanted or needed.[40] People wanted to ensure that there was an element of national fairness and protection via minimum standards, but also the flexibility to provide services in the way that best met local needs.

3.96   This appetite for what I call 'managed difference' is reflected in the survey results. There was a strong sense of disagreement with a proposition that levels of service should vary until the concepts of local consultation and satisfaction with the services were introduced. The proportion of respondents who agreed that service levels could differ changed from 26 per cent to 77 per cent once these conditions were added.

3.97   Striking the right balance in managing differences between areas and across services is a difficult challenge. It is particularly hard to conduct clear local discussion of priorities when people do not understand the true cost of local services. This will impact on negotiations of the different standards of service that can be expected for different levels of cost. However, local and central government need to confront this challenge in order to develop a better understanding of what taxpayers are buying or people's dissatisfaction with local government will continue.

---

[40] *Lyons Inquiry – Public Deliberation Events: Final Report for the Lyons Inquiry Team*, Lyons Inquiry, 2006.

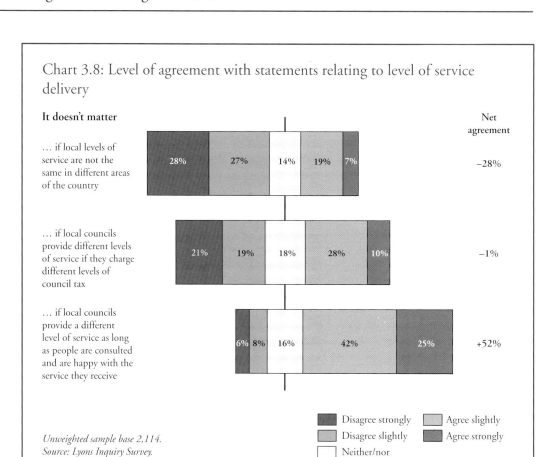

Chart 3.8: Level of agreement with statements relating to level of service delivery

It doesn't matter

Net agreement

... if local levels of service are not the same in different areas of the country — 28% | 27% | 14% | 19% | 7% — −28%

... if local councils provide different levels of service if they charge different levels of council tax — 21% | 19% | 18% | 28% | 10% — −1%

... if local councils provide a different level of service as long as people are consulted and are happy with the service they receive — 6% | 8% | 16% | 42% | 25% — +52%

Disagree strongly   Agree slightly
Disagree slightly   Agree strongly
Neither/nor

Unweighted sample base 2,114.
Source: Lyons Inquiry Survey.

Lack of trust in the system of local government

3.98   Trust is the other crucial, but perhaps often understated, factor that is necessary for local government to be able to lead effective place-shaping. As Chapter 2 reports, local institutions and representatives tend to be more trusted than national institutions. In 2005, 58 per cent of people said they trusted their council a lot or a fair amount, whereas in contrast just 37 per cent of people said they trusted parliament.[41] In a survey for the Committee on Standards in Public Life in 2006, 48 per cent trusted their local MP and 43 per cent their local councillors, compared to 23 per cent trusting government ministers and 29 per cent trusting MPs in general (see Chart 3.8).[42] These figures do not offer room for complacency by either local or central government.

[41] Kitchen et al., 2005, *Citizenship Survey: Active Communities Topic Report*, CLG, 2006.
[42] Ipsos Mori, *Survey of Attitudes Towards Conduct in Public Life 2006*, Committee for Standards in Public Life, 2006.

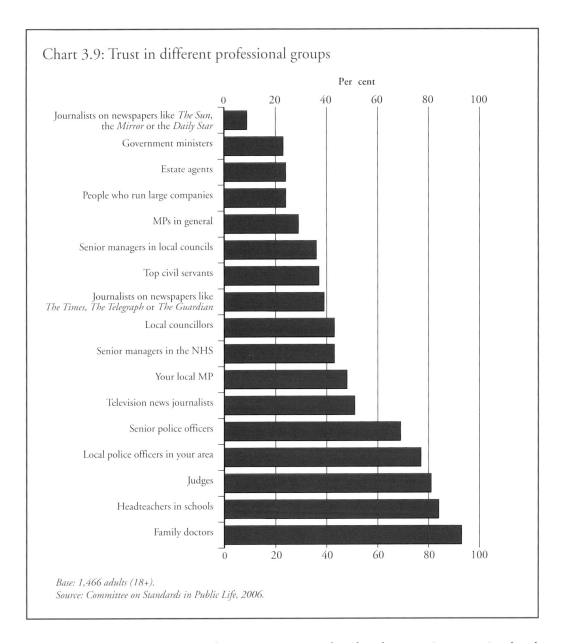

Chart 3.9: Trust in different professional groups

Per cent

Base: 1,466 adults (18+).
Source: Committee on Standards in Public Life, 2006.

3.99   Encouraging trust is a complex activity as trust is based at the same time on rational and emotional responses, yet it is a necessary aspect of dealing with the complex problems that face local services.[43] I believe that a major factor limiting trust in the system is the confused accountability described above. However, there are other issues limiting trust in local government:

• the concern about council tax and its fairness;

• an adversarial relationship between central and local government; and

• a disempowered local government sector leading to a lack of confidence in its relevance and ability to make change happen.

Concern about council tax and its fairness

3.100   Over the past ten years, as shown in Chart 3.10, there have been instances of steep increases in council tax. Media coverage, submissions to the Inquiry and the Inquiry's research have shown that there is ongoing public concern about overall percentage increases but there is also anxiety about the fairness of council tax, particularly in terms of ability to pay, which is most often equated to income.

[43] Taylor-Gooby, P., *The Efficiency/Trust Dilemma in Public Sector Reform*, ESRC, 2006.

3.101   This issue has been particularly picked up by older persons' representative groups but, as demonstrated in Chapter 7, it is not a simple task to decide what a fair tax would look like as different groups describe fairness in different ways.

3.102   Indeed, our survey work has analysed three different types of response to council tax. Nearly half of the respondents could be characterised as 'dissatisfied payers' of council tax but, more surprisingly perhaps, a third were characterised as 'accepting payers' with the other 20 per cent being more satisfied non-payers, as they were receiving benefits. So, although no tax will ever be 'popular', and non-payers have obvious reasons to feel benign towards council tax, these responses do show that compared to some of the perceptions of council tax portrayed in the media, the tax is not vilified by all payers.[44]

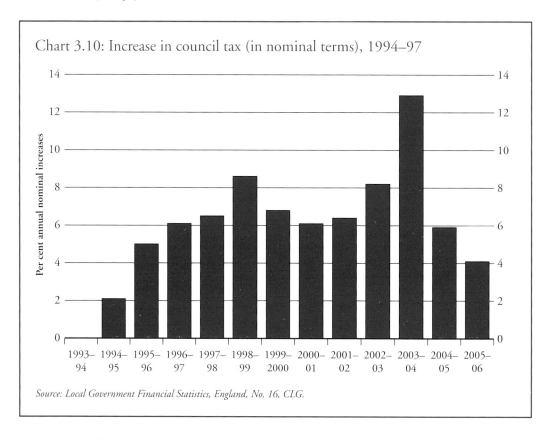

Chart 3.10: Increase in council tax (in nominal terms), 1994–97

Source: Local Government Financial Statistics, England, No. 16, CLG.

3.103   That said, I am concerned about the impact of the perceived lack of fairness of council tax and the damage I believe it has caused to the relationship between local authorities and their communities. This may in part be, as Peter Smith argued in 1991, one of the legacies of the poll tax which he argued "brought into question the legitimacy of local taxation in the United Kingdom".[45] Whatever the cause, the survey work for the Inquiry shows that only a minority consider that council tax represents value for money. This is important because the second most important driver for satisfaction with local government is perceived value for money.[46]

---

[44] *Lyons Inquiry Survey*, Lyons Inquiry, 2007.

[45] Smith, P., Lessons from the British Poll Tax Disaster, *National Tax Journal*, Vol. 44, no. 4, (December, 1991.)

[46] *What drives public satisfaction with local government*, Local Government Association, 2004

3.104 Central government has a responsibility, alongside its overall responsibility for the finance and taxation framework for the country, to maintain a trusted, viable tax for local government. An impression can be gained too often, that council tax is a local problem which can be solved through ad hoc solutions and changes, rather than recognising that many of the pressures and unfairnesses associated with the tax require national action.

An adversarial relationship

3.105 Another key factor contributing to a lack of trust in our institutions of government is the current relationship between central and local government – at least as played out in public – which can be characterised as adversarial. It may be that this is an aspect of the generally adversarial nature of British politics. As Chapter 4 discusses, such poor central–local relations are not a clear feature of all other countries. As well as damaging accountability, the wider fall-out is a sense that poor relations damage the standing and credibility of both local and central government and politicians as a group.

3.106 The focus of attention in recent decades, as set out above, has been the performance of the local authority and the delivery of service improvements. These are undoubtedly important issues but this focus has arguably neglected the need to improve the relationship between central and local government, which is still allowed to be seen as one of competition and criticism. As John Stewart from the University of Birmingham argues:

> *The nature of central–local relations is critical to building effective local government, yet there were no proposals to modernise central–local relations alongside the proposals for modernising local government.*[47]

Lack of confidence and capability

3.107 The Inquiry's councillor engagement events were marked by a general sense of disempowerment among the councillors who attended, reflecting the argument that one of the reasons people do not engage with local government as much as they might is because local councillors are perceived as having only limited powers. Some councillors argued that their credibility was undermined since, as they see it, they could not deliver for local people because central government overrides them. There was concern that central government's lack of trust in local government had undermined public confidence and felt that they were often seen as merely doing the will of central government:

> *Unless the public see local councillors as having real power to make a difference, then they feel 'what is the point?'.*

3.108 This is further evidenced in research on councillors' and former councillors' views on their own role. In the IDeA's last 'exit survey' of councillors standing down, one in four respondents cited the erosion of local government influence as their reason for leaving.[48] Recruitment of councillors, in particular younger people, is also proving difficult, with nearly half of all councillors over the age of 60.[49] This serves to reinforce the reputation of local government as unrepresentative and out of touch. This is an issue that the Government is rightly concerned about and is at the heart of the recent announcement to set up a new commission, led by Dame Jane Roberts, the former leader of the London Borough of Camden, to look at how local democracy can be revitalised and made both more representative and more responsive to local people.

---

[47] Stewart, J., *Modernising British Local Government: An Assessment of Labour's Reform Programme*, 2003.

[48] *Exit Survey of Local Authority Councillors*, IDeA, 2003.

[49] *National Census of Local Authority Councillors*, Provisional 2006 results, Local Government Analysis and Research, 2006.

3.109 The case study research reinforced this sense of disempowerment; some councillors felt that at times, middle managers paid more attention to the direction given to them by central government departments and national inspectorates than they paid to the aspirations of the elected members in their local authority. There was a questioning of the worth of standing as a local councillor if such a role cannot make a difference.

3.110 Specific examples were raised by councillors of regulatory regimes being so heavily circumscribed – for example, planning and licensing – that decisions could not sufficiently reflect local considerations and concerns, leading to public disillusionment with local government. They cited the example of local people wanting new approaches to licensing to help tackle street drinking. They took the view that the detailed national framework restricts the scope for local tailoring, making engagement frustrating and sometimes pointless.

3.111 Later chapters discuss how to tackle this lack of trust in local government in detail, however I believe the two important factors for increasing trust in local government are improved understanding and clearer accountability. I am convinced that better engagement between local government and the public – at both political and managerial levels – is the key to improving understanding of local government, the frameworks in which it operates and the tough trade-offs which require decisions. This will, in turn, help to improve the accountability of authorities to local communities for decisions over which they have control.

Effective engagement

3.112 Chapter 2 argued that the key to making best use of resources for the well-being of local communities is to enable communities to make their own choices where possible and include them in the design and delivery of services through co-production. These will help to obtain better outcomes and improve understanding and satisfaction. This, in turn, relies on local government engaging with local communities to understand their preferences for services and other aspects of local government activities. This is currently limited by:

- central and local government frameworks on engagement having a focus solely on service improvement against formal targets at the expense of overall satisfaction and wider understanding of community needs and preferences; and

- too great a focus on the centre in terms of performance reporting and target setting, rather than a focus on the community.

Engagement too focused on service-specific improvements

3.113 Recent research has concluded that central government initiatives to enhance engagement and participation through initiatives such as Best Value have improved services.[50]

3.114 However, there is a question of whether the current focus of community engagement enables the broader understanding that is required to judge whether the right services are being delivered in the first place, as opposed to services being delivered in the right way. This is essential to achieving the broadest type of 'allocative efficiency' needed to maximise well-being. Recent developments have moved the dynamic for participation towards individuals' interaction with services as consumers, rather than gaining an understanding of community needs through the wider forms of democratic participation that are important to develop social capital and community cohesion. As Wilkes-Heeg and Clayton argue:

---

[50] *Long-term Evaluation of Best Value Regime: Final Report*, Communities and Local Government, 2006.

The limitations of the more consumerist approaches to participation must ... be underlined. Substantial investment in market research, focus groups, consultation events, survey questionnaires and so on, has clearly not prompted participation in electoral politics Indeed, there is little reason to suppose that 'individualised' approaches help enhance more collective forms of democratic participation or serve to reinvent, or even sustain, notions of democratic participation.[51]

Too great a focus on the centre 3.115 Some commentators have raised concerns about levels of central control damaging local engagement. They argue that people will not engage with organisations that have no authority. The Electoral Commission's research into the 2002 local elections concluded that 60 per cent of respondents would be encouraged to vote at local elections if the council had more scope to make local decisions and 51 per cent if councils had more scope to determine taxes and spending.[52] Such concerns can be typified in the following quote:

The public is unwilling to engage with councils which they see as delivery agents of national government with little room for manoeuvre and therefore unable to make a real difference locally.[53]

3.116 Central controls also govern consultation and engagement processes. These often cover both the topics on which consultation must take place and, at times, the methods that should be used. This has had benefits in raising the priority of such activities and has led to methodological advances. However, it produces risks; central priorities are put above those of localities and the focus is on the centre – the Communities and Local Government work on performance measurement estimated that councils spend about 80 per cent of their reporting effort on reporting 'upwards' aimed at Government departments and ministers and less than 20 per cent on their local systems which are aimed at electors and taxpayers.[54]

POOR INCENTIVES IN DISTRIBUTION OF NATIONAL RESOURCES

3.117 The place-shaping council should be clearly focused on the needs and wishes of its local community. In contrast, the current model in England is characterised by a centralised form of governance both with regard to finance and levels of control. This affects the behaviour of local government, particularly through the distribution of national resources through the grant system which can distract local government away from the concerns, needs and future prospects of its citizens and its local areas.

Impact of balance of funding 3.118 The impact of grant is sometimes articulated as part of the balance of funding issue, with commentators arguing that central government's provision of a large proportion of funding to local government in itself creates risks of dependency. This issue is summarised well in the following quote:

In a system where local government was responsible for, say, 50 per cent of all public expenditure without commensurate local tax raising responsibility, the impact of changing levels of central support would be far greater than when the figure was, say, five per cent.[55]

---

[51] Wilkes-Heeg, S. and Clayton S., *Whose Town is it Anyway? The State of Local Democracy in Two Northern Towns,* 2006.

[52] *Public Opinion and the 2002 Local Elections,* Electoral Commission, 2002.

[53] *Implications of Local Devolution for Efficiency and Effectiveness in Service Delivery,* Martin, S., Lyons Inquiry Seminar: Greater Devolution: Evidence in Support, June 2005.

[54] *Mapping the Local Government Performance Reporting Landscape,* CLG, 2006.

[55] Travers, T., *International Comparisons of Local Government Finance: Propositions and Analysis,* Lyons Inquiry, 2005.

Impact on central and local relations

3.119 However, the amount of funding provided by central government is not the only determinant of the effect of the grant system on central–local relations. The structure of that funding – the incentives it produces and the consequences that it has for control and for accountability – shapes the interface between local and central government and, by implication between local authorities and their communities.

3.120 The objective of both central and local government should be to obtain the best results and outcomes from existing resources without being distracted from striking the right local deal over taxation. Instead, the current process fosters, and is supported by, local government behaviours which are focused on lobbying government for changes to data, formulae and grants in order to gain marginal extra revenue from the centre. This absorbs energy amongst council members, officers, civil servants and ministers. It contributes to a sense that resources are seen not as citizens' money to be used in their best interests but somehow as the property of central government handed out by ministers. There is a strong sense that lobbying for more grants is also free of political cost to local authorities.

3.121 It also results in local authorities being in competition with each other, individually or through representative bodies such as those that promote the case of different types of local authorities. I doubt it is possible to design a distribution system that is completely competition-free but it is useful to contrast our experience with that of other countries, such as Denmark and Germany, that operate horizontal equalisation systems. In these countries, authorities with high tax bases share their resources more directly with low tax base authorities, through arriving at consensus, without the need for the centre to become involved in orchestrating the transfers.[56]

Current objectives of the grant system

3.122 The current grant system balances two objectives, which can often be in tension with one another. On the one hand, it seeks to deliver equity by taking local needs and local council tax resources into account when allocating grant, thus providing more generous grants to areas with the highest needs and lowest local resources.

3.123 On the other hand, the grant system also seeks to deliver some stability in grant allocations for local authorities. This objective has been given substantial weight in recent years through a system of damping. The emphasis has been put on minimum, or floor, levels of grant increase for all authorities, imposing ceilings and scaling back of grants to other authorities to pay for those floors. An example of the impact of damping can be seen in 2006–07, when 71 out of the 150 local authorities with responsibility for personal social services were protected by the 'floor' which was set to guarantee all authorities a minimum two per cent increase for this aspect of their budget. Further information about damping is set out in Annex A.

3.124 Clearly, a degree of stability is important to allow local authorities to plan. However, there is evidence that this focus on stability is also about controlling council tax increases as council tax may have to increase to compensate for shifts in grant. In doing this it limits the ability of the grant system to react to needs, which for those areas with high or increasing needs means that they need to put further pressure on council tax. In consequence, Government's concern to control council tax without resolving how to deal with the underlying pressures on the tax risks distorting other aspects of the finance system.

---

[56] Loughlin, J. and Martin, S., *Options for Reforming Local Government Funding to Increase Local Streams of Funding: International Comparisons*, Lyons Inquiry 2005.

Limited incentives for growth

3.125 Such concerns need not be an issue, if one considered that the current grant system was delivering all that could be asked of it. However, examples from international systems suggest that grant should not be just about insulating local authorities from their particular circumstances or from change, or indeed from an unpopular local tax. The grant process should also be about providing incentives to support positive activities, as argued by the OECD:

> *full equalisation removes the incentive to increase jurisdictional tax base by attracting new economic activity ... [as such] full compensation of differences in tax or service capacity may compromise the incentive to expand the tax base and should be avoided.*[57]

3.126 As the above quote suggests, the question of incentives is of particular importance when considering the role of local authorities in pursuing and enabling economic prosperity and housing supply in their area. These are important aspects of their place-shaping role and so a link between the health of the economy and the size of local tax base is a key motivation for local authorities to take growth seriously.

3.127 Outside specific initiatives, local authorities can only share in the general growth of housing or business tax bases in a limited way. Neither growth in council tax nor business rates in England are rewarded in any way through the funding of the authority because the grant system automatically takes into account any growth in tax base. Housing growth does have some benefit for the local community in that it allows council tax increases to be spread across a larger tax base but the residents' use of services produces costs as well. Local government can only see a very long-term benefit from growth in business tax base in the form of more resources for central government to allocate.

3.128 The special initiatives that have been introduced to create incentives mainly relate to development, including Section 106 contributions and the proposed Planning-gains Supplement. There are proposals for a Housing and Planning Delivery Grant to provide incentives for the delivery of new housing and the recently introduced Local Authority Business Growth Incentives scheme aims to provide local authorities with general financial gains from a growing business tax base.

3.129 Such systems are important, but a concern remains that they are special schemes that operate outside the main local government finance system and are subject to specific and, at times, complex allocation criteria and changes by the Government. These factors reduce the degree to which authorities can successfully rely on such schemes and make long-term decisions. I discuss options for improving incentives in Chapter 9.

CONCLUSION

3.130 This chapter has identified the key problems limiting local government's contribution to place-shaping and local well-being as deeply engrained systemic issues affecting the confidence of people in local government, and the confidence of local government to act in the interests of its communities. Local government's own responses and behaviours are, of course, key to achieving change and these are discussed in Chapter 5. However, change is needed at central government level too.

---

[57] *Intergovernmental Transfers and Decentralised Public Spending*, OECD Network on Fiscal Relations Across Levels of Government, 2005.

3.131 As this chapter has shown, problems with council tax and the balance of funding for local government are important issues. The causes of council tax pressure, lack of trust in the system of government and the constraints holding local government back lie in a system which is over-centralised, which offers too little local flexibility and in which accountability is unclear and confused. Tackling such large-scale problems is a major task and will require central government working to support and maintain a trusted and viable local tax and, crucially, to create more space to respond to local choice.

3.132 The Government has made a real move forward in the Local Government White Paper and associated Bill. I share much of the Government's analysis of the problem, but believe that the objectives for reform are profound and broad, including:

- **clearer accountability** over who is responsible for what, including clarity over who controls tax and spending decisions so enabling a clearer understanding of the costs of services and who can and should be held to account. I see this as a good in its own right but also a necessary condition for local communities to fully engage in the process of determining priorities and choices within limited revenues;

- **greater flexibility** – this includes: financial flexibility, enabling local authorities to have more control over managing their budgets, raise revenue and take spending decisions to best meet the needs and preferences of their local communities; and flexibility to enable local government to manage local services in response to local needs and work with partners in new and innovative ways to improve how well services work for local communities;

- **better incentives** for local government to own and grow their tax bases and for both central and local government to develop a more productive relationship over time which recognises their shared objective for improvements in the system;

- **tackling perceived unfairness**, in order (along with other objectives) to improve satisfaction and trust in the system of local government as a whole. This is a difficult but important area and, in assessing my reform options, I have attempted to balance: competing views of fairness in terms of concerns about particular groups such as pensioners; issues around ability to pay, wealth and the link between the level of tax and the value of the property; and consideration of the benefit principle – that recipients of the service should bear the costs of that service; and

- **continued improvements in efficiency** – the overall efficiency of local public services is a key factor which could help to relieve pressures on council tax under the current system. It is therefore essential that public services are delivered in the most cost-effective way possible. However, in seeking to improve the well-being of local communities and manage pressures as effectively as possible it is also essential that public expenditure is allocated to best meet the needs and preferences of the community: delivering the right local priorities rather than just doing them as cheaply as possible. Both of these objectives require greater scope for local choice.

3.133 All these objectives need to be addressed if we are to move towards a more sustainable system of local government and local government funding. That means being able to adapt to changes and manage pressures caused by demographic, societal and global challenge as well as those brought about by policy and political changes, locally, nationally and internationally.

3.134 These themes will form the objectives against which I will appraise reform options presented in subsequent chapters.

4 Central government's contribution to reform

Summary

This chapter examines what central government can do to improve the framework within which local government operates, enabling it more fully to take on its place-shaping role. It recognises the significant step forward represented by the proposals in the recent Local Government White Paper and subsequent Bill, but argues, that in delivering the ambitions which the Government has set out, it faces significant risks and challenges, which will need to be addressed if the potential benefits of the White Paper are to be fully realised.

It argues that a key priority is to sharpen and clarify the accountability of the current system, particularly by:

- clarifying the respective roles of both central and local government, including what local government is best placed to do;
- streamlining the performance management framework with a clearer local focus;
- allowing local government to improve its own governance; and
- improving the transparency and accountability of the funding system for the public and Parliament. This may require an independent and authoritative source of evidence to inform the debate about local government funding. It also means that the system of council tax capping should end – while born out of understandable motives, it confuses accountability and can have perverse effects.

The White Paper sets a welcome path towards a system which provides greater local flexibility and choice, particularly through the proposals to reduce central targets and burdens through the new performance framework. In order to ensure flexibility is protected over time, central government will need to achieve a shift in attitudes and behaviour to ensure that:

- soft controls in the form of new types of conditional funding, guidance and central government pronouncements do not take the place of formal targets – moreover, the chapter argues that the Government should make a firm commitment to further reductions in conditional funding;
- funding flexibility is preserved and joint working with other partners is made easier;
- local government's convening role is more formally recognised and supported by the system;
- local government is recognised and rewarded for improving allocative efficiency – delivering the right priorities for local people – as well as for driving forward managerial efficiency;
- local government's sense of ambition and powerfulness on behalf of local people is encouraged by central government as well as from within the sector;
- arrangements for working at the level of the functional economy (across authority boundaries) should be flexible and based on what works in the local area.

The chapter also considers what this means for a range of different services, including adult social care, domestic waste collection and disposal, health and well-being, children's services, community safety and economic development.

INTRODUCTION

4.1   Central government has responsibility for the overall framework within which local government operates, and therefore bears a significant responsibility for the performance of the system of local government as a whole. However, central government can only ever be responsible for part of that system; it shares responsibility with local government to make it work as well as it can for our citizens. Indeed, the previous chapter argues that some of the problems currently afflicting local government and its funding system are due to central government's attempts to take *too much* responsibility for matters which should be appropriately left for local decision.

4.2   This chapter sets out where I think the government's approach will need to change if local authorities are to be able to play their place-shaping role, and respond flexibly and efficiently to the needs of communities. Later chapters propose detailed and specific changes to the funding system, and also changes which local authorities will themselves need to make to fulfil the potential of their place-shaping role.

4.3   In my May 2006 report, *National prosperity, local choice and civic engagement,* I argued the need for greater local flexibility and choice to enable local government to rise to this challenge, and emphasised in particular the weight of the range of central controls on local authorities, which has tended to distract their attention upwards, towards central government and away from their local communities.

4.4   The recent Local Government White Paper, *Strong and Prosperous Communities,* and the resulting Bill, responded directly to many of the proposals in my May 2006 report and set out a very positive direction of travel. I particularly welcome the intention to streamline dramatically the number of targets imposed by central government, and the performance management framework governing local authority performance. The emphasis on greater engagement by local government is also key to improving accountability, public satisfaction and trust. The White Paper and its implementation plan also include a wide range of other proposals and changes, which should help to reinforce the shift towards greater flexibility and choice at the local level, and greater responsiveness by local government to the communities and individuals it serves.

4.5   I do not set out in detail here all those aspects of the White Paper and other developments which I endorse. The next section points to areas of concern or risks which could hold back delivery of the objectives reflected in the White Paper, and which will need to be addressed in future to provide the space for local choice, the right conditions for local energies and leadership to flourish, and continued momentum towards making the most of what local government has to offer. The chapter also considers how local government can play a role in fostering economic prosperity, and discusses implications for a number of specific services.

IMPROVING ACCOUNTABILITY

4.6   In the current system, responsibility for both local public services and the way in which they are funded is complex and confused. As set out in Chapter 3, this fundamental problem leads to confusion and mistrust in the system as a whole, since it creates incentives for central and local government to blame the other for failings and to claim credit for success themselves, rather than focusing on providing the greatest contribution they can to the well-being of our citizens.

4.7   There is therefore an urgent need to improve accountability throughout our system of local government, and to create incentives so that each tier of government has every reason to improve their own contribution to well-being, and to support others in doing so as well. This requires improvements across a range of issues:

- greater clarity about the respective roles of central and local government – this means being clearer about where central and local government can each add most value, as well as maintaining the commitment to pursue a much smaller number of nationally set central priorities, leaving real space for local choice;

- ensuring the new regulatory regime for local government is focused on the right issues, and allows enough space for local choice and priorities to be taken forward, while minimising burdens across the sector;

- improving the framework for local governance in order to promote effective local leadership and engagement, and to better inform local choices which help manage public expectations and service pressures; and

- seeking to clarify how local services are funded to provide greater transparency over what local services cost, and how decisions on spending and resources have been made.

Clarity over roles and responsibilities

4.8   A key challenge for government at all levels is that political and popular ambitions for public services are arguably greater than ever before. We demand high-quality, responsive and increasingly tailored services while the majority of us (55 per cent) do not think it is acceptable for standards of service to vary between different parts of the country.[1] I will not attempt in this report to debate the appropriate size of the state nor the appropriate level of total investment in public services; different governments will always need to make judgments about these political questions. However, there is a critical need to manage public expectations of public services against what people are willing to pay for, otherwise I believe that trust and satisfaction in the system as a whole will suffer. This is a challenge for both central and local government.

4.9   Chapter 2 argued that local government is best placed to engage with local communities to understand their needs, priorities and preferences in order to make well-informed choices about how resources should be spent in the best interests of local people. Councils are also best placed to manage the difficult trade-offs which inevitably have to be made when making choices about what should be spent, where, how and on whom in the light of local priorities. Explaining those choices to the public is crucial to achieving well-being and satisfaction. But, when accountability is blurred, clear explanation becomes difficult, as local people may be uncertain as to who is responsible for success or failure in their area, or who to lobby for change. Blurred accountability can also lead to local service providers being pulled in different directions, making it very difficult to develop a clear set of shared priorities to which they can develop joint solutions.

4.10   The most obvious way to clarify accountability would be to make a definite distinction between those services which are national and those which are local responsibilities, but it is clear that such a formal separation is not possible. Public services are by their nature complex, both in terms of what they do and how they aim to do it. Most services include some elements which are

---

[1] BMG Research, *Lyons Inquiry Survey,* 2007.

appropriately centrally determined and some which should be locally determined, and some have regional or sub-regional aspects, suggesting decision-making should take place at different levels.

4.11   Despite this complexity, it is possible to point to some services where greater or lesser degrees of local choice would be appropriate. Although I argue that greater local flexibility and choice are needed across the range of local government activity, I fully accept that there will always be a range of services and priorities where national government will want to set national standards and ambitions. In those areas where a sense of national entitlement is very strong, or where central government has a specific democratic mandate to deliver particular improvements (for example on health or education), I can see the merits of formalising this 'national promise' through a clearer definition of local and national responsibility, backed up by clearer financial arrangements. There is, however, a challenge in defining and funding a national promise in a way that ensures it can be afforded everywhere, and that focuses on what should be achieved, not how it should be delivered. This reinforces the need to balance the desire for national standards with that for local flexibility and choice. Chapter 2 set out the principles which could be used to inform decisions on the balance of local and national determination, which I first introduced in my May 2006 report.

Recognising the potential contribution of local government

4.12   A shift in approach is needed from both central and local government, to recognise the contribution each can make to the shared agenda for improving the well-being of all our communities. This means recognising that central government should not expect to do some things which local government is well equipped to do, and vice versa. For example, local government is, by virtue of its closer connection with citizens, better placed to engage with them about what they want, to manage expectations about what is possible, and to work with service users to improve the effectiveness of local public services, by influencing behaviour and reviewing service design and delivery. Such co-production is a key potential contribution of local government that is not adequately recognised or developed in the system as a whole.

4.13   I recognise that there are many areas where local government performance (like central government performance) needs to improve substantially. However, the key challenge for the system as a whole is to recognise that every level of government has a comparative advantage which determines what it is better placed to do than the others. All of our governments need to make the most of that potential in pursuing better outcomes for citizens.

4.14   There is also a need to recognise the fact that central government – like local government – has limitations in terms of what it is best placed to do. Some of these will be intrinsic – a function of the very fact it is a central, rather than a local, organisation. Others may be a function of current skills, behaviours and organisational arrangements. There is widespread interest currently in how government departments and 'the centre' of government can collectively be made more effective.[2] There is also an ongoing programme of reform, drawing on a number of Government-commissioned reviews which have made recommendations that aim to improve efficiency and effectiveness, and the ongoing round of Capability Reviews explicitly examine questions similar to those asked about local government, including about the leadership, skills and capacity of government departments.[3] Some of these exercises explicitly question the fitness for purpose of various aspects of the centre, and there is an ongoing debate about some large-scale concerns, for example the National Health Service and some Home Office functions.

---

[2] See for example Darwall, R., *The Reluctant Managers,* December 2005.

[3] See for example, Gershon, P, *Releasing Resources to the Front Line: Independent review of public sector efficiency,* HM Treasury, 2004; Lyons, M., *Well Placed to Deliver? Shaping the pattern of government service,* HM Treasury, 2004; Varney, D., *Service Transformation: A better service for citizens and business; a better deal for the taxpayer,* HM Treasury, 2006.

4.15   I do not seek to answer the specific questions or concerns raised by this ongoing work as it is outside the scope of this Inquiry. But questions about the capability of central government departments will remain highly relevant to considerations of the future role of local government – since the key challenge, as I have set it out, is to ensure that the system as a whole can make best use of the relative advantages of each tier of government. So in what follows, I seek to bear in mind that:

- it is right to ask questions about what central and local government are each best-placed to do; and whether we are making the best use of the talents, energies and resources available at each level under the current system;

- questions of performance relate to all tiers of government – and it is therefore wrong to assume that a centrally designed and implemented solution will necessarily always be better than a local one; and

- it is reasonable to ask whether the centre is trying to do too much, and whether this contributes to confused accountability.

4.16   Future Capability Review processes might usefully assess how well equipped central government departments are to work in partnership with local government while protecting and enhancing local flexibility. This might take account of my recommendations in later sections about central government behaviours and soft controls.

Identifying areas of local discretion   4.17   The Government has announced that it will in future set a much smaller set of key national performance measures, and the overall approach to an area's priorities and objectives will be negotiated through the Local Area Agreements which are being introduced across the country. This will require central government to be much clearer about those areas in which responsibility should be firmly local, and to resist calls to intervene in them. This in turn will require an acceptance that variability between areas is not only inevitable but also desirable.

4.18   This is a challenge for central government, but it could help significantly to improve local accountability. The centre will need to respect the value of local communities being able to make choices that the centre might not recommend or welcome – it will need to value local difference. It is also a significant challenge for local authorities and other local partners, who have in many cases contributed to the development of the current system by pressing the Government for national targets, strategies or ring-fenced funds as a signal that their area or their particular interest features on the list of national priorities. If both central and local partners can overcome these old ways of working, the prize is greater efficiency, well-being and satisfaction as local services are more closely matched to local needs and wishes.

Greater consistency within central government   4.19   For those issues where central government takes responsibility, or shares it with local government, there is a need for greater consistency in the behaviour and messages coming from departments. A number of submissions to my Inquiry from local authorities have raised this issue, typified in the following quote:

Lack of co-ordination within Whitehall or between Whitehall and its agencies can lead to further difficulties. For example, the Department of Health pushing adult education and the Department for Education and Skills withdrawing funding for it, or the Home Office recognising the importance of alcohol treatment compared with drugs treatment, but being unwilling to sustain funding to support this. (Surrey County Council)

4.20   Delivering on the promise of this model depends on the expectation that Local Area Agreements will be based on a genuine negotiation between local partnerships, led by the local authority, and central government. This requires government to act corporately in the negotiation, which will depend to a great extent on the behaviour of ministers and their departments.

**Role of
Government
Offices**

4.21   Given the proposed key role for the Government Offices in negotiating Local Area Agreements on behalf of the government, it will be important to be clear about their negotiating power and to ensure they have the right skills and capability to perform that role. My case study research found a sense of frustration within councils at being obliged to go through Government Offices in their dealings with central government, as they perceived that the decision-making powers lay in the departments themselves, not the Government Offices.[4] Some councils questioned whether Government Offices currently have the capacity and local knowledge to make judgements about local priorities. Others argued that their role often appeared to involve administering central government programmes and second-guessing central departments, at the same time as constraining and second-guessing local choices. Many expressed concerns about whether the Government Offices have the skills to meet the increasingly strategic role that is expected of them:

> *I have to say that I am yet to be persuaded of what the added value of regional government is to these issues really. We know the city and the police know the city and we know what the priorities are. If regional government is to interpret what central government says well then I'd rather have it straight from central government.* (Senior local government officer, community safety)[5]

4.22   This suggests that the role of the Government Offices needs to be much more clearly defined and focused on areas where they can add most value. I strongly support the recommendations of the review of the Government Offices published last year.[6] I particularly welcome the recommendations to streamline the Government Offices' role in order to secure a more strategic approach and a more appropriate staff skills mix. However, behaviour will again be a key determinant of the strength of the new arrangements. Government Offices must clearly recognise matters which are wholly for local determination and resist encouragement (whether local or central) to become inappropriately involved.

4.23   The review also recommended that Government Offices should challenge government departments to ensure policies are joined-up and capable of being delivered effectively. While some key government departments are not represented in the Government Offices (notably the Department for Work and Pensions), this role could in my view add real value. The Government Offices could play a part in helping to develop a stronger corporate style in central government by reflecting back to individual departments and central government as a whole the challenges that their own behaviours (however well-intentioned) can create at the local level. Over time this could help to improve relationships with local government, and the functioning of the system as a whole.

Streamlining the performance framework

4.24   Chapter 3 argued that the Government's performance framework has tended to distract councils from an outward focus on their communities, instead creating a focus on upward reporting lines to central government.

[4,5] Entwhistle, T., et al., *Perspectives on Place-shaping and Service Delivery: A report of case study work conducted for the Lyons Inquiry,* 2007 – summarised in Annex H.

[6] HM Treasury and Department for Communities and Local Government, *Review of Government Offices,* 2006.

4.25   The Audit Commission's report on the future of regulation pointed the way forward on the regulation of local authorities.[7] From April 2008 the Audit Commission will operate as the single local services inspectorate, and a radically reformed performance framework is likely to be implemented in the form of the new Comprehensive Area Assessment from the following year.

4.26   The Local Government White Paper's objectives for the new performance framework are that it should:

- strengthen accountability to citizens and communities;

- give greater responsibilities to local government and its partners to secure improvements;

- provide a better balance between national and local priorities;

- improve coordination between the various inspectorates;

- relate inspection more closely to risk; and

- streamline the process for providing improvement support and intervention.

4.27   I welcome all of these objectives. If implemented fully they will mark a step change in the performance framework, providing a much more streamlined system of regulation which will provide much greater space for local flexibility and choice.[8] In implementing the new regime a number of issues need to be borne in mind.

4.28   First, and most important, the regulatory regime needs to be clear about who is responsible for what. This has two aspects:

1.   Being clear about what the local authority is responsible for. The Comprehensive Area Assessment will of course need to take account of performance in relation to the 53 local targets (made up of 35 locally negotiated targets and 18 mandatory ones in early years) for each local area and the 200 national indicators (to be agreed at the Comprehensive Spending Review). However, the new regime will need to find a way of recognising the appropriate balance of accountability for the local authority as convenor, leading the Local Area Agreement in partnership with a wide range of other providers. It will also need to recognise the local authority's wider place-shaping role, which will be reflected in the targets and ambitions developed locally. These are not a matter for central control, but will impact on the satisfaction of local people, which will be an element of the new framework.

2.   Being clear about what is the responsibility of each inspectorate. Overlapping responsibilities would add to confusion and not aid the objective of aligning the regimes across all local public services. The role of central government in setting expectations about performance beyond the targets agreed in the Local Area Agreement also needs to be clear. We need to avoid the risk that taking forward government ministers' public pronouncements about particular services or issues become seen as the responsibility of the inspectorates.

---

[7] Audit Commission, *The Future of Regulation in the Public Sector*, 2006.

[8] By this I mean the wide range of activities undertaken by central government and inspectorates to regulate the behaviour and performance of local authorities. The performance framework incorporates not only regulation but also a much wider range of activities, such as peer review and support, and other mechanisms included in the Local Government White Paper.

4.29   Second, the regime must be proportionate. This is clearly reflected in the move to risk-based inspection. Across most services, the framework should allow for intervention in local affairs only where there are significant failures which demonstrably risk harming the well-being of local people. The proposed regime will look across the 200 national indicators in judging risk, but I hope it will also take account of local priorities and the fact that while a particular service may be crucial for well-being in one area it may be much less important in another.

4.30   Third, arrangements for inspection and assessment need to focus on supporting change by the authority itself. I welcome the Improvement and Development Agency (IDeA) and the Local Government Association (LGA)'s developing work on self-assessment against an externally agreed community plan, and 'peer challenge' to examine progress against the commitments agreed with partners. While peer-group support is unlikely to provide adequate public assurance on its own, this is an important demonstration of the capacity and willingness of local government to embrace improvement. But the system must recognise that there is only so much that even well-targeted and well-intentioned support, advice and intervention by peers or regulators can achieve. Real improvement in performance must be the explicit responsibility of, and must be driven by, the council itself. I therefore welcome the emphasis on self-assessment and stakeholder views.

4.31   Fourth, inspection needs to be joined-up. Even after the merger of eleven public service inspectorates into four, there are still real challenges for the smaller number to work together effectively and to reduce the burden they place on inspected bodies. I look forward to the outcome of Michael Frater's work on reducing the burdens of the reporting systems, which will help achieve a reduction in the burden of inspection.[9] The new Comprehensive Area Assessment needs to take full account of local partnership working and shared priorities through the Local Strategic Partnership and Local Area Agreement – so that inspection and assessment can be genuinely joined-up across agencies and the public services they deliver. This means putting greater effort into ensuring that the separate performance frameworks for primary care trusts, schools, the police and Jobcentre Plus are as consistent as possible with each other and with the Comprehensive Area Assessment framework for local government.

4.32   Regulation must of course be well informed. The promised smaller and clearer set of outcome-based national indicators should constitute the bulk of the performance information required from local authorities. It is particularly important that they are available to the public, who must be the key judges of performance. I accept that there may be a need for some further monitoring information, for example on satisfaction (despite the challenges in using such measures robustly), and local authorities will of course want to monitor management information themselves. However, it is important that the requirements for publication of extra information should not be used as an indirect way of imposing additional national standards.

4.33   Finally, I strongly support the notion that local people should be the ultimate judges of how well local authorities perform their place-shaping role, how well they deliver locally determined services, and how well they undertake their role as convenor across all local public services. The performance framework should support the ability of local people to do this – but it should not prescribe how, as the best approach will vary in different places. It is for local authorities to design transparent and effective mechanisms to engage with their citizens, to inform and challenge policies and decisions, and to explain how their views have been used.

4.34   Local government already recognises the value of external challenge and peer support to improve performance. The chairman of the LGA, Lord Sandy Bruce Lockhart, recently argued, that "there should be no hiding place for poor performance" within local government, as he

---

[9] Audit Commission, *Assessment of Local Services Beyond 2008,* 2006.

launched the LGA's Raising our Game initiative.[10] Although there will always be a need for public assurance in some services that cannot be delivered through self regulation, I believe this is a very helpful message. The more strongly the local government family takes steps to improve the performance of the sector as a whole, and the more individual authorities are clearly seen to actively improve their own performance on an ongoing basis, the less reason there will be for central government to intervene.

4.35   There is of course a critical need for local authorities themselves to take on this challenge individually, to engage with their communities and to put every effort into improving their place-shaping role as well as their role as service commissioners and providers. I discuss this further in Chapter 5. If they fail to do so, there remains a legitimate role for regulation to protect against and mitigate failure – but this should be recognised as regulation of last resort.

Recommendation 4.1

The burdens and effectiveness of the new Comprehensive Area Assessment and other aspects of the performance framework should be independently evaluated, and a report published, two years after its introduction.

This should examine:

- how well the new system is achieving its objectives, and in particular how much space it leaves for place-shaping, local innovation and responsiveness;

- whether other external assessment and inspection frameworks are adequately supporting joint agendas; and

- whether the framework effectively assesses and supports the community empowerment agenda.

Improving the framework for local governance

4.36   Democratic processes are not the only means by which citizens can hold their representatives and the local authority to account. They do however have the strong advantage that they provide representation for all local citizens – whether taxpayers, service users or residents. It is this which gives local authorities the unique remit to act in the interest of the whole community. This is particularly important when making difficult decisions, which have to weigh different interests against each other, taking into account the needs and wishes of the community as a whole – for example in decisions about where development activity should take place and, when necessary, which schools or other facilities should close.

4.37   It is therefore important for all of us that local democratic processes work well. Low levels of civic interest and engagement and a low electoral turnout, at local elections in particular, are a matter of local and national concern. Local and central government share an interest in sharpening local accountability, re-engaging communities and revitalising interest and improvements in the way we are governed.

4.38   Such improvements rely to a large degree on local government changing its approach and behaviours, as I set out in Chapter 5. The challenge for central government is to design a framework which encourages and enables local authorities to take responsibility for how their communities are governed, to design and prove the value of governance structures that work

---

[10] New Local Government Network conference, 17 January 2007.

for their own locality.[11] No single model will work everywhere, and too much central prescription over models and approaches could result in the wrong local solution and could also damage innovation.

Local leadership   4.39   The framework within which councils operate can constrain or enhance their ability to improve the governance of their area. I therefore welcome the recent decisions to enable councils to move to a four-year election cycle where all councillors are elected simultaneously. This was an option strongly supported by the Electoral Commission in its submission to me. Equally, I welcome the proposal that councils can ask the Electoral Commission to undertake a review to move to single member wards. These changes should help to enable authorities to experiment with new approaches and to find the one that works best in their area.

4.40   The Government has emphasised the role of strong and clear local leadership in providing accountability – in particular placing an emphasis on elected mayors and the role of the council leader. I agree that leadership is important, but in setting the national frameworks for local government we must acknowledge that effective leadership is not a simple concept, and should not be reduced to a simple prescription that requires the same arrangements everywhere.

4.41   There is a risk in placing too heavy an institutional reliance on the ability and effectiveness of a single person. Elected mayors are argued to have benefits in terms of visible and accountable leadership, with international examples of effective mayoral leadership being cited in support. I too have seen and been impressed by examples of strong leadership, and their achievements, in some American and European cities. However, this is often in a very different context, and it often involves other complex forms of leadership. For instance, the mayor of Chicago has a wider set of powers (particularly in terms of taxation) than local government in this country, and success has been built to a significant extent on building strong coalitions of interest and 'striking a deal' with residents and businesses to invest in the reshaping of the city and its economic role.

4.42   I am also concerned more generally that relying on the leadership of one individual for every area risks losing some of the strengths of the current system, in terms of collective leadership and the ability of the system to represent diverse interests. Communities are complex and a broad-based leadership, based on a number of people across a number of institutions may be preferred.

4.43   Given such variations in the 'best' governance models for different communities, it is crucial to recognise that local areas may need to change their model of leadership from time to time. We should learn lessons from the effects of the Local Government Act 2000 which – though beneficial in a range of ways – prescribed models of governance that have failed to make best use of non-executive or frontline councillors and alienated many of them in the process.[12] This might have been avoided if there had been greater freedom for councils to choose how to achieve the goals of reform.

4.44   It is therefore important that if local areas opt for a directly elected mayor or executive, under the new governance arrangements provided for in the current Bill, this should not be set in stone. If local people feel that their experiment with a mayoral or other model has failed, they should have the right to make a further choice in favour of an indirectly elected model, which they prefer and which may work more effectively for their area. The Government's current proposal requires local authorities to wait for ten years after the original referendum that gave rise to a

---

[11] This builds on an argument put by Sue Goss, Principal at the Office of Public Management, at the SOLACE conference in October 2005.

[12] Gains, F., *Early Outcomes and Impacts: Qualitative research findings from the ELG evaluation of new council constitutions*, Department for Communities and Local Government, 2006.

directly elected mayor before local communities can choose to move back to an indirectly elected model. A decade is a long time to tolerate a particular model of leadership if people do not consider it is benefiting their area.

> **Recommendation 4.2**
>
> The Government should ensure that local communities retain the flexibility to choose models of leadership that best suit their circumstances, and to adapt them as and when they judge appropriate.

Less central definition of officer and councillor roles

4.45   Central government has also prescribed that there must be a lead member and director of children's services and a director of adult social services, as well as in the latter case specifying certain elements of how those roles must be fulfilled. While most councils manage to organise these roles successfully, building their local structures to fit around them, some have argued to me that this prescription can constrain their ability to structure their organisations and processes in the most efficient way for their area.

4.46   There is of course no simple or unique way to divide up the responsibilities of a council. The strong interest in joining-up has produced a trend to focus on client groups, such as children's services and adult services, to encourage a client focus. But any structure will suffer from some problems. For instance the division between children's and adults' services raises new challenges in managing the transition from childhood to adulthood. This raises issues for the education and skills training of young adults in particular. Similarly, social services for children and adults need to work very closely together in relation to vulnerable families, particularly where there are child protection concerns.

> **Recommendation 4.3**
>
> The Government should not seek to define any further lead councillor and officer roles and structures, and existing prescriptive models should be kept under review.

Funding an accountable system

The debate about whether funding is adequate

4.47   The complexity of the current finance system and its lack of transparency is a barrier to clear accountability, as discussed in Chapter 3. It is, I believe, virtually impossible to come to a definitive view about whether funding is 'adequate' even to fund central government commitments under the current system. This is in part a reflection of the intrinsic difficulty of assessing pressures on spending which amounts to more than £140 billion a year – however it is also a design feature of the current system.

4.48   While reforms in the early 1990s were designed to ensure that all areas of the country could provide the same level of service for the same level of council tax, recent models of formula grant funding have sought to avoid an explicit objective that grant distribution should allow the same level of services everywhere. However, it is far from clear that this was ever achieved, and it required a high level of stipulation by central government over 'appropriate' levels of local spending. Recent models of funding have therefore sought to avoid this objective. The move to a new system of distribution in 2006–07, commonly known as the Four Block Model (described in Annex A), ensures that annual changes to grant are now explicitly determined by relative need and resources, rather than by absolute figures.

4.49   However, while the grant system appears to recognise the practical impossibility and policy costs of central determination of 'correct' levels of spending in individual areas, government announcements and statements still often imply that the public should be able to expect the same high standards of services everywhere – across a wide range of services. The raising of such unrealistic expectations makes it difficult to manage pressures effectively at the local level, and it raises questions about whose 'fault' council tax increases are, which are impossible to answer definitively.

4.50   Aggregate pressures on local government are assessed through the Spending Review process, with contributions made by a wide range of stakeholders, including local government. However, final decisions on the total amount of grant, and the finance settlement that determines how the grant is distributed, are not wholly transparent. It is not therefore possible to judge whether the funding allocations are intended to ensure a level of funding regarded as adequate for local government. This issue was highlighted in the Audit Commission report on the causes of the 2003–04 council tax increases, and in submissions received:

> *It has always been impossible to show in practice that money provided nationally has reached local councils ... now it is impossible to show theoretically too. ... Formula Grant has moved somewhat closer to being a general subsidy to the council tax payer and away from being a means of allocating resources of individual service blocks so that each council can provide a similar level of service for a similar level of council tax.* (Society of London Treasurers)

4.51   The Government does have a clear policy that any new burdens imposed by central government departments on local government should be funded through the grant regime. The principle behind the policy is a good one, though this is necessarily a blunt instrument, and many submissions received from local authorities argue that it does not always ensure adequate funding for every local authority (particularly after grant allocations are 'damped', as discussed in Chapters 3 and 9). However, it only deals with marginal change in central government's demands rather than with overall pressures on local authority budgets.

4.52   It may never be possible to create a system in which anyone can determine precisely whether the total funding available to local authorities is enough to enable them to achieve all the ambitions set out for them. I would not promote a funding system which simply focused on inputs and actual costs rather than outcomes. Nevertheless, it is crucial that if central government makes promises about what local government will deliver, the funding system should provide some certainty that sufficient money will be available to do that – in a way that helps local people to hold local and central government to account for their actions much more clearly.

4.53   In the short term, the most straightforward way to move towards this goal is to reduce the extent and ambition of the national promises made by central government which have to be met by local government funding. The commitment to reduce the number of targets and indicators set by central government, and my recommendations to improve local flexibility and choice set out below, will help to do that. This should at least make it easier than at present to be confident that total funding for local services is sufficient to deliver what government has promised nationally – though it may never be possible to identify the point at which there is 'enough money in the system'. I am not seeking to eliminate the scope for debate but rather to encourage a more productive debate between central government and local government on priorities for the system as a whole to ensure we get value for money for our citizens.

Improving transparency

4.54   It is understandable and entirely appropriate that central government should want to ensure that monies provided to local government should be well spent and achieve value for money. Indeed, I would argue that local government explicitly shares this objective. My aim is to improve the ability of the system not only to deliver that goal but also to help both central and local government, Parliament and the public to understand more clearly how well it is being delivered for the system as a whole.

4.55   Many submissions to my Inquiry have argued for the need to improve the transparency of the funding system, its objectives, and how well it is achieving them, in a way that improves understanding and the quality of debate.

4.56   One way to do this is to introduce a more independent and authoritative voice to provide an expert and unbiased view on the issues. It could comment on the claims and counterclaims made by both sides of the debate, so that the public could better understand the issues at stake, and they and Parliament could have a consistent source of independent and balanced evidence. The Audit Commission's analysis of the 2003–04 council tax rises arguably provided this type of role. Issues on which comment would be useful include:

- whether the cumulative impact of new mandates on local government has over time been greater than or less than the funding made available to pay for them;

- what evidence is available about future pressures on local services and what might be reasonable assumptions to make about their impact on costs; and

- whether the funding system is meeting its objectives, particularly in terms of delivering national promises made by central government.

4.57   This could help contribute to a better-informed and more constructive debate about the funding of local government and its priorities. It might even help us to move towards the more consensual position that other countries, such as Denmark and Spain, seem able to achieve in their distribution of local government funding. Part of the situation in England can perhaps be ascribed to our national political culture being based on challenge and adversarial debate, rather than consensus, but it may also be due to the lack of neutral assessments and lack of independent attempts to explain how grant and settlement decisions are made.

An independent commission

4.58   One mechanism that might be used to help to provide greater transparency in the funding system is an independent commission. Some commentators have proposed an independent commission to provide a range of roles.[13] The LGA's final submission to my Inquiry proposed that a commission should:

- maintain the stewardship of overall funding regime(s), including management of the distribution and equalisation mechanisms;

- keep data and tax base valuations up to date, in the latter case by commissioning contract work from valuation offices;

- regulate a devolved regime of fees and charges, and to investigate and advise on new or alternative charging regimes;

- provide the regulatory framework for the relocalisation of business rates; and

- provide research and advice, to support the integrity of the system.

---

[13] For example McLean, I., *The Fiscal Crisis of the United Kingdom*, ESRC, 2005; McLean, I. and McMillan, A., *New Localism, New Finance*, 2003; also explored by the Audit Commission in *Passing the Bucks: The Impact of SSAs on Economy, Efficiency and Effectiveness*, 1993.

4.59   While there is a case for each of these roles to be undertaken, I do not believe they could or should all be undertaken by an independent commission. A key aspect of an independent body's work is that it should be very clearly defined, and not asked to second-guess or undermine decisions which are properly the domain of central or local government. I therefore believe that it would be inappropriate for a commission to make political judgments about the priorities for funding. However, it could usefully provide an independent voice in commenting on the extent to which funding objectives are achieved in practice, or might even be given the job of implementing them through the distribution of grant between authorities. The Australian Commonwealth Grants Commission provides a possible model – it advises on the relative distribution of general revenue to the states from national government, against terms of reference set by the federal government.

4.60   If decisions by a commission were transparent this model could help to improve joint understanding of how funding decisions are reached on the basis of clearly articulated ambitions about what central government should pay for. This could, I believe, help to secure greater trust and confidence in the allocation process and its reliance on objective criteria. It would provide an independent perspective on the distribution of funding to local government, and could involve verifying whether the criteria governing allocations achieve the desired equalisation, highlighting anomalies or distortions and ensuring that allocations were supporting central government's aims.

4.61   Such objectives are supported by Organisation for Economic Cooperation and Development (OECD) work on this area, which recommends that:

> *Decision-making about the general principles* [for the revision of grant systems] *should be reserved to national authorities on the basis of neutral expertise. The views of sub-national authorities are important, but should be developed in a setting that encourages objective debate, for instance, in a consultative council that is informed by neutral expertise. Also, the advice of sub-national representatives should focus on the technical aspects of the grant systems, such as the estimation of relevant variables and the quality of statistical data, rather than on principles.*[14]

Clarifying the cost of new burdens

4.62   One of the most important of the potential roles that a commission could play would be to provide evidence on the actual cost of new burdens imposed on local government by central government, to improve the confidence of both central and local government, Parliament and the public that new burdens have been adequately funded, but not over-funded.

4.63   However, it is possible that this role could be undertaken by existing independent bodies, such the National Audit Office or the Audit Commission or a joint team drawn from both organisations. The evaluation expertise already resides in those bodies and it may be most cost-effective to ask them to take on this new role. However, they would need to report formally, either to a joint board, or to an independent or joint body such as a parliamentary committee or the Central Local Partnership.

4.64   If a commission was introduced either to advise on the distribution of grant or to comment on the actual cost of new burdens, it would be essential for it to be seen to be an independent and non-partisan body with the status to engage with and be respected by both local and central government and by Parliament. Careful consideration should therefore be given to its status and appointment procedures in light of its role.

---

[14] OECD, *Intergovernmental Transfers and Decentralised Public Spending*, 2005.

Recommendation 4.4

Mechanisms should be put in place to improve the transparency of the objectives of the local government funding system, in particular central and local government should agree:

- what central government requires of local government and how it should be funded;
- the ways in which central government should appropriately influence other aspects of local government activity and the extent to which such influence should be limited.

This should be formalised in a written agreement.

Recommendation 4.5

The Government should consider ways to improve independent information available to the public and Parliament about:

- the actual costs of new burdens imposed by central government;
- actual burdens of targets, performance management and soft controls imposed on local government by central government and its agencies;
- whether the cumulative impact of new mandates on local government is over time greater than, or less than, the funding made available to pay for them;
- what evidence is available about future pressures on and efficiency opportunities in local services and what might be reasonable assumptions to make about their impact on costs and savings; and
- whether the funding system is meeting the agreed objectives in terms of enabling local government to deliver what has been agreed with central government.

Options considered should include an independent commission.

4.65   Chapter 9 discusses other questions of accountability in relation to which groups of taxpayers (or charge payers) pay for which public services, and also the question of which resources should be seen as 'local' and 'national'.

Capping of council tax

4.66   A key confusion in the current system is the question of who is responsible for setting council tax levels. Chapter 3 argued that council tax capping contributes to the confused accountability in the finance system, by overlaying heavy central controls on a tax that is supposed to be a matter of local responsibility. Survey evidence for my Inquiry suggests that the public believes councils should have the most say in setting council tax levels; after that local people themselves, and after that central government.[15] Capping damages that sense of local ownership.

4.67   Capping is a sign that central and local government have together failed to make the system work. It represents a short-term response to council tax increases that are a symptom of problems elsewhere in the system – namely the pressure on local budgets and hence council tax, combined with a lack of local flexibility and unclear accountability. I argue elsewhere in this report that these underlying problems need to be tackled urgently.

4.68   Both the taking of the powers and the Government's recent use of them reflect the genuine concerns in central government that they must be able to ensure moderate rate increases, following the high average increases in council tax in 2003–04 and given the strength of the media's and the public's concerns and calls for central government to intervene. It is less often recognised that local government is also concerned about the impact of large increases on council tax payers and tries hard to minimise council tax rises – a message which was made strongly by many councillors and local government officers during the course of my Inquiry.[16]

---

[15] BMG Research, *Lyons Inquiry Survey*, 2007.
[16] Chapter 3 includes a fuller discussion of the causes of council tax increases.

4.69   However, it is also true that the current system provides an opportunity for local authorities to raise council tax without full accountability. Capping reflects the extent to which accountability for local services has become centralised. If ministers feel that any blame for problems in local services are likely to be laid at their door, then taking control of the finance that supports them may seem relatively logical. I have commented on how far this centralisation has led to central control of local spending; capping is partly an extension of this control to local taxation as well, but it tends to be presented as an instrument to tackle wholly local failings rather than central behaviours.

4.70   It is clear that council tax increases have the potential to distract public attention away from the good work that local government does, and thus to undermine the case for devolution over time. However, I believe that the harm to local accountability, incentives and flexibility created by the system of capping greatly outweighs the benefits of keeping council tax increases at an artificially uniform level. With greater local flexibility to manage pressures more effectively and less central control over local government's activities, the pressures on council tax should lessen over time. The recommendations in this report aim to achieve that goal. As part of that package, I believe it is critical that the Government should cease to use its capping powers in order to reinforce local accountability for managing pressures and for setting council tax locally. This will of course require some courage from the Government, but there could be no clearer and more fundamental sign that devolution is a key part of the agenda for the 21st century than this.

> **Recommendation 4.6**
>
> The Government should cease to use, and then abolish, its capping powers as pressures on council tax reduce, forming part of a package of measures to re-establish local accountability for tax and spending decisions.

Precepting   4.71   Chapter 3 identified the complexity of the funding system as a barrier to accountability. This complexity is added to by the system of precepting. Precepting authorities are mainly county councils, the police and fire authorities, which instruct the billing authorities to collect council tax on their behalf to finance their expenditure (see Glossary for a full list). Council tax bills can therefore include numerous precepts and levies from various local authorities. There may be a case for seeking to further clarify the information which is presented on the council tax bill, which is tightly constrained by legislation. This issue is covered in Chapter 9.

4.72   Most precepts are subject to the capping regime, with the exception of the parish precept, which has led to concerns expressed by some respondents. This has been particularly raised in the context of responsibilities transferred to parish level. A view expressed by a few parish respondents and Isitfair was that some non-statutory, upper tier authority services and functions were increasingly being carried out by parish councils, which had led to significant rises in their precept on the council tax bill:

> *In a growing number of cases across the entire country, towns and parishes are now picking up the costs for such* [non-statutory] *functions – and imposing huge percentage increases in their share of council tax bills; increases which are pushing the total increases in council tax bills through the five per cent cap.* (Isitfair)

4.73   Others argued that devolution of responsibility could be used as a means of passing costs on to parish councils and away from upper tiers:

> *At this moment in time local councils can take on the provision of services to their residents if the principal authority is in agreement but there is no pressure on the principal* [council] *to ensure that funding follows the service. Keynsham Town Council would like to see more services devolved to local levels, ensuring that finance follows function.* (Keynsham Town Council)

4.74   The available data provide some support for this argument, suggesting that the significant increase in parish spending since 1998–99 – from £154 million to £260 million – was partly due to the creation of over 150 new parishes since 1998, but also partly due to increases in activity in existing parishes.[17] However, there are no centrally held data on parish finances that would enable this argument to be tested robustly. Moreover, parish councils cannot be 'forced' to take on responsibilities from the tiers above. They have no mandatory functions apart from the management of allotments, and any discretionary functions that they take on from another council would need to be subject to agreement beforehand. It is therefore important that parish councils and upper tiers work closely together to ensure that functions are undertaken by those best placed to do them, and that the means of funding new activities are clearly agreed.

4.75   Even supporters of capping would understand how impractical it would be to bring 8,700 parish councils within the capping regime. The key to ensuring this tier of government is more responsive to the wishes of its citizens is to build strong local accountability backed up by a strong relationship with councils at higher tiers (building on my arguments for stronger joint working set out below). The Young Foundation argued that more flexibility and some additional fund-raising powers at local levels would enable first tier – or community – councils to make a distinctive contribution to place-shaping at very local level, in particular where they are presented with incentives for a constructive relationship with the strategic tier of local government.[18]

4.76   I remain convinced that a voluntary approach together with maximum flexibility is the right one; parish councils should be encouraged to take an active view as to whether their community might wish them to take on a service that might otherwise be discontinued. The precept is an important local flexibility which supports communities' abilities to take action themselves. I discuss the need for the other tiers of local government to take active steps to devolve responsibilities where appropriate in the next chapter.

PROTECTING FLEXIBILITY

4.77   The Local Government White Paper sets a welcome path towards a system that gives the potential for greater local flexibility, particularly by reducing central targets, with a focus on outcomes rather than outputs and processes. This responds directly to concerns that I outlined in my May 2006 report and is very welcome.

4.78   The challenge will be to deliver this through the Comprehensive Spending Review 2007, and to maintain this approach over time. There is a risk that the process of cutting centrally determined targets and indicators will not be fully reflected in a reduction of central controls, and that some central controls will instead 'leak' into either separate mechanisms, such as ring-fenced grants, or soft controls, which are less transparent and less easy to measure.

4.79   I believe this is a risk, not because I suspect the Government of having malign intentions, but because of the huge change in mindset it requires, not only for local and central government but also for citizens and the media. It is the wish to deliver improvements to everyone in the country; the wish to prevent a problem observed in one area from happening in others; the well-intentioned wish to take responsibility for things which cannot possibly all be controlled from Whitehall, which I fear may undermine the White Paper's ambitions over time. There may of course be incentives in the system which worsen these tendencies. For instance, the ability of junior ministers, or indeed officials, to develop and deliver new eye-catching national initiatives is seen by some as a badge of success, and has been a key objective of many in government for many years.

---

[17] *Local Government Financial Statistics England,* Communities and Local Government, 2005.
[18] Hilder, P., *Where's the Money? Neighbourhood governance and the future of local finance,* Young Foundation, 2006.

4.80   This requires a shift towards a situation where ministers respond to issues of local discretion by referring them to the local council; and where central government resists encouragements to meet the particular objectives of lobby groups, professional organisations and representative bodies through central action, and instead encourages such groups to work with local government. This will require a change in mindset not only by those individuals but by Parliament itself. In a country so preoccupied by fears of a 'postcode lottery' we should not underestimate the challenge this poses.

Resisting the temptation of soft controls

4.81   All parts of government – ministers, departments, a range of agencies and Government Offices – have a part to play in minimising soft controls, and avoiding simply replacing formal control with informal influence by other means. Central government must restrict use of all of its tools, not just targets, in a way that respects and values local choice and therefore difference. When space is left open for local decisions, the temptation is often to fill it with central guidance, reinforcing the idea that local actors must have their choices edited and influenced by the centre at all times. This can create a culture of dependency, which I have witnessed first hand during the course of my Inquiry, for instance in the form of local authorities suggesting they cannot use the power of well-being or their charging powers more fully without better guidance from the Government.

4.82   As set out in Chapter 3, many of these things are almost wired into government departments' ways of working and will take time to overcome. When an initiative is called for, civil servants will naturally wish to have answers to any question a minister might ask about the detail of its impact and implementation, leading them to second-guess and thus proscribe decisions that should really be taken on the ground. I want to see a world in which civil servants can confidently advise ministers that those decisions are best left to local councillors – and that the councillors will therefore be accountable for them.

4.83   Additional changes are required to deal with the lesser aspects of central controls which relate to the preponderance of guidance, reporting requirements and central exhortations to local government to act in certain ways. I am concerned that such controls undermine local government's confidence that they are best placed to take many decisions, and further reinforce the sense that the centre is in control – confusing both responsibility and accountability for local actions. The Government intends that guidance needed to implement the Local Government White Paper will be 'consolidated and light-touch', developed in consultation with those affected. This is welcome. However, this commitment should be extended to all of the guidance issued by all the departments of central government, not just this recent White Paper or policies led by the department of Communities and Local Government. I fully recognise that local government also needs to examine its own behaviours in requesting central government guidance on issues that are properly matters of local discretion, as I discuss in Chapter 5.

4.84   There is a parallel here with the approach taken by the Better Regulation Executive to the regulation of the private sector. The Government has committed to reducing administrative burdens imposed by regulation by at least 25 per cent by 2010, and this is being implemented through a series of simplification plans to deregulate, consolidate existing regulation, rationalise sector specific measures and reduce the burden of existing regulations. While the nature of regulation and direction over local government is often very different to that affecting the private sector, a similar degree of respect for the burdens imposed on local government from central government should be reflected in the Government's approach to soft controls. This can draw on the work of the Lifting the Burdens task force, which was established last year to examine the burdens of performance management and monitoring regimes on local government.

> **Recommendation 4.7**
>
> As well as reducing the number of targets and performance indicators in the revised performance framework set out in the recent White Paper, the Government, its agencies and the inspectorates should also reduce the wider data burdens and reporting requirements that local authorities face, drawing on the work of the Lifting the Burdens task force.
>
> **Recommendation 4.8**
>
> The Government should set a target to reduce these burdens, and progress against the target should be monitored transparently by an independent body such as the Audit Commission.
>
> **Recommendation 4.9**
>
> The Government, its agencies and the inspectorates should reduce the levels of guidance in areas of local concern and responsibility. The Government should also develop a code of practice for departments and agencies which clarifies the limited circumstances under which it is appropriate to place conditions on funding streams for local government.

4.85   The new Local Area Agreement (LAA) framework is intended to free up local energy to focus on local priorities – though there is of course a risk that the 200 planned national indicators, along with the shared targets to be negotiated in each LAA will still absorb all the energies of local authorities, leaving little room for place-shaping. It will be important to monitor how this plays out in practice – and for local authorities as well as central government to review how they are approaching the new system.

> **Recommendation 4.10**
>
> Local Area Agreements should be developed in a way which leaves enough space for local priorities. New central government priorities which emerge between negotiations over the LAA should be incorporated into the framework on a strictly 'one in, one out' basis in order to avoid gradual regrowth of central control.

More flexible finance system to enable local choice

4.86   Chapter 3 argues that the inflexibility of the current funding system inhibits local responsiveness. Chapters 6 to 9 cover detailed analysis and recommendations on local government finance, but there are other ways of improving financial flexibility, by enabling resources to better reflect local priorities and to support partnership working.

Reducing ring-fenced and conditional funding

4.87   One of the most powerful tools at central government's disposal has been the ability to influence local government behaviour through ring-fenced or specific grants which come with specific targets or other conditions attached. While the use of ring-fenced grants has reduced over recent years, the use of specific grants has increased dramatically, as noted in Chapter 3, and the introduction of the Dedicated Schools Grant was criticised in submissions to my Inquiry from a number of authorities for constraining local choice:

> *Take for example the demographic pressures we have in Shropshire. We have a rapidly growing population of elderly and very elderly people and falling pupil numbers in our schools. The recent settlement gave a rise of 6.7 per cent to schools and 2.1 per cent to all other services. From an economic perspective, we are not getting the same utility from that last £1 million spent on schools as we would if we were free to make the choice to spend it on services for older people that can keep them at home and out of expensive hospital places.* (Shropshire County Council)

4.88   The Government's intention to provide a single pot LAA grant is welcome – and will mark a really significant step forward if it incorporates the vast majority of current specific and ring-fenced grants and is genuinely unconstrained. Central government will need to avoid introducing over time new specific grants to re-exert control over specific funding streams if the extra flexibility promised by LAAs is to be delivered in practice.

4.89   As set out in Chapter 3, there are many specific grants which, while not formally ring-fenced, come with strict conditions on how the money should be spent and accounted for. These still make up a high proportion of local government spending and reduce the flexibility to respond to local priorities and place-shape. I recognise that service providers in local authorities often lobby for such grants to provide extra funding for their services, but the impact of tightly constrained grants on local authorities can skew behaviour out of all proportion to the financial benefit to the area.

4.90   Such controls also contribute to the difficulty that local partners experience in pooling resources in order to work towards joint objectives or to jointly fund projects or teams. Reducing the ring-fencing, formal and informal, of grants given to local agencies will allow more effective partnership working and joining up of local activity.

4.91   One of the frequent messages in evidence to my Inquiry was that while the ability to pool budgets between health and social services had in some circumstances been useful, it was limited by the need to account separately for the streams of funding. For instance, the Inquiry's case study research heard evidence that the separate reporting arrangements to different government departments makes it more difficult for health and social services to work together productively:

> *On a purely financial basis it is a real barrier to pooling resources and working together because you've got separate funding streams, separate reporting requirements, separate accountability. So you might, as two organisations, pool a source of money to achieve something, but then you have to disentangle it to take it back apart for separate reporting requirements, which is just an administrative nightmare. And while we are reporting to different places on different timetables under different requirements, I don't see how that's going to happen.* (Senior local government officer)[19]

4.92   Such constraints may be unavoidable in a system where accountability for spending taxpayers money is (understandably) seen as of the highest importance. But if the pooling of budgets cannot be made to work effectively to support joint initiatives between partners by making reporting arrangements more flexible, it makes it more important that the constraints on the use to which those funds can be put are loosened.

4.93   I accept that in some cases specific grants are seen as essential to deliver new national priorities which require a kick-start. However, the conditions for grant should be based on achieving desired outcomes which are clearly defined, not on prescription about how local government should spend the money to achieve those ends.

---

[19] Entwistle, T., et al., *Perspectives on Place-shaping and Service Delivery: A report of case study work conducted for the Lyons Inquiry*, 2007.

Recommendation 4.11

The Government should commit to significant further reductions in the amount of conditional, ring-fenced and specific grants to local government and its partner agencies and set clear targets and a timetable for achieving them. It should ask the Audit Commission to audit and report on progress in an annual public report.

Where conditional and hypothecated funding remains central government should:

- consider ways in which reporting arrangements for pooled budgets could be more flexible to support joint working; and

- focus on outcomes not process with flexibility on how the money is spent to enable it to fit better with local priorities and circumstances.

Enabling joint investment in prevention

4.94   One of the key gains from allowing greater financial flexibility in partnership working could be through improving the incentives to invest in prevention locally. One of the strongest messages which came up in evidence from service providers during the course of the Inquiry was that incentives to spend money on preventing problems later are weak or even perverse.

4.95   This is not a new issue of course. Initiatives such as Sure Start and a range of crime prevention initiatives were put in place partly because of the lack of incentive for public agencies to invest in prevention, even though such investment may be very cost-effective. A key problem is the time taken for savings to be seen:

> *Where we're not investing is around prevention ... The problem is of course, you need to have a little bit of an act of faith around that because you may not see results for three or four years if things are going well because you are investing heavily in prevention of crime.* (Senior stakeholder)[20]

4.96   A further problem is that the savings accruing from investment in early years support, public health, co-production to change behaviour towards healthier lifestyles, or intensive support for families with severe problems are likely to benefit the National Health Service or the police rather than local authorities. Strong partnerships which share clear common goals focused on the well-being of local citizens will help to align incentives here, and LAAs could provide a real opportunity to develop those shared goals. But there remain some barriers to local authorities and partners working closely to invest in tackling key local problems early on.

4. 97   As argued in Chapter 3, differences in the budget cycles and predictability in the budgets of major partners can make it difficult for local partner agencies to work together effectively. My case study work suggests that this is a particular issue in relation to primary care trusts and local authorities – and I welcome the Government's commitment to align the planning and budgetary cycles of local government and the health sector.

4.98   Enabling longer-term planning through three year settlements should also help – as preventative work is often the activity which gets squeezed out by short term budget cuts. This was one of the strongest conclusions from the expert seminar I held on children's services.[21]

---

[20] Entwistle, T., et al., *Perspectives on Place-shaping and Service Delivery: A report of case study work conducted for the Lyons Inquiry*, 2007.

[21] Summarised in Annex H.

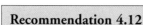

> **Recommendation 4.12**
>
> Central government departments should:
>
> - ensure that the budget cycles of major local agencies are aligned to enable joint planning; and
>
> - move to put all local agency budgets on a three-year basis to reflect the introduction of three-year settlements for local government.

Managing pressures

4.99   I have argued that greater local flexibility and clearer accountability are essential to enable local choices to be made in light of local priorities and within what people are willing to pay for. These elements are crucial to improve the management of pressures on local services. I argued in Chapter 3 that increases in total local government spending, and the ability of local government to drive out overall efficiencies, will be important determinants of the implications for council tax, as well as revenues from other sources.

4.100   The constraints that I have identified on cost effectiveness and value for money become more pressing if the pressure on public services increase. The notion that these can be addressed through central action, particularly with the central tendency to want to promise equal standards irrespective of local priorities and choice, is very concerning. In these terms the requirements for local flexibility and communities really being able to hold local – and national – decision-makers to account are essential.

4.101   However, this will mean different things for different services:

- **Central responsibility:** For issues on which national government is committed to certain standards of service or certain performance measures across the country, it is appropriate that central government should ensure adequate funding to deliver those. This is of course the case for the National Health Service, but is also true to some extent for schools. In this circumstance, central government has the incentives to manage pressures on the service – though not always all the levers to do so;

- **Local responsibility:** In contrast, for those issues which are left wholly to local discretion, local authorities have the right incentives and should be responsible for managing pressures and expectations, and for making decisions about local priorities in light of what people are willing to pay for; and

- **Shared responsibility:** For many services, however, central government may wish to specify some minimum standards or levels of service, with local flexibility beyond those standards. In such services, local authorities have strong incentives to manage pressures and maximise efficiency, but they also need the levers and sufficient local discretion to be able to do so effectively.

4.102   Many services arguably have some 'local' and some 'central' components, and therefore could be seen as 'shared' under this definition. Recognising this may help us to acknowledge the complexity of the ambitions we have for services, and also the contribution which both central and local government can make in shaping them. However, it raises complex challenges when seeking to determine who is accountable for what, and – particularly for those services which face increasing pressures in the future – raises the risk that pressures will not be managed effectively by either central or local government.

4.103   I discuss pressures in waste and social care specifically in later sections. But the key point here is a more general one – while it is right to design the system governing local public services so that they can each be managed as well as possible in light of their specific characteristics, local government's job must be to manage overall pressures by working with local communities to work out what is most important in each area. This reinforces the need for local authorities to own and drive forward efficiency improvements, to engage effectively, take a strategic view and work cooperatively with partners, as discussed in the next chapter. They also need to be able to take a wide view across local public services so that, if necessary, they can inform difficult judgments about those things which are of least value, where savings can be made, as well as about those things which are most important. And crucially they need the flexibility to be able to manage demand, improve effectiveness and work with partners to make best use of resources across the whole area.

Reorganisation

4.104   Reorganising or restructuring local government, particularly in two-tier shire areas as set out in the Local Government White Paper, is proposed as a solution to a number of problems. Some commentators have argued that restructuring can provide greater efficiency by creating larger authorities, which are able to benefit from economies of scale in provision, or through the elimination of a tier of administration; while others see it as a way of improving accountability to the citizen by simplifying a system in which responsibilities and community leadership are divided between two elected bodies. Although it did not form part of my remit, this issue has been raised on a number of occasions during the Inquiry, and the Government's invitation of bids for reorganisation has sparked considerable debate in some communities. Given the ongoing nature of this debate, I do want, briefly, to consider the issue, in the context of this chapter's wider discussion about what central government can do to enable more effective place-shaping local government.

4.105   This is by no means a simple question, and there is no 'right' scale for local authorities – any sensible size or design of authority has to trade off between a number of tensions which cannot be entirely reconciled. There is very likely to be a tension between economies of scale and the need to engage citizens and provide services that are tailored to their needs – the same problem as exists at a higher spatial level when considering the role of local authorities compared with that of national government. For multi-purpose authorities, as we have in England, different services are also each likely to have a different level of efficient scale of production, making it more difficult to identify the 'right' scale. In addition, there is the complex question of community identity and the degree to which local authorities should reflect a sense of place and community. Evidence about the balance between these different factors is inconclusive and contested, and the picture is further complicated by the growing opportunities to take advantage of economies of scale, without changing the scale of the commissioning unit, by commissioning services from external providers.[22] International experience, particularly in Europe, certainly shows that authorities smaller than our districts can form the basis of effective systems of local government, for example in France, and that multi-tier systems do work. Results from the Comprehensive Performance Assessment show examples of excellence in service provision and leadership at both county and district levels (though it should be acknowledged that a higher proportion of county councils are judged as reaching the highest levels of performance, and that the tests are qualitatively different).

4.106   That said, it should be acknowledged that research and practical experience do suggest some limitations. Some of the smaller unitary authorities created in the reorganisation of the 1990s have questioned whether they are large enough to attract scarce skills and to carry out the complex

---

[22] On debates about economies of scale, see for example the recent debate between Raine, J., et al., *An Independent Review of the Case for Unitary Status*, INLOGOV, 2006, and Chisholm, M., *Local Government Reform: A critique of the April 2006 INLOGOV Document*, 2006.

commissioning necessary for the effective provision of services such as social services. On the other hand, many authorities, particularly in the big cities, are seeking to find ways to establish more local structures to reflect local difference and bring some decisions closer to neighbourhood level in an attempt to practice double devolution.

4.107   The past experience of reorganisation in this country provides some warnings about the risks of poorly developed or executed change, and it shows that it is by no means the straightforward panacea that some would suggest. Reorganisation can also often be costly, and more importantly disruptive, siphoning officer and member resources away from actual priorities. Added to the very public expressions of inter-authority hostility which can result – and which marked the reorganisation debate in the 1990s in particular – this does not help to create or maintain public trust in local government, nor does it suggest that the welfare of the citizen is at the heart of local decision-making. It is also by no means clear that reorganisations have actually always been able to deal with some of the most pressing problems – as can be seen in the failure to address the tight boundaries of some authorities at their creation, for example in the case of the City of Nottingham.

4.108   It is my opinion that reorganisation is not, in most cases, likely to provide either a theoretical or practical solution to the challenges we face, and there are other approaches that authorities should seek in preference. I put a much stronger emphasis on the responsibility of authorities to develop effective and flexible coalitions, which transcend boundaries and seek joint solutions to problems where those offer the potential advantages. The recommendations I make in the next section on how authorities in two-tier areas can work more effectively together are intended to support this.

4.109   There are a number of areas in which joint action by local and regional authorities will be important. Under the present arrangements, regional assemblies are not elected, so the vehicle for engaging with the public is often through partnerships with local authorities. If local funds are to be invested at a regional level, this must reflect the outcome of a bottom-up process of community choice, mediated through local authorities as the elected representatives of those communities.

4.110   My original remit also asked me to consider the prospects for financing of elected regional assemblies. That debate has obviously changed significantly since 2004, and the financing of such assemblies would therefore need to be considered alongside any future decisions on their likely role. There is a precedent for financing elected assemblies through a precept on council tax bills, as in the case of the Greater London Authority; however, this would need to be given careful consideration given the existing pressures on council tax.

Strengthening the convening role

4.111   Many local services are provided not by councils but by other arms of the public sector – in particular, schools, colleges and universities, primary health care through GPs and NHS trusts, and policing through local police authorities and benefits, employment and skills through a combination of Learning and Skills Councils and Jobcentre Plus – which have their own relationships with central government.

4.112   Central government behaviour, systems and legislation can all have an impact on the ease with which local partnerships develop and operate. However well intentioned, mechanisms such as ring-fenced grants, centrally determined targets, budgetary and performance mechanisms which drive and constrain the behaviour of local service partners, combined with frequent changes to policy and funding regimes, all make it more difficult to work together coherently at the local level.

This reinforces the need for Government ministers to be restrained in the number of targets and ambitions they set out which require local government and other local agency input, and the frequency with which they introduce new initiatives.

4.113 The Government's intention to ensure that relevant targets for other local agencies are aligned with one another through Local Area Agreements is very welcome. It will of course be made easier if the targets and indicators adopted by government departments are as consistent as possible. This may require closer cooperation between government departments, though this should be easier to achieve if the number of targets and indicators set by central government are dramatically reduced in number as planned. I hope that the process will also provide for sufficient flexibility for frontline staff and managers in such services to enable them to respond to problems which arise during day-to-day activity. This is critical to ensure the continued effectiveness of the system and to deliver cost efficiencies.

4.114 There are many examples of successful partnership working across wide fields of activity, including success in developing local strategic partnerships, though the picture is variable.[23] In some service areas, partnership and convening roles have been enshrined in legislation: for example through the development of Children's Trusts and Crime and Disorder Reduction Partnerships. However, it is not only in the provision of mainstream public services that the convening role is important. Local authorities have an increasingly important role in leading all local agencies on issues such as emergency planning – particularly important in some areas of our major cities due to concerns about terrorism, but important for every area in terms of coping with natural or other disasters.

4.115 The Local Government White Paper acknowledges the convening role of local authorities in taking responsibility for outcomes across an area even when they are most directly affected by other agencies. It notes that local strategic partnerships should be coordinated by local authorities and should prepare the Sustainable Community Strategy in consultation with others. The Government's intention is to ensure elected members are fully involved in the local strategic partnership processes, that named partners are under a duty to cooperate with the local authority to agree and have regard to targets in the local area agreement, and local government has enhanced scrutiny and overview arrangements.

4.116 Under the terms of the Local Government and Public Involvement in Health Bill, the duty to cooperate would include health trusts but not schools and GPs. The introduction of the duty to cooperate reinforces the crucial need for local authorities to work with partners right across public services. There is a particular need for strong links between providers of universal services such as primary healthcare and schools and the communities which they serve where there are opportunities for co-production to improve outcomes (e.g. working to change behaviour to reduce health risks through tackling smoking, sexually transmitted diseases and obesity; or work with carers and parents to improve educational outcomes and the life chances of children). There is therefore, I believe, a need for formal recognition of the need for local authorities to be able to influence such key bodies in delivering important local outcomes – an issue which has been debated particularly strongly in relation to child protection and the 'Every Child Matters' agenda.

4.117 One obvious option is to extend the duty to cooperate under Local Area Agreement to these bodies. I recognise that in each authority area there can be hundreds of schools and doctors' surgeries, and that this would be a blunt instrument; it would therefore be important that such a duty reflect the different nature of the relationships between those bodies and the local authority compared to other local partners. This is discussed further in the section on services.

---

[23] *National Evaluation of Local Strategic Partnerships: Formative Evaluation and Action Research Programme 2003-2005*, Office of the Deputy Prime Minister and Department for Transport, 2006

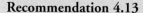

> **Recommendation 4.13**
>
> The Government should:
>
> - seek to ensure that changes to the performance frameworks, guidance and funding systems affecting local government and its partner agencies are kept to a minimum, to help provide a more stable environment within which to develop joint strategies and actions;
>
> - seek to ensure the suite of targets and national indicators for local government is internally consistent and outcome-focused. A priority in the negotiation of Local Area Agreements should be to allow the local alignment of targets across all local public services; and
>
> - acknowledge the role of local authorities in having lead accountability for local outcomes across all local agencies.

4.118 These changes need to be reflected in the performance framework as reflected above. It is important that comprehensive area assessment truly supports the drive for better joined-up working, more alignment and more recognition of local authorities' responsibility for place. It is, however, important that expectations are realistic in light of the resources which the local authority can influence, as well as focusing on the outcomes and satisfaction of local people that will be such an important focus of future performance reporting.

Making two-tier government work more effectively

4.119 For this approach to work and for accountability to be clear in two-tier areas, county and district authorities will need to put considerable effort into their working relationships and behaviours. There are of course already many positive instances of partnership working, and in my case studies I heard of good and improving relationships between counties and other tiers of local government and with other partners:

> *I think the county's attitude to the districts has changed dramatically ... In the old days it was the case that we're the county so we know best, you know, do as you're told otherwise we'll clip you round the ears. Now it's much more of a partnership, they are much, much more willing to listen to what we have to say and understand.* (Case study council)

4.120 Nevertheless there remains a need to improve two-tier working in many areas and I welcome the Government's nuanced approach to proposals for unitary local government, which seeks to change current arrangements only where there is a strong case for change and a broad cross-section of support. As noted above, too often in the past proposals for reorganisation have distracted local government, with authorities devoting their energies to battles about boundaries rather than to delivering effective outcomes for local people.

4.121 However, I agree with the Government that improved working is needed in two-tier areas, and that authorities in these areas need to aspire to operate as 'virtual' unitaries with greater efficiency through shared back-office functions and integrated service delivery mechanisms as discussed in Chapter 5. Some authorities have already made great progress towards this.

4.122 I also support the recommendation from the evaluation of Local Strategic Partnerships that there should be greater district representation on county partnerships and vice versa (or streamlined arrangements agreed by both tiers), to improve the common understanding of their respective strengths and roles, and to make it easier to deal with cross-boundary issues. Plans to apply the duty to cooperate between tiers in two-tier areas are also welcome.

4.123   These aims for two-tier government are welcome in terms of improving the user experience, enabling efficiency and promoting the development of an area. I would however be concerned if the delivery of this ambition became a question of designing rigid models of how two-tier working should operate. These are issues of local discretion that need to reflect differences in political and service dimensions and improving joint working is at least as much about behaviour as about structure. There must be room for different areas to design their own arrangements, recognising that they are likely to be distinctive.

4.124   I am also concerned that joined-up working between tiers, while undoubtedly beneficial, should not dilute the accountability of local councils. The ambition in the Local Government White Paper that service users should have "no need to understand whether the county, district, or other service provider is responsible" will only be to the benefit of local people if there is a clear accountability mechanism through one of those bodies, or through some other clearly defined part of the local strategic partnership. This ambition should therefore not be over-emphasised as district councils will retain a useful role and strong advantages in terms of engagement with local people which should not be lost. In the same way that there needs to be greater clarity about central–local relationships, there needs to be clarity about county–district relationships.

4.125   The recent award of Council of the Year to Wychavon and High Peak Councils is a welcome statement of the important role of district councils. The Government Offices have a role to play in this as well – by engaging directly with district councils on issues relating to the contribution of the lower tier. I would expect that they, and colleagues in county councils and other partners, should welcome the potential that districts bring in terms of having agencies that are closer to local communities in terms of the intelligence and ease of engagement that this brings. As some recent research pointed out:

> *Local residents' relationships with the respective borough councils are far stronger than with any other public agency in town. In comparison to other public bodies, local residents are far more likely to have attended a borough council meeting, to have responded to a borough consultation exercise and to have made a formal complaint to the borough council.*[24]

4.126   As I stress elsewhere, the opportunity to engage more effectively with the public should be seized by every council. This issue is discussed further in Chapter 5.

Working with other sectors

4.127   Most local authorities already recognise the value that the voluntary and community sector – the third sector – brings to place-shaping activities, particularly in engaging with users who have multiple or high needs, and in developing approaches to co-production. It is often more flexible and seen as more approachable than statutory services. A research report prepared for the Department of Health in February 2007 estimated that 35,000 third sector organisations currently provide health and/or social care in England.[25] Most of these are well established; 72 per cent have been operating for over 10 years. In general, local authorities were positive about services provided by third sector organisations, with overall levels of satisfaction high (over 80 per cent). Local authorities felt the organisations provided good value for money, high quality and responsive services compared with other external service providers – although a small number of authorities had concerns about a lack of experience among some third sector organisations.

---

[24] Wilks-Heeg, S. and Clayton, S., *Whose Town is it Anyway? The state of local democracy in two northern towns*, Joseph Rowntree Foundation, 2006.
[25] Department of Health, *Third Sector Market Mapping*, 2007.

4.128 Full recognition of the convening role of local government should take account of the complex relationship which local government has with the third sector – key partners who play a significant role in service delivery, but who also act as pressure groups on local and central government for particular interests. Lobbying of national government will rightly continue, and indeed in some instances there is the need for national standards and frameworks, for issues such as the equalities agenda. In other instances central government should resist encouragements to meet the particular objectives of individual third sector and lobby groups through central action and instead focus on encouraging the third sector and lobby groups to work with local government.

4.129 Local government cannot and should not take responsibility for everything which happens in a locality. My May 2006 report discussed the appropriate circumstances for intervention. However, it is legitimate for local government to take an interest in the actions of businesses and other organisations where their activities have a significant impact on the wider community. Local authorities already play an important role in this field, working with, advising and regulating such wider activities, for example through the planning process and its various licensing and inspection roles.

4.130 In their submission to the Inquiry, the Centre for Public Scrutiny has argued that a duty should be placed on external agencies to cooperate and respond to local authority scrutiny. The Government intends to legislate to extend scrutiny powers to cover all bodies subject to the duty to cooperate, to strengthen the role of overview and scrutiny committees to examine a wider range of place-shaping issues.

4.131 I have considered the merits of calling for a further formal extension of local government's scrutiny powers to cover organisations such as the Post Office, GPs and retailers. However, I do not believe this is necessary given the fact scrutiny powers appear to operate widely and to good effect already in many authorities. Scrutiny committees examine a diverse range of issues across a wide range of sectors on a voluntary basis; issues have including examinations of councils' budgets, Post Office closures, campaigns to promote healthy eating and physical activity, and fly-tipping, though existing powers could be used to better effect by local government, as discussed in Chapter 5.

Efficiency and choice

4.132 Chapter 3 distinguished between two different types of efficiency. First, public services need to be delivered in the most cost-effective way possible. Second, the system should be designed to enable what economists call 'allocative efficiency', ensuring that public expenditure is allocated to best meet the needs and preferences of each community. These concerns about efficiency are likely to become more important if public finances become more constrained in the future. There may sometimes be a tension between improving cost-effectiveness to find financial savings, and prioritising the right activities in each area, but ensuring value for money in the broadest sense is likely to become an even greater necessity.

Managerial efficiency

4.133 A forthcoming report by the Audit Commission identifies the innovative use of hand-held computers by the London Borough of Sutton to conduct financial assessments. This allows benefit payments to be calculated and agreed on-site, reducing the time taken for assessment from six weeks to a few hours. This has led to a significant reduction in back-office processing and realised efficiency savings of £300,000 – 50 per cent more than predicted at the outset of the project.

Customer Service Centre, Bunny Hill, Sunderland

A new £7.8 million customer service centre at Bunny Hill, which opened on 26 June 2006, provides one of the most comprehensive ranges of services available under one roof in the country. Sunderland City Council developed this project in conjunction with its strategic partners, including Sunderland Teaching Primary Care Trust, Sunderland Housing Group, a local GP Practice, a local pharmacy company, the voluntary sector and Sunderland North Community Business Centre. The project is the latest in a new generation of customer service centres giving people access to the kind of services which meet the essential elements of their everyday life, such as health, housing, education and welfare – all under one roof. Services at Bunny Hill include:

- a new Council Customer Service Desk and associated interview facilities;
- a Wellness Centre, with a gym and confidential consulting rooms;
- a GP's surgery, an NHS primary care centre and a pharmacy;
- a community library and electronic village hall;
- a Sure Start Children's Centre with facilities for parents and the under-fives, including a neighbourhood nursery and crèche;
- an adult education centre;
- Sunderland North Community Business Centre's Community Suite with a café, community hall and meeting rooms; and
- a neighbourhood housing office.

The project is funded by Sunderland City Council and its strategic partners with assistance from grants given by the Neighbourhood Renewal Fund, Sport England, the Big Lottery Fund, the Learning and Skills Council, the European Community and Sure Start. Bunny Hill serves communities across the Castletown, Town End Farm, Downhill, Hylton Castle and Hylton Red House areas to help address problems of illness and deprivation in the area, but also the needs of the whole community. The Council has now opened seven new Customer Service Centres with a further five planned for Ryhope, Southwick, Washington, Ford & Pennywell and Doxford Park.

Leader of Sunderland City Council, Cllr Bob Symonds, said: "This is a milestone in our efforts to revolutionise the way in which council services are delivered in Sunderland, with customer service at the core of that programme".

4.134   There has been significant improvement by local government, with the support of central government, in driving cost effectiveness in the delivery of local services. This has been achieved through a variety of means including greater service collaboration, exploiting technology, better procurement and understanding of local government's role as commissioner of services – so driving innovation and broader improvement across the sector. Figures released in December 2006 suggest that local authorities will deliver £1.3 billion of efficiencies in 2006-07 – well in excess of the £1 billion target set by central government, and building on performance in previous years.

4.135   I am pleased that the Local Government White Paper is seeking to build on these successes while recognising that local authorities are best placed to decide how to improve efficiency. However it is important to recognise that cost-effectiveness is as much about productivity and the quality of service as it is about cashable savings.

4.136 Even with these achievements, local government needs to locate itself more fully as a champion of cost effectiveness. The need to improve local government behaviours in this regard is explored further in Chapter 9. The focus group work for my Inquiry illustrated concerns about the efficient use of public resources where respondents called for the more careful targeting of funds and the more efficient use of existing revenue. In particular, local authorities were criticised for not managing public money efficiently. One participant commented: "If all we put in was used properly and it was managed properly then I bet everyone would be better off".

4.137 The framework in which local government operates needs to encourage a more entrepreneurial spirit. This can only be achieved if local authorities are given more flexibility to manage and by making local government more clearly accountable to the local communities upon whom the burden of any inefficiency will fall, either in terms of reduced outcomes for services or higher tax requirements. I strongly encourage an approach which locates responsibility for improving efficiency firmly with local authorities themselves, rather than developing expensive central initiatives which are unlikely adequately to reflect local needs and circumstances.

4.138 I am, however, concerned that there has not been more recognition that the current level of centralised control still restricts scope to improve cost effectiveness. My case study work and submissions received argue that central government requirements constrain public agencies from making sensible choices about how to shape and deliver their services. This occurs both within and between services.

4.139 Sir David Varney's report on service transformation argued that "providing joined-up services designed around the needs of citizen or business will yield efficiency savings by reducing duplication across the public sector".[26] Restrictions described in earlier sections that hinder joint working and flexibility have a cost in efficiency terms which has not been fully recognised. The tighter the constraints on how funding has to be used within local government, the NHS, police and other partners, the more difficult it is for those partners to work jointly to improve efficiency. This is particularly important in fields such as emergency planning, which requires very close working between agencies, and a degree of flexible capacity to respond which can be squeezed out by an overemphasis on cost effectiveness.

4.140 However, this joining-up role is already being led by local authorities in many areas – we must not ask local authorities to wait for a centrally designed initiative to find the 'correct' answer as to how best to join up; rather, the system should encourage them to find ways of making these savings, give them the flexibility to innovate, learn from their experience and allow them to continuously improve.

Innovation 4.141 One obvious cost of inflexibility is the inability of local government to innovate. Overemphasis on setting frameworks which have to work in every area can mean that the whole country is forced to go at the pace of the slowest area. But equally, overexperimentation runs the risk that many areas spend time reinventing new approaches and wasting time and resources. The challenge here is to strike the right balance, allowing those communities who are ready to innovate to do so, and ensuring that appropriate support and guidance based on best practice and evaluation evidence is available to support those who are not. This does not mean central government should issue guidance on innovation – rather the family of local government should take responsibility for this, building on work already ongoing, with organisations such as IDeA and LGA leading on the provision of information and reference sites which provide genuine examples of good practice. There are several examples of where councils have used current powers flexibly to achieve real benefits.

---

[26] Varney Report: *Service Transformation: a better service for citizens and businesses, a better deal for the taxpayer*, 2007.

Flexibility and innovation in Wakefield[27]

Section 2 of the well-being power has been used in Wakefield to purchase houses on an estate in rapid decline to facilitate speedy clearance of the site and afford reasonable recompense to residents and owners, without going through the lengthy compulsory purchase process. This estate – which was split equally between owner-occupied, housing association-owned and private landlord-owned residences – was overwhelmed by antisocial behaviour and drug-related problems, resulting in many unfit or vacant homes and leading to reduced market value of the remaining habitable houses. The council was keen to acquire and demolish the houses and rehouse the remaining occupants. The prevailing rationale was that use of the well-being power would facilitate appropriate action relatively quickly and effectively, and without this it was difficult to see how any action could be taken quickly enough.

To achieve property acquisitions, intensive negotiations took place directly with owners, based on criteria of current market value and considerations of community gain. This meant some properties were purchased over the current market value to achieve the development strategy in the most cost-effective manner for the council. There were criteria for the people living in the estate. If they kept their home in good order the local authority would give them the full market price plus recompense for disturbance and relocation. Agreements were made with the housing association which agreed to demolish their properties and rehouse their tenants. If the property was privately owned and it was abandoned the landlord would be given £3,000 to give over property rights to the council.

The initiative was driven by the then head of housing, supported by the local authority lawyer and led politically by the cabinet member for social care and housing.

The well-being power was used innovatively to enable the council to act outside the more restricted compulsory purchase process and to take over the responsibility for regeneration from others. (It should be noted that the legal basis of this initiative has recently been overtaken by a change in legislation, which would allow the activity without reliance on the well-being power.)

4.142 The proposal in the Local Government White Paper that national targets will focus on outcomes rather than processes is helpful. The performance framework must recognise the benefits of innovating and trialling new approaches, even if (as is inevitable in a creative, risk-taking approach) not all of these deliver improved results. There may be scope for the role of research and development to be given greater emphasis in relation to innovation. The Audit Commission's current inspection framework emphasises local authorities' ability to learn from experience and it is important that this is carried through into the new Comprehensive Area Assessment framework, with a stronger emphasis on innovation.

The value of difference

4.143 The submissions I have received from local authorities reflect a sense that managerial efficiency or cost effectiveness is too frequently emphasised in the public sector at the expense of allocative efficiency or broader value for money – we tend to care more about doing things cheaply rather than delivering the right priorities locally; those which have the greatest impact on well-being. Central government messages, supported by processes and monitoring mechanisms, are focused on the need to drive down costs in existing services. This means that the prior questions of whether the right services are being delivered have not been considered.

4.144 I believe the biggest cultural challenge we face as a country in delivering the promise of real devolution is in understanding, accepting and celebrating the fact that difference and distinctiveness between our communities is a good thing and is important for raising satisfaction and well-being.

---

[27] Taken from *Formative Evaluation of the Take-up and Implementation of the Well Being Power – Annual Report 2006*, CLG, 2006.

4.145   Central government, local authorities and communities need to place greater value on the ability of local authorities to exercise choices and establish priorities on behalf of their communities. As I argued in Chapter 2, there is no universally accepted measure of well-being that we can use to judge how well local authorities are doing in enhancing the well-being of their communities. It is essentially a subjective judgement, which will vary between places and over time, and it is for that reason that, across a range of services, the ability of local communities to make choices themselves about how to improve their own communities is the decisive factor.

4.146   Despite concerns about a 'postcode lottery' so evident in the media, my analysis in Chapter 3 suggests people would welcome greater – but managed – difference if this accorded with local needs and priorities. I believe the public understand the need to set priorities locally in order to afford what we want – there is already a great deal of variation in standards in practice, and getting that variation right is, I believe, the key to managing pressures effectively and improving satisfaction in the future.

4.147   There are clearly some core services, including aspects of education, health and the emergency services, where people want to be assured that all areas get the same high level of services. Even these will often prove difficult to achieve. However, there are many other policy and service areas where fairness could be better understood in terms of managed difference which enables the diversity of communities and their different aspirations to be properly recognised and reflected in the services they get.

> **Recommendation 4.14**
>
> The Audit Commission should ensure the Use of Resources judgement in the new performance framework includes delivering the right priorities to meet the needs and wishes of the local community.
>
> **Recommendation 4.15**
>
> Central and local government should together challenge the presumption that difference between areas – the 'postcode lottery' – is always a bad thing.
>
> **Recommendation 4.16**
>
> The Government should explicitly recognise that for a range of local services the best way to improve well-being is to enable greater local choice.

Engagement and responsiveness

4.148   Local government is ideally placed to operate as the key mechanism of local choice by engaging with the public as citizens – crucially through the work of frontline councillors, but also by virtue of local government's responsibility for a wide range of services and for the well-being of all its citizens.

4.149   There is inevitably a need for local authorities to make difficult decisions – which benefit some people and disappoint others – and therefore a critical need for local authorities to engage with communities to inform and validate those choices, and to explain them so people can understand why they were made. Understanding the difficulties involved in making choices locally can help citizens to feel the decisions themselves are fair ones, even if they are not the choices they themselves would like to have seen. Effective civic engagement can also provide the connections for community cohesion by developing trust and mutual respect within the wider community.

4.150   Greater engagement will not in itself directly improve satisfaction with local services or with local government. It depends on local government's ability to ask the right questions, listen to the answers and respond in the best way, involving people from a diverse range of backgrounds in the design and delivery of services and broader place-shaping activity. It is clear that engagement efforts by local government need to improve, as discussed in Chapter 5, but local government's ability to respond to the needs and wishes of citizens also depends on the flexibility offered by the system within which it operates. This determines whether or not local councillors can respond to local concerns – and be seen to make a difference – by taking steps to improve not only services provided by the council, but also the wider factors affecting the places people live in, the facilities and services they use.

4.151 This role will, I believe, become more important if pressures on local services increase. For those services and roles which are appropriately subject to local discretion, local government needs to have an ongoing dialogue with local people about what they want, what they are willing to pay for through taxes and charges, and what services or activities they might be willing to spend less on over time in order to pay for more important local priorities. This means creating realistic expectations and explaining difficult decisions, but ultimately it should help to manage the pressure on council tax and on local services in a way which better meets the needs and wishes of local people. The action here lies with local, not central, government, but this role needs to be valued and encouraged by the system as a whole.

Co-production 4.152 Chapter 2 argued that local government is well placed to engage with local communities and service users to improve the effectiveness of services through what can be termed co-production. Sue Goss from the Office for Public Management comments:

> *Many of the new priorities – 'respect', an end to 'binge drinking', 'recycling', 'improved public health' – cannot be achieved by a smart government delivery machine; they require changes in behaviour from the public. This means not simply considering how to deliver using public or even private resources, but how to access the 'free' resources of public energy, engagement and action.*[28]

The case studies below provide some examples of local authorities undertaking this role.

Sheffield Partnership for Older People Project

Sheffield Partnership for Older People Project (POPPs) is a partnership led by Sheffield City Council comprising older people, carers, Sheffield Teaching Hospital Trust, Sheffield Care Trust, Sheffield Primary Care Trust and key voluntary organisations. POPPs is part of a national programme working with older people to promote health and independence and prevent hospital admissions.

The programme, which started in September 2006, promotes the integration of services in the neighbourhood designed to support and promote older people's independence and sustain their health and well-being for longer. The project focuses on issues that older people say make the most difference to their lives. This means listening to older people, engaging with them as citizens, and identifying and addressing their concerns and about the communities in which they live and responding appropriately.

A key part of delivery has been the development of the Expert Elders Network. The Network is made up of older people who sign up to be involved in the planning, design, delivery and evaluation of services. They can choose how they would like to be involved, from attending strategic planning boards to commenting on job descriptions. It is designed to transform services for older people by harnessing the expertise of older people themselves, strengthening planning at a neighbourhood level, simplifying access to services and making it easier to tap into preventative services. Training is available to give older people the skills and confidence to contribute in their chosen area of interest.[29]

---

[28] Hassan, G. (ed.), *After Blair: Politics after the New Labour decade,* 2007.

[29] Entwistle, T., et al., *Perspectives on Place-shaping and Service Delivery: A report of case study work conducted for the Lyons Inquiry,* 2007.

Southampton's Binge Drinking Design Campaign

Students at Southampton Solent University have joined forces with Southampton City Council, Southampton Police and the Tackling Alcohol Partnership to challenge the issue of binge drinking in the city. The aim of the project was to listen to and learn from what young adults had to say about tackling alcohol misuse, enabling young adults to help each other.

Second-year HND Advertising and Media Communication students were asked to create a campaign that challenges attitudes towards drinking alcohol to excess among young adults. To devise their design-based campaigns, the students conducted eight months of research and analysis into the issue of binge drinking to consider the type of campaign needed and the best ways to get their message across to young adults.

The campaign gives information on local and national services that provide support, advice and guidance on issues relating to alcohol using a variety of media, including A3 posters suitable for noticeboards, and smaller media such as postcards and discreet credit card size information. Designed by students for young adults, the campaign seeks to tackle the problem in an engaging and understanding way.[30]

4.153 Mechanisms such as these can help prevent poor outcomes and higher costs later on, and in other contexts, such as recycling, can help to manage the pressures on local services more directly.

4.154 The ability of local government to work with local people and to innovate and respond flexibly to local needs together provide opportunities for local government to significantly improve the efficiency and effectiveness of public services and to manage pressures more effectively.

4.155 These possible benefits have, however, been increasingly lost over recent years as a result of increasing dependence by local government on central direction, and I believe a loss of self-confidence. The current reform process needs to recognise the value that local government can bring in this area, and to encourage local government to seize the opportunities presented by those reforms to work with local people to find ways to improve services and well-being in every area of the country.

Powers and powerfulness

4.156 One of the questions which has arisen persistently in my Inquiry is whether local authorities already have sufficient powers to undertake their place-shaping role. The overwhelming message from authorities who presented submissions to my Inquiry was that a lack of local flexibility to do what was needed locally, as a result of the burden of central controls and performance management was the key problem, rather than a lack of powers.

4.157 Local authorities already have wide legal powers, extended significantly by the introduction of the power of well-being in section 2 of the Local Government Act, 2000 which enables authorities to "do anything which promotes or improves the economic, social and environmental well-being of their area". There is still some way to go to ensure that all local authorities are aware of and able to use their existing powers fully. Early evaluation of the well-being power highlighted that many local authorities need to take a more active and confident approach to the use of the

---

[30] Entwistle, T., et al., *Perspectives on Place-shaping and Service Delivery: A report of case study work conducted for the Lyons Inquiry,* 2007.

power.[31] The experience of Local Area Agreement negotiations has shown that in a number of cases local authorities have requested enabling measures from Government departments that they are already legally able to undertake.[32] Chapter 5 considers this issue in more detail.

4.158 However, there is a need for some changes in local government's powers in specific areas where local authorities are constrained by the way in which existing powers are drafted or used, and where powers and resources are potentially located at an inappropriate level of government. Later chapters discuss specific funding powers and make recommendations for these to be extended. The next section examines powers with respect to specific services.

4.159 But it is important to recognise an equally important point, which is often missed in discussions about whether local government has sufficient powers. Local government has become dependent on central government not only financially, but in many cases also for guidance, encouragement and permission to innovate, across a wide range of fields. This culture of dependency has, I believe, been driven by increasing central direction over the detail of local government activity, which has tended to distract it from focusing on the local community, sapping its sense of direction and confidence. While I believe increasing confidence and capability must be driven from within the local government community itself, central government needs to encourage an increasing sense of powerfulness through not only devolving powers but also by expecting local decisions to be taken locally.

4.160 One of the suggestions put to me during the course of my Inquiry was that a duty should be placed on central government to cooperate with local government on matters of local importance. Such a mechanism might encourage local authorities to identify those matters which are properly for local determination – and could give them a lever to influence central government's behaviour and legislation to ensure it will not inappropriately interfere with local choice in a way which could reduce the well-being of people in that area. This of course would raise a number of very difficult legal and perhaps constitutional questions, but I am attracted to the spirit of the proposition because it emphasises the importance of the locality in determining well-being and has the potential to help shift the relationship between central and local government towards a more explicit partnership where power over the locality is shared between the tiers of government more equally.

Promoting economic prosperity

4.161 The concept of place-shaping underlines the importance of communities taking responsibility for their own economic fortunes, and for striking the right balance between economic, environmental and social objectives and concerns. It highlights the need for governmental interventions and action to be joined up by local authorities in order to tackle problems and exploit opportunities at a local level. While, as Chapter 3 acknowledged, patterns of economic activity do not match the administrative boundaries of local authorities, and sub-regional working by groups of local authorities is a necessity if they are to effectively address economic issues, resolving this issue in a way which undermines or cuts across the place-shaping role risks disengaging local government from the economic prosperity agenda. That could have damaging implications for both effective delivery of economic objectives, and for relationship between communities and government.

---

[31] ODPM, *Formative Evaluation of the Take-up and Implementation of the Well Being Power, 2003-2005*, 2006.
[32] *Local Area Agreements Research: Round 2 negotiations and early progress in Round 1*, CLG, 2006.

4.162 It would be desirable to locate a greater proportion of relevant resources and decision-making power on economic issues at the sub-regional level by devolving more powers. That would help to ensure that decisions are aligned with the needs of the local economy, and that the trade-offs and interactions between such decisions can be fully considered. It is the clear message which emerges from recent work, such as the *State of the English Cities* report, the LGA's *Prosperous Communities II*, and the work of Kate Barker and Rod Eddington. The challenge is to develop effective institutional arrangements as the Government will, entirely properly, want to ensure that any sub-regional arrangements that seek to wield greater resources and decision-making power have robust and accountable mechanisms for making difficult decisions and implementing long-term strategies. There are a number of different options for securing this.

Voluntary partnerships

4.163 One potential approach is to build on existing patterns of cooperation between local authorities. Such arrangements have the advantage that they leave discretion to local communities as to when to collaborate and the exact form of collaboration. Arrangements can be devised to respond to different challenges, which may not always need to follow the same spatial boundaries – for example where a joined-up approach is needed along transport corridors. Many authorities are already building such partnerships, often working in collaboration with Regional Development Agencies, such as the Partnership for Urban South Hampshire, the work of the authorities in the Greater Bristol Area, the Association of Greater Manchester Authorities, the Milton Keynes South Midlands arrangements, and joint working between Nottingham, Leicester and Derby. All the former metropolitan county areas also have such arrangements, though some are stronger than others.

4.164 However, there are limitations to a purely voluntary partnership approach. A system with many different bodies requiring unanimity for decisions has some structural drawbacks. Discussing and negotiating decisions between many partners can incur substantial transactions costs. The fact that each body has an effective veto is seen as risking decision-making taking place on a 'lowest common denominator' basis, which requires all partners to benefit equally, rather than on the basis of the most beneficial overall decision for the area as a whole. A partnership approach may find it difficult to create enhanced political leadership at the level of the body as a whole, and will not be directly accountable for its actions to the people of the partnership area. The fact that each constituent body will continue to face its own political and financial challenges and priorities may mean that such arrangements are not as robust or long-lasting, with authorities able to join or leave at relatively short notice (though these tensions do not disappear under dedicated arrangements). This might militate against making the long-term decisions on policy and funding that are necessary for some economic decisions, for example on transport and other infrastructure investments.

New sub-regional authorities

4.165 An alternative, suggested by the Centre for Cities and others, would be to create new authorities to take on powers over key economic levers such as transport, planning, skills and regeneration, led by a political leadership explicitly elected to use those powers. This approach does have certain attractions. It provides a clear and transparent model, with a clear set of responsibilities and direct accountability through election for the leadership of the new authority (which might be a council or a directly elected mayor). However, there are a number of potential drawbacks, and the creation of new institutions should not be seen as a simple solution to what is a complex issue.

4.166 While it is possible to devise new boundaries which better reflect economic geography than current administrative boundaries, no boundary will ever be perfect. The appropriate area will be different for different aspects of economic activity, and we can expect them to change over time, as economic, social and technological factors change. For example, we have longer commuter flows now than prevailed when current transport arrangements were established in the late 1960s, making those arrangements less appropriate in their current form. There are also a number of areas which are linked into more than one economy. Coventry, situated within the West Midlands urban area, and sharing many interests with the other parts of that area, is also engaged in the sub-regional economy around Warwickshire, for example. Barnsley, linked to the economies of both Sheffield to the south and Leeds to the north, is another example. Any solution must offer a means for this complex reality to be acknowledged and responded to, not simplified and ignored.

4.167   At the practical level, developing sensible boundaries for any new arrangements will need to deal with the vexed question of local authority boundaries. Local government reorganisations in the recent past have not displayed local government at its best, and have often diverted energy and attention away from the business of working with citizens and delivering improved services. The experience of the referendum on the North East Elected Regional Assembly showed the public is also sceptical about new tiers of government. While the Greater London Assembly and the Mayor of London have been successful and popular, we should be careful not to generalise from the re-establishment of city-wide government in London to the very different situations in other places, with different histories and identities. Other European countries have also found collaborative approaches more effective than formal changes – the *State of the English Cities* report concluded that:

> *There is substantial evidence regarding the problems of using formal institutional or constitutional changes to achieve sub-regional collaboration ... The majority of places* [in Europe] *are attempting to collaborate informally on policy issues across boundaries and with partners where they can.*[33]

Safeguarding place-shaping   4.168   In the debate on developing sub-regional arrangements, I am concerned to emphasise the need not to cut across or undermine the place-shaping role of local authorities. Drawbacks in current institutional arrangements – for example the fragmentation created in transport planning in our larger cities by arrangements which only cover public transportation, do not include the full commuting geography and are institutionally separated from local decision-making – already risk this, though many areas are trying to overcome these problems.

4.169   Linking all the different issues involved in sustainable economic development together – planning, housing, transport, skills, education, social inclusion and so on – is an essential place-shaping task. To attempt to divide responsibilities, to suggest that economic issues and the responsibility for pursuing prosperity can or should be separated from the core objectives of a local authority is potentially damaging. There is a danger within these arguments that the move to aggregate upwards, towards a larger spatial level which captures all of the possible different boundaries, can create pressures for uniformity rather than responsiveness, and disempowers local effort and understanding. That could create longer term problems for public trust and confidence. It is therefore important that local authorities are responsible for making the links, and building the coalitions, necessary for them to fully pursue the task of place-shaping. Any one locality may need to be part of different coalitions at the same time, depending on the issue and the context. The example of Lille, overleaf, describes how the creation of effective coalitions has supported economic development across an area.

---

[33] Parkinson, M., et al, *State of the English Cities*, vol. 1, ODPM, 2006.

Metropolitan Lille and the regeneration of Roubaix[34]

The Metropolitan Lille authority (now called Lille Metropole Communaute Urbaine) was established in 1967, as part of the French government's policy to devolve power from Paris and to encourage the creation of metropolitan authorities in larger urban areas. It is controlled by an Assembly whose members are appointed by the elected municipalities. Initially seen as a device for providing services more efficiently, it has, particularly since 1989, enabled joint working between the municipalities to promote economic growth across the metropolitan area. Lille has been able to reposition itself as a significant European city through its position on new high-speed rail lines (including the Channel Tunnel link to London), investment in a major new commercial and shopping centre, and other projects to re-orient the local economy towards growth sectors.

Working at the metropolitan level has also supported regeneration and redevelopment in within former industrial towns within the conurbation, such as Roubaix. Lille's leaders realised that it could not attract in the people and investment that it needed to become a leading European city if it was still associated with major areas of deprivation such as those found in Roubaix. Over the past 20 years, substantial investments have therefore been made in transport, housing, cultural facilities and economic development in Roubaix, including the revitalisation of the town centre. The access to the wider tax base of the metropolitan area as a whole and funding channelled through the metropolitan authority from other public and private sources have been important contributions to that process. While there is still a long way to go (unemployment, for example, although down from 33 per cent in the late 1980s is still over 20 per cent) it is widely agreed in France that Roubaix has turned the corner decisively and is making significant – and somewhat unexpected – progress. In the process, the gaps between French provincial cities like Lille and the capital have been narrowed, and their economic performance has outstripped their British equivalents.

An alternative approach

4.170 The Government has accepted these arguments and is rightly not pursuing a structural reorganisation to address them. Nevertheless, it understandably wants to be confident that approaches are in place to ensure a proper emphasis on economic prosperity, enable effective decision-making with public accountability, avoid unhelpful competition and cost, and to be credible with investors and the business community.

4.171 In the light of these issues, I believe that an approach which marries some of the benefits of a voluntary approach with some of the rigour of a structural solution is necessary. Establishing a framework in which proposals for sub-regional working are developed and owned locally and then considered against a clear set of tests and expectations set by the Government would ensure that the partnerships have clear objectives, can take a long term view and are sufficiently strong to support the greater responsibilities that would then be provided. This offers a developmental solution to the problem, with the capacity for improvement and change as the relationships between different groups of authorities, and between local and central government grow.

---

[34] Based on a case study prepared by URBED as part of Joseph Rowntree Foundation's *Making Connections: Transforming people and places in Europe* project.

Possible tests for sub-regional arrangements

The Government's tests for any new arrangements might include an expectation that they would:

- reflect a sensible definition of the prevailing economic geography;

- have appropriate arrangements for offering voice and accountability to all of the communities affected;

- be able to set clear outcomes and objectives, underpinned by a robust evidence base;

- include robust decision-making machinery, capable of making hard choices, building local support and agreeing clear priorities. That suggests a presumption in favour of a tight board structure with delegated powers, but connected to and accountable to leadership arrangements for all relevant councils, with scope for non-executive members to be drawn in to bring additional skills and experience;

- be clear about how decision-making will be connected across key issues, including transport, spatial planning, infrastructure investment and skills;

- be able to demonstrate support from the public and the business community;

- show the ability and intent to attract the key technical skills necessary; and

- have clear and well-signed ports of entry for would-be investors to access, and clear policies governing the speed and nature of decision-making processes.

4.172 The development of Multi Area Agreements, as signalled in the Local Government White Paper, provides a possible model for such an approach, whereby local authorities could establish arrangements between them and enter into a discussion with central government on the objectives of that agreement and what central government could contribute by way of devolved powers and resources to its success. This would meet the recommendations of the Barker and Eddington reviews that such powers are wielded at that level where appropriate arrangements exist.[35]

4.173 The objectives of empowering place-shaping and taking a holistic approach to issues of prosperity suggests that it is also important to align existing governmental and delivery arrangements in order to reduce the scope for conflicting policies and decisions. While delivery agencies may well need to have boundaries designed around variable spatial patterns for different services – perhaps strengthened by strong executive boards – the strategic direction and accountability for that needs to be clear and located with local authorities and their leadership. That should be the case unless the agency is unequivocally the agent of central government.

4.174 New arrangements between collaborating local authorities provide one way to redistribute and devolve responsibilities and funding (including those of existing Passenger Transport Authorities) in order to ensure the alignment of local decision-making powers. Others, including Eddington and Barker and the LGA, have undertaken detailed analysis of the most appropriate responsibilities and funding to be managed at the sub-regional level, and following their analysis, these could include:

- strategic planning powers currently held partly by the individual authorities within the arrangement and partly by central government;

- resources and land currently administered or owned by Communities England;

- power over some strategic roads currently administered by the Highways Agency;

---

[35] Entwistle, T., et al., *Perspectives on Place-shaping and Service Delivery: A report of case study work conducted for the Lyons Inquiry*, 2007.

- ability to make some adjustments to the quality and frequency of rail services, and perhaps to commission or decommission some sub-regional services;

- allocation of some proportion of current regional transport and housing funding and regional economic development spending;

- powers and revenues allocated to local authorities in relation to road pricing; and

- depending on existing arrangements and the views of local employers, a role in convening the work of an area-wide Employment and Skills Board.

Recommendation 4.17

Reflecting the importance of working at the level of the functional economy in pursuing economic prosperity, the Government should:

- use Multi Area Agreements as a way of engaging with local authorities to develop locally determined sub-regional arrangements to address issues related to economic prosperity;

- set clear tests and expectations for arrangements in order to ensure that they would be robust enough to make challenging decisions and trade-offs;

- detail which powers, responsibilities and funding would be devolved from national and regional level to sufficiently robust and capable groups of authorities, and align existing governmental and delivery arrangements with new sub-regional arrangements; and

- avoid the creation of new institutional structures where these do not currently exist unless a consensus exists at the local level, or local authorities fail to put in place adequate arrangements through collaboration.

WHAT THIS MEANS FOR SERVICES

4.175 The analysis for my Inquiry used a range of techniques to assess the problems facing local government and possible solutions. Although my work was never intended to provide an exhaustive analysis of all the services which local government provides or influences, I have examined a range of specific services in order to inform my work. They were selected to cover different issues in terms of pressures, degree of central control and role in place-shaping, and included economic development, children's services, social care for older people, waste and recycling, health and well-being and community safety.

4.176 I used these services to provide a focus for my case study work, public deliberation events, and a series of expert seminars.[36] In these I examined a range of questions about the role of local government, relations between central and local government and local partners, pressures and funding arrangements.

4.177 This section draws out issues which emerged in relation to specific services. It focuses first on the analysis of the Barker, Eddington and Leitch reviews and my analysis of economic development to draw out implications for planning, transport and skills. It then summarises the most prominent issues which have emerged in relation to housing and other specific services.

---

[36] A summary of which is provided in Annex H.

Economic development

4.178 Local authorities already have wide responsibilities and powers to act on issues related to economic development and prosperity. Finding new ways to develop sub-regional arrangements and to devolve responsibility and resources – as set out above – will expand the influence of the local level in making decisions on economic issues. There are also some specific issues, arising from my work and my consideration of the Barker, Eddington and Leitch reviews, which I wish to discuss further.

Planning   4.179 Land use planning is an important aspect of place-shaping, perhaps the most immediate tool that authorities can use to influence the physical aspects of localities. It has important links to environmental, economic and social issues, to quality of life and to the distinctiveness of communities. In developing local plans, and in making planning decisions, a host of sometimes conflicting views and interests have to be balanced – between the environment and the economy, the interests of existing investors and those of future investors, and between the interests of local communities and wider regional and national interests. There is not necessarily a 'right' answer here – the ability to take a nuanced approach, and to recognise the validity of different views within and between communities, is essential. I agree with Kate Barker's conclusion that a return to the previous generalised presumption in favour of development is not appropriate, and that a more balanced approach is required which takes account of local plans and the likely costs and benefits of development proposals.

4.180 The Barker Review of Land Use Planning argues that decisions should be made at the level where the impact is felt, and that this is most often the local level. There are some areas of planning policy and guidance where the Government can make this clearer and give more discretion and responsibility to local authorities to make those decisions themselves, and the Government should take steps to reduce inappropriate central oversight, prescription and intervention where that does exist. It may be appropriate to set some targets or guidance where there are priorities of national significance, but these should be focused on desired outcomes rather than the means by which they are accomplished. Some planning and decision-making might well sensibly take place at a sub-regional level within the locally led arrangements described above. This should enable local authorities better to manage some of the physical attributes of place, and support local distinctiveness where desirable. A side-effect of this should be to make planning a more rewarding career and thus to enhance its reputation and attractiveness.

4.181 The Secretary of State's call-in powers are the ultimate means by which the Government can influence or change local planning decisions. While there will be circumstances in which it is appropriate for national considerations to override local decisions, it is imperative that these powers are used in a transparent way, and only where issues of genuinely national significance are involved.

> **Recommendation 4.18**
>
> The Government should pursue devolution and clarification in the planning system as set out by Kate Barker in her review of the land use planning system and in particular:
> - reduce the complexity and detail of directions which provide for central control; and
> - set out clearer criteria on the use of call-in powers.

4.182 Both Barker and Eddington propose changes in the way major infrastructure projects are dealt with in the planning system, most notably through the creation of an independent Planning Commission to make the final decisions on such projects. The objective behind this is – along with related recommendations on Statements of Strategic Objectives – to simplify, clarify and speed up the processes that exist for making decisions on projects of national significance. This proposal has been contentious, and sparked discussion, both in submissions from stakeholders and in my Inquiry's seminar on the Barker Review.[37] However, I think that there are attractions to the proposal, which could provide a clearer and more transparent discussion and decision-making process for issues of national importance.

4.183 It is right that decisions of national importance, where the national interest is overwhelming, are ultimately made at a national level. Current planning arrangements do already seek to deliver this through the use of ministerial call-in powers, and through legislation which gives secretaries of state the powers to determine applications for certain types of infrastructure. However, the system can be complex and time-consuming for both those seeking to develop major infrastructure projects and for the local communities who quite legitimately want to have their say – with multiple stages at which 'final' decisions are made, which are later amended. Reforming the system to make it clear from the start who will make the final decision, and what factors will influence them, would make it simpler for individuals and communities. There was a wide variety of opinions on this issue in submissions to the Inquiry, though a number took the view that it could help to provide greater clarity.

> *The establishment of an independent planning commission could streamline the consideration of projects of national significance provided the strategic objectives are clear. However, it needs to be linked to the process of policy making. In particular, each phase of the planning process needs to take forward delivery by establishing the need, and principles to be adopted.* (West Midlands Shire Councils)

4.184 Just because a decision has national benefits does not mean that the perspectives of local people, and the impact on their community or quality of life, should not be taken into account. It will be imperative that these implications are considered, both by the Government in its preparation of the national Statements of Strategic Objectives and during the Planning Commission's deliberations, on the basis of representations from individuals and communities. The Barker and Eddington proposals acknowledge this.

4.185 Once decisions have been made, the Commission, the Government and local authorities will also need to put effort into communicating those decisions and the reasons for them. Communication is something at which our institutions of government have traditionally been poor, but it is essential if communities are to have trust in government at all levels. There is a challenge here for both local and central government.

Recommendation 4.19

In taking forward reforms to the planning process for major infrastructure projects, the Government should ensure that:

- the new arrangements apply only to issues of unambiguously national importance, subject to clear and published criteria;
- local individuals and communities are informed of the process and have an opportunity to make their views known; and
- a clear process for reporting back to local communities is established.

---

[37] A summary of which is provided at Annex G.

Transport 4.186 There is substantial debate about how decisions on transport investment and prioritisation should be made, and many local authorities perceive that the current system does not give them sufficient influence over the decisions taken in their area. The sub-regional governance proposals I set out earlier in the chapter should provide an opportunity for local authorities and the Government to develop approaches which will enable greater devolution and effective local decision-making.

4.187 There is also one particular aspect of transport provision where the capacity for influence by either local or central government is weak. That is in buses, which were deregulated in all areas outside London in 1986. Lack of influence over buses outside London is felt by many to have led to falls in ridership, rises in fares, and to have weakened the ability of local authorities to maintain effective integrated public transport systems. London, where regulation remained, has shown substantially better performance and higher usage in the intervening period, partly, it is argued (including by the Audit Commission and National Audit Office) as a result of the different regulatory system, which has allowed Transport for London to manage provision better in London.[38] However, it is important to note that the substantially higher subsidies now provided for bus operation in London are also a factor, and that other parts of the country have also seen improvements in local provision, often helped by effective working relationships between bus operators and local authorities.

4.188 The Government has acknowledged the problems associated with the current approach and has recently announced plans to enhance and extend the powers and options at the disposal of local authorities.[39] This is a welcome step, which should expand the ability of local authorities to ensure that local public transport provision is appropriate and integrated. The Government's proposals were supported by the vast majority of submissions to the Inquiry on this subject.

> *The ability for local authorities to be able to plan and secure new bus services to a level it considers necessary to secure broader objectives, including economic regeneration, free from the constraints of the current legislation, would be invaluable. This does not mean a return to prescriptive regulation but empowerment to local authorities to work more flexibly to meet local needs.* (Essex County Council)

Recommendation 4.20

The Government should implement its plans for local authority powers to regulate bus services as soon as practicable.

Skills and employment 4.189 The UK's competitive position is now, and will increasingly in the future be, dependent on the level of skills of its workforce. The Leitch Review of Skills sets out powerful arguments for further investment in the skills of both our existing and future workforce if we are to maintain and improve our prosperity. To a significant extent, it is for individuals and their employers to assess and pursue their own skills needs. However, there is also an important role for government in setting the appropriate framework, providing funding and addressing social issues associated with a lack of skills or access to training. The Leitch Review proposes a new demand-led model for adult skills and a simpler framework for employer engagement, in order to make the system more responsive and competitive. It also calls for greater integration between skills and employment services, drawing together existing services such as Jobcentre Plus with a new adult careers service.

---

[38] National Audit Office and Audit Commission, *Delivery Chain Analysis for Bus Services in England*, 2005.
[39] Department for Transport, *Putting Passengers First: The Government's proposals for a modernised national framework for bus services*, 2006.

4.190   The vital contribution that skills can make to economic development makes it essential that local authorities in their place-shaping role, engage with these issues. They will be particularly concerned to ensure that the public funding and planning/commissioning of training and skills provision, which are the responsibility of the Learning and Skills Council (LSC), are responsive to local conditions and the needs of local employers and individuals. The Leitch Review's recommendations would replace the current system of planning and commissioning with a demand-led skills system, driven by individual and employer requirements, though the Government's initial response envisages a continuing role in the short term for some planning and commissioning, at the regional level, including to deal with identified gaps in the provision available.[40]

4.191   I think that in any system, there is likely to be a need for the employer voice to be tested with high quality local intelligence to consider whether it provides a complete picture of the needs of the area. Where a planning and commissioning approach is retained, that needs to be tested to ensure that it is responsive to the conditions of the labour market. There is also a need to challenge and monitor the activity of public sector employment and skills support. All of these activities must engage employers and reflect the functional economy, rather than being bound by the administrative boundaries of local authorities or the region.

4.192   The Employment and Skills Boards recommended by the Leitch Review (and being developed in a number of areas at present) could perform such a role. Local authorities should have an appropriate role in any such boards, both as substantial local employers, but also as the representatives of the wider community with an interest in the future prosperity of the area. Many local authorities already have, or are in the process of developing, arrangements with local employers, and where these are effective they should be allowed to continue. It would also be desirable to link activity on skills with any other joint city or sub-regional activity being taken forward by partnerships of local authorities, as described earlier. Skills issues need to be considered alongside the complex mix of other issues which impact on local economic prosperity and the economic opportunities of individuals.

4.193   Local authorities also have a role to play in addressing other employment and skills issues, particularly for those furthest from the labour market. Authorities' contributions in this area are a good example of their convening role, working with Jobcentre Plus, the LSC, employers and others, including the voluntary sector, to address the variety of different factors, including childcare, transport and housing, as well as skills, that can affect the ability of individuals to enter the labour market. A number of authorities made this clear in their submissions.

> *It is sensible to link employment and skills issues together in a way that enables more effective planning and delivery arrangements to reduce worklessness. The creation of clear progression routes from unemployment into work that involves a range of local service providers is a key challenge for City Strategy. In addition to formal learning and training, greater links need to be made with other public services... This includes health services, housing providers, adult learning and adult social care services etc.* (Manchester City Council).

4.194   Reforms to the welfare system in this areas, following David Freud's report *Reducing Dependency, Increasing Opportunity: Options for the future of welfare to work*, which recommends regionally based contracting of support for those facing multiple disadvantage and long-term benefit dependency, are likely to have implications for local authorities.[41] As his report identifies, it

---

[40] Department for Education and Skills and Learning and Skills Council, *Delivering World-class Skills in a Demand-led System,* 2007.

[41] Freud, D., *Reducing Dependency, Increasing Opportunity: Options for the future of welfare to work:* an indepedent report to the Department for Work and Pensions, 2007.

will be important to ensure that any new framework strikes the right balance between large-scale contracting and local, sub-regional control, providing local authorities with appropriate influence, and contractors with the incentives to work closely with them.

4.195 Funding and responsibility for 14–19 education and skills provision is currently shared between local authorities and the LSC, with local authorities expected to play a strategic role.[42] The implementation of the new 14–19 diplomas, and the expansion of more complex and innovative forms of provision which cover the traditional school-leaving age of 16, make it essential that authorities and the LSC, as well as schools and other providers, work closely and effectively together.

4.196 There is a debate about whether merging funding and responsibilities within local authorities would help to secure more seamless provision. There are certainly some potential advantages to such a move, though as has been pointed out, integrating responsibilities in the local authority could simply create a new division at 19, and the Leitch Review recommended against further structural reorganisation in this area. The Government will want to keep current arrangements under review, especially if it decides to require all young people to remain in full or part time education or workplace training up to the age of 18, as discussed in the Leitch Review.

Recommendation 4.21

In taking forward reforms following the Leitch Review, the Government should:

- ensure that there is sufficient scope and resource to enable the Learning and Skills Council and local partners to tailor provision appropriately at the local level;

- enable local authorities to play an appropriate role in Employment and Skills Boards; and

- seek to build on existing arrangements between employers and local authorities where possible.

Housing   4.197 Patterns of housing development and mobility, the availability and condition of housing and the willingness of individuals and developers to invest in it are all important influences on, and reflections of, the health of our communities. That applies as much to social housing as it does to privately rented and owner occupied housing. Policy objectives from school attainment to the cohesion and sustainability of communities are affected by the type, quality and affordability of housing available.

4.198 Housing is not simply a matter for national policy – its influence on local communities is too direct and material for that, and the reality of the different housing markets across England are clearly evident. The challenges for national policy in responding to very different market conditions and issues in the North, South East and East, and South West have been evident in recent years.

4.199 As such, looking at housing issues in a strategic context is an essential part of the place-shaping role of local authorities. Local government has traditionally been focused on its role as municipal landlord, and some authorities who have transferred their stock to the social sector no longer see themselves as interested in housing issues. However, that will need to change if local

---

[42] Department for Education and Skills, *Further Education: Raising skills, improving life chances*, 2006

authorities are to perform a full place-shaping role. The new role is very different, however, and is essentially strategic – using powers and influence to shape local markets and the contribution of other players. Local authorities have already demonstrated their ability to engage and develop innovative solutions through creative use of public land and Section 106 negotiations with developers to respond to the issues in their areas.

4.200 I have identified the following as issues that local and central government will need to pursue in the future:

- a clear challenge to local government to take a strategic view of housing provision in their area across the piece, including market as well as social and affordable housing;

- a question mark over whether local government will have to take a more active role in supply, given the difficulties of provision for older people, and continuing problems in supply, especially of affordable housing and in some rural communities;

- the importance of ensuring that investment in social housing delivers the best value for money, both with regard to local action, and to the impact of the Housing Revenue Account Subsidy arrangements. Authority-owned housing is still a £98 billion asset, and one which needs to be used to full effect; and

- a danger that current arrangements are too fragmented both locally and nationally, and a need to engage housing associations, particularly the larger organisations, more fully in place-shaping. The Government should consider whether extending the duty to cooperate to housing associations would have advantages.

Recommendation 4.22

The Government should ensure that local authorities have appropriate influence over housing issues in their place-shaping role and should consider whether to extend the duty to cooperate to housing associations and other social landlords.

Social care for adults

4.201 Local authorities have a range of responsibilities to provide social services to all age groups. In both adult social care and child protection there is a strong sense of a national entitlement, perhaps due to concerns about the need to protect both our vulnerable older people and vulnerable children in ways which offer equal standards of protection across the country. Participants at the public engagement events strongly argued for national standardisation in the funding of social care, particularly for older people and the supply of residential care.[43] However, in these services, as in others which are even more strongly nationally controlled – such as schools and the NHS – the need for local tailoring to meet local needs, to engage with those receiving the service and their carers, and to link with other services, is still significant. My recommendations on the convening role of local government set out earlier are therefore relevant.

---

[43] OPM, *Lyons Inquiry – Public Deliberation Events,* 2006.

4.202   Social care is not what economists term a local public good, such as street lighting or public health, which provide benefits to the whole community equally. It is a publicly provided private good, provided specifically to those who need a range of care but on a means-tested basis. It has clear benefits to the people supported and their families, but few direct 'spillover' effects on the wider community – and the rationale for public provision is based on a sense that society should provide care to those who need it and cannot afford to pay for it themselves.

4.203   I focus my comments here on social care for older people. Local authorities are responsible for commissioning and delivering adult social care to national standards.[44] Local authorities have the flexibility to vary who is eligible to receive care (across four different categories of need defined by government), and for non-residential care they can decide whether, and how much, to charge for services.[45] This has a range of advantages – particularly in terms of the ability to determine locally how many people are eligible for care. However, it means that while the standards of social care are intended to be uniform across the country, whether or not people are eligible to receive it, and the charges they have to pay, can vary greatly across the country.

4.204   This poses one of the most difficult questions facing our public services today: who should pay for adult social care, and how should it best be managed? Derek Wanless sparked the latest debate on this important issue and raised profound questions about the role of the state in providing private goods and about who is best placed to decide who is entitled to what.[46] There now needs to be an open debate involving central and local government, service users, private sector providers and current and future tax payers if the best solution is to be found.

4.205   The Comprehensive Spending Review 2007 will examine some of the challenges in the future provision of adult social care. It will need to consider whether there is scope to clarify responsibility for adult social care, in order to improve the ability of the system to manage pressures more effectively. It should take account of the factors affecting the appropriate balance between central and local control. These include the principles in Chapter 2, but the following are particularly relevant to adult social care for older people:

- How strong is the sense of national entitlement?

- Is central government or local government best placed to manage pressures?

- How much do costs, needs and the most effective form of delivery vary between different areas?

- How much scope is there for co-production and innovation?

- How extensive are the benefits of joining up locally?

4.206   I examine each of these questions in turn in relation to adult social care for older people.

National entitlement

4.207   In my survey work social care was clearly seen as a service that is, and should be, subject to the shared responsibility of central and local government. However, some aspects of adult social care – particularly older people's residential care – increasingly raise concerns about uniform entitlements and there appears to be little appetite among the public for local difference in this

---

[44] There are national minimum standards against which all core providers are inspected and regulated by the Commission for Social Care Inspection (CSCI).

[45] The need categories are called the Fair Access to Care (FACS) eligibility bands.

[46] Wanless, D., *Securing Good Care for Older People; taking a long term view*, King's Fund, 2006.

service, despite wide variations already on a number of dimensions. Participants at the public deliberation events run for my Inquiry tended to see social care for older people particularly as 'a national issue'. They were conscious that needs varied widely in terms of the size and needs of local populations of older people, many of whom moved to certain areas after retirement, which they felt meant it should not be funded from local taxation.

Managing pressures

4.208   Derek Wanless' detailed analysis showed that future pressures are likely to be driven by the greater number of older people living longer and requiring intensive support. Increases in unit costs, particularly wage costs, which make up the great majority of the adult social care budget are also important pressures.[47] My case study research also identified the rising expectations of adult social care service users, who are demanding higher standards and increased flexibility in the services they use:

> *As people move into older age they have different changing expectations. Our generation and generations behind will have a very different expectation to the generation who are currently service users. We need to make sure our services are absolutely modernised for current service users ... so where you've got the need, you've got increasing demand, the need to improve services for hard to reach communities like black and ethnic minority communities, the need to modernise services.* (Senior local government social care officer)[48]

4.209   A recent survey commissioned by the LGA into people's expectations of social care and charging policies found that only ten per cent of people expected to pay for all home care, and 49 per cent expected to make a contribution, but that over one third (32 per cent) still expected to receive all home care for free.[49]

4.210   There is scope to better manage these pressures though considering how people are supported in their old age, which may affect the point at which people need more intensive or residential care. Unit cost pressures could arguably be managed more effectively at the local level, particularly because wage pressures and the markets for social care provision vary between different parts of the country. Meeting service users' changing expectations is also arguably better achieved at the local level. However, central government determination of standards, particularly for residential care is a clear driver of the costs of provision.

4.211   More generally, there is a need for the system to support increased cooperative working between the NHS and local authorities, as discussed earlier. This means, as a minimum, aligning budget and performance management cycles to enable better joint planning. But joint working would also be supported by changes that increase flexibility on both sides, as discussed in earlier sections.

4.212   I would argue strongly that responsibility for determining the eligibility for social care should be as closely aligned as possible to responsibility for (and levers to enable) the management of pressures. The current hybrid model whereby local authorities set eligibility criteria and bear the cost, but central government sets the standards and the means testing criteria for residential care, gives local government limited tools but arguably much of the responsibility for managing pressures. An increasing number of authorities are already restricting care to those with the highest levels of need, as this form of rationing is one of the limited number of ways in which they can respond to pressures.

---

[47] Wanless, D., *Securing Good Care for Older People; taking a long term view*, King's Fund, 2006.
[48] Entwistle, T. et al., *Perspectives on Place-shaping and Service Delivery: A report of case study work conducted for the Lyons Inquiry*, 2007.
[49] LGA, *Without a care?* 2006.

4.213 Aligning responsibility for determining who is eligible with the management of pressures might also encourage a greater focus on outcomes rather than inputs – which came through as particular issues in my case studies:[50]

> *The performance agenda is driven by numbers and not necessarily by quality and... the things that social workers on the ground actually see are the most appropriate numbers to be counting.* (Senior local government officer)

4.214 There may also be scope for local authorities to become more efficient in the commissioning and provision of social care services and to take on a greater role in shaping the market in their area, which could help to manage cost pressures. Procurement practice and markets vary significantly across the country, and Chapter 5 discusses local government's role in using commissioning and 'market-shaping' practices to deliver value for money.

Variation in needs and costs

4.215 Differences in culture, the age profile, levels of wealth and whether an area is urban or rural mean that the needs for adult social care vary greatly between areas. This means not only that demands on social services will vary greatly, but that the best means of meeting those needs is likely to look very different in different places. This suggests the need to allow for variation, to respond to local needs in a tailored way, which must be balanced against the widespread view that social care is a national entitlement demanding uniform standards.

Co-production and innovation

4.216 Achieving some of the objectives of adult social care – for instance, helping older people to remain independent and in their own homes – depends on working with individuals themselves and with carers and the local community. Designing services which help people to remain self reliant for as long as possible requires the involvement of service users and the local community in service design and delivery. This can also lead to innovation – finding new mechanisms which, for example, prevent falls and help people live safely at home for longer. The Partnerships for Older People Projects (POPPs) have been found to provide flexibility at the local level for local authorities to work in partnerships with other organisations and their citizens in the design and delivery of services. An example from Sheffield is outlined earlier.

Joining up

4.217 The crucial role of other local services in supporting the objectives of social care suggests that social services must remain rooted in the local community to be effective. This is particularly important for children's services, and for support for adults and non-residential care for older people. It is important for local authorities to work across their boundaries and join-up effectively with local PCTs.

4.218 There is also a key role for co-production in the effective provision of support for vulnerable people, through working with and supporting carers and neighbours who provide day-to-day assistance. Developing strong relationships with carers is crucial not only for ensuing the best possible care for those receiving social services, but also in managing pressures into the future.

4.219 The case for making adult social care a more clearly 'national' or 'local' service is therefore finely balanced. It suggests there is a case for it to remain a shared responsibility between central and local government, reflecting both the sense of national entitlement and the need for local flexibility to cope with varied needs and to make the most of links with other services and carers. This is a clear example of a service where central and local government together need to operate a system of 'managed difference' (discussed in Chapter 3) in order to maximise the well-being of service users and the local community.

---

[50] Entwistle, T., et al., *Perspectives on Place-shaping and Service Delivery: A report of case study work conducted for the Lyons Inquiry,* 2007.

4.220 However, there is a clear need for reform to enable the system to cope more effectively with future pressures. Reforming the system of social care to align incentives for efficiency – balancing costs against outcomes and satisfaction – with the ability to control eligibility and pressures as effectively as possible is a huge challenge. In my view it can only be solved by a well informed and honest debate about the challenges the system faces and the difficult questions they raise.

4.221 There needs to be a clear, shared agenda between central and local government about the care and support we provide for older people. A critical outcome from the Comprehensive Spending Review 2007 should therefore be to ensure that the solutions for managing the future of social care effectively are properly debated by central and local government, service users, carers, private and third sector providers and taxpayers. Following questions raised by Derek Wanless, this should ask whether the current system has got the balance right in terms of who should bear the costs of care, and to what extent: should it be taxpayers through local taxation or national taxation, or individuals themselves; and who should make decisions about levels and standards of care provided by the state. Any shared agenda needs to ensure individual needs are met in the most cost-effective way possible, particularly gaining an understanding of who pays – the balance between NHS and social care, and the role of co-payment in providing better individually focused care.

4.222 If Government makes a 'national promise' about future adult social care, local government must be adequately funded to enable it to deliver that part of the promise for which it is asked to be responsible. As part of this, it is important that responsibility for managing pressures lies with those who are able to do so most effectively.

> **Recommendation 4.23**
>
> The Government should lead a clear national debate about how we want to manage and pay for social care for older people, which should cover:
>
> - what, if any 'national promise' central government wants to make for the whole country;
> - what local government is to be responsible for, and who is best placed to manage pressures; and
> - who should pay for social care: state or service user, and how incentives can be aligned to ensure competing demands are managed appropriately.

Domestic waste collection and disposal

4.223 Waste is the other area of significant cost pressures that I examined in my case studies. Rising costs in waste management are a widespread problem, as our dependence on cheap landfill must be reduced in line with EU legislation. The UK faces substantial financial penalties if it fails to meet targets on reducing the amount of waste sent to landfill, which may be passed on to local authorities through the Landfill Allowance Trading Scheme. The Scheme provides for fines if authorities exceed their landfill limits, including any extra allowance they may buy from other councils. Local authorities must therefore invest in alternative means of disposing of waste, including increasing recycling. The continuing rise in the volume of waste, together with rising targets for recycling and composting and increasingly strict regulations for the treatment and disposal of waste, all contribute to the growing cost pressures on local authorities.

4.224   In many ways, waste collection is one of the most local of services, however the issues and challenges described by case study interviewees showed more consistency than any other service area.[51] This may reflect the fact that the current policy agenda in waste has been set at European and central government levels. Respondents in my case studies saw solutions to the problems facing them as lying in improved county and regional partnerships and significantly increased capital investment. They also saw a critical role for central government in incentivising collaboration through carefully chosen performance targets and the introduction of new economic instruments.

4.225   An issue which emerged clearly in discussions on waste was the confusion over responsibility for managing the waste stream, including over crucial issues such as minimising our production of waste in the first place. All tiers of government have different, though overlapping, roles to play in making sure we meet our international obligations, each of which is essential to the delivery of the whole. Even within central government, a range of departments have relevant responsibilities including Defra, who lead on the development and implementation of waste policy, the statutory framework and most waste negotiations at EU-level. Defra and DTI have joint responsibility for responding to some EU waste directives. CLG lead on planning for waste management facilities and waste from the extraction industries as part of their wider responsibility for planning policy, and HM Treasury, CLG and Defra have responsibility for adequately funding waste management.[52]

4.226   Local government leads the way in some areas of waste minimisation – which should be the 'first best' option for managing waste pressures in the future. Work with communities and households to encourage such changes in behaviour through co-production is one of the key advantages in ensuring waste collection remains a properly local service. Many local authorities are already taking forward innovative initiatives in this area, and many are building waste reduction messages into their existing literature on recycling and composting. However, despite the introduction of the recycling credits scheme, authorities which push ahead on waste minimisation may not always reap the benefits themselves, partly as a result of the complex and shared responsibility for waste.[53] Chapter 6 discusses ways in which local authorities can be given more levers to manage pressures in waste through charging mechanisms.

4.227   Despite some notable successes in partnership working, interviewees still complained about the complexity of institutional arrangements for waste management:

> *Effectively we're doing it* [working in partnership with the districts] *but that's taken a hell of a lot of hard work and many years to achieve.* (Senior local government officer)[54]

> *The first* [priority] *for me would be the abolition of two-tier working because on waste management, I think it's an anomaly.* (Senior local government officer)[55]

---

[51] Entwistle, T., et al., *Perspectives on Place-shaping and Service Delivery: A report of case study work conducted for the Lyons Inquiry,* 2007.

[52] *Review of England's Waste Strategy – a consultation document.* Defra, February 2006.

[53] Waste collection authorities have a duty to encourage householders to recycle and compost more of their waste, through initiatives such as sorting waste before it is collected. To incentivise this activity, the Government introduced recycling credits in 1990. Because recycling and composting waste diverts that waste from normal disposal routes, action at the collection end of the waste stream saves money at the disposal end of the operation. Recycling credits allow waste collection authorities to claim some of the revenue that their recycling and composting activities save waste disposal authorities.

[54, 55] Entwistle, T., et al., *Perspectives on Place-shaping and Service Delivery: A report of case study work conducted for the Lyons Inquiry,* 2007.

4.228 Some interviewees were also concerned about whether responsibilities at the regional level were working as well as they could:

> *It's interesting because I do quite a lot of work at a regional level and the regional agenda is completely dominated by the regional spatial strategy work and planning and housing numbers and things like that. And waste doesn't appear very high up the agenda ... Transport comes higher up, but the overall thing is housing at the moment and housing numbers and again that's responding to government agendas.* (Senior local government officer)[56]

4.229 For some officers, real progress required the establishment of unitary local authorities responsible for collection and disposal. However, other consultees argued that effective waste management can be achieved through effective multi-agency working:

> *Having a critical mass for partnership working is more important than restructuring change, for instance through unitary status.* (Representative, Lincolnshire County Council, waste seminar)[57]

4.230 Others argued for the Landfill Allowance Trading Scheme and recycling targets to be brought together as part of a coherent package of measures to provide incentives for districts to work with their disposal authorities:

> *need more incentives (including financial incentives) to get two tier areas working together. Partnership working really requires a shared decision-making structure, pooled funding, and a clear precept on local taxes.* (Representative, Kent County Council, waste seminar)[58]

4.231 The introduction of the duty to cooperate between tiers should help to encourage joint working – discussed earlier in this chapter – but there is a need also for central government to be clearer about its own responsibilities for managing the waste stream. Waste offers a good example of a service area in which there is a need to find ways to make the system as a whole work better, based on a clearer understanding of what each tier is best placed to do.

4.232 For instance only central government – or in some cases the EU – can legislate for initiatives to improve the incentives on businesses and the packaging industry to reduce the amount of waste we produce in the first place. But only local government can manage the collection of domestic waste in a way which recognises the different challenges of different types of community – for example, rural areas compared to blocks of flats – working with communities to find the most cost-effective ways of minimising waste and increasing recycling. Other tiers also have a contribution to make. The need to find solutions must be explicitly recognised as a shared responsibility between central and local government, and the challenge is to ensure that all tiers contribute what they are best placed to do to make the system work as well as possible.

4.233 This means, for example, being clearer about which drivers of waste production and disposal costs can most appropriately be managed by central government (such as the negotiation of international obligations), which should be managed at the regional level, and which are appropriately subject to local action (such as mechanisms to influence the behaviour of households). It also means finding ways to improve the way in which objectives and incentives are aligned between the various tiers of government, and to make it possible for authorities to work constructively together to manage waste pressures.

---

[56] Entwistle, T., et al., *Perspectives on Place-shaping and Service Delivery: A report of case study work conducted for the Lyons Inquiry,* 2007.
[57, 58] A summary of this work is provided at Annex H.

4.234 The Government recently announced its intention to legislate for Joint Waste Authorities in those areas where local councils wished to establish such formal partnership structures. This is a positive step in a context where joint working may make it easier for authorities to procure alternatives to landfill and streamline their dealings with private sector firms. It will, however, be important that there is room for structures to be tailored to, and driven by, local partnerships, and not imposed according to a central template.

4.235 There may also be a case for examining the tools local authorities have to influence not just how waste is disposed of, but also the volumes emerging in the first place. To this end, Chapter 7 considers the case for giving local authorities greater powers to influence the behaviour of local people through a variable charge for the collection and disposal of domestic waste.

> **Recommendation 4.24**
>
> The Government should give greater recognition to the fact that effective waste management is a shared responsibility between central and local government and consider ways to provide greater local flexibility to manage the waste stream locally (including waste production), particularly through a new power to charge for domestic waste (see Chapter 7).

Community safety

4.236 Community safety offers a very good example of a set of concerns and activities which can only be delivered effectively where there is a strong local element – particularly to influence behaviour, working very closely with local communities. It is key to supporting social cohesion, which is one of the most important roles for local government in modern society, as discussed in Chapter 2.

4.237 One of the clearest messages to emerge from my case studies was the need for more stable funding for community safety to enable strategic planning and to encourage partnerships to grow.[59]

4.238 The community safety interviews exhibited high levels of consistency across the case study areas. Respondents described very similar issues; they provided a largely positive account of partnership working, identified problems with the prevailing system of central–local relations, primarily for excessive dependence on national performance targets, and almost unanimously criticised current funding arrangements for the dysfunctional effects of short-term project funding. They complained that national targets required them to focus on issues of questionable local significance, crowding out what were perceived to be more pressing local priorities.

4.239 Two points were particularly emphasised. The first was focused on their dependence on short-term project funding. Interviewees complained particularly that short-term initiatives – very often introduced with their own detailed regulations – antagonised local communities, as services they supported were axed when the funding dried up:

> *Short-term funding is always a difficulty with communities because if they think this is just short-term fix they don't buy into it. They get quite upset in fact ... what's going to happen at the end of the year then – don't know – well what's the point of us committing if you're going to pull them out? That is a difficulty and you need that longer-term strategic approach to this kind of subject if you're going to get communities really engaged and supported because they will see through it.*

---

[59] Entwistle, T. et al., *Perspectives on Place-shaping and Service Delivery: A report of case study work conducted for the Lyons Inquiry*, 2007.

Many of them have been round this bidding process many many times. And it does take up a lot of time and energy ... there's a bit of money here and a bit of money there. The time it takes to actually pull that together you have to sometimes think well is it actually worth it? (Senior police officer)[60]

You want to get a grant to start up a youth club to hire the hall – which kids are you going to involve? How do you demonstrate they're from Area 6? Well actually some of them are from Area 5 and some of them go to the school in Area 3. Oh well we're not going to pay for them they're not our kids you need to go to Area 3 and Area 5 and they'll give you a proportion of the grant. Well if that was me I would've given up wouldn't you? (Senior local government officer)[61]

4.240   Second, our respondents complained more broadly about the uncertainty of funding arrangements. They argued that short-term and tightly hypothecated funds made it difficult to focus on key local priorities, including prevention, as emphasised earlier:

The real problem is the funding keeps changing ... if they want us to do a three-year strategy, then give us three years' funding, because otherwise it's pretty pointless in my view, (Senior stakeholder)[62]

There isn't spare money to pick up all these government initiatives ... because they're done on grants you never know quite how long it's going to go on for. So security of funding is the essential thing for the development of partnerships because then you'd never get one partner reneging on a deal because ... they've run out. (Senior local government officer)[63]

4.241   This problem may have emerged in relation to community safety more strongly than other services, because of the strong reliance on focused, time-limited grants provided through a range of channels. A key role for Local Area Agreements should be to allow the funding and flexibility for those sources of funding to become more streamlined and stable over time. Other evidence on community safety supported the broader findings of the Inquiry in terms of the need for greater local flexibility both in terms of function and funding, reflected in earlier sections. Police funding did not emerge as a particular issue from my case studies, although a number of submissions raised it as an issue as discussed in Chapter 3.

> **Recommendation 4.25**
>
> The Government should simplify funding streams and targets, particularly for community safety.

Health and well-being

4.242   The protection and improvement of public health is a role which clearly benefits from local determination, arguably to an even greater degree than social care – since the benefits of enhancing health and well-being can accrue to the local community as a whole, and the health needs of each community (and therefore what needs to be done) vary dramatically. Priorities range from the need to reduce smoking and obesity, to tackling sexually transmitted illnesses, all of which can require quite different local emphases depending on the local population, and different strategies to tackle them.

[60-63] Entwistle, T., et al., *Perspectives on Place-shaping and Service Delivery: A report of case study work conducted for the Lyons Inquiry,* 2007.

4.243   Some of the targets which have proved most intractable to the Government relate to health and well-being – particularly in terms of tackling inequalities in health outcomes, for example childhood obesity and life expectancy. It is clear that there are great difficulties in improving the health of some groups, with poor health being strongly linked to deprivation and determined very strongly by cultures, behaviours and wider environments. This raises the importance of local services, such as schools, colleges, children's services and social services, libraries, leisure, transport and environmental health, since they can all influence health either directly or indirectly by influencing behaviour.

4.244   These links are not new – public health was one of local government's first responsibilities – but they are increasingly being recognised again. For example there is a shared 'healthier communities' aspect of the Corporate Assessment part of the performance framework, and the Joint Annual Review framework also examines 'being healthy' as an aspect inspected. The recent consultation by the Commission for Social Care Inspection on a new Adult Outcomes Framework includes improved health and emotional well-being and an emphasis on Healthy Communities.[64]

4.245   However, funding for health and well-being activities comes mainly through PCTs, plus some small specific grants to local authorities. Strong arguments have been put to me that such activities therefore get 'squeezed out' by acute healthcare needs, which are subject to more stringent management controls and targets, and findings from my case studies supported this.[65]

4.246   In my case studies, health and well-being were not seen by interviewees as a current core role for their local authorities. Roles within councils were varied, and case study interviewees often had responsibility for health and well-being in addition to a 'main' role. That said, some councils are embracing the health and well-being agenda through their local strategic partnerships, and through joint appointments with health services, including joint Directors of Public Health.

4.247   Some consistent messages emerged from the interviews. Accounts of partnership working with the NHS served largely to underline the difficulties of collaboration, with difficulties in aligning performance management frameworks and different budget cycles. As with community safety, respondents claimed that a collaborative approach to health and well-being was crowded out by the hierarchical emphasis on acute care in the NHS. In terms of funding, as in other areas, respondents experienced problems with short-term project funding and the current funding pressures in the NHS. In particular this reduces flexibility to channel funding into preventative approaches.

4.248   Given the importance of health for every other aspect of people's well-being, I would expect this emphasis on public health to grow over time – exploiting councils' advantages in using co-production to work with communities and individuals to improve outcomes – as they are given greater flexibility in place-shaping. The key issues in moving this agenda forward are set out below:

- health is a key issue for place-shaping and needs councillors to take the approach to convening that I recommend in Chapter 5, taking ownership of the overall health challenge, seeing the health impact of the services which the council controls and joining up with NHS services. The new duty for health trusts to cooperate will assist with this;

- cooperation on health would be assisted by better and explicit alignment of aims, performance frameworks, inspection and budget regimes between councils and health trusts;

---

[64] *A New Outcomes Framework for Performance Assessment of Adult Social Care: Consultation document*, CSCI, 2006.
[65] Entwistle, T,. et al., *Perspectives on Place-shaping and Service Delivery: A report of case study work conducted for the Lyons Inquiry*, 2007.

- local health commissioning at GP surgery level has the potential to fit well with councils' work to localise services to smaller community areas, but this would be greatly assisted by the duty to cooperate or similar mechanism being extended to GPs. This would of course need to take account of the particular status of GPs within the public sector, as many are effectively independent – albeit publicly funded – businesses; and

- local authorities, through scrutiny but also as partners, have the ability to challenge health services in a constructive way, as well as to consider how their services can better support health outcomes. Councils are well placed to engage with local communities to help encourage healthier behaviours and approaches for all age groups. At my seminar on public health, contributors also pointed out the role which councils could play in ensuring local service users can engage with and help to shape services which can tend to be producer-led and focused on national targets.[66]

Recommendation 4.26

The Government should support a stronger and more explicit role for local government as convenor in the realm of health and well-being, building on the proposals in the Local Government White Paper to strengthen partnership working.

Recommendation 4.27

The Government should ensure the commitment to harmonise budget and performance management cycles in health and social services is delivered.

Children's services

4.249   Children's services have seen dramatic reforms in recent years. The Children Act 2004 introduced a significant reorganisation of children's services, bringing services and partners together with the aim of promoting better outcomes for all children and improving the child protection system. By 2008 every council is expected to lead the creation of a Children's Trust, bringing together strategic oversight of all services for children and young people in an area. The reforms aim to introduce an approach to child well-being, welfare and safeguarding based on early intervention and prevention, rather than simply through improved child protection procedures.

4.250   Another significant area of reform in recent years relates to schools funding, and increased central direction of that funding through, first, passporting of increases in budgets directly to schools and then ring-fencing in the form of the Dedicated Schools Grant. These changes, and their implications for local government, are discussed in other chapters.

4.251   My Inquiry's case studies particularly focused on issues related to vulnerable children and child protection.[67] Although the issues raised by respondents in the area of children's social care showed some local variety, the key challenges appeared common across different authorities. A common statutory framework means that these services are delivered in a very similar fashion and case study respondents tended to support these arrangements. They welcomed clear central

---

[66] This work is summarised in Annex H.
[67] Entwhistle, T., et al., *Perspectives on Place-shaping and Service Delivery: A report of case study work conducted for the Lyons Inquiry*, 2007.

guidance and called for more dedicated funding for their area of work. The only problems they reported about the system of central–local relations were focused on the resource requirements of the existing inspection and performance management systems. They called for a more joined-up approach to target and indicator setting, which would facilitate inter-agency collaboration. I recognise that a holistic approach to child protection does not only depend on a consistent focus on the child identified as at risk; it also requires links to a wide range of other responsibilities, in particular certain aspects of community cohesion, housing availability, employment opportunities, educational standards and even road safety.

4.252   Councils should not be tempted to 'opt out' of educational issues because of the constraints imposed by the funding framework and the increasing independence of schools (through the introduction of academies, trust schools and so on). Bringing together education and other service providers across all sectors for different age groups is a key part of place-shaping, and is critical to strengthening community cohesion, community safety and enhancing employment and health outcomes.

4.253   Schools provide a service directly to the community, and therefore provide a vital link between local communities and the local authority, crucial to any place-shaping agenda which focuses on improving the well-being of families. No other service provider, except arguably GPs, plays such a role. Furthermore, schools play a vital role in helping to determine the life chances of local children, and potentially have a huge part to play in local preventative strategies which work with families and children. It is therefore critical that they should be able to work closely and flexibly with local partners, particularly on issues around prevention, which are demonstrably cost effective and can dramatically improve life chances for those children, as well as reduce the costs that fall to other services through crime and poor health later on.

4.254   These issues are widely recognised, but schools have been excluded from the duty to cooperate applied to local partners with respect to Local Area Agreements under the Local Government and Public Involvement in Health Bill, as they were from the Children Act 2004 duty to cooperate with strategic bodies locally to promote the well-being of children in the local area. This is on the grounds that:

- the duty to cooperate would be too onerous on both schools and local authorities and it would be impractical for every school to be actively engaged with the Local Strategic Partnership on a regular basis; and

- local authorities already have a direct relationship with schools (though this has been weakened in recent years). Schools are now also to be placed under a new duty under the Education and Inspection Act 2006 to promote the well-being of their pupils. The Government intends that by 2010 all schools should be extended schools, working more effectively with other services in their local area.

4.255   It is also clearly the case that schools are much more likely to play an active role in a local strategy if they have been consulted and agree with the priorities being pursued by the local authority, and I understand concerns that prescribing the relationship with the Local Area Agreements could create perverse effects in some areas.

4.256   Schools are, however, required to have regard to the Children and Young People's Plan, which informs and is informed by the Sustainable Community Strategy. Nevertheless I am concerned at schools being excluded from the arrangements for other partners when they play such a critical role in the place-shaping agenda, and am concerned that this link may be too weak to ensure a high degree of cooperation on place-shaping issues. The Government should consider more formal mechanisms to ensure greater collaboration on place-shaping issues.

> **Recommendation 4.28**
>
> The Government should consider more formal mechanisms, such as an extension of the duty to cooperate or a duty to have regard to the LAA or Sustainable Community Strategy, to encourage greater collaborative working between Local Strategic Partnerships and GPs and schools.

CONCLUSION

4.257　The Local Government White Paper and subsequent Bill signalled a welcome and strong move towards a more devolved system of local government, responding directly to a number of the recommendations I made in my May report. In this chapter, I have argued that in order to make the most of the opportunities offered by these changes, we may need to tackle a number of risks, many of which require profound and sustained behavioural change on the part of central (as well as local) government, and those who work within it. In my May report, I argued that to deliver and sustain change over time a programme of reform may need to be underpinned by a formal constitutional settlement to ensure it has cross-party support and provides a long-term and sustainable basis for change. This is discussed further in Chapter 10.

4.258　Central government determines the framework and much of the detail in the current system, and it is from central government that much of the change has to come. While the recent Local Government White Paper and Bill are a significant step forward, further change is essential if momentum is to be maintained towards greater local choice and flexibility. The key changes needed are in behaviour and approach, to ensure that the devolution the Government is committed to is not undermined by additional controls over time.

4.259　Clearly, local government is responsible for its own behaviours, ambitions and achievements, and only local government can improve itself and its efforts on behalf of its communities. Chapter 5 discusses changes which local government needs to make. But there is a shared responsibility to ensure the system of local government works well.

4.260　We need to ensure our system provides the conditions necessary for local government expertise and energy to be released to find the best way in each community to maximise value for money and well-being. This will mean different things for different services as discussed above. However, in general this requires:

- greater clarity over who is responsible for what – this is particularly important for social care, given future pressures – and the need to be very clear about who is responsible for managing or funding which aspects of those;

- delivering on promises of a performance management system which is streamlined, and more clearly focused on the needs of whole communities rather than individual services;

- a funding system which is much more transparent, with clear objectives agreed between central and local government;

- behavioural change on the part of government to ensure that promised reductions in targets and central controls are maintained over time, not replaced by indirect or 'soft' controls. This may require a shift in mind set in some areas – and possibly a requirement to report regularly on progress to Parliament – to ensure all parts of government act in the spirit, and not just the letter of the Local Government White Paper;

- greater flexibility over how local authorities can use existing resources, particularly by pushing forward on the Government's commitment to reduce the use of specific and ring-fenced grants;

- stronger acknowledgement and support for local government's convening role;

- greater acknowledgment that well-being depends on a broader definition of efficiency, i.e. greater emphasis on doing the right things for local communities rather than just doing them as cheaply as possible. This means encouraging innovation, making the most of local government's ability to engage with local communities and supporting co-production to get better outcomes; and crucially it means supporting local government to make the right decisions to manage pressures on local services as effectively as possible in the light of local circumstances; and

- recognising and encouraging the need for local government to make best use of its powers, and to develop the confidence and capability to deliver its place-shaping role for all communities.

4.261   In order to underpin and sustain change into the future, the relationship between central and local government must itself improve. Chapter 10 discusses the ways in which a more formal constitutional basis could be established to underpin that relationship. Key issues which need to be the subject of agreement between central and local government include the agreed roles and responsibilities of each tier of government and greater transparency about the objectives and performance of the funding system. These elements are essential to encourage a more mature and negotiated relationship between central and local government, and through that to build the public's trust in the system and our institutions of government over time.

Local government's contribution to reform

This chapter explores what local government's own contribution to reform should be, arguing that greater local flexibility presents as significant a challenge to councils as it does to central government.

Opportunities for reform present a complex challenge for the leadership of local authorities, requiring long term vision and the ability to build coalitions to achieve that vision. This challenge falls to both political and managerial leaders.

An important role for the modern local authority is that of convening across all local services. To fulfil that role effectively, it needs to adopt a leadership style that engages local partners, facilitating, advocating, arbitrating and influencing rather than dominating.

The national voice of local government is important in supporting both improvements across the sector, and the growth in confidence of all councils as place-shapers. The Local Government Association (LGA) should continue to develop its role with partners, to provide leadership to local government and to challenge underperforming councils.

Political parties and political groups are also key players in the process of improving leadership, particularly in improving councillor recruitment and in making the role of councillor, especially frontline councillor, more rewarding. Political parties can play their part by refreshing their approach to recruiting councillors, while political groups should enhance performance management of their members and consider circumstances when use of the party whip may not be appropriate.

Improving public engagement is also very important and should be supported by better information for the public, developing scrutiny and through more creative approaches.

Finally, councils need to consider how they could use existing powers more innovatively, making best use of Local Area Agreements (LAAs) and the development of their commissioning role to build their capacity to innovate. This can build on local government's success to date in securing efficiency, developing approaches which focus on outcomes in terms of their value to the local community.

INTRODUCTION

5.1   Chapter 3 argued that the centralisation of governmental and public service functions has confused the accountability for local service delivery. This has generated a relationship that 'crowds out' local government's role in responding to local needs and priorities, and limits local government's contribution to the kind of society we want. I believe also that this downgrading of the local has contributed to a sense of powerlessness among some local politicians and officers, which needs to be reversed if local government is to deliver its full potential in helping to meet the challenges we face in the 21st century.

5.2   Chapter 4 set out the changes that I believe central government needs to make and I will go on to describe how local government funding should be reshaped to ensure that local government can play its full role. However, responsibility for changing the dynamic of local-central relationships and re-energising the relationship between the citizen and their locality also rests with local government itself. This chapter therefore looks at the changes needed in the behaviours and attitudes of local government – both for individual local authorities and for local government collectively. I do not want to downplay the progress that many local authorities have made already but, while there is no comprehensive blueprint for success, I am convinced that major changes of approach are needed if councils are to embrace the place-shaping role in all our communities and rise to the challenge that ambition presents. My recommendations concentrate on those changes which are most urgent.

PLACE-SHAPING – THE CHALLENGE FOR LOCAL GOVERNMENT

5.3   In Chapter 2, I identified place-shaping as capturing the central role and purpose of local government, defining it as the creative use of powers and influence to promote the general well-being of a community and its citizens. I went on to argue that shifting the relationship between central and local government by reducing central control and prescription will enable local government to respond better to local need and to manage pressures and expectations of public services more effectively. There is also, however, a clear need for local government to step up to the place-shaping challenge, and develop its style, skills and behaviours in order to make the role a reality.

5.4   The term place-shaping covers a wide range of local activity – indeed anything which affects the well-being of the local community. It will mean different things in different places and at different levels of local government, informed by local character and history, community needs and demands, and local politics and leadership. The powers and freedoms which local government can exercise are an important part of enabling councils to play this role. However, I am clear that effective place-shaping is as much about the confidence and behaviours of local government as it is about statutory powers or responsibilities.

5.5   In my May 2006 report, *National prosperity, local choice and civic engagement,* I cited diverse examples of place-shaping behaviours in local government, including Gateshead, Middlewich, Lewisham, Woking and Wakefield. These authorities and many others have made space for this even with current constraints on local flexibility. However, experience is patchy and I have identified a 'dependency culture' in many areas of local government – and all could do more. In the remainder of this chapter I will concentrate on the behaviours that I consider need to be developed by local government to ensure that all authorities can become effective place-shapers.

Focusing on the future

5.6   Place-shaping requires local government to be more consistent in raising its sights beyond the immediate delivery of services, the short term political cycle and the timetables of funding and performance management – and to do this with greater ambition. It needs to focus on developing a vision for an area and its communities, a vision owned by those communities and by local businesses.

5.7   Such vision for the future requires:

- having a sense of where a place should be in five, ten, 20 and even 30 years' time;

- awareness, of long-term trends locally as well as in the world beyond their geographic boundaries – for example the changing economy and workforce, demographics and diversity, and environmental challenges;

- a sense of how the local area can be prepared and well placed to respond to these challenges;

- an ability to be responsive, as influences and trends will change in unforeseen ways, and local government and its partners will need to be prepared to adapt and change direction as required; and

- strategies for achieving all of this.

5.8   The pressures to focus solely on the shorter term are very strong, even for those councils with four-yearly all-out elections. For councils with more frequent elections, these pressures are even greater. Long-term planning can be challenging to achieve in the face of short-term demands but some local authorities have realised that it is only by shaping a strong vision for the long-term future that they can create a truly cohesive community. The residents of a single local authority can have very diverse needs and interests varying between people living in urban and more rural settings, between people distinguished by ethnicity or by other social or demographic factors. In the short term, such difference can generate seemingly insuperable conflicts. A longer term view, which emphasises common interests, future economic prosperity, environmental sustainability and a harmonious, secure community is more likely to overcome divisions and secure support for some of the more difficult, immediate decisions a council has to take.

5.9   The best authorities are already taking this longer term strategic approach to securing sustainable strategies that address the issues facing their communities. They are scenario-planning for the future, drawing on information about national and international trends as well as engaging with local partners and residents concerning their priorities and aspirations. They are using their community strategies as tools for engagement and working with local partners to articulate local ambitions and identify joint approaches to meeting future challenges.

Black Country Consortium

The four local authorities of Dudley, Sandwell, Walsall and Wolverhampton are working together to counter the process of decline across their region and deliver lasting change. They were instrumental in setting up the Black Country Consortium to help engage the private sector and other public bodies in decisions which affect the whole community, and are jointly developing a Core Strategy which will provide a common set of strategic policies to be applied consistently across the whole of the Black Country.

The strategy will require significant investment by each local authority in the economy, town centres, housing, education, the environment and transport. The Black Country Study commissioned by the Consortium, sets out an ambitious long-term vision which has been agreed with over 150 civic and business leaders, community representatives, educationalists and young people. Their vision statement says:

> By 2033, we aim to make the Black Country a confident 'we can do it' place, where our skills, work ethic and diversity are key to our prosperity. The Black Country will be made up of a polycentric network of four centres – Wolverhampton, Walsall, West Bromwich and Brierley Hill/Merry Hill – each offering a distinct, wide range of shopping, leisure and cultural facilities, office employment and housing. A transport revolution will have taken place with our bus, Metro, rail and road networks making it easy to move around ... Our manufacturing companies will be prospering, at the cutting edge of technological innovation but our high quality environment – not our industrial legacy – will dominate the urban landscape... Our canal system, linking our communities together, means we are known as Britain's Venice... All Black Country citizens will have a deep sense of belonging and will be enabled to contribute actively to the social, economic and physical well-being of the area ...

5.10   However, despite many strong examples of long-term planning, I have detected a sense that some local authorities have developed a tendency to wait and see where central government will go next, rather than setting out their own long-term strategic plans. In some cases this reflects political instability or other obstacles to making difficult decisions, but also insufficient confidence about the long-term budgetary position of the authority. Sometimes this is linked to too narrow a focus on service delivery rather than a wider strategic view of service provision within the locality.

5.11   I recognise that proposals have been made in the White Paper, *Strong and Prosperous Communities* for leaders with a four-year mandate to assist this shift to longer term thinking. I welcome this, but it will not be enough by itself to generate the change needed. I discuss the need for flexible models of leadership in Chapter 4, and local authorities need to find ways to manage their own governance which work locally. Clearly councils need to avoid a protracted, inward-looking debate about any change. Some may be concerned that less frequent elections will reduce the viability of local party political machinery by reducing the need for regular canvassing and campaigning. I would argue, however, that parties should anticipate this challenge and consider how they can motivate their supporters to engage with the electorate outside election time, participating in activities such as the identification and training of the councillors of the future to aid succession planning.

5.12   As I set out in Chapter 4, stable three-year funding and fewer specific grants will support the development of a long-term approach. This is largely a matter for central government, but local government also needs to recognise that too often it has been complicit in supporting initiative-based funding as a means of securing additional resources for their area – only then to complain about the lack of flexibility in its use, the burdens of accounting for it separately and its time limited nature. I hope that a reduced dependency by government on funding through these streams will enable local authorities to be more strategic. The incentives I identify in Chapter 9, which will enable councils to benefit from economic growth in their area, should also support the long-term approach.

5.13   I am also concerned that the performance and inspection framework should support a long-term approach, as I have already highlighted in Chapter 4. I believe that the new post-CPA performance framework signalled in the White Paper should consider the extent to which indicators measure longer term outcomes rather than simply short term impact. Councils, too, should focus their planning and performance management around these long-term outcomes and the ultimate public value of their activities, rather than solely concentrating on narrow output measures.

> **Recommendation 5.1**
>
> In their forward planning, local authorities should look further ahead than even the ten-year time frame of the community strategy and therefore should:
>
> * make best use of intelligence and evidence of future demographic and other changes;
> * take account of national and international trends and forecasts;
> * engage local partners, businesses and residents in a debate about the long-term aspirations for the area; and
> * focus their performance management on long-term outcomes.

Leading communities and places

5.14   Leadership in local government is complex and I am convinced that there is no standard recipe for success. Councils as different as Kent, Camden, Tameside and High Peak have demonstrated they can provide strong local leadership, but do so in ways that are specific to their local circumstances. Leadership is also rarely just about a single leader; it is undertaken at several levels and by a variety of players – including individually by frontline councillors, council leaders and mayors, and collectively by the cabinet and the council as a body across the whole area and on behalf of the entire community. Good leadership extends far beyond the walls of the town hall. It involves harnessing the expertise and energy of diverse groups of local people, public and third sector partners and local businesses and engaging them as leaders in their own fields.

5.15   There are numerous theories of leadership, many derived from the business world. The IDeA Leadership Academy and the Leadership Centre for Local Government have done much to identify which aspects of leadership are most relevant to the local government context[1]. The Commission which established the Leadership Centre defined leadership as "creating and making happen what would not otherwise happen. Above all, it is getting significant new things done or improvements made." This captures well the energy and dynamism that is required in providing leadership in the complex environment of local government. There is clearly a shift in the understanding of councillors' leadership in the local government family from one of exercising that leadership principally through the formalities of decision-making in the council chamber to an approach based on coalition building and developing popular support outside the town hall among residents, partners and opinion formers.

5.16   Leadership of place is an inherently political role, involving the setting of clear priorities and making difficult choices, resolving conflict and balancing differing demands and views. The process of arbitrating between competing local interests tests community cohesion, so requires leaders to bring together an inclusive vision of ambitions for the future, persuading others to support a shared direction, and shifting public opinion as well as responding to it. It also involves effective engagement before decisions are taken, and communication to ensure that decisions have been well understood by those they affect. Local leaders have a key role in developing trust in local government and in local institutions generally.

5.17   Leadership also operates at an organisational level, through the actions of both elected members and senior managers, at a very local community level through the representative role and the actions of frontline councillors, and at a strategic level through partnerships and the convening role of local government.

---

[1] Funded by the department for Communities and Local Government and formed following recommendations by the Leadership Development Commission (comprised of ODPM, the LGA, the Audit Commission, the IdeA, the Society of Local Authority Chief Executives (SOLACE), the Employers Organisation (EO), the Society of Personnel Officers (SOCPO), the Cabinet Office (OPSR) and HM Treasury) set up in 2002 to improve leadership within local government.

Improving waste management in Mid Bedfordshire

In 2002, Mid Bedfordshire District Council identified recycling as both a major performance issue and a concern for local people (through a MORI survey). As well as putting capital investment into rolling out kerbside recycling and retendering all waste management with a 12 year contract, the leadership of the council realised that a more radical approach was required to deliver the required step-change in performance.

Research showed that the most effective way of increasing participation, driving up recycling percentages while minimising cost, would be to move to alternate weekly collection (AWC) of waste and recyclables, combined with the innovative use of split back vehicles for the collection of dry recyclables and garden waste to minimise the numbers of collection vehicles and crews required. This had some risks, since at that time only a small number of authorities had adopted AWC, many on a partial basis and with a couple having backtracked and returned to weekly collections following public dissatisfaction.

The Leader of the Council identified that, while the environmental and financial benefits of the AWC system were attractive, seeking to change the behaviour and expectations of 53,000 householders was a significant challenge.

The Leader set out her vision and all her tenacity and resilience was required to respond to intense political and public scrutiny of the proposals with waste management, rats and maggots becoming topics of conversation in parish councils and public houses. A vociferous minority of residents who opposed AWC sought to challenge the council at every opportunity and gained significant and disproportionate media coverage.

The Leader took a personal interest and personal responsibility for the communication of this change to residents. She maintained a single voice across the majority group despite different views and steered the proposals through the council's decision-making process. She took phone calls and answered letters from residents personally, sending a letter to all households, and delivered a post-implementation survey. She also made appearances in local media to put the case for AWC, emphasising the wider benefits to the community in terms of sustainability.

Post-implementation, surveys show that this leadership has shifted public attitudes, showing 84 per cent satisfaction with recycling. Performance has also improved markedly, with recycling increased to 20.2 per cent, composting to 9.35 per cent giving a total of 29.5 per cent against a statutory target of 18 per cent and a previous total of only 12 per cent. It is also estimated that this approach has saved the authority an initial £750,000 per annum and up to £12 million over the life of the new contract.

Providing political leadership

5.18   As with the rest of Britain's constitutional framework, local government structures have been created and adapted over the years in response to contemporary issues and circumstances. Leadership in local government has moved from appointed magistrates through various models of appointed and elected bodies. Complexity is nothing new, and through much of local government's history, leadership has had to be forged within a tangled patchwork of overlapping tiers of government. Successive local government Acts have sought to secure a local government system that combines effective service delivery with local leadership and accountability, but much of the complexity remains and local government continues to operate at different tiers and to co-exist with numerous appointed bodies. In particular, recent developments such as the development of New Deal for Communities, city academies and Foundation NHS Trusts have seemed to create new forms of local governance which can impact on the role of elected councillors and make accountability less clear.

5.19   I am convinced that structure is less important than the spirit in which it is implemented and the attitudes of those in leading roles, but I do welcome the recent focus on developing leadership in local government whether through structural change within councils or otherwise. My concern about the reforms of the Local Government Act 2000 is that it prompted councillors to focus too much on internal issues and neglect their outward facing, community engagement and leadership role.

5.20   Visibility of leadership is very important and a key component of accountability. Where people know who is in charge, they know whom to call to account. This is important in terms of public recognition, but also in building the personal networks and relationships with key local partners. If leading councillors, whatever the leadership model being used, adopt an outward looking approach, communicate and engage local people with energy and enthusiasm and also develop credibility with their partners, they can be excellent place-shapers, even where leadership is not focused on a single individual. A summary of these place-shaping behaviours, which apply as much to small localities as major cities, is set out below.

Political leadership behaviours that support effective place-shaping include:

- anticipating future challenges and opportunities for the local area;
- building coalitions and looking outside community boundaries for knowledge and collaboration;
- advocating powerfully on behalf of the local community with the credibility to negotiate across all sectors;
- arbitrating between competing local interests and supporting community cohesion, taking tough choices where necessary;
- listening to the views of local residents and stakeholders, being accessible and visible;
- communicating effectively with local residents and other stakeholders and building trust in local institutions;
- being open with information and ensuring transparency in decision making;
- demonstrating a high level of understanding of local issues and having a strong evidence base which shapes policy priorities;
- focusing on service performance for its impact on the community rather than to meet government requirements, looking outward rather than upward; and
- championing efficiency and service innovation – getting the best value from public expenditure and maximum impact from private investment in their area.

Recommendation 5.2

In reviewing their structures and leadership arrangements local authorities should focus on securing visible and accountable leadership with the capacity to take a long-term, outward-looking approach and build credible relationships with local partners.

Managerial leadership   5.21   In my May report, I emphasised political leadership as key to place-shaping. I should also stress the importance of managerial leadership. Research has identified that councils with CPA 'excellent' ratings had strong leadership, both political and managerial. The Tavistock Institute and Warwick Business School identified one of the preconditions for local government improvement as "political ambition supported by professional excellence.[2]" High calibre managerial leadership also requires a high quality team of directors, not just a chief executive.

5.22   The consequences of the recent emphasis on strong managerial leadership has not always been fully thought through, however, with a risk that roles may overlap and that expectations may be confused. This may be especially the case where there are changes of political leadership. On the one hand, the convening role and role as head of service for thousands of staff requires a courageous leader who, with the other members of the corporate management team, has a profile and commands respect. Indeed, a glance at advertisements for chief executives in the local government media confirms this expectation. On the other hand, a chief executive should not be seen as a rival to, or usurper of, elected members as community leader, acquiring a public and media profile which consistently outstrips that of their leader or mayor.

5.23   This can be a very difficult balance to achieve:

> *Only those who have had the privilege of managing in a political environment can know how exciting, exhilarating, exhausting and, at times, quite frightening it can be. Politics (with a small 'p') is an intrinsic part of management but 'politics' (with a big 'P') adds a whole different dimension to the job of managing.* (Cheryl Miller, former President of the Society of Local Authority Chief Executives (SOLACE)).[3]

5.24   Good chief executives should, however, be able to express their wider duty to the area's stakeholders by being able when necessary to challenge members to maintain an outward focus and strong ambition for improvement – for example, in a complex hung council. In an unstable environment, chief executives must also have the confidence and status to maintain separate dialogues with a range of partners, including with representatives of government departments as well as Government Offices.

5.25   One of the key roles of managerial leadership is to develop the organisation in terms of competencies, behaviours and understanding including the ability to build coalitions outside the organisation. I am convinced by Jim Collins's argument that the flywheel of public sector achievement is the development of "brand reputation – built upon tangible results and emotional share of heart – so that potential supporters believe not only in your mission, but in your capacity to deliver on that mission."[4] Again, I feel strongly that facilitating this role of local government is not a matter of legislation or formal frameworks, it is primarily a question of behaviours. The next box sets out the managerial behaviours which I think best support councils' place-shaping role.

---

[2] The Tavistock Institute and Warwick Business School for the LGA *Beyond Competence: Driving Local Government Improvement* 2005.

[3] Foreword to the report of the SOLACE Commission on Managing in a Political Environment 2005.

[4] Good to Great and the Social Sectors: A Monograph to Accompany Good to Great, Collins, J. 2006.

Managerial leadership behaviours that support effective place-shaping include:

- negotiating roles, remits and boundaries with the political leadership;

- understanding and demonstrating genuine enthusiasm for the full scope of place-shaping and its tensions;

- supporting elected decision-makers with the ability to recognise the need to invest in purposeful engagement and challenge which helps to underpin the elected role rather than displacing or subverting it;

- supporting councillors in their frontline role and developing structures and processes for effective public engagement;

- negotiating room to manage the resources of the organisation, especially to commission external resources where necessary and to deal with staffing issues, including having a strong voice in all top level appointments;

- achieving visibility to staff and to partners as part of the nexus of community leadership, personally capable of reinforcing the links with other public bodies and the private sector;

- articulating an emphasis on knowledge and evidence, efficiency and professional expertise in preparing the council for its 'primus inter pares' role; and

- questioning the performance and ambition of the organisation, acting as a champion for value for money and ensuring that the council is able to challenge itself.

Convening 5.26 Effective local leadership is not simply a question of getting the political management arrangements right. It is also about the ability of the council, collectively, to exercise leadership of the whole community, creating a shared agenda that recognises the roles that different partners can play in bringing it to life. As with wider political leadership, convening requires local government to be able to identify a direction of travel, articulate a sense of the future and enthuse others to be part of a common mission.

5.27 This role, too, has been a major focus of change and improvement in recent years, although, as noted in Chapter 4, progress has been variable. Many local authorities have grasped the opportunities offered by Local Strategic Partnerships (LSPs), local public service agreements and, more recently, Local Area Agreements, to take significant steps in developing the convening role and the skills and behaviours which make this effective.

5.28 However, despite the very significant progress that has been made by many local authorities in their convening role, I believe that local government still has further to go and I set out here a series of criteria for successful partnerships.

Strong partnerships have:

- a good strategic capacity;
- a clear understanding of their role and purpose;
- shared goals;
- effective sharing of information and data;
- inclusive and relevant membership;
- a focus on external impact rather than internal processes; and
- partners with mutual trust, willing to put aside their own interests to focus on the wider interests of the partnership.

5.29   I believe that, as yet, too few existing partnerships meet these tests. In addition, elected members need to be better equipped to participate in and lead partnerships.[5] Local government needs to work with local partners to ensure that partnership structures are fit for purpose. Many are legacies of past initiatives and in some areas there is a proliferation of partnerships with overlaps and duplications. This often makes poor use of partners' time and undermines coherence in partnership working. In many areas a rationalisation of existing partnerships with greater clarity about links to key strategic bodies such as the LSP would ensure more effective working.

Recommendation 5.3

Local authorities need to take the lead in ensuring local partnership structures are fit for purpose, streamlining and reducing the number of bodies and groups where necessary, ensuring that the structures are genuinely local in character and meet the criteria outlined above.

5.30   The most effective local leadership makes a virtue of the fact that councils have several roles to play at once: balancing the role of community strategist and visionary with that of champion of the local community and scrutineer of partner agencies, while having a particular interest as one of the area's key service providers. Embracing and enhancing the convening role also involves a recognition on the part of local government of the importance of influencing outcomes in services which are being directly delivered by others. This form of leadership requires a consensual approach, new skills and strong, shared knowledge and understanding of local needs and priorities. It is principally a matter of building broad coalitions and consensus about the direction of travel for an area, reaching out to citizens, partners, businesses and stakeholders from within and beyond the geographical boundary and being open to the contribution of others, valuing their expertise. Too often key partners find local government tending to confuse leadership with dominance, where partners feel that their views are not sufficiently valued.

5.31   Good leadership for prosperity, as part of economic place-shaping is particularly challenging and complex, since it requires work with partners and independent organisations including private businesses at a regional, national or even international level. The council has to have the leadership and influencing skills to assert the interests of its residents, while having the credibility to be taken seriously as a negotiating partner.

---

[5] Joseph Rowntree Foundation, *New roles for old: local authority members and partnership working*, 2002.

Cumbria County Council leading the recovery programme following the Foot and Mouth outbreak.

In March 2001, England was hit by an outbreak of foot-and-mouth disease (FMD). The worst affected county in the UK was Cumbria. Cumbria County Council led the area's recovery strategy. They set up and chaired an FMD taskforce from early on in the crisis, bringing together key stakeholders from the public, private and voluntary sectors to provide a collective voice for the county.

The Council established a Rural Action Zone (RAZ). To help members of the public follow the progress of the initiative, Cumbria RAZ produced a monthly newsletter, the first of which saw 2,000 distributed to individuals and organisations. The 'First Steps' strategy involved implementing short-term measures – allocating £500,000 to provide immediate support to community led projects tackling social, environmental and economic recovery. The 'Next Steps' strategy went on to set out a programme for maximising the use of existing rural regeneration programmes, as well as harnessing increased external resources. The council secured a £42 million rural recovery programme in Cumbria from the North West Development Agency for the period 2003–2008 and established a new independent company – Rural Regeneration Cumbria – to manage the programme from April 2003.

The Council led a Cumbria FMD Inquiry, published in September 2002. This included far-reaching proposals. Secretary of State for the Environment, Food and Rural Affairs, Margaret Beckett commented "the thinking behind these imaginative ideas has been welcomed by the Government ... we'll be seeking to assist their successful implementation."

Cumbria County Council Leader Rex Toft commented:

> *Securing so much money to boost the rural economy in Cumbria is significant as it's the largest grant of its kind ever to be given. This funding will be spread over a five year period and will have a tremendous impact on the worst affected areas. It will help to broaden the economic base of rural Cumbria as well as benefiting the agriculture and agricultural support industries and contribute towards strengthening Cumbria's tourism industry.*

Cumbria County Council continue to lead on the rural regeneration of Cumbria in partnership with Rural Regeneration Cumbria and, since 1 September 2006, Cumbria Vision. Over the past four years 1,000 new jobs have been created and many hundreds of others safeguarded.

Recommendation 5.4

Local authorities need to adopt a leadership style that engages local partners, builds alliances and secures support for delivering joint priorities. It should facilitate, advocate, arbitrate and influence rather than dominate.

Making two-tier local government work

5.32   While the 'pathfinder' programme instigated following the Local Government White Paper appears to have attracted a number of proposals to move towards unitary status, it is important to recognise here the value of good two-tier local government.[6] At the same time as the virtues claimed for unitary government are expounded, many urban areas are trying to find ways of getting the right balance between local and city-wide governance. Voluntary two-tier arrangements are being formed and councils are exploring area and neighbourhood dimensions to governance. Furthermore, the examples of local government elsewhere in Europe and beyond – which are often offered as good examples, are frequently multi-tiered. Two-tier local government has a future and

---

[6] Invitations to councils in England to make proposals for future unitary structure and to pioneer, as pathfinders, new two-tier models, CLG 2006.

a key aspect of the convening role is the challenge for those tiers to work productively together, as 'pathfinders' or otherwise.

5.33   It is self-evident that, alongside the development of a new relationship between central and local government, there should be an improved partnership between tiers. In the best county-wide partnerships, time and effort are invested in building strong relationships and an understanding of different perspectives as well as the investment in joint governance arrangements for LSPs. These are most effective when they have an outward focus, making the most of the frontline engagement of the districts and viewing all as equal partners rather than a hierarchy. I have seen good examples of place-shaping at district and county level and am convinced that this is not the sole prerogative of any one type of council.

The Cambrian Visitor Centre – place-shaping in Shropshire

During the 1960s, the Cambrian Railway in Shropshire fell into disuse. The former railway station, the headquarters of the Cambrian Railway Company in the town of Oswestry, gradually decayed over three decades. This dilapidated building provided a harsh first impression of Oswestry for anyone visiting the district.

The Community strategy for Oswestry, led by the Council, identified the Old Station building as key to regeneration. In 2002, Oswestry Borough Council began consultation with its partners, Advantage West Midlands, Oswestry Borderlands Tourism, Cambrian Railway Society, Cambrian Railway Trust and Oswestry Town Council on how they could regenerate the former headquarters.

The consultation had several aims: to investigate how the area could achieve economic regeneration and to look at the strengths and identity of the past and build them into the new regeneration programme. The Council also wanted to identify gaps in business accommodation for the town, to maximise the availability of high quality produce and local craftsmanship, to ensure appropriate visitor infrastructure and to support the voluntary sector to develop a sustainable social enterprise.

Oswestry Borough Council secured funding from Advantage West Midlands Rural Regeneration Zone, Objective II European Regional Development Fund, the Market Town Initiative, Shropshire Tourism Action Plan, Heritage Lottery Fund and the Townscape Heritage Initiative, amounting to £2.1 million to renovate the building. The funding secured the building, now managed through a charitable trust, and allowed the Council to create the Cambrian Visitor Centre, an informative and interactive craft and visitor area, together with a modern Tourist Information Centre, and 'Porters Fine Food,' a restaurant utilising local produce. The upper floors have been converted into high quality office accommodation and are now home to a number of high profile technology and media companies.

The project has truly met its aims and objectives; a major building in the town has been restored to economic use creating a sense of place for the area. Above all, it has restored a sense of pride to the people of Oswestry who are proud to see this once dilapidated, significant landmark restored to its former glory. The building was recently awarded joint first place in the National Heritage Railway Awards sponsored by Network Rail.

5.34   From the perspective of the public, it is important that they receive a seamless service and do not have to work through the complexities of individual responsibilities in order to access public services. In practice, this can involve establishing a single access channel as well as remodelling service delivery around the user, making 'joins' invisible.

To achieve effective two-tier working, councils should ensure:

- a shared agenda across councils in both tiers but with room for preservation of local identities and differing priorities;

- a common understanding of respective roles and responsibilities, without 'turf wars';

- strong leadership of place, at different levels, with different partners taking the lead at different times;

- a sense of accountability which accepts shared responsibility, without any blame culture, with the ability to make difficult decisions and tough choices, for example about resource allocation;

- governance and service provision designed to support effective external partnerships, with issues being discussed at the right tier;

- easily accessible service provision which is fully transparent to users and utilises shared, locality-based access channels; and

- efficient operations in both front and back office, avoiding duplication and accepting that savings may accrue in a different tier to where the action (and even initial investment) is undertaken.

Leading neighbourhoods and parishes

5.35 Many parish and town councils thrive, contributing to place-shaping and some non-parished areas have developed successful neighbourhood arrangements. I argue elsewhere in this report that devolution to local government can improve efficiency. A progression of this argument suggests that, for some services, even more local management arrangements and devolution of decision making may help to deliver more efficient use of resources, in terms of meeting need in a more targeted way and harnessing co-production to engage users in delivering services in a way which works best for them. This is particularly the case in services related to 'liveability'.

5.36   Past experience of local councils in developing neighbourhood or local area governance arrangements is, however, mixed and brings risks with it. While strongly identifying the benefits of localisation, a recent report by the Young Foundation notes:

> *Community control over finances, services and assets brings with it the threats of fragmentation, mismanagement of public goods, the politicisation of neighbourhood issues, and the potential for localised power to create or exaggerate community divisions.*[7]

5.37   In the light of these risks but also the benefits of neighbourhood governance, I believe that if councils have more flexibility to act and greater space to reflect local choices in their place-shaping activities, they are more likely to respond productively to bottom up-pressure. This should help to improve the incentives for developing new neighbourhood arrangements, working with them and devolving decision making where appropriate. Conversations with communities about their needs are more likely to lead to action where the council has the discretion to act, space to reflect on the best solution for local people and a clear focus on the local community, rather than central government, as the primary customer.

5.38   Effective neighbourhood working is also partly a matter of style and behaviour. Using models of neighbourhood governance which include participatory democracy involves taking further steps towards accepting a strategic leadership role where at least as much is achieved through influence as through direction. Effective place-shaping councils are more likely to recognise the value to be gained through devolving decision making to neighbourhoods or areas better placed to deliver the community's strategic goals, having the confidence, in some circumstances, to 'let go'.

---

[7] The Young Foundation, *Managing the Risks of Neighbourhood Governance*, 2006.

5.39 There is no fixed prescription for effective accountability at neighbourhood level. There are numerous different models and, despite the work of the Young Foundation and others, still not enough evidence on what works.

Wakefield: developing new neighbourhood engagement and governance models

As part of the Wakefield Local Area Agreement – 'Families and Neighbourhoods', the Council is rolling out three Neighbourhood Management pilots with its partners.

The pilots form an integral part of the LAA, not just in terms of the development of neighbourhood level service delivery and governance models, but also in terms of the wider LAA outcomes framework and in achieving its associated outcomes and targets. The pilots are also one of the projects being used to put into practice the broader place-shaping community strategy for the district – 'Knowledge Communities'. The Knowledge Communities approach supports local people sharing information and developing shared solutions to local problems, both to increase local quality of life and to allow communities to shape their own destinies.

Each neighbourhood has its own model for governance and engagement. This ensures that the Council and partners take advantage of the opportunity to identify good practice on the ground and test out new approaches.

The three models being deployed in Wakefield are:

'**Community Leadership**' – this entails strengthening the roles and responsibilities of currently elected representatives, in particular Local Ward Councillors. Local members are working with communities and their representatives through neighbourhood forums, to identify local needs and desires, and influence services and partners to achieve desired outcomes;

'**Collective Governance**' – this approach establishes new representative neighbourhood bodies and partnerships to influence and deliver services, including through the formation of new delivery organisations. The approach builds on existing community capacity and groups, especially in the voluntary and community sectors, and seeks to broaden the base of neighbourhood community activists; and

'**Realtime Democracy**' – this approach seeks to involve local people in day-to-day decisions about their neighbourhood and services using different methods that go beyond the traditional meetings-based approach. The approach is being supported by the innovative and wide scale use of new technology, e.g. telephones, text voting, digital video production ('citizen journalism'), as well as more traditional engagement and communication mechanisms, e.g. bulletin boards, neighbourhood newsletters, citizen forums and staggered voting.

The Wakefield approach is not exclusive, but is identifying what works, be it modern or traditional, and assessing which approaches can be effectively employed on a larger scale.

Recommendation 5.5

Local authorities need to identify where they can make space for neighbourhood or parish activity, particularly to address liveability issues, and to encourage participation and innovation.

Building leadership capacity

5.40 The extent of the local leadership challenge I have set out above demands a complex mix of skills and competencies from both elected members and senior officers. The Improvement and Development Agency (IDeA) and the Leadership Centre for Local Government have undertaken excellent work with local government to develop the skills of local government so they can more effectively deliver their local leadership and convening role. However, as I argued in my May report, I believe that there remains a need for councils, and for organisations that represent and support local government, to develop the personal leadership skills within authorities, along with raising the accountability and visibility of leaders, mayors and frontline councillors.

5.41   The current provision for improvement and development support in local government is overly complex and not sufficiently demand-led and thus there is a risk of confusion amongst councils about who does what and where to seek the most appropriate support. The combined resources allocated to supporting and driving improvements in local government is significant – more than £1.6 billion over three years from 2005 to 2008.[8] Although much of this work is undoubtedly having an impact, local government collectively needs to review regularly whether it is achieving maximum value from this important resource. It is also important to look beyond the local government community, to what local government can learn from the business and third sectors, through initiatives like Common Purpose.[9]

5.42   I am convinced that local government collectively, through the Local Government Association (LGA) and its partners, needs to take responsibility for its own improvement and ensure that maximum value is being secured from the resources, including those in IDeA, and CLG available to support it. While the work by these organisations is vital in developing local government leadership, I believe that a fundamental shift in the balance between central and local government will be most important in delivering change. If local government works effectively to recover public trust and a stronger sense of powerfulness, and central government becomes clearer in its recognition of the contribution councils should be making to well-being, I am convinced that a wider range of people will be willing to contribute to local leadership.

Local government's national voice

5.43   The leadership challenge in local government is primarily about councils gaining the confidence and sense of power to speak for their local communities, but there is also a need for the local government community to be represented and led nationally. The development of the LGA in 1997 significantly strengthened local government's national voice and there has been important progress in recent years through approaches such as the central – local partnership, to generate a more equal relationship between local and central government. Nonetheless, local government still finds it difficult – particularly in the public's perception – to be regarded as having sufficient stature in many debates with central government.

5.44   While the debate with central government is important, I believe that the LGA is making positive progress in seeking to move away from the continual negotiation and wrangling with the machinery of central government. Instead, it is beginning to embrace more strongly its key role of communicating with the public about local government, its value, its challenges and its successes. To lead this public debate, it needs to ensure it makes best use of good quality and timely research. As part of the process of building confidence in local government, it must also lead the sector in developing its own benchmarks for good practice. Rather than looking for a national badge of recognition, local government should be able to identify its own 'reference sites', with the LGA perhaps developing the capacity to make testing judgements about local authority performance. I welcome the LGA's review of its role and relationships through the Best Commission.[10] The LGA is likely to have a critical role in reshaping local government and developing the relationship between local government and central government, particularly in terms of its work with partners to provide leadership and challenge underperforming councils, alongside contributing to debate on major policy issues of the day.

---

[8] CLG (unpublished) *Vfm Review of Programmes Aimed at Incentivising Improvements in Service Delivery and at Capacity Building,* 2006.

[9] Common Purpose run educational programmes and activities for leaders of all ages, sectors and backgrounds http://www.commonpurpose.org.uk

[10] Established by the LGA in September 2006, but working independently.

5.45   Regional partnerships between councils are also becoming more dynamic and successful in increasing voice and co-ordination. A good example is the Association of Greater Manchester Authorities where councils of different political complexion work together successfully in joint bidding and in procurement.

> **Recommendation 5.6**
>
> The LGA should continue the development of its work with partners to provide leadership to local government and to challenge underperforming councils as well as continuing to strengthen its performance in contributing to debate on major policy issues and improving its communication with the public.

The democratic framework

5.46   The Local Government White Paper proposals will make it easier for local authorities to opt for four-yearly all-out elections and I welcome this. I am mindful of the Electoral Commission's research findings that indicate high levels of public confusion about partial elections. All-out elections would allow more concerted campaigning on voter registration and voting, help to promote the profile of local elections and make the local election process more transparent. While I understand that more frequent elections are valued in some authorities for historical and other reasons, the gains to be made in terms of more visible and strategic leadership under a four year mandate are great enough to make this change attractive for many local authorities.

5.47   I am also pleased to see that the White Paper proposes to enable local authorities to ask the Electoral Commission to review the warding of their area, to move to single member wards. There is a need to balance carefully the benefits of single member wards in terms of greater transparency of local leadership with the potential for less representation. Given this trade-off, I would strongly support the Electoral Commission being very explicit that, when embarking on a review of this kind, it requires councils to make evidence-based proposals on the basis of a full and meaningful debate with the public on how they should be represented.

The role of political parties

5.48   I believe there is also an important role for political parties in contributing to reform. As I identified in Chapter 2, patterns of political engagement have changed and continue to do so. Traditional party membership has declined while willingness to be involved in single issue campaigning has increased. Perhaps one of the most striking messages I received from many councillors, including at the councillor engagement events I held across the country, was an acknowledgement that political parties need to change if local government is to rise to the place-shaping challenge since this depends so heavily on the calibre and commitment of councillors. As one attendee put it: "All political parties should have a much more rigorous system in their sorting of candidate panels to promote quality of candidates". Public confidence in councils will only be reclaimed over time and will be dependent on the ability of local government to deliver results, to build a local profile and to connect with their communities and local partners in the pursuit of a shared vision and common objectives.

5.49   A recent Leadership Centre survey found that 62 per cent of chief executives and 48 per cent of leaders thought that attracting high calibre candidates for political office was their top priority in developing leadership capacity.[11] The performance (real and perceived) of local councillors needs to be improved, as does the extent to which they reflect the diversity of the communities they seek to represent, and the major onus here is on political parties to improve their recruitment practices.

---

[11] Leadership Centre, *Chief Executives – Leaders: What You Really Think,* 2005.

5.50   In order to improve the calibre and performance of councillors, parties need to be prepared to attract a wider pool of potential candidates from which to select and train in advance of elections, including considering people who do not necessarily wish to sign up to an entire political programme. At my councillor engagement events, some councillors argued (along the lines suggested by some local government commentators) for political parties to operate a much more open recruitment process with systematic talent scouting amongst both members and supporters alongside active support to encourage under-represented groups to put themselves forward for selection.[12] Parties could even consider the approaches used by the voluntary sector to recruit non-executive directors, for example that used by the charity Crisis, using executive search techniques to seek out talent for closely defined roles. I welcome the work which Dame Jane Roberts' Commission will be undertaking to examine these issues.[13]

> **Recommendation 5.7**
>
> Political parties should refresh their approach to recruiting local councillors, actively seeking out talent and reaching out beyond their traditional activist base.

5.51   I also believe that there needs to be much greater clarity about expectations and the time commitment involved in being a councillor (and greater discipline about how members' time is used). This should, as a minimum, include clear job descriptions and a thorough induction process. There are some useful examples here from recruitment to public bodies. For example, there may be some lessons to be learnt from the NHS non-executive director model, where there is greater clarity about the role and commitment expected of directors and a regular evaluation of performance.

5.52   The case for greater performance pressures on councillors is strong. The basic legal criterion for retaining the position of councillor is attendance at a council meeting once every six months. While this hardly provides transparency about what councillors do or accountability for their activity levels, I do not think that the answer lies in making the formal criteria more stringent. I support the use of qualitative criteria such as those set out in the IDeA's Political Skills Framework.[14] The pressure to meet these criteria should come from the political groups, with support from officers and national bodies. Some party group leaders within councils are already working on developing far clearer job descriptions and objectives for members of their executive and are carrying out appraisal-style reviews of performance either with individual members or collectively as an executive. Some are also looking beyond the executive to a self-evaluation of the performance of the group as a whole, learning from the approach now used on most company boards, informed by the Higgs Review.[15] This form of self-review and evaluation demonstrates a commitment to challenge performance and to the continuing development of members' skills. It would be useful, however, if the tools used in any one council could be developed and agreed on a cross-party basis.

---

[12] Wheeler, P., Joseph Rowntree Foundation, *Political Recruitment: How Local Parties Recruit Councillors*, 2006.

[13] Councillors Commission announced by CLG Secretary of State, Ruth Kelly on 8 February 2007 to look at what barriers are preventing everyday people from becoming councillors and what steps can be taken to get more people involved, to be chaired by Dr Jane Roberts, DBE.

[14] Silvester, Prof. J *'Political Skills Framework'* with the Work Psychology Foundation for the IDeA available at www.idea-knowledge.gov.uk

[15] Higgs Review: *An Independent Review Into the Role and Effectiveness of Non-executive Company Directors*, 2003.

5.53   I also take the view that accountability can be enhanced by, as many councils do, producing information about councillors' attendance at meetings. I commend the practice of some party groups in requiring councillors to place regular reports of their activity on the council's website as a means of getting their members to focus on their effectiveness and holding them more widely to account for their performance. A number of councils are well-developed in this approach which also reinforces public engagement. For example in Luton, Tameside and Stockport every councillor produces an annual report which is then published on the council's website.

> **Recommendation 5.8**
>
> Political groups, mainly at local level, but supported at national level, should place stronger performance management pressures on councillors, including performance appraisal and mechanisms to provide the public with information about their activities.

5.54   Political groups should also reflect on how they are organised and should consider how to reach the right balance between enforcing the party whip and allowing councillors to represent local issues. This is very difficult where a council has a fine political balance. While the party system has many obvious strengths, automatic adherence to a party line can undermine councillor credibility with ward constituents and discourages many, in this individualistic age, from coming forward to be a councillor in the first place. At my councillor engagement events, some councillors were asking for more freedom to pursue ward issues, even if it sometimes conflicted with party views, arguing that this would make the role of councillor far more attractive. As one argued: "Party politics makes my job as a councillor very frustrating – national party policies have little relevance to issues in my ward". Perception is important, and Ipsos MORI found that only 25 per cent of people surveyed believed that in general councillors put the interests of their local area first compared with 32 per cent believing that they put the interests of their party first.[16] Councillors told me that their constituents and potential future councillors found 'political bickering' off-putting and they saw the value of good cross-party working complementing strong party working: "we should have the local relationships to focus on ambition and delivery rather than process".[17] This suggests that greater freedom for councillors might help to improve recruitment and retention.

> **Recommendation 5.9**
>
> All political groups should:
>
> * organise themselves so that all councillors feel valued;
> * consider giving ward members more freedom, limiting whipping to a narrower range of decisions and employing more flexible processes for group discipline; and
> * develop skills in cross-party working.

Developing the role of frontline councillors

5.55   My May report emphasised that the reforms to political management arrangements introduced by the Local Government Act 2000 gave insufficient attention to the frontline role of councillors. The frontline role is one of the keys to effective engagement with the local community and one which receives insufficient attention and support. It is important to emphasise that I do not just mean non-executive councillors here, I mean all (including executive) councillors in their

---

[16] Ipsos MORI, for the Standards Board for England, *Public Perception of Ethics,* 2005.
[17] At Councillor engagement events – Report on councillor engagement events – Lyons Inquiry, 2006.

role of engaging with the public to research opinion, test options and explain decisions. Clearly, whether or not a councillor is a member of the executive or not will influence the way they carry out this task – but it remains an important role for all councillors. I believe that the White Paper and Local Government Bill provide an opportunity for all councils to reflect on how they can encourage their members to be outward facing and on how the balance of working time can be shifted towards engagement with the community.

5.56   I believe there is a role for the local government family, including the LGA, Local Government Information Unit and IDeA, to develop new models for frontline councillor working. Local government itself should be more innovative, experimenting with redefining the frontline councillor role, developing new forums for engagement with citizens, empowering them to influence or make decisions locally, and developing scrutiny to ensure input on longer term strategic issues. This will involve making the best of new provisions such as the community call for action and considering individual ward councillor budgets. It is also likely to include consideration of how the time of councillors is best spent and some rationalisation of existing time commitments.

5.57   Local government must also work to support councillors in their frontline role, providing administrative and IT support. Above all, councils should ensure that each frontline councillor has the information they need to do their job. They must also have clear channels to influence policy decisions. Again there are many examples of effective practice within local government, but I am concerned that this role is often undervalued and that too often councils are overly cautious about supporting councillors in their frontline role, fearing that this is too close to their party political role. There are tensions and risks here, but there are also real benefits from supporting councillors in their public engagement role, encouraging them to be more effective in the communities they represent and particularly in supporting more effective two-way communication with their constituents.[18]

Ward councillor information in Westminster

Westminster City Council has identified greater access to information as a significant factor in empowering ward councillors – not in the legal sense, but in terms of convenience. Too often, ward councillors have heard of matters that will affect their wards too late in the process. The council has, therefore, set up and is about to lauch an 'online neighbourhood information grid', targeted primarily at councillors and accessible by them. Information on planning, highways and other initiatives is accessible by ward in a graphical format, with scope for further development, including information sharing with partners.

5.58   In developing more localised arrangements for management and decision-making, the role of individual councillors is absolutely crucial and must be part of the equation from the beginning. I do believe, as suggested in the White Paper, that it is good practice for local authorities to provide individual councillors with budgets and devolved powers where appropriate. This also has the potential to support councillors in their engagement with local people. For example, a ward councillor's ability to direct funding towards improvements to a local community hall could help to generate resident participation in wider discussions about the regeneration of the area.

---

[18] Gardiner, T., Joseph Rowntree Foundation, *Frontline Councillors and Decision Making: Broadening their involvement*, March 2006.

Staffordshire County Council's Local Members Initiative Scheme (LMIS)

The LMIS gives each of Staffordshire's county councillors a maximum of £10,000 to spend on a project or projects in their constituency, based on applications from community groups or organisations in consultation with the community. The £10,000 is specifically earmarked for the promotion of the well-being of those people who live in that part of the county. County Councillors can also choose to team up to spend their allocations on joint projects.

The scheme has a number of criteria:

- that the proposal supports one or more of the County Council's corporate and service priorities;
- that the expenditure is lawful and will be properly allocated;
- that the proposal does not conflict with the county council's policies; and
- that it does not lead to a financial commitment into future years.

The maximum annual LMIS allocation for each county councillor is £10,000.

All proposals for funding, although put forward by councillors, have to be approved by Staffordshire County Council's Cabinet.

Since LMIS began in 2001 more than a million pounds has been spent through this scheme, helping around 1,600 projects across Staffordshire, including Community First Responder schemes, churches and vulnerable young people.

> *This is a scheme that is aimed at giving everyone living in communities across the county a say in how together we can enhance their local community. LMIS plugs local members directly into community organisations and is a fantastic way for people to deal directly with their county councillor. People comment that LMIS is the most effective and least bureaucratic way of getting resources for local initiatives and recognise that their county council is their champion. (County Council Leader Terry Dix).*

Recommendation 5.10

Every council should improve the support it provides councillors in their frontline role by:

- ensuring that they have the information they need to do their job effectively;
- putting in place role descriptions, training and development specifically for the ward member role as part of a wider commitment to member development;
- ensuring that support for elected members in their community leadership role is properly thought through, given sufficient priority in the work of the council and is resourced appropriately, with full use being made of IT;
- considering the use of individual ward member budgets but assessing what works best in local circumstances; and
- ensuring clear routes for frontline councillors to influence policy decisions.

IMPROVING LOCAL ACCOUNTABILITY

5.59   While local government's status as a body chosen by the community gives it a special mandate to speak and act in the interests of the community, I argued in Chapter 2 that councils need to go further, beyond elections, to seek an ongoing mandate. Changing expectations about the accountability of government mean that councils need to earn the confidence of local people: that they are responsive to their views and that they understand their needs and priorities. To do this, they need to develop forms of accountability which refresh their council's knowledge of local issues and provide ongoing public input. I believe that for local government to be credible in the new, wider place-shaping role, it must develop much stronger accountability to local people and partners.

5.60   The White Paper makes clear that central government expects that a shift in powers and flexibility to local authorities must be accompanied by greater local accountability and I support this 'deal'. Local government can go a long way to improve its accountability to local people within the current framework and has no need to await further legislation.

Developing social capital 5.61   It is important to remind ourselves why accountability is so important. In Chapter 2, I identified local government's role in developing social capital, both bonding capital within communities and bridging capital between communities. As part of local leadership, the best councils already ensure they have a knowledge and understanding of levels of social capital in their area and take responsibility for increasing those levels. The London Borough of Camden's work with the Institute of Public Policy Research (IPPR) has shown that a local authority can monitor levels of social capital using proxy indicators and data that many local authorities collect already.[19] It has also shown the ways that a council can develop social capital:

- through service delivery which promotes social capital, involving and engaging people themselves and bringing different communities together;

- through the information which the council gives out via elected members and staff, plus through its publicity, publications and campaigning;

- by engendering public debate on issues in a way that improves understanding, promotes cohesion rather than division (particularly where difficult decisions are being taken) and makes people feel positive about getting involved; and

- by recognising that the council, even in partnership with other agencies, is not an all-powerful service provider which can solve every problem. Many solutions require 'co-production', the contribution of citizens themselves.

5.62   There is also an increasing realisation that councils are in the best position to create the climate where citizens can debate among themselves and with partners how they may need to change, accept constraints and contribute to prioritisation – for example to tackle a high death rate from coronary heart disease. This approach is more likely to result in changes in behaviour than a more top-down approach.

Improving information to the public 5.63   One key way of improving engagement and developing social capital is through improving information. The Ipsos MORI evidence on public attitudes to local government consistently shows higher levels of satisfaction where people feel that they are kept informed. Among residents of 150 upper-tier councils, 89 per cent of those who regarded themselves as well-informed by their council were satisfied with the way it runs things, while only 23 per cent of those who felt completely uninformed were satisfied.[20] Good information can also enhance trust. People respond especially well to regular feedback informing them how their views have been taken into account.

5.64   The White Paper rightly emphasises the importance of informing the public on service standards, on the council's plans and on its achievements.

[19] IPPR and LB Camden. *Sticking Together – Social Capital and Local Government – the results and implications of the Camden social capital surveys 2002 and 2005, 2006.*
[20] Ipsos MORI, *Best Value User Satisfaction Surveys 2006, General Survey: initial topline report for single and upper-tier local authorities,* CLG, 2007.

5.65   I was pleased to see in my case studies and in my councillor engagement work that most councils who participated were strongly committed to informing the public and understood the value of doing this well. Many have regular newspapers, magazines or newsletters and have worked to improve their websites. Councils across the country have signed up to the LGA's Reputation Campaign, which is working to tackle councils' credibility gap. Informing the public is not the same as engaging the public, but it is an absolute prerequisite to it.

Recommendation 5.11

The main steps forward which councils still need to take in informing the public are:

- working with partners across the LSP to present a common set of key messages for the area;

- identifying through research and customer feedback what really works in reaching the public and focusing resources on those channels; and

- using new channels to target particular groups in the population, especially young people, with relevant messages in an imaginative and entrepreneurial way.

Improving public engagement

5.66   I believe that local government's ability to engage local people lies at the heart of its place-shaping role. If local government is to act in the interests of its community, influence its partners and respond to local priorities, it must build stronger engagement with its citizens as the foundation for place-shaping.

5.67   Many of the democratic and structural changes discussed in Chapter 4 require action by central government. However, local government can also go a long way to improve its engagement of local citizens and must demonstrate it can embrace this challenge. Ipsos MORI research shows us that most people do not want to spend time in wider political debates about their locality, with consistently less than five per cent of the population taking part in political campaigns of any kind.[21] They do, however, want to know to whom they should go if they have a complaint or concern, and they do want to be clear about who is responsible for making decisions – and when they do raise something they want feedback. Research shows that there is a strong correlation between the extent to which people perceive that there are opportunities for participation and their satisfaction with their council.[22]

5.68   There is strong evidence of innovation by local government in public engagement and of increasing use of a range of engagement tools to involve geographically defined groups or communities of interest in:

- developing services of which they are recipients, for example involving older people in developing and tailoring the 'meals on wheels' service;

- representing a particular hard-to-reach group's views, for example establishing a youth parliament;

- developing policy or strategy, for example through participatory budgeting; and

- problem solving at a local level and tasking local services, for example addressing community safety at a very local level through Safer Neighbourhood Teams.

---

[21] Ipsos MORI; *Analysis of Socio-political Activism – 1996-2006*, 2006.

[22] Ipsos MORI; *Best Value Performance Indicators 2006 (70 district, county and single tier authorities)*, 2007.

Innovative engagement with citizens

One mechanism being piloted to enable councils to better engage with their citizens is the participatory budgeting process, first developed in Porto Alegre in Brazil in the 1980s. Its core purpose is to involve citizens and local communities in decision-making processes around the local authority budget every year. Priorities for spending a proportion of the mainstream budget are identified through a structured and timely dialogue between the council and its citizens. Key to its success is devolution of an element of the budget to neighbourhoods so that service delivery and spending decisions are influenced and shaped by local needs. The Power Inquiry research report *Beyond the Ballot,* issued in May 2005, concluded that participatory budgeting had particular resonance for the UK.

In England, participatory budgeting projects are being delivered by Church Action on Poverty and the Community Pride Initiative, with the active support of Oxfam's UK Poverty Programme.

Other organisations have also worked with councils to carry out tailored public budget consultation work. Ipsos MORI's work with Oxfordshire County Council is one example. The modelling approach used in Oxfordshire has enabled residents to become the Council's 'Cabinet for the day' and to make 'decisions' on real-life scenarios. Oxfordshire Council Leader Keith Mitchell, who attended a workshop with colleagues from all parties, concluded:

> *I was impressed by participants' interest and enjoyment of the day. We found it invaluable to hear at first hand what they had to say. There is no doubt in my mind that the workshop influenced the Executive in setting their budget'.*

Residents who participated also found the process involving and informative, with the following quotes being typical:

> *Very enjoyable – showed us how difficult it must be for councillors to make these life-altering decisions. I now have a lot more confidence in the way the budget is handled.*

5.69   Some local authorities however still tend to use more passive forms of engagement, using more traditional consultation techniques, and are less good at feeding back to local people.[23]

Recommendation 5.12

Local government needs to make a step-change in the quality of its engagement work, building on the effective communications and engagement practice already being used and also ensuring that its application is much more systematic and rigorous. In particular, councils need to:

- focus on what matters in their engagement work, being selective about where resources are targeted;

- follow best practice in engaging all sectors of the community, particularly those voices which are not always heard, including vulnerable people, and black and minority ethnic groups;

- avoid allowing statutory requirements for consultation to limit their approach to consultation and engagement;

- accord higher status to the skills set needed by officers and councillors to engage effectively with the public; and

- ensure they explain to participants how the results of engagement have been used, including how they influenced councils' or partners' plans.

---

[23] ODPM, *New Localism – Citizen Engagement, Neighbourhoods and Public Services: evidence from local government,* 2005.

5.70   The stronger emphasis placed on LSPs in the White Paper reinforces the importance of coordinating engagement activities. By bringing together all local partners, LSPs offer the opportunity to coordinate and plan consultation, engagement and feedback activities. Asking the public for their views on a wide range of public services and outcomes, for example, including health and policing, is more efficient and more likely to generate responses and ultimately involvement.[24] This would ensure that the public has a much more coherent sense of what is happening locally and that partners have a stronger shared understanding of local priorities and views.

Developing scrutiny   5.71   Local government has succeeded in making scrutiny part of the local governance landscape since its introduction in the Local Government Act 2000. Scrutiny by non-executive councillors of the executive's decisions, policies and strategies is increasingly playing an important role in the accountability of local government, strengthening public engagement and improving council performance. I want to stress that I see scrutiny as having a core role in place-shaping. Done well, evidence from the many case studies and examples from the Centre for Public Scrutiny shows that scrutiny can provide a key focus for community and stakeholder engagement, harness local expertise, challenge current performance and service priorities and secure changes that mean services better meet local needs.[25]

5.72   Councils have, with the help of the Centre for Public Scrutiny and others, learned lessons about what constitutes effective scrutiny, the level of resource it needs and how it can play a role in strategic decision-making. Where it is most successful, scrutiny also has a positive impact on service delivery and contributes to better outcomes for local people. Strong overview and scrutiny complements strong executive leadership, and the two have been identified in analysis of Comprehensive Performance Assessment scores as being associated with good performance.[26]

5.73   I am encouraged that there are already many examples of effective scrutiny by local government. It requires councils to be selective about the issues it considers and to focus on strategic questions. Although scrutiny bodies do not make decisions, examples of effective scrutiny demonstrate that they can influence strongly the decisions that are made by others and ensure that local services are responsive to local priorities. Effective scrutiny also provides an opportunity to be inclusive, drawing on skills and different views within the local community. With the introduction of health scrutiny in the Health and Social Care Act 2001, local government has also begun to develop scrutiny as a means of considering issues of community interest beyond its own services, and its use as a means to hold other agencies to account; the White Paper offers further welcome scope for this.

---

[24] For example, Birmingham's Commissioning Strategy for services for people with physical disabilities www.birmingham.gov.uk/

[25] Centre for Public Scrutiny www.cfps.org.uk.

[26] John, P. and Gains, F., *Political Leadership Under the New Political Management Structures.* ELG Research, 2005.

Successful health scrutiny by Richmondshire District Council

The Yorkshire Dales area covered by Richmondshire District Council is over an hour away from the nearest accident and emergency hospital. The council's Community and Environment Overview and Scrutiny Committee has a broad remit, covering issues ranging from health and well-being to the physical environment. Prior to a proposed change to general practitioner out-of-hours services, and despite district councils having no formal scrutiny powers in relation to health matters, the Overview and Scrutiny Committee decided to undertake a review into how residents of Richmondshire perceived the out-of-hours service and what effect doctors opting out of this service would have on local residents. The committee also wanted to try and guide the primary care trust (PCT) in its future plans on this issue.

Prior to the introduction of the new out-of-hours scheme, the Committee publicised its intention to review current service provision, received a presentation from Richmond and Hambledon PCT and heard evidence from residents, the North Yorkshire Emergency Doctors Service and other health care professionals. As well as raising public awareness of the issue, the main outputs of this initial review were to check the operating procedures of the PCT, register the concern of patients that current service levels be maintained and ensure that any future new patient centre should be located in the local practice areas to reduce patient travel time. The recommendations were endorsed by the full council and passed on to the North Yorkshire Health Scrutiny Committee and the Tees Health Service Review.

Following the introduction of the revised service, and having recognised the original service review, the County Council asked Richmondshire's Overview and Scrutiny Committee to carry out a second review. This involved multi-agency meetings and site visits.

The majority of the recommendations of the second review were endorsed by the County Council's Scrutiny Committee and have now been implemented, including: the relocation of the emergency ambulance permanent station; provision of an initial patient assessment centre and out-of-hours waiting room, staffed by paramedics and/or emergency nurses at a local ambulance station; and the availability of better information to raise awareness of the complaints procedures. This case study demonstrates the contribution that effective council scrutiny can make on behalf of its community, even where they have no formal control over the service being scrutinised.

> *With North Yorkshire County Council endorsing the review we were a stronger body, therefore, we were able to successfully improve the out-of-hours service.* (Cllr Yvonne Peacock, Former Chair, Community and Environment Scrutiny Committee, Richmondshire District Council)

> *District councils have a vital and meaningful role to play in the scrutiny of health and healthcare on behalf of their communities.* (Tim Gilling, Health Scrutiny Programme Manager, Centre for Public Scrutiny)

Taken from *Successful Scrutiny 3* published by Centre for Public Scrutiny 2007 and available at http://www.cfps.org.uk/successfulscrutiny2007.

5.74   However, there is evidence that the practice and use of scrutiny as a tool for local accountability is mixed, with some councils performing better than others.[27] There are also major differences in the extent to which councils prioritise and resource the scrutiny role. I am pleased that the White Paper is extending councils' scrutiny role as I believe that scrutiny will become an increasingly important tool for local accountability in a more devolved system. The wider remit set out in the White Paper offers councils a further opportunity to shape the full range of services delivered locally and to act as a powerful advocate and champion of local people's interests.

5.75   As local government takes hard decisions in order to balance the needs of different communities and to manage local pressures, scrutiny offers a means by which to take into account the views of local people and to involve councillors in the policy-making process. For example, if councils are exploring a hard local choice where different interests must be weighed against each other, scrutiny can be part of that process so that backbench councillors and the wider community share ownership of the problem and contribute to the solution in a deliberative way, rather than merely reacting and responding to proposals which have already had political, if not formal council, agreement.

5.76   I believe that scrutiny also has a major part to play in supporting other tasks and behaviours that I consider essential to developing local government's place-shaping role:

- it offers a means of supporting local government's convening role through the consideration of strategic issues and, particularly through the role of frontline councillors, provides a means for the local community to hold partners to account; and

- it has the potential to play a key role in the self-assessment process of local authorities as part of the new performance management regime, and in strengthening the accountability of local partnerships such as the LSP and Crime and Disorder Reduction Partnership as partnership models become more important in the delivery of local outcomes and services.

5.77   The proposals in the White Paper for the introduction of a Community Call to Action and local petitions also introduce new demands on the scrutiny process. It proposes scrutiny involvement at a smaller neighbourhood level, about which I am cautious. I believe it may sometimes be appropriate for scrutiny to focus on smaller, localised issues, particularly those with cross-cutting implications, but this must be within a strong strategic context, without diluting scrutiny's strategic role, and in a way that fully recognises the overriding need for councils to manage competing demands.

> **Recommendation 5.13**
>
> Scrutiny needs to be seen as a core strand of local government's place-shaping role. Councils and other participants must resource it appropriately and link it to local partnership work.

INNOVATIVE, LOCAL SOLUTIONS TO PUBLIC SERVICE CHALLENGES

5.78   I have no doubt that councils can and do provide adequate and even outstanding services without fully embracing their place-shaping role. I am convinced, however, that they cannot achieve optimum performance without a strong sense of place which is needed for services to be relevant

---

[27] Stoker, G., et al, *Operating the New Council Constitutions in English Local Authorities: A Process Evaluation,* ODPM, 2004.

and tailored to the needs of the local area. For services to be provided in this way, innovative local solutions are necessary which may, in some cases, mean taking carefully judged risks. A recent study from the Tavistock Institute argued this would create greater diversity and difference within and between communities – the key challenge of local political leadership would be to both celebrate and respond to that difference and diversity.[28]

Creative use of powers

5.79   In order to innovatively and effectively carry out a place-shaping role, local government should make fuller use of the powers already at its disposal. This means actively considering the full range of levers available to achieve the council's goals in the short and longer term. Such powers can be used to support effective local services and outcomes, to innovate and respond to local needs, but there is also a credibility argument here. If local government is to be given new powers and freedoms, it is essential that it also demonstrates its ability to be ambitious and innovative in using both the new powers and the existing ones.

Use of the well-being power to set up an employment brokerage and training agency in the London Borough of Greenwich

Greenwich Council established Greenwich Local Labour and Business (GLLaB) as a mechanism to link local people to the thousands of new jobs being created by an unprecedented level of regeneration in the Borough. The challenge for the Council has been to maximise the local benefits of this investment by giving local residents, particularly those who are traditionally less successful in the labour market, access the new job opportunities and help to overcome barriers to employment caused by decades of structural unemployment and social exclusion.

Working with a wide range of local partners, GLLaB offers a highly customised job brokerage and training service that matches local residents to new job opportunities with contractors and end-user employers on all major development sites in Greenwich.

GLLaB's achievements since its establishment 1996 include:

- 7,000 local residents trained in skills relevant to new job opportunities;
- 7,200 people placed into work;
- 44 per cent of job placements from ethnic minorities;
- 75 per cent of job placements previously unemployed; 34 per cent long-term unemployed;
- 56 per cent of people placed into work were from the Borough's most disadvantaged wards.

GLLaB has been acknowledged as an example of good practice by the Joseph Rowntree Trust and the Audit Commission and has recently been awarded Charter Mark for the second time. GLLaB's success helped Greenwich achieve Beacon Council status in 2003–04 for Removing Barriers to Work.

5.80   I believe that the limited use of the well-being power in the Local Government Act 2000 is a powerful example of local government failing to make best use of the powers available to it. Long campaigned for by local government, the introduction of the well-being power could have represented a significant shift in the constitutional position of local government. Rather than being restricted to roles and functions specified in statute, the well-being power offers local government a much less constrained role in leading their communities. However, the evidence shows that the knowledge and understanding of the power is patchy and very few councils are using it actively in their community leadership role.[29] There appear to be several reasons why local government is not using all the powers available to it. It is too often perceived to be a legal or technical issue and therefore

---

[28] Tavistock Institute, commissioned by ODPM, *All Our Futures, a study of local governance in 2015*, 2006.
[29] CLG, *Formative Evaluation of the Take-up and Implementation of the Well Being Power Annual Report, 2006.*

not widely understood. As a result, rather than being seen as an integral part of a council's powers, it is being introduced as means of giving comfort where the adequacy of other powers is unclear. The evidence also indicates that councils that are more experienced and confident in working with a wide range of partners are also more likely to be making use of the power as are councils that have a greater capacity for looking at cross-cutting issues. Perhaps this is because this approach tends to take councils into areas of work which are less circumscribed by other primary legislation.

5.81   There are also cultural and behavioural reasons why local government does not widely use its current powers. Government research has found that the main barrier to the use of the power seems to lie in local government attitudes and the absence of an entrepreneurial approach to problem solving.[30] While part of the explanation for this lies in the over-centralisation identified in Chapter 3, it is local government itself which must take responsibility for raising its game in the future. This needs to be part of the behavioural shift in local government from being constrained by thinking within the confines of a service provider to being a catalyst for wider innovation and change for the community as a whole.

> **Recommendation 5.14**
>
> Local government needs to think widely and creatively about how to use its existing powers to the full and take a more entrepreneurial approach to problem solving, as part of the place-shaping role.

5.82   In Chapter 3, I also identified central government's tendency to issue detailed guidance to councils, I am also aware of councils' own tendency to request guidance from central government. Indeed, evidence has been put to me on several occasions asking for central government guidance or funding. I emphatically believe that this is not the solution to local government's problems. In terms of recovering its own sense of powerfulness, local government must reduce its dependency on central government guidance and its default position should be to find solutions from within and seek support and guidance from its peers rather than seeing government departments as its first port of call.

> **Recommendation 5.15**
>
> Local government should itself develop mechanisms to provide peer guidance to councils and filter requests for guidance to government. The LGA could play a gatekeeper role.

Local Area Agreements

5.83   I have discussed the potential advantage and risks faced in delivering what LAAs promise in the future in Chapter 4. However, I also identify a challenge for local government in terms of its attitudes and behaviours in relation to LAAs. The concerns I have heard voiced about the current generation of LAAs during my consultation indicate that many authorities see them as an exercise in conforming to a central government requirement (and a means of 'earning' potential rewards) rather than a negotiated or contractual agreement between partners. As a consequence, few LAAs currently reflect a very strong local perspective and many authorities feel unable to challenge the steer they get from Government Offices, which represent government departments in this dialogue.

5.84   The explicit link made in the White Paper and the Local Government Bill between Community Strategies and LAAs as their delivery plans, may be helpful here. Community Strategies, when done well, are strongly grounded on the views and priorities of local people and are rich in evidence about local needs and opportunities. A stronger link with LAAs may help councils take a more robust stance in terms of their knowledge and evidence about local needs and priorities and support an approach to LAAs that shifts the balance of negotiation to one between more equal partners.

---

[30] CLG, *Formative Evaluation of the Take-Up and Implementation of the Well Being Power – Annual Report 2006.*

5.85 Local government needs to be particularly robust in identifying those matters which may be important priorities but which are for local determination. These may require significant negotiation with a whole range of local partners – but the Government Office should not be holding sway in these discussions. Unless LAAs are focused on those matters which truly need a national contractual arrangement, the approach will tend to be devalued. There is a key challenge for local government in making best use of LAAs as intended in the White Paper. This means negotiating the 'right' 35 targets with central government and selecting an appropriate set of local targets with partners. These should reflect a proper strategic discussion of priorities, resisting any temptation to fall back on a standard list.

Recommendation 5.16

Local government needs to emphasise the 'local' in Local Area Agreements, tailoring them to, and using them as a stimulus, for identifying key local priorities, seeing them as a tool for local improvement rather than a matter of mere compliance with central government.

Securing efficiency

5.86 Improving efficiency and value for money will continue to be a major driver for local government, not least because of the imperative for councils to manage pressures on public expenditure and to secure the trust and confidence of both their local population and central government. Local government, in its role as an effective place-shaper, is in a strong position to improve efficiency. It should be able to harness local knowledge, and shape local markets and align its partnership and collaborative capacity to secure the best use of resources locally.

5.87 While local government needs to position itself more clearly as a champion for efficiency, its record is far stronger than common perception would suggest. It has led the way in using technology to re-shape the delivery of public services and provides a wide range of examples of innovative procurement and partnership models. Local government is comfortably meeting its Gershon efficiency target of 7.5 per cent: it is a year ahead of target and is producing 75 per cent, as opposed to 50 per cent, cashable savings.[31] Nonetheless local government still has a way to go in embedding an entrepreneurial mindset: it still sees itself too much as a prisoner of external factors and constraints rather than as shaping its own future. It is my belief that a reduction in central government direction will help councils to increase their sense of powerfulness and bring a clearer understanding of the distinctive role of local government, where it can be the unequivocal local champion of value for money.

5.88 Views expressed to me during the Inquiry reflect a sense that too frequently in the public sector, managerial efficiency is emphasised at the expense of allocative efficiency and its potential to improve user satisfaction and well-being. Pursuing allocative efficiency involves attempting to maximise general well-being by addressing the most important priorities for each area rather than seeking uniform standards. It needs, however, a really good understanding of local needs and aspirations, together with good engagement to both inform and explain hard choices. This in turn helps to manage pressures.

5.89 It is important to note that this tension between managerial and allocative efficiency plays out not only between central and local government, but also at a local level where councils are reluctant to devolve their powers to local or neighbourhood bodies, which may be in a better

---

[31] Gershon, P, *Releasing Resources to the Front Line – Independent review of public sector efficiency*, 2004.

position to understand and meet local demands. Local government needs to have the confidence to judge where economies of scale and managerial efficiency secure better outcomes at an authority-wide level, and where a more locally responsive approach may lever wider benefits and satisfaction and deliver stronger overall efficiency. Following on from Gershon's valuable emphasis on joining up back-office functions, the recommendations of the Varney Report build on exciting work already led by local authorities to join up front-line service delivery in line with user need.[32]

Sharing good practice

5.90   Central government does have a role in spreading best practice and supporting innovation. However, the collective role of local government in driving this agenda is also important and may not require any support from central government in many instances. Bodies such as the LGA and IDeA need to ensure that they are capturing the knowledge and experience of local government effectively and supporting the exchange and spread of effective practice. I welcome the LGA's commitment to developing cross-sector responsibility for challenging performance and supporting improvement and there are already good examples of stronger local authorities supporting improvements in weaker authorities outside of any formal inspection or accountability process.[33] I do, however, remain concerned that there has been huge investment in the identification and dissemination of best practice, for example Warwick University's wide-ranging evaluation of the Beacon scheme,[34] but there is still sometimes a tendency in local government to continually reinvent the wheel.

> **Key aspects of efficiency include:**
>
> - **service innovation:** reshaping the way in which public services are delivered through business process improvements and greater innovation in delivery models;
>
> - **co-production:** working with service users themselves to improve outcomes;
>
> - **effective commissioning:** a stronger understanding of needs (including related needs across service providers where joint commissioning may be appropriate), effective use of competition through strategic market management and flexibility about delivery options;
>
> - **smarter procurement:** changing approaches to procurement including the use of e-procurement, aggregating demand and tracking spend patterns far more closely;
>
> - **effective management of contracts:** adopting a 'one team' approach to working with partners providing services to achieve a smaller, leaner client side, less administration and a more creative approach to problem solving;
>
> - **E-Government:** using technology to help deliver information and access to services more efficiently and to secure gains in terms of better information and data sharing and the accessibility of services;
>
> - **partnership working:** collaboration where economies of scale or the sharing of expertise provide better more cost-effective services;
>
> - **asset management:** rigorous challenge to the current and future use of assets, including joint consideration of future asset needs with local partners. Asset planning should be fully integrated with the long-term strategic plans for the area; and
>
> - **delivering the right priorities:** efficiency in its broadest sense means finding the right local solutions, in light of local needs and wishes and setting priorities accordingly.

---

[32] Varney Report: Service transformation: a better service for citizens and businesses, a better deal for the taxpayer, 2007.

[33] LGA Closer to People and Places 2006 http://www.lga.gov.uk

[34] htttp://www2/warwick.ac.uk/fac/soc/wbs/research/lgc/research/beacons/reports/

Asset management in Rotherham

In 2005, Rotherham reviewed a selection of its assets, and had used a database and geographic information systems to look at staff satisfaction and the demographics of properties, mapping other public service organisations alongside service properties and key commercial centres to consider if the right buildings were in the right places.

This approach helped the authority to develop a 'hub and spoke' approach to fit the needs of effective service delivery for its users. As a result, six outer borough service centres are being set up to enable services users to gain access to multiple services from one place. Existing accommodation was used to focus on customer needs in the town centre, but new facilities areas also being funded, designed, built and run. The primary care trust is a major partner for these developments.

Time-elapsed studies of building occupancy (carried out with another partner, BT) revealed that during an extended day, desks were only occupied for 41 per cent of the measured time and 30 per cent of space was used for hard-copy filing. Rotherham Work Style has now been introduced to maximise use of work space, resulting in savings through freed-up space.

Council-wide asset reviews are both sensitive and contentious, therefore in Rotherham they are overseen by the Regeneration and Asset Board, which is itself part of the Cabinet. This model is set to be extended to deal with Community (Buildings) Governance as set out in the Local Government White Paper. The current review has examined 250 assets, generating £32.7 million in capital receipts, and has produced significant revenue savings.

Rotherham operates a series of framework agreements to ensure a timely response to funding and other opportunities. Land ownership has been used as leverage, by lease or sale, to the extent that £900 million of development has been raised from assets worth £40 million. New civic and cultural centre projects, worth around £90 million, are a further example of innovative asset redeployment and reinvestment.

Choice and co-production   5.91   Public engagement too, can help councils to develop innovative solutions which can deliver more effective outcomes by bringing in the perspective of users. Councils should involve users in the design and delivery of services, to find ways to enhance user choice and harness the benefits offered by co-production.

Hartlepool's Healthy Food Co-operatives

Hartlepool Borough Council's Healthy Food Project is a new scheme designed to promote health and well-being in the borough by supporting the creation of fruit and vegetable co-operatives across the town.

The project has been developed by the Council in close partnership with health professionals and local communities. While the council is taking the lead role in supporting and overseeing the project, the co-ops have been set up by local people for local people with the intention of each co-op becoming owned and controlled exclusively by their members. Granting local people ownership of their own co-ops promotes independence and self-sufficiency within the community through co-production.

There are five food co-operatives operating in Hartlepool at present, two are completely independent. The first was set up in Heronspool in 2002 in response to a survey that showed residents, particularly the elderly within the area, had very limited access to fruit and vegetables. The co-op now serves the needs of 98 sheltered bungalows. The Elm Tree Park Co-operative serves the needs of a static home park in Seaton Carew. The co-op is open to all 100 residents as well as the wider community. The scheme was created with the help of the Healthy Food Initiative but now operates completely independently.

One resident said:

> *I've had a triple bypass and have diabetes as well. I couldn't do without the [co-op] now. I love the fact that it is so local, right in the middle of our community. I used to have to get taxis all of the time but now I don't have to rely on anyone, I can do it myself.*

The co-ops also play an important social role for both the users and the volunteers, promoting a sense of community within the borough. One local resident commented:

> *the shop means we have independence. We get to choose the food we want in the quantities we can use and at a reasonable price. We can meet up with our neighbours, do our shopping, have a cup of tea and find out what's going on. It gives back the feeling of community.*

Commissioning role

5.92   The need for innovation applies not only to local government's traditional role as service provider. The future also requires councils to reflect further on whether they are the optimum provider of services or whether they should more fully develop their commissioning role, working in partnership with the private and third sectors and with other public bodies. Evidence in recent years from service delivery partnerships with the public, community, voluntary and private sectors has demonstrated that commissioning models often provide valuable new ways of delivering services.

5.93   Such commissioning has a number of benefits. It can bring new expertise, skills and experience from other sectors to bear on traditional and sometimes, outdated services. The community and voluntary sector in particular can bring the added benefits of community capacity building alongside service delivery. The process of commissioning lends itself particularly to bringing user involvement into determining the nature of the service to be provided. It can also draw in local users as co-producers of their services, for example where local social enterprises grow up to take action to improve and maintain green spaces on disadvantaged estates.

5.94   The stronger emphasis on the commissioning role can help refocus the role of local government in relation to services, changing the dynamic from provider of local services, with a tendency to be defensive about service quality or responsiveness, to one of 'market-shaper', using stronger community advocacy and taking a strategic view of the needs of the community. This should bring the desired outcomes and impact of a service to the fore and mean that delivery mechanisms flow from this rather than simply building on historical arrangements. Rethinking of established service delivery and business process improvement can deliver both efficiencies and a more responsive service.

5.95   Councils have a role, as commissioners and as convenors, in developing local markets, creating an environment where the third sector and social enterprise can flourish and supporting local business growth. By using its purchasing power strategically, local government can achieve the double benefit of securing services that are relevant and sensitive to local needs and support their local economy thus bringing broader community benefits.

5.96   Work with the private sector can also bring new solutions to long-standing problems or challenges in service provision, involving them as real partners rather than merely as providers of services. For example, Staffordshire County Council's partnership with Accord is built on a 'one team' approach, rather than on a rigid definition of client and contractor roles. The focus on outcomes and a shared performance culture is improving efficiency, service quality and budget management. Staffordshire was ranked in the top ten of highways authorities for achieving efficiency gains in 2005–06 and consistently ranks at the top of national league tables in reducing serious road casualties. These partnerships can enable councils to explore better forms of cooperation that enable big complex changes to be made which are driven by local interests and ambitions, rather than the demands of central government.

5.97   There are many examples in local government of where this type of innovative commissioning is taking place, but I believe that there is far greater potential that has still be realised across the sector as a whole. I believe that the principal barrier to this happening is the behaviours and attitudes of local government. It is still too often the case that historic patterns of delivery go unchallenged and opportunities to fundamentally reshape the approach to delivering services are missed. Skills are a factor here and there needs to be greater capacity within local government to lead and manage strategic approaches to commissioning. This may involve actively working to shape and manage the market, as well as the development of effective procurement arrangements that avoid overly elaborate or lengthy bidding processes.[35]

> **Recommendation 5.17**
>
> Local government needs to develop its capacity to commission innovative service solutions, to develop markets for services and to think more creatively about delivery options.

Partnership and cross-boundary working

5.98   Improving efficiency at a local level should not preclude partnership and cross boundary working. Large-scale partnership working and collaboration across administrative boundaries can make services less local and reduce flexibility. However, most supply markets are not local in character and increasingly local government is recognising this in its approach to procurement. Rather than trying to manage the market for goods and services in a very localised way, many councils now purchase goods and services through collaborative links and working with the Regional Centres of Excellence (RCEs) funded by CLG and the Office of Government Commerce. This enables councils to benefit from the economies of scale and lower overall transaction costs that can come from aggregated purchasing.[36] Councils' work to develop shared services should also focus strongly on service integration at the local level. The White Paper's support for RCEs and proposals to further develop support for effective procurement are welcomed.

---

[35] CLG, *Developing the Local Government Services Market to Support the Long-term Strategy for Local Government*, 2007.

[36] For example, the Better Services Better Systems programme was set up to examine the way the infrastructure for social care was delivered in Worcestershire County Council in order to improve the service to callers and to reduce the time spent on paperwork by social workers.

> **Recommendation 5.18**
>
> Local authorities should ensure that their overall approach to efficiency:
>
> - places a value on outcomes in terms of their value to the local community;
> - values the additional inputs generated though co-production;
> - allows them to consider where it may be appropriate simply to do less of a particular service or activity in balancing local priorities;
> - considers all options available including use of charging or other powers to reduce costs, raise revenues and change behaviour in the interest of the local community; and
> - considers where it may be possible to encourage market solutions to local needs and so reduce the pressures on the tax base.

Performing for the community

5.99   I have referred in Chapter 3 to the damaging effect of the upward focus of local government performance management, welcoming fewer targets as proposed by the White Paper. Chapter 4 also discussed how best to ensure the new performance framework and inspection regimes minimise burdens on local government and focus on the right questions. None of this should be taken to imply that local authorities should focus any less on performance. Indeed, I argued that the performance framework should encourage a focus on improvement by the authority itself, while also recognising the need to provide public assurance and make best use of external and peer support.

5.100   Local government needs decisively to take ownership of its own performance. Too often, the accountability for performance has run primarily between local government professionals and the central agencies inspecting or directing them, with councillors being insufficiently involved in monitoring and reporting more widely on performance. There is an opportunity under the new performance framework to follow the best of local government. Under the new model, outstanding service performance should be driven by outcomes which the public can understand and identify with. Internally, the whole organisation, managerially and politically, should be clearer about exactly how it is working for the good of the local community, whether it is achieving its aims and what more it needs to do to reach its own targets.

> **Recommendation 5.19**
>
> Local government should continue to focus on performance, using the reduction in central targets and inspection as an opportunity to:
>
> - re-orientate its performance management towards public accountability; and
> - work with other councils to support service improvement, through peer review, challenge and benchmarking.

CONCLUSION

5.101 My starting point was that local government must recognise its responsibility for changing the dynamic in its relationship with central government. In this chapter, I have tried to demonstrate that this is primarily about behaviours and attitudes rather than new powers or structures. In all the areas I have identified above, there are examples of excellent practice already within local government, so there are no fundamental barriers to making change happen. Nevertheless there is a great challenge in ensuring the energies and talents in all local authorities can be released to make the most of the potential of local government. Sharing good practice is a key aspect to achieving effective place-shaping.

Part III

Funding

6 Funding reform – an introduction

Summary

This chapter introduces a series of issues around reform of the local government funding system, and sets out my objectives for reform.

My recommendations on funding reform are guided by a series of broad objectives, in the context of the wider vision of place-shaping local government described in earlier chapters. Reform will often need to strike a balance between competing aims, and take account of tensions between different parts of the funding system.

Achieving a change in the balance of funding is not of itself a driving objective of this Inquiry. Recent changes to schools funding demonstrate that altering the headline balance of funding may have little impact on local authorities' freedom to set locally appropriate spending plans, and can in some circumstances reduce their ability to do so. Instead it is important to focus on the underlying causes of pressures on local budgets, and to ensure flexibility and accountability in both tax and spending at the local level.

Tax policy should have regard to a set of general principles for good taxation, and should consider the elements that contribute to a good local tax. Taxes on property (and land) have particular advantages as local sources of revenue.

There is however no 'golden key' to reform of local government funding. Reform will require a series of complementary measures, implemented over time, both to deal with the immediate challenges facing the funding system and to pave the way for wider choices in the future.

OBJECTIVES FOR REFORM

6.1   I have said that my overriding objective is to enable all local authorities to become strong, effective, place-shapers; confident in their role and direction, actively engaged with citizens and communities, and ready to contribute to our development as a prosperous, cohesive and fair society.

6.2   In that context, reform of the local government funding system should aim to do two things. Firstly, funding reform should complement my recommendations on changes to the role and function of local government. Secondly, it should address those aspects of the current funding system which may act as a barrier to local choice and effective place-shaping, including those elements which contribute to strained central-local relations, or undermine public trust in local government.

6.3   Funding reform has the potential to contribute to the empowerment and renewal of local government in England. However, it is also important to recognise the limitations of what can be achieved through reform of local government finance. No reform can alter the reality that local government (indeed all government) is about making tough choices, and dealing with competing demands on finite resources. As I set out in my May report, *National prosperity, local choice and civic engagement,* it is my strong view that many of those tough choices are best made locally, through engagement with local people to achieve the best possible fit between their ambitions for local services, what they are prepared to pay for through taxes and charges, and what they are prepared to do for themselves. Funding reform must underpin a world in which councillors can both engage the community in that conversation and respond to what they hear.

6.4   With those things in mind, my objectives for reform of local government funding are consistent with those for reform of local government as a whole. My work on the role and function of local authorities has convinced me of the importance of:

- greater local **flexibility** and choice;

- stronger national and local **accountability** based on clearer responsibilities; and

- better **incentives** for local government.

6.5   I am also clear that any reform of local government funding must, as a basic requirement, ensure that councils have access to the necessary funds to deliver against a sensible set of expectations and promises, and that they are able to spend them in a way which ensures the best value for money. To that end, I will be looking at reforms which promote:

- **efficiency** in local tax and spending; and

- better **management of pressures**.

6.6   Finally, funding reform must address the crucial issue of fairness, to ensure that the right balance is struck between the interests of different groups, and to underpin the future viability of the funding system.

6.7   I believe that by using these objectives to shape a package of reforms, we can ensure local government finance is sustainable not just in the immediate future but for the long term.

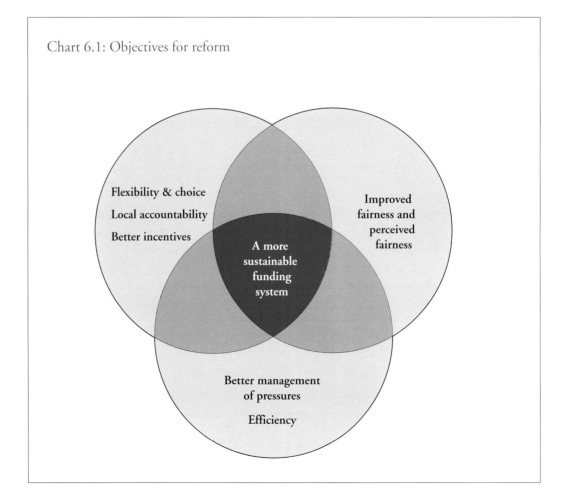

Chart 6.1: Objectives for reform

Flexibility & choice

Local accountability

Better incentives

A more sustainable funding system

Improved fairness and perceived fairness

Better management of pressures

Efficiency

6.8   As set out in Chapter 4, some of these objectives are best pursued not through reform of the tax system as a discrete entity, but through wider reform to create greater flexibility for local authorities to direct resources to local priorities, to tailor services, and in doing so, to manage the inevitable pressures on their finances. The recommendations in that chapter reflect the fact that for reform to deliver a sustainable funding system, it must consider expenditure as well as taxation.

6.9   This chapter and the ones that follow will focus on the revenue side of the equation, as follows:

- the rest of Chapter 6 will discuss some general principles on tax policy and local taxation in particular;

- Chapter 7 will discuss the elements of local revenues that come from direct taxes and charges on local residents and service users;

- Chapter 8 will consider the business contribution to local government finances; and

- Chapter 9 will look at the way central government uses national revenues to fund local government.

6.10   I have also considered the implications of my recommendations for the other parts of the United Kingdom. A discussion of the implications is provided in a separate section at the end of the report.

Tensions and trade-offs

6.11   It will be important, in arriving at a series of reforms, to consider how different objectives for reform may pull in different directions. The current funding system represents a particular balance between the objectives I outline above. I will explore where, in my view, a rebalancing is called for.

6.12   Important judgements include:

- what is the right balance of fairness between different groups of taxpayers?

- who do we want to target support (in the form of reliefs and benefits) towards?

- what is the right balance between taxpayer subsidy and user-charge?

- do we want a simple system for the sake of accountability, or a more complex one for the sake of fairness or local flexibility?

- how much equalisation between areas is appropriate, and how far would we be prepared to reduce it to improve the incentives acting on local government?

- which is preferable in local funding: buoyancy, or stability?

6.13   The recommendations that follow will aim to be clear about where I have taken a judgement on these issues, and where they remain open as political choices for government in future.

Reform and the balance of funding

6.14   The reform objectives outlined above do not take finance as their starting point, but rather they are informed by the kind of place-shaping local government that we want to see. For some, the list should also include an objective to change the balance of funding between central and local government, making local authorities more reliant on locally raised revenues and less dependent on funding from central grants.

> *In our view, the calibration of the balance of funding [is one] important factor for the strategic role of local government. A significant increase in the proportion of expenditure that is raised locally would assist in the revitalisation of local democracy and its strategic role.* (Chartered Instituted of Public Finance and Accountancy)

I have considered the arguments for this but have not included 'changing the balance of funding' as a separate objective for reform, for the reasons that follow.

6.15   The Balance of Funding Review argued in 2004 that the proportion of revenues raised locally was important for two reasons. Firstly, they considered that the centrally-weighted balance of funding at the time resulted in heavy dependence on central grant, which weakened local accountability. This picked up the argument advanced by Layfield in 1976 that "the first requirement of a financial system for local government is accountability: whoever is responsible for incurring expenditure should also be responsible for raising the necessary revenue."

6.16   Secondly, the Review argued for a shift towards local revenues to lessen the so-called 'gearing effect', which they explained as follows:

> *Local authorities' dependence on Government grant means that for every one per cent increase in spending they need, on average, to increase council by four per cent, a 'gearing ratio' of 4:1 ... Because of the gearing effect, comparatively small spending pressures can lead to some big increases in council tax for individual taxpayers.*[1]

6.17   I agree that accountability for local decisions, including decisions about tax, is an essential part of meaningful local government. Equally, it is important that the finance settlement does not put local authorities in a position where local choices about tax rates are continually overridden by external pressures. However I have some doubts about whether changing the balance of funding would, of itself, solve these problems.

Tax as a basis for local accountability   6.18   There is no consensus around the importance of local taxes for locally accountable government. For example, the report of Sir Peter Burt's independent Local Government Finance Review Committee in Scotland recently argued that accountability does not pertain only to taxation.

> *To us, the principal distinction between local government and local administration does not turn solely on the extent or otherwise of tax-raising powers. Accountability depends on how well the services delivered by the local authority meet the community's needs and the power that the authority has to prioritise and shape local services, as well as to deliver them.*[2]

6.19   The Scottish Executive itself is a good example of accountability that does not rest on tax-raising powers. While the Executive does have a limited power to vary the standard rate of income tax, as yet this has not been used. Instead the Executive's accountability attaches to its spending decisions and its legislative powers on devolved matters. Its autonomy from the UK Government is based not on fiscal independence, but in the constitutional settlement set out in the Scotland Act 1998.

6.20   The position of local authorities in England is rather different: they do raise taxes, and should rightly be accountable for them as well as for their spending decisions. As discussed in Chapter 3, accountability for council tax is highly confused, and the division of central and local

---

[1] *Balance of Funding Review – Report*, ODPM, 2005.
[2] Local Government Finance Review Committee, Scotland, *A Fairer Way*, 2006.

responsibility for the spending it supports is unclear. However, it is not obvious that a new or larger local revenue stream would of itself create greater independence from central government. Indeed, greater responsibility for painfully accountable revenue-raising, if it came without greater discretion about the services and outcomes being pursued, might be the worst of all worlds.

The impact of the 'gearing ratio'

6.21   Similarly, the 'gearing' problem may in fact be a secondary issue: a symptom of the limited scope councils have to manage spending pressures, rather than the root cause of those pressures. The New Local Government Network have suggested that in some circumstances, changes to the balance of funding or 'gearing ratio' (the proportion of the total budget that is raised locally) will not have the desired effect on either local accountability or local discretion over budget increases. For example, changes that notionally reduce the weight of central funding in the system will have little impact on gearing if local authorities are still restricted in their ability to prioritise and cannot exert a deciding influence over the level of budget increases.

> *The gearing ratio is a symptom of a deeper failing. It is the lack of local discretion and flexibility that must be removed.*[3]

6.22   I agree that finance reform should aim to tackle the underlying objective of greater local flexibility to deal with pressures, and that focusing on the gearing ratio itself might not achieve the right result. This view is informed by the fact that the ratio itself is susceptible to different definitions. Council tax represents a different proportion of total revenues depending on what classes of income are included, and importantly, recent changes to schools funding show clearly that altering the ratio may do very little to relieve pressures on council tax.

Schools ring-fencing and the new balance of funding

6.23   In the past, funding for education was provided to local authorities as part of their Revenue Support Grant (RSG). Over the years however it became increasingly earmarked for schools spending, and in 2006-07 was formally ring-fenced as Dedicated Schools Grant (DSG), allocated directly to authorities by the Department for Education and Skills, rather than through the Revenue Support Grant system run by the department for Communities and Local Government.

6.24   Since specific grants are traditionally omitted from the definition of local budgets used to assess the balance of funding, the removal of Dedicated Schools Grant appears, on the face of it, to radically alter the composition of local budgets. The balance of funding has, on the face of it, changed in local government's favour: council tax now provides around half of all local revenue, in theory reducing the gearing effect by half.

Table 2: Balance of funding before and after ring-fencing of Dedicated Schools Grant[4]

	2005-06 Pre-DSG £ billion (%)	2006-07 DSG removed £ billion (%)
Council tax	21.0 (32)	22.0 (51)
Business rates	18.0 (27)	17.5 (41)
Revenue Support Grant	26.7 (41)	3.5 (8)
Total	65.7	43.0

Source: Public Expenditure Statistical Analyses 2006, and Budget 2006.

6.25   Yet my discussions with local authorities do not suggest that this change in the gearing ratio has made pressures feel any lighter. Indeed, pressures may now be more acute, since local flexibility

---

[3] New Local Government Network, *Pacing Lyons: a route map to localism,* 2006.

[4] Balance of funding here defined as in the Balance of Funding Review 2004: council tax as against business rates and RSG.

over budgets has been further reduced by the introduction of a new ring-fence. It may be that the pressures which have driven council tax increases were not driven by schools spending anyway – that area has seen generous support from many local authorities and from central government, and its funding was heavily protected even before ring-fencing, and could not generally be diverted to other services.

6.26   I recognise that the Government's decision to ring-fence schools funding was not taken in isolation, but was the culmination of a longer process aimed at reflecting education's status as a national priority. Education funding was already being 'passported' directly to schools, reflecting ministers' concern that announcements of new funding for schools should feed through to them directly. Ring-fencing may have been the natural conclusion of that process. However it has undeniably reinforced a world in which local communities' flexibility to determine spending plans continues to be highly constrained.

6.27   The example of DSG ring-fencing shows that gearing is not, of itself, the cause of pressures on council tax; it is rather a symptom of, and a way of expressing the nature of that pressure in relation to council tax and the wider budget. Changing the wider budget without changing the pressure does not make any real-world difference to council taxpayers, who are still faced with the same percentage increase in their bills.

6.28   The key question for this Inquiry is therefore not "how can we alter the gearing ratio". Instead the primary concerns are: understanding where pressures come from; being clear where central government has some responsibility for them as well as local government; and asking what options are available locally for managing them. My recommendations will consider the impact of change not just on the headline balance of funding, but on the wider financial flexibility that councils need in order to be able to manage pressures and be accountable for the decisions they make about spending levels and tax rates.

The principles of good taxation

6.29   My objectives for reform are rooted in my analysis of what needs to change in order for local government to become more empowered and effective. Any tax change must of course also take into account the wider impact of tax policy on the UK's economic stability and competitiveness, and on the government's fiscal balances. These are primarily matters for central government, and beyond the scope of this Inquiry. However my recommendations will have regard to some other general principles on taxation, which should apply equally to local as to national taxes.

6.30   Broadly speaking, taxes can serve two purposes: raising revenue, and providing incentives to alter behaviour in line with policy objectives. The balance of these two purposes will differ between taxes. For example, duty on cigarettes or alcohol may have as a key objective reducing consumption of those goods, but will also represent a source of revenue, whereas the design of income tax systems will generally seek to raise revenue, while minimising the impact of the tax in terms of discouraging people from working.

6.31   Despite the significant changes to the structure of local taxes over the past twenty years, both council tax and business rates exist, in their present forms, primarily to raise revenue, and together support a large proportion of local authority spending. I have received a number of submissions arguing that other policy objectives might be integrated into these local taxes: for example, supporting environmental policy by offering homes and businesses a financial incentive to install energy-efficient features. I will consider some of these measures in the chapters that follow. However I am clear that my recommendations must leave local government with an adequate and sustainable revenue base, and that revenue generation is likely to remain the central purpose of the main local taxes. I will look at whether supplementary sources of revenue might be used to influence behaviour or create incentives to support wider policy.

6.32 Beyond this, recommendations on taxation will consider the impact of change in terms of:

- economic efficiency – avoiding unintended consequences, including those which impact unacceptably on the taxbase itself, minimising negative tax competition, and ensuring macroeconomic stability is not compromised;

- equity – so that taxpayers in similar circumstances pay similar amounts (horizontal equity) and differences in circumstances are reflected in tax liabilities (vertical equity); and

- administrative value for money – so that the compliance costs of paying or collecting a tax are not unacceptably onerous.

6.33 Of course, balancing these objectives requires political judgment: good taxation should follow these principles but tax setting will never be a wholly objective, value-neutral process. For example, deciding what sort of equity to aim for is a matter of judgement. Taxing on the basis of 'similar circumstances' might reflect income, wealth, property value, business turnover or other factors, and might be assessed in a single year or over time and between generations. In making my recommendations, I will aim to be clear about where they leave room for such political judgements (at national or local level) to be made by those elected to that responsibility.

What makes a good local tax?

6.34 Within these broad parameters it is also necessary to consider which taxes are particularly suited to local control. Submissions to the Inquiry have suggested a wide range of possible sources of supplementary revenue for local authorities, and it is beyond the scope of this report to do justice to them all in detail. In focusing my analysis on a few lead options, and weighing their suitability, I have been guided by some general criteria on what makes a sensible local tax.

Breadth and evenness of the tax base

6.35 If a local tax is to operate primarily as a revenue-raising tool, it may be desirable that the tax is broadly based, so that a large section of the local population are liable to pay. This provides less scope for individuals and businesses to avoid tax, and may help ensure that citizens' preferences about service provision are also informed by their willingness, as taxpayers, to meet the costs of services. It can also ensure that local authorities' revenue streams are less subject to cyclical or structural changes in society and the economy, creating more certainty about future revenues.

6.36 It may also be desirable that the taxbase is spread relatively evenly across the country, minimising the need for equalisation between areas. It is a matter for judgement how much variation is sustainable: for example taxbases for council tax are relatively variable between areas, but council tax does still provide substantial revenues for all local authorities.

Tackling local externalities

6.37 There is a strong case for local fiscal instruments where they can be targeted in ways that deal with locally-concentrated problems, especially those which are not apparent in the market cost or price paid (what economists term 'externalities'). This particularly applies to taxes that are aimed at changing behaviour. If the problems, or the actions necessary to solve them, are unlikely to respond to local taxation, then they should properly be targeted through other means. For example problems such as congestion might respond to local financial incentives. Others may require action on a wider scale; for example packaging of consumer goods, which may not be so susceptible to action at local authority level. In some circumstances, it might be appropriate that use of a local tax is concentrated in only some areas, for example, where it aims to change behaviour in particular groups, or to deal with an externality that is not present everywhere.

Avoiding distortions

6.38   Local taxation should operate in a way that minimises distortions, particularly where locally variable taxation might create unfair competition between different areas. Ideally, local taxes should be levied on taxbases which cannot migrate easily (property being a good example), and which avoid creating perverse incentives.

6.39   For example, sales taxes operate successfully at the local level in some countries, including in many cities in the United States. However, there is not a tradition of variable sales taxes at the level of English local authorities, and it would be reasonable to ask whether, at that spatial level, they might create some unwelcome effects, such as creating incentives for particular kinds of retail developments, or altering traffic patterns between areas with different tax rates.

6.40   In practice, the UK's existing tax on consumption of goods and services, Value Added Tax (VAT), is subject to a number of restrictions in European Union law and could not be legally adapted to allow for local variation. Any local sales tax would therefore need to operate alongside VAT, which introduces a range of wider questions about the appropriate balance of different taxes in the national economy and on particular goods and services, which is a matter for ministers. In light of these obstacles, I have not pursued local sales taxes as an option in this report.

Land and property taxation

6.41   In the chapters that follow I consider a number of different types of tax that could contribute to local government revenues. Two of the most important local taxes (council tax and business rates) are both forms of land and property taxation, and are examined more fully in Chapters 7 and 8. In order to set that discussion in context it is useful to summarise the benefits and drawbacks of these types of tax, based on the very wide literature on these issues.

Taxation of economic rent

6.42   Most economists would agree that there is a strong case for levying taxes on land. Land is in fairly fixed supply, and much of its value will therefore be what economists call 'economic rent', which can be taxed without altering the incentives to use the land.[5] The fact that much of the value of land is the result not of the actions of the owner, but the activity and investment of the wider community – for example, by providing transport connections, desirable schools or accessible markets – makes the case for such taxation even stronger. Taxing only the value of the land, not the use to which it is put, or the buildings and other improvements constructed on it, could also ensure that there is no distortion created by the tax system between the types of activity that might be undertaken on the land.

6.43   Land value taxes have been proposed on a number of occasions in the past, perhaps most notably in the Budget of 1909, because of these advantages. A number of groups, from the Land Value Taxation Campaign to the British Retail Consortium, supported the idea of a land value tax in their submissions to the Inquiry. For example, the BRC argued that:

> *Land Value Tax (LVT) has a number of advantages. These include not distorting behaviour in the same way as taxes on income and profits do, LVT's potential effectiveness in incentivising the efficient use of land (as all land would incur a charge even when it was not being used for productive activity) and taxing land values could also enable local governments to profit from some of the increase in value as a result of a prosperous local economy.*

---

[5] Economic rent is a complex economic concept and definitions vary. Broadly speaking it means the difference between the return made by a factor of production (i.e. land, labour or capital) and the return necessary to keep the factor in its current occupation.

Taxing property to widen the tax base

6.44   There are also some arguments in favour of taxing the property built on the land, as well as its basic value as land. In general, taxes should be applied to as broad a base as possible in order to reduce the tax rate needed, and thus the potential distortions created. Taxing the value of improvements as well as land values can help to expand the size of the property tax base, and a number of land value taxes used around the world actually levy a tax on improvements for this reason.[6] On the negative side, however, the taxation of the value of property as well as the land value could distort activity by discouraging investment in development and improvements.

Economic stabilisation

6.45   Well-designed taxes on the use of land and property can in theory contribute to the stability of the property market, and thus to the stability of the economy overall. With a flat rate tax on up-to-date property values, tax bills would tend to increase during periods of growth, and fall during downturns. In an upturn, the cost of consuming a particular amount of property would therefore tend to increase, reducing demand for it, and motivating property owners to make full use of their property (for example by renting out a room). In a downturn, the opposite would occur, helping to soften the impact, and these effects should reduce the magnitude of changes in property prices.[7]

Reducing other taxes

6.46   Raising tax revenues through land and property taxes has the additional advantage that it could allow for reduced taxes on profits and incomes, thus reducing the disincentive to effort and success that such taxes can create.

Administrative advantages

6.47   There are also a number of advantages to land and property taxes from an administrative perspective, related to the fact that land and property are in the main immobile, and relatively straightforward to identify for taxation purposes. As a result, they are difficult to avoid and cost-effective to collect because those liable to tax cannot move their property elsewhere to avoid taxation, or hide their property to evade taxation. Indeed, some tax experts argue that the ability of large multinational companies to reduce their liability to taxation on their profits by moving profits between different countries will make property taxes increasingly important in the future because they are less easy to avoid.

6.48   A further advantage cited is that the yield from property taxes is predictable and stable, due to the fact that the tax base can be measured reasonably easily and is unlikely to change rapidly from year to year. This is particularly true of council tax in its current form; other property taxes, particularly if they reflect changes in actual property values, might fluctuate more.

Advantages as local taxes

6.49   Land and property taxes are used around the world as local taxes, and there are a number of reasons for this. The relative simplicity of assessment and collection and the difficulty of evasion, mentioned above, are all important. In addition, taxing property locally has the advantage that it can provide a strong connection between the tax people pay and their residence in an area. Taxes on property value reflect residents' (and owners') financial stake in a community and its prosperity, and their interest in local services and investment, which themselves impact on the desirability of property in a given area.

6.50   There can be tensions between the different possible purposes of land and property taxes. For example, the regular revaluations needed if the tax is to remain up-to-date may make bills and revenues less predictable for taxpayers and tax authorities, and create administrative costs, and the variable rates of tax needed to fund local authorities' different spending choices could be in conflict with the consistent rate of tax desirable to perform a market stabilisation function. These tensions need to be borne in mind when considering reforms.

[6] NERA Economic Consulting, *Options for Reforming Local Government Funding,* Lyons Inquiry, 2005.
[7] Muellbauer, J., *Property, Land and Taxation after the Barker Review,* 2004.

FRAMING A PACKAGE OF REFORM

6.51   As set out in Chapter 3 there is, I believe, a strong and growing case that change is necessary. The 'no change' option is itself a painful one: the pressure on local services, on council tax as the only local tax, and hence on council tax payers, will not disappear and may indeed sharpen in some areas as growth in total public spending slows down in the coming years. I believe there is enough evidence to justify action to make the finance system more sustainable into the future.

6.52   However, although it is true that the status quo is problematic, it is very clear that there are no easy options for change, and no simple 'golden key' that will unlock the problems of the funding system. Taking the pressure off council tax, or reducing the burden on a group of taxpayers, implies a cost to some other group or part of the system. If less tax is collected locally, then either services must be cut back, or other taxpayers must contribute more, either through local or national taxation. Any change in taxation creates 'winners' and 'losers', with those who pay more tending to react much more strongly to change than those who benefit. Deciding whether any change is acceptable is therefore a highly political decision.

6.53   Efficiency will always have a part to play in getting the balance of tax and spending right, and I wholeheartedly endorse the push for greater efficiency and value for money in local spending. However, it is not clear that efficiency gains alone can absorb the pressures on local government in the medium term, or at least not without some cuts to services which may run counter to local preferences. The question, then, is what wider structural changes to the finance system may be necessary.

6.54   My central proposition is that a mosaic of changes, implemented over time, is the best way to move forward. My work has convinced me that no single change could of itself deliver a sustainable finance system. And, given the tensions I outline above, a package of complementary measures will be crucial if we are to balance the impact of change on different groups in an acceptable way.

6.55   Equally, I believe that a developmental approach to reform is the right way to proceed. While a 'big bang' reform has been urged by some, I think that this would be unacceptably disruptive, and unlikely to find the public support which would be critical in order to create space for ministers to successfully pursue reforms. In that context, the difficulty of agreeing a single package might lead to those reforms which could otherwise be made quickly being delayed.

6.56   In the following chapters I will examine a range of options for reform of the local government finance system. In doing so I will outline the changes that I think should be implemented in the short term to address the most urgent problems in the system, but also with a view to paving the way for greater ambition in future. Chapter 10 will draw together my recommendations to show how a developmental model might allow for reform to be taken forward over time.

7 Household taxation and local charges

Summary

This chapter assesses the merits of different forms of household taxation and charging, and the role that they should play in local government finance in England. It argues that council tax is not 'broken', and should be retained as a local tax either on its own, or alongside other local taxes. However, improvements to council tax benefit are crucial in the short-term, to improve the perceived fairness and sustainability of council tax. This should happen alongside measures to increase local flexibility over spending described in Chapter 4, to help take the pressure off council tax.

There also remain a number of options, including a local income tax and assignment of national taxation, which could be used to supplement, or fully or partially replace council tax, and thus further help to reduce the pressure on it over time. While these are not likely to be realistic options for the immediate term, they have a number of advantages and remain possibilities for the future.

In detail, the chapter argues that:

Council tax remains a broadly sound tax, though it has become overloaded within the present system. In the short term, action is needed to both improve the perceived fairness of council tax by improving the take-up and design of council tax benefit, and to take the pressure off council tax through greater local flexibility over spending.

'Fairness' means different things to different people; however the most common concerns about the perceived unfairness of council tax relate to 'ability to pay', or income, particularly with regard to older people. Other important dimensions of 'fairness' in this context include the link between tax and property value, and the perceived benefits of local services to taxpayers.

There are limits on the extent to which reform of the council tax bands can make it less regressive to income. Nonetheless, there are advantages to revaluation and reform of council tax to make it a better property tax. Revaluation of properties is an important part of maintaining a viable and up-to-date local tax base, and should go ahead in the medium term. At that point the Government should create new bands at the top and bottom of the existing structure.

Council tax benefit (CTB) has the potential to significantly reduce the burden of council tax on the poorest households, In practice, however, up to £1.8 billion in CTB entitlement was left unclaimed in 2004-05, much of it by older people.

Since the primary purpose of CTB is to adjust households' liability for council tax, it should be renamed 'council tax rebate'. Moreover, the Government should urgently pursue measures to simplify the claims process, as well as more ambitious work towards automated, proactive delivery of entitlements to taxpayers, with a view to achieving a step-change in take-up.

Some pensioner households pay a relatively high proportion of their income in council tax but are not eligible for CTB. The government should increase the upper savings limit for pensioner households, and eventually abolish it, in line with savings thresholds for Pension Credits. These reforms would address some of the main problems with council tax. Other problems, such as its lack of buoyancy, would require more fundamental changes.

Local income taxes were discussed in many submissions to the Inquiry, and are a possible option for inclusion in the local government finance system in the future.

Local income taxes are more progressive than council tax (even with full take-up of CTB) and popularly seen as fair, but some people may underestimate the amount they would pay under a local income tax compared with council tax. A local income tax would be naturally buoyant in that revenues would rise in line with earnings growth, but it would still be crucial to manage the pressures placed on local taxes if rate increases were to be avoided.

It would be feasible to implement a local income tax in England, but further detailed work would be needed to resolve complex questions around its precise design and operation. It is likely that the process of implementing a local income tax would take approximately six to seven years from the point at which the government decided to work towards it. There are some similarities with assignment of national taxation to local government, which I discuss in Chapter 9.

Charges for services are already a significant source of revenue for local authorities. New flexibilities to charge and trade were introduced for some authorities in 2003, but appear not yet to have been widely used. Local authorities need to develop confidence in taking a strategic approach to charging and trading, and should seek to engage their communities in a wider debate about the role for user charges in pursuing policy objectives and in meeting service costs, including as an alternative to council tax.

I do not at present see a case for a further extension of general charging powers, though the charging and trading powers in the 2003 Act should be made available to all local authorities.

There are significant emerging pressures on waste services as the UK aims to reduce its dependence on cheap landfill in the face of growing waste volumes. The Government should create powers for local authorities to charge for domestic waste collection, as a means by which incentives can be created to reduce household waste and manage costs, and to help ensure that the remaining costs may be shared in a way that is perceived as fair.

INTRODUCTION

7.1   Local residents are substantial contributors to local authority revenues, through council tax and through a range of fees and charges for local services. The financial dimension to local government's relationship with its citizens is crucial and, unsurprisingly, often fraught with tension. I will consider how the current system lends itself to supporting local choice and engagement whilst having regard to concerns about fairness in local taxation, and will make recommendations on:

- the role of domestic property taxes in local government finance, and the future of council tax and council tax benefit;

- the potential for a local income tax to be implemented in England; and

- the part played in the finance system by local service charges.

COUNCIL TAX

A hybrid property tax and service charge

7.2   Since its inception in 1993, council tax has been the only locally levied tax on households in England, and the only tax whose rate is decided by local authorities. With a total yield of over

£22 billion in 2006-07, council tax makes a significant contribution to the funding of local public services: chart 7.1 below shows that on average, around 16 per cent of local authorities' total budgets are funded from council tax. While council tax payers also contribute to the costs of local services through other taxes, redistributed as grant by central government, survey evidence shows that council tax is particularly well known, with public awareness of the tax at 99 per cent.[1]

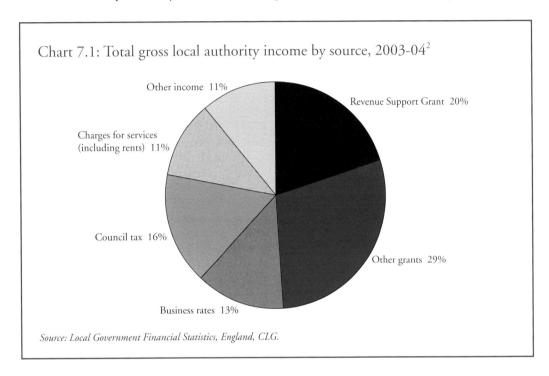

Chart 7.1: Total gross local authority income by source, 2003-04[2]

Other income 11%

Charges for services (including rents) 11%

Council tax 16%

Business rates 13%

Revenue Support Grant 20%

Other grants 29%

Source: Local Government Financial Statistics, England, CLG.

7.3   This chart represents gross local authority income, making it possible to take into account charges for services (other definitions often show revenue and expenditure net of this income). However, it should be noted that the latest available data on this definition relates to 2003-04 and so does not take into account the changes to schools funding. A similar chart for 2006-07 would be expected to show a larger proportion of income from "other grants", including Dedicated Schools Grant, and a smaller proportion from the unhypothecated Revenue Support Grant.

[1] BMG Research, *Lyons Inquiry survey,* 2007

[2] Chart 7.1 shows gross local authority income as published in *Local Government Finance Statistics no.16,* 2005 (latest published data). Previous discussion on local government funding, for example the Balance of Funding Review, have focused on local authority revenue income, and more frequently refer to the 'balance of funding' in terms of revenue expenditure, which includes Revenue Support Grant, business rates and council tax. Under this definition, council tax provides around 25 per cent of net revenue expenditure.

Council Tax

Council tax was introduced in England, Wales and Scotland in 1993. It replaced the community charge (commonly known as the poll tax), which had in turn replaced domestic rates in 1990.

Residential properties were assigned to one of eight council tax bands, from A to H, according to their assessed capital value in 1991. Properties built since 1993 are assigned an estimated value at 1991 prices to put them in a council tax band.

Billing authorities decide each year on the level at which band D bills will be set in their area, with bills for all other bands then charged at a fixed proportion of the Band D amount.

Average council tax in 2006-07

A	B	C	band D	E	F	G	H
£846	£987	£1,128	£1,268	£1,551	£1,833	£2,115	£2,538
or							
£16.27 per week	£18.98 per week	£21.69 per week	£24.38 per week	£29.83 per week	£35.25 per week	£40.67 per week	£48.81 per week

Because more properties are in the lower bands than the higher ones, the average bill per dwelling is lower than the band D average, at £1,056.

Where there is more than one local authority in an area, one of them acts as the billing authority for council tax (for example, District Councils in two-tier county areas) and is responsible for tax collection, though the council tax revenues are shared between those authorities.

All residential properties are liable for council tax, but some discounts and exemptions apply, including:

- a 25 per cent discount for households with only one liable resident;

- exemptions for certain classes of unoccupied dwelling; and

- exemptions for certain groups of people including students.

Full details on council tax in England, including discounts and exemptions, can be found at www.communities.gov.uk, and on local authority websites.

7.4   Council tax is an unusual hybrid: both a property-based tax, and a charge on local service users. An individual household's bills do not perfectly reflect the value of their home, but neither do they pay a flat charge for services. Households with only one liable resident receive a 25 per cent discount on their bill, partly reflecting the expectation that they will have lower service needs.

7.5   Council tax benefit (CTB) was designed as part of the council tax system to protect those on low incomes. In effect, it means that for eligible households on low incomes, council tax also acts as a hybrid property and income tax, as changes in earnings alter benefit entitlement. I will discuss this point in more detail later in this chapter. The idea of offering income-related reliefs against property tax is not new and the Layfield Commission noted in 1976 that the rebates used to adjust the property tax liability of the poorest under the old domestic rates were "a necessary feature of rating".[3]

7.6   As a hybrid of this kind, council tax is unique among local taxes. There is nothing inevitable about the design of council tax – in fact it is in many ways a very pragmatic compromise between a property tax and a service charge. In considering whether council tax should be reformed, I have looked at whether this particular hybrid remains the right model for England's main local tax, and compared the advantages and disadvantages of a range of alternatives.

[3] HMSO, *Local Government Finance: Report of the Committee of Inquiry*, 1976.

The problem with council tax

7.7   When I was first asked to conduct this Inquiry, my remit was clearly focused on local government funding and, in particular, building on the findings of the Balance of Funding Review and preparing for a revaluation of all residential properties.[4] Also at that time, in 2004, England had just been through a round of particularly steep average increases in council tax, and the Government would soon resume use of 'capping' powers to restrict the rate of increase in bills. My remit therefore has its origins in a period of increasing sensitivity about council tax: its overall size, the rate at which it was increasing, and its sustainability into the future.

7.8   I suggested in Chapter 6 that property taxes have a number of things to recommend them. Since council tax incorporates a property tax element, it shares many of these advantages. It is relatively easy to collect and difficult to evade; collection rates have risen steadily to their 2005-06 levels of nearly 97 per cent. Since properties do not move, tax bases are stable and revenues relatively predictable, allowing local authorities a degree of certainty in their financial planning. Property taxes are widely used around the world as a source of finance for local government, reflecting the crucial link between residents of an area and the services that are provided there.

7.9   These factors lead me to the view that council tax remains broadly sound, and should be retained as a local tax. It does however have some important shortcomings, some of which can be mitigated through reform in the short term, and others which may require more radical or longer-term reforms.

7.10   Concerns about council tax have several dimensions, all of which are exacerbated by the highly visible nature of the tax. A solution to "the council tax problem" must address:

- the perceived fairness of the way council tax distributes the tax burden, particularly in relation to people on low and fixed incomes, and especially older people;

- the burden of expectation and spending pressures that have been placed on council tax, with consequences for the rate of increase in bills; and

- concerns about the continued reliance on a single local tax which is not naturally buoyant.

7.11   Not all of these problems will respond to reforms which look at local tax in isolation. Tax reform alone will fail to take the pressure off local budgets unless it is accompanied with reform of the spending side of the equation. Chapter 4 set out recommendations to introduce greater local flexibility to manage pressures, by ensuring that resources can follow priorities in the most efficient way possible.

7.12   The chapters that follow focus on the options for reform of local government's revenues. In the short term, the fairness and sustainability of council tax could be improved through reform of council tax and council tax benefit. There are, however, underlying concerns about the lack of natural buoyancy and whether popular support for council tax can be improved adequately through these and other short-term reforms. In the longer term, therefore, there are a number of possible options, including a local income tax, which could be used to supplement, or fully or partially replace council tax, and thus further help to reduce the pressure on it over time.

7.13   This chapter considers the options for reform of local taxes and charges on households. Chapter 9 will go on to consider wider options for central government's funding of local services, including through assigned national taxes.

---

[4] ODPM, *Balance of Funding Review – Report*, 2004.

Fairness and property taxes

7.14   I suggested in Chapter 6 that there is a strong economic case for retaining a local property tax in some form. Council tax has some great advantages, not least that it is a predictable source of revenue for local authorities, with high and rising collection rates.

7.15   Nonetheless, during the course of my Inquiry I have been struck by the strength of feeling that residential property taxes provoke. My research found real resistance to the idea that tax bills should reflect property values, and to the idea that they should rise when property values rise, as shown in chart 7.2 below. When homeowners benefit from growth in the equity in their property, it appears that this is often seen as a 'reward' for their diligence as investors, rather than the product of housing market conditions, including constraints on the supply of new housing.[5] This is often expressed in the idea that 'an Englishman's home is his castle' and as such, treating it as a taxable asset is something of an affront to privacy – though this phenonomenon is by no means confined to England; property taxes have also been controversial in other countries at various times.

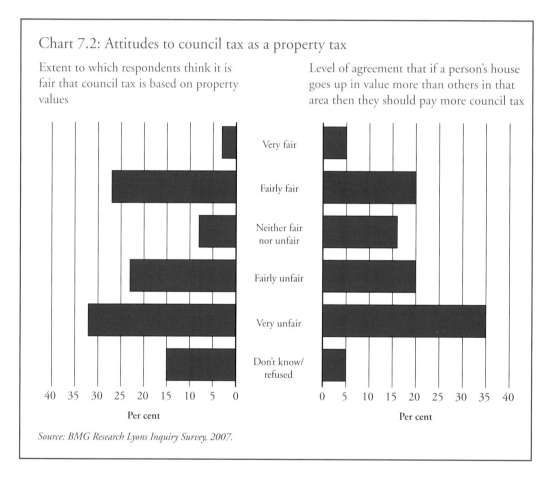

Chart 7.2: Attitudes to council tax as a property tax

Extent to which respondents think it is fair that council tax is based on property values

Level of agreement that if a person's house goes up in value more than others in that area then they should pay more council tax

Source: BMG Research Lyons Inquiry Survey, 2007.

7.16   Concerns about fairness most commonly centre on the relationship between property taxes and ability to pay, generally measured in terms of household income. In this context there is particular concern about the impact of property taxes on those households who are asset-rich but income-poor, and may find it difficult to pay a tax based on the value of their home rather than their income. I will go on to look in some detail at the relationship between property value and income, and the impact of different reform options on 'fairness' in terms of progressiveness to income.

---

[5] For detailed discussion of housing supply, see Barker Review of Housing Supply *Delivering Stability: securing our future housing needs* 2004.

7.17   However, income is not the only measure of fairness. Arguably, fairness in relation to income could in fact be the wrong question to ask of a property tax, since some property taxes by nature aim to tax the consumption or return on property. Taxes should therefore reflect the value of the good – in this case property – rather than the overall income of those consuming it. Fairness in these terms would mean that those in the most valuable properties would pay the most tax, and vice versa. It is worth remembering that the community charge was unpopular not just because it was regressive to income, but also because it did not reflect the type or value of home being occupied – one MP observing in 1989 that "under the poll tax two pensioners living in a flat will be paying more than a millionaire living in a mansion".[6]

7.18   In assessing the scope for reform of council tax it is therefore worth considering both these dimensions of fairness. Reform might be used to achieve greater progressiveness to income, or to property value, or a combination of both.

Property taxes and household income

7.19   I will return to the question of income taxes later in this chapter, but first want to consider the extent to which it is possible or desirable for property-based taxes to be designed to be progressive (or avoid being regressive) in relation to income.

7.20   Chart 7.3 overleaf shows that council tax, as it is designed at the moment, is regressive to income before council tax benefit is applied. That is, in terms of the pure structure of the tax itself, the highest-income households are liable to pay the lowest proportion of their income in tax, while lower-income households are liable to pay greater proportions of their total income in tax before CTB.

7.21   Once eligibility for council tax benefit is taken into account, council tax liability appears to be a relatively constant proportion of people's incomes throughout the income distribution, becoming relatively progressive to income for those on the lowest incomes, and regressive only in the top three income deciles. However, the current system of CTB does not achieve this result in practice – something I will discuss later in this chapter.

---

[6] Hansard, 19 January 1989.

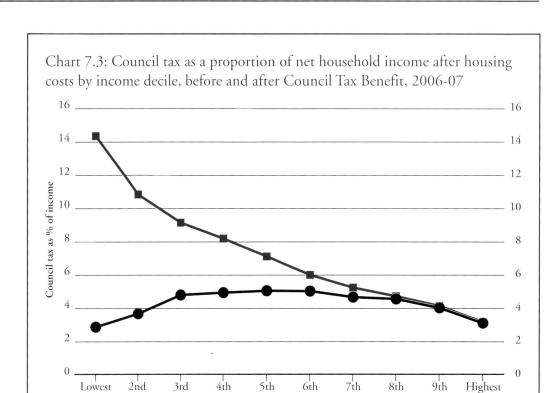

Chart 7.3: Council tax as a proportion of net household income after housing costs by income decile, before and after Council Tax Benefit, 2006-07

Source: Lyons Inquiry analysis.

7.22   In December 2005 I published some analysis of options for redesigning the council tax band structure alongside revaluation of properties. This included options such as regional bands, and adding extra bands at the top and bottom of the present band structure, which had been suggested in a number of submissions to the Inquiry. There was a strong view in many submissions that council tax should be made fairer in relation to ability to pay; I was therefore particularly interested in the impact of these sorts of changes on households in terms of the tax burden relative to their income.

7.23   The results of that analysis, as I said in my Interim Report, were somewhat surprising.[7] As shown in Chart 7.4 overleaf, this demonstrates that even options which significantly improved the link between property value and tax paid (such as adding extra bands at either end of the scale) did not have a significant impact on the overall relationship between council tax bills and household income. It remained the case that those on the lowest incomes paid the greatest proportion of their incomes in tax (before CTB) and vice versa. This regressiveness was not noticeably altered by any of the reform options examined (either before or after CTB).

7.24   I concluded that this unexpected result reflects the fact that people living in houses within a specific band tend to have widely different income levels, so changes to bands do not have a clear impact on the overall progressiveness of council tax to income. The options modelled, though not of course exhaustive, point towards the conclusion that structural change to council tax as a property tax will have very limited success in delivering greater 'fairness' to income.

[7] Lyons Inquiry into Local Government, *Consultation Paper and Interim Report*, 2005.

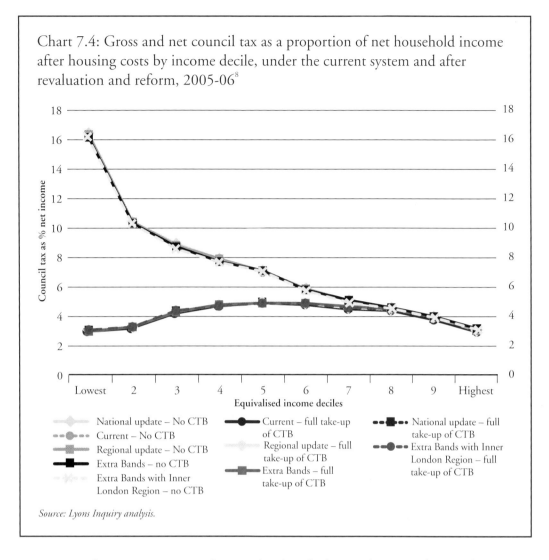

Chart 7.4: Gross and net council tax as a proportion of net household income after housing costs by income decile, under the current system and after revaluation and reform, 2005-06[8]

Source: Lyons Inquiry analysis.

7.25   Since the Interim Report I have undertaken further work to test that conclusion. For example, some commentators have argued that perhaps more radical reform options would have greater success in making council tax 'fairer'.[9] I have therefore looked closely at the relationship between property values and income in England, and some key trends emerge.

7.26   Chart 7.5 overleaf shows the range of values of properties occupied by households in each income group. This demonstrates a positive and statistically significant correlation between income and property value.[10] However, there is also substantial overlap in the value of property occupied by all but the top income decile.

---

[8] This chart shows a slightly higher average proportion of income paid in council tax in the lowest income group compared with other similar charts in this chapter (approximately 16 per cent compared to approximately 14 per cent in charts 7.3, 7.9 and 7.14). This reflects methodological changes in the treatment of outlying values in the modelling.

[9] I am grateful to the New Policy Institute and the Local Government Information Unit for their valuable challenges on this point, and their help in examining the scope for council tax reform.

[10] English Household Condition Survey data gives an overall correlation between income and property value of 0.4.

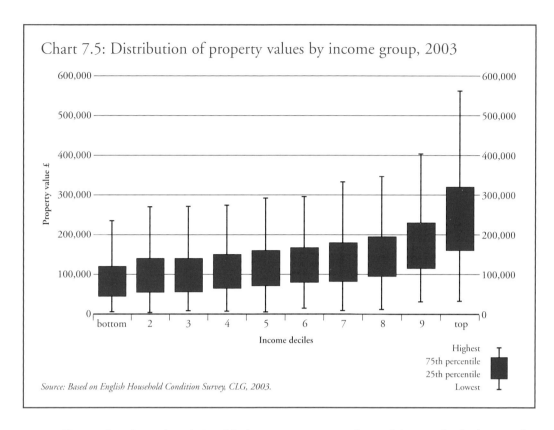

Chart 7.5: Distribution of property values by income group, 2003

Source: Based on English Household Condition Survey, CLG, 2003.

7.27   Chart 7.6 explores the relationship between property value and income by looking at the range of income groups in each council tax band, based on work by Michael Orton for the Joseph Rowntree Foundation.[11] This further demonstrates that the correlation between income and value is strongest at the top end of the scale, with nearly all band H households having high or above average incomes. Low and modest-income households are generally concentrated in the lower bands. However all bands also contain significant numbers of households with above average incomes, weakening the overall correlation between income and property band. A small but significant minority of low-income households are in bands F, G and H, of which over half are pensioner households.

7.28   Orton rightly points out, however, that these asset-rich, income-poor households are a minority in the population overall. The total numbers of households in the top bands are relatively small: over 80 per cent of all households in England are in bands A to D, including over 90 per cent of all low-income households. Nonetheless the mix of income groups in each band suggests that the burden of council tax in relation to income will vary widely between households.

---

[11] Orton, M *Struggling to pay council tax: new perspectives on the local taxation debate* Joseph Rowntree Foundation, 2006.

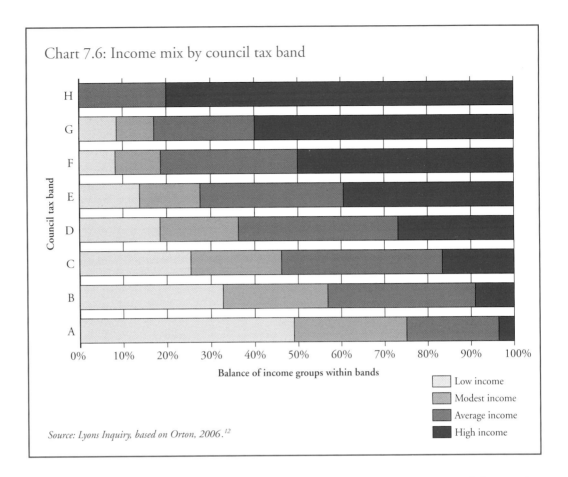

Chart 7.6: Income mix by council tax band

Council tax band (vertical axis): H, G, F, E, D, C, B, A

Balance of income groups within bands (horizontal axis): 0% to 100%

Legend:
- Low income
- Modest income
- Average income
- High income

Source: Lyons Inquiry, based on Orton, 2006.[12]

7.29   The evidence indicates that the nature of property markets in this country, and the complex factors influencing people's choice of home mean that there is not a simple relationship between a household's income and the value of their home, beyond the trends outlined above. I therefore remain of the view that while changes to the design of council tax can have some impact on its overall progressiveness, it is likely that a property tax will remain regressive to income overall, before council tax benefit is applied.

7.30   This is not to say that I consider property taxes to be inherently 'unfair', or that I see no point in reforming council tax. While the reforms I have examined do not produce the kind of income-related "fairness" that many hoped would emerge, they may still have advantages in terms of improving the link between council tax and property value, and may in some circumstances reduce, though not eliminate, the regressiveness to income of council tax as a property tax.

Options for reform of council tax

7.31   I have suggested that council tax should be retained, but that there may be a case for reforms of the tax aimed at improving its perceived fairness. In the short term, the key problems for council tax fairness relate to its impact on those with low incomes. Given the weak overall correlation between income and property value, it is likely that the main solution to this lies outside the design of council tax itself, in council tax benefit.

---

[12] Data from the Family Resources Survey. Income groups defined as: low Income – less than 60 per cent of median income; modest income – between 60 per cent of median income and median; above average – between median and twice median income; high income – more than twice median income.

7.32   However, it is within the scope of this Inquiry to consider not just how to resolve those immediate issues, but to look at how to make council tax a sensible and sustainable tax in the future. Solving its short term problems may create the space for a wider look at council tax in the medium term, and I consider elsewhere options for other local taxes and for assignment of national taxation which could play a role in the future.

7.33   This section summarises the options examined for reform of council tax as a property tax. It includes options examined in my Interim Report in 2005, as well as further analysis conducted since then.

Reforming the council tax bands at revaluation

7.34   I first looked at the options for council tax reform in the context of a planned revaluation exercise. Revaluation of properties presents an opportunity for reform by redefining the council tax bands, and then allocating properties to bands based on their current values. In my Interim Report, I published the results of modelling on a range of options of this kind.

Extra bands at top and bottom   7.35   Council tax bills are bounded by the current banding structure, which sets an effective floor and ceiling on the amount a household will pay, before benefits. Adding one or more extra bands at the top and bottom of the band structure would move that floor and ceiling, and widen the variance in bills.

7.36   This has the advantage of focusing reform on the very top of the band structure, where the correlation between property value and income is strongest, and on the bottom band, where many of the poorest households are concentrated. So while adding extra bands might not dramatically alter the overall link between tax bills and income, it would reduce council tax (before CTB) for many of the poorest while ensuring that the increased bills for the new higher bands are largely targeted at those with above-average or high incomes.

7.37   I have assumed that a reform of this nature would be revenue-neutral, so that the same amount of council tax (gross of CTB) is raised overall, but with the tax burden distributed differently between households. The bills for some taxpayers would therefore be increased, allowing others to pay less. The effect on individual households is complicated somewhat by CTB. Significant numbers of households who would, in principle, enjoy lower bills might not feel a change in practice since their bills are already paid wholly or partially by CTB. In that case, some of the benefit from a reduction in bills would accrue to the Government, rather than to the taxpayer, through a reduction in the costs of paying CTB to those households. Adding extra bands at revaluation would be expected to reduce total CTB costs, assuming full take-up, by approximately £130 million.

7.38   Since not all entitlement for CTB is taken up, in practice the savings to the Government would be less than this gross figure, and the savings to households slightly greater.[13] None the less, if the Government so chose, it could use any savings to pay for measures to help those still paying a large proportion of their income in council tax, for example through changes to the eligibility criteria for CTB.

---

[13] The statistical model used by the Inquiry is not adapted to forecast actual take-up levels after policy change. Broadly speaking however, if take-up of CTB entitlements remained at around 65-71 per cent (on an expenditure basis), cashable savings after reform might be around the same percentage of the gross figure given above.

Regional bands 7.39   The modelling around revaluation did however expose that the impact of such reforms would vary around the country. In particular, revaluation would be likely to generate significant, 'turbulence', with around half of all households changing band under the Extra Bands option (and about 36 per cent even under revaluation without reform). Properties in London and the southern regions, where house prices had, on average, risen the fastest since 1991, were most likely to move up at least one band.

7.40   In response to this I considered whether there might be lower turbulence if different band margins were applied to the nine English regions, reflecting different average property values around the country. This option had been suggested to the Balance of Funding Inquiry, and was modelled to consider the case for a sub-national banding scheme.

7.41   In fact, about as many properties changed bands under the regional option as under the national one. Furthermore, the regional option created a number of sub-regional 'hotspots' where property values had grown faster than average for the region, meaning that a large proportion of homes would be likely to move up one or more bands. It therefore appears that regional bands would not be an attractive option under the current distribution of house prices.

Separate bands for Inner London 7.42   A further variant of this approach would be to operate a distinct set of regional bands for Inner London, where properties were most likely to move up the bands under national and regional reform options. The number of Inner London households moving up at least one band was more than halved by the introduction of special bands for Inner London, without creating significant impacts on band movements in the rest of the country. The Government should consider introducing special bands for Inner London at the next revaluation, to reflect the unique circumstances of the Inner London property market relative to the rest of the country and to reduce the turbulence associated with revaluation there.

Limited upward band movement 7.43   Under the different options modelled, up to 11 million households would have been expected to move to a different council tax band (around half of all households in England). The majority of these would have moved by only one council tax band, with a minority of up to 400,000 households (two per cent of the total) expected to move up two or more bands, and a similar number moving down two or more bands. Given that most of the benefits of revaluation, in terms of a more up-to-date property tax base, can be achieved by properties moving only one band in either direction, there may be a case for limiting upward band movements to avoid sharp increases in individual households' bills. The Inquiry modelled an option in which properties' upward movement was limited to only one band, which would have resulted in approximately 370,000 households (two per cent of all properties) being held down one or more bands. The Government could consider implementing a limitation of this kind at the time of any revaluation.

The case for revaluation

7.44   The Government decided in 2005 to postpone revaluation of properties for council tax, for at least the life of this Parliament. While I understand the Government's reasons for postponing the revaluation exercise, it is my view that there are advantages to revaluing the property base that have not been adequately explained so far. It is also worth noting that postponement itself created 'winners' and 'losers' – 3.7 million households (or 17 per cent of all households in England) that would have been moved down the bands by revaluation are arguably paying too much council tax, subsidising those who would be paying more because their properties had grown in value more quickly.[14]

---

[14] Lyons Inquiry into Local Government, *Consultation Paper and Interim Report*, 2005, figures refer to national update option.

7.45   Revaluation would have two significant benefits: it can help underpin the credibility of a property tax by maintaining a meaningful relationship between relative property values and bills; and it creates an opportunity to make structural changes to council tax of the kind outlined above and later in this section. It is a matter for the government whether they are sufficiently attracted by any reform options to look at revaluation as an opportunity for change. However it is clear that significant reform is impossible without updating the tax base.

7.46   As for credibility, evidence from elsewhere does show that it is possible to use very outdated valuations as a tax base. The domestic rates in England lasted from 1973 to 1990 without revaluation, and Northern Ireland's rates have been, until this year, based on a 1976 valuation exercise that used rental data from the 1960s.

7.47   However, other successful property taxes are based on frequent revaluations. For example, property taxes in Washington DC are based on market valuations updated for all properties on an annual basis. These taxes are different from council tax in that bills represent a certain percentage of values, so revaluation allows public authorities to capture any increases in property values (which can itself be contentious). Revaluation has also happened closer to home. While England's revaluation exercise has been postponed; the Welsh Assembly Government went ahead with revaluation in Wales, demonstrating that revaluation, while difficult, is possible without undermining the sustainability of council tax. Moving to more frequent revaluations would promote stronger public understanding of the importance of accurate valuations, and introduce greater clarity to the system.

7.48   Substantial work was done in preparation for a 2007 revaluation in England (based on 2005 values), including the development of new valuations software in the Valuation Office Agency (VOA). This technology provides the opportunity to undertake a revaluation exercise, should the Government choose to go ahead, more cost-effectively than was possible in the past with manual valuations. It is also likely that subsequent revaluations would become more cost-effective over time if such exercises were fairly regular, as each revaluation would improve the accuracy of information on which properties are valued. More regular revaluations could also reduce the need for, and cost of, transitional schemes to phase in changes in tax bills.

7.49   In making the judgement about whether and when to revalue, government must weigh the risks to council tax from a turbulent or painful revaluation, against the risks of allowing the tax base to fall further into disrepair. There is no doubt that a first revaluation, some distance from the original valuation exercise, would be a challenging exercise, and some form of transitional arrangements might well be appropriate to ensure that any significant changes in liability for individual households – for example upward movements of more than one band – can be implemented in stages.

7.50   Even so, it is my view that the Government has a responsibility for maintaining the foundations of such an important revenue stream, since an out of date tax base will mean that the credibility of council tax as a property tax will gradually be eroded. There is a real risk that failure to revalue only makes it more difficult ever to do so, whereas an expectation of regular revaluations (as is already the norm in business rates) would contribute to the long-term sustainability of a property tax.

Revaluation of properties for council tax

Some submissions to the Inquiry have raised concerns about what a revaluation exercise might mean in practice. There are some common misconceptions about how revaluation would take place, and what might happen to the tax paid by people living in properties that have increased in value.

Assessment of properties by the Valuation Office Agency

Some people have been concerned that the valuation process might be intrusive, or that valuers might be given new and wider-reaching powers in order to conduct a revaluation of properties for council tax. In fact:

- the Valuation Office Agency (VOA) is a central government agency responsible for valuing homes for council tax purposes. It has the same powers now as it did when council tax was introduced in 1993;

- the VOA has a duty to maintain up-to-date information on properties in order to ensure they are in the right band for council tax. It only takes into account features of a property which affect its overall value. It does not collect any personal information about the residents of properties;

- in the minority of cases where the VOA need to visit a property, they will generally gather the information they need from outside. Valuers may only enter properties with the permission of the householder – the VOA has no powers to forcibly enter homes;

- fewer than one per cent of all homeowners are visited by VOA staff each year, and then often at the householder's request: for example when they have challenged the council tax banding of their property and have asked for a review.

A general revaluation of properties for council tax would not imply any new powers for the VOA.

Growth in property prices and revaluation

Most properties in England have increased in value since the date of the last valuation in 1991. The Government's stated aim, when revaluation was being considered, was that it should not increase the overall amount of money raised from council tax in England. There is no presumption that because house prices have gone up, tax should go up too. This means that revaluation would simply change the way the council tax burden is shared out across the country.

Which band a property is assigned to after revaluation would depend on its relative growth in value since 1991. Homes that have grown in value more quickly than the average would tend to move up the bands, while those whose value has grown more slowly than average would tend to move down. Since the current bands are relatively wide, a large number would stay in the same band as now.

The Government has stated that revaluation of properties for council tax will not take place within the life of the current Parliament.

Further options for reform

7.51   The postponement of revaluation obviously restricts the scope for reform of the council tax bands in the short term. I have therefore considered the options for reform in the absence of a revaluation exercise, as well as some more radical options for reform of council tax as a property tax.

Reform of Band H   7.52   The existing design of council tax contains a number of elements of judgement, some of which might reasonably be revisited. One such element is the current cap on council tax liability that is imposed by the ceiling on band H. Under the current system, the top band contains all properties worth at least £320,000 in 1991 (equivalent to approximately £900,000 in 2005 prices), right up to the most expensive property in the country at that time. Because of the way band ratios are set at present, the most valuable properties can only pay twice the tax paid by a band D home, and only three times as much as the least valuable home in band A, despite being at least eight times more valuable than band A homes in 1991.

7.53   There may therefore be a case for raising the ceiling on council tax liability by adding new top bands. This would be possible in theory without revaluation; properties could be assigned to the new higher bands based on their assumed value in 1991. This is the method already applied to any homes built since 1993, for which an estimated 1991 value is calculated to assign them to a council tax band.

7.54   Such reform would have the advantage of producing a stronger link between property value and tax bills for the most valuable homes, who currently pay a relatively small proportion of their value in tax. While the majority of households would not be affected, as a first step to reform improving this link at the very top of the scale could send an important signal that reform of the property tax element of council tax could be viable, and be a first step away from treating the current banding structure as inevitable and fixed. It would also, as noted above, be consistent with a definition of fairness based on ability to pay, since it would target those households where the correlation between income and property value is strongest.

7.55   The financial impact of raising or removing the ceiling on band H would depend on the new structure introduced at the top of the scale. The Inquiry modelled a scenario based on introducing several new top bands, including one for properties worth more than £1 million in 1991 (it is estimated that the latter would contain only around 800 homes).[15] It was estimated that this option would raise approximately £75 million in additional revenue compared with the current council tax bands. Again this extra revenue, while modest, could conceivably be used to offset the costs of other measures aimed at those paying a high proportion of their income in council tax.

7.56   Less than 0.6 per cent of all households in England are in the top band, so in practice, reform of band H would only affect a very small minority of properties. However, most band H properties are concentrated in a relatively small number of authority areas – almost a quarter of all band H properties are in Kensington and Chelsea or Westminster – so implementing such a change might be challenging in those areas. Any extra yield would also be highly concentrated in a handful of authorities, though under the present system of grant equalisation the gain would be redistributed through grant to other areas.

---

[15] See Annex C for full details of the options modelled.

Extra bands at 1991 values

7.57   A more far-reaching reform in the absence of revaluation would be to alter both the floor and the ceiling on council tax by creating new bands at both the top and the bottom of the scale, again by allocating properties to bands based on their assumed value in 1991.

7.58   The advantage of this option is that it allows for some relatively significant reform of council tax as a property tax, introducing a stronger link between bills and property value (albeit 1991 values) at either end of the scale, but without creating the large-scale turbulence of a full revaluation exercise. Approximately 2.5 million households would move into the new lower band and see their tax reduced, but the vast majority – over 85 per cent of all households – would not change bands.

7.59   The Valuation Office Agency advise that measures of this kind would be possible without a full revaluation, but practically challenging in some respects. For example, it would be difficult to re-band properties consistently in areas whose relative desirability had radically altered since 1991, and it would be necessary to decide how to take account of improvements made to properties since 1993. There are also drawbacks to a method which does not allow those properties which, at revaluation, would have moved down into band A, or up into band H, to do so. Ultimately it may be better to implement reform alongside revaluation.

7.60   None the less, even an imperfect reform of this kind would be expected to increase the overall progressiveness of council tax to property value at either end. This would increase bills for some households, and reduce them for others, including for many low-income households in band A. Since many of those households receive full or partial CTB, some of the reduction in bills would translate into reduced costs in the CTB bill for government. It is estimated that adding new bands in this way could reduce total CTB costs by around £110 million (assuming full take-up).

Widening the band ratios

7.61   Another alternative would be to leave the band structure unchanged, but alter the ratios applied to each band. This would effectively redistribute the tax burden by requiring the higher bands to pay more, and the lower bands less than now as a proportion of band D bills.

7.62   Widening the band ratios would have the advantage of reforming council tax to strengthen the link between bills and property values, without any properties having to move bands. Reform would therefore be possible without revaluation of any kind, if it were decided that this was the best way forward in the short term.

7.63   Again, this would be expected to reduce council tax bills (before CTB) for a large number of low-income households. As before, part of that saving would accrue to the Government through reductions in the costs of paying CTB to those households. Total CTB costs could be reduced by up to £570 million, based on the band ratios in the options modelled and full take-up of CTB.

7.64   However, this would be a significant reform affecting bills for nearly all households, albeit without their having to change bands. It would therefore only be attractive in the context of a wider commitment to fairer, or at least more progressive, property taxes in relation to value.

Point value property tax

7.65   Finally, I said in my Interim report in 2005 that I was interested in looking at the experience of other parts of the UK and international examples of different local taxes.[16] In that context I have considered what the impact might be of eventually replacing council tax with a so-called 'point value tax', under which bills would be based on a set percentage of property value each year.

---

[16] Lyons Inquiry into Local Government, *Consultation Paper and Interim Report*, 2005.

7.66   Property taxes in many other jurisdictions are directly related to property value in this way. For example, Northern Ireland's domestic rates are to be replaced by a point value tax this year, with bills based on capital value as determined by the Valuation and Lands Agency. The Northern Ireland context is of course very different to that in England, and decisions about local taxes there are entirely separate from decisions about reform in England. It is, however, an interesting example of a property tax very different to council tax. Many US states also operate 'real' property taxes, based on annually updated capital values.

7.67   Analysis by the Inquiry shows that based on 2005 values (the most recent detailed data available to the Inquiry), a point value tax would need to be levied at approximately 0.64 per cent of capital value in order to raise the same amount as council tax (before CTB). More households would gain than would lose under this reform option, with almost 60 per cent of households paying at least £1 per week less than now. Around 40 per cent would pay at least £3 per week (or £156 per year) less than now. However more than a quarter of all households would pay at least £1 per week more than now, and around 18 per cent would pay more than £3 per week more than now.

7.68   A point value tax has some theoretical attractions in the longer term. As Sir Peter Burt's Committee noted last year, a tax of this kind would have the potential to act as a more effective stabiliser of the property market than council tax.[17] If properties were regularly revalued, it could even be a source of buoyant revenue for local government, as yield from a particular multiplier would rise (or fall) with house prices, and embed incentives for local authorities to invest in the desirability of their area for residents, in terms of the service quality and wider well-being which can be reflected in property prices.

7.69   Applying a fixed multiplier to property value would be the logical extension of the idea that fair property taxes should not tax expensive homes more lightly than cheaper ones. It would also result in significantly greater progressiveness in relation to income, though a point value property tax would remain regressive overall before benefits are taken into account. Compared with the current system, this would significantly reduce the costs of council tax benefit. Analysis by the Inquiry suggests that a point value tax might reduce the average burden of tax as a proportion of income for the poorest by around 15 per cent, and so could also reduce total CTB costs by up to £1 billion (assuming full take up).

7.70   However, this would be a radical change and could not be contemplated in the short term, or until such time as public support for such reform could be established. There is also a tension between on the one hand achieving a perfect relationship between tax and property value, and on the other allowing for local variability, which is an important part of the system at present. In light of these drawbacks, I am not recommending point value tax as a replacement for council tax, but it remains a viable option for future governments.

Weighing the case for reform

It must be considered that there is nothing more difficult to carry out, nor more doubtful of success, nor more dangerous to handle, than to initiate a new order of things. For the reformer has enemies in all those who profit by the old order, and only lukewarm defenders in all those who would profit by the new order. (Niccolo Machiavelli)[18]

---

[17]   Local Government Finance Review Committee, Scotland, *A Fairer Way*, 2006.

[18]   Machiavelli, N., *The Prince*, 1513, with thanks to Peter Watt, University of Birmingham.

Winners and losers

7.71 My work on options for reform of council tax further exposes that there is no 'golden key' that will make it a perfect tax, or universally accepted as fair. There are advantages to reforming the property tax element of council tax, but these must be weighed against its drawbacks, not least that any redistribution of the tax burden inevitably creates 'winners and losers'.

Impact on local tax bases

7.72 Reforming the property element of council tax also has implications for local authorities' tax-raising capacity. The current council tax bands limit the amount that bills can vary by compressing properties towards band D, rather than reflecting the full range and variability of house prices within and between areas. If local taxes more closely reflected real property values, and the relative desirability of areas, this would mean that the grant system might have to work much harder to equalise for the differences between authorities' local tax-raising capacity. The extent of this impact would, however, vary over time, as relative property prices between regions may diverge at some times and converge at others. The extent to which reform made tax bases more variable would partly depend on the point in the housing cycle at which revaluation took place.

7.73 Some authorities might also find that their tax bases shrink after reform, shifting their balance of funding towards greater dependence on central revenues. The government would therefore want to consider the implications of reform for authorities, while recognising that reform might still be justified in terms of its impact on taxpayers.

Ability to pay, and CTB costs

7.74 There are arguments in favour of some reform of the current design of council tax, in the medium term. Reform of the property tax element can help make council tax less regressive to income, though it would still be regressive overall, before benefits. Such reforms are particularly successful in reducing the burden on many low-income households, creating consequent savings in council tax benefit. The Government would have to decide how to spend any such savings, but they could help contribute to the long-term sustainability of council tax and CTB, for instance if used to strengthen the ability of council tax benefit to reach those paying a high proportion of their income in tax.

'Fair' property taxes

7.75 Strengthening the link between property value and tax can also be justified in its own right. Some submissions to the Inquiry express fairness not just in terms of income but also in relation to property value.

> *Council tax is not even a fair property tax. It was oversimplified... this ensures that the richest people in the biggest houses pay proportionately much less.* (Bristol Older People's Forum)

7.76 There is a case for altering the bands in recognition of the fact that the present, very compressed, bands impose a lower effective rate of tax on expensive homes than on cheaper ones, not least with a view to the potential for property taxes to stabilise house prices in theory, as discussed in Chapter 6. I do not have detailed evidence on which to judge the likely macroeconomic impact of the reforms outlined above. However, it is clear that the current design of council tax does not lend itself to acting as a stabiliser of property prices, and that reform could in theory improve it in this respect.

7.77 In particular, reform should recognise that the current band structure is the product of judgement rather than natural law. The floor and ceiling on current eligibility are the products of a series of choices in the early 1990s, and might reasonably be revisited now. Adjusting the relationship between bills and value at either end of the scale would go some way to capturing the benefits outlined above.

> **Recommendation 7.1**
>
> Council Tax should be retained as a source of revenue for local government. The option of change in the longer term to shift the balance towards other taxes and charges remains open.
>
> **Recommendation 7.2**
>
> While not the most urgent priority, the Government should conduct a revaluation of all domestic properties for council tax. Transitional arrangements to ensure households do not face steep tax increases from one year to the next should be considered at the point of revaluation.
>
> **Recommendation 7.3**
>
> Subsequent revaluations should take place regularly and automatically at intervals of no more than five years.
>
> **Recommendation 7.4**
>
> At the revaluation the Government should introduce new property bands at the top and bottom of the current structure. It could also consider the introduction of separate bands for Inner London to reflect the unique shape of the property market in that region and to reduce turbulence there.

The fairness of a service charge

7.78   While income or ability to pay is often the focus of discussions around council tax fairness, other submissions to the Inquiry have focused on the fairness of charging occupiers of property, based on their status as service users. Council tax liability currently applies mainly to occupiers rather than owners, partly reflecting its roots in the community charge, under which all residents of an area were asked to make a contribution to the funding of local services. For some, fairness means paying according to the benefits received from services, perhaps on an individual rather than household basis.

> *What do you get for it? I have lived in London ten years and it has gone up by about 200 per cent. In ten years there hasn't been a 200 per cent increase in services... that is the thing that I think is unfair.* (Focus group participant)[19]

> *[An] anomaly exists where a household of two old aged pensioners have to provide say £600 per head to pay Council Tax of £1,200 and the household next door which is occupied by four tax payers who only have to provide £300 per head to fund Council Tax of £1,200.* (T.R. Troughton)

7.79   It appears that the emphasis on the service-charge element of the council tax may have contributed to the expectations people have of a very direct return on their payment for local services. When we pay VAT, or even income tax, we are aware that we are contributing to the pool of 'general taxation'. We do not calculate the fairness of our VAT payments (if we are aware of them) in terms of how many times we have used the local hospital that year, nor do we expect to pay more income tax during the years when our children are at school. Council tax, on the other hand, is often described as unfair to those who do not make heavy use of local services.

---

[19] Gfk NOP Social Research, Qualitative Research on Public Attitudes to Taxation and Public Services, 2005, Lyons Inquiry.

7.80   In practice, an expectation of a direct return from local services is unrealistic. For example, local government provides social and care services which are by nature likely to directly benefit a particular group of people, with many of the benefits to the wider community being indirect. There is perhaps a need for a more open debate about how we fund such services, so that people's expectations of what local government provides, and what council tax pays for, can be more realistic.

7.81   It is worth noting that the balance between the tax people pay and the services they use will vary over time. Chart 7.7 below shows how, on average, people consume most services when they are young and when they are old, and pay most tax during their working lives. So, while council tax functions partly as a service charge, it is clear that not every taxpayer will use services in proportion to their payment every year – if they did, then all services could be provided simply by charging at the point of use.

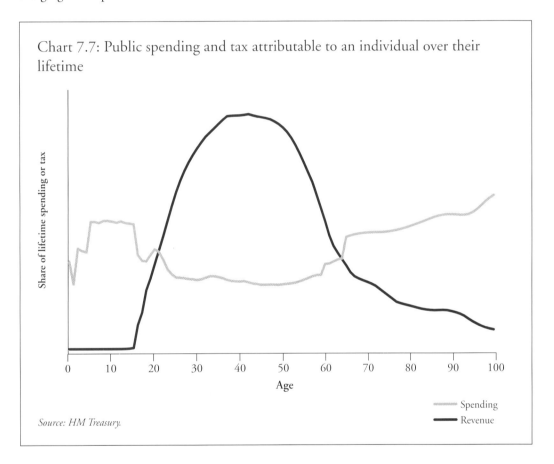

Chart 7.7: Public spending and tax attributable to an individual over their lifetime

Share of lifetime spending or tax

Age

Source: HM Treasury.

Spending
Revenue

7.82   In practice, public services are more complex than that sort of simple transaction; the costs of services extend beyond the product 'used' on the day to include longer-term investment in provision, often with large overheads that do not obviously relate to individual service users. By providing services through taxation, we must accept a degree of shared responsibility for financing them as distinct from our personal use of those services. In my view, it is important to be clear that this holds true for local services financed partly by council tax as much as for national services financed by other taxes.

7.83   Different kinds of 'service charge' also speak to different sorts of fairness. For example, pure service charges might mean direct payments in proportion to the services used by each individual. The community charge is often discussed in the language of a service charge, because it represented a shift away from a local tax on households towards one on adult individuals, thus reflecting an assumption about per-head service use. However this made it a broadly flat universal charge, rather than one which varied according to the actual amount of services consumed by each person. These complexities show that taxes introduced as service charges, like property taxes (and indeed most other forms of tax), are subject to some debate about how 'fairness' ought to be defined.

7.84   I believe it is right that council tax should continue in the short to medium term to incorporate elements of both a property tax and a service charge. The service charge element of council tax is well understood by the public, and reflects an important link between residence in an area and a household's interest in local services and local prosperity. However, retaining a hybrid model, which also reflects the different value of people's homes, ensures that the service charge element is balanced by a reflection of households' different circumstances. A move towards local taxes based solely on service use would not address concerns about fairness in relation to ability to pay, and might in fact worsen them.

7.85   Nonetheless, there is room for a debate about the balance between taxes and user charges in paying for local public services. Charges already operate across a wide range of services, from parking to social care. Local authorities already make decisions about whether council tax increases or charges are the best outlet for a spending pressure, particularly at a time when the ability to increase council tax is restricted by capping. I will return to the issue of charging later in this chapter, and consider how charges can be used alongside local taxes to spread the costs of services in a way that is perceived as fair.

Fairness to older people

7.86   Submissions to my Inquiry, and other evidence, suggest that there is particular concern about the impact of council tax on pensioners, linked particularly to concerns about the council tax burden on households who are asset-rich but income-poor. Many retired and older people wrote to the Inquiry, often expressing deep concerns about the impact of council tax on them, and about the likely impact of tax increases in the future.

> *Many older people inhabit homes which might have been in their family for, in some cases, generations. These homes do not necessarily reflect their present circumstances, but there is no need for them to move, other than the cost of "running" that home. Therefore, relating local taxation to size of home is unfair.* (Mr M Napier)

7.87   Concerns about fairness to older people are perceived by many as central to the council tax debate. In surveys conducted for the Inquiry, three quarters of all respondents agreed that the elderly should automatically pay less council tax even if they own a property without a mortgage. There was substantial though lower support for the idea that elderly people should pay less even if they have a lot of savings, pensions or investments. However, up to a quarter of respondents thought it would be unfair for other households to pay more to relieve the burden on pensioners or retired people, expressing concern that working people should not have to pay more tax, or suggesting that a degree of means-testing would be fairer.

7.88   These issues speak to our wider expectations about the tax we will pay and the benefit we will take from public services over our lifetimes. Survey respondents prepared to pay more so that pensioners paid less were likely to cite the fact that older people "have paid into the system and are entitled to help".[20] As shown above, it is already true that on average, people are net beneficiaries of public services when they are older (and when they are young), and net contributors during their working lives. Older people benefit substantially from public expenditure, and overall pay less tax as they get older. Chart 7.8 shows that council tax is, however, an exception to this rule, with most people continuing to be liable for the same council tax (before benefits) in retirement as when they worked. Nonetheless the overall picture is one of declining tax contributions into old age.

---

[20] BMG Research, Lyons Inquiry Survey, 2007.

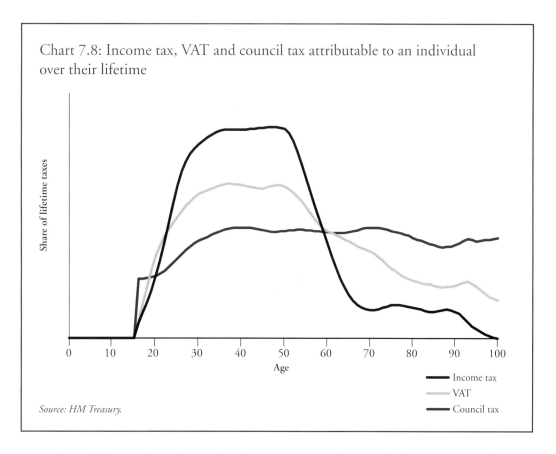

Chart 7.8: Income tax, VAT and council tax attributable to an individual over their lifetime

Share of lifetime taxes

Age

Income tax
VAT
Council tax

Source: HM Treasury.

7.89   One of the tensions facing the Government in reforming local taxation is addressing people's concerns about the unfairness of council tax to older people, within a tax system that already puts much of the burden of taxation on working-age taxpayers. With an ageing population, transferring the burden of council tax towards younger households might become unaffordable in the future. I will explore these issues further in looking at the role of council tax benefit, and the arguments around a local income tax.

Council tax liability: ownership, occupation, discounts and exemptions

7.90   My view is that it is right in principle that all residents of an area should contribute in some way to the cost of local services (though I recognise that council tax benefit meets up to 100 per cent of some households' bills in practice). I am however interested in whether the tax system can also reflect the fact that non-resident property owners have a stake in the desirability and wellbeing of an area, and will benefit from place-shaping and local services which contribute to the value of their property. It is interesting that some other countries levy separate taxes on occupation and ownership; for example, in France the occupier of a property pays a locally-set "taxe d'habitation", while the owner pays a separate tax based on the value of their property and land, which is assessed annually.

7.91   Council tax effectively combines these elements in one hybrid tax, so that liability falls either to the owner or the occupier. In the case of rented accommodation, tenants will generally pay council tax, with liability reverting to the landlord if the property is empty. While I am not making a general recommendation in this area, a number of submissions to the Inquiry have suggested that the Government might look again at the tax liability of particular groups of owners and occupiers, particularly students, owners of properties let to students, and second home-owners.

Students' exemption from council tax

7.92   Full-time students are currently exempt from paying council tax for the duration of their course of study. Some submissions to the Inquiry have questioned whether this exemption is fair, given that students are likely to make substantial use of local services but do not currently make a contribution to the costs of providing them.

7.93   Some submissions have also raised wider concerns about the impact on communities of having a high concentration of student accommodation.

> *Every student conversion brings with it increased costs to refuse collections, street cleaning and the administration of residents parking schemes. All of these costs are paid for by the remaining council tax payers. It is a source of massive grievance and aggravation as well as of financial loss to the local authority.* (Alan Simpson MP)

7.94   However other submissions, including from the National Union of Students, have argued for the retention of the exemption, pointing out that unlike other households, students are not usually eligible for benefits and so could not claim CTB.

7.95   There might be a case for bringing students into liability for council tax, reflecting their interest in local services and their stake in the community. However, such a move would need to be accompanied by making council tax benefit available to students on low incomes. A large proportion of the student population would be likely to be eligible for CTB, and processing their claims would be a significant addition to local authorities' CTB caseload in some areas.

7.96   I am attracted to the principle that students should make some financial contribution to the services provided in the area in which they study. However, on balance I am not convinced that the benefits of bringing students into the council tax and CTB system would be enough to outweigh the administrative costs involved. I therefore am not recommending a change to the student exemption.

7.97   Another possibility might be that liability for council tax should revert to the landlord when all tenants are exempt students. At present, the student exemption covers the dwelling itself, so the landlord does not become liable to pay tax. I am attracted in principle to the idea that owners of such properties, which in some areas represent a large section of the total community, might make a contribution to the costs of services in those areas. However, in practice this would put treatment of student landlords out of line with that of other landlords, and might have perverse consequences, potentially driving up rents or creating disincentives to let to students. I am therefore not recommending a change to the student exemption, but have looked for other ways that the impact of highly concentrated student populations might be reflected through the local government finance system.

Student populations and local tax base numbers

7.98   Formula grant to local authorities reflects, among other things, the number of council tax-paying households in the area in a given year (the tax base). Authorities submit information on tax base to the department for Communities and Local Government (CLG), including the number of households subject to discounts or exemptions, providing a snapshot of the tax base on a given day once a year.

7.99   At present the timing of the grants settlement means that a snapshot is taken in September. For authorities with student populations beginning courses at that time, many student households may not yet have registered for an exemption, meaning that authorities may overestimate their tax base in the data they provide to CLG. In some cases authorities may therefore receive a lower grant settlement than would have been the case had the snapshot been taken at a different time of year, possibly leaving some of the costs associated with student populations to fall on council tax.[21]

7.100   I recommend that the system be adapted to allow authorities to submit more realistic data on student numbers to inform the grant settlement. This could be done either by taking a snapshot of student numbers on a different date (for example, six months earlier) or by submitting data based on outturn figures from the previous year. Data submitted in 2007 will be particularly important as they will inform grant settlements for three years going forward. The Government should seek to resolve this issue before then.

> **Recommendation 7.5**
>
> The Government should ensure the grant system reflects realistic data on the number of student households exempt from council tax in their areas. This should be done in time to inform the forthcoming negotiations on three-year settlements.

Second homes   7.101   Other submissions to my Inquiry have raised questions about the tax treatment of second homes, particularly in rural communities. At present, second homes are eligible for a discount on their council tax of up to 50 per cent, although since 2002 billing authorities have had the power to reduce the discount in their areas to a minimum of 10 per cent and locally retain any revenues over the 50 per cent amount.

7.102   The availability of a discount for second homes is based in the service charge element of council tax, and reflects their assumed lower consumption of local services. However the new flexibility indicates that the discount can also be seen in the wider context of local authorities' place-shaping role, and the fact that second homes can have a variable impact on local communities, particularly where they represent a large proportion of the total housing stock.

7.103   The report of Elinor Goodman's Affordable Rural Housing Commission last year suggested I consider whether local authorities should have the power to levy a 'second homes impact tax', particularly in areas in which the concentration of second homes had become "disproportionate".[22] I am attracted to the idea that in their place-shaping role local authorities should have the power to decide whether any discount should be available, and indeed whether a supplementary levy might be an appropriate way of coping with high-concentrations of second homes in their areas, which may have implications for community cohesion and prosperity.

7.104   I am aware however that there may be some practical barriers to implementing such a power. At present, second home-owners identify themselves to councils to register for a discount – if that discount were removed, or a supplementary tax imposed, their incentives to do so would be weak. This in turn might make it harder to identify the part of any revenues that should be locally retained. Nonetheless, if local solutions could be found to this problem, greater flexibility over tax rates for second homes could be a valuable policy tool for rural and some other communities, and I would urge the Government to consult local authorities on these issues.

---

[21] The relationship between student numbers and grant levels is not a straightforward one: final settlements will be affected by a range of relative needs and resource measures, and any 'floors' applied to grant increases. See Annex A for full details on the grant system. However the numbers of exempt households is a component of authorities' grant allocations.

[22] Defra, *Affordable Rural Housing Commission – final report*, 2006.

7.105   It has been suggested to me that council tax benefit might be adjusted so that no household receives 100 per cent relief against their tax bill. Advocates of this idea argue that it would ensure that every household makes at least a symbolic contribution to the cost of local services, and might create stronger democratic pressure for low council tax and efficient services by avoiding there being a constituency of people unaffected by rate increases.

> *Everyone in the community should pay [the] local tax... This would mean everyone has an interest in how efficiently the community is run. So when someone drops some litter they cannot only say, "someone is paid to pick it up" but also "and I help to pay his wages".* (Mr A Coulthurst)

7.106   I am attracted to this idea for its accountability benefits, and on the principled basis that all citizens have a stake in the community that might properly be reflected in local taxes. The same argument might equally apply to groups currently exempt from council tax, such as students. However, I am concerned that the costs of collecting small amounts of council tax from households currently receiving full CTB – and of prosecuting non-payment of those small amounts – might outweigh the benefits of its collection. I would also be concerned that such a move should not lead to an unfair burden on the very poorest households. I am therefore not recommending it.

Not broken but overloaded

7.107   This chapter has outlined a range of options for reform of the way council tax is designed, particularly with a view to addressing the perceived fairness of the tax. Any reform carries significant difficulties and redistributing the tax burden inevitably creates winners and losers. However the prize, if reform were successful, might be a tax that is more widely perceived as broadly fair, and potentially a better property tax. I will go on to explore the role of council tax benefit in achieving the link to income that is clearly crucial to perceptions of fairness.

7.108   However, as outlined at the beginning of this chapter, the sustainability of council tax also depends not just on its inherent fairness as a tax, but on its relationship with the rest of the local government finance system. I have argued that giving local authorities the tools to manage pressures more effectively is a key element of addressing the rate of increase in council tax.

7.109   I have suggested that the key to controlling the rate of increase in council tax bills is equipping local authorities to better manage spending pressures. Doing so will require central and local government to promote more realistic public expectations of local services, engaging with the public on making realistic trade-offs between the services people want and the taxes or charges they are willing to pay. I have also argued that management of pressures would be facilitated by more transparent financial settlements from central government, which most of all fully fund those mandates which are central government priorities, both to avoid unfunded burdens on local authorities and to incentivise a more mature relationship between central and local government.

7.110   Above all it is my view that the solution to the rate of increase in council tax lies not in constraining local authorities' powers to raise revenue, for example through capping, but in providing real flexibility to set spending plans in a way that reflects local choice about service provision and tax rates. Chapter 4 set out a range of recommendations to increase local authorities' financial flexibility, by reducing ring-fencing and making room for reprioritisation within budgets, to enable authorities to pursue not just managerial efficiencies but a more efficient use of public funds across their service responsibilities by tailoring spending plans to local preferences and circumstances.

7.111 A further dimension to these concerns about council tax relates to its overall size, and the type and proportion of local services it is asked to support. Many council taxpayers perceive the tax primarily as a charge for services, with their views on 'value for money' in council tax informed by the perceived benefit they take from those services. There is evidence to suggest that people are most conscious – and accepting – of local spending on services which visibly relate to their property or the physical area such as waste collection, parks, street cleaning and physical regeneration.

7.112 This is not unique to England; for example a recent study of attitudes to local property taxes in New Zealand showed that people see services such as waste collection and town planning as essentials which should be paid for by local ratepayers, but place social services, and arts and cultural services in the category of "luxuries" which should not be paid for through local rates.[23]

7.113 It appears that property taxes in particular may hit an 'acceptability threshold' beyond which they generate public resistance. The high visibility of property taxes, perhaps combined with their overall regressiveness to income, may make it difficult for property taxes to support very ambitious spending programmes, particularly where tax increases are not perceived to deliver benefits in the most visible service areas or those of direct benefit to residents, and homeowners in particular.[24] The threshold of acceptability may not be a fixed cash amount, so much as the point beyond which service improvements are not perceived to have significant benefits to local property.

7.114 This has implications for the way in which pressures impact on council tax and its public perception. For example, it may be right that pressures on waste services are met by council taxpayers, since most households make use of, and contribute to the cost of running waste services. By contrast, social care services are used by a minority of local citizens, making pressures on, or improvements to those services, less visible to taxpayers.

7.115 In this context, I have considered the options for reducing the overall size of council tax as a source of revenue, either through a one-off measure (by increasing funding from another source) or over time (by introducing greater buoyancy into another element of local revenues). I will explore in this chapter whether a local income tax might be an attractive option for introducing natural buoyancy to local revenues, or as an alternative source of revenue for local authorities. In Chapter 9 I will consider a range of wider options for ensuring the contribution made by central government to funding local services is sustainable.

Conclusions

7.116 It is my judgement that council tax is not broken, and remains a broadly sound tax. Council tax benefit is, in my view the key to ensuring the burden of council tax on the lowest-income households is appropriately reduced. If fully taken up, CTB can have a substantial impact on 'fairness' in terms of the link between council tax and ability to pay. I will look at the current impact of CTB in practice, and whether reforms in that area may be called for.

7.117 The rate of increase in council tax has placed a growing burden on many households and could put at risk the sustainability of council tax in the long term. Capping of local authority budgets fails to address the underlying causes of high tax increases. I suggest in Chapter 3 that council tax tends to bear the strain of pressures in the whole local government finance system. Its acceptability therefore rests not just on the way council tax is designed, but on whether service expectations can be managed and met in a way that does not continue to put council tax under unsustainable pressure.

---

[23] Commissioned by Local Government New Zealand, *Improving the Reputation of Local Government a survey of Perceptions of Rates*, 2006.

[24] Fischel, W *The Homevoter Hypothesis* 2001.

7.118 Reform of council tax, and council tax benefit, are a key part of the picture and should be the priority in the short term. There are also wider possibilities for change in the future. In that light I will look further at whether, in the medium term, other taxes and charges including a local income tax, or assigned national taxes, could be an alternative or additional source of revenue for local authorities. I will also consider the interaction between local taxes and central government support for services, which is important in understanding how pressures on council tax might best be managed in future

7.119 While council tax is broadly sound, reform of its structure could be desirable in order that the relationship between bills and property value be brought out more strongly, and to deliver some greater progressiveness to income. In the medium term, revaluation combined with reform to add extra bands at the top and bottom would remove the distorting effect of the current ceiling on council tax, as well as reducing bills for many low-income households and cutting the overall cost of CTB.

COUNCIL TAX BENEFIT

7.120 As shown above, my analysis suggests that while council tax could be reformed to make it a better property tax, it is the nature of the relationship between property and income in England that no property tax could deliver a close enough relationship between bills and household income to satisfy those most concerned with income as a measure of ability to pay. This does not, in my view, mean that council tax is 'broken': however, it does suggest that a mechanism for dealing with inability to pay for those on the lowest incomes is important for the perceived "fairness" and therefore the continued acceptability of the tax.

The key to fairness? 7.121 Council tax benefit (CTB) has been designed specifically for this purpose, and if council tax is retained, I believe that reform and more effective delivery of CTB is the key to dealing with council tax 'unfairness' for the poorest households.

> **Council tax benefit**
>
> Council tax benefit is available to some households on low incomes, and may cover all or part of their council tax bill. It is administered by local authorities, but can also be accessed through agencies including the Pension Service.
>
> Eligibility for CTB depends on the circumstances of each household, and takes into account:
>
> - household income including earnings, occupational pensions and some benefits and tax credits;
> - income from savings above £6,000 (the lower capital limit); and
> - the composition of the household (for example eligibility thresholds are different for lone parents, pensioners and other groups, in line with other parts of the benefit system such as Income Support and Pension Credit).
>
> Savings above £16,000 (the upper capital limit) mean that a household will not usually be eligible for CTB.

Rebate, not benefit 7.122 It has been suggested to me, including by the IsItfair? campaign group, that a tax which must be accompanied by a benefit must be flawed. I disagree; there is no difference in principle between a tax against which a benefit is paid in certain circumstances, and a tax against which rebates or discounts are available. I tend to agree with those who argue that it is particularly the term 'benefit' which is unwelcome to some taxpayers, with the result that CTB is perceived differently to the single person discount, for example. The term has a particular resonance which may prevent some people (many of whom might be sure to claim an income tax rebate owed by the Inland Revenue) from taking up their entitlements. Similar issues have also been identified by a joint working group on council tax benefit in Wales. A paper shared with the Inquiry by the Welsh Assembly Government observes that among other barriers to claiming CTB, "pensioners were sometimes averse to claiming because of pride – 'I've never claimed benefits in my life and I'm not about to start now'."

7.123 It is noteworthy that take-up of the rebate available against the old domestic rates was higher than that for council tax benefit, at around 75 per cent. Pensioners were then the group most likely to claim, with take-up rates at around 90 per cent.[25] It is possible that among other things, the rebranding of what had been a rebate as a benefit has impacted on its ability to reach certain groups.

7.124 I am strongly of the view that CTB's primary purpose is not to provide income support per se, but rather to adjust each household's liability for council tax according to their ability to pay. In that light, I suggest that the Government should address the perception problem around CTB by explicitly recognising it as a rebate, and re-naming it 'Council Tax Rebate', to reflect its unique place within the tax and welfare system.

Recommendation 7.6

Council tax benefit should be recognised as a rebate rather than a benefit, and re-named 'council tax rebate', to properly reflect its main purpose: adjusting households' liability to council tax.

Take up of council tax rebates

7.125 I believe that renaming CTB is justified in its own right, given the particular links between council tax benefit and council tax, which already give it a somewhat different purpose to other income-related benefits. However renaming CTB is not purely a question of presentation, but implies a wider recognition that steps should be taken to ensure rebates reach those households who are entitled to them. Ideally, CTB would therefore be renamed alongside the announcement of measures to improve take-up and delivery of entitlements.

7.126 Chart 7.9 demonstrates that council tax rebates have the potential to fulfil what is, in my view, their main aim: alleviating the burden of council tax for low income households. If current entitlement to rebates were fully taken up, council tax would be progressive to income overall for the poorest households. However this graph also shows that CTB is not yet fully achieving that aim in practice, because not all entitlement is being claimed. In particular, for the poorest ten per cent of households council tax remains a large average burden relative to income.

---

[26] HMSO, *Local Government Finance: Report of the Committee of Inquiry*, 1976.

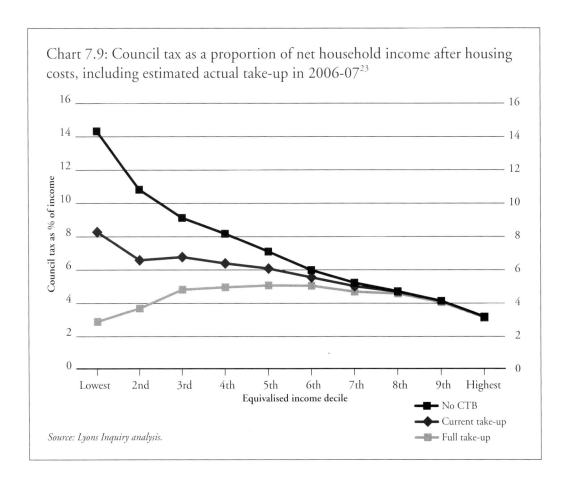

Chart 7.9: Council tax as a proportion of net household income after housing costs, including estimated actual take-up in 2006-07[23]

Source: Lyons Inquiry analysis.

7.127 CTB is the means-tested benefit with the highest number of claimants, but the lowest level of take-up. Overall take-up of CTB in 2004-05 was between 62-68 per cent, and has been falling in recent years, down 8-10 percentage points since 1997.[26]

7.128 Take-up is lower than average among pensioner households at 53-58 per cent, which represents an 11 percentage point drop since 1997. The National Audit Office has estimated that a ten per cent increase in pensioner take-up of CTB would lift approximately 47,000 pensioners out of poverty. Crucially, it appears that most of the money unclaimed is owed to pensioners; the Department for Work and Pensions (DWP) estimate that up to £1.36 billion in CTB entitlement is left unclaimed by older people each year.[27]

---

[26] Estimates of current take-up are based on latest published figures (which relate to the year 2004-05) as against income and council tax data for 2006-07.

[27] Department for Work and Pensions, *Income Related Benefits, Estimates of Take-Up in 2004/2005* (table 4.2), 2006. Take-up figures shown here relate to caseload, not expenditure. Decreases in headline take-up partly reflect the fact that some recent policy changes have increased the number of eligible households, not all of whom have claimed, which reduces headline take-up. Even after adjusting for this however, the Department for Work and Pensions estimates that overall CTB take-up has dropped by up to five percentage points since 1997.

[25] All figures from DWP, above.

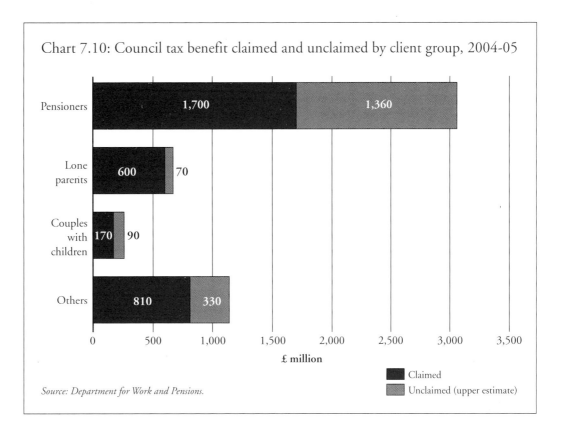

Chart 7.10: Council tax benefit claimed and unclaimed by client group, 2004-05

Pensioners: 1,700 (Claimed), 1,360 (Unclaimed)
Lone parents: 600 (Claimed), 70 (Unclaimed)
Couples with children: 170 (Claimed), 90 (Unclaimed)
Others: 810 (Claimed), 330 (Unclaimed)

£ million

Claimed
Unclaimed (upper estimate)

Source: Department for Work and Pensions.

Barriers to claiming

7.129 Low take-up has a number of causes: people may be unsure whether they are entitled to a rebate, or may have an aversion to becoming a benefit claimant. The effort involved in filling in application forms and pursuing claims is itself a barrier for many, despite efforts at simplification.

7.130 Help the Aged have done extensive work to identify the barriers to pensioners' claiming their CTB entitlements. Their work suggests that while for some older people the barrier may be aversion to benefits or uncertainty about whether they are entitled, for a significant number the barriers are more practical, and in many cases:

> *…the individual knows they ought to find out whether they could get council tax benefit but does not get round to actually claiming. This group may include people who have been sent the forms to fill in but who have left these languishing among other paperwork.* (Help the Aged)

7.131 Help the Aged suggest that the effort involved in making a claim (filling in a 28 page form, providing proof of income, savings and other relevant information) may put older people off applying for CTB. They call for a redesign of the system so that CTB is much more proactively delivered to entitled taxpayers. Age Concern have also expressed interest in measures to make CTB delivery more automatic, including in the context of wider efforts to join up services and benefits for older people.

7.132 Local authorities administer CTB, and Government statistics show significant variation in, for instance, average time to process new claims and percentage of claims decided within 14 days. In part this will reflect local circumstances. But local authorities have also worked in many instances to improve take-up of entitlements within their communities, often as part of wider efforts to make services more joined-up and accessible. Local action in this area can make a valuable contribution to ensuring CTB is successfully delivered.

7.133 Improving take-up is not straight-forward. For example, home visits, while very effective in improving take-up in some cases, may be perceived as intrusive in others. Local action in this area reveals some good examples of client-friendly services, which can help to ensure people receive any rebates they are eligible for. The box below gives some examples of this.

Local action to improve take-up of council tax benefit

Halton Borough Council's 'Benefits Express' is a high-tech, mobile, door-step service dealing with benefits claims which helps to greatly reduce the time it takes to apply for benefit.

The purpose of the service is to:

- reduce the time it takes to process benefits claims;

- simplify the application process for claiming benefit through face to face contact with the customer;

- make information available about other benefits to residents;

- maximise benefits up-take within the borough; and

- work with other key partners in the borough to add value to the services offered via the Benefits Express.

The Benefits Express operates as a mobile office connected to the Council's computer systems and tours the borough offering a range of services.

Since the service began in 2004, processing time for claims has reduced from an average of eight weeks to less than 48 hours for customers using the service. The service works through officers visiting customers at home, collecting all the necessary information and processing the claim on-line, thereby giving the customer an instant decision on their claim. Lengthy delays associated with dealing with customers via postal correspondence are now avoided, thereby reducing frustration for both customers and staff.

Milton Keynes Council has worked to achieve a customer-focused and friendly approach to delivery of benefits, by training staff to put customer needs first and to resolve the customer's demands at that first point of contact wherever possible. This involves the whole service being focused on customers' individual needs rather than on bulk or batch processing.

This approach has been backed up by changes within the organisation that allow the council to focus more staff on dealing with claims, and fewer on back office functions, for example by reducing unnecessary paperwork.

The council succeeded in reducing the average time for dealing with benefit claims from 63 to 25 days within a six-month period, moving from the bottom quartile to the top quartile of local authorities in the country on this measure.

7.134   In Wales, many authorities are also taking innovative steps to ensure entitlements are taken up, including a joint project by four authorities, in conjunction with their software supplier, to telephone taxpayers and proactively offer them a benefit eligibility check. Others are working with the voluntary sector to reach groups such as pensioners or ethnic minority groups, among whom take-up of council tax benefit is low. There is scope for more action at the local level in England, in particular for some authorities to learn from the experience of the best performers.

7.135   Nonetheless, with up to £1.8 billion per year in CTB entitlement going unclaimed, it is clear to me that low take-up is a systemic as well as a local issue, and as such requires a structural change in the way rebates are administered.[28] Local authorities will always have an important role to play in reaching their citizens and connecting them with services and other entitlements, but

---

[28]   Department for Work and Pensions, *Income Related Benefits, Estimates of Take-Up in 2004/2005*, (table 4.2), 2006. Amounts unclaimed are published in ranges: estimated at £1.33 billion – £1.80 billion in 2004-05. Includes Scotland and Wales.

they cannot be solely responsible for the successful delivery of CTB; central government has a prior responsibility for getting the framework right.

A joined-up approach to delivery through the Pension Service

7.136 Some steps have already been taken to simplify the claims process and improve take-up. The Pension Service already aims to ensure that callers to its telephone line are means-tested for CTB and housing benefit alongside pension credit. Details of callers' circumstances are entered into a short form, which is then posted to the caller to sign and forward to their local authority. This removes the need for claimants to enter the same information into a separate form for CTB.

7.137 This is a welcome innovation: it avoids people having to provide the same information several times, and moves towards the kind of joined-up services that the Government is pressing for and that the public increasingly expects. Last year, over 120,000 pension credit claimants received a pre-completed CTB form from the Pension Service in this way.

7.138 However these measures do not at present simplify the claims process for up to 1.2 million pensioners who are not eligible for pension credit but are entitled to, and not claiming, CTB. At present those people cannot claim CTB via the Pension Service, since calls end at the point pension credit eligibility is ruled out. Although many of the personal details needed for a council tax benefit claim have been given during the course of the call, if no pension credit claim goes forward those details are not currently retained by the Pension Service's systems, and cannot be entered into the simplified forms for CTB.

7.139 I agree with Help the Aged that this represents a missed opportunity to deliver CTB more effectively, and I understand that the barriers to change are partly technical, and could be solved through the adaptation of the software used to log calls. In that case the Government and the Pension Service should work together to adapt their systems so that all callers can be assessed for all three benefits at once, regardless of whether they qualify for Pension Credit.

7.140 These are positive measures, which can and should be implemented in the short term. However, it is likely that while the onus remains on taxpayers to activate claims, the government will continue to face some difficulty in dramatically improving take-up. For example, of those pensioners who received a completed form from the Pension Service, around half still failed to forward their claim to their local authority for processing.

7.141 I understand that the Department for Work and Pensions is considering whether this claims process could be further simplified by The Pension Service passing CTB information directly to local authorities, instead of sending a short claim form to the taxpayer to forward. This seems a sensible step and, given that the Pension Service will have verified callers' personal details and satisfied themselves that pension credit can be paid, there seems little value in claimants having to re-sign a form to verify the same details for CTB.

Recommendation 7.7

The Government should build on recent efforts to streamline delivery of council tax rebates by adapting IT systems so that the Pension Service can act as a portal to rebates for all callers, regardless of pension credit eligibility.

Recommendation 7.8

Further improvements to the claims process should be pursued to allow the Pension Service to liaise directly with local authorities in processing rebate claims.

7.142 It is right that the Government should take steps within the current system to ensure that rebate entitlements are delivered as effectively and as fully as possible. However, given the particularly low take-up of CTB compared with other benefits, and the very significant barriers to take-up identified above, I believe there is also a need to look at a more radical overhaul of the way council tax rebates are delivered, in the medium-term.

Automated delivery of entitlements

7.143 In 2006, a joint team of DWP and local authority officials began a 'blue skies' project to look at the scope for automated delivery of CTB. They envisaged a model in which government agencies would share data, including some currently held by HM Revenue and Customs, to assess households' eligibility for CTB and initiate claims on that basis. Instead of individuals being required actively to apply for benefits, they would be asked to verify their assessed details after which benefits would be paid. Requirements to provide proof of circumstances would be minimised through a risk-based approach to claims, so that full verification would only be carried out where people were on the borderline of eligibility, or there was greater uncertainty about their status.

7.144 DWP officials are now working on a project with the Pension Service to consider the possibilities for gathering data and using it in CTB, pension credit and housing benefit claims processes. The ultimate extension of this approach would be that in theory households could be billed for council tax net of any rebate entitlement, but with a responsibility to inform the Government if the details on which it was calculated were incorrect.

7.145 More automatic delivery of entitlements would not be without risk. More streamlined checks of people's status as claimants might expose the Government to some increased risk of fraud, including if similar processes were applied more widely than to council tax benefit alone, for example to housing benefit. The Government would want to weigh these risks carefully given its responsibility for ensuring benefit fraud is not tolerated.

7.146 Nonetheless, there is a balance to be struck between concerns about preventing fraud, and equally valid concerns about the system failing genuinely entitled households. The current system appears to favour 100 per cent precision over easy accessibility for taxpayers, which may be the wrong balance to strike in the case of CTB, given its importance for the sustainability of council tax. An automated and risk-based system would be more user-friendly, and though a risk-based approach might allow for error in some cases, it would help to achieve the step-change in take-up that is in my view necessary for council tax rebates to successfully underpin a local property tax.

7.147 I strongly endorse the direction of this early work on automation, and urge the Government to pursue it as a matter of urgency. I recognise that this would also represent a philosophical change in the Government's treatment of CTB. Instead of it being an elective benefit with the onus on the claimant (as is appropriate in other benefits such as Jobseekers' Allowance) CTB would become an automatic entitlement. I believe that this shift is justified and necessary: as an elective benefit CTB is currently failing to reach a large number of entitled people, which undermines the perceived fairness of council tax itself.

7.148 Increasing take-up in this way would also not be without costs to the Government. The amounts currently unclaimed are large (up to £1.8 billion in 2004-05) and additional money spent on increased CTB take-up would clearly reduce the amount of money available to spend elsewhere. Nonetheless, I am clear that the success of the system of council tax rebates – and particularly its success in reaching entitled pensioners – is critical to the sustainability of council tax, and should be considered a priority.

Recommendation 7.9

Ministers should examine the scope for data sharing between agencies to proactively deliver council tax rebates to those who are entitled, with a view to achieving a step-change in the take-up of council tax benefit.

CTB eligibility criteria: options for reform

7.149 Achieving high levels of take-up would be a real step forward. However, even with full take-up of current entitlements, some households would still face a relatively high council tax burden as a proportion of income. Estimates for the Inquiry suggest that a significant number of ineligible pensioner households face a high council tax burden. Around 200,000 pay more than 10 per cent of their net household income in council tax but do not qualify for benefits. Of those households, 70 per cent are in the bottom two income deciles, of which a quarter of have savings under £25,000.

7.150 Work by Michael Orton's work for the Joseph Rowntree Foundation[29] has suggested that two million households are struggling to pay council tax. These are mostly low-income households in bands A-C. However, low-income households do exist in all bands, including a small but significant minority of band F-H households who have below-average incomes and may struggle to pay. Orton's estimate is based on the number of households receiving a council tax summons, which is only one possible indicator that households find it difficult to pay council tax. This approach will necessarily exclude those who struggled to pay but nonetheless did so by some means, and may include some who are able to pay but choose not to. Nonetheless it suggests that at present the burden of council tax may still be too high for some households.

7.151 There is, in my view, a strong case for more generous CTB eligibility criteria for some groups. It is clear that council tax can be a relatively large burden on households that fall outside the current thresholds for CTB, either because their income is over the 'applicable amount', or because their savings exceed the CTB 'capital limit'.

7.152 I have considered a number of options for reform of the current eligibility thresholds, including:

- **Increasing or abolishing the upper capital limit for pensioners**, to reduce the number of pensioner households excluded from eligibility for a rebate by their savings. This could also help reduce the extent to which benefit eligibility may act as a disincentive to save for retirement by ensuring that the capital thresholds do not penalise those who have saved;

- **Increasing the lower capital limit**, so that the first £10,000 in savings, and any income from it, would be disregarded for the purposes of benefit entitlement; and

- **Increasing the 'applicable amounts'** or income thresholds for both pensioners and working age households, so that liability for council tax would begin at a slightly higher level of income. The examples modelled increase applicable amounts by five per cent and ten per cent.[30]

---

[29] Orton, 2006.
[30] The cash value of "applicable amounts" varies between different groups; see Annex C for details.

Alignment with other benefits

7.153 In implementing any changes to CTB eligibility criteria, the Government would need to consider the knock-on implications for the other income-related benefits. At present CTB is considered part of a wider suite of policies aimed at tackling poverty, and in that context thresholds for housing benefit, income support and pension credit are mostly aligned with those for CTB. However there is already some difference between the thresholds applied to different benefits: notably, pension credit where no upper capital threshold exists.

7.154 Keeping eligibility criteria aligned has the advantage of providing a degree of consistency across the benefits system. There could be a risk that moving to different criteria for different benefits might be confusing for claimants, which could act against attempts to simplify the system to improve take-up.   In practice however, increasing the thresholds for all benefits together would be much more expensive than reforming council tax rebate criteria separately. The Government would have a very pragmatic choice to make about balancing the financial costs of continued alignment against the risk of added complexity. The example of capital thresholds for Pension Credit also shows that in some cases policy considerations, such as providing incentives to save for retirement, may outweigh concerns about keeping thresholds perfectly aligned.

7.155 I am primarily concerned with CTB as a specific mechanism to alleviate the burden of council tax. Recognised as a rebate, rather than a benefit, it could legitimately be detached from the rest of the suite of income-related benefits though it is currently administered alongside Housing Benefit by local authorities. The fact that other mechanisms can be used to address poverty among specific groups should not become a brake on any reform of CTB – I believe reform here is justified in its own right, to improve the sustainability of council tax.

Savings thresholds and pensioners

7.156 My primary focus in considering changes to eligibility criteria has been on pensioners, as the group most likely to be on fixed incomes, and about whom I have received by far the greatest number of submissions expressing concern. Evidence from survey and public deliberation work carried out for the Inquiry also supports a focus on older people as the group around whom concerns about council tax fairness are strongest.

7.157 Changes to capital limits have the potential to deliver benefits to significant numbers of pensioner households. Table 7.1 shows the likely costs of altering capital thresholds in different ways, and the amounts by which households would be expected to gain, on average, as a result. The options shown here concentrate on savings limits for pensioners, as modelling showed that since older people hold the majority of all savings, only a very small number of working-age households would benefit from changes to capital thresholds. Full details of this modelling, including on other options considered are provided in Annex C.

Table 7.1: Cost and impact of reform of CTB savings thresholds for pensioners[31]

	CTB costs:	Likely to benefit:	Average weekly gain:	
			households already entitled to full or partial CTB	newly-entitled households
Increase upper capital limit to £50,000 for pensioners	£195 million	370,000 pensioner households	n/a	£10.10
Increase upper capital limit to £50,000 and increase lower limit to £10,000 for pensioners	£260 million	1,040,000 pensioner households	£1.20	£10.00
Abolish upper capital limit for pensioners	£220 million	420,000 pensioner households	n/a	£10.00

7.158 The evidence suggests that raising the upper savings limit to £50,000 could have a significant impact for many pensioner households whose savings currently make them ineligible for CTB, who would gain rebates of around £10 per week on average. Around 370,000 pensioner households would be brought into eligibility for CTB by such a change, including 135,000 of the poorest pensioner households. Abolishing the threshold brings approximately a further 50,000 pensioner households into eligibility for a rebate worth similar amounts on average. Adjusting the lower limit makes a small difference to a large number of households who are already entitled to a partial rebate on their bills. Approximately three times as many households' gain by this measure compared with altering only the upper limit; however the benefits to many of them are small, at just £1.20 per week on average, suggesting that the extra costs of moving the lower limit might not be justified in terms of the impact on individual households.

7.159 The costs of these changes would be significant, though the extent to which they are realised would depend on take-up rates. However they would target significant support to households currently bearing a relatively large council tax burden, and would cost much less in any one year than the £800 million devoted to a £200 one-off payment to pensioner households in the 2005 Budget.

Income thresholds and working age households

7.160 Some submissions to the Inquiry suggested that reform should also look at the impact of council tax and benefit eligibility criteria on working age households. For working age households, the income thresholds on rebate entitlement are most important, with council tax liability beginning at a relatively low level of income.[32] Some measures for working age households have been modelled in this light. Again, full details of this modelling can be found in Annex C, including some options not pursued here.

---

[31] All costs based on full take-up of new entitlement compared with full take-up of current entitlement (see Annex C). Costings on a Great Britain basis since CTB changes would also affect eligibility in Scotland and Wales.

[32] The level of income at which council tax liability begins will vary depending on the composition of the household. For example, the income threshold for a single person under 25 is approximately £45 per week; for a pensioner couple, approximately £175 per week; and for a couple with two children, approximately £200 per week.

Table 7.2: Cost and impact of reform of CTB income thresholds for working age households[33]

	CTB costs:	Likely to benefit:	Average weekly gain:	
			households already entitled to full or partial CTB	newly-entitled households
Increase applicable amounts for working age households by 5 per cent	£60 million	980,000 working age households	£1.20	£0.90
Increase applicable amounts for working age households by 10 per cent	£130 million	1,100,000 working age households	£2.30	£1.70

7.161   The options shown above represent a one-off increase in the level of income at which council tax liability begins. Changes of this nature have the potential to reach large numbers of households, though the amounts gained by each would be very small. It may be more important that the thresholds are uprated in a way that ensures eligibility for rebates keeps pace with earnings growth. Pensioners and lone parents have seen particularly generous uprating of income thresholds in recent years.

7.162   It may also be that council tax rebates is not the best vehicle for addressing poverty and work incentives in working age households. These are issues that go much wider than council tax and are beyond the scope of this Inquiry, so are likely to be best considered in the context of wider welfare policy including the tax credits system. I am therefore not recommending changes to the applicable amounts.

Recommendation 7.10

The Government should increase the savings limit on council tax rebate eligibility to £50,000 for pensioners.

Recommendation 7.11

The Government should, over time, abolish the savings limit in CTB for pensioners, so aligning council tax rebate thresholds with the criteria for eligibility to the pension credit.

Other options for relieving the burden of council tax

7.163   CTB is the primary mechanism by which households' liability for council tax can be adjusted to take into account their circumstances, making reform of CTB the option of first-resort for dealing with council tax-related hardship. However the government could also consider other options to help those struggling to pay council tax. If the costs of benefit reform proved a barrier to implementation, these other options might deserve serious consideration.

Rebates linked to income   7.164   For instance some US states use a "circuit breaker" rebate to ensure no household pays more than a set proportion of their income in property tax. I have considered whether a similar scheme might be possible in England. A rebate of this kind would probably have to operate similarly to income tax reconciliations, with the taxpayer applying for a rebate after the end of the financial year once total income was known. It would probably have to apply to gross household income,

---

[33] All costs based on full take-up of new entitlement compared with full take-up of current entitlement (see Annex C). Costings on a Great Britain basis since CTB changes would also affect eligibility in Scotland and Wales.

since taking into account housing costs and other factors would make the scheme extremely complex and perhaps open to abuse. In the US such schemes tend not to exist alongside a CTB-type mechanism. However in England it could be available as a supplement to council tax benefit, so that a household would first have to claim any CTB entitlement. This in itself could be an advantage of a 'circuit breaker' scheme, which would be reasonably explicable to the public and could be used as a lever to encourage take-up existing entitlements.

7.165 A rebate of all council tax above 10 per cent of gross household income would cost approximately £100 million in 2006-07 and benefit over 350,000 households, of which 70 per cent are in the bottom two income deciles. Around 55 per cent of households receiving a rebate would be pensioners. If council tax continued to rise faster than average earnings, one would expect the costs of a rebate also to rise over time.

Deferred payment for pensioner homeowners

7.166 Deferred payment schemes are used in some countries to allow pensioners with equity in their homes to postpone property tax liability until their property is sold. For example, the Canadian province of British Colombia has operated a deferral scheme for over-60s and some other homeowners since 1974, with 11,000 households currently making use of the option to defer tax. Householders must have at least 25 per cent equity against the property's assessed value, and pay interest on the amount deferred when the property is sold.

7.167 Equity release products are already available from a range of private sector lenders in this country and could in theory be used to pay council tax or for any other purpose. The Financial Services Authority regulates equity release products, providing assurance to those who take this option up. However commentators have raised concerns about the suitability of those schemes to older people, particularly if the amounts to be released are relatively small, in which case transaction costs might outweigh the benefit of equity release. The Institute for Public Policy Research suggests that in some cases the quality of advice from providers on equity release can be poor, creating a risk of mis-selling.[34] There is some doubt over whether markets are currently able to provide the right opportunities for equity release for low-income homeowners struggling with council tax.

7.168 Equity release might not be the right option for all households, and should be a matter of individual choice on take-up. However the Joseph Rowntree Foundation suggest that attitudes to inheritances are changing, and that people are increasingly prepared to draw down wealth for spending during their lifetime.[35] For some, releasing housing equity might be an attractive way of coping with tax liabilities in old age.

7.169 Equity release schemes linked to council tax could in theory be operated locally, but there might be economies of scale in running a national scheme, perhaps in collaboration with the financial services industry. There are modest precedents for this, including in existing provisions to allow homeowners moving into residential care to defer some fees until their property is sold. It would be important that equity release for council tax were considered carefully alongside government policy on social care, charges for which are partially determined by a person's assets including housing equity.

Conclusions

7.170 I concluded above that council tax is not broken. While it has some significant weaknesses, it also has some important strengths and should be retained, either alone or, in the longer term, alongside other local taxes and charges. To an extent, that conclusion rests on the premise that CTB

[34] Maxwell, D and Sodha, S, ippr, *Housing Wealth: first timers to old timers*, 2006.
[35] Joseph Rowntree Foundation, *Attitudes to Inheritance in Britain*, 2005.

can be used to achieve an acceptable link between tax liability and ability to pay for the lowest income households.

7.171   CTB is only partly succeeding in that role at present, mainly because of low take-up, with take-up among pensioners a particular concern. A new approach to the delivery and presentation of council tax benefit is therefore required. The Department for Work and Pensions, working with local authorities and the Pension Service, has made a promising start on work in this area, but this must now be pursued further and implemented as rapidly as possible.

7.172   There is also a case for some reform of CTB eligibility criteria. As a first priority the government should act to increase savings limits for pensioners, which are currently set at modest levels and may penalise those who have saved for their retirement.

7.173   Both increased take-up and an extension of eligibility would carry costs to the government (and hence taxpayers). However, I see these as necessary if the problem of perceived unfairness in council tax is to be addressed. In the medium term, reform of council tax as discussed earlier could produce offsetting savings in the benefit bill by reducing the liability of many low-income households.

LOCAL INCOME TAX

Local income taxes in other countries

7.174   I have argued in this chapter that council tax remains a sound local tax and should be retained, though it should be reformed and valuations updated in the medium term. This does not rule out further reform of the local government finance system, in the longer term. While the immediate focus should be on council tax benefit and management of pressures to stabilise council tax, it may be that in future, a developmental approach to reform could allow for a wider look at the balance of local taxation.

7.175   It is part of my remit to consider both alternatives to council tax and possible sources of supplementary revenue for local government. In respect of both these questions, local income tax (LIT) has been a prominent feature of the debate about local government finance, as part of formal submissions and in focus groups and survey responses. I have therefore explored in some detail the potential for a local income tax to be deployed in England, either alongside council tax or as a full or partial replacement to it.

7.176   In this section I will:

- consider the high level implications of a shift from property to income taxes, in terms of both the impact on taxpayers, particularly with regard to public perceptions of fairness, and the implications for local revenues and the local government finance system;

- discuss a number of questions around the detailed design of a local income tax, and explore some of the complexity of designing such a tax;

- present the outcomes of some modelling work on a local income tax in England, including the likely rate needed to fully or partially replace council tax; and

- address questions around the practical implementation of a LIT, including likely costs and timescales.

7.177   This chapter will focus on the potential for introducing a locally-variable income tax, with rate-setting powers for local authorities. However it would be possible to design a model in which income tax revenues contributed to financing local government without going as far as the locally-variable model described below. I will consider other options in Chapter 9, as part of a wider look at central government's financing of local services.

Background to the local income tax debate

7.178 Local income taxes are a relatively widely-used source of local government funding in other countries, and were present in two thirds of the EU's then fifteen member countries in 2004, as well as Japan, Canada and all but seven US states. As chart 7.11 demonstrates below, it is also relatively uncommon for local government to be entirely dependent on a single local tax, whether property-based as in the UK or income-based as in Sweden.

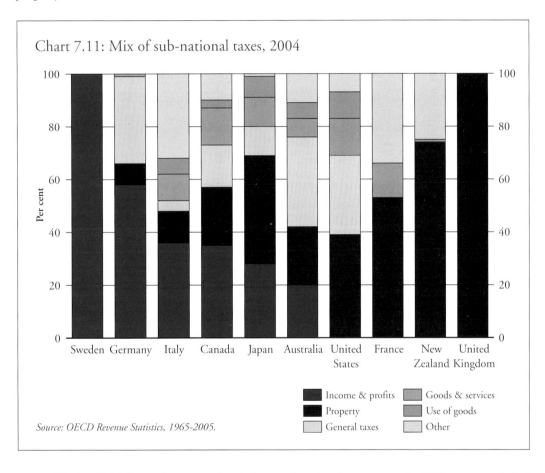

Chart 7.11: Mix of sub-national taxes, 2004

Legend: Income & profits, Property, General taxes, Goods & services, Use of goods, Other

Source: OECD Revenue Statistics, 1965-2005.

Local income tax in the UK

7.179 The Layfield Committee considered the case for a local income tax in 1976, and concluded that it was "the only feasible major new source of income" for local authorities, should the government judge that a new source of local revenue was necessary. Prior to Layfield, such taxes had been under consideration at various points during the 20th century, but had been rejected by previous bodies such as the Royal Commission on Local Taxation of 1901 and the Kempe Committee of 1914.

7.180 The Balance of Funding Review also pointed to LIT as the chief option, besides relocalisation of business rates, for achieving a shift in the balance of funding towards local revenues. Both Layfield and the Balance of Funding Review saw advantages in using a local income tax as a new local tax, on top of property taxes, so that more money could be both raised and spent locally, giving councils more direct accountability for their finances. In a sense there is nothing special about a local income tax for creating accountability (in fact, if administered via the PAYE system LIT might be less visible than council tax and so would arguably have less impact in terms of accountability); but it could be implemented in a way that could have some accountability benefits.

7.181 Other studies have raised doubts about the application of a local income tax, either for practical or principled reasons. Local income tax was considered again by the 1981 Green Paper on local taxation, which suggested that administering a local income tax through the national income tax system might be costly and highly complex.[36] More recently, Sir Peter Burt's independent committee in Scotland concluded that it would not be appropriate to introduce a LIT there because of concerns including the impact on incentives to work, and in light of the fact that taxes on income already contribute a relatively large share of total UK tax revenues.[37]

7.182 Supporters of local income taxes have tended to highlight three potential benefits of introducing them into the local government finance system. Firstly, it has been suggested that income taxes would be 'fairer' than property taxes in that liability should more closely reflect ability to pay. Secondly, those interested in achieving better local accountability and flexibility through a shift in the balance of funding have argued that introducing local income taxes alongside property taxes would be a positive step towards making local authorities less dependent on central grant. Thirdly, it has been suggested that introducing a naturally buoyant local tax would help make local government finance more sustainable in the long term.

7.183 I have considered all these high-level arguments, as well as some of the detailed practical questions around how a local income tax might operate in this country.

Fairness and the implications of a LIT for taxpayers

Public opinion on local income tax

7.184 Survey evidence suggests that, in principle, many people like the idea that council tax should be replaced with a local income tax, with nearly half of all respondents to an Inquiry-commissioned survey saying that council tax should be partly or fully replaced by LIT. However it may be that this support is not based on a true understanding of what local income tax would mean for respondents' own bills. Almost four in ten respondents did not have a view on local income taxes, suggesting the arguments around it are not widely familiar to people. And, while people recognise that pensioners would probably do well from a move to income-based taxation, relatively few (just 13 per cent) think that they would pay more themselves.

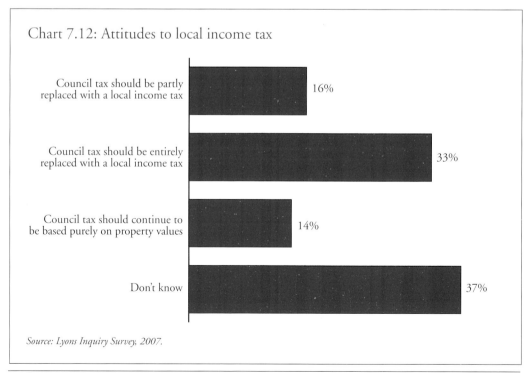

Chart 7.12: Attitudes to local income tax

Council tax should be partly replaced with a local income tax — 16%

Council tax should be entirely replaced with a local income tax — 33%

Council tax should continue to be based purely on property values — 14%

Don't know — 37%

Source: Lyons Inquiry Survey, 2007.

[36] *Alternatives to Domestic Rates*, HM Stationery Office, 1981.
[37] Local Government Finance Review Committee, *A Fairer Way*, 2006.

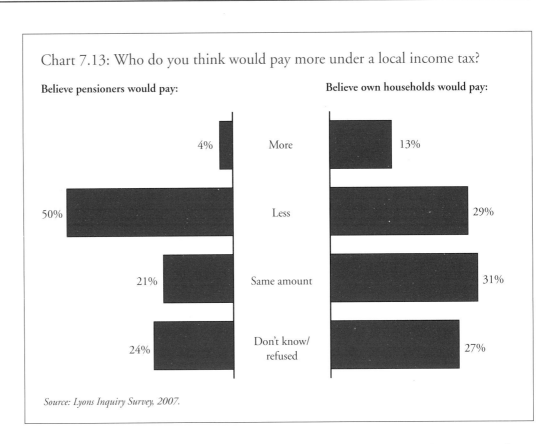

Chart 7.13: Who do you think would pay more under a local income tax?

Believe pensioners would pay: Believe own households would pay:

More — 4% / 13%
Less — 50% / 29%
Same amount — 21% / 31%
Don't know/refused — 24% / 27%

Source: Lyons Inquiry Survey, 2007.

Fairness

7.185   In fact, moving away from a property-based tax to an income tax would mean a significant rebalancing of the tax burden away from retired households and onto the working-age population. As shown earlier in this chapter, council tax liability is spread throughout adult life, while an individual's income tax and VAT liability is typically concentrated during their working life. Any decision to replace council tax with income taxes would therefore require a political judgement that retired households should, on average, pay a reduced burden, and younger working households a larger one.

7.186   Again, the crucial issue is what definition of fairness, or 'ability to pay' is applied. If income were the only measure of ability to pay then this shift would arguably be a fair one. However, I am concerned that this would neglect other relevant factors. I am not convinced, for example, that a pensioner household with a relatively modest income but significant savings or housing equity, is less able to pay than a young family with a larger income but no other assets. In this light I have some concerns about whether abandoning property taxes for income taxes would be fair; in practice this might simply replace one sort of perceived unfairness with another.

Convenience of collection versus visibility

7.187   Participants in focus groups for the Inquiry also raised issues around the practical experience of paying income taxes compared with council tax. Some felt collecting tax at source would be simpler than the present system of council tax, which required individuals to actively decide and organise the most appropriate method of payment for them. The way that income tax is paid made it less perceptible as a call on people's weekly or monthly resources than council tax:

> I don't consider it [income tax] an outgoing because you do your outgoings after your net pay... so everyone forgets the tax. You know you are not getting it, so it is not like an outgoing. (Focus group participant)

7.188   Others were concerned that a LIT might operate as a 'stealth tax', particularly if introduced alongside council tax. Nonetheless, the fairness of income and property taxes was the overriding theme in these discussions.

Implications of a LIT for local government finance

A buoyant local tax?

7.189   Moving from a property tax to an income-based tax could have profound implications for local government finance. Firstly, income tax yield could introduce natural buoyancy into the system, potentially removing the need for rate increases each year: instead yield would grow as people earned more, or if more people moved into work. However this would, by the same token, expose authorities to more uncertainty than in the past – tax income might go down in the bad times. To capture the benefits of buoyancy, authorities would also be exposed to risk.

7.190   If a LIT were introduced, the government of the day would want to consider the scope for measures to allow local authorities to budget sensibly around this risk, including embedding full end-year flexibility, and multi-year grant settlements. Other countries manage this risk successfully: for example in Denmark the annual negotiations around grants from central government take into account the expected growth in local revenues, with an expectation that the government may provide 'top up' resources during downturns.

7.191   It is important also not to overstate the extent to which a local income tax would be buoyant. My research indicates that while the natural buoyancy of an income-based tax would be an advantage, it would not make a local income tax immune to the pressures that are felt in council tax. Modelling for the Inquiry suggests that in fact the revenues from basic rate income tax may even tend to grow more slowly than council tax.[38] If spending requirements outstripped the amount of yield produced by this natural buoyancy, the rate of local income tax would come under pressure to increase.

7.192   It might therefore be unrealistic to expect a local income tax to support the kind of spending growth that has been supported by council tax in recent years, since doing so would be likely to require successive rate increases. Upward pressure on LIT rates would no doubt be just as controversial as increases in council tax bills, so it would still be crucial that the overall finance system were managed in a way that did not put the local tax under unsustainable pressure, whether based on income or property.

7.193   Revenues from all income tax as well as the individual higher and starting rates of tax, do tend to grow more strongly than revenues from the basic rate alone. Income tax revenues could potentially be assigned to local authorities as a buoyant income stream. This possibility is explored more fully in Chapter 9.

Adapting the grant system to a LIT

7.194   Moving from council tax to income taxes, or a combination of the two, would have consequences for the amounts of money different authorities could expect to raise in tax. For example areas with many retired or low-income households might have a smaller-than-average income tax base, while those with many low-banded homes might find income a stronger tax base than property. Any change in local taxes will tend to change the pattern of authorities' tax-raising capacity. This could have implications for the amount of grant equalisation that might be required if central government wished to continue compensating for tax base disparities.

7.195   The Balance of Funding Review suggested that income tax bases were less evenly distributed between areas than the council tax base, and that equalisation grant might therefore be expected to work harder if local taxes were based on income. Moreover, because authorities with high council tax bases also tend to be those with high income tax bases, if a LIT were introduced in a way that shifted the balance of funding towards local revenues, one might expect the differences between local authorities' tax bases to be amplified.

---

[38] See Annex C for full details of this modelling.

Designing a local income tax

7.196   As well as considering the theoretical case for a local income tax, I have also looked in some detail at whether it could be made to work in practice. In this context, there are a number of key issues to consider. While I have not sought to exhaustively cover every element of the design of a new local income tax, nor definitively solve all the elements discussed below, this section aims to draw out the complexity of these issues, and highlights some of the key questions that would need to be answered in order for a local income tax to be implemented.

Constraints   7.197   In introducing the power to raise local taxes on income, it would be necessary to decide how those powers might be appropriately defined and what limits might be placed on them. For example, the Scottish Executive has a limited power over the basic rate of income tax, which it can choose to vary by up to three pence above or below the UK basic rate.

7.198   A locally-variable LIT might appropriately be subject to similar constraints, to ensure a minimum level of revenues and prevent unfair tax competition between areas, or to reassure taxpayers that rate increases would not be excessive. For example, local authorities might be given powers to vary either side of a standard local rate, or could be given a limited menu of local rates to choose from. Central government would however retain the powers to set certain variables nationally, such as thresholds and allowances, which could affect the actual revenues raised by a given rate of LIT.

Level of the rate-setting authority   7.199   It would also be necessary to decide which authorities would have rate-setting powers, particularly in two-tier areas. I am inclined to the view that upper tier authorities, which are responsible for most local spending, should hold rate-setting powers: not least because a system in which around 150 authorities set income tax rates would certainly be less complex than one in which around 350 did so, which could be particularly important for employers if they were to administer the new tax through payrolls.[39] However this would alter the current role of district councils as the billing authority for local tax, and a mechanism for ensuring they would still be able to influence rate-setting decisions would be important. It would also be necessary to consider whether precepting authorities should have a claim on the revenues from a new tax, and if so, how this would operate.

Place of taxation   7.200   Property taxes are clearly applicable to a given authority area, based on the location of taxable property. In taxing income and particularly wages, it would be necessary to decide whether liability would apply according to the taxpayer's residence, or their place of work. My analysis is based on the presumption that taxpayers would be liable for LIT at the rate set by the authority in which they live. Since the options modelled assume that a local income tax would replace all or part of council tax, they also assume that local income tax might aim to retain one of the benefits of that tax: a strong link between tax paid and services delivered in the area in which people live and vote. I recognise that some authorities might feel disadvantaged by this – particularly those with large numbers of commuters coming into the area to work. This is, however, a criticism that could be levelled at any residence-based local tax, including council tax, so need not undermine the case for a local income tax based on residence as such.

---

[39]   Shire Counties, Metropolitan Districts, Unitary Authorities and London Boroughs = 150 authorities in total ('Upper tier refers to County Councils in two-tier areas, not in this case the Greater London Authority). Shire Districts, Metropolitan Districts, Unitary Authorities and London Boroughs = 354 authorities in total.

Defining taxable income   **7.201**   Income tax is levied on a number of different forms of income, the most obvious being wages from employment. However, national income tax also applies to a variety of other sources, including self-employment income, pensions, some benefits, income from savings and dividends and income from renting out property. It would be necessary to decide which of these types of income would be subject to a new local income tax. It would also be important to consider the impact this could have on incentivising tax-motivated incorporation.

7.202   In the present system, income from savings and dividends is dealt with through deduction at source by financial institutions, so that for the majority of taxpayers the process happens automatically. Higher rate taxpayers pay any additional amount due through self-assessment. However, to deduct a variable amount according to local rates would either require financial institutions to have variable deduction systems, which would be extremely complex, or would need taxpayers to fill in individual tax returns. CIPFA concluded in 2004 that the only way to tax income from savings and dividends would be to introduce universal tax returns, which would be a significant change to our current system of deduction at source for most taxpayers.[40] CIPFA further concluded that the additional revenue to be raised from taxing savings and dividends would probably be outweighed by the additional cost of moving to universal tax returns, and I have seen no evidence to contradict this.

IT bracket to which LIT would apply   **7.203**   Different commentators have made various suggestions about the element of income tax which might be increased by a LIT. Some assume an increase in both the basic and higher rates of tax locally; others focus on the basic rate only. Both approaches have some merits: in particular increasing the higher rate might be a way of introducing some progressiveness to income at the top end of the scale, which is arguably a weakness of the council tax at present.

7.204   However, for the purposes of the Inquiry's own analysis local income tax is applied only to the basic rate of income tax. This reflects a judgement that since higher-rate taxpayers are not evenly distributed throughout the country, local authorities' ability to benefit from higher rate revenues would be highly variable. If LIT rates were not to vary too greatly, the grant system would need to adjust for those differences, implying quite ambitious equalisation between areas. Basic rate income taxpayers are distributed much more evenly across the country, creating fewer disparities between areas' tax-raising capacity and therefore making it a better local tax base.

7.205   The advantages of a local stake in higher rate income tax might be realised without local rate-setting powers through assignment of national revenues to local government, as discussed in Chapter 9.

Modelling a local income tax

7.206   The options explored below apply a LIT as an addition to the current 22 pence basic rate. Two scenarios were modelled:

- **full replacement LIT**, which would take the place of council tax, raising the full £22 billion raised in council tax (gross of council tax benefit) in 2006-07. An average local rate of 7.7 pence on the basic rate of income tax would raise the full amount necessary to replace council tax; and

- **partial replacement LIT**, which would replace approximately half of council tax. Council tax would be retained but reduced so that it raised approximately £11 billion (gross of council tax benefit) in 2006-07. An average local rate of 3.9 pence on the basic rate of income tax would replace half the current yield from council tax, and allow band D council tax to be reduced to an average of £629.

---

[40]   CIPFA, *Reviewing the case for a Local Income Tax* Balance of Funding Review Paper 19, 2004.

Impact by income group

7.207 A local income tax would be more progressive to income overall than council tax, even with full take-up of benefits. Chart 7.14 shows some reduction in the average burden on the bottom half of the income distribution, with the burden remaining progressive for all but the top income group. This reflects the fact that the top income decile contains many higher-rate taxpayers. The modelling also confirmed that, on average, pensioners and one-parent households would pay less under a local income tax than under council tax, with other working-age households paying more.

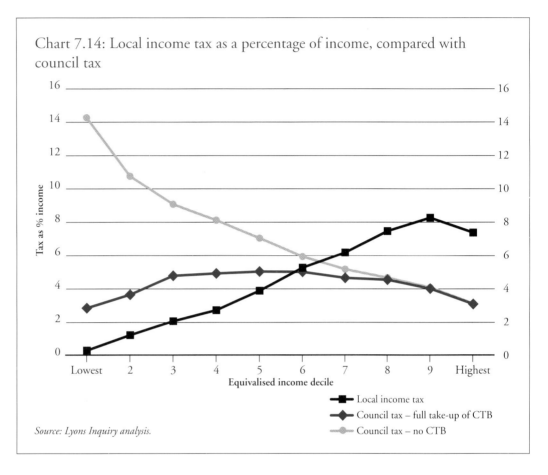

Chart 7.14: Local income tax as a percentage of income, compared with council tax

Tax as % income

Equivalised income decile

— Local income tax
— Council tax – full take-up of CTB
— Council tax – no CTB

Source: Lyons Inquiry analysis.

The impact of CTB savings on LIT rates

7.208 These rates of local income tax are based on the assumption that the new tax would replace council tax, including the element of council tax that is paid by the Government as council tax benefit. If local income tax were to replace both of these there would, on the face of it, be a saving to the Government, which would no longer have to pay council tax benefit in the case of a full replacement LIT, or would pay less under a partial replacement LIT.

7.209 It would be a matter for the Government to decide how best to use those savings, but it could choose to use them to hold down overall rates of tax. If council tax benefit savings were paid back to local government as grant, the overall amount of local tax necessary would be lower. A full replacement LIT offset by the £3.15 billion currently paid in CTB (at current levels of take-up) could be set at 6.6 pence on the basic rate. A partial replacement LIT could in theory be set at 3.3 pence.

7.210 In practice it is likely that CTB savings would be somewhat lower than these headline figures. By increasing income tax rates, households' net income would be reduced and they might become eligible for new or increased support through tax credits or other benefits. In that case, the extra social security expenditure would to some extent offset the savings made in council tax benefit; however without detailed data it is not possible to test the precise impact of these effects.

LIT as a supplement to council tax

7.211   A further element of my remit was to consider whether Local Income Tax might have a role as a source of supplementary revenue for local government. Key questions are the scale of revenues that might be raised through a supplementary tax on income, and the public acceptability of such a levy.

7.212   A supplement levied at 1 pence on the basic rate of income tax would raise £2.87 billion in 2006-07.[41] A supplement of this size would therefore be a substantial new source of revenue, roughly equivalent to total budgets across the country for cultural services.

7.213   The yield from a one pence supplement would be equivalent to, on average, about 13 per cent of the average authority's budgeted council tax yield for 2006-07. This proportion would vary widely across the country, with the supplement raising an amount equivalent to just 7.6 per cent of the council tax take in West Somerset, up to 28.8 per cent in Wandsworth and 47.8 per cent in the City of London. This variation in the amounts raised by authories partly reflects the differences in incomes between areas, as well as the proportion of the population in work. The national average amount levied per head of population would be £57, varying from £33 (Barrow-in-Furness) to £88 (Surrey Heath).[42] The Government would need to consider how far this unevenness would be compensated for by the grant system.

7.214   However, focus group work conducted on behalf of the Inquiry has suggested a lack of public appetite for LIT as a supplement to council tax, because of a concern among respondents that they might be paying twice for the same services.

> *Having it alongside [council tax] is too much. To us it would just seem like another tax.* (Focus group participant)

7.215   If the motivation for introducing an income tax supplement were to relieve the pressure on council tax, strong public support for such a move would be essential. While I have made no presumption in my work about what the revenues from a supplement might be used for, I am clear that local authorities would need to communicate its purpose to their communities, and be able to reassure citizens that the new tax would deliver tangible benefits according to local preferences. Under those circumstances, a supplementary LIT might be an option for the medium term.

Implementation

7.216   For a local income tax to be adopted in England, the Government would need to be satisfied that it was not only desirable in principle but achievable in practice. Introducing any new tax throws up a raft of complex and often minutely detailed problems, and while it is beyond the scope of this Inquiry to resolve them all, it is worth exposing some of those complexities and understanding their implications for how, and how soon, a new tax might realistically be implemented.

Collection mechanisms

7.217   Most income tax is collected at the time wages are paid via the Pay-As-You-Earn (PAYE) system. Unlike in many other countries where local income taxes exist, UK taxpayers do not, in the majority of cases, fill in annual tax returns. A LIT which required a move towards tax returns for all would be unattractive to the Government and more complex for many taxpayers, whereas a system which integrated a LIT with PAYE would retain the convenience of that system for taxpayers.

---

[41] Based on data from HM Revenue and Customs. See Annex C for more details.

[42] Excludes City of London.

7.218 I have explored two specific options for the collection of locally-variable income taxes:

- The "**Tax tables**" approach seeks to use the present system of employers withholding tax from pay. At present employers use a set of tax tables (which are published by the Government) to calculate how much of each employee's pay to withhold and pay to HM Revenue and Customs (HMRC). A local income tax could be implemented by creating new tax tables for the new local rates of tax. Employers would then need to be told by HMRC which set of tables to use, depending on which authority area the employee lived in.

- The "**Coding adjustments**" approach (suggested by CIPFA in one of their later proposals on this topic) uses adjustments to each person's tax free allowance to collect the local element of income tax. In this option we assume that HMRC would need to use data on earnings to calculate each person's expected local tax liability and subtract this from their tax free allowance for the year, so that over the year they should pay the right amount of local and national tax.[43]

7.219 For the self employed, higher rate taxpayers and people with more complex tax affairs the self assessment system would continue to operate and could be used to collect local tax liability.

7.220 These two approaches have different advantages and disadvantages. The tax tables approach would be the most consistent with the current principles of the PAYE system. Employees would pay their local tax over the course of the year as they do with their national tax, and most people should have paid the right amount of tax by the end of the year, in most cases avoiding the need for adjustments at year-end. That would reduce the complexity of the system for individuals, and for HMRC (for whom a large number of end-year adjustments would be a substantial additional burden).

7.221 However, the tax tables approach does have some disadvantages. While convenient for taxpayers (and thus potentially less visible and painful than council tax), taxes collected in this way might lack transparency. Separate itemisation of local taxes on payslips would help, though this would require legislation to make it possible.

7.222 Crucially, the tax tables approach would be likely to impose a substantial administrative burden on employers. Variable rates would make the operation of payroll systems much more complicated, and the greater the variance permitted, the greater the complexity. It should be possible to design software to cope with much of the practical work of processing variable tax rates; however there would be initial costs associated with buying in that software and adapting systems to it. For small businesses, and particularly those without computerised payroll systems, the burden of implementing the new tax would be particularly heavy.

7.223 Operating the alternative system of coding adjustments would not impose that administrative burden on employers, who would continue to operate the system as they do now. Local tax would be collected via the national income tax system by altering each employee's tax code in HMRC. There are some limited precedents for this: coding adjustments are used for some taxpayers at present to collect small amounts of underpaid tax from previous years.

---

[43] A variant on this option has been suggested by the Liberal Democratic Party, which would involve deducting local income tax at a standard rate from all taxpayers and settling up at the end of year, depending on the actual LIT rate that a taxpayer should have faced.

7.224 However, this approach has some substantial drawbacks. Individuals' tax codes are calculated some months in advance of the beginning of the tax year, and to use them to collect LIT in this way HMRC would have to make estimates of individual incomes for the forthcoming tax year at that point. Any change in an individual's income, or the local tax rate to which they were subject (for example if they moved to an authority area with a different rate), during the course of the year would mean that they paid the wrong amount of tax. It is therefore likely that a very large number of taxpayers would pay the wrong amount of tax during the year, and would have to enter a process of end-year reconciliation with HMRC, creating a substantial new administrative burden for them. Some taxpayers already have to engage in such reconciliation, but the number is fairly small. It could also create confusion and difficulties for taxpayers, including the possibility of unexpectedly owing tax at the end of the year.

7.225 On balance, I consider that of the two systems, the tax tables approach is the better, as it would be much easier for taxpayers to understand, require fewer end-year corrections (which can also create hardship for those on modest incomes) and less burdensome to operate overall. However, I recognise that there would be potentially significant new burdens on employers. Should the Government wish to implement a local income tax in the future, further detailed work would be needed to assess the costs to business of running such a system, and what steps might be taken to minimise that burden.

Timing of local budget decisions

7.226 Council tax increases are decided as part of authorities' annual budgeting process, which generally takes place in February and March. Once rates have been decided, bills can be sent out, with all the effort of collection being handled locally. The collection mechanisms for local income taxes would necessitate big changes to the timetable for local decision-making about tax rates.

7.227 For example, the tax tables approach would require HMRC to have full information about local income tax rates in every authority by the Autumn, when tax tables are published. The coding adjustment approach would require several months' work on calculating tax liabilities ahead of the start of each financial year. Either method would bring forward local decision-making by about six months compared to now, which could in turn require a radical change to the timing of grant settlement decisions. The Government would need to consider how this could be accommodated, perhaps by building on the practice of three-year settlements.

Costs of implementation: HM Revenue and Customs

7.228 There would undoubtedly be significant costs involved in moving to a new system of taxation. The scenarios above assume that HMRC would remain the body with responsibility for income tax collection, so many of those costs would fall to them. It is not possible to arrive at precise estimates of the costs of collecting a LIT without specifying in much greater detail how it would operate, and any costings would be highly susceptible to change according to decisions about some of the complex issues outlined above, and many other operational questions.

7.229 However, a preliminary and indicative estimate of possible costs to HMRC suggest a range of £125 – 200 million for set up costs, with ongoing costs potentially in the order of £10 million per year, for the tax tables option, and a range of £340 – 520 million for set up costs, with ongoing costs of £30 – 45 million per year, for the coding adjustments approach.[44] Given the broad range of new activities that it would be necessary for HMRC to design and implement – including additional staffing, new IT systems, enforcement activity, and establishing processes with both local authorities and businesses – in order to support the introduction of a LIT, these estimates clearly remain subject to significant variation.

---

[44] HMRC, based on Lyons Inquiry specifications; not indicative of Government policy.

| Costs to employers | 7.230 It is important to recognise that the costs of implementing a LIT might not be confined to government. It is difficult to estimate the likely costs to employers of administering a LIT, not least because the available technology at the time of implementation will have a big impact on the initial costs of changing to a new system. The government of the day would of course be expected to conduct a full assessment of the likely impact on business of the new tax. Work for the Balance of Funding Review by CIPFA suggested start-up costs to business in the order of £100 million and this remains a reasonable estimate, though it would obviously be affected by the timing and detailed implementation of any changes. As noted above, it is likely that small and medium-sized enterprises would be particularly affected, and the government might wish to consider schemes to mitigate initial costs for small businesses. |

Costs to local authorities

7.231 Separately from these costs there would also be financial implications for local authorities. If LIT were to be introduced as a full replacement for council tax it could generate significant savings to local authorities, who currently bear the costs of council tax collection and enforcement, of around £340 million per year, and to central government who bear the costs of most council tax benefit administration through a grant to authorities of around £280 million per year.[45] There would be a role for local authorities to assist HMRC in collecting and enforcing payments of a LIT, and this would have cost implications for authorities.

7.232 At present the responsibility for collecting council tax (and consequent revenue risk) is local. Local and central government would also need to reach an understanding on who would bear the risks of default on local income taxes, and who would prosecute non-payment.

Timetable for implementation

7.233 Preparing for the implementation of a new local income tax would be a complex process, and as such would require a long-enough lead time to ensure the tax were robust and sustainable once introduced. Preparations would be expected to include:

- a policy design phase, including consultation with the public and with businesses, to explore detailed questions around the type of scheme that could be supported;

- passage of legislation providing for the tax change;

- development of new IT software for tax collection. It is likely that IT development could not be progressed until after policy had been fixed and legislation passed; and

- roll-out to business payroll systems if required, and integration with the local government finance settlement process.

7.234 Initial views from HMRC suggest a total lead time, depending on the complexity of the scheme being introduced, of approximately six to seven years from the point at which the government decided to work towards a LIT.

Implications of a LIT for the devolved countries

7.235 If a local income tax were introduced in England this might also have implications also for the devolved countries, where I know these issues have attracted some political interest. Council tax does at present exist in Scotland and Wales; and Northern Ireland has a system of local and regional rates, on which the Government has implemented a separate review. Local taxation is devolved in Scotland, although Wales is governed by the same system of primary legislation as England. Since I am not recommending that a local income tax be implemented in England in the short or medium term, it would be speculative to go any further into the possible implications for the devolved countries of a future LIT. If the Government were attracted to a local income tax in future, it would need to consult the devolved administrations in Scotland, Wales and Northern Ireland on any consequences for them of such a change.

---

[45] CLG, figures for 2005-06.

Conclusions

7.236 Local income taxes were seen as a positive option in many submissions to the inquiry, demonstrating the resonance of the idea that 'fair' taxation is based on ability to pay, or income. Income-based taxes could introduce greater progressiveness to income both for the poorest households and at the top of the income scale, in a way that council tax presently cannot, even with full take-up of council tax benefit. They could significantly reduce the burden of local taxes on those groups with the lowest average incomes, notably pensioners and lone parents.

7.237 However, it is important to recognise the limitations of local income taxes. A LIT would be progressive to income but might mean substantial increases in tax for the working population. There is evidence that the public may have unrealistic expectations of what a local income tax would mean for them, so it is not clear that in-principle support for taxes based on income would translate into support for a local income tax in practice.

7.238 Local income taxes are naturally buoyant, though not infinitely so. In practice a LIT on the basic rate might deliver less buoyant funding than the existing streams of revenue to local government, while introducing a risk that local tax revenues could go down as well as up. It would therefore be wrong to assume that income taxes could withstand pressures that property taxes cannot: managing pressures effectively will be essential if any local tax is to remain sustainable in the long term, and requires discipline from both central and local government.

7.239 I am satisfied that a local income tax could be feasible in England and could viably replace all or part of council tax, or operate alongside it. Implementation of a LIT would however require thorough preparation to ensure that it could be properly integrated with existing PAYE and Self-Assessment systems, and that local authorities and HMRC were given adequate time to prepare for a transition.

7.240 Particular attention should be given to the likely costs to employers, and particularly small business, of administering locally-variable income tax rates. The Government might wish to consider options for providing financial support to help businesses meet the initial costs of administering the new tax. If a LIT were introduced as a full or partial replacement for council tax, savings in council tax benefit might be a source of funding for such a scheme.

7.241 The desirability of a LIT is a matter of political judgement, particularly in view of the substantial lead times involved in implementing a new local tax. The Government would also want to consider broader questions about the overall balance of the tax system, the load on different tax bases and overall incentives, in considering the implementation of a LIT. My analysis suggests that a preparatory period of more than one parliamentary term should be assumed, making a LIT a significant undertaking and an option for the medium to long term.

LOCAL SERVICE CHARGES

7.242 While council tax is the largest revenue stream controlled by local authorities, other sources of income are available in the form of fees and charges for some local services. While not all charges are locally set, and a variety of conditions apply to their use, charging nevertheless represents a key financial flexibility for local authorities.

7.243 I have argued that greater flexibility is a key part of equipping local authorities to deal with pressure on budgets. Equally, it is right that if local communities wish to invest in the improvement of their area, or in improving a service, they should have the means to do so. While council tax provides one option for raising funds in support of local ambitions, in many cases a charge on the users of a particular service may be an appropriate and more popular way of financing those choices.

7.244 Charges also have the potential to be a significant policy tool, if used strategically. Place-shaping in an area should include the judicious use of charges; for example, to pay for improvements which directly benefit services users who are willing to pay for them, to subsidise services for a particular group such as children or older people, and to support wider policy objectives such as changing behaviours or moderating demand for a particular service.

7.245 I will consider how far the current framework for charging allows for financial flexibilities to support local choice and place-shaping. My recommendations will focus on the general use of charging and on any specific areas where new powers might be called for.

The current picture

7.246 Income from charges already represents a significant part of local authorities' revenues. In 2003-04 (the latest year for which published data in this form is available), local authorities received approximately £10.2 billion from sales, fees and charges, which comprised 8.5 per cent of all income.[46] Over a quarter of all councils raised more income from sales fees and charges than from council tax. The amount of money raised from fees and charges has grown steadily and in line with total spending, making charging income a relatively stable proportion of local revenues.

7.247 There is a high degree of variation between areas, and between services, in the use of charging. In cash terms, revenue from charges is highest from social services, education, and highways. As a proportion of all funding for different services, charging income is most significant in highways and transport spending.

7.248 Chart 7.15 shows that charging as a proportion of service expenditure varies significantly between types of authority, whose powers will differ, but also between authorities of the same type. Since authorities' spending levels also differ widely, this means that there is also significant variation in the level of charges raised per head of population in different authorities.

---

[46] Some outturn data on revenue from fees and charges is available for 2004-05 and 2005-06; however comparable data on the overall proportion of local authority income derived from charging is not available beyond 2003-04.

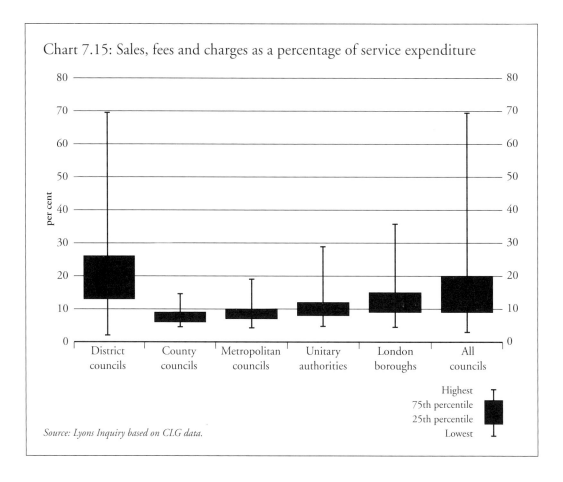

Chart 7.15: Sales, fees and charges as a percentage of service expenditure

Source: Lyons Inquiry based on CLG data.

Legislative powers on charging

7.249 Local authorities have a variety of powers to charge for different services, many of them enacted as individual provisions attached to a particular local government function. The Audit Commission's 1999 paper *The Price is Right* noted the wide variance in councils' discretion to charge for different services, from those which could be charged for at levels set locally, to those which councils were required to provide and prohibited from charging for. At that time the Audit Commission recommended that government should undertake a review of the logic and consistency underpinning the framework of charging powers, and consider introducing a general power to charge for discretionary services, to encourage local innovation.

7.250 In 2003 the Government introduced such a charging power, and new powers to trade commercially (see box for more details). These changes were to some extent the financial corollary of the well-being power in the 2000 Local Government Act, which enables authorities to take any steps they consider likely to promote or improve the economic, social or environmental well-being of their communities but did not extend to raising taxes or charges. Following the 2003 Act, local authorities have been able to take innovative action in support of local well-being, alongside relatively widely-drawn charging powers around non-core services. Taken together these provisions represent significant new local flexibilities.

Charging and trading powers in the Local Government Act 2003

Section 93 of the 2003 Local Government Act conferred a new power on 'best value authorities' to charge for some services.[47] Certain conditions apply to this power:

- authorities may only use this power to charge for "discretionary services". This excludes services that the authority has a statutory duty to provide, but covers improvements to statutory services that go beyond the level of provision required by law;

- authorities may only set charges up to the level that is deemed to "cover the cost of provision" – that is, they may not make a profit through the use of charges under this power; and

- if another legal power to charge already applies to a service, or an authority is expressly prohibited from charging for a service, this power may not be used.

Authorities can continue to charge for statutory services or charge at levels above cost-recovery where there were already legal powers to do so.

Section 95 of the 2003 Act makes provision for the Secretary of State to empower best value authorities to do for a commercial purpose anything that they are authorised to do to carry out their ordinary functions, by trading commercially through a company. This provision allows for such companies to trade at a profit, which may be returned to the local authority through dividends and shares. A local authority must prepare a business case and risk analysis before using trading powers.

Full details and guidance on the use of charging and trading powers under the 2003 Act may be found at www.communities.gov.uk

---

7.251 However, early evidence on use of these new powers suggests that take-up of these new flexibilities has been limited. A survey by the Local Government Association in 2004[48] showed that 77 per cent of councils were not using the new charging powers and had no plans to do so. Around 80 per cent were not using the new trading powers and had no plans to do so.

7.252 That survey was conducted when the new powers were still relatively new and untested; as yet there is not enough data to judge how far their use has since moved on. A recent CLG paper suggested that:

> *trading and charging powers, while welcomed 'in principle' by some authorities and deployed by others, are perceived by most authorities to be having a marginal impact..; this is an area where a small number of 'innovating authorities' are keen... but where most authorities are reluctant to explore the limits of the powers available to them.*[49]

7.253 It is disappointing that local authorities, many of whom lobbied strongly for the wellbeing power and for greater financial flexibility, have not embraced the new charging and trading powers more enthusiastically. It is therefore important to understand what barriers, either internal or external, might prevent local government from innovating in this area.

---

[47] Authorities in the top three categories in their Comprehensive Performance Assessment:: 'excellent', 'good' or 'fair'.

[48] LGA, *Loosening the reins: a survey of local authority approaches to prudential borrowing, charging and trading*, 2004.

[49] CLG, *Evaluation of Freedoms and Flexibilities in Local Government: Baseline study*, 2006.

Barriers to wider use of charging and trading powers

7.254 Early work by the Audit Commission to investigate the latest picture on use of powers suggests a number of possible barriers to charging and trading:[50]

- public acceptance of charging schemes can be difficult to secure. The Audit Commission suggest that high quality engagement with the public is crucial to securing support for charging schemes, by providing clarity about the policy aims being pursued, and the likely benefits to service users. Poor engagement risks public suspicion that charges are in place only to raise revenue, and that they may be paying twice for the same services;

- political willingness to consider charging or trading is crucial. Some councils express a preference for taxation over user charges, seeing this as a fairer way of providing 'free' services. This is a legitimate debate and should be subject to local choice: however the Audit Commission suggest that this debate has some way to go in engaging local service users and taxpayers:

  > There would seem to be little public appetite to fund increasing proportions of council activity through direct charging. This may simply reflect the fact that no one has yet made a convincing case to the public for changing the balance of funding from taxation to charges. (Audit Commission)

- capacity constraints can be a problem, particularly in smaller councils for whom developing charging policies that take account of information about service costs, local markets and the likely impact of charges may be challenging. Trading is regarded by some councils as complex and risky, or peripheral to councils' core role as a provider of public services. There is also a perception that guidance from central government on local authority trading has been cautious, which does not encourage innovation or risk-taking;

- information on the cost of service provision may not be available or well understood. Some councils cite difficulty in discerning the true costs of services as a barrier to making use of the 2003 power, which requires that charges do not exceed cost-recovery; and

- European Union procurement rules may be a particular barrier to local authority trading, since they will impact on councils' ability to award contracts to their special-purpose trading companies. The complexity of the rules in this area may deter councils from entering the fray.

Local behaviours

7.255 It is striking that while some of these barriers are structural, such as the interaction between trading powers and EU legislation, the majority are linked to local government confidence and behaviours. I have not found evidence that central government has got the legal framework drastically wrong, nor that the powers conferred on authorities are too tightly drawn to permit action. However this apparent lack of capacity and confidence to innovate perhaps further demonstrates that local strategic decision-making has been 'crowded out' by local authorities' perceived core role as service deliverers against a centrally-allotted budget. There is perhaps a need to both make space for local action, and to create an appetite for it.

---

[50] Audit Commission, *Charging for local services: submission to the Lyons Inquiry based on scoping research for a national study*, 2006.

7.256 Some councils are making innovative use of charging to pursue policy objectives and help meet costs in a way that is perceived as fair. For example, Cornwall County Council has used charging powers to finance the investment needed to upgrade facilities at Newquay Airport. The council-owned airport encourages inward investment to the region and supports local tourism. Though unpopular with some airlines, the £5 per passenger charge ensures the Council's share of the £44 million improvement costs are borne largely by airport users and not local council taxpayers.

7.257 However, the general picture if one of reticence on the part of authorities to make wider use of charges. 'The Price is Right' suggested in 1999 that only 12 per cent of local decisions about charges were the result of tariff redesign or a wider review of charging policy. The vast majority of charges were simply increased with inflation or were not changed at all. This is a significant missed opportunity, since it suggests councils are not taking a strategic approach to making charges and services work together. The Audit Commission make the valid point that 'doing more' on charging need not always mean higher charges – one council in their study suggested that reducing charges could increase service use, which could mean greater efficiency against fixed overheads.

7.258 The Local Government Association (LGA) and Improvement and Development Agency (IDeA) published advice for councils on getting the best from charging and trading, including a checklist of key actions including:

- conducting an internal review of charging and trading activity;

- adopting a policy on charging and trading in line with the council's strategic aims;

- taking forward an appraisal of the options available to the council; and

- agreeing and implementing a business case and change programme that take into account both practical and cultural steps needed to charge or trade successfully.[51]

7.259 These seem to me the right tests of whether authorities have explored the possibilities that charging might offer, and I endorse them fully, but would add that significant changes must be informed by, and communicated through, effective engagement with the local community, including citizens, businesses and the voluntary sector, as appropriate.

The legal framework for charging

7.260 A wide range of legal powers to charge already exist, and I do not yet see a case for more widely drawn general powers than the 2003 Act provides, though the discretionary power in the 2003 Act should be made available to all local authorities. Powers to charge should be a means by which councils can exercise strategic management of local budgets, not a reward scheme for those who have already done so.

7.261 Some submissions argued that the removal of the 'cost recovery' restriction would free up local authorities to charge. However it is not clear that councils have yet exhausted the opportunities available to them within the cost-recovery restriction, and it may be appropriate to reflect on those powers after several years of use before judging them inadequate. Developing a good understanding of real service costs should in any case be part of sound financial management and should be part of the evidence underpinning decisions about charging for services.

---

[51] IDeA, *Enterprising councils: getting the most from charging and trading*, 2005.

7.262 However there may be a case for a review of local authorities' scope to charge for statutory services, where provisions have evolved piecemeal and may not represent a coherent whole. As discussed in Chapter 3, it is not obvious why, for example, councils are permitted to charge (often significant amounts) for social care for the most vulnerable, but may not charge for other services such as waste collection or the lending of library books. Greater coherence across these powers might help provide greater clarity to both local authorities and to the public, though further detailed work, such as that being undertaken by the Audit Commission, will be needed to explore this more fully.

> **Recommendation 7.12**
>
> The powers to trade and charge conferred on 'best value' authorities in the Local Government Act 2003 should be extended to all local authorities.
>
> **Recommendation 7.13**
>
> The Government should carefully consider the wider framework of charging powers for statutory and discretionary services, including in the light of the Audit Commission's work when published later this year.

7.263 I am not recommending changes to the general framework of charging powers, but would encourage central government to make space for local innovation in this area, and to focus guidance in areas where central expertise can add value: for example in relation to EU procurement rules. There are however some specific areas in which new powers may be called for: particularly in relation to waste services, and around developing policy on congestion charging and road pricing.

Charging for waste services

7.264 Local authorities may not, at present, charge for the collection and disposal of household waste, with some exceptions, for example the collection of bulky items. Local authorities also have powers to fine residents if, for example, they contaminate recycling or do not comply with compulsory recycling schemes. Local authorities already have the right to charge businesses for the collection of waste.

7.265 As set out in Chapter 4, waste policy in future will have to meet the challenge of reducing the volume of biodegradable municipal waste sent to landfill, in line with EU legislation. Councils now have 'landfill allowances' which they can trade with other local authorities, but which they may not exceed. If excess waste goes to landfill, heavy fines can be imposed on the authority, creating a risk that council taxpayers might have to bear these punitive costs.

7.266 Increasing the amount of waste that is recycled is a key part of managing these challenges, as is action to reduce waste volumes 'upstream'. There is already evidence of significant local variation and innovation in this area.

Action by councils to encourage recycling

Blaby District Council is one of a large number of councils that provide an integrated refuse and recycling service. Residents are provided with two wheeled bins, one for refuse with a black lid, and the other for recycling paper and card with a green lid. Also provided are two smaller containers for recycling. Garden Waste is also collected separately.

The standard bins are both 140 litres and are of a slim line design to minimise the space required to store them. Bigger bins are available upon request, but larger refuse bins usually require an additional payment, except in medical circumstances. For households who only need extra capacity occasionally, 'Blaby District Council Extra waste sacks' can be purchased from local outlets.

The refuse bin is emptied on a weekly basis. The recycling containers are optional and are emptied every fortnight. Garden waste can be collected in either special garden waste wheeled bins, or 'Blaby District Council garden waste sacks' available from local outlets again for an additional charge.

Since the scheme became fully operational in January 2005 the recycling rate looks set to increase from 29 per cent to a projected recycling rate of 39 per cent in 2006/7. In addition, the chargeable bags/bins system has proved to be a substantial income generator for the Authority, which in turn keeps the overall costs of the service to an acceptable level. A further noticeable benefit is a 3 per cent reduction in the total amount of household waste generated.

Barnet, in London, has adopted an innovative approach to recycling – by making it compulsory. Under the Environmental Protection Act 1990, local authorities may require residents to use particular containers for different waste materials. In this new scheme, the council requires residents not to put glass, paper or cans, in the black wheeled bin for general waste but instead provides a black box for these items to be collected separately for recycling.

A trial compulsory recycling scheme ran in four wards from April 2004, and was expanded across the Borough from March 2005. The compulsory recycling scheme does not apply to those in households who have shared refuse facilities, such as flats.

Monitoring of compliance is based on the use of recycling boxes by households. Recycling assistants visit households who do not regularly recycle in order to further explain the scheme and encourage people to participate. Residents who persistently and deliberately fail to recycle receive warnings and formal notices. Only as a last resort will the council prosecute the most persistent offenders – this has not been necessary so far. As a result of the scheme, resident participation in recycling has risen from a low of 40 per cent to around 85 per cent and resulted in a 28 per cent increase in tonnage of waste recycled in 2005-06.

7.267   During the course of my Inquiry I have received a number of submissions – including from local authorities, environmental groups and waste management organisations – detailing the advantages and disadvantages of various waste charging schemes. A key theme through these submissions and at Inquiry engagement events has been that introducing a charging regime would act as a powerful incentive on householders to reduce the amount of waste they produce and encourage them to recycle and compost more of that waste. It might also be seen as a fairer way of spreading the costs of waste disposal, with the heaviest waste-producers contributing most.

> *You only have to look at a landfill to know that it's bad to continue in this way.* (Shropshire resident engagement event)

In [another area] the size of your bill is set by the size of your bin. Small bin, small bill. I live alone so I don't throw away the equivalent weight of a small child every week, so why should I pay for people who do? (Barnet resident engagement event)

7.268   Given the severity of the pressures likely to arise in the waste system – both financial and environmental – I can see that a power to introduce variable charging for household waste could have a significant role to play in reducing the waste we produce and recycling more of that waste, and might be a sensible addition to councils' financial 'toolkit'.

7.269   Local authorities would need to ensure that any new scheme addressed a number of potential problems. The submissions I have received and the evidence I have gathered make it plain that a poorly thought out variable charging system would have the capacity to impact most harshly on those people least able to afford it, particularly young families. Some respondents also raised the issues of fly tipping and 'waste tourism', which would need to be addressed as part of a new system.

7.270   In addition, there would need to be clarity about the purpose of any new charge, and how it interacts with council tax. My public perceptions work clearly demonstrates that people consider waste management to be a key local authority activity, and that many feel they already pay for this service through their council tax bill.

Variable charging – if introduced – needs to be part of a greater system, not a solution in its own right. In particular, people will need to be able to avoid charges by being able to easily access recycling facilities. (Green Alliance, waste seminar)

Recycling should get you a discount off your council tax. We already pay for the bins and we shouldn't have to pay more for not recycling. (Shropshire resident)

Fining encourages you to do it, but it's a bit big brotherish – we don't want the bin police. (Essex resident)

7.271   These perceptions will have an impact on the design and development of any variable waste charging scheme, and its acceptability to local people. Public understanding of the principles behind a charging scheme is essential, putting a premium on effective public engagement to secure local support for new policies on waste.

7.272   There is evidence of emerging pressures on waste budgets as we reduce our dependence on landfill, in the face of an upward trend in waste volumes. Charging powers in this area would represent a significant new flexibility to manage pressures on budgets according to local preferences.

7.273   I am clear that charging should be a matter for local choice, and am not proposing that it be rolled out nationally or in a way that does not reflect community preferences. However if tailored to local circumstances, variable charging might be a means by which incentives can be created to reduce waste and thereby reduce costs – and could help ensure that the remaining costs are shared in a way that may be perceived as fair.

Recommendation 7.14

The Government should take new powers to allow local authorities to charge for domestic waste collection, developed in close consultation with residents and other key stakeholders.

Road pricing and congestion charging

7.274   Congestion charging and road pricing have been raised by a number of submissions to the Inquiry as a possible source of revenue for local authorities. Powers to operate congestion charging schemes were introduced for authorities outside London in the Transport Act 2000, in instances where charging would support the Local Transport Plan. These are still relatively new powers, and local authorities face a considerable challenge in building the public understanding of, and support for road pricing that would be necessary for schemes to go ahead. In light of that, and given the long-term nature of much transport investment it is perhaps not surprising that powers in this area are still largely untested, with the notable exception of London's congestion charge.[52]

7.275   Road pricing therefore represents an area of developing policy, in response to congestion and associated concerns about the environmental impact of road travel. It is important, in my view, that the debate about road pricing can be taken forward in the communities that are affected by congestion and the citizens and businesses that would be affected by charging schemes.

A local role in road pricing

7.276   Many of the negative impacts of congestion are felt locally: while carbon emissions are obviously of wider significance, congestion also impacts on the local environment through air pollution, and on local homes and businesses, with consequences for the prosperity of local economies. Equally, many of the causes of, and solutions to congestion are local, making local knowledge a key advantage in designing charging schemes that can tackle congestion while avoiding perverse consequences.

7.277   On a more pragmatic level, local engagement and buy-in would are important to the wider road pricing agenda. Local councillors have a key responsibility in building public support for charging schemes through engagement with their communities, and would be held accountable for unpopular schemes.

7.278   Under the 2000 Act, it is likely that the difficult engagement necessary to get a road pricing scheme off the ground would be delivered locally. In that context, it is right that locally accountable bodies should also have the freedom to invest revenues according to the 'deal' communicated to and agreed with local citizens. Without this, councils' incentives to engage with road pricing and be locally accountable for its success would be undermined.

> *Retention of the revenue raised from road pricing is a major incentive towards using this as a demand management measure where this is an appropriate element of a local transport strategy... If local schemes become established, there will be a steady demand for spending the funds on transport schemes at a local level to meet local needs.* (Norfolk County Council)

Hypothecation of congestion charging revenues

7.279   Under the 2000 Act, local authorities that introduce congestion charging schemes before 2011 can keep the revenues and must spend the revenues on improving transport in their areas for the first ten years of the scheme's operation. Similarly in London, congestion charging income has been used to support investment in public transport, particularly buses.

7.280   I have a general presumption against ring-fencing funds, which can restrict the scope for local choice and produce incentives to make priorities follow funds, rather than the other way around. Place-shaping local government requires room for manoeuvre; decisions about how to make use of congestion charging should properly be a matter of community choice. I recognise that in some circumstances hypothecation of funding streams can help build public support for a charging scheme by making the benefits of that new public investment appear more tangible or targeted. However when revenues are raised locally it is reasonable that responding to public

---

[52]   The London congestion charge is based in powers in the Greater London Authority Act 1999.

concerns about the benefits of charging schemes, including by deciding what the revenue should be spent on, should be a matter for local accountability.

7.281   In that light, the Government should consider removing restrictions on the use of road pricing revenues, and as a minimum should ensure that any hypothecation operates at a strategic level that allows local authorities to take a broad view of their investment priorities, and the views of their communities.

Developing national and local policy together

7.282   If national road pricing were to be rolled out in future, it would be important that the advantages of local schemes were not lost. Given the importance of transport policy for local authorities' place-shaping role, and in recognition of councillors' accountability for charging schemes in their areas, local government might properly have a role in national road pricing. While recognising that the government will want to consider these issues in the context of wider national policy on road pricing, ministers will need to continue to be mindful of the incentives for, and benefits of local action in this area.

Conclusions

7.283   Charges are a widely used and significant part of local authorities' financial landscape. While take-up of the new powers has been relatively limited, in time one would expect to see greater innovation under these new provisions, and indeed take-up of older powers is much more widespread. There is substantial variation between areas in their use of charging powers, and it seems likely that while some of that variation reflects local choice or circumstances, it also partly reflects the level of councils' willingness to engage with charging and take a strategic approach to its use.

7.284   Some councils are at the forefront of innovation in this area. Well-designed charging schemes can help to manage demand for services, influence behaviours, or build in equity by using charges on some users to subsidise others. As such they form an important part of local authorities' policy toolkit.

7.285   There is room for a much fuller conversation with local service users and taxpayers about the best way to fund local services. Stephen Bailey argues convincingly that public support for charges is unlikely to be secured if they are perceived as purely revenue-raising rather than as supporting a policy goal.[53] Equally however, many responses to the Inquiry's consultation on council tax expressed a perception of fairness in terms of the 'benefit principle', whereby those who use services would also pay for them.

7.286   I would suggest that given the pressures on council tax, a move towards services users meeting some costs directly, rather than allowing the costs to fall on council tax, might itself be a policy aim, and one which councils could legitimately open up for public debate. User charges have a valid place alongside local taxation, and in some contexts may be perceived as fairer. As a minimum, when local authorities face a choice between increasing charges or council tax, or reducing service provision, that trade-off should be made transparent to citizens, with charging presented as one of the options where available. I would encourage all local authorities to take a strategic approach to the use of charges, including as part of the range of levers available for managing pressures on budgets and on council tax.

---

[53]   Bailey, S. published by CIPFA Technical Information Service, *User Charges for Services – a response to the Lyons Inquiry interim report*, 2006.

8

Business taxation

Summary

This chapter argues that changes to business taxation can provide greater local flexibility for communities to invest in themselves and in the infrastructure needed to support growth, and improved incentives for the efficient use of land.

Both local authorities and businesses are keen to engage in a constructive dialogue about how best to foster economic development and growth at the local level. In order to support the positive signs of a developing relationship I recommend the RPI cap on business rates should not be removed and business rates should not be relocalised.

I also recommend introducing a power for local authorities to levy a local supplement in order to increase local flexibility and support the continued investment in infrastructure that both businesses and local authorities have called for, subject to detailed consultation with, and a strong voice for, the business community.

Better incentives for the efficient use of land could be provided through reforms to the empty property relief and by the possible taxation of derelict and previously developed land. The other reliefs and exemptions from business rates also need to be reviewed.

In taking forward a possible Planning-gain Supplement the Government should ensure it is designed as a local tax with an appropriate regional share, not as a national tax, in order to maintain the necessary local connection.

There are some arguments in favour of new taxes to reflect tourist pressures in some areas. The Government should conduct wider consultation before considering the introduction of permissive powers to allow local authorities to levy such taxes.

INTRODUCTION

8.1   Businesses are important stakeholders in the debate on local government. Over the course of my Inquiry I have received many detailed and constructive submissions from businesses and business organisations, keen to engage both with taxation issues, and also with wider questions about the role of local authorities and their potential contribution to economic growth and a successful business environment. My description of the place-shaping role of local government has been welcomed by local government and business (most notably in the recent joint statement by the Local Government Association (LGA) and the CBI, *Making 'place shaping' a reality*), and I believe that there is real potential for better and closer engagement between businesses and local authorities in the pursuit of their mutual interest in successful and prosperous places.

8.2   Taxation has, unsurprisingly, been an issue of immediate and significant concern to businesses during the Inquiry and there are some difficult and contentious issues to be addressed. Though not all will agree with my conclusions, I think it is important that we approach the subject with the objective of enhancing relationships between businesses and local authorities, and providing authorities with the tools and incentives they need to engage effectively in fostering economic prosperity. As one business in Leeds put it, I believe we need to create "a debate on investment, rather than a debate on taxation."[1]

8.3   This chapter considers three different existing or potential local taxes which are paid, in the main, by businesses. It concentrates on business rates but also discusses the proposed Planning-gain Supplement (PGS) and taxes on tourist pressures.

BUSINESS RATES

8.4   Business rates (formally called 'national non-domestic rates') are an important part of the local government finance system, providing billions of pounds each year to support public services delivered by local government. They are at one and the same time both a contested part of the system – with recurring arguments over the last 17 years over whether the tax rate should be set locally or nationally – and a tax which in its fundamentals seems to be little questioned. This section:

- discusses business rates both as a tax and as a part of the local government finance system;

- considers whether the current level of tax and contribution from business is appropriate;

- assesses how changes to the business rates system could provide greater local flexibility; and

- looks at the efficiency and fairness of rates as a tax, including the exemptions and reliefs within the tax.

Business rates in local government   8.5   Property taxes on non-domestic property have been part of the English local taxation system for many hundreds of years, for most of that time as part of a combined tax on all property. This is an experience repeated in most other countries around the world including Germany, France, Denmark, Ireland, New Zealand and across the United States, where some form of business property tax (either as a separate tax, or as part of a general property tax) forms part of the local tax base.

---

[1] Lyons Inquiry Business Engagement Events, 2006.

Business rates

Business rates are a property tax for which the occupier or owner of most non-domestic land and property is liable. This applies to shops, factories and offices, but also includes public buildings, pipelines and advertising hoardings. Some land and property, including agricultural land and associated buildings, derelict buildings or unoccupied land, and churches and other places of religious worship, are exempt from rates. Other types of property receive reliefs, including small businesses, charities and empty properties.

Each property has a rateable value based, broadly, on the annual rent that the property could command on the open market, with revaluations conducted every five years. The amount of money to be paid each year is a proportion of the rateable value, determined by a tax rate known as the multiplier. Prior to 1990 this was set separately by each local authority, but it is now set by the Government on a national basis. The multiplier for 2006-07 in England is 42.6p for small businesses and 43.3p for larger businesses. It is adjusted each year so that between revaluations the tax rate rises only in line with Retail Price Index (RPI) inflation (new properties and improvements pay this tax rate, and do therefore contribute to an increase in overall yield). At each revaluation the tax rate is recalculated to maintain the yield from the tax in real terms, taking account of likely appeals.

The vast majority of revenues from rates are collected by local authorities, though some properties are administered through a separate central list.

Full details on business rates can be found at www.mybusinessrates.gov.uk, www.voa.gov.uk and on local authority websites.

8.6   Until 1990, business rates were set by local authorities alongside domestic rates. Indeed, it does not seem to be widely understood today that business and domestic rates were actually aspects of the same tax. In principle, business and domestic properties faced the same rate of tax, though in practice central government provided resources through grant (the Domestic Element of Rate Support Grant) to reduce the tax rate on domestic properties by 18p in the pound. It is not, therefore, true to say that prior to 1990 local authorities were able to choose to place a greater weight of taxation on businesses rather than residents. This mistaken view does, unfortunately, seem to have become the accepted wisdom in debates on local business taxation.

8.7   In 1990 business rates were separated from domestic rates, and the latter were replaced by the community charge. Since then the status of business rates has become more complex. They remain fundamentally the same tax, and local authorities continue to collect the revenues. Authorities also have some discretion over the level and granting of reliefs, for example, to charities and for hardship. However, since 1990 the tax rate has been set centrally and levied at a national rate, with the locally collected revenues redistributed centrally as part of the government grant system. It would perhaps be most accurate to call the present system of business rates a national tax, but one that is assigned to the funding of local government. It does mean that there is some confusion about the purpose of the business rates system – because of its history and the way it is collected, it is still perceived by many businesses as a local tax, but it is actually used in great part to fund the provision of services according to national expectations and requirements. Since the removal of schools funding from Revenue Support Grant (RSG) in 2006-07, business rate revenues have become an essential source of the funding needed to allow equalisation between authorities for needs and resources.

The contribution from business rates   8.8   Businesses as a whole have been protected from real-term increases in rates, because of the way in which legislation lays out how the tax rate is to be calculated (as described in the above box). As local government grants and council tax revenues have risen significantly faster than both inflation, and increases in the number of business properties, business rates have provided a falling proportion of local government spending over time. In 1990, when the national business rates system was introduced, business rates raised £9.6 billion and provided 29 per cent of local government revenues. In 2006-07 business rates are expected to provide around £17.5 billion or 20 per cent of local government spending.[2] The changes in the mix of funding over time is shown in the chart below.

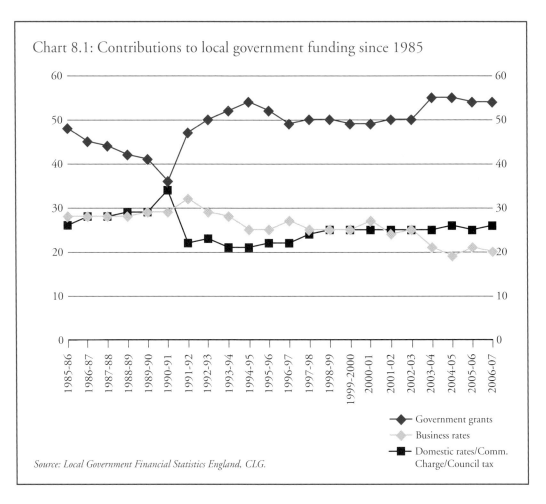

Chart 8.1: Contributions to local government funding since 1985

Source: Local Government Financial Statistics England, CLG.

Legend:
- ◆ Government grants
- ◆ Business rates
- ■ Domestic rates/Comm. Charge/Council tax

Business rates in the wider tax system

8.9   Business rates are a significant tax for businesses – in 2006-07 they are expected to raise around £18.4 billion in England (£20.3 billion across the UK), compared to £47.5 billion (net of tax credits) in UK corporation tax on business profits. Research suggests that for most businesses, rates account for around three per cent of turnover, although this can vary substantially between companies in different parts of the country and different sectors of the economy, and be much higher for small businesses.[3]

8.10   Some, particularly those for whom property is a substantial part of their costs, challenge the weight of taxation levied on property through business rates. In my discussions with businesses, concerns were expressed by some in the retail and manufacturing sectors about the greater burden they perceived from business rates because of their significant property usage. This was a significant issue during the 1970s and 1980s, though it has been more muted in recent years, as a result of the more prominent debate about whether the tax rate should be set nationally or locally. The growth of e-commerce retail businesses with little need for property, particularly in expensive city centre and high street locations, also raises questions about how the tax burden falls across business sectors, and how that may change in the future.

---

[2] This figure is lower than the £18.4 billion total expected yield from business rates mentioned below because of the way in which the business rates pool manages fluctuations from year to year.

[3] IFF Research Ltd, *The Impacts of Rates on Businesses*, Department of the Environment, 1995.

8.11   It is true that business rates are a more significant tax on business property than comparable taxes in most other European countries. Analysis in 2001 showed that the rate of property tax on business in the UK was second-highest in the EU15, as shown in the chart below.[4]

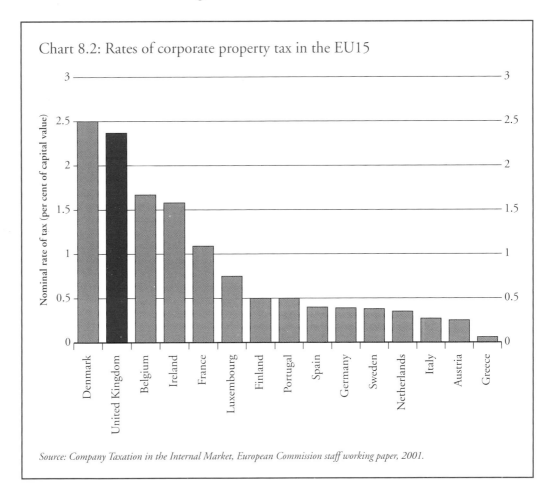

Chart 8.2: Rates of corporate property tax in the EU15

Source: Company Taxation in the Internal Market, European Commission staff working paper, 2001.

8.12   At the same time however, the UK had lower levels of corporate income taxes and social security contributions than other countries, something that clearly needs to be taken into account in assessing the overall position for business taxation in the UK. This is illustrated in the charts overleaf.

---

[4] EU15 refers to 2001 at which time the European Union had only 15 members.

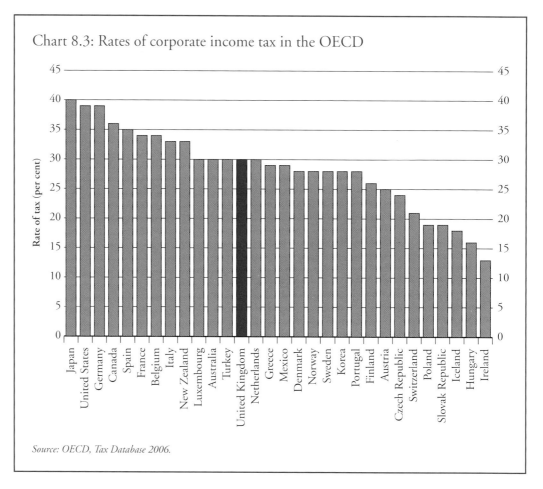

Chart 8.3: Rates of corporate income tax in the OECD

Source: OECD, Tax Database 2006.

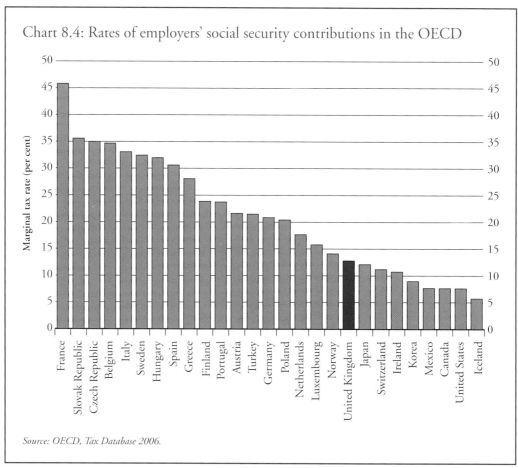

Chart 8.4: Rates of employers' social security contributions in the OECD

Source: OECD, Tax Database 2006.

Reforms to business rates

8.13   Business rates are a successful and stable property tax, with a wide tax base, and while the rate can be unpopular, the principles of the tax do not excite significant opposition from ratepayers. Properties have been successfully revalued for the purposes of business rates every five years since 1990, which is a great success when compared with council tax, and with historical experience. Compelling arguments would therefore be needed to make significant reforms to the current system.

8.14   However, there have been calls for business rates to be abolished and replaced by other forms of taxation. Some believe that it would be better to tax businesses entirely on the basis of profits, a position supported by one small businessman in the regional events who argued that "you could abolish, or reduce, business rates and instead get that tax from other business taxes such as corporation tax. This would shift the burden across to those who are able to pay." However, very few stakeholders (and none of the business representative organisations) who made submissions to the Inquiry expressed any support for this proposal. Abolishing business rates and making up the shortfall in revenues through an increase in corporation tax would require a very substantial increase in that tax.

8.15   Chapter 6 showed that other stakeholders have called for the replacement of business rates with tax on land values. As noted there, land value taxes have some clear theoretical advantages. Nevertheless, given that business rates already have some of the attributes of a land value tax, strong arguments would be needed to support a wholesale change. A consideration against the principles of a land value tax can help to suggest areas for reform and suggests that reform, rather than replacement, is the most pragmatic approach.

8.16   One significant difference between business rates and pure land value taxes are that business rates are a tax on property as well as land. As noted in Chapter 6, the taxation of property can have some distorting features, but it increases the width of the tax base, which enables a lower tax rate to be charged (and in practice many land value taxes in other countries include at least an element of tax on property for precisely this reason). Another difference is that business rates are a tax on current use value, rather than the optimum use of the land, which potentially means that they do not provide the same incentives for underused property or land to be redeveloped for another use. To change this would be a substantial alteration in the principles of business rates as they currently stand.

8.17   Not all non-domestic land and property is liable for business rates. There are a number of reliefs and exemptions which have been introduced over the years, for a variety of economic and policy reasons, which I identified in my interim report and are considered further later in this chapter. The existence of reliefs and exemptions means that, for a given level of revenue, the tax rate is higher than it would otherwise need to be. They also potentially create distortions between different types of business and uses of land. The most significant exemptions and reliefs in terms of revenue given up are empty property relief, charity relief and the exemption of agricultural land and buildings. The exemption of derelict brownfield land is also an important omission in theoretical, though not necessarily in value, terms.

8.18   Business rates differ from a purist model of property tax in the way that the rate is set. Following the 1990 reforms, the tax rate is now recalculated at revaluation to maintain the yield in real terms and increased in line with the RPI between revaluations. Although the fixed yield approach is predictable, which has advantages for both government and business, it does potentially have some negative economic consequences. In particular it means that the tax rate (expressed as a proportion of current rental value) will increase if the commercial property market weakens and rents fall, but conversely that the tax rate will fall when commercial property increases in value. This has a pro-cyclical effect on the commercial property market – the tax take increases as a percentage of value in downswings, and falls in upswings. This is an inevitable consequence of the design of the tax, where yield is not related to property values. This also makes business rates a rather unusual tax in comparison with almost all others – not only is the tax rate set in legislation, with no flexibility for the government to alter it as part of its decisions about the overall tax system, but it means that there is no buoyancy in the yield, and increases in property values, reflecting economic growth and greater prosperity, do not lead to any additional revenues.

8.19   One further potential criticism comes from the fact that business rates are levied on occupiers rather than owners. Some of those who made submissions to the Inquiry, particularly in the context of Business Improvement Districts (BIDs) argued that it is landowners, not occupiers, who benefit from increases in the value of land that greater economic activity and public investment can create. However, economic theory suggests that the person who really ends up paying the tax is not necessarily the same as the person who hands over the money initially. In the case of property taxes, we would expect the owner to bear the final burden, because he or she will receive lower rents where taxes and other occupation costs are higher. There is some discussion on the market conditions necessary for this to happen – Kay and King argue in their classic work on the British tax system that outside city centres and areas where land is in high demand, some of the impact might fall on employment, prices or profits.[5]

8.20   However, the available empirical evidence on business rates supports the theory and suggests that it is landlords who bear the cost (or receive the benefit) of changes in rates. For example, in the Enterprise Zones (a policy introduced in the 1980s in which properties in certain areas were given a complete exemption from rates for a ten year period) the evaluation shows that rents in the zones tended to rise to reflect the absence of business rates, thus transferring much of the benefit of the exemption from the occupier to the owner.[6] In the short term, tenants do face the cost of higher rates because their rents do not respond quickly, due to multi-year rent agreements and upward only rent reviews, but in the medium to long term almost all of the impact will fall on landlords in terms of lower rents. This means that, all other things being equal, a rise in business rates will lead to a fall in property values to reflect the reduced value of future rental streams, and that a reduction in rates will lead to a rise in property values. These are issues that I will return to later, as they are relevant to some of my proposals for the reform of the tax.

The rate of tax

8.21   I highlighted earlier in the chapter the fact that the proportion of local government spending funded by business rates has fallen over the last 17 years from around 29 per cent of local government spending before 1990 to 20 per cent in 2006-07. Some of those who made submissions to my Inquiry – particularly local authorities, but also some commentators and experts – felt that this was unfair. They pointed out that while business rates had been constrained by the RPI cap on the tax rate, council tax bills had increased substantially in real terms since the introduction of that tax. One analysis in 2004 suggested that if the contribution from the domestic and non-domestic sectors had risen at the same rate over the period since 1989-90, business rates would now raise around £1.5 billion a year more.[7] There have therefore been calls for an increase in business rates, either to rebalance the current burden, or to spread the load more widely in the future, and thus reduce council tax increases.

---

[5] Kay, J. and King, M., *The British Tax System*, 1990.

[6] Institute for Fiscal Studies, *The Relationship between Rates and Rents*, Department of the Environment, 1993; Mehdi, N., *The Capitalisation of Business Rates: An Empirical Study of Tax Incidence in Six London Boroughs*, PhD thesis, 2003; PA Cambridge Economic Consultants, *Final Evaluation of Enterprise Zones*, HMSO, 1995.

[7] Hale, R., *The Relocalisation of the Non-Domestic Rate – A Discussion Paper*, CIPFA & Rita Hale Associates, 2004.

The current arrangements for the increase in business rates – currently limited to RPI by law – should have been more in line with the Government's own planned increases in council tax, thereby sharing the proceeds and burden of growth. (East Sussex County Council)

8.22 A small number of members of the public also felt the same way, including the Devon Pensioners' Action Forum:

[our] strongly held view is that the burden of Devon County Council's tax rises should, at the very least, be spread evenly between the business sector and private householders instead of over 80 per cent of these increases being piled onto the County's hapless council tax payers.

8.23 Businesses and their representative organisations strongly resisted this line of argument. They felt that increases to the level of business rates would be damaging to the economy, particularly given the relatively high level of property taxation in the UK. The CBI and British Chambers of Commerce (BCC) both argued that the national tax burden on business had increased in recent years, and that they were therefore making a contribution through the government grants funded from national taxation. Finally, some argued that many of the increases in local government spending have been targeted at areas from which they perceive little benefit, such as social services and domestic waste management, while some of the services they are more concerned about, such as highways maintenance, have not been prioritised. Some business bodies, for example, London First and the Federation of Small Businesses, called for business rates to fall over time.

We propose... gradually reducing the annual increase in the national business rate i.e. by RPI minus. This would have the consequence of reducing grants to London boroughs in real terms and at the same time require them constantly to seek efficiency savings. (London First)

8.24 There are pressures on local government spending which need to be funded or managed in some way, which I discussed in Chapter 3. Raising more money from business rates, either as a one-off rise in the rate of tax, or through a gradual increase (for example, changing the way in which the tax rate is adjusted from year to year to use general growth in the economy, rather than the change in the RPI) would be a way of raising additional resources to take pressure off council tax. Using business rates would have advantages in this regard, as they are an accepted and robust form of taxation, and they apply across a wide tax base.

8.25 However, I have concluded that for the present, the national business rate is not an appropriate way to raise additional resources to fund general local government activity and services. The most pressing need is to develop much more constructive relationships between local authorities and businesses, focused on joint interests in fostering economic prosperity and investment in local infrastructure. A general national tax rise to support local government funding could put the development of those relationships in jeopardy, particularly given the high level of taxation on property that business rates represents, by international standards. Future governments might wish to review this arrangement, and consider some of the other options discussed later in this chapter.

Recommendation 8.1

The RPI cap on the national level of business rates should be retained.

Greater flexibility for local communities

8.26 Earlier chapters of this report have argued that local communities need greater flexibility over how they use existing revenues. I believe that they also need more power to choose to raise new local revenues to invest in themselves. Businesses have identified a need to invest more in the infrastructure needed to support future growth – the CBI for example "has estimated that projects worth at least £300 billion should be initiated in the next ten years to deliver a better transport system" – and an appetite for greater engagement with local authorities on economic development, including a willingness to discuss how the revenues for investment might be found.[8]

8.27   That concern can perhaps most easily be exemplified by reference to the debate in London on Crossrail, but examples exist across the country. Rod Eddington's Transport Study showed that there are a large number of projects – some with relatively modest overall costs – that could provide substantial benefits to local economic growth if resources could be found to support further investment.[9] Where spending is targeted to such projects it should support an expansion in the number and success of businesses and the value of the properties in an area. Thus, combined with effective incentive for local communities – which Chapter 9 considers in more detail – greater flexibility over raising revenues to invest at the local level should allow communities to strengthen their own economies and tax bases over time.

8.28   This section considers whether business rates could provide some of that flexibility, and the ability to fund new investments, whether through existing arrangements, or through other reforms. Such arrangements need to be transparent and accountable, helping to develop greater trust between businesses and local authorities.

Existing flexibilities

8.29   Business Improvement Districts (BIDs), based on a model from the United States and introduced in the Local Government Act 2003 (but operated on a voluntary basis in a number of areas prior to that Act) do already provide some additional flexibility. Many businesses and business groups including the BCC, the CBI and the British Retail Consortium have expressed their support for BIDs. BIDs schemes have been welcomed because they are business led, have addressed business priorities and provided genuinely additional resources, alongside accountability to those paying the extra tax. In my business engagement events, the strengths of BIDs were identified as "the ability they gave local businesses to make decisions and initiate service improvements, and the clarity of the planning, delivery and benefits realisation sequence."[10]

8.30   It is very positive that these new measures have been welcomed. They show that, with the right proposals and engagement, local authorities and businesses can develop effective relationships and mutually advantageous proposals for the improvement of places.

8.31   However, BIDs have a number of limitations and they are not the answer to all problems. First, their purpose is specific and limited. They are intended as a way for local businesses to raise collective contributions for specific improvements and services, and can run only for a maximum of five years without an additional vote. Although there is significant local variation, BIDs mainly spend their money in tightly defined local areas on marketing and safety and security, and sometimes on cleaning and local improvements. Even the more substantial plans for Coventry's 'city-wide' BID focus on providing specific services such as information technology and crime reduction measures to tenants in a number of dispersed locations rather than on measures of general benefit to the city as a whole. Second, some concerns were raised during my discussions with businesses and BID operators that the costs of developing and administering BIDs reduced their impact and effectiveness – noted for example in the Inquiry's business engagement events.

[8]   CBI, *Transport policy and the needs of the UK economy*, 2005.

[9]   Eddington, R., *Transport's role in sustaining the UK's productivity and competitiveness*, 2006.

[10]   OPM, *Report of Business Round-Tables,* 2006.

Third, as BIDs build on the existing structure of business rates there is a concern that their priorities can be skewed towards short-term issues rather than longer-term investments, because they can only compel contributions from occupiers (though in some cases landowners are also making contributions).[11]

8.32   While BIDs are an important part of the package, these drawbacks suggest that other flexibilities are needed, particularly if we are to be able to address, in a locally flexible and accountable way, larger projects and needs, including infrastructure investment.

Localisation   8.33   Transferring business rates revenues and decisions over tax rates to local control has been suggested by many local authorities and some other commentators. This would give local authorities a new locally controlled revenue source (although, as business rates revenues are currently devoted to local government funding there would be no increase in available resources) and some flexibility to raise additional revenue by changing the tax rate, depending on the approach adopted to equalisation.

8.34   In principle I have considerable sympathy with this view, and am of the opinion that the nationalisation of business rates in 1990 was not a positive change. However, there are two key issues to be addressed in the consideration of this proposal. First, there are concerns in the business community about the implications for them of greater local discretion over tax rates. They fear increases in taxation without a greater say over local priorities and spending, and are concerned at the potential additional complexity of a number of different local rates. For example, the BCC said that:

> *The BCC has significant concerns about this suggestion, which we fear would lead to an increase in business rates. Because business does not have a vote, the fear is that local authorities would be tempted to increase business rates, because they could enhance their spending power without enduring the political pain associated with increases in council tax.*

8.35   Second, there are wider concerns about the impact of localisation on the Government's ability to equalise resources between authorities. Following the decision to move schools funding into a separate ring-fenced grant, business rates now provide the bulk of the revenues needed to equalise between authorities for differences in needs and council tax resources. To maintain current levels of equity under a localised business rates system, 65 authorities would need to pay some of their local tax revenues to central government to support other authorities with smaller tax bases and higher needs.[12] Chart 8.5, overleaf, illustrates this graphically, comparing council tax and local business rate revenues with budget requirements in 2006-07. This chart shows only upper tier authorities, as these are the authorities most affected by localisation, though in this modelling all tiers and classes of authority were allocated a share of local business rates. It shows that a large number of authorities would raise far in excess of their current spending, while others would be substantially under-funded. The limited sum of revenues available through RSG (not shown here) would not be sufficient to compensate for this.

---

[11] Communities and Local Government, *Review of the Role of Property Owners in Business Improvement Districts*, 2006.

[12] This is based on one possible way of localising business rates – there are numerous others models, which would show slightly different patterns, but a similar overall picture.

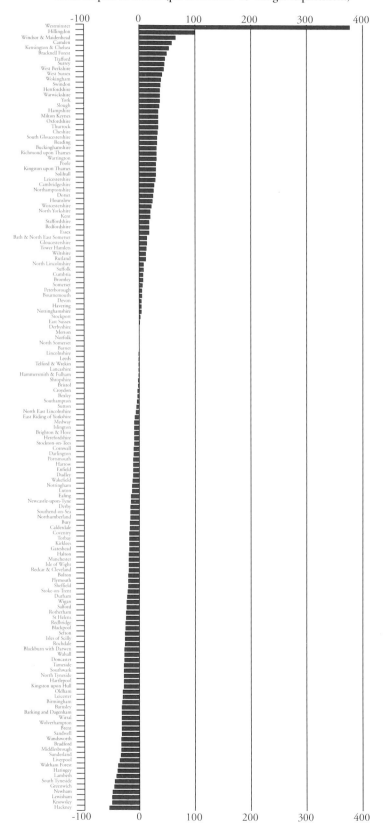

Chart 8.5: Surplus/deficit in council tax and local business rates revenues compared to 2006-07 budget requirement

Note: This chart shows upper tier authorities only (excluding City of London)
Source: Lyons Inquiry

8.36   Such a system can work, with richer authorities pooling some of their resources to support authorities with smaller tax bases. Some other countries, such as Sweden, take this kind of approach, and before the reforms of the late 1980s, some rates revenues were redistributed through the London Rate Equalisation Scheme in a similar fashion. As Tony Travers has argued in a recent paper for the LGA, there is little technical reason that this approach could not be used to enable business rates to be localised without reducing equity.[13] It would require the Government – or some other institution – to decide on the appropriate level of equalisation, and therefore the amount of revenue that authorities in surplus would need to surrender for redistribution, but that is a process which (in a sense) occurs already through the national pooling and redistribution of business rates, and should not therefore pose substantially more significant technical or administrative challenges.

8.37   Despite the fact that it is technically possible to operate such a scheme, I am not attracted to this approach. I believe that it would be confusing, and would not help to create the direct and accountable relationship between local authorities and businesses needed if new local flexibility is to be used effectively. In many areas businesses would be paying taxes to their local authority that would seem to be local revenues, but would then be reallocated elsewhere in the country. Changes to the calculations for that reallocation could have effects on local taxation levels without providing local benefits. That would not be a very transparent system.

8.38   In addition, I do not think that the time is right for such a substantial change to be introduced. Local authorities and the business community still have to work on developing trust and shared objectives, and I am therefore concerned to avoid changes which could put developing that shared agenda at risk. This does not imply that full-scale relocalisation might not be possible and appropriate at a later date. However the conditions are not yet right for such a change.

Supplementary powers   8.39   An alternative option for reforming the business rates to provide additional flexibility would be to introduce a power at the margin for local authorities to levy a supplement on the national business rate within their area. The Corporation of London already has the power to raise a supplement on business rates, in consultation with local businesses, which it has used to generate resources to invest in additional security and other measures. A similar power has been discussed in the past for local authorities more generally, most notably when the Government consulted on reforms to business rates in 1998.[14] While many business groups expressed concern at any change in the current arrangements, greater local flexibility is supported, subject to appropriate constraints and arrangements for voice, by a number of others.

> *[Subject to certain conditions] we could see the benefit to the local economy of re-localisation... we believe that i) businesses as customers will pay a fair price for a quality, efficient service ii) conversely businesses will become disillusioned as customers if they have no recourse, remedial options or leverage to counteract poor services iii) allocations of central and local funding need to be better balanced, particularly in the light of changing economic drivers.* (Leeds Chamber of Commerce)

> *...we wish to see the return to Surrey County Council of control over the business rate. This would give the business community a stake in the running of the County and enable it to express its views about the balance between tax raising and investment. For example businesses would be empowered to argue for an increase in the business rate on the understanding that the proceeds would be invested in measures to reduce congestion.* (Surrey Chambers of Commerce)

---

[13] Travers, T., *Would it be possible to re-localise the NNDR? The technicalities of achieving reform*, LGA, 2007.

[14] Department of Transport, Local Government and the Regions, *Modernising Local Government: Business Rates*, 1998.

8.40   A supplement would provide local authorities with a more limited flexibility to raise revenues for new investment, but it would also have a more limited impact on businesses. It would require authorities to make a transparent decision to change their local rate from the national rate, and that decision could more easily be made subject to greater consultation and constraints than a general power to set tax rates. It would also avoid the need for other complex changes to the finance system such as the equalisation noted earlier.

8.41   Given the need to develop relationships between local authorities and businesses, and my concern to ensure that any new local flexibilities provide genuinely and measurably additional local revenues, agreed with the local business community, I have therefore concluded that a supplementary power would be the most sensible step forward.

> **Recommendation 8.2**
>
> The existing national arrangements for business rates should be retained at present, but a new local flexibility to set a supplement on the current national business rate should be introduced.

Proposals for a local supplement

Principles   8.42   To work effectively, and to help develop trust between authorities and businesses, I think that some limitations on the new power and requirements associated with its use need to be established for both local and central government.

8.43   Getting these constraints right will be essential for the credibility of any new supplement. The business community will need to be able to have confidence that the introduction and use of the power to raise a local supplement is in their interests. Equally, the new power needs to provide genuine flexibility so that local communities can make investments in their future. The British Retail Consortium argued that:

> *In the event that a supplementary business rate be introduced it is vital that such a levy be clearly labelled as additional funding, ring fenced to be spent only on agreed initiatives of benefit to business, and measured against clearly defined evaluation criteria.* (British Retail Consortium)

8.44   There will need to be a debate about where the balance should be struck. However, there are four key criteria that I believe need to be borne in mind in developing a supplement, drawn from business views about the basis on which a larger local contribution might be acceptable.

8.45   The supplement should be:

- local, both in the decision to levy a supplement and in the decisions about how it is to be spent;

- additional, with any new revenues available to spend on new infrastructure or projects rather than taken into account in central government grant allocations;

- transparent, so that businesses and other local taxpayers understand how much money is being raised and what it is being spent on; and

- agreed within the local community, with the local business community having a strong voice in the final decision on whether there should be a supplement, and the purpose to which the proceeds are put.

8.46   This proposed supplement is intended to contribute to greater flexibility for local communities – residents, businesses and their representatives – to invest in themselves and in the future. They are not intended to provide greater powers for general taxation.

8.47   Businesses have also emphasised that any reforms should, wherever possible, build on the simplicity and predictability of the current business rates system. I set out my recommendations on this subject below.

Potential size of a supplement

8.48   The potential size of a supplement is the most clear limitation that could be imposed. In doing so, a balance needs to be struck between providing sufficient flexibility to enable local communities to make a real difference to local investment, and ensuring that tax rates remain within acceptable limits. A one pence supplement across England would raise something over £400 million each year, assuming no impact from the higher tax rate on rateable values (although in practice one might expect some impact, depending on how the supplementary revenue was used). The amount that would be raised by individual authorities would vary substantially depending on the size of the authority and the number and value of properties in the area. Chart 8.6 over shows revenues at upper tier level from a one pence supplement.

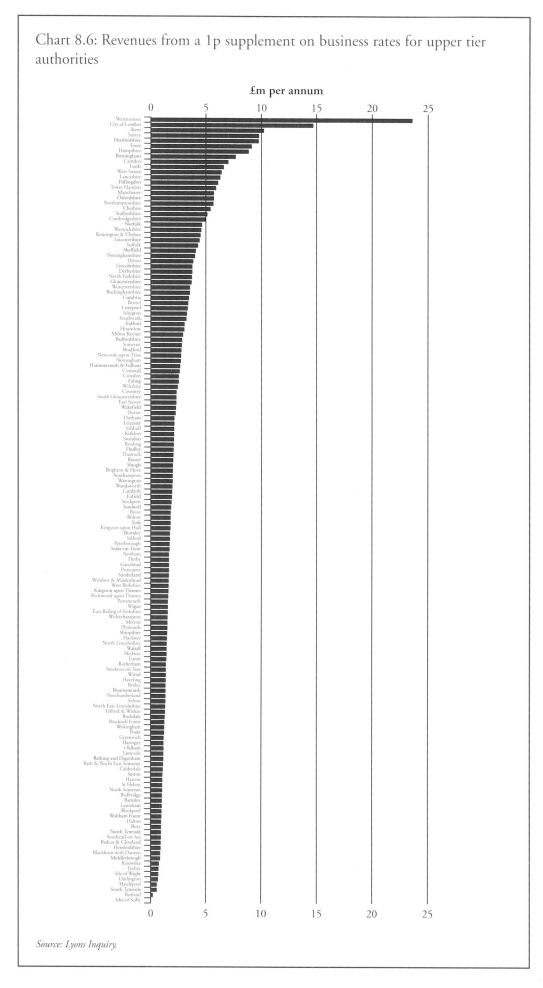

Chart 8.6: Revenues from a 1p supplement on business rates for upper tier authorities

£m per annum

Source: Lyons Inquiry.

8.49   Different levels of supplement would enable different kinds of projects to be undertaken, and there is thus no 'right' answer to this question. At the upper end, some BIDs (for instance in Rugby) have levied supplements equivalent to as much as four pence. This would provide substantial local flexibility and revenues to support investment. A lower limit on the supplement would provide less revenues and less flexibility, though it might enable confidence in the new arrangements to develop more gradually. There might be a case for a lower limit to be applied in general, with a higher limit used for particularly significant projects – and probably subject to more stringent approval processes.

8.50   The table below illustrates the revenues that a supplement of one pence and one of four pence could raise in selected local areas, and the amount of borrowing for capital purposes that these revenues could support over a ten-year period.

Table 8.1: Using a supplement for borrowing

All figures £m	London	Greater Manchester	Birmingham	Kent	Cornwall
1p supplement					
Yield	109.5	20.3	7.7	10.2	2.6
10 year loan of	839.4	155.6	59.0	78.2	19.9
4p supplement					
Yield	438.0	81.2	30.8	40.8	10.4
10 year loan of	3357.6	622.5	236.1	312.8	79.7

Borrowing figures based on a loan from the Public Works Loan Board, at an interest rate of 5.15 per cent repaid on an annuity basis.
Source: Lyons Inquiry analysis

Decision-making processes

8.51   An upper cap on the supplementary rate is an important part of my recommendations. However, with or without it, local proposals will stand or fall on the details of arrangements and discussions between local authorities, business taxpayers and the wider community. It is therefore important that such arrangements should be introduced in a transparent and accountable way, which enables businesses to have greater trust in the desire and ability of local authorities to prioritise the issues of greatest concern to them. In my discussions with businesses I have found an appetite for greater engagement with local authorities on economic development issues, and a willingness to discuss how the revenues for investment might be found, provided there is effective and genuine discussion.

8.52   One approach would be to establish a set of national rules and ring-fences, requiring the resources only to be spent in certain ways or on certain kinds of project. However, I am wary of creating detailed formal requirements at national level for the governance and use of locally raised supplements, because of the risk of restricting genuinely additional activity that local businesses and authorities would both want to sign up to. For example, ring-fencing revenues from supplements to capital expenditure or physical infrastructure would prevent its use for the provision of services (such as security, cleaning, or town marketing) which we know from successful BID schemes are valued by businesses, and which may be an important part of making a place an attractive and successful business location.

8.53   I believe that a better focus is on bottom-up accountability to local taxpayers. This has the merit of encouraging a stronger partnership between local authorities and business. It also provides scope for a better reflection of the particular interests and needs of different types of businesses – such as the SME population. Their ability to absorb the impact, and their priorities for spending, are likely to differ from larger businesses. Local Accountability can and should take into account these differing interests and ensure they are effectively addressed. There are two main options here for ensuring that those affected by a supplement have a voice.

8.54   The first is a voting mechanism. In discussions, many business groups highlighted the benefits they saw in the BID management and voting arrangements, and London First suggested similar arrangements on a much larger scale as the most appropriate way of funding major projects such as Crossrail. A voting mechanism has the advantage that it provides a clear mandate for an increase in taxation from those affected. The support received from the business community suggests that a model could be developed which would command consensus. It would offer a way to ensure that the projects brought forward by authorities are likely to address issues that businesses also perceive as requiring action and investment.

8.55   On the other hand, a voting mechanism could make it difficult to finance projects which may not be in the short-term interests of those affected, but which have widespread benefits in the longer-term. Such projects may well involve funding streams other than a supplement, and in such cases a voting system could add complexity and bureaucracy. Finally, it would not be consistent with the accountability arrangements for other taxes, including council tax and other, national, business taxes. I am also keen to avoid abortive proposals which burden the council tax payer, and fear that this risk would be greater with a prescriptive voting system.

8.56   The second alternative is a statutory consultation process. Such a process would require authorities to consult on raising a supplement for a specific purpose, with a clear economic assessment of its likely impact. This would provide greater flexibility to pursue projects with long-term, as well as short-term, benefits. It would allow local government a genuine freedom. However, in this proposal the control exercised by business rate payers would be weakened. This might make support among the business community more difficult to build.

8.57   On balance, I do not recommend that the use of this new power should have to be subject to a vote, though such a course should be open to local authorities if it is appropriate to the local situation.

8.58   Under either model, revenues from the supplement would be hypothecated to the approved purposes. In order to provide a contribution to infrastructure investments, which can be financed over many years, I do not propose that there should be a universal limit on the time for which a supplement can run, but the proposal to introduce the supplement should include a clear timetable. For a supplement to run beyond this period, the authority would need to gain new approval.

8.59   Whatever model is pursued, if it is to work effectively, both local authorities and local businesses will need to work hard to establish constructive and effective relationships, and to build trust and mutual understanding and respect.

Types of authority   8.60   Businesses have made clear to me that, in addition to being accountable, any new arrangements should maintain the predictability and stability of the current business rates system where possible. Retaining a standard national rate, and implementing changes as the power to set a local supplement on this rate, should aid in this. I also think that it is necessary to keep the number of different possible supplements manageable in order to minimise the administrative burden for businesses and to make the system as simple as possible.

8.61   A supplement could in theory be levied at any tier of local government – all, including parishes, used to set rates before 1990, and all charge council tax directly or via a precept. The numbers of authorities involved is set out in the table below:

Table 8.2: Number of different types of authority

Authority type	Number
Upper tier authorities (unitary, met district, county, London borough, City of London	150
District councils	238
Police and fire authorities	67
Town and parish coucils	Circa 8,700

8.62   I have reservations about giving supplementary powers to a large number of authorities, given the business community's concerns about complexity. There is an opportunity, however, to marry a concern for simplicity with an encouragement to collaborative decision-making and the coalition building that is essential to effective place-shaping. I propose that only upper tier authorities should levy supplements. In two-tier areas, those proposals should be the subject of discussion and agreement between the county and the district councils, with a joint plan for the use of the revenues raised to meet the overall needs of the area. This reduces the number of possible different rates to 150, providing a less complex system for businesses, and acknowledges the interest of all levels of elected local government in the revenues raised through the use of the supplementary power.

8.63   The governance arrangements in London are rather different from elsewhere, with a division of responsibility between the 32 boroughs and the Corporation of London, which are responsible for most local government services, and the Greater London Authority (GLA), which has various strategic powers and functions including for transport, planning and (subject to the passage of the Greater London Authority Bill) skills. The size of the business tax base varies enormously, from areas of inner London with some of the most expensive business properties in the world, to areas of more deprived outer London boroughs with among the lowest tax bases in the country. I believe that it is important that the respective roles and voice of the Mayor and the boroughs are reflected in the approach taken, but that approach must facilitate city-wide action on infrastructure issues and acknowledge the wide variations in the size of the tax base between different parts of the city. The places where infrastructure is required may well not match the pattern of revenue raising.

8.64   This need for city-wide action suggests that it would not be desirable for all powers over business rate supplements to rest solely with the boroughs, but it is also important that the boroughs are involved in any proposals. I therefore propose a more flexible and collaborative arrangement under which a single, London-wide supplementary rate would be set through agreement between the GLA and the boroughs, and in consultation with the business community, with a joint plan for the use of the revenues collected from that rate. This approach recognises the joint interest that the GLA and the boroughs have in any proposals for additional taxation and investment in London, and the need for a city-wide approach to ensure that investment is targeted in the appropriate areas. This London-wide supplement would be in addition to the Corporation of London's current powers, which should continue to operate as at present.

8.65   Although the governance arrangements in London are unique, discussions in other areas, particularly large urban areas and city regions, might come to the conclusion that a similar joint approach would also be desirable in those places.

High tax base
authorities

8.66   The power to levy a supplement will not be equally valuable in all areas and the revenues that individual areas could raise would vary substantially, as shown in chart 8.6. This raises the concern that it might appear unfair to other parts of the country that these areas could raise substantially greater revenues, and in the past (for example in the Government's consultation on supplementary rates in 1998) it has been proposed that special arrangements should apply to these areas.

8.67   However, introducing special arrangements would constrain the ability of local authorities and businesses to choose how to use resources they had chosen to raise, and reduce the accountability of local authorities for the use of locally raised money. Given that this supplement is designed to enable greater local flexibility where there is local support, it would arguably be perverse to apply an equalisation or limitation scheme to it. In addition, comparing the revenues from a supplement on a per head of population basis shows that most of the authorities with very large tax bases per head are in London, where the differences should be dealt with through the joint approach between the GLA and the boroughs suggested above. I have therefore concluded, in line with the principles I established at the beginning of this section, that all of the revenues should remain local.

Table 8.3: Authorities with largest revenues per head

Local authority	Revenues from 1p supplement (£ per head)
City of London	£1655.70
Westminster	£94.88
Camden	£31.70
Tower Hamlets	£27.69
Hillingdon	£24.01
Kensington & Chelsea	£23.32
Islington	£17.74
Slough	£17.00
Hammersmith & Fulham	£15.14
Reading	£14.45

Source: Lyons Inquiry

Small businesses

8.68   Small businesses pay a higher proportion of turnover in rates than larger businesses, and reflecting this the Government has recently introduced Small Business Rate Relief to reduce bills for small businesses. There is therefore a question as to whether small businesses should receive any discount or exemption from a business rates supplement. The smallest 90 per cent of properties only represent a little over 30 per cent of rateable value, so a discount or exemption for smaller businesses would not in most places substantially reduce the yield from a supplement. On the other hand, it might well be considered unfair by larger businesses that they should effectively have to subsidise smaller businesses, simply on account of their size.

8.69   Central government may wish to set the overall framework and how national exemptions and reliefs apply in relation to the supplement. In particular, it may wish to protect the smallest businesses through setting a threshold below which small businesses do not pay a supplement. However I think it is also important that there is flexibility to manage these issues at a local level. Local authorities and local businesses should be able to consider whether additional discounts or exemptions from a supplement are justified for small businesses, taking into account the purpose of the supplement and local economic conditions. A number of BIDs alter their levy depending on the size of the business involved. Authorities will also wish to consider whether these discounts or exemptions should apply to all small properties, or whether to apply a more complex test (as with the Small Business Rate Relief) to ensure that only small businesses benefit by excluding smaller properties owned by larger businesses from any relief.

Borrowing powers 8.70 In order for this new flexibility to be used efficiently and effectively, it is important that local authorities have appropriate powers to use the revenues to support borrowing. The prudential borrowing powers introduced by the Government in 2003, which allow local authorities to borrow for capital purposes, provided that they are satisfied that such borrowing is prudent and affordable, have been warmly welcomed, and should provide the flexibility required.

8.71 Some authorities did raise concerns during discussions that the current Minimum Revenue Provision requirements, which require authorities to set aside four per cent of net outstanding debt out of their revenue resources to redeem their debts, are too complex and rigid and reduce their ability to use borrowing powers. However, the Government has already acknowledged this issue and is addressing it through new regulations and by taking new powers in the Local Government and Public Involvement in Health Bill.

Recommendation 8.3

Local supplementary powers should be designed in a way which can gain credibility with business and the wider community. The key issues to be considered are:

- the appropriate scale of the supplement. At the upper end, some Business Improvement Districts have levied supplements as high as four pence. A lower limit would provide less revenue and less flexibility, but might enable confidence in new arrangements to develop more gradually. In that situation, there might be a case for allowing a higher limit in some cases subject to more stringent approval mechanisms;

- retention of revenue, where I believe all revenues should be retained locally;

- the right form of accountability to business taxpayers. The most obvious options are some form of voted approval or a statutory consultation process. On balance, I propose that there should be a requirement to consult local businesses, and the wider community, before introducing a supplement, with a clear proposal and timetable. Revenues from a supplement should be hypothecated to the purposes agreed through consultation;

- how to ensure that supplements contribute to, rather than detract from, the local economy. I propose that authorities should be required to make an assessment of the impact of a supplement on the local economy, and the potential economic benefits of the spending they propose to finance from the revenues generated;

- the authority by which supplements should be levied. I recommend that supplements should be levied by unitary authorities and metropolitan districts, and in London and areas with two-tier local government, a single rate should be set through agreement between the relevant authorities, with a joint plan for the use of revenues. Where arrangements develop for collaborative working between authorities elsewhere in the country this could usefully include cooperating around supplements. Powers to introduce Business Improvement Districts should remain with shire districts and the London boroughs;

- whether authorities should have a degree of flexibility over which sizes of business pay the levy, which I would support; and

- whether there should be a threshold below which small businesses do not pay the levy.

The wider impacts of a supplement

8.72   The way business rates work, and the interaction between rates and rental values, raises a number of issues that it will be important for the Government and local authorities to take into account in implementing these recommendations.

8.73   In the short term a local supplement on business rates will increase the cost of property occupation for tenants and owner-occupiers, who will have to pay higher taxes, as well as (for tenants) their current rent. In the longer term, as set out earlier in this chapter, the evidence suggests that business rates will be passed on to owners in lower rents. Depending on the use to which the revenues from a supplement are put, owner-occupiers and landlords may see some reduction in the capital value of their property compared to what would otherwise have happened without a supplement, as a result of the value of future rents being reduced.

8.74   The reduction in rental values that a supplement could lead to will have other implications for the Government and for taxpayers. I have recommended that for the present the existing method of calculating the national business rate multiplier should remain as it is. The Government will therefore continue to set the multiplier at revaluation so as to generate the same national revenue in real terms as before the revaluation. Since the introduction of local supplements may reduce rateable values compared with what they otherwise would have been, the national tax rate may need to be slightly higher than it would otherwise have been in order to continue to raise the same amount of money.

8.75   My analysis suggests that if the supplement was fully absorbed by reductions in rents, the resulting fall from a one pence supplement levied across the country would be around 0.7 per cent of total rateable value, though in practice the effect might be lost in other, more significant changes in rateable values. The chart below shows the likely impact on overall rateable value under a range of assumptions about the degree to which the increase is passed through to rental values (where zero is no impact on rents and one is where the increase in tax is fully compensated by a fall in rents). This is a potentially significant impact for property owners and investors, although small compared to recent increases in the value of commercial property.

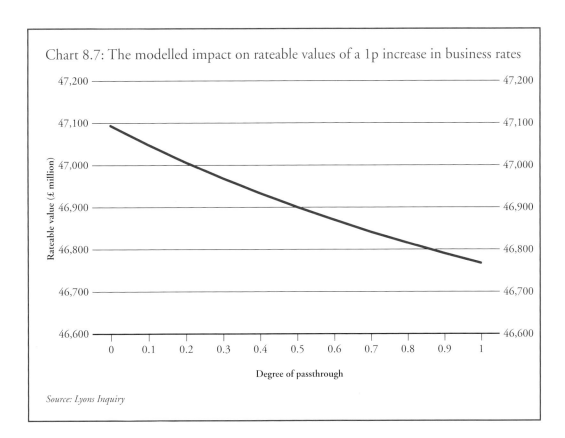

Chart 8.7: The modelled impact on rateable values of a 1p increase in business rates

Rateable value (£ million)

Degree of passthrough

Source: Lyons Inquiry

8.76   However, it is important to remember that the objective behind introducing greater local flexibility is to enable authorities to invest in infrastructure and other activities, which enhance local quality of life and the distinctiveness of places, and support economic development and growth. Where spending is targeted well on such areas it should support an expansion in the number and success of businesses and the value of the properties in an area, offsetting the negative impact of the supplement. This makes it especially important that in proposing supplements, local authorities consider the purpose to which they intend to put the resources raised, and consult fully with businesses and other local stakeholders to ensure that they will create value in the local economy.

8.77   Changes to business rates will also have wider impacts on the public purse. Business rates are considered as a cost for tax purposes, which means that an increase in business rates liability, for a profitable company, can be partially offset against its tax bill. Public sector buildings are also liable for business rates, and public sector organisations will therefore have to pay higher rates where supplements are levied – there should not be any relief or exemption for the public sector. This will affect local and central government, as well as other public institutions such as the health service. Although no definitive figures on the rate bill of the public sector exist, a basic analysis suggests that they make up around ten per cent of the gross value of non-domestic properties.[15] Local authorities will need to consider these impacts when developing their proposals on supplements.

---

[15] The total rateable value of public sector properties as at 1 April 2006 is estimated at £4.1 billion. This is derived from information published by HM Revenue and Customs. The main components (with estimated rateable values shown in brackets) are: Local authority schools & colleges (£1.3 billion); Medical facilities (£0.8 billion); Other properties (£0.7 billion); Police stations & courts (£0.3 billion); Community centres & halls (£0.3 billion); Local government offices (£0.2 billion); and Libraries & museums (£0.1 billion).

Improving the efficiency and fairness of business rates

8.78 There are a number of different types of land and property which receive a partial relief, or are completely exempted, from business rates, for a variety of historical and policy reasons. The main exemptions and reliefs are set out in table 8.4, below, together with their cost in terms of revenue given up. Exempt land and properties are not valued for business rates, and the data on reliefs is therefore far better than the data on exemptions.

Table 8.4: Costs of business rate reliefs and exemptions

	2006-07 cost/estimated cost (£m)
Reliefs	
Empty property	1333.1
Charity (mandatory relief)	724.3
Partly occupied property relief	40.8
Community Amateur Sports Clubs	7.1
Rural shops (mandatory relief)	5.9
Former agricultural premises	0.9
Transitional relief	Revenue neutral over revaluation cycle
Small Business Rate Relief	Revenue neutral
Exemptions	
Agricultural land and buildings	300-450
Derelict/brownfield land	Uncertain

Other smaller uncosted exemptions include places of religious worship, fish farms, sewers, and public parks

Sources: CLG; Lyons Inquiry analysis

8.79 While there are reasons behind the existence of these reliefs and exemptions, it is sensible to cast a critical eye over them in order to ensure that they remain fit for purpose. The existence of reliefs and exemptions can create distortions, or weaken incentives to take positive actions. In addition, they represent a cost in terms of revenue foregone – money which could otherwise be used to cut the overall rate of tax or fund additional spending.

8.80 In my *Interim Report and Consultation Document* in December 2005 I noted my interest in considering areas in which business rates falls short of functioning as a full land and property tax, and I have therefore specifically considered the empty property relief and the exemption of vacant land and derelict property. These are subjects on which, in the intervening period, the Barker Review of Land Use Planning has also made recommendations.

Empty property 8.81 Empty property relief provides a substantial relief from taxation for all empty property, and full relief for some types. Most property receives 100 per cent relief for the first three months, and 50 per cent relief thereafter, and warehouses or factories receive 100 per cent relief at all times. At an annual cost in terms of revenue foregone of £1.3 billion it is the single most significant relief in the business rates system. Some stakeholders called for the relief to be reduced, or removed entirely.

> *Empty properties should pay full business rates as an incentive to encourage local business growth, with exceptions allowable for any property owner who can prove that they are doing all they can to fill the property and are delayed by means beyond their control.* (Federation of Small Businesses)

> *Leeds supports the case for the reform of empty property relief...and agrees that reform could be used to encourage early redevelopment and re-use particularly in urban areas.* (Leeds City Council)

8.82   There are some arguments in favour of the existence of empty property relief. It can be argued that a general relief shares the risks of a property not being able to earn a return between government and the owner.[16] A relief for property that is only empty for a short time supports an active property market, as it means that owners do not pay tax while tenants move. Relieving empty property of taxation also reduces the incentive for owners to make their properties derelict in order to avoid taxation.

8.83   In the main, the prospect of commercial returns from the property should ensure full use of properties. However, the risk of not earning a return does not just result from external factors, but is also determined by the actions of the owner. For example, they might not maintain the property properly and let it fall into disrepair, be uninformed about better uses for it, or might keep it empty for speculative reasons. Empty properties can also impose additional costs on communities by rendering areas less safe and attractive, and still require some public services such as policing and fire protection.

8.84   Demand for land for development is growing as a result of economic change and household growth, and it is clear that, more than ever, need to ensure that all previously developed land is used most effectively.[17] Analysis shows that vacant property is found in areas of high demand as well as in areas of low demand and former industrial areas.[18] Finding ways to raise the opportunity cost of holding unused land and property in areas of high demand at such a time would be desirable. Reforming the empty property relief would help to provide this, and thus assist local authorities in their place-shaping role.

8.85   The existence of different levels of relief for different types of property distorts the market. It creates a sectoral imbalance within the system, providing a greater level of benefit to one sector than to others, and it does not provide any pressure from within the tax system to encourage the reuse of such land or the property for alternative uses, including redevelopment of the site and conversion to another use. This imbalance should be rectified by balancing the relief currently provided to factories and warehouses with that available for office and retail premises.

8.86   Changes to the empty property relief would have a number of implications for businesses. The increased taxation would encourage the owners of empty property to find ways to make better use of it, either through using it themselves, attracting new tenants (perhaps by reducing rents) or redeveloping the site for a new use. The effect across the economy would probably be a fall in future rents that would benefit property occupiers. This might be accompanied by a fall in capital values, which would have no impact on current owner-occupiers (assuming that they wanted to continue using the same or more property in the future) and a positive benefit for future purchasers.

8.87   No national breakdown exists of how much of the £1.3 billion of empty property relief is accounted for by the different elements of the relief. However, in a small sample of local authorities who were able to provide the Inquiry with data, 80 per cent of the relief was accounted for by the full relief for factories and warehouses and the partial relief on longer term empty property.[19]

---

[16] Atkinson, A.B., and Stiglitz, J.E., *Lectures in Public Economics*, 1980.

[17] Doing so helps to protect open spaces and the countryside, promotes urban regeneration, and supports the viability of services like public transport which rely on dense populations.

[18] Office of the Deputy Prime Minister, *Commercial and Industrial Floorspace and Rateable Value Statistics 2005*, 2006.

[19] Based on data for 2005-06, kindly provided by Birmingham, Stockton, Oldham, Bury, Manchester and Rochdale.

Existing data on the value of empty property in all local authority areas, and additional detailed analysis of the speed at which property falls empty, and the time it takes to be re-let or sold (currently in the process of being compiled by Communities and Local Government) paints a similar picture.[20] Together these sources suggest that the reforms I am proposing could raise potentially significant additional resources, alongside providing improved incentives for the efficient use of land.

8.88   Rating organisations who commented on the Barker Review of Land Use Planning's recommendations on this issue noted that measures had been introduced in the 1970s to provide better incentives for the reuse of empty property and that these had not been successful. They pointed out that when faced with penal rates of tax, owners often found it easier to make the property derelict rather than to bring it back into use. This is an instructive lesson. Any proposals for reform should seek to avoid this problem through limiting taxation to 100 per cent of liability, rather than imposing penal rates of tax. However, it remains a concern that some owners may find dereliction an attractive route to escape taxation. A tax on previously developed land, considered next, provides a possible solution to this problem.

Recommendation 8.4

The Government should reform and reduce the empty property relief by:

- retaining the existing 100 per cent relief for short-term empty property (up to three months);

- reducing the rate of empty property relief thereafter; and

- providing factories and warehouses with the same level of relief as other properties.

Derelict property and brownfield land

8.89   Land that is not 'capable of beneficial occupation' is not subject to taxation through business rates. However, the arguments set out above about the possible role of the tax system in ensuring an efficient use of land also apply to derelict property and previously developed land, and could thus support the place-shaping role of local authorities. The potential for a tax on such land to close a possible loophole in the system is also a reason for considering it seriously.

8.90   However, introducing such a tax would be a much more complex matter than reforming the empty property relief, for a number of reasons. Defining, identifying and valuing the land would be a significant task, as the land is not currently identified or taxed for the purposes of business rates. Valuation would be a particularly challenging task, given that this land does not, almost by definition, have a rental value. An approach which imputed a rent from the capital value of the land might be necessary, which would be a significant change from the normal principles of business rates, which is a tax on occupation and the consumption of property rather than its ownership.

8.91   It is difficult to calculate what the revenue from this tax would be. Although an estimated 36,500 hectares of previously developed land in England are vacant or derelict, most of this land will be worth comparatively little, and therefore the revenues from a tax on it is be unlikely to be very substantial.[21] However, the purpose of the tax would not primarily be revenue generation, but rather to provide proper incentives for re-use and to prevent some owners exploiting the loophole in the system that would otherwise exist.

---

[20] Office of the Deputy Prime Minister, *Commercial and Industrial Floorspace and Rateable Value Statistics 2005*, 2006.

[21] Office of the Deputy Prime Minister, *Commercial and Industrial Floorspace and Rateable Value Statistics 2005*, 2006.

8.92 These proposals are not yet fully developed, and further work will be needed to test whether this is a feasible proposition and how implementation and administration could be undertaken. The Government will need to consider a number of issues, including:

- whether it is economic to incur the costs of valuing and administering a new tax on this land given the potential yield;

- avoiding development pressure on green spaces and other public amenities. There may be a case for an exemption for such land;

- how to treat land that is uneconomic to develop (though such land should have a very low or zero value and thus little or no tax liability in any case);

- how to avoid reducing rather than increasing development because of any interaction between a new levy on previously developed land and the Planning-gain Supplement, or other aspects of the taxation system; and

- whether there are any legal circumstances or cases of reserved strategic capacity where incentives should not apply, as noted by Kate Barker.

Recommendation 8.5

The Government should develop proposals for the taxation of derelict property and brownfield land and consult on those with stakeholders.

8.93 There are myriad other reliefs and exemptions in the business rates system. The most substantial in terms of revenue foregone are the reliefs for charities, and the exemption for agricultural land and buildings. The transitional relief available to cushion the impact of revaluation and the small business rate relief are also important, though they are intended to be revenue neutral.

Agricultural land and buildings

8.94 Agricultural land and buildings have been completely exempt from business rates since 1929, although they had enjoyed some level of relief since the late 19th century because of economic difficulties in the sector. This situation no longer applies to the same extent, and there would seem in principle to be little reason to maintain the special treatment, which gives agriculture a tax benefit that no other business sector enjoys. Farms and other agricultural businesses are generally liable for a range of other taxes in the same way as other businesses (although there are some specific differences, for example in inheritance tax). That said, agriculture does have some unique characteristics, including the role of farmers in land stewardship as well as agricultural production, and the sector has been the subject of significant ongoing reforms of agricultural subsidies and support.

8.95 My analysis suggests that the exemption is worth in the order of £450 million a year in revenue foregone. This is not an exact figure as agricultural land and buildings are not currently valued for business rates by the Valuation Office Agency (VOA). In addition, we would expect agricultural rental values to fall as a result of the re-introduction of rates. If rental values fell so as to completely offset the impact of taxation, this would reduce the expected income from rates on agricultural land and buildings to around £300 million. The impact of taxation would also be to reduce the capital value of agricultural land.

8.96 There are precedents for large-scale changes in the rating system in the return of industrial property to full rating in England and Wales in 1961, having enjoyed a 75 per cent exemption from

1929, and more recently in the re-rating of industry in Northern Ireland. However, re-introducing rates on agriculture would undoubtedly be a significant step, and a tax liability of £300 million – £450 million a year would represent a substantial proportion of the income from farming (which totalled £1.9 billion in 2005 in England and Wales, as measured by the Department for the Environment, Food and Rural Affairs' Total Income from Farming assessment). Adjustment by farmers, and the agricultural sector as a whole, to a range of powerful long run economic pressures is a normal, ongoing process, but it is also the case that UK farmers are still responding to the implications of 'decoupling', and that significant further Common Agricultural Policy reform is likely over the next few years.[22] Ultimately, the incidence of business rates falls on the owners of business assets, but policy on reforming exemptions to business rates needs to be sensitive to the broader economic context of the affected sectors, and in respect of farming (particularly tenant farmers) it needs to be sensitive to the realities of the agricultural adjustment process. If the Government was to re-introduce rates there would therefore certainly need to be a period of transition to allow the sector to adjust, and there might well be a case for some continuing level of relief, for example to avoid a situation where otherwise viable and environmentally beneficial agricultural business activity is curtailed. In particular, I believe that marginal agricultural land should continue to receive full relief from business rates. Other land, including that used for 'lifestyle', rather than agricultural purposes, would legitimately face taxation.

Charities 8.97   The relief for charities is the second most significant relief after the empty property relief. The 80 per cent mandatory relief was worth £724 million in 2006-07, and local authorities also provided further discretionary relief. Charities are generally not liable for tax, such as income tax, corporation tax and capital gains tax, and this relief arguably extends that approach to the business rates system. However, as we have seen earlier in this chapter, in general the evidence suggests that a fall in rates will lead to an increase in rents, and we would expect at least some proportion of the charity relief to accrue to the owners of the properties, in the form of higher rents. Some business organisations, such as the Forum of Private Business, feel that the existence of this relief helps some charities to unfairly undercut other high street businesses.

New reliefs 8.98   Some of those who made submissions to my Inquiry called for new reliefs. The Social Market Foundation have suggested new reliefs to support the environmental agenda, for example by reducing the rates payable on energy efficient buildings.[23]

8.99   Such incentives might have a part to play in this country's approach to greater environmental sustainability and lower energy use. Following the publication of the Stern Review on the economics of climate change, it is clear that as a society we will have to take new steps to deal with the impact of climate change.

8.100   I do not recommend business rate based measures at this stage. It is beyond the remit of this Inquiry to consider all of the possible measures for addressing climate change, and while there is the potential to use business rates as part of an overall strategy, it is unclear whether a business rate relief would be the most effective and value for money approach. An energy efficient property will have reduced costs for the occupier, which means that there is a business case for investment in energy efficiency by owners and occupiers without public subsidy. Such a property would also therefore command a higher rent than a comparable energy inefficient property, transferring the benefit of the relief from the occupier to the owner. The concern of many of those involved in the rating system, that new reliefs would increase the complexity of an already complex system, also needs to be given some weight.

---

[22] See for example the Government's *A Vision for the Common Agricultural Policy*, 2005.
[23] Blackwell, T. and Gough, B., *Turning business rates green: How to make the Uniform Business Rate fit for the future*, Social Market Foundation, 2006.

8.101 In the light of this, I recommend that the Government should undertake its own review of the reliefs and exemptions in the system. That review should have a number of objectives:

- to consider the current reliefs and exemptions and to judge whether they remain justified in terms of their cost, their contribution to policy objectives and the potential distortions they create to a level playing field for all property users;

- in particular, to review the case for the continuing existence of the agricultural exemption, and to consider the costs and benefits of undertaking a valuation of agricultural land at the 2010 revaluation in order to accurately assess the value of the exemption; and

- where practicable, to remove or merge existing reliefs and exemptions.

8.102 When considering any new reliefs as part of this review, the Government should consider the following principles:

- the benefits of the introduction of the relief should exceed the costs, including the costs to the Government, and to businesses, of administering a more complex system, the distortions to the property market that reliefs can create, and the fact that providing one type of property with relief might necessitate a higher tax rate on other property to maintain the overall yield; and

- since the value of any relief is likely to accrue in substantial part to the owners rather than the occupiers of the property, reliefs should only be introduced where this is a desirable end.

> **Recommendation 8.6**
>
> The Government should conduct a review of exemptions and reliefs to consider the scope for removing inappropriate subsidies and distortions, and to simplify the system.

Local discretion 8.103 In reforming reliefs and exemptions, there will be a choice about whether any changes should be made across the country, or whether there should be an element of local discretion. Local discretion, particularly on the empty property relief, would give local authorities new tools with which to pursue local regeneration and development, and enable them to take an approach sensitive to local economic and property market conditions. On the other hand, a national approach would have the advantage of ensuring a consistent and predictable approach across the country for property owners and developers, and it would also provide additional revenue at national level.

Use of additional 8.104 Changes to reliefs and exemptions will have an impact on total yield. This will obviously be revenues subject to the outcome of the review. However, if the net result of any changes was an overall increase in yield then this could be used to reduce business rates for all businesses. This could assist with the introduction of a discretionary supplementary power by reducing the impact of national business rates on businesses, and on the Government's other tax receipts. Final decisions on this will be for ministers to make, in the light of the wider review of reliefs, the overall fiscal position, and other calls on available revenues.

Implementation

8.105   Many of the changes I have recommended in this chapter will require primary legislation to implement them. The timescale on which they can be introduced will therefore depend on when the Government can bring forward a bill and when Parliamentary time can be found. The Government would also need to undertake further consultation with stakeholders and experts on detailed proposals and technical issues.

8.106   New powers for local authorities to levy a local supplement on business rates should be introduced as soon as possible after primary legislation, allowing sufficient time for local billing authorities and their suppliers to deal with any necessary amendments to software and information systems.

8.107   In order to remove exemptions a large number of properties which do not fall within the system at present must be valued, and it would be sensible to integrate this valuation process with the VOA's cycle of valuation work. Depending on the size and complexity of the task involved, it might be possible to remove exemptions from the beginning of the 2010 list in April 2010.

Options for future governments

8.108   The key options for the future of business rates centre on changes to the process and frequency of revaluation, and to the way in which the tax rate is set. A number of these options were considered by the Government's review of revaluation in 1999-2000. The Government will also need to keep the overall level of business rates under review, as part of its general approach to considering the appropriate level and method of taxation on businesses and on other sectors.

Revaluation   8.109   From a theoretical point of view, there is much to be said for increasing the frequency of revaluations. More frequent revaluation would mean each property paid a bill more related to its actual value (relative to other properties) – whereas in the present system property values can be almost seven years out of date (revaluations are implemented every five years, but published lists use assessments of rateable value from two years before the implementation date). This would make the tax more responsive to the actual state of the property market and could have economic advantages by reducing the burden of taxation on businesses in economic downturns. Since the changes in rateable value, and hence in tax bills, would vary less if updated each year, rather than every five years, it might also be possible to scale back or remove transitional relief, which would remove some complexity from the system.

8.110   Increasing the frequency of revaluations would have some drawbacks (including possible increases in administration costs). By updating values more frequently, it would remove some of the stability of the current system, which enables a business to calculate its likely rates bill for five years at a time. The impact of this would affect different sectors in different ways, and might be particularly challenging to sectors which are not valued using the normal rental value approach. In addition, though such a system would improve the link between business taxation and the state of the property market, this might make things harder for businesses during upturns if they had difficulty of rapidly adjusting the use of property as its price changed.

8.111   There are a variety of options for increasing the speed of revaluation. With the improvements in information technology now available it seems likely that annual revaluations would be possible in the not too distant future, though with some cost implications. Another option would be to adopt a system of rolling revaluation in which only a certain proportion of properties would actually be revalued each year, while the others were uprated using statistical analyses of property price changes.

Setting a fixed multiplier

8.112 Under the current system the tax rate is set at the beginning of a revaluation cycle in order to generate the same level of revenue from the new tax base, and updated in line with RPI each year to maintain the value of the revenue in real terms. This creates a stable and predictable system for both government (which knows how much revenue it is going to collect) and for businesses (who can estimate their bills for five years in advance, subject to any appeals and the impact of transitional relief). However, as I mentioned earlier, there are potential disadvantages as it means that the weight of business rates is heavier during times of economic downturn when rents are low, and lighter during times of growth.

8.113 An alternative possibility – probably in conjunction with more frequent revaluations – would be to fix the tax rate and allow the yield from the tax to change from revaluation to revaluation depending on the state of the property market. More revenue would be raised during periods of growth, and less during periods of downturn. This system should have economic benefits as it would make taxation better linked to the market situation, helping to ease demand during growth periods and support it during downturns. It might also have advantages from the perspective of the local government finance system, as it would make it easier to provide financial incentives which would encourage local authorities to enhance the value of business properties in their area, as well as supporting growth in the number of properties. This is also noted in Chapter 9.

8.114 However, it would make business bills more variable from revaluation to revaluation, and businesses might find it difficult to renegotiate their rent or adjust their use of property appropriately between revaluations depending on the extent and predictability of fluctuations. It would also expose central and local government to greater variability in their revenues.

Setting rates at local level

8.115 My recommendation for the introduction of a local supplementary power is a limited new power for local authorities to alter the rate of tax paid by businesses in their area. In the longer term, those limits should be reviewed, taking account of how relationships evolve between local authorities and businesses, and the evidence on the economic impacts of better local authority engagement with economic development issues. The localisation of revenues and power for local authorities to set the tax rate for themselves in the light of local circumstances, including making the choice to set a lower tax rate, could be considered. Businesses have made clear their concerns about such a radical step in the short term, but it is a decision future governments may wish to consider as new arrangements evolve.

SECTION 106 AND PLANNING-GAIN SUPPLEMENT

8.116   To complete the review of local land and property taxation, it is worth a brief reflection on Section 106 (S106) contributions and the proposed Planning-gain Supplement (PGS). Both have been extensively reviewed by Kate Barker in her work on housing supply and land use planning, and the Government has set out proposals for reform, but these raise issues relevant to my remit.

8.117   These two sources provide (or could in future) a substantial source of revenues linked to development. They have two purposes – firstly, to provide community infrastructure to meet the needs of residents in new developments and/or to mitigate the impact of new developments upon existing community facilities. This is the stated purpose of S106, which is used to fund new roads, schools and so forth. Secondly, PGS is intended to capture some of the excess profits received by landowners when planning permission is granted for new developments. There are some who argue that where S106 is used to its fullest extent by local planning authorities it can in fact capture some of those profits, even though it is not strictly intended to do so, which has at times complicated the situation, and created delay and uncertainty. However, the extent to which authorities are successful in using S106 varies considerably around the country.[24]

8.118   The Government's proposed reforms would retain a scaled back S106 to mitigate direct impacts from development and to fund immediate local infrastructure necessary to that development. It would also continue to be used to support affordable housing targets. The PGS would then be available as a general revenue source to support wider infrastructure development, and be allocated between local and regional spending with at least 70 per cent kept locally.

8.119   I support that approach in general. However, given that these revenues are linked to local planning decisions and the infrastructure needed to support and enable growth, it is important that the links to local authorities and the local community are made explicit, clear and substantial. The PGS should be seen as a local tax with a regional share, not a national tax, and the Government should not seek to direct the way in which it is spent. S106 will remain important as a source of negotiated local revenues to support development.

8.120   There is also an unresolved question about how revenues from PGS will be allocated between districts and counties in two tier areas. District authorities are responsible for making the ultimate planning decisions and engaging with developers, but it is county councils which are responsible for much of the infrastructure necessary to support development. It is also important to consider whether either tier has advantages from the perspective of ensuring that individuals and local communities perceive the financial and infrastructure benefits that development is bringing with it.

8.121   Providing appropriate infrastructure to support development is a shared issue for both tiers. I therefore think there is merit in pursuing a joint option for the management of the revenues, in which county and district councils would be jointly responsible for developing and implementing a plan for the use of the revenues from PGS in their area. That should help to give a genuine local connection, but also the opportunity to use the revenues across a wider area in order to support necessary strategic infrastructure.

---

[24] University of Sheffield and Halcrow Group, *Valuing Planning Obligations in England: Final Report*, Communities and Local Government, 2006.

> **Recommendation 8.7**
>
> If the Planning-gain Supplement is introduced, the Government should:
>
> - design it primarily as a local revenue source, with a regional share of an appropriate scale, not as a national source which may or may not be allocated to authorities. It is imperative that a transparent and predictable link between local development and local resourcing exists if development is to take place, or incentive effects are to be realised; and
>
> - consider whether in two-tier areas, it could be managed through plans jointly developed and implemented by county and district councils.

TAXES ON TOURIST PRESSURES

8.122 The Local Government Association, in its submissions to the Government's Balance of Funding Review and subsequently to me, have suggested that local authorities could be given a discretionary power to levy a tourist accommodation tax in their areas. Some interest in such taxes was expressed by a small number of authorities during the Inquiry, though on the whole local authority enthusiasm for new taxes of this kind was less than might have been expected. The proposal understandably generated significant debate within the tourism industry and beyond.

8.123 Accommodation taxes have been deployed in a number of places around the world, with varying degrees of success. For instance, an accommodation charge is levied on all overnight stays in France, with the level of the charge largely left to local determination. I also received evidence of voluntary schemes operating in England.

> *For over a decade the Tourism and Conservation Partnership has operated a very successful and entirely voluntary visitor payback scheme in the Lake District and more recently the wider county of Cumbria... for example, Heart of the Lakes accommodation company automatically adds £2 to every invoice they raise. Guests are given the option of opting out of paying this, but rarely do... Many guests make a voluntary contribution in excess of the requested £2.* (The Tourism and Conservation Partnership)

8.124 The submissions I have received make clear the importance of weighing the merits of a tourist contribution against the costs they impose against the likely impact on the tourist industry and local economies. The impact of tourism on local communities can include tourist use of local transport networks; community safety; the local environment; local arts, sport and culture; and redevelopment activity. The societal costs imposed by tourists include pollution (for example increased CO_2 emissions), degradation of place, land use and use of public utilities (additional use of water, electricity and sewage). However, it should be noted that the evidence base relating to the economics surrounding tourist accommodation choices is still being developed; in particular there is currently insufficient data to assess the impact of a proposed local scheme at the level of individual authority areas' local economies. It is also important to remember that tax revenues are already raised from tourist activity – VAT from spending, and the business rates and other taxes from businesses which rely on tourists – and government grant to local authorities does take some account of the costs imposed by visitors.

8.125 Some submissions have articulated concerns about the likely impact of a tourist tax, including the concern that it would damage local economies by driving tourists elsewhere in the country or to other parts of the world. Local authority submissions recognised the complexity of the situation:

The economy of the Borough of Restormel is heavily dependent on tourism. Accordingly, special note was made of the concept of a tourist accommodation tax. The additional costs created by large seasonal influxes of visitors could potentially be offset by such a charge, but only if it was locally administered. However, the significant disbenefit is the potential for a loss of competitive advantage – tourists will simply go elsewhere. (Restormel Borough Council)

8.126   Many of those who wrote to me, including a substantial campaign from the hotel industry, were concerned that I might recommend a blanket tax on tourist accommodation across the country, regardless of the characteristics of the area or its economy. However, I have concluded that no single mechanism or economic instrument is likely to fit the needs of circumstances of all local authorities. I do not recommend a generally applicable 'bed tax'. However, in some areas there may be a case for a tourist related tax, developed in partnership with local businesses and residents – possibly through an annual bed licencing scheme levied on operators, or alternatively by directly levying the tax on overnight visitors.

8.127   I do not support the introduction of any new taxation powers for the sake of it. In my view, a local accommodation tax is only likely to be acceptable if a local authority can demonstrate that:

- there is a robust evidence base that the local economy could support the introduction of the tax, including the likely start-up, collection and enforcement costs;

- existing alternatives, such as Business Improvement Districts, have been fully considered;

- there is local support for the tax; and

- the scheme has been developed in partnership with local businesses and residents, who should continue to have a voice in the evolution and review of the scheme.

8.128   In practice the impact of a levy of this kind would vary greatly between areas. A tax that would have very little impact on tourist numbers in one place might be more damaging in another, and there is not at present sufficient evidence on which to assess this at a fine-grained local level. Local authorities would therefore need to undertake rigorous analysis of the likely economic costs and benefits of levies in their areas before implementing any such scheme. Decisions about the viability of local tourism levies would need to be taken on a case-by-case basis.

8.129   It is also not clear that there is significant local appetite for new powers to tax tourists, and before extending such powers it would be important to establish that local authorities would wish to make use of them, and to undertake the necessary analytical and engagement work that would pave the way to any tax being implemented. A wider consultation with local authorities and the tourism industry would be necessary to examine this fully.

> **Recommendation 8.8**
>
> The Government should consult on the costs and benefits of providing a permissive power for local authorities to levy taxes on tourism, including a possible tax on accommodation, and whether local authorities would use such a power. It should use the results of that consultation to examine the case for extension of such powers to local authorities.

9

The funding system and incentives

Summary

This chapter argues that the current grant system should be re-balanced to improve incentives for local areas to grow their tax bases. This could offer a direct financial benefit to local communities which are weighing up difficult decisions over residential or economic growth. Along with the other benefits that growth may provide, a financial incentive that allowed authorities to retain more of the extra tax raised locally as a result of their efforts could go some way to compensating local communities for any wider costs.

The chapter examines a number of possible options for reform to link funding more directly to the local tax base. However, it is very difficult to create such incentives in the current 'four block' grant distribution system. Therefore more substantial reform may be needed.

The chapter also explores ways to improve the transparency of the funding system by seeking ways to reflect more explicitly the shared nature of revenues coming from central and local government which support local services. It considers options for the assignment of part of a national tax such as income tax to local government.

Depending on how it is designed, an assigned tax could not only help to improve transparency by making it clearer that a proportion of national taxation also contributes to local services but might also pass on some buoyancy from the national tax base to local government, which could help to keep pressure off council tax.

There are some disadvantages: any income from buoyancy of a tax assigned to local government would not then be available to support central government priorities delivered through agencies other than local government. Also, local government might have to bear the risk that income tax revenues (unlike council tax) can fall in a recession – they are not necessarily buoyant in every year. This raises questions about the capacity and willingness of local government to manage with a fluctuating and unpredictable tax base.

The chapter concludes that:

- the grant system should be changed to introduce incentives to support growth and, in the short term, the Local Authority Business Growth Incentives scheme should be simplified; and

- in the short term, better information should be provided on the extent to which nationally collected taxes are used to support local services in addition to council tax. In the medium term the Government should consider a more formal direct assignment of part of income tax to support local services.

INTRODUCTION

9.1   This chapter considers ways to make the funding by central government of local public services more transparent, and to improve the incentives it creates for local government. These reforms should support the desire for a stronger, clearer and more mature relationship between central and local government which is at the heart of my recommendations on a new constitutional settlement in Chapter 10.

9.2   The first section examines ways of reforming the grant system to clarify its aims and improve incentives on local authorities to be more self-reliant in expanding their tax bases. The second section examines ways of sharing revenues to improve public understanding of how local government services are funded, to improve accountability and enhance confidence in local government.

INCENTIVES, EQUALISATION AND GRANT

9.3   Chapter 3 argued that grant is at the centre of the relationship between central and local government. It examined the effects on incentives of the equalisation process which, while having aims that I support, acts to control the effects of differences in local tax bases and growth. The effect of this is that while local authorities see it as a core part of their concern to pay attention to local prosperity, and the needs and future prospects of its citizens and its local areas, there are no coherent or systematic financial incentives that encourage growth either for them or, more importantly, for their communities.

9.4   There is a strong case for equity and stability to remain key objectives of the grant system. Equity – pursued in the current system through the equalisation processes – is important to ensure that communities with high levels of socio-economic need or low tax raising abilities are not left behind. Indeed there are economic arguments that public resources are better targeted at such areas as they can have more of an impact on the outcomes which are national priorities than if distributed to affluent areas.

9.5   I have also argued in previous chapters that a degree of stability in the funding system is essential to allow local authorities to plan. Having said that, I am concerned that the focus on stability – pursued in the current system through grant damping – appears to be over-emphasised due to central government's concern about council tax levels. A more effective solution would be to deal with the pressure on, and public concern about, council tax through proper reform rather than using other parts of the system to control the pressure on the tax.

9.6   However, in order for local authorities to be able, and encouraged, to perform their place-shaping role to the full, I believe that a further objective needs to be considered for the funding system: providing financial incentives for local authorities and communities to promote economic prosperity and residential growth, and to take into account their benefits and costs fully.

9.7   Financial incentives should give local authorities more reward for owning and growing their own tax bases without such growth being immediately equalised away, and enable them to benefit from growth more directly, either in terms of population or more business activity in their areas. Such changes would, as argued in Chapter 3, support areas in taking action to respond to the social and economic pressures on our country and align the incentives they face more closely to these objectives.

9.8   My proposals are not intended to dramatically reduce equalisation, or to increase stability in a way that impacts on local government's ability to plan. Rather I want to find a way to provide space – at the margins, but with enough weight to change local government behaviours – to incentivise local government to grow their tax bases and crucially enable local communities to receive some reward for allowing their area to develop and grow.

9.9   I recognise that there may be concerns about such incentives benefiting areas which are growing at the expense of needy areas. The distinction may be more appropriately made on the differing ability of areas to grow, rather than just their current level of need. Some of the most deprived areas of the country including Manchester and areas of East London have experienced major increases in residential and business development as shown in Table 9.1 below.

Table 9.1: Authorities with largest growth in council tax and business rate tax bases, 1999-2004

Largest council tax base growth	Largest business (rateable value) growth
Tower Hamlets	Westminster
Westminster	Tower Hamlets
East Riding of Yorkshire	City of London
Hackney	Camden
Lambeth	Birmingham
Leeds	Southwark
Manchester	Leeds
Milton Keynes	Milton Keynes
Islington	Sheffield
South Gloucestershire	Hillingdon
Wandsworth	Islington
Bradford	Bristol
Liverpool	Hounslow
Newham	Manchester
Wakefield	Nottingham

9.10   In contrast, it is unlikely that some of the less well-connected and more economically weak areas of our country will see such change unless there is concerted policy effort – beyond changes to the grant system – by national and local government. Ensuring that support for these types of area does not fall away is one of the main reasons that I have discussed changes in terms of marginal, rather than whole-scale terms. I explore in the more detailed discussion of particular incentive schemes, a method by which the degree to which the incentive impacts on different types of area could be controlled. In the design of any eventual scheme there will need to be decisions made on where the resource to fund incentives should come from. If the choice was between equalising less, or damping less, I would favour the latter. As, in principle, I believe that with proper reform the pressure can be taken off council tax and in pragmatic terms, the authorities who will find it most difficult to grow are already not the main beneficiaries of damping which impacts most positively on more affluent areas.[1]

---

[1] See Annex E for a further discussion of this issue.

9.11   In summary this will mean the grant system balancing three aims, as set out below.

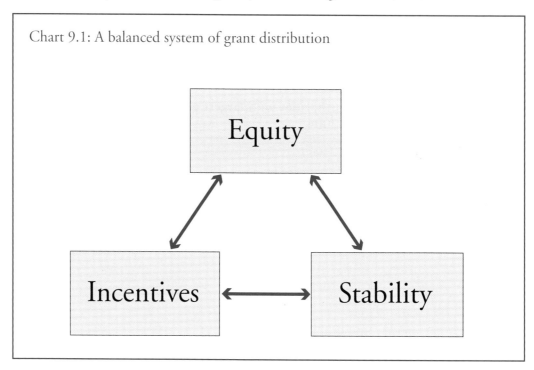

Chart 9.1: A balanced system of grant distribution

Incentives

9.12   Providing incentives to grow local tax bases could serve three purposes, they could:

- aid a more balanced decision making process, because financial benefits for the community could be used to compensate those affected either through improved services or reductions in tax bills. In this sense incentives could help to rebalance the costs and benefits of economic or housing growth by providing clearer local benefits to offset the costs of this growth, such as additional congestion and pressure on services – to the current residents;

- help to influence local authority behaviour in general by providing a more direct relationship between local authority finances and the health of the local economy through its investment to make the area attractive to businesses and also to attract a good skills base of local employees to the area; and

- provide a potential source of revenue which could be used for local investment in growth-enabling measures, such as infrastructure, which may need long-term planning and greater certainty over funding mechanisms.

9.13   It is important to note that all of these relate to long-term issues: planning and development decisions, relationships with and support to the business community and making investments to secure long-term gains. Incentives are therefore required which can operate on long timescales and which are sufficiently clear and transparent to enable councillors and local communities to understand their potential benefits. It is also important that any revenues from incentives should not be ring-fenced, nor have restrictions on their use. The costs of growth impact on different communities in different ways, and therefore local authorities and local communities should be able to use the financial benefits as they wish, whether that be to support investment, to provide additional services, or to meet other priorities.

Mechanisms for providing incentives

9.14   Incentives for local authorities need not be introduced through changes to the grant system. The Government could, for example, allocate specific reward grants to authorities on the basis of local changes in any indicator it chooses, including housing or economic growth. Indeed, as set out in Chapter 3, this is the approach it has chosen in recent years to respond to the identified problems caused by a lack of local incentives to support growth.

9.15   The Barker Review of Housing Supply identified housing growth as an area where new incentives are required for local authorities. Following this, the Government has consulted on a new Housing and Planning Delivery Grant (HPDG), which will allocate funds to 'reward' authorities for housing growth. In relation to business and economic growth more widely, the Government introduced the Local Authority Business Growth Incentives (LABGI) scheme in 2005, intended to distribute around £1 billion over three years to reward local authorities for growth in business rate revenues above pre-determined thresholds.

9.16   As the discussion of alternative and more systematic incentives below sets out, there are different ways of delivering incentives beyond special schemes such as LABGI and HPDG. Such schemes are steps in the right direction as they emphasise incentives although they remain controlled by central rules rather than supporting local decision making processes. This may be particularly the case for LABGI which has some specific drawbacks.

9.17   The criteria used to allocate resources through LABGI are complex – though they need not be in principle. This means that they are not transparent and are open to being amended and revised, as policy makers seek to refine the incentives provided and the pattern of distribution of resources. While such objectives may be valid, complexity and changes to criteria have reduced the ability of local authorities to predict their likely gains from the scheme, constraining the degree to which they are able to make decisions that rely on future financial benefits being realised and making it difficult to demonstrate the benefits to their citizens.

9.18   A key property of a good incentive scheme is predictability which provides a clear relationship between the effort and reward. However, LABGI includes special equalisation arrangements which blunt its incentive effect and add a further layer of complexity. The complexity and special nature of this scheme means that it produces a new set of transaction and compliance costs which falls most heavily on central government.

9.19   However, there are other issues that apply more generally to incentives that are delivered through special schemes:

- they reinforce the sense that authorities are following Government wishes and being rewarded. More systematic incentives could open up processes for local government to make the right local decisions, based on the local costs and benefits, and responding to general economic and social pressures; and

- reflecting the Spending Review cycle, grants are usually only allocated on a one to three year basis. This means that they are less likely to be able to motivate long-term changes in behaviour, or influence decisions which take more than three years to have an impact, as there is no guarantee that the scheme will continue to exist to provide the financial benefits expected.

9.20   Together, these can limit the extent to which specific reward schemes will actually influence authorities' long-term plans and decisions. This is of particular concern when we are seeking to influence decisions related to development and infrastructure planning, which are by their nature usually long term. LABGI, while welcomed by many stakeholders in principle, has suffered particularly from criticism that it is too short-term to influence behaviour, and too complex to be transparent and predictable, particularly given concerns about managing its distributional impact. Complex specific grants based on ministerial priorities can also reinforce a particular type of central-local relationship in which local authorities have to wait for central government judgments rather than basing change on the needs and aspirations of their local communities.

9.21   Incentives rooted in the wider system of local government finance could have the potential to be a more constant feature of local-central relations and could over time embed a different relationship between authorities and their tax base, creating better incentives to support growth and prosperity. However, particularly with the current grant system, the creation of such incentives is not straightforward. I have considered a number of illustrative options for council tax and business rates, all of which are based on the current government model of grant distribution – the 'four-block' model.

The four-block model

The distribution of national resources to local government impacts on all local authorities. No local authority in England is independent of central resources and indeed it can be considered an aim of the distribution system that all areas get a positive grant. However, the other key aim in distributing national tax resources is equalisation of needs and local tax resources.

Equalisation is the process by which national resources are used to supplement local revenue to support areas with high socio-economic needs and/or low local tax-raising potential. It is this process which requires the distribution of grants to local government to be based on detailed formulae and processes which allow these two elements to be identified.

The current English model of equalisation is recognised as one of the most complex in the world, and seeks to achieve one of the highest levels of equality compared to other advanced nations. Equalisation in England can be traced at least as far back as 1929, when block grant was introduced. The process developed in later decades, with the introduction of an explicit Exchequer Equalisation Grant in 1948.

Equalisation calculations have usually involved an 'approved' measure of expenditure which involves an assessment - based on demographic, economic and social data – of the appropriate share of revenue spending for each local authority, within a fixed national total. Similarly, account has usually been taken of a local authority's capacity for raising tax locally. In recent years, this has been done by using information on each authority's tax base and multiplying it by an assumed national average council tax for the appropriate class of authority. The capacity for raising other income – such as fees and charges – is not taken into account.

The current model was introduced for 2006-07 onwards. Its aim was partly to get away from what the Government regarded as the widespread misinterpretation of some of the components of the previous system, particularly that it was allocating resources based on actual rather than relative need.

The core components of the current system are four blocks carrying out the following roles in distributing Revenue Support Grant and redistributed business rates:

1. The **Relative Needs block** takes account of the variation in spending needs across authorities, covering the major services which they provide. As with the previous system, formulae are used to quantify relative, rather than absolute, spending needs, based on various factors which affect local authorities' costs locally. The national Relative Needs Amount for 2006-07 was £14.82 billion which was allocated to give each local authority a separate figure.

2. The **Relative Resource block** is a negative figure which takes account of each local authority's capacity for raising money locally through council tax. The total Relative Resource Amount for 2006-07 is -£5.13 billion. This is calculated to give a separate figure for each local authority. It can then be set against the Relative Needs Amount to give a further figure for each local authority which takes into account their relative needs and relative resources.

3. The **Central Allocation block** is the amount left in the overall grant pot for local authorities once account has been taken of the Relative Needs and Relative Resources of each authority. It totals £11.19 billion for 2006-07 and is allocated on a 'per head of population' basis. There was no exact parallel to the Central Allocation block in the previous system.

4. The **Floor Damping block** is self-funding (i.e. sums to zero nationally). It reallocates the amounts calculated in the previous three blocks to ensure that each authority receives a guaranteed minimum percentage increase in grant over the comparable figure for the previous year. Different minimum percentage increases are set for different groups of authorities. In practice, floor damping has a significant effect for many authorities, eclipsing large changes in grant that would otherwise result from applying the first three blocks.

Grants calculated under the four-block model depend upon a combination of analysis and the exercising of policy and political judgment. Judgment is applied in the following areas:

- in setting the national control totals for each category of services;
- in some of the relative needs formulae, such as those for Environmental, Protective and Cultural Services; and
- in setting the level of the damping floors.

Further details of the four-block model are given in Annex A.

Council tax incentives

9.22　The Inquiry team modelled three different methods for changing the way grant is equalised for council tax base, in order to provide an incentive to grow the numbers of properties in an authority's council tax base.

Partial equalisation

9.23　The first method is 'partial equalisation'. Effectively this means disregarding a proportion of an authority's tax bases when calculating their grant. In theory, this would provide stronger incentives for growth because a part of council tax revenues would be 'retained' and not offset by grant reductions.

9.24　However, my modelling showed that in practice this option would not produce any change in authorities' grant allocations. This is because the current way the grant system is administered does not treat each authority separately, but allocates a fixed pot of grant between them, based on the relative size of their council tax bases. Scaling back authorities' tax bases to make them appear smaller would have an equivalent impact on all authorities, so would not change their relative standings, it would therefore not affect the amount of grant received, and would have no effect on financial incentives.

Differential equalisation

9.25　The second option I have looked at is 'differential equalisation' – disregarding part of the tax base only for certain classes of authority. In theory this would mean that resource equalisation could be used to create stronger incentives to grow the tax base in designated housing growth areas, for example.

9.26　Ultimately however, such a mechanism would be relatively complex, and subjective judgements would need to be made on the degree to which different classes of authorities would have their tax base disregarded. I am cautious about such schemes since this could be open to regular amendment in light of changing policy priorities – in much the same way as a specific grant. Authorities could benefit or lose out according to the priority given by ministers to different types of council, rather than according to their own approach to growing the tax base. It would not therefore have the key benefit of promoting a different relationship between central and local government, and might become similar to 'just another needs formula' or another specific grant. In practice it might even be less transparent than most specific grants, further weakening any incentive effects.

Equalising for
'lagged' tax bases

9.27   Finally, I have considered equalising for 'lagged' tax bases, similar to the proposal by Kate Barker in her report on housing supply – that is, basing the 'relative resource allocation' on data from previous years.[2] This should mean that authorities whose tax base is growing still receive grant according to their older, smaller tax base, resulting in more generous funding for growing authorities than would otherwise have been the case. Authorities which have the fastest rate of growth would expect to have the greatest benefit from this scheme. Those with slower rates of growth and a shrinking tax base would lose out in relative terms.

9.28   Of the options modelled, this appears the most viable within the constraints of the four block grant system. The modelling suggests that if grant had been allocated in 2006-07 on the basis of tax base figures from three years ago, the distribution of funding would have been rather different overall. In particular, it suggests:

- a modest shift in grant away from metropolitan areas (-0.4 per cent overall) to shire areas (+0.2 per cent overall);

- a more significant shift in grant from Outer London (-1.1 per cent) to Inner London authorities (+1.1 per cent), whose tax bases have grown more quickly on average over the three years; and

- a modest benefit, overall, to the Government's designated Growth Areas (+0.2 per cent).

9.29   However, while the modelling shows that an incentive of this kind would be technically feasible, it would still require some significant changes in the way the government approaches grant settlements. Most significantly, it would require a different treatment of 'damping', as indeed would any incentive scheme, in order for the incentives to take effect. The current system of damping is designed so that grant changes are controlled by putting in 'floors' below grant decreases and scaling back increases in other authorities' grants by applying 'ceilings' to their grant increases to pay for it.[3] Such damping can override the effects of equalisation for both resources and needs, eliminating any incentive effect. Stronger incentives would require a political choice to reconnect authorities with their tax bases, even if this means moving away from the aim of stability that is currently prioritised through damping.

9.30   Providing some levels of protection for areas of declining population and high need is, rightly a concern of central government. As set out in Chapter 3, there are concerns that the current focus on stability is driven more by a concern to control council tax increases. I am concerned that the solution to pressure on council tax should – and can – be dealt with on its own terms rather than affecting other parts of the system and limiting positive reforms such as the introduction of financial incentives.

9.31   Once issues about the extent of damping are resolved, a practical solution for the current system may be to allow incentives to impact after damping had, taken place for all other factors; essentially to add a fifth block to the grant distribution system. This would, however, require the impact of damping to be more predictable then it currently is – perhaps moving to being announced along with the three year settlement – allowing local government to focus on gaining more of the benefit from the extra tax base they create rather than the degree of damping.

[2] Barker, K., *Review of Housing Supply: Delivering Stability: Securing our Future Housing Needs,* 2004

[3] An example of the impact of damping can be seen in 2006-07, when 71 out of the 150 local authorities with responsibility for personal social services were protected by the 'floor' which was set at guaranteeing all such authorities a minimum 2% increase for this aspect of their budget. Further detail about damping is set out in Annex A.

9.32   There is a question about how fire and police authorities should be treated under any incentive scheme. On the one hand, it could be argued that they are less connected to either residential or economic prosperity than councils. On the other hand growth – residential or commercial – would stretch police and fire services. In this regard these organisations might also be more supportive of development if the costs on their services were offset to some degree and I believe that they should be subject to any incentive as well.

Business rates incentives

Local Authority
Business Growth
Incentive Scheme

9.33   The Government has already introduced the LABGI scheme to provide better incentives for business rate growth through increases in the number of properties. Most stakeholders, including both local authorities and the business community, have welcomed the scheme in principle. More than 300 local authorities benefited in the second year of the scheme, receiving over £300 million between them. However, its complexity and short-term nature are felt to reduce the incentive effect of LABGI, though the scheme is only in its second year.

9.34   A significant part of the scheme's complexity can be ascribed to the objectives the Government set when designing it. The Government wished to develop a scheme which would:

- give all local authorities an incentive to maximise local economic growth;

- provide incentives that are consistent with its aims for growth in all regions of the country and reductions in the persistent gap in performance between regions; and

- distribute resources in a way which reflects relative performance not relative circumstances.

9.35   As a result of these objectives, LABGI attempts to redistribute resources for policy reasons at the same time as providing a growth incentive based on the size of the tax base, and in seeking to do so has become extremely complex. It does this through the use of historical growth rates to set each local authority a target growth rate that they have to meet before they receive incentive payments. Those target rates are calculated using the average historical growth rates for eight groups of authorities (with authorities with similar historical growth rates grouped together). This approach means that authorities with historically high growth need to continue to grow quickly if they are to receive incentive payments, and that those with historically low growth have a less difficult target to meet before they are rewarded.

9.36   It may be that now those targets are set and known, the system will become more effective, as it is clearer to authorities what level of performance they have to meet to gain revenues. However, it will still suffer from the fact that it is only a short-term scheme, constrained to the time horizon of government grants, and is still not closely linked to changes in the tax base so blunting its impact on local decision-making and producing a confused incentive.

Improving
incentives

9.37   I strongly support the Government's objective, to which the LABGI scheme is intended to contribute, to provide better incentives to local authorities to support economic prosperity, and the use of the business rates system as a way of doing so. However, reform to the current system is required to deliver a more transparent and long-term incentive scheme.

9.38   One issue that needs to be considered is whether the present attempt to use the LABGI scheme both to provide financial incentives that are applicable to all authorities, and to create a 'fair' distribution of resources, makes it too complex and unpredictable, and weakens the incentives it provides. It would be worth considering whether to separate the incentive element of the scheme from the desire to provide a reward for all areas. That would tend to give greater benefits to areas with high levels of growth and high value properties than the LABGI scheme does. In doing so it would help to develop much clearer and more transparent incentives.

Simplified LABGI

9.39 A number of the drawbacks of LABGI could thus be addressed through substantially simplifying the way in which local allocations are calculated, by removing the historical basis for calculations, and allowing local authorities to keep all, or a proportion of growth. This would address concerns about the arbitrary and unpredictable nature of rewards. It would still, as with the current system, ensure that no local authority actually lost resources as a result of the scheme, since it would still be paid out as a grant (though some authorities would get less than they might have done under the current LABGI system and others may gain more).

9.40 Such a system would help to provide clearer short-term incentives to authorities. It would not achieve the objective of creating a more permanent link between authorities' tax base and their income as the grant available would still be dependent on central government decisions as to the level of resource to be distributed through the scheme.

Property value-linked incentives

9.41 No simple reforms would enable LABGI to provide long-term incentives to enhance the value of properties in an area. At present the only additional revenue received (in real terms) from business rates comes from new properties being added to the rating list. There would be considerable merit in finding ways for local authorities to benefit from growth in the value of properties in their area as well as from the number of properties. That would give them an incentive to consider the wider business environment, and the needs of existing as well as potential new businesses. It might also provide the opportunity for authorities to invest in projects which enhance the value of properties in the area (for example new transport infrastructure in an already developed area) whereas the incentives under existing models are likely to be geared more towards unlocking new land and the construction of new properties.

9.42 Two further options I have considered could provide value-linked incentives and be made a more inherent part of the overall system.

Partial assignment of business rates

9.43 One option would be to explicitly share the business rates tax base or revenue between the local authority and national government – a partial assignment, or partial localisation, of the revenues (but without the power to change the tax rate). Rather than pay all of the business rates collected locally to central government, authorities would keep a proportion of the money and have their grant from central government reduced. From then on local authorities would be responsible for their share of the tax, and could benefit (or lose) from changes in revenues at the local level, including those created from the increased value of properties identified during revaluations.

9.44 My analysis shows that up to 16 per cent of business rates revenue (with the City of London excluded) could be retained at local level without leaving any authority 'over-funded' in the first year of such a scheme. For this proposal to provide clear incentives, it would then be necessary to maintain the local share at 16 per cent, and not to take changes in the local share of revenues into account when setting government grant.[4]

9.45 Under this system, authorities would gain increased resources over time if their tax revenues grew, and authorities with a falling tax base would lose in cash terms. If no additional resources were provided for the overall local government funding system, then there would also be some authorities that lost relative to the current system, depending on how the growth in revenues would otherwise have been allocated through the grant system.

---

[4] For such a system not to alter funding levels in its first year, the maximum amount of revenue that could be assigned to individual local authorities is determined by the point at which one authority becomes fully self-funding from council tax and its share of business rates. Up to that point Revenue Support Grant can be reduced to compensate for any increased business rates revenue, and thus ensure that – in the first year of the scheme – no authority is better or worse off.

9.46   This option has the advantage of being clear and transparent, and could in theory be separated out from the rest of the grant distribution system, providing a new, explicitly local tax base not subject to equalisation. It could also be maintained from year to year without the need for government decisions about how much money to allocate to providing incentives.

9.47   However, though there might be some transparency benefits, the total value of the incentives provided might well be lower than is currently being provided by the LABGI scheme. LABGI is intended to provide £1 billion over three years, whereas a 16 per cent share of growth in revenues over the period from 2004-05 to 2006-07 would have totalled under £450 million.

Lagged retention of business rates

9.48   Another option would be to adjust the operation of the business rates system so that local authorities keep the proceeds of growth in the business rate base for a fixed number of years, before eventually paying it into the national pot. A local authority's required contribution to the national pool would be based, not on the amount of revenue they had collected in that year (as now), but on the revenue they had collected a number of years before, as described in the lagged tax base model for council tax incentives. That would mean that if an authority had managed to grow the tax base in the intervening period, they could keep that additional resource for local spending and investment but that, if there was decline or low growth, they could lose resources either in absolute or relative terms as described, again, in the option of lagging council tax bases.

9.49   This approach would have some advantages in terms of transparency, as local authorities should be able to identify the amount of money that they would expect to pay in to the national pot in advance, and thus use any growth for their own purposes. It would present some challenges to local authorities, in that they would have to forecast their growth in revenues and compare that with the amount they needed to pay to the pool. This would produce a level of uncertainty, particularly in the early years, as they might not know until the end of the year whether their forecasts were right or not.

Constraints within the current system

9.50   These options could be pursued further as the Government develops proposals for the future of business rates incentives following the LABGI scheme. However, the current business rates system creates significant challenges for such schemes because of the national cap on revenues and the way that the national multiplier is calculated, as explained below. Consideration of the more radical forms of incentives described here would need to be considered alongside other changes to the business rates system.

9.51   As discussed in Chapter 8, at the national level increased property values do not lead to additional revenues being collected. This is because the multiplier is recalculated after each of the five-yearly revaluations (the next one is due in 2010) to maintain the overall yield in real terms. Increases in property values are used to reduce the overall tax rate for all businesses (and conversely, during downturns in the property market, the tax rate will rise). This feature of the system means that there is no additional business rates revenue at a national level arising from increased property values that could be used to give local authorities more of a benefit from any growth in the tax base that they may create.

9.52   The cap on yield also means that the revenues raised from business rates in a given local authority area are apt to change substantially at revaluation, so that the possible benefits from an incentive scheme would be much less easy for individual local authorities to predict. This would reduce the degree to which the scheme could provide effective incentives for long-term decision making. This is explained further in the following box.

The impact of the national cap on local revenues and incentives

The revenues collected in a local area from business rates are – simplifying the system substantially – the result of applying the national tax rate (the business rate multiplier) to the tax base (total rateable value).

In a simple system with a fixed tax rate, at a revaluation, if property values have increased then the total revenues raised in the area will also increase – the same tax rate is applied to a larger amount of total rateable value in the area. If the authority retained a proportion of revenues, this would provide an incentive for it to seek to bring about an increase in the value of properties in the area.

However, under the current business rates system, the tax rate falls if the national tax base rises, in order to raise the same overall revenue in real terms. The impact on revenues in any one area will therefore depend on the change in property values across the rest of the country, because it is changes elsewhere that will determine whether the multiplier falls, rises or stays the same.

In the example below there are only two areas in the country, both with the same initial tax base. By the time of revaluation both areas have seen increases in property values. Both might expect to gain some revenues as a result of this success. However, because the national multiplier is reduced to maintain the yield at a national level, from 45 pence in the pound to 40 pence, the revenues raised in area B fall. The revenues in area A rise, but not by as much as might otherwise have been expected. The fact that for each authority the impact is determined partly by what happens somewhere else, makes it harder to predict what will happen to their revenues.

	Local area A	Local area B	National
Rateable value	1000	1000	2000
Multiplier	0.45	0.45	0.45
Revenue raised	450	450	900
After revaluation			
New rateable value	1175	1075	2250
New multiplier	0.40	0.40	0.40
New revenue raised	470	430	900
Change on previous	20	–20	0

9.53   In the short term, reform of LABGI seems likely to be the most effective way to continue to provide incentives to local authorities, though even here decisions will need to be made about how the scheme should operate at the time of a revaluation. In the longer term, this analysis adds weight to the options for longer term reform of business rates set out in Chapter 8, including considering a future localisation of the tax or setting a fixed national tax rate.

> **Recommendation 9.1**
>
> In the short term, the Government should simplify Local Authority Business Growth Incentives scheme in order to provide sharper incentives. Reform should focus on providing transparency and predictability through reducing the emphasis on distributional objectives.
>
> **Recommendation 9.2**
>
> In the longer term, the Government should consider wider reforms to business rates, such as localisation, which would make it possible to design longer-term incentives for local authorities.

Conclusions

9.54   Table 9.2 summaries the options I have considered for introducing tax base incentives into the local government finance system.

Table 9.2 Summary of incentive schemes

Council tax base incentive schemes	Business tax base incentive schemes
Partial equalisation	Simplified LABGI
Differential equalisation	Partial assignment of business rates
Lagged retention of growth from council tax	Lagged retention of growth from business rates

9.55   Improving the incentives facing local authorities is a crucial aspect of changing behaviours and bringing about stronger local decision making. As the above analysis demonstrates there is potential to introduce incentives into the grant system to ensure better reward for growing both residential and business tax bases. However, the current design of the grant distribution system through the four-block model, based as it is on relative measures of tax raising capacity, means that it is difficult to implement such schemes for residential growth through council tax. Incentivising authorities through business rates, as well as dealing with the constraints placed on them by the interaction with the national cap on the multiplier, will mean changes to the way in which Formula Grant is calculated as allowing authorities to keep growth will either mean that further resources are needed from national taxation, or a more constrained level of grant in the overall pot. This means, therefore, that changes to the grant system would need to be considered to accommodate incentives on business rates.

9.56   A choice needs to be made about whether to continue to develop special schemes, or to consider wider changes to the grant system to enable incentives to be built in. I very much support the second of these. There needs to be a much stronger and longer-term link between local authorities' tax bases and the revenues they receive if they are to face strong incentives and rewards to grow the housing stock or the local economy. Both of these goals are key to enable local authorities to take on place-shaping roles on behalf of their local communities.

9.57   Reviewing grant distribution was not part of my remit and therefore I have not devoted time to reviewing in detail this aspect of the local government finance system. It was only through attempting to improve the incentives facing local authorities that I have concluded that the current design of the grant distribution mechanism is acting as a barrier to doing so.

9.58   During this consideration of incentives attention must be paid to making sure that local authorities – and their communities – would be able to understand the incentive being offered to them. Time must be taken to consider the clarity of messages on issues to do with:

- what actions will secure positive reward;

- the size of the reward and over what timescale; and

- the consequences of not acting.

Recommendation 9.3

The Government should consider ways in which the incentives in the grant system could be improved. In particular it should focus on:

- how far the grant system should be re-balanced to accommodate a greater focus on incentives;
- what changes will need to be made to the current grant system to support residential property tax base incentives;
- how to deliver business rate incentives, and whether these should be funded through additional resources or through redistribution within the current grant total; and
- clarity of messages to local authorities to ensure that they understand, and therefore can act on, any incentives.

SHARED REVENUES TO SUPPORT LOCAL SERVICES

How local services are funded   9.59   As set out in Chapter 3, local authorities derive part of their funding from council tax, but the majority from sources of revenue that are not in local control. Chart 9.2 shows what contribution different taxes make to the totality – local and national – of public finance. Council tax is used directly for local services. All business rate revenues plus funding derived from other general revenues such as income tax, VAT and corporation tax go towards Formula Grant which is the other major element of funding for local services. The total amount of grant to local government is decided by central government as part of its regular Spending Reviews. That total is then shared between authorities according to a set of formulae owned by the department for Communities and Local Government but contributed to by other policy departments. A sizeable proportion, 23 per cent of revenue is given to local government in the form of ring-fenced and other specific grants which may have conditions attached.[5]

---

[5] See Chapters 3 and 4 for a fuller discussion of this issue together with recommendations for lessening the impact of such grants so giving local authorities more flexibility to manage pressures and deliver services in line with local priorities and needs.

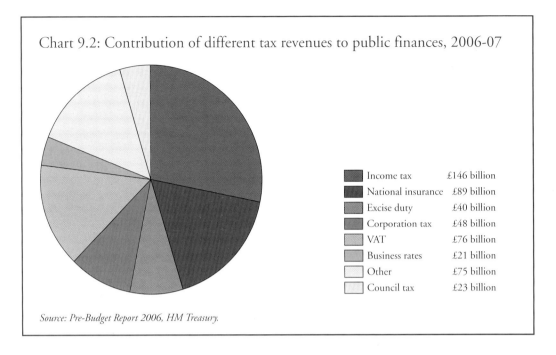

Chart 9.2: Contribution of different tax revenues to public finances, 2006-07

■	Income tax	£146 billion
■	National insurance	£89 billion
■	Excise duty	£40 billion
■	Corporation tax	£48 billion
■	VAT	£76 billion
■	Business rates	£21 billion
□	Other	£75 billion
□	Council tax	£23 billion

Source: Pre-Budget Report 2006, HM Treasury.

9.60   Formula Grant is commonly referred to as the 'central' part of local authorities, funding. However, in reality, this funding is not central government money but citizens' and businesses' money, collected by central government and distributed by them to local government, who are then responsible for spending it alongside council tax. This is an important distinction, and often missed by both local government, who may lobby ministers for more grant without adequate reference to the impact on taxpayers, and by ministers and their departments who, at the extreme, may view grant as a gift to local authorities which entitles them to a high degree of control. As set out in Chapter 3, these perceptions of funding can result in an adversarial relationship between central and local government, where different layers of government often complain about and blame each other for actual or perceived injustices and failings in the funding system. In that context, it is difficult for the public to understand how local government is funded or, to see who is responsible for decisions about tax and spending.

Shared revenues to support local services   9.61   Chapter 3 argued that there is a need for greater clarity about local and central responsibilities so that local communities can better understand who to hold to account for tax and spending decisions. Greater clarity is also needed about who is paying for public services. There are some services which are clearly driven by a national promise and there is a case, in principle at least, for arguing that these should be funded from national taxation to make clear that central government is, in some sense, responsible for these services. In some instances, these are appropriately supported through specific grant, though these are too great a feature of the current financing of local authorities. Conversely there are issues that are rightly local, in principle, and so in theory would best be delivered from local resources. In practice, the effect of such a simple split between responsibilities would be very difficult to achieve and could lead to greater inflexibility in local government finance.

9.62   As recognised in Chapter 4, there are also many service areas where it is not possible to distinguish clearly between national and local responsibilities. Such services can be considered a shared responsibility and, given this, there is benefit, in terms of accountability, in such services being funded more explicitly from a shared source of revenue.

9.63   I am particularly interested in such an option if it improves the poor public understanding of the costs of services (which as Chapter 3 sets out is low at the current time), of how they are funded and of the degree to which national taxation supports local services. A system which was more transparent, and enabled citizens and local businesses to better understand how their taxes pay for services, should make it easier to manage expectations and pressures and to have a more honest discussion about them, both locally and nationally.

9.64   Such clarity would illuminate some potentially difficult issues. For instance, as set out in Chapter 3, many people believe that council tax pays for the majority of local services but also feel that it does not represent value for money. There is, therefore, a risk that greater clarity about the actual cost of services will come as a shock to some, unless balanced by an equal understanding of the full range and value of public services delivered through local government. However, without this knowledge, local government's ability to engage with their communities to discuss priorities and trade-offs is limited as there will be unrealistic expectations about what can be afforded.

Assigning taxes

9.65   These concerns, about accountability, clarity, and central-local relations, have led me to consider an assigned form of taxation which would set out more explicitly the current reality that many local services are paid for by a shared source of revenue. If designed correctly this could clarify how local services are funded.[6] This is an issue that I have been considering for some time, and on which the New Local Government Network has done some interesting and useful work.[7] It was not an option that was considered in depth by the Balance of Funding Review and therefore may appear to some readers as a new option. However, as set out in Chapter 1, assigned revenues were an important part of local government funding at the end of the nineteenth and beginning of the twentieth centuries. It is also a form of local government funding that is used elsewehere in the world. For example: in Germany, income, corporation and sales taxes are used jointly by federal, state and municipal governments; and in Austria, a number of federal taxes are allocated for use by local government according to population.[8]

Types of assignment   9.66   Taxes can be assigned either at the national level, so that a proportion of an overall national tax is allocated to support local services, or at the local authority level, where a proportion of a national tax collected in each local authority area is assigned to the relevant local authority. For either of these options decisions will need to be made as to whether the proportion of the tax that is assigned is fixed over time or variable over time. The next sections of this chapter discuss national assignment and local assignment in more detail.

Stewardship of the tax system   9.67   Before starting on the detail of assignment, I consider it important to stress that central government would remain responsible for the overall stewardship of the taxation system. Assignment would not change this, but would impact on the relationship between local and central government.

---

[6] International evidence suggests that if designed incorrectly assignment with complex tax systems and various levels sharing tax bases could confuse accountability. Loughlin, J., and Martin S., *Options for Reforming Local Government Funding to Increase Local Streams of Funding: International Comparisons,* Lyons Inquiry, 2005.
[7] New Local Government Network, *Pacing Lyons: a route map to localism,* 2006.
[8] King, D., *Report on Statistical Work for the OECD Network on Fiscal Relations Across Levels of Government,* OECD, 2005.

What is assignment?

An assigned revenue is a national tax stream which is dedicated, in its entirety or in part, to a particular purpose – in essence a form of tax hypothecation. Business rates are an example of an assigned national tax, in that the rates and bases are set nationally, but are used in their entirety to support local spending through Formula Grant.[9]

Assignment does not change the amount of tax that anyone pays. At its simplest, it is more about how nationally controlled taxation is used. At the current time most national taxation – income tax, VAT, excise duties, stamp duty, corporation tax and many other major tax revenues – is paid to central government and is treated as a single pot of money, which is then used to pay for public services. This approach maximises national government's ability to direct taxation to its current priorities and respond to pressures in how it manages and allocates public expenditure. In doing so it retains more flexibility to prioritise spend rather than simply raise taxes or borrowing.

With an assigned tax there is greater clarity about the use of particular revenues, including which taxes are assigned to support particular activities. In some ways this is similar to National Insurance Contributions which support the National Health Service and other forms of social insurance.

The analysis of assignment

9.68   The following sections examine a range of options for assignment of taxes to local government. Given that assignment would represent a radical departure from the current system of local government finance, the analysis I present is in the main illustrative. It includes some interesting findings which will be of use to any future work on assignment. However, the main aim of this discussion is to stimulate thinking and debate about whether assignment could be a viable and positive part of the funding system for local government in the future, as a supplement or partial replacement for council tax.

9.69   All the analysis that follows is based on assigning two amounts of revenue: £3.4 billion and £13.1 billion. In the analysis of a national fixed assignment these are equivalent to assigning 3 per cent and 12 per cent of 1996 income tax respectively.[10] In the analysis of a local fixed assignment this equates to some 7 per cent and 28 per cent of starting rate income tax.[11]

9.70   I will discuss the reasons for basing my analysis of national assignment on income tax revenue and local assignment on starting rate tax later in this chapter. However, to aid understanding it is important at this juncture to explain the rationale for choosing £3.4 billion and £13.1 billion. The first represents the 2006-07 amount of Revenue Support Grant, that is the element of Formula Grant that is paid from general national taxation rather than business rates. The second is what Revenue Support Grant might have been if schools' funding had not been ring-fenced only in Revenue Support Grant, but had instead also taken part of business rates. This has an in-principle appeal to me, as I consider it a better reflection of what businesses would expect their rates to be used for, rather than being used as the major source of revenue for equalisation.

Buoyancy

9.71   In addition to the potential transparency benefits of assignment, I have become interested in it because, depending on how it is designed, it could enable local government to access a

---

[9] In recent years business rates have been increasingly used to equalise resources for high need and low tax base authorities, which has produced concerns – as outlined in Chapter 3 – about the relationship between businesses and local authorities.

[10] The way the model works is to assign £3.4 billion and £13.1 billion as their equivalent proportions of income tax in 1996-97 and then apply the real changes in income tax yield in the 10 subsequent years to illustrate the impact of assignment.

[11] The local fixed assignment modelling is based on forecasts rather than historic time series. The reasons for this are explained in Annex E.

buoyant source of revenue. In tax terms, buoyancy refers to increases and decreases in yield from a tax caused by 'automatic' changes in the tax base, either in terms of the numbers of tax units, or in the value of the tax base. Many national taxes are designed to have buoyant revenues, and some tend to grow every year – for instance income tax and VAT – because incomes and consumer sales tend to grow each year and tax is paid as a proportion of these figures. Conversely, there are downside risks associated with buoyant taxes, as there can be slower or negative growth in specific tax revenues either through specific shocks to tax bases (for example, from fraud) or through broader impacts on the economy (for example in the event of a downturn). Buoyancy also comes from the design of national taxes as central government reforms them to keep pace with economic and political developments, including making changes to limits and rates, and wider policy changes to move the overall burden of taxation to change behaviours rather than raise revenue. These could have year to year implications for the value of any assigned revenues and could result in decreases in the value of income taxes. This presents a further risk for local government of having grant linked to specific tax receipts.

9.72   Council tax is not a naturally buoyant tax and, apart from when there is major residential development, council tax rates must be put up every year if revenues are to grow even in line with inflation. If local government 'owned' a buoyant source of revenue, then in years when its revenue from that source was increasing at a faster rate than the pressure on local tax, it could be used to offset pressure on council tax or relieve funding pressures on services.

Comparing increases in buoyant taxes to local taxation

9.73   There have been increases in yield from local tax almost every year since 1981. As discussed above this has been achieved through annual increases in the rate of local tax. Such increases are very apparent to tax payers. Income tax and VAT have risen at least in line with, and at times faster than, local tax. By contrast, however, these increases have been, for the most part, achieved through buoyancy, so that in general tax payers do not feel that they are paying more.

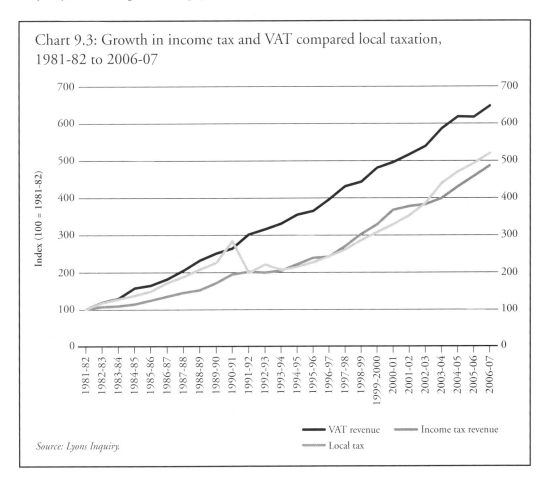

Chart 9.3: Growth in income tax and VAT compared local taxation, 1981-82 to 2006-07

Source: Lyons Inquiry.

National assignment

National assignment

Under national assignment a proportion of a national tax - such as income tax or VAT - would be allocated to replace some or all of the grant allocated to local government.

This assigned proportion of tax could be fixed over time, for example, each year three per cent of the yield from income tax could be assigned to local services. As the yield from income tax varies over time, this would mean that a different amount of money would be available to local services each year.

In tax jargon this variation is called the 'buoyancy' of the tax as on average it rises each year. So, for instance a fixed national assignment of income tax would allow any benefits from the buoyancy of the tax to support local services.

The level of the assigned proportion of a tax could also vary year on year, to reflect choices about the amount of national taxation that should be used to support local services. For example, in one year it might equate to three per cent of income tax revenues, but in the next year, if there was an increase in the amount of national taxation that central government decided should be used to support local services, it might equate to 3.5 per cent of income tax.

Potential effects of a national assignment

9.74   Table 9.3, sets out the main effects of national assignment, depending on whether the assigned proportion of the tax is fixed or variable over time. This would be one of the key decisions in moving to an assigned form of taxation. It determines whether the changes are aimed at being clear about the actual contribution of national taxation to support local services (which would be the focus of an assignment that is variable over time) or whether they have the additional aim of capturing the buoyancy of a tax stream for local government.

Table 9.3: Potential effects of national assignment depending on whether proportion of assigned tax is fixed or variable over time

	Fixed over time	Variable over time
National assignment	Greater transparency	Greater transparency
	Local government access to a buoyant tax stream	
	Constraints on central government's control over, and use of, national taxation	
	Local government revenues partially reliant on fluctuating tax base	

9.75   A fixed assignment that is designed to allow local government to retain automatic increases in revenue from any positive buoyancy of the tax, would potentially enable authorities to use this to offset pressure on council tax or relieve funding pressures on services. There may be benefits to central government in such an approach. For instance, it could reduce the need for central government to deal with the impact of council tax, either through one-off support to specific groups such as pensioners, or through annual, painful exercises to find money from existing central government budgets to try to keep council tax down through extra grant to local government.

9.76   All forms of assignment would have transparency benefits, because they provide greater clarity over how services are paid for. This would be of benefit to both central and local government, as well as enabling communities and citizens to better understand how their local services are financed.

9.77   Fixed assignment would have disadvantages for central government in that it allocates any gains from growth (or losses from reduction) in the assigned tax base to local government, so constraining central government's room for manoeuvre. Any additional revenue through buoyancy provided to local government from assigning a fixed amount over time would be 'lost' to central government and could not be spent on other national services. This would need to be balanced against how far central government chose to devolve additional functions to local government.

9.78   Access to buoyant taxes would expose local government revenues to fluctuations both in terms of predictability and in actual tax yield, which would be a particular concern at times of economic downturn, both for local and central government. Essentially a small element of the risk which is currently being borne by central government over the economic cycle could, in the case of fixed assignment, be transferred partly to local government. This is an issue that is returned to in considering implementation issues below.

An assigned tax that is variable over time

9.79   Introducing a form of assignment that is variable over time may be considered a limited option, as it does not improve the buoyancy or incentives in the local government finance system; it would still be for central government to determine the level of resources allocated to local government. However, it would provide a greater degree of transparency over how local services are actually funded – with a more direct recognition that it is tax payers' money that is being used rather than an abstract notion of central resources – and it better clarifies the actual costs of services which, as set out above, could help to enable a more realistic and effective level of engagement with local communities.

9.80   In essence, a variable assignment option could be introduced through an annual statement that set out the amount of national taxation that supported local services. This could be done at either a national aggregate level or at a local authority level. There would obviously need to be consideration as to how this was best communicated, with an option being to ensure that council tax bills make clear the extent to which national, as well as local taxes, are used to support local services. This could be presented as the proportion of the relevant national tax that is raised in each local authority, which has benefits in that it reinforces the link to the local area. An alternative would be to present the amount as a proportion of overall national taxation, which is a simpler calculation but omits any reference to the local tax base.

Designing a fixed national assignment

9.81 Key questions in considering a national assignment option that is fixed over time are how many taxes to assign, and which are the most appropriate for assignment.[12] Assigned taxes, ideally, need to be buoyant, large and have a broad tax base. This last criterion is important as to ensure that the tax is paid by a sizeable proportion of the population so that there is a good understanding of the tax and a strong sense that most people are contributing.

9.82 I commissioned analysis based on assigning revenue from income tax. I decided to concentrate on a single tax for the sake of clarity and simplicity. Both income tax and VAT fit the criteria for assignment as they are generally buoyant, widely paid and sizeable forms of taxation. However, there are currently some practical concerns about VAT being more unpredictable than income tax due to recent evasion and non-compliance. More importantly, research and representations to the Inquiry gave a strong sense that people consider income tax to be a fair tax from which to pay for local services. Assigning income tax could be expected to have a greater resonance with the public than VAT.

Potential impact on local revenues

9.83 If there had been a direct assignment of income tax to local services in 1996-97 the buoyancy in income tax over the ten years since then would have provided benefits to local government in the form of additional revenue compared with Formula Grant in that period. This is shown in Chart 9.4 which shows the additional revenue from assigning different proportions of income tax. This further shows that the greater the proportion of revenue assigned, the greater the 'return' for local government in terms of buoyancy supplying additional revenue.

9.84 It is important to stress that this is not 'free money' but would represent a transfer of control over the buoyancy from the assigned tax from central government to local government. If central government wanted to recoup the buoyancy to maintain the same overall level of revenue and funding to all other it would need to increase the national rates of income tax or other national taxes.

---

[12] The technical issues associated with designing and modelling a fixed national assignment are covered in depth in Annex E.

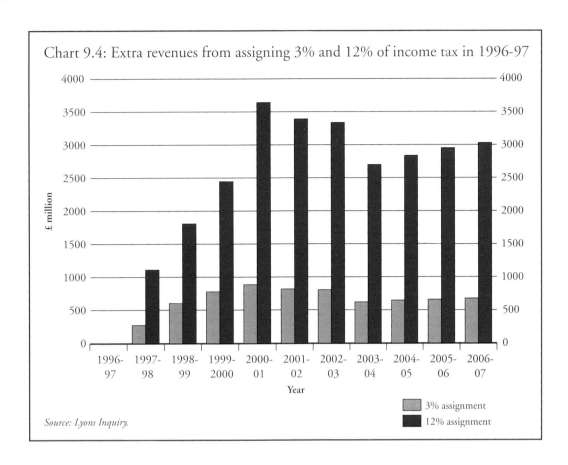

Chart 9.4: Extra revenues from assigning 3% and 12% of income tax in 1996-97

Source: Lyons Inquiry.

- 3% assignment
- 12% assignment

Implementation of a national fixed assignment

9.85   A national fixed assignment would be a major departure from the current system by which local authorities receive funds from national taxation. It would require some major practical and behavioural changes on the part of both local authorities and central government, and could also have implications for local taxpayers. These are discussed below.

Use of additional revenue

9.86   Local authorities would need to consider how to use any additional resources from buoyancy to best meet the needs and aspirations of their local communities. The different purposes to which these resources could be put will be extremely varied. However, as an illustration I have commissioned analysis to understand what the impact of an assignment could be if local authorities chose to use any additional resource, in full, to offset pressure on council tax.

9.87   If there had been a fixed assignment of income tax in 1996-97 there could have been lower council tax bills in each of the ten years since then. As Chart 9.5 shows, the larger the assigned proportion of income tax the greater the effect. For example, in 2001-02 actual average band D council tax bills were £989 per year. Assigning three per cent of income tax could have lowered this by £53 per year while and assigning 12 per cent of income tax could have lowered bills by £218. As set out previously this is not 'free' money; any lower rises in council tax result from the transfer of resources – in the form of buoyancy – from central to local government. This would mean lower central government investment in other services.

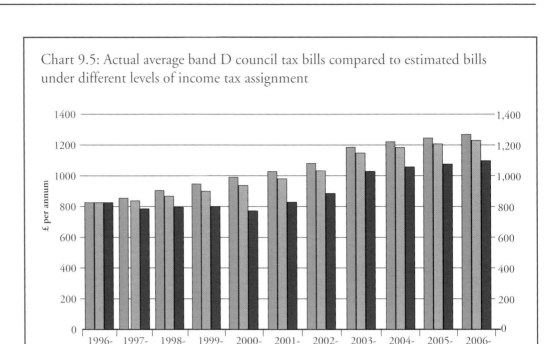

Chart 9.5: Actual average band D council tax bills compared to estimated bills under different levels of income tax assignment

Source: Lyons Inquiry.

Accessing a fluctuating source of taxation

9.88   If it was decided to implement a national assignment based on income tax, consideration would need to be given to how local authorities could best manage the fluctuations that are inherent in such a tax base.

9.89   One option would be for local authorities to vary the rates of council tax to offset the fluctuation in the assigned income tax. However, the analysis I commissioned showed that this could result in major fluctuations in council tax.[13]

9.90   I am clear that such fluctuations would need to be managed given people's existing concerns about council tax increases. Whatever method was eventually chosen its aim would be to 'smooth' large changes between years. In the short term this may be a task for national government, but this task could be transferred to local authorities in the medium term as their experience of working with an assigned tax develops.

Changes in central-local relations

9.91   A national fixed assignment would mean central government losing some control over the buoyancy from a source of national taxation. This is only likely to be achieved as part of an ambitious 'new deal' which sought to change the relationship between central and local government. If central government was willing to pursue a national fixed assignment, it might argue with some force that local government should, for its part, be more self reliant and less concerned about the

---

[13] The modelling work conducted for the Inquiry shows that if council tax was used to offset the variability in the revenue from an assigned income tax there would be a lot of variation in yield from one year to the next reflecting the pattern of growth in income tax. In years of good growth in income tax yields, the model shows small percentage increases in council tax: for example, in 1999-2000 and 2000-01. In years of more limited growth in income tax yield, the model shows very sharp increases in council tax – higher than any actual increase: for example in 2002-03 to 2003-04. This is caused by council tax compensating for the low income tax revenue increases, but is also partly driven by previous small and negative percentage increases in council tax, meaning that the level of revenue available to local authorities is lower than would have been the case if council tax had been rising more quickly. It is also the case that the larger the proportion of funding assigned, the more significant the volatility and fluctuation in terms of its overall impact on local authority finances. Further details are given in Annex E.

detail of the grant settlement. A more constructive relationship between local and central government would also be required to reflect the shared interest they would have in a common tax.

Funding new mandates
9.92   There is a further question of whether the percentage of assigned tax should alter if the functions that local government are responsible for change, to reflect the fact that the shared revenue is supporting more or fewer services. I believe there would still need to be consideration of the need for central funding of new mandates, and whether and to what extent central government could expect any of the buoyancy from assignment to contribute to them. It would be important that this was the subject of agreement between central and local government.

9.93   Questions such as how best to get the balance right over these issues could be decided as an aspect of the new constitutional settlement between local and central government, discussed further in Chapter 10.

Distribution of additional revenue
9.94   There are also questions about how any additional revenue from buoyant taxes should be distributed to local government. I can see that there are strong in-principle arguments for this revenue continuing to be allocated according to a nationally determined process of grant distribution. I would strongly contend, however, that wherever possible this should be in the form of unhypothecated grant that is, therefore, under local rather than national control.

Local assignment

Local assignment

Under local assignment a proportion of a national tax – such as income tax or VAT – collected in each local authority area is assigned to each local authority, replacing some or all of the differing levels of grant they receive from central government. These differing levels of grant reflect the fact that each local authority receives different amounts of revenue from national taxation depending on the needs of their communities and how far they can raise their own resources from council tax.

Again there would be a choice over whether this assignment should be a proportion that is fixed over time, that is the same proportion of the tax is available to the local authority year-on-year ,so enabling any buoyancy in the tax to be captured locally.

Fixing the proportion of tax that is assigned at the local level could also produce incentive effects for local authorities to grow their local tax base, since they would keep a proportion of any growth in yield, and would also face the consequences of a shrinking tax base. For instance, if a fixed amount of income tax was assigned to each local authority, then the local authority could also keep this proportion of any increase in the tax base collected in its area. For example, if an authority had been assigned five per cent of the income tax collected in its area, it could keep five per cent of any growth caused by new jobs or increased incomes.

Alternatively, the amount that each local authority received in assigned tax could be varied year-on-year. This would, as is set out in the box above on national assignment, express the actual

Potential effects of a local assignment
9.95   As shown in Table 9.4, fixed and variable local assignments have much the same effects as national assignment. The important difference is that a local assignment that is fixed over time also offers an incentive effect, as local authorities would be able to keep part or all of any revenue that is produced from growing or protecting the relevant tax base. The nature of this incentive effect would depend on which tax base was assigned. For example: assigning income tax would give an incentive around job creation or protection whereas if it was possible to locally assign VAT based on the site of sales it would give local authorities an incentive to increase sales of goods or services.

Table 9.4: Potential effects of local assignment depending on whether proportion of assigned tax fixed or variable over time

	Fixed over time	Variable over time
Local assignment	Greater transparency	Greater transparency
	Local government access to a buoyant tax stream	
	Incentives on local communities and local government to grow local tax bases	
	Constraints on central government's control over, and use of, national taxation	
	Local government revenues, partially reliant on fluctuating tax base	

Designing a local fixed assignment

The best tax for local assignment

9.96   As with national assignment, I believe a local assignment should ideally be based on a single tax. It would produce the greatest clarity for local communities, and also would help to give clear messages to local communities about what the incentive effects of assignment would be. This differs somewhat from NLGN's work, which has as its starting point the local assignment of a wide range of taxes. Such an approach is attractive from the perspective of the local community having the first 'slice' from a wide range of nationally controlled taxes, but was outweighed by my concerns about the need for clarity to the tax payer.

9.97   In determining the best tax for local assignment all the national assignment criteria apply: the tax must be sizeable, buoyant and paid by a large proportion of the population. In addition, consideration needs to be given to how evenly yield is spread across different areas of the country, to prevent major differences in the impact of assignment on local finance. Finally, the tax base needs to be one that is based on something which enhances well-being if local authority attempts to increase it are successful so it creates the right incentive effects. This also assumes the tax base is something upon which local authorities can have a positive effect.

9.98   I have again chosen income tax as the best tax base on which to examine local fixed assignment in more detail. This is because it has clear and more positive incentive effects, in that and assigning part of this tax base could encourage local authorities to create or protect local jobs and incomes. VAT was the only other form of taxation that was seriously considered, but this raised a number of concerns in relation to the rate of VAT not being uniform across all goods and services, which could lead to local authorities competing to attract businesses from sectors with high VAT revenues to the detriment of businesses from other sectors. There were also challenges with local assignment of VAT regarding whether it would be conducted on an area of residence or an area of purchase basis.

Assigning the starting rate of income tax

9.99   The starting rate band of income tax best meets the criteria for an evenly spread tax base on which local assignment could operate, as all people that have taxable incomes above the personal allowance will pay this rate.[14] Analysis for the Inquiry also suggests that starting rate tax has been quite buoyant.[15]

---

[14] New Local Government Network, *Pacing Lyons: a note map to localism,* 2006
[15] This compares to the concerns about the buoyancy of the more modest basic rate tax raised in the discussion of local income tax in Chapter 7.

Assigning to
area of residence
or area of
employment
9.100   In locally assigning a local income tax, there is an important question as to whether it is done on the basis of the taxpayers' area of residence, or their place of employment. Some taxpayers will live in one local area and work in another. I recognise that such a decision is open to debate and that assigning income tax based on the area of residence could have the effect of encouraging some authorities, particularly those that are close to major conurbations, to attract tax payers to live in their areas rather than create or protect jobs.

9.101   However, as set out in the discussion of local income tax in Chapter 7, I consider that basing a tax on the area of residence helps to retain local accountability to residents and link tax to the interests of residents in local services. The decision to assign starting rate of income tax, rather than basic or higher rate tax, would limit any incentive for local authorities to attract taxpayers but not jobs. This is because an incentive based on starting rate tax will apply equally to both low and high earning taxpayers, and low income groups are less likely to commute long distances for work, and so are more likely to work in their area of residence.[16]

Type of
authority
9.102   Following the same logic as in my consideration of a local income tax, I have limited local assignment to upper tier and unitary authorities, as these are responsible for the majority of spending on local services.

Dealing with
divergence
between areas
over time
9.103   A key decision in implementing local assignment which is fixed over time is how to deal with the divergence in local authorities' tax bases which may occur over time. In principle there should be no equalisation for assigned revenues to allow the incentive effect of a local fixed assignment to act on the behaviours of local authorities. For this reason the analysis presented here has not included any equalisation.[17] I believe, however, that in practice government will need to strike a balance between the equalisation that is needed to support areas with high socio-economic needs and low tax bases against its negative impact on the incentive effects.

Outcome of a local fixed assignment

9.104   In summary, my analysis of the impact of a locally-assigned income tax shows that even assigning a relatively high proportion of starting rate income tax, and applying an optimistic forecast of growth at the local level, only has a small impact. Not all local authorities gain and all changes, both positive and negative, are very small.

9.105   Assigning 28 per cent of starting rate income tax as discussed above, using an optimistic forecast model, alleviates pressure by 2007-08 on council tax for 38 per cent of authorities by an average of 0.5 per cent. The impact on bills of such an assignment would be minimal, equating to a saving of some £5.00 on an average band D bill. Assigning the more modest amount of seven per cent of starting rate income tax produced, on the optimistic forecast model again, additional revenue also for 38 per cent of local authorities. If this was all used to offset pressure on council tax it would provide an average saving of 0.13 per cent per year.

---

[16] Harding, M., and Robson, B., *A Framework for City-Regions*, ODPM, 2006.

[17] The model does attempt to limit divergence by, at the time of inception, preventing any local authority from receiving more money through assignment of starting rate income tax than it would receive from the current levels of grant. The Inquiry's analysis is based on applying the same proportion of starting rate income tax across all local authorities, and this is determined by fixing the proportion assigned at the highest percentage which could be assigned before any authority received more than they would have otherwise received in grant. This requirement does place major constraints on the design of a local assignment.

Implementation issues

9.106   Implementing a fixed local assignment could present challenges to our current system of income tax. Some of these are similar to those for local income tax, such as the requirement for HM Revenue and Customs (HMRC) to be able to assign the tax revenue to the appropriate authority (and how to deal with in-year changes in tax band or people moving areas). This and other implementation issues are similar to those involved in a full local income tax and are discussed in detail in Chapter 7. The overall conclusion is that changes to support a local income tax, and therefore a local assignment, would be feasible but with significant costs and would require careful and lengthy preparation.

Conclusions

9.107   My analysis of local assignment, based on the relatively restrictive parameters that I have set, shows that it has a limited buoyancy effect.

9.108   However, this does not mean I consider that a locally fixed assignment based on starting rate income tax is an unattractive option. Even with the restrictive parameters that I have set, the incentive effects still remain. While these are not exceptionally large each job a local authority created would produce a receipt of a percentage of the starting rate which in 2006-07 was £2,150 per year. Therefore, a seven per cent starting rate assignment would equate to approximately £150 per job, and a 28 per cent assignment would mean about £600 per job accruing to the local authority. There is a question about whether this would be large enough to change a local community's attitudes to growth and local government behaviour, though it is equally worth noting that if incentives are too large that can raise problems as well, as they can distort decisions excessively. It may be that these incentives are unlikely to change behaviour in relation to individual jobs, but they could influence decisions that relate to large employers and could go some way to compensating the community for economic expansion.

9.109   In addition, a move to funding local services, even to a limited degree, through an alternative form of fluctuating taxation could be a first step to helping local authorities to become accustomed to having more than one tax base at their disposal and developing their skills in managing a fluctuating form of tax. Both of these could provide useful experience relevant to the consideration of possible local income tax options if considered at a later date.

Assignment recommendations

Variable assignment

9.110   As an immediate step, a form of variable assignment could be introduced to improve understanding of how local public services are financed. As set out above, this should be in the form of an annual statement to local residents setting out the amount of national taxation that is used to support local services, in addition to what they pay in local taxation. This could be done at the national aggregate level or at a local authority level. The former would be the easier option but not would not have the benefit of a specific relevance to each local authority. Such a statement could also include information on what is spent in total on different services in the area so that citizens can gain a better sense of the cost of services.

9.111   There are many ways in which this could be communicated and I look to local and central government to come up with creative ways of achieving this aim. The obvious route is to use the council tax bill or the accompanying leaflet to convey this information. However, the information that can go on these documents is currently prescribed by regulations which would need to be relaxed so that local authorities could use council tax bills and accompanying leaflets to convey this information if they chose.

Recommendation 9.4

The Government should relax the regulations that govern the information that can be included on council tax bills and the accompanying leaflet. This is to enable local authorities to use this communication route, if they chose, to make clear:

- the level of national taxation that they each receive to support local services set out in absolute amounts; and

- how that is used to support the overall expenditure on services in that area.

A fixed national assignment

9.112   A fixed national assignment is an attractive option to me as it better reflects the current processes by which local services are resourced, through both national taxation and council tax. As set out in the discussion of the implementation of a national assignment, it could also precipitate a new relationship between central and local government, based on a change in mind-set in both. It would mean ensuring that local government was equipped to cope without significant central support in managing a buoyant, but fluctuating tax base, in return for the sector becoming more self-reliant. It would also require central government to give up some control over elements of national taxation in return for a more mature local government sector that looked less to central government to resolve local funding issues.

9.113   Recognising that such changes will take some time to be implemented my recommendations on a fixed national assignment are more for the medium term. Realistically they could not be implemented until after the current Comprehensive Spending Review period, at the earliest.

Recommendation 9.5

The Government should consider, in the medium term, assigning a fixed proportion of income tax to support local government services. This would need to be done in the context of a new constitutional settlement between central and local government providing for greater self-reliance on the part of local government.

Central and local government should agree as to how far buoyancy from assignment should be used to support new mandates and how much central support should be given to local government in times of downturn.

CONCLUSION

9.114   This chapter argues that the way central government supports local services should be re-oriented. Incentives to support growth should be an important element of the grant system, allowing communities to take balanced judgments and receive some financial compensation for growth in their areas.

9.115   Greater transparency over the use of national taxation in delivering local services can also be advanced: in the short term by greater clarity over how far national taxes pay for local services at the current time. Over time this could be developed with the possibility of an element of income tax being directly assigned to local government, which would help to provide greater flexibility to manage pressures (including potentially offsetting pressure on council tax) or to improve local services.

9.116   I recognise that some of these changes will present real challenges to local and central government. It is for these reasons that I have set out these, and my other recommendations, in a developmental framework in Chapter 10, the conclusion to this report.

Part IV

Conclusions

Chapter 10   **A developmental approach**

Overall conclusions and proposals for a developmental approach in implementing the report's recommendations.

A developmental approach

Summary

This chapter argues that a developmental approach to reform is required, in order to build relationships and trust, and increase public confidence in local government over time.

Changes in behaviours will be important for both central and local government, including:

- for local government, the recognition of the place-shaping role and a greater focus on engagement with citizens and being recognised as a champion of efficiency; and

- for central government, providing greater flexibility for local authorities and the space for local decisions on priorities, with a reduction in centrally determined and monitored targets.

The Government needs to take action in the short-term to ensure a more sustainable finance system, including:

- making council tax fairer through changes to council tax benefit, including increased take-up, and increasing local flexibility to manage pressures on council tax;

- a package of measures on business rates to promote economic prosperity, provide local flexibility and support improved relationships between local authorities and businesses;

- enabling local authorities to show clearly on council tax bills what proportion of national taxation is being used to support local services;

- other measures to support the place-shaping role.

Council tax should be retained as a local tax. In order to underpin its sustainability, the Government should conduct a revaluation of properties in the near future – with appropriate transitional protection – and introduce a process of regular revaluation for the future.

However, even a reformed council tax would still have some problems, such as lack of buoyancy. Over time, more radical reforms could be considered to take further pressure off council tax, to improve the fairness of the local taxation system and to further increase local flexibility and choice.

A proportion of income tax could be assigned to give local government access to a buoyant form of taxation, and in the longer term a local income tax would be a feasible option. Further reforms to business rates could also be considered, such as the full relocalisation of the business rate.

In order to reinforce and support this process of change central and local government should negotiate a contractual agreement which sets out what central government requires of local government, how it should be funded, and the ways in which central government should appropriately influence and control other aspects of local government activity. That agreement should be open to external and parliamentary scrutiny.

INTRODUCTION

10.1 Throughout this report I have sought to describe a vision of local government as part of a single system of government, playing a place-shaping role, engaging with citizens to build an understanding of their needs and preferences, and contributing to satisfaction and the efficient use of resources, by enabling collective choices to be made at the local level. To go back to the question that the Layfield Committee posed, I do believe that many of the decisions of government can and should be taken in different places, by people of diverse experience, associations, background and political persuasion. Enabling different communities to take governmental decisions and set priorities for themselves can contribute to a more effective overall system of government which is better able to tackle the difficult issues we face as a society.

10.2 Achieving this vision will take time. It requires not just the development of new relationships between local and central government, but a strengthening of public understanding of, trust in and support for local government (and indeed, to a significant extent, government in general). For some of the more radical possibilities discussed during the report to be feasible, a much greater level of public confidence in local government will be needed.

10.3 Reflecting this, I therefore want to set out an approach that is explicitly developmental – that acknowledges that trust and relationships need to be built, and seeks to use a wide-ranging but reasonably modest set of short term changes to create the space and the mutual understanding needed for wider reforms in the future. If the opportunity is seized by local and central government, I believe that there is the potential to create a virtuous circle, where increased local choice and accountability reinforce one another and create greater public trust and understanding. The unattractive alternative is further central prescription and a reduction in the scope for local accountability. Chart 10.1 shows a stylised version of these alternatives.

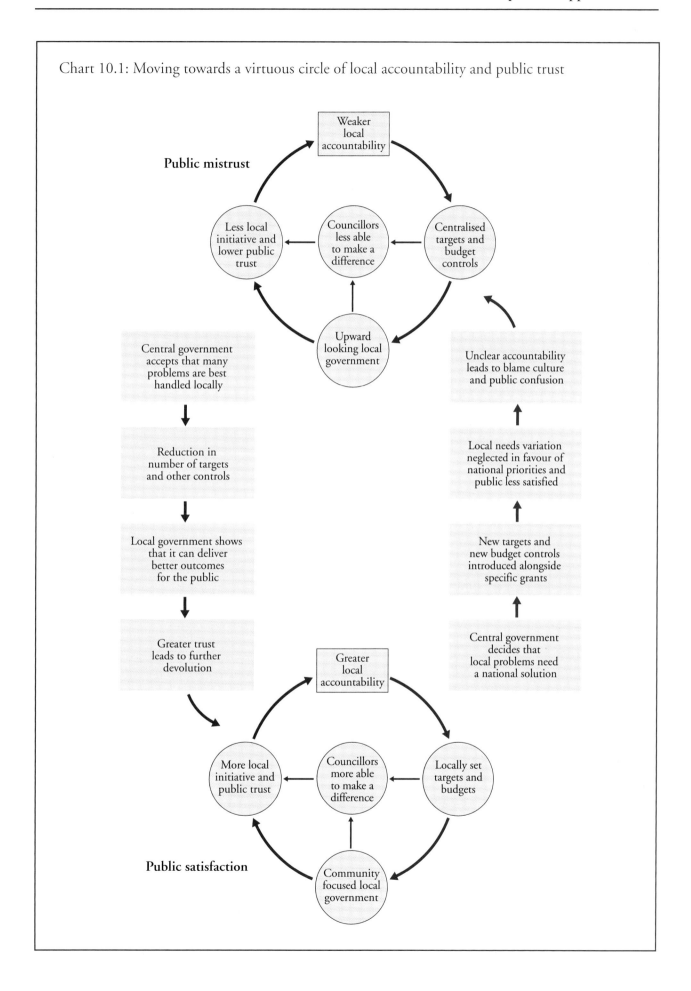

Chart 10.1: Moving towards a virtuous circle of local accountability and public trust

Weaker local accountability

Public mistrust

Less local initiative and lower public trust

Councillors less able to make a difference

Centralised targets and budget controls

Upward looking local government

Central government accepts that many problems are best handled locally

Unclear accountability leads to blame culture and public confusion

Reduction in number of targets and other controls

Local needs variation neglected in favour of national priorities and public less satisfied

Local government shows that it can deliver better outcomes for the public

New targets and new budget controls introduced alongside specific grants

Greater trust leads to further devolution

Central government decides that local problems need a national solution

Greater local accountability

More local initiative and public trust

Councillors more able to make a difference

Locally set targets and budgets

Public satisfaction

Community focused local government

10.4   This chapter describes how my recommendations can provide this developmental approach, looking at:

- the behavioural changes that both central and local government can make in the short term, using opportunities such as the implementation of the White Paper and the associated Local Government and Public Involvement in Health Bill, and the forthcoming Comprehensive Spending Review;

- short term changes to the funding and legal powers of local authorities, and medium term measures to underpin a sustainable finance system, both for the Government to implement through legislation and other means;

- the longer term funding choices that future governments might face, subject to the successful implementation of these short term reforms and changes to behaviours; and

- how this process of developmental change might be supported and underpinned by a more formal agreement or constitutional settlement between local and central government.

CHANGING BEHAVIOURS

10.5   One of the conclusions that I have drawn from my work is that legal obstacles are not, in the main, the major hindrance to local government performing its place-shaping role. Whilst I have made a number of recommendations for substantive legal and policy changes for the Government to implement, more important is that local authorities develop a sense of powerfulness and capability to perform the place-shaping role, and change their behaviours to pursue those objectives.

10.6   The Government needs to support this process, by enabling greater local flexibility and more space for local choices to be made. To do so it will need not just to make changes to legislation, but also to its corporate behaviours, and those of individual departments. This should be to the advantage of both central and local government – our system of government as a whole will be most effective if the comparative advantages of its constituent parts are used to their full effect in addressing service challenges and difficult 'wicked issues'.

10.7   All of these changes can be set in motion in the short term, though I do not pretend that they can be introduced instantly everywhere. It will take time for them to come to fruition as local authorities and government departments assess their own situation in the light of my recommendations and make the changes that are appropriate.

Local government   10.8   Local government can begin immediately to change its behaviours to enhance its ability to perform the place-shaping role, building on the steps that have already been taken. Some local authorities are further along the road than others, though all need to act, and the local government family has a collective responsibility to respond to the challenges and opportunities presented by this agenda. It is local authorities who must lead the process of enhancing public trust and understanding, demonstrating their ability to engage with citizens, to respond to their concerns and aspirations through managed difference, and to make full use of the potential of co-production.

10.9   Key issues that local authorities need to address include:

- taking the task of place-shaping seriously and focusing on the future of their communities, both the places and the people, in order to describe and agree a vision with the public and other partners and to use their powers to pursue it;

- developing the skills and confidence to convene and lead the activities of the local public sector, and to draw in the energy of the voluntary and business communities, through appropriate partnership and contractual arrangements;

- demonstrating the ability to work with other authorities across boundaries and between tiers in a way which delivers a better service to the public, and building relationships to address longer-term economic, social and environmental challenges;

- engaging effectively and closely with local citizens through a range of methods, including ensuring that the role of all councillors as frontline representatives and advocates is acknowledged and supported, and making use of co-production;

- acting as a champion of efficiency and value for money in the procurement and delivery of services and the use of assets; and

- taking responsibility for their own opportunities, challenges and problems and the means of solving those.

10.10   This change in attitudes and approach must come from within local authorities themselves. If local government is to be trusted by the public and accepted as an important and essential part of our overall system of government, then authorities must recognise their problems and the areas where they need to improve, and take their own steps to address them. The Local Government Association (LGA) and other parts of the local government family, such as the Improvement and Development Agency (IDeA), do however have a part to play. This has been on their agenda for the last few years, and the Best Review offers the opportunity for the LGA to take steps to further enhance its ability to promote improvement within local government. Other recent steps by the LGA, such as its new 'Raising our Game' campaign to challenge and assist local authorities to improve, are welcome.

Central government   10.11   There is much for the Government to do here as well, to improve the interface between local and central government and to ensure that both play their full part in addressing the key challenges both face. The positive direction set out in the Local Government White Paper and the developing experience of Local Area Agreements offers an encouraging start. In particular, central government departments – ministers, civil servants and their colleagues in the Government Offices – need to act to reduce the substantial levels of control, both hard controls such as ring-fencing and soft controls such as prescriptive guidance and monitoring requirements that have grown up over time. This will require focus and self-discipline to reduce targets and expectations and to ensure that new controls do not come into being to replace old ones. The Local Government Bill currently going through Parliament, and the work of the Lifting the Burdens taskforce, are both opportunities for developing this approach.

10.12   The Comprehensive Spending Review (CSR), later this year, offers a key opportunity to implement changes, and particularly to ensure a corporate approach across government to the necessary prioritisation and resourcing. The Government could use the CSR and subsequent discussions to:

- reduce targets and ensure a focus in those targets that are necessary on key issues of central priority, supported by appropriate resources;

- Set a clear and measurable target to reduce conditional, specific and ring-fenced grants; and

- work with local government to develop deliverable targets and priorities, with monitoring processes that do not pose undue burdens on authorities or on the front line, and also avoid soft controls where services and priorities are for local discretion.

LEGISLATIVE AND POLICY CHANGES

10.13   I have made recommendations for a number of changes to legislation and policy on finance and function issues which I recommend the Government should implement in the near future through changes to policy or, where necessary, through legislation. These are intended to:

- address problems in the system that preclude constructive debate and political space for wider changes;

- provide additional local flexibility and the ability to pursue the place-shaping role; and

- focus accountability for decisions clearly at the local level where that is appropriate.

10.14   There is no 'golden key', no single change that will meet all these objectives. Rather, a mosaic of changes is needed, and my recommendations are intended to form a single package, rather than a menu from which specific choices can be selected.

Council tax   10.15   It is my judgement that council tax is not broken, and should be retained as a local tax. Short-term reform is needed to deal with the immediate concerns about the pressure on, and fairness of, council tax. This will, in turn, help to create the space for a wider look at reform in the medium term – at the moment debate on council tax overwhelms any other discussion about the role and financing of local government. Improvements to council tax benefit must be pursued as a matter of urgency to improve the perceived fairness and sustainability of the council tax, by:

- more accurately reflecting the unique status of council tax benefit as an adjustment to households' liability for a single tax according to ability to pay, by re-naming it council tax rebate;

- substantially increasing the current low level of take-up by pursuing work on more automated delivery of benefit entitlement, with a view to achieving a step-change in take-up, particularly for pensioners; and

- increasing the savings limits for pensioners, and over time seeking to abolish them, aligning council tax rebate with Pension Credit.

10.16   There also remain a number of options, including the assignment of a fixed proportion of a national tax, or a local income tax, which could be used to help reduce pressure on council tax further over time. While these are not likely to be realistic in the immediate term, they have a number of advantages and remain possibilities for the future.

Capping   10.17   For local government to take responsibility for making local choices, and be held accountable for them, it must be clear which decisions are a local responsibility and which are a national. This is essential to the developmental process.

10.18   Council tax capping confuses accountability in the finance system by overlaying heavy central controls on a tax that is supposed to be a matter of local responsibility. Central government has a right to expect careful use of public resources and judicious decisions on tax rates, as do the public, but I am not convinced that capping currently guarantees either. If the cause of high council tax increases is based in pressures on local public services and a lack of local flexibility to deal with them, the solution must lie in greater local flexibility to allow pressures to be managed and controlled. Thus, having made recommendations designed to provide greater local flexibility and space for local decisions, I recommend that central government should cease to use, and then abolish, its capping powers as pressures on council tax reduce. This will of course require some courage from the Government, but there could be no clearer and more fundamental sign that devolution is a key part of the agenda for the 21st century than this.

Transparency 10.19 Some of the pressures on local government come from central government requirements and expectations. If local authorities are to be held responsible for taxation decisions, it is important that the spending pressures and requirements placed on them are manageable. Reducing the scope of central requirements and expectations, and providing greater scope for local choice, will be an important contribution to that. In order to support that process and to provide greater transparency and challenge, I have also recommended that the Government should consider how it can enhance the amount and quality of independent information available on the requirements placed on local government, and the pressures on local services, in order to enable more effective public and Parliamentary scrutiny.

10.20 To aid transparency at the level of the citizen, I also recommend that councils should – supported by the Government relaxing restrictions on the layout of the bill – provide a clear statement on council tax bills which shows the level of support from nationally raised taxation they are receiving, and what that represents as a percentage of locally collected income tax.

Business rates 10.21 To make the place-shaping role a reality, local authorities need greater flexibility and space to act, and to build stronger relationships with the business community. Reforms to business rates need to contribute to this. There are already positive signs in this area, with support from businesses for the place-shaping role of local authorities and joint work between the CBI and LGA. However, I do not think that the time is right for substantial changes to the business rates system to be introduced. Local authorities and the business community still have to work on developing trust and shared objectives, and I am therefore concerned to avoid changes which could put the developing shared agenda at risk.

10.22 My short-term recommendations on the reform of business rates therefore include:

- retaining the current national system and Retail Price Index (RPI) cap;

- introducing the power for local authorities to levy a local supplement in order to increase local flexibility and support the continued investment in infrastructure that both businesses and local authorities have called for, subject to effective accountability; and

- reforms to business rates exemptions and reliefs, through reform of the Empty Property Relief and a wider review of reliefs and exemptions.

Incentives 10.23 Changes to the funding system can also help to connect local communities and authorities to the health and prosperity of their local economy. Incentives could both enhance the focus of authorities on the economic aspects of place-shaping, and enable those local communities who choose to support development and expansion to receive some of the financial benefits of those changes. I have recommended that these objectives be pursued through reforms to the Local Authority Business Growth Incentives (LABGI) scheme and a wider review of the grant system, where the current structure at present precludes the delivery of clear, transparent and long-term incentives.

Economic prosperity 10.24 Local government has an important role to play in fostering economic prosperity, and balancing it with the need for environmental sustainability. Much of what is needed here revolves around local authorities' own sense of powerfulness and place-shaping role, and their ability to build coalitions with neighbouring authorities and others. However, the Government can support this through:

- ensuring that the Sub-National Economic Development and Regeneration Review and the Comprehensive Spending Review, bring forward proposals for the devolution of resources and powers to local authorities working across sub-regional areas and with regional bodies; and

- implementing the measures it has proposed on the regulation of bus provision and on other issues related to planning and skills provision.

Revaluation 10.25 Council tax is currently based on property bands established in 1993 on the basis of property values in 1991. The lack of a revaluation makes the tax increasingly arbitrary and precludes most meaningful reform of the tax itself. Although it is not the most pressing priority, in order to provide the opportunity for reform, and to underpin the future sustainability of the tax, the Government should conduct a revaluation of properties in the near future – with appropriate transitional protection – and introduce a process of regular revaluation thereafter. At the time of the revaluation exercise I recommend that new bands should be introduced at the top and bottom of the distribution to begin to address the current weaknesses of council tax as a property tax.

Assignment 10.26 In the medium term, the Government should consider whether the assignment of a proportion of income tax revenues to local government, to replace current grant allocations, would have advantages. It might provide a better reflection of the fact that local services are funded from both national taxation and council tax, and help to develop a new relationship between central and local government, based on a change in mind-set in both local and central government. However, it would be a significant change, requiring central government to cede control over some elements of national taxation, and greater self-reliance on the part of local government.

OPTIONS FOR FUTURE GOVERNMENTS

10.27 The combination of changes to behaviours, and the implementation of a package of legislative and policy measures which provide greater flexibility, accountability and address fairness, should contribute to providing the space for a wider and more constructive debate. In the longer term, therefore, the success of these measures could give future governments the opportunity to consider possible further reforms to local government funding and taxation, should those seem desirable.

The basis of local taxation 10.28 One of the most important issues to consider will be whether the current basis of local taxation is the right one. Property taxes, of which the council tax is a form, certainly have a number of advantages. Future governments might wish to move towards a rather purer system where liability is more closely linked to the actual value of a property in order to make the local tax more effective as a property tax. An alternative option would be to introduce a local income tax to replace part of council tax or some proportion of grant.

10.29 Both of these approaches are technically possible at present, but my conclusion is that a combination of factors (particularly the length of time it would take to implement, and public ambivalence about the ideas) make them only a realistic option in the long term. Radical changes to taxation such as this require greater consensus than is currently in place.

Business taxation   10.30 Depending on the way in which the relationships between local government and the business community develops, future governments will wish to consider the best approach to business rates. The supplementary power I have recommended could be developed into a locally controlled tax through the possible future localisation of revenues, and increased local discretion over the rate (including the ability to lower as well as raise it).

10.31 There are also some good arguments for looking again at the business rates system once relationships have bedded in, particularly in terms of providing more effective incentives on local authorities to foster local economic activity and enhance the value of the local area.

UNDERPINNING THE DEVELOPMENTAL APPROACH

10.32 Beginning and maintaining a developmental approach relies on effective engagement between, and constructive behaviours from, both local and central government. I am confident that both will respond positively to this challenge, and there are structures already in place to support this, including amongst others:

- the machinery of the Central Local Partnership, and the Framework Document between the LGA and the Government which underpins that, enabling dialogue and debate about local and central priorities and issues of mutual interest;

- the signing and ratification of the European Charter of Local Self-Government;

- a considerable degree of transparency in the processes and data used to allocate the local government settlement between authorities, with strong engagement between local government officers and central government officials on technical issues;

- the work of the Audit Commission, aided by the Chartered Institute of Public Finance and Accountancy (CIPFA), in promoting debate about public services and encouraging the refinement of information for comparison;

- a substantial programme of rigorous research and evaluation commissioned by the department of Communities and Local Government into local government and local public services; and

- the development of innovative approaches to setting targets and allocating resources, such as Local Public Service Agreements and Local Area Agreements.

10.33 However, the changes we need to see, if local government is to play its full place-shaping role everywhere, will take some years to undertake. We therefore need to build relationships between local and central government for the long term, beyond the lifetime of any one government, and to cement the position of local government within a single system of government. It is not clear that current arrangements, and processes of debate and discussion, are sufficient to do that. In my May 2006 report, *National prosperity, local choice and civic engagement*, I suggested that some kind of formal agreement between central and local government might be needed, which would need to address the following issues:

- clarify roles and responsibilities;

- ensure central government expectations of local government are fully funded;

- ensure greater local flexibility and reinforce local government's convening role across local public services;

- formally recognise the place-shaping role of local government;

- enhance local accountability through reforming the role of councillors;

- reform the performance management framework; and

- provide a clear timetable for reform.

First steps 10.34 The first steps towards addressing these issues have already begun. The White Paper acknowledges the place-shaping role of local government and proposes a number of changes to the framework of expectations and targets on local government. If implemented successfully, these should enhance flexibility and strengthen the convening role. Local Area Agreements, particularly as the White Paper envisages they should be developed, also have an important part to play. Creating a clear single negotiation about the resources being provided to individual areas and local authorities, and the limited number of central government priorities that they are intended to deliver, alongside appropriate space for local discretion, will be an important step forward. The White Paper also sets out criteria for a new performance framework that, if implemented fully, will mark a real step change in the performance framework, providing a much more streamlined system of regulation which will provide much greater space for local flexibility and choice.

Contractual agreement 10.35 There remains a question as to whether a more formal arrangement between central and local government is needed to underpin these changes, to inform future policy development and to support scrutiny. There are profound behavioural changes being required of central government both by the White Paper and by my recommendations, which may need some external support and scrutiny to be delivered. A number of stakeholders, supported some kind of formal settlement, arguing for example that:

> *It would demonstrably improve local governance if there was a clear statement of purpose in the form of a written settlement between central and local government specifying the powers, responsibilities, duties and freedoms of the signatories.* (Mayor of London)

10.36 I do think there should be greater clarity over what central government requires of local government and how that commitment should be funded, and a much clearer understanding of the appropriate extent of central government influence or control over other aspects of local government activity. Without a clear shared understanding of these fundamentals, we cannot hope to tackle the sense of confusion and mutual blame which characterises our system and undermines the public's trust in our institutions of government.

10.37 The definition of those objectives should, I believe, be agreed between central and local government, and reviewed transparently on a regular basis. The existing Central Local Partnership, which involves Government ministers and representatives of local authorities, could take on responsibility for agreeing those objectives. They should then be made public in the form of a contractual agreement, and should be clear enough to enable an independent assessment of how well they are being met. This needs to be supported by the improved provision of independent information, as mentioned earlier, to inform the public and Parliament about the cost of new burdens on local government and the pressures on local services.

10.38 These changes would ideally encourage a more mature approach to negotiations between central and local government, focusing on the outcomes desired from the system as a whole, to inform the hard decisions about spending priorities which follow.

Formal constitutional change 10.39 There are further steps that could be taken. In other countries formal constitutional or legal measures protecting the existence and the powers of local government form part of the basis of central-local relationships. For example, in Sweden the first article of the Instrument of

Government (part of the constitution) says that:

> *All public power in Sweden emanates from the people. The Swedish democracy is founded on freedom of opinion and on universal and equal suffrage and shall be realised through a representative and parliamentary polity and through local self-government ...*[1]

10.40 Whether such an approach is directly relevant to the UK's constitutional system can be debated, but a number of options have been proposed. For example, the Local Government Information Unit (LGIU) have called for legislative recognition of the position of local government in line with article two of the European Charter on Local Self Government. Others have suggested that Parliament be given a role in the process, for example through a parliamentary committee (as suggested by the House of Lords Select Committee on Relations between Central and Local Government in 1996), or as part of the wider process of House of Lords reform (recently suggested by the New Local Government Network and the LGIU).

10.41 I am not seeking to enshrine the constitutional position of local government in law. Laws and agreements do not necessarily create relationships, and the initial steps towards the developmental approach need to be given time to bed in. Nevertheless, I am attracted to a model which in time provides greater Parliamentary oversight, because of the contribution which that could make to developing and sustaining a wider consensus about the respective roles of central and local government.

Recommendation 10.1

Local and central government should pursue a developmental approach to reform, in order to develop relationships, trust and public confidence in government. This should be based on a new constitutional settlement between central and local government, which in time would enable greater scrutiny and parliamentary oversight. As short-term reforms take effect the Government should consider building on them to further increase local flexibility and choice and consider longer term and more radical reforms to the funding system.

CONCLUSION

10.42 There is no simple solution, no golden key, which will unlock the problems of local government or local government finance. These are profoundly complex and difficult issues which have their roots not only in legislation, but also in behaviours and deeply ingrained expectations on the part of local government, central government and the public they serve. Any reform will involve political trade-offs and widespread impact, and requires a strong case for change. I have sought throughout my work, and throughout this report, to take a sophisticated approach which recognises the genuine choices we have to make in developing and maintaining our systems of government.

10.43 The current system of local government, and the relationships that exist between citizens and their local authorities and between local and central government, has many strengths, but it is not sustainable. However, changing views, approaches and competences will take time. New political, professional and working relationships and alliances need to be built. That is why I have proposed a developmental approach, which gives time for those relationships to grow within a strong view of the necessity for, and the potential of, local government.

---

[1] Scottish Office Central Research Unit, *The Constitutional Status of Local Government in Other Countries*, 1998.

Summary of recommendations

CHAPTER 4 – CENTRAL GOVERNMENT'S CONTRIBUTION TO REFORM

Performance framework   4.1   The burdens and effectiveness of the new Comprehensive Area Assessment and other aspects of the performance framework should be independently evaluated, and a report published, two years after its introduction.

This should examine:

- how well the new system is achieving its objectives, and in particular how much space it leaves for place-shaping, local innovation and responsiveness;

- whether other external assessment and inspection frameworks are adequately supporting joint agendas; and

- whether the framework effectively assesses and supports the community empowerment agenda.

Leadership   4.2   The Government should ensure that local communities retain the flexibility to choose models of leadership that best suit their circumstances, and to adapt them as and when they judge appropriate.

4.3   The Government should not seek to define any further lead councillor and officer roles and structures, and existing prescriptive models should be kept under review.

Transparency of the funding system   4.4   Mechanisms should be put in place to improve the transparency of the objectives of the local government funding system, in particular central and local government should agree:

- what central government requires of local government and how it should be funded;

- the ways in which central government should appropriately influence other aspects of local government activity and the extent to which such influence should be limited.

This should be formalised in a written agreement.

The Government   4.5   The Government should consider ways to improve independent information available to the public and Parliament about:

- the actual costs of new burdens imposed by central government;

- actual burdens of targets, performance management and soft controls imposed on local government by central government and its agencies;

- whether the cumulative impact of new mandates on local government is over time greater than, or less than, the funding made available to pay for them;

- what evidence is available about future pressures on and efficiency opportunities in local services and what might be reasonable assumptions to make about their impact on costs and savings; and

- whether the funding system is meeting the agreed objectives in terms of enabling local government to deliver what has been agreed with central government.

Options considered should include an independent commission.

Capping 4.6 The Government should cease to use, and then abolish, its capping powers as pressures on council tax reduce, forming part of a package of measures to re-establish local accountability for tax and spending decisions.

Soft controls 4.7 As well as reducing the number of targets and performance indicators in the revised performance framework set out in the recent White Paper, the Government, its agencies and the inspectorates should also reduce the wider data burdens and reporting requirements that local authorities face, drawing on the work of the Lifting the Burdens task force.

4.8 The Government should set a target to reduce these burdens, and progress against the target should be monitored transparently by an independent body such as the Audit Commission.

4.9 The Government, its agencies and the inspectorates should reduce the levels of guidance in areas of local concern and responsibility. The Government should also develop a code of practice for departments and agencies which clarifies the limited circumstances under which it is appropriate to place conditions on funding streams for local government.

4.10 Local Area Agreements should be developed in a way which leaves enough space for local priorities. New central government priorities which emerge between negotiations over the LAA should be incorporated into the framework on a strictly 'one in, one out' basis in order to avoid gradual regrowth of central control.

Flexible finance 4.11 The Government should commit to significant further reductions in the amount of
system conditional, ring-fenced and specific grants to local government and its partner agencies and set clear targets and a timetable for achieving them. It should ask the Audit Commission to audit and report on progress in an annual public report.

Where conditional and hypothecated funding remains central government should:

- consider ways in which reporting arrangements for pooled budgets could be more flexible to support joint working; and

- focus on outcomes not process with flexibility on how the money is spent to enable it to fit better with local priorities and circumstances.

4.12 Government departments should:

- ensure that the budget cycles of major local agencies are aligned to enable joint planning; and

- move to put all local agency budgets on a three-year basis to reflect the introduction of three-year settlements for local government.

Convening 4.13 The Government should:

- seek to ensure that changes to the performance frameworks, guidance and funding systems affecting local government and its partner agencies are kept to a minimum, to help provide a more stable environment within which to develop joint strategies and actions;

- seek to ensure the suite of targets and national indicators for local government is internally consistent and outcome-focused. A priority in the negotiation of Local Area Agreements should be to allow the local alignment of targets across all local public services; and

- acknowledge the role of local authorities in having lead accountability for local outcomes across all local agencies.

Efficiency and choice   4.14   The Audit Commission should ensure the Use of Resources judgement in the new performance framework includes delivering the right priorities to meet the needs and wishes of the local community.

4.15   Central and local government should together challenge the presumption that difference between areas – the 'postcode lottery' – is always a bad thing.

4.16   The Government should explicitly recognise that for a range of local services the best way to improve well-being is to enable greater local choice.

Economic prosperity   4.17   Reflecting the importance of working at the level of the functional economy in pursuing economic prosperity, the Government should:

- use Multi Area Agreements as a way of engaging with local authorities to develop locally determined sub-regional arrangements to address issues related to economic prosperity;

- set clear tests and expectations for arrangements in order to ensure that they would be robust enough to make challenging decisions and trade-offs;

- detail which powers, responsibilities and funding would be devolved from national and regional level to sufficiently robust and capable groups of authorities, and align existing governmental and delivery arrangements with new sub-regional arrangements; and

- avoid the creation of new institutional structures where these do not currently exist unless a consensus exists at the local level, or local authorities fail to put in place adequate arrangements through collaboration.

Planning   4.18   The Government should pursue devolution and clarification in the planning system as set out by Kate Barker in her review of the land use planning system and in particular:

- reduce the complexity and detail of directions which provide for central control; and

- set out clearer criteria on the use of call-in powers.

4.19   In taking forward reforms to the planning process for major infrastructure projects, the Government should ensure that:

- the new arrangements apply only to issues of unambiguously national importance, subject to clear and published criteria;

- local individuals and communities are informed of the process and have an opportunity to make their views known; and

- a clear process for reporting back to local communities is established.

Transport	4.20	The Government should implement its plans for local authority powers to regulate bus services as soon as practicable.

Skills and employment   4.21   In taking forward reforms following the Leitch Review, the Government should:

- ensure that there is sufficient scope and resource to enable the Learning and Skills Council and local partners to tailor provision appropriately at the local level;

- enable local authorities to play an appropriate role in Employment and Skills Boards; and

- seek to build on existing arrangements between employers and local authorities where possible.

Housing   4.22   The Government should ensure that local authorities have appropriate influence over housing issues in their place-shaping role and should consider whether to extend the duty to cooperate to housing associations and other social landlords.

Social care   4.23   The Government should lead a clear national debate about how we want to manage and pay for social care for older people, which should cover:

- what, if any 'national promise' central government wants to make for the whole country;

- what local government is to be responsible for, and who is best placed to manage pressures; and

- who should pay for social care: state or service user, and how incentives can be aligned to ensure competing demands are managed appropriately.

Waste   4.24   The Government should give greater recognition to the fact that effective waste management is a shared responsibility between central and local government and consider ways to provide greater local flexibility to manage the waste stream locally (including waste production), particularly through a new power to charge for domestic waste.

Community safety   4.25   The Government should simplify funding streams and targets particularly for community safety.

Health and well-being   4.26   The Government should support a stronger and more explicit role for local government as convenor in the realm of health and well-being, building on the proposals in the Local Government White Paper to strengthen partnership working.

4.27   The Government should ensure the commitment to harmonise budget and performance management cycles in health and social services is delivered.

Children's services   4.28   The Government should consider more formal mechanisms, such as an extension of the duty to cooperate or a duty to have regard to the Local Area Agreement or Sustainable Community Strategy, to encourage greater collaborative working between Local Strategic Partnerships, GPs and schools.

CHAPTER 5 – LOCAL GOVERNMENT'S CONTRIBUTION TO REFORM

Long-term planning 5.1 In their forward planning, local authorities should look further ahead than even the ten-year time frame of the community strategy and therefore should:

- make best use of intelligence and evidence of future demographic and other changes;

- take account of national and international trends and forecasts;

- engage local partners, businesses and residents in a debate about the long-term aspirations for the area; and

- focus their performance management on long-term outcomes.

Leadership 5.2 In reviewing their structures and leadership arrangements, local authorities should focus on securing visible and accountable leadership with the capacity to take a long-term, outward-looking approach and build credible relationships with local partners.

5.3 Local authorities need to take the lead in ensuring local partnership structures are fit for purpose, streamlining and reducing the number of bodies and groups where necessary, ensuring that the structures are genuinely local in character and meet the criteria outlined in the report.

5.4 Local authorities need to adopt a leadership style that engages local partners, builds alliances and secures support for delivering joint priorities. It should facilitate, advocate, arbitrate and influence rather than dominate.

Devolution 5.5 Local authorities need to identify where they can make space for neighbourhood or parish activity, particularly to address liveability issues, and to encourage participation and innovation.

5.6 The Local Government Association should continue the development of its work with partners to provide leadership to local government and to challenge underperforming councils, as well as continuing to strengthen its performance in contributing to debate on major policy issues and improving its communication with the public.

Recruitment and support of councillors 5.7 Political parties should refresh their approach to recruiting local councillors, actively seeking out talent and reaching out beyond their traditional activist base.

5.8 Political groups, mainly at local level, but supported at national level, should place stronger performance management pressures on councillors including performance appraisal and mechanisms to provide the public with information about their activities.

5.9 All political groups should:

- organise themselves so that all councillors feel valued;

- consider giving ward members more freedom, limiting whipping to a narrower range of decisions and employing more flexible processes for group discipline; and

- develop skills in cross-party working.

5.10 Every council should improve the support it provides councillors in their frontline role by:

- ensuring that they have the information they need to do their job effectively;

- putting in place role descriptions, training and development specifically for the ward member role as part of a wider commitment to member development;

- ensuring that support for elected members in their community leadership role is properly thought through, given sufficient priority in the work of the council and is resourced appropriately, with full use being made of IT;

- considering the use of individual ward member budgets but assessing what works best in local circumstances; and

- ensuring clear routes for frontline councillors to influence policy decisions.

Informing the public 5.11 The main steps forward which councils still need to take in informing the public are:

- working with partners across the Local Strategic Partnership to present a common set of key messages for the area;

- identifying through research and customer feedback what really works in reaching the public and focusing resources on those channels; and

- using new channels to target particular groups in the population, especially young people, with relevant messages in an imaginative and entrepreneurial way.

Public engagement 5.12 Local government needs to make a step-change in the quality of its engagement work, building on the effective communications and engagement practice already being used and also ensuring that its application is much more systematic and rigorous. In particular, councils need to:

- focus on what matters in their engagement work, being selective about where resources are targeted;

- follow best practice in engaging all sectors of the community, particularly those voices which are not always heard, including vulnerable people and black and minority ethnic groups;

- avoid allowing statutory requirements for consultation to limit their approach to consultation and engagement;

- accord higher status to the skills set needed by officers and councillors to engage effectively with the public; and

- ensure they explain to participants how the results of engagement have been used, including how they influenced councils' or partners' plans.

Scrutiny 5.13 Scrutiny needs to be seen as a core strand of local government's place-shaping role. Councils and other participants must resource it appropriately and link it to local partnership work.

Use of powers 5.14 Local government needs to think widely and creatively about how to use its existing powers to the full and take a more entrepreneurial approach to problem solving, as part of the place-shaping role.

5.15 Local government should itself develop mechanisms to provide peer guidance to councils and filter requests for guidance to government. The Local Government Association could play a gatekeeper role.

5.16 Local government needs to emphasise the 'local' in Local Area Agreements, tailoring them to, and using them as a stimulus for, identifying key local priorities, seeing them as a tool for local improvement rather than a matter of mere compliance with central government.

Innovation 5.17 Local government needs to develop its capacity to commission innovative service solutions, to develop markets for services and to think more creatively about delivery options.

5.18   Local authorities should ensure that their overall approach to efficiency:

- places a value on outcomes in terms of their value to the local community;

- values the additional inputs generated through co-production;

- allows them to consider where it may be appropriate simply to do less of a particular service or activity in balancing local priorities;

- considers all options available including use of charging or other powers to reduce costs, raise revenues and change behaviour in the interest of the local community; and

- considers where it may be possible to encourage market solutions to local needs and so reduce the pressures on the tax base.

5.19   Local government should continue to focus on performance, using the reduction in central targets and inspection as an opportunity to:

- re-orientate its performance management towards public accountability; and

- work with other councils to support service improvement, through peer review, challenge and benchmarking.

CHAPTER 7 – HOUSEHOLD TAXATION AND LOCAL CHARGES

Council tax 7.1   Council tax should be retained as a source of revenue for local government. The option of change in the longer term to shift the balance towards other taxes and changes remains open.

Revaluation 7.2   While not the most urgent priority, the Government should conduct a revaluation of all domestic properties for council tax. Transitional arrangements to ensure households do not face steep tax increases from one year to the next should be considered at the point of revaluation.

7.3   Subsequent revaluations should take place regularly and automatically at intervals of no more than five years.

7.4   At the revaluation the Government should introduce new property bands at the top and bottom of the current structure. It could also consider the introduction of separate bands for Inner London to reflect the unique shape of the property market in that region and to reduce turbulence there.

Student 7.5   The Government should ensure the grant system reflects realistic data on the number of households student households exempt from council tax in their areas. This should be done in time to inform the forthcoming negotiations on three-year settlements.

Council tax 7.6   Council tax benefit should be recognised as a rebate rather than a benefit, and re-named benefit 'council tax rebate', to properly reflect its main purpose: adjusting households' liability to council tax.

7.7   The Government should build on recent efforts to streamline delivery of council tax rebates by adapting IT systems so that the Pension Service can act as a portal to rebates for all callers, regardless of Pension Credit eligibility.

7.8   Further improvements to the claims process should be pursued to allow the Pension Service to liaise directly with local authorities in processing rebate claims.

7.9   Ministers should examine the scope for data sharing between agencies to proactively deliver council tax rebates to those who are entitled, with a view to achieving a step-change in the take-up of council tax benefit.

Capital limits   7.10   The Government should increase the savings limits on council tax rebate eligibility to £50,000 for pensioners.

7.11   The Government should, over time, abolish the savings limit in council tax benefit for pensioners, so aligning council tax rebate thresholds with the criteria for eligibility to the Pension Credit.

Charging powers   7.12   The powers to trade and charge conferred on 'best value' authorities in the Local Government Act 2003 should be extended to all local authorities.

7.13   The Government should carefully consider the wider framework of charging powers for statutory and discretionary services, including in the light of the Audit Commission's work when published later this year.

Waste charging   7.14   The Government should take new powers to allow local authorities to charge for domestic waste collection, developed in close consultation with residents and other key stakeholders.

CHAPTER 8 – BUSINESS TAXATION

Business rates   8.1   The RPI cap on the national level of business rates should be retained.

Supplementary powers   8.2   The existing national arrangements for business rates should be retained at present, but a new local flexibility to set a supplement on the current national business rate should be introduced.

8.3   Local supplementary powers should be designed in a way which can gain credibility with business and the wider community. The key issues to be considered are:

- the appropriate scale of the supplement. At the upper end, some Business Improvement Districts have levied supplements as high as four pence. A lower limit would provide less revenue and less flexibility, but might enable confidence in new arrangements to develop more gradually. In that situation, there might be a case for allowing a higher limit in some cases, subject to more stringent approval mechanisms;

- retention of revenue, where I believe all revenues should be retained locally;

- the right form of accountability to business taxpayers. The most obvious options are some form of voted approval or a statutory consultation process. On balance, I propose that there should be a requirement to consult local businesses, and the wider community, before introducing a supplement, with a clear proposal and timetable. Revenues from a supplement should be hypothecated to the purposes agreed through consultation;

- how to ensure that supplements contribute to, rather than detract from, the local economy. I propose that authorities should be required to make an assessment of the impact of the supplement on the local economy, and the potential economic benefits of the spending they propose to finance from the revenues generated;

- the authority by which supplements should be levied. I recommend that supplements should be levied by unitary authorities and metropolitan districts, and in London and areas with two-tier local government, a single rate should be set through agreement between the relevant authorities, with a joint plan for the use of revenues. Where arrangements develop for collaborative working between authorities elsewhere in the country, this could usefully include cooperating around supplements. Powers to introduce Business Improvement Districts should remain with shire districts and the London boroughs;

- whether authorities should have a degree of further flexibility over which sizes of business pay the levy, which I would support; and

- whether there should be a threshold below which small businesses do not pay the supplement.

Empty property relief 8.4 The Government should reform and reduce the empty property relief by:

- retaining the existing 100 per cent relief for short-term empty property (up to three months);

- reducing the rate of empty property relief thereafter; and

- providing factories and warehouses with the same level of relief as other properties.

Derelict and brownfield land 8.5 The Government should develop proposals for the taxation of derelict property and brownfield land and consult on those with stakeholders.

Reliefs and exemptions 8.6 The Government should conduct a review of exemptions and reliefs to consider the scope for removing inappropriate subsidies and distortions, and to simplify the system.

Planning-gain Supplement 8.7 If the Planning-gain Supplement is introduced, the Government should:

- design it primarily as a local revenue source, with a regional share of an appropriate scale, not as a national source which may or may not be allocated to authorities. It is imperative that a transparent and predictable link between local development and local resourcing exists if development is to take place, or incentive effects are to be realised; and

- consider whether in two-tier areas, it could be managed through plans jointly developed and implemented by county and district councils.

Taxes on tourist pressures 8.8 The Government should consult on the costs and benefits of providing a permissive power for local authorities to levy taxes on tourism, including a possible tax on accommodation, and whether local authorities would use such a power. It should use the results of that consultation to examine the case for extension of such powers to local authorities.

CHAPTER 9 – GRANT AND THE USE OF NATIONAL TAXATION TO SUPPORT LOCAL SERVICES

Incentives 9.1 In the short term, the Government should simplify the Local Authority Business Growth Incentives scheme in order to provide sharper incentives. Reform should focus on providing transparency and predictability through reducing the emphasis on distributional objectives.

9.2 In the longer term, the Government should consider wider reforms to business rates, such as localisation, which would make it possible to design longer term incentives for local authorities.

9.3 The Government should consider ways in which the incentives in the grant system could be improved. In particular it should focus on:

- how far the grant system should be re-balanced to accommodate a greater focus on incentives;

- what changes will need to be made to the current grant system to support residential property tax base incentives;

- how to deliver business rate incentives, and whether these should be funded through additional resources or through redistribution within the current grant total; and

- clarity of messages to local authorities to ensure that they understand, and therefore can act on, the incentives.

Assignment 9.4 The Government should relax the regulations that govern the information that can be included on council tax bills and the accompanying leaflet. This is to enable local authorities to use this communication route, if they choose, to make clear:

- the level of national taxation that they each receive to support local services set out in absolute amounts; and

- how that is used to support the overall expenditure on services in that area.

9.5 The Government should consider, in the medium term, assigning a fixed proportion of income tax to support local government services. This would need to be done in the context of a new constitutional settlement between central and local government providing for greater self-reliance on the part of local government.

9.6 Central and local government should agree as to how far buoyancy from assignment should be used to support new mandates and how much central support should be given to local government in times of downturn.

CHAPTER 10 – A DEVELOPMENTAL APPROACH

10.1 Local and central government should pursue a developmental approach to reform, in order to develop relationships, trust and public confidence in government. This should be based on a new constitutional settlement between central and local government, which in time would enable greater scrutiny and parliamentary oversight. As short-term reforms take effect, the Government should consider building on them to further increase local flexibility and choice, and consider longer-term and more radical reforms to the funding system.

Terms of Reference and Acknowledgements

LYONS INQUIRY TERMS OF REFERENCE

Original terms of reference

1   On 20 July 2004, the Deputy Prime Minister and the Chancellor of the Exchequer asked me to:

- consider, in the light of the report by the Balance of Funding Review, the detailed case for changes to the present system of local government funding;

- make recommendations on any changes that are necessary and how to implement them; and

- take evidence from stakeholders.

2   And, in particular, to:

- make recommendations on how best to reform council tax, taking into account the forthcoming revaluation of domestic property;

- assess the case both for providing local authorities with increased flexibility to raise additional revenue, and for making a significant shift in the current balance of funding;

- conduct thorough analysis of options other than council tax for local authorities to raise supplementary revenue, including local income tax, reform of non-domestic rates and other possible local taxes and charges, as well as the possible combination of such options; and

- consider the implications for the financing of possible elected regional assemblies.

3   I was also asked to consider, as appropriate, any implications that my recommendations may have for other parts of the United Kingdom.

Extended terms of reference

4   On 20 September 2005, the Deputy Prime Minister and the Chancellor of the Exchequer extended my work to allow me to consider issues relating to the functions of local government and its future role, as well as, and prior to, making recommendations on local government funding. This work was intended to inform the Comprehensive Spending Review 2007.

5   In particular, I was asked to:

- consider the current and emerging strategic role of local government, in the context of national and local priorities for local services; and the implications of this for accountability;

- review how the Government's agenda for devolution and decentralisation, together with changes in decision making and funding, could improve local services, their responsiveness to users, and efficiency;

- in light of the above, consider in particular: how improved accountability, clearer central-local relationships, or other interventions could help to manage pressures on local services; and changes to the funding system which will support improved local services;

- publish a report or reports, as appropriate, in time for the Comprehensive Spending Review 2007.

6   I have worked closely with a full range of stakeholders including local and central government in delivering this remit.

Barker, Eddington and Leitch   7   On 6 December 2006, the Chancellor announced that he and Ruth Kelly, Secretary of State for Communities and Local Government, had asked me to consider the implications for local government of the Eddington transport study, the Barker report on planning and the Leitch review of skills in the final report of my Inquiry into the role, function and funding of local government, and to make appropriate recommendations to government.

ACKNOWLEDGEMENTS

8   I am grateful to the numerous organisations and individuals that have provided invaluable input throughout the course of my Inquiry. I would like to take this opportunity to thank all of those who have submitted formal responses and case studies, and to extend my thanks to the large number of people who have given both their time and expertise in a range of ways throughout my Inquiry.

9   At every stage of this Inquiry, I have sought to ensure that my work has been informed by a diverse range of stakeholders. This has meant ensuring that my research, public engagement, business, and councillor events were conducted to include the experience and attitudes of men and women, different age groups and people from white, and Black Minority Ethnic backgrounds. In organising my regional events, the Inquiry team endeavoured to invite a mix of people representative of the communities in the different regions.

Submissions received   10   All those who have provided formal submissions to my Inquiry are listed at the end of this Annex. All submissions from organisations are also available to view on the Lyons Inquiry website and in hard copy in the Communities & Local Government main library. Many of these contributors followed up their submissions in further conversations and meetings with me and the Inquiry team.

Panel of experts   11   I formed a panel of experts to provide input at different times over the length of my Inquiry, and I would like to thank them for their highly valued contributions, which have informed my deliberations. The group included at various times – Kate Barker, Bank of England; David Bell, Pearsons Group; Tom Bentley, Demos; Glen Bramley, Herriot-Watt University; Sir Brian Briscoe, Local Government Association; Steve Bundred, Audit Commission; Paul Coen, Local Government Association; Lucy DeGroot, Improvement and Development Agency; Steve Freer, Chartered Institute of Public Finance and Accountancy; Alan Gay, Leeds City Council; Sue Goss, Office of Public Management; Amanda McIntyre, Accord Plc; Iain McLean, Nuffield College Oxford; Mary Mitson-Woods, Suffolk Associations of Local Councils; Phil Swann, Tavistock Institute; and Tony Travers, London School of Economics.

Other key contributors   12   The Local Government Association Group Leaders – Lord Bruce-Lockhart; Sir Jeremy Beecham, Richard Kemp, Margaret Eaton and Keith Ross – also made regular, helpful input to my deliberations, for which I am grateful. I would also like to express my appreciation to the following individuals who have all provided valued contributions, some of them on a personal basis, at various times over the length of this Inquiry: Sir Rod Eddington; Sir Simon Jenkins; Lord Sandy

Leitch; Councillor Sir Simon Milton, Leader of Westminster City Council; Professor John Stewart, Birmingham University; Professor Gerry Stoker, now Southampton University; Matthew Taylor, now Chief Executive, Royal Society of Arts; Dr Peter Watt, Birmingham University; Ed Balls MP, Economic Secretary to the Treasury; Ed Davey MP; Rt Hon David Miliband MP, now Secretary of State for the Department of the Environment, Food & Rural Affairs; John Healey MP, Financial Secretary to the Treasury; Eric Pickles, MP; Rt Hon Nick Raynsford MP; Caroline Spelman MP and Andrew Stunell MP. I would also like to thank my clients, the Deputy Prime Minister, the Chancellor of the Exchequer and the Rt. Hon. Ruth Kelly, Secretary of State for Communities and Local Government.

Case study councils 13 I would like to thank the leaders, chief executives, councillors and officers of my nine case study councils: Barnet; Bristol; Essex – and within the County, Braintree, Brentwood, Colchester and Tendring; Hartlepool; Nottingham; Sheffield; Southampton; Shropshire – and within the County, Oswestry and South Shropshire; and Trafford.[1] Thanks also go to the numerous local authority officers, councillors, business representatives and members of the public who gave up their time to attend my engagement events over the course of the summer. This work is available on the Lyons Inquiry website.

Speakers and lead contributors at events 14 I would also like to thank all of the individuals who attended various events throughout my Inquiry and, in particular, the following people who spoke, chaired or led the debate:

Greater Local Devolution Seminar – June 2005

Professor Vivien Lowndes, De Montfort University; Professor Steve Martin, Cardiff University; Professor Martin Smith, University of Sheffield; Professor Gerry Stoker, University of Southampton; Professor Ivan Turok, University of Glasgow; Professor Perri 6, Nottingham Trent University.

Rockpools Annual Local Government Seminar – April 2006

Gillian Beasley, Peterborough City Council; Jonathan Brearley, Communities and Local Government; Hamish Davidson, Rockpools; George Krawiek, North East Lincolnshire Council; Susan Law, Doncaster Metropolitan Borough Council; Claer Lloyd Jones, Rockpools; Mary Ney, London Borough of Greenwich; Ben Page, Ipsos/Mori; Barry Quirk, London Borough of Lewisham; Nick Raynsford MP; and Steven Taylor, Local Government Leadership Centre.

Public Finance Round Table – April 2006

Neil Kinghan, former Director General, Local Government, Communities & Local Government; Sir Simon Jenkins, Guardian; Sarah Wood, formerly of the Local Government Association; and Frank Wilson, Deloitte.

Councillor Engagement Events – July 2006

Councillor Richard Kemp, Liverpool City Council; Councillor Sir Simon Milton, Westminster City Council; and Councillor Bryony Rudkin, Suffolk County Council.

Cleaner & Greener Environments Seminar – July 2006

Nicola Beach, Essex County Council; Chris Butcher, LGA; Dr Tom Entwhistle, Cardiff University; Bryn Griffiths, Suffolk County Council; Dr Dominic Hogg, Eunomia Consulting; Michael Hynes, Enterprise Plc; Councillor Nicholas Paget-Brown, Royal Borough of Kensington & Chelsea; Neil Thornton, Defra; and David Wilson, WRAP.

---

[1] Entwistle, T. et al., *Perspectives on Place Shaping and Service Delivery: A Report of Case Study Work,* conducted for the Lyons Inquiry 2007. Available on http://www.lyonsinquiry.org.uk
Lyons Inquiry Public Deliberation Events – Office of Public Management, November 2006. Available on http://www.lyonsinquiry.org.uk

Future Options for Adult Social Care Seminar – September 2006

Dr Stephanie Allen, PriceWaterhouseCoopers; Professor David Bell, Stirling University; Stephen Burke, Counsel & Care; Councillor Barbara Clare, Shropshire County Council; Dr James Downe, Cardiff University; Jonathan Ellis, Help the Aged; Dr Julien Forder, London School of Economics; Anne Mcdonald, Department of Health; and Anne Williams, Association of Directors of Social Services.

Economic Prosperity – The Local Contribution Conference – September 2006

Stephen Bates, Angle UK; James Braithwaite, South East of England Development Agency; Tom Bloxham, Urban Splash; Lord Sandy Bruce-Lockhart, LGA; David Frost, British Chambers of Commerce; Felicity Goody CBE, Salford Regeneration Company; John Healey MP, Financial Secretary to the Treasury; Professor Mark Hepworth, Birkbeck College; Sir Digby Jones, now Skills Envoy; Rt Hon Ruth Kelly, Secretary of State, Communities & Local Government; Sir Robert Kerslake, Sheffield City Council; Professor Michael Parkinson, European Institute of Urban Affairs; Elizabeth Reynolds, Industrial Performance Centre MIT; Michael Snyder, City of London; Jay Walder, Transport for London; and Rob Wye, Learning and Skills Council.

Health and Well-being Seminar – September 2006

Robin Clark, Office of Public Management; Tony Elson, Consultant; Sharon Grant, Commission of Patient & Public Involvement in Health; Jane Martin, Centre for Public Scrutiny; Sara Williams, London Borough of Tower Hamlets and Professor Gerald Wistow, London School of Economics.

Driving Efficiency Seminar – October 2006

Dr Neil Bentley, CBI; Councillor Mike Fisher, London Borough of Croydon; Roger Latham, Nottinghamshire County Council; Bruce Melizan, Interserve; Sue Reid, Communities & Local Government and Ian Smith, Rotherham Borough Council.

Local Government's role in Community Safety Seminar – October 2006

Zoe Billingham, Audit Commission; Councillor Bob Jones, Association of Police Authorities; Professor Gloria Laycock, University College London; Ray Mallon, Mayor of Middlesbrough; and Dr John May, Consultant, Metropolitan Police Authority.

Local Government's role in Children's Services – November 2006

Susanna Cheal OBE, The Who Cares? Trust; Councillor Peter Dowd, Sefton Borough Council; Paul Fallon, Association of Directors of Social Services; David Hill, Director of Social Services, London Borough of Merton; and Clare Tickell, National Children's Homes.

Visionary leadership in Housing – a new future for local housing strategy – hosted by the Chartered Institute of Housing – November 2006

Richard Capie, Housing Corporation; Grenville Chappel, Beacon Community Partnership Regeneration; Nick Hooper, Bristol City Council; Roger Jarman, Audit Commission; Ian Richardson, Chartered Institute of Housing; David Rosser, SW CBI; Councillor Roger Symonds, LGA; David Trethewey, Bath & North East Somerset Council; and David Warburton, English Partnerships.

Effective Public Engagement – November 2006

Shane Bartley, Chelmsford Borough Council; Paul Coen, LGA; Hilary Cottam, RED Design; Jude Cummins, Office of Public Management; Lucy de Groot, Improvement and Development Agency (IDeA); and Ben Page, Ipsos MORI.

Barker Round Table Event – January 2007

Sir Howard Bernstein, Manchester City Council; John Best, Milton Keynes Council; and Adrian Penfold, British Land.

Eddington Round Table Event – January 2007

Michael Frater, Nottingham City Council, Professor Steven Glaister CBE, Imperial College London; and Adam Marshall, Centre for Cities.

Leitch Round Table Event – February 2007

Graham Badman, Kent County Council; Pam Meadows, National Institute of Economic and Social Research; and Marion Seguret, CBI.

Visit to Denmark

15 I am also keen to acknowledge those who I met and were involved in my visit to Denmark including: Marianne Hedegard and Wendy Wyver at the British Embassy; Niels Jorgen Mau Pedersen, Ib Kok Hansen and Jann Larsen from the Ministry of the Interior and Health; Jorgen Lotz, Ministry of Finance; Jens Lunde, Associate Professor, Copenhagen Business School, Department of Finance; Henrik Plougmann Olsen, and Mikkel Elkjaer, City of Copenhagen; and Per Schollert Nielsen and Frank Johansen from the Association of Municipalities.

Central government

16 In addition, I am grateful for the assistance that I, and my team, have received from various central government departments – most notably the Department for Communities and Local Government and HM Treasury, but also from the Department for Culture, Media and Sport; the Department for Environment, Food and Rural Affairs; the Department for Education and Skills; the Department of Health; the Home Office; the Department of Trade and Industry; the Department for Transport; the Valuation Office Agency; the Department of Work and Pensions; and the devolved administrations of Scotland, Wales and Northern Ireland.

Inquiry team

17 Finally, I would like to express my gratitude to Sally Burlington, team leader, for her support and to the other members of my team. They include Lee Burge, Ben Day, Alison Morris and Rik Roots who have been part of the Inquiry team since its inception, and others who have contributed to major parts of my remit: Kate Alexander; Nicola Croden; Charlotte Ellis; Stephen Evans; Sarah Phillips; Anna Randle; Mel Rich; Madeleine Rudd; Jane Todorovic; and Sara Williams.

18 I am also grateful to several others who have provided more short-term or part time support at various points during the Inquiry, including the following; Martyn Ayre; Tom Callagher; Miguel Castro Coelho; Katie Donnelly; Richard Field; Alice Gamm; Krupa Kothari; Guy Lever; Bente Nielsen; Andrew Presland; Rob Robinson; Laura Rowley; and Jo Sparkes.

ORGANISATIONS

Academy for Sustainable Communities

Accord Plc

Action in Rural Sussex

Advantage West Midlands

Age Concern England

Age Concern Essex

Alnwick District Council

AMICUS – the union

Appleby-in-Westmorland Town Council

Arun District Council

Ashford Borough Council

Association of Charity Shops

Association of Chief Police Officers of England, Wales and Northern Ireland

Association of Convenience Stores

Association of Greater Manchester Authorities

Association of Licensed Multiple Retailers

Association of North East Councils

Association of Police Authorities

Association of Second Homeowners

Association of Valuation Office Valuers

Association of Wiltshire Towns

Audit Commission

B&Q plc

Babergh District Council

Bank of England

Barking & Dagenham Retired Members Assoc, T&GWU

Barnsley Metropolitan Borough Council

Basingstoke and Deane Borough Council

Bath and North East Somerset Council

Bay Court Resident's Assocaition

Bed & Breakfast Association

Bedfordshire Police

Belfast City Council

Better Government for Older People

Biffa Waste Services

Big Wide Talk Children's Project

Birmingham City Council

Blackpool Borough Council

Blyth Valley Borough Council

Boots Group Plc

Borough of Telford & Wrekin

Boston Borough Council

Bournemouth Area Hospitality Association

Bournemouth Borough Council

Bracknell Forest Council

Bradford Chamber of Commerce

Bradford City Council

Braintree Borough Council

Branksome Park, Canford Cliffs & District Residents' Association

Breckland District Council

Bridgnorth District Council

Brighton & Hove Older People's Council

Brighton and Hove City Council

Bristol City Council

British Association for Monetary Reform

British Chambers of Commerce

British Holiday & Home Parks Association

British Hospitality Association

British Property Federation

British Resorts and Destinations Association

British Retail Consortium

Bromsgrove District Council

Broxtowe Borough Council

Buckinghamshire Association of Local Councils

Buckinghamshire County Council

Burnley Borough Council

Burnley Wood One Stop Shop Ltd

BUPA

Bury Metropolitan Borough Council

Business in Sport and Leisure

Butlins

Calemcal Ltd

Cambridge City Council

Cambridgeshire County Council

Campaign for the Protection of Rural England

Campaign of English Regions

Canterbury City Council

Caterer and Hotelkeeper

Central London Partnership

Centre for Cities

Centre for Public Policy Seminars

Centre for Public Scrutiny

Centro – West Midlands Passenger Transport Executive

Chaddesley Corbett Parish Council

Chartered Institute of Environmental Health

Chartered Institute of Housing

Chartered Institute of Public Finance and Accountability

Chartered Institute of Wastes Management

Cheltenham Borough Council

Chequers Inn Country Hotel & Restaurant

Cheshire Association of Local Councils

Cheshire County Council

Chester City Council

Chesterfield Borough Council

Chichester District Council

Chief Economic Development Officers Society

Chief Executives London Committee

Chief Fire Officers Association

Chorley Borough Council

Christchurch Borough Council

Citizen's Advice Bureau

Citizens Say Forest of Dean

City and Guilds

City of York Council

Civil Service Pensioners Alliance

Councillor Clinkscales, Southend on Sea

Councillor Guest, Billericay South West Ward

Councillor Wood, Kennett District Council

Councillor Menell, Uttlesford District Council

Colchester Borough Council

Colchester Pensioners Action Group

Colliers Robert Barry

Colney Heath Parish Council

Commission for Rural Communities

Commission for Architecture & the Built Environment

Commission for Social Care Inspection

Confederation of British Industries

Confederation of British Industries, Wales

Coniston Parish Plan

Core Cities

Cornish Association of Holiday Home Agencies

Cornish Constitutional Convention

Cornwall Commercial Tourism Federation

Cornwall County Council

Corporation of London

Council for National Parks

Council of European Municipalities and Regions

Council of Mortgage Lenders

Country Land & Business Association

Countryside Agency

County Councils Network

County Surveyors Society

County Treasurers Department

Crawley Borough Council

Crewe and Nantwich Borough Council

Civil Service Pensioners' Alliance

Cullumpton Town Council

Cumbria County Council

Cyngor Gwynedd Council

Darlington Borough Council

Dedicated Data Systems

De Montford University (Lowndes)

Demos

Denbighshire County Council

DentonWildeSapte

Derby City Council

Derwentside District Council

Destination Performance UK

Devon & Cornwall Police

Devon County Branch UNISON

Devon County Council

Devon Pensioners' Action Forum

Dorset County Council

Dover District Council

Dunwich Parish Meeting

Durham County Council

Easington District Council

East Midlands Chamber of Commerce

East Midlands Regional Assembly

East of England Development Agency

East of England Regional Assembly

East of England Tourist Board

East Riding of Yorkshire Council

East Sussex County Council

Eastbourne Borough Council

Eden District Council

Edinburgh Tourism Action Group

EEF Yorkshire & Humberside

Elcena Jeffers Foundation

Electoral Commission

Elevate East Lancashire

Ellesmere Port & Neston Borough Council

Empty Homes Agency

Energy Networks Association

Englands Regional Development Agencies

Equalities Review

Essex County Council

Evening Standard

Exeter City Council

Exmouth Town Council

Family Holiday Association

Fareham Borough Council

Federation of Small Businesses

Forest Heath District Council

Forum of Private Business

Freight on Rail

Gateshead Council

Glasgow Caledonian University (Bailey)

Global Olivine

Gloucestershire County Council

Greater London Authority

Greater Manchester Chamber of Commerce

Greater Manchester Police Authority

Growth Areas Special Interest Group

Growth Coalitions

Gwynedd Council – Independent Group

Hambleton District Council

Hampshire County Council

Harborough District Council

Harpenden Town Council

Harrogate Borough Council

Hartlepool Borough Council

Hastings Borough Council

Havant Borough Council

Help the Aged

Hereford & Worcester Fire & Rescue Authority

Herefordshire Council

Herriot-Watt University (Bramley)

Hertfordshire County Council

Hertsmere Community Partnership

Higher Education Funding Council for England

House of Commons:

    Graham Allen MP

    Candy Atherton MP

    Tony Baldry MP

    Celia Barlow MP

    Andrew Bennett MP

    Sir Paul Beresford MP

    Clive Betts MP

    Graham Brady MP

    Tom Brake MP

    Annette Brooke MP

    Rt Hon Stephen Byers MP

    Ian Cawsey MP

    David Cleland MP

    Vernon Coaker MP

    Patrick Cormack MP

    John Cummings MP

    Tony Cunningham MP

    Edward Davey MP

    Jonathan Djanogly MP

    Tim Farron MP

    Linda Gilroy MP

    Julia Goldsworthy MP

    Nick Harvey MP

    Ivan J Henderson MP

    Nick Herbert MP

    David Irvine MP

    David Kidney MP

    Eleanor Laing MP

    Shona McIsaac MP

    Fiona Mactaggart MP

    Chris Mole MP

    George Mudie MP

Bob Neill MP

Bill O'Brien MP

Bob O'Brien MP

Rt Hon Nick Raynsford MP

Chris Ruane MP

Christine Russell MP

Adrian Sanders MP

Grant Schapps MP

Alan Simpson Mp

Andrew Smith MP

Caroline Spelman MP

Andrew Stunell MP

David Taylor MP

Stephen Williams MP

Mark Williams MP

Housing Corporation

Hull and Humber Chamber of Commerce

Hull City Council

Humber Economic Partnership

Humberside Fire Authority

Improvement and Development Agency

Institute of Chartered Accountants

Institute of Community Cohesion

Institute of Local Government Studies Birmingham University

Institute for Political and Economic Governance University of Manchester

Institute of Revenue, Rating and Valuation

Institute for Employment Research, Warwick University

Institute for Public Policy Research

Institute for Transport Studies, University of Leeds

Institute of Directors – West Midlands

Institute of Payroll and Pensions Management

Ipsos MORI

Ipswich Borough Council

IRATE (Irate Ratepayers Against Tax Excesses)

Isitfair

Isle of Wight Council

Joseph Rowntree Foundation

Kent County Council

Kent Fire & Rescue Service

Kerrier District Council

Kettering Borough Council

Keynsham Town Council

Kingston University (Connellan)

Kirklees Metropolitan Council

Knowsley Metropolitan Borough Council

Local Authority Co-ordinating Office on Regulatory Services

Labour Land Campaign

Lancashire Constabulary

Lancaster City Council

Land Research Trust London

Land Securities Group PLC

Land Value Taxation Campaign

Law Society

Leadership Centre for Local Government

Learning & Skills Council

Leeds City Council

Leicester City Council

Leicestershire County Council

Leicestershire Economic Partnership

London Fire & Emergency Planning Authority

Liberal Democrat Action on Land-value Taxation & Economic Reform

Liberal Democrat Group at Oxfordshire County Council

Lichfield District Council Taxpayers Association

Lincolnshire County Council

Local Government Association

Local Government Association Independent Group

Local Government Association Liberal Democrats

Local Government Association New Zealand

Local Government for Yorkshire & Humber

Local Government Information Unit

Local Government Ombudsman – The Commission for Local Administration in England

Localise West Midlands

London Borough of Barking & Dagenham

London Borough of Barnet

London Borough of Brent

London Borough of Bromley

London Borough of Camden

London Borough of Croydon

London Borough of Hammersmith & Fulham

London Borough of Harrow

London Borough of Haringey

London Borough of Havering

London Borough of Hillingdon

London Borough of Hounslow

London Borough of Islington

London Borough of Lewisham

London Borough of Redbridge

London Borough of Richmond-upon-Thames

London Borough of Southwark

London Borough of Sutton

London Borough of Tower Hamlets

London Borough of Waltham Forest

London Borough of Wandsworth

London Chamber of Commerce and Industry

London Councils (formerly ALG)

London First

London Leaseholder's Network

London Luton Airport

London Tenants Federation

Lone Pine Residents Association

Long Ashton Parish Council

Low Incomes Tax Reform Group

Luton Borough Council

Maidstone Borough Council

Malvern Hills District Council

Manchester City Council

Mansfield District Council

Mebyon Kernow – The Party for Cornwall

Medway Council

Melton Borough Council

Mersey Travel

Metropolitan Police Authority

Microsoft Ltd

Mid Devon District Council

Mid Yorkshire Chamber of Commerce & Industry

Mill Farm Residents Association

Milton Keynes Council

Much Wenlock Town Council

National Association of Local Councils

National Assembly for Wales

National Association for Voluntary and Community Action

National Audit Office

National Council for Voluntary Organisations

National Federation of Arms Length Management Organisation

National Hairdressers' Federation

National Institute of Adult Continuing Education

National Landlords Association

National Pensioners Convention

Neath Port Talbot County Borough Council

New Economics Foundation

New Forest District Council

New Local Government Network

New Policy Institute

New West End Company

Newark and Sherwood District Council

Newcastle City Council

Norfolk Constabulary

Norfolk County Council

Norfolk Police Authority

North Cornwall District Council

North Dorset District Council

North East Assembly

North East Chamber of Commerce

North East Derbyshire District Council

North East Lincolnshire Council

North Kesteven District Council

North Lincolnshire Council

North Lincs. Seniors Forum – Ancholme Area Branch

North Norfolk District Council

North Somerset Council

North Tyneside Council

North Wales Police Authority

North West Federation of Town & Parish Councils

North West Regional Assembly

North Wiltshire District Council

North Yorkshire County Council

North Yorkshire Police

Norwich City Council

Notting Hill Housing Trust

Nottingham City Council

Nottinghamshire County Council

Nuffield College, Oxford (McLean)

Nuneaton & Bedworth Borough Council

Oadby & Wigston Borough Council

Office of Fair Trading

OneNortheast

OpenStrategy (UK) Ltd

Optimum Communications Development Ltd

Organisation for Economic Co-operation and Development

Orrest Head House

Oxford City Council

Oxfordshire County Council

Passenger Transport Executive Group

Pensioners Forum Wales

Peterlee Town Council

Plymouth City Council

Plymouth Senior Citizens Forum

Pm Group Plc

Policy Exchange

Policy Studies Institute

Poole Tourism Partnership

Portsmouth City Council

Preston City Council

Prudhoe Older People's Forum

Public & Commercial Services Union

Purbeck District Council

Ratings Surveyors Association

Reading Borough Council

Redbourn Parish Council

Regional Cities East

Renew North Staffordshire

Restormel Borough Council

Retired Members Section of the Devon County Branch of UNISON

Royal Institute of Chartered Surveyors

Rotherham Metropolitan Borough Council

Royal Borough of Kensington & Chelsea

Royal Borough of Kingston-upon-Thames

Royal Borough of Windsor and Maidenhead

Royal Commission on Environmental Pollution

Royal Town Planning Institute

Ruschliffe Borough Council

Salford City Council

Sands Resort

Sandwell Metropolitan Borough Council

Scarborough Borough Council

Selby District Council

Sevenoaks District Council

Sheffield City Council

Shrewsbury & Atcham Borough Council

Shropshire Association of Senior Citizen Forums

Shropshire County Council

Sidmouth Town Council

Slough Borough Council

Small Business Council

Smith Institute

Society of London Treasurers

Society of Local Authority Chief Executives

Society of Local Authority Chief Executives, Wales

Solihull Metropolitan Borough Council

Somerset County Council

South Bank Employers Group

South East County Leaders

South East England Development Agency

South Hams District Council

South Holland District Council

South Norfolk Council

South Northamptonshire Council

South Ribble Borough Council

South Somerset District Council

South Somerset Homes

South Tyneside Council

South West Conference of Local Council Associations

South West Local Government Association

South Yorkshire Joint Secretariat

South Yorkshire Police Authority

Southampton City Council

SPARSE (Sparsity Partnership for Authorities delivering Rural Services) & Rural Services Partnership

Special Interest Group of Municipal Authorities

St Albans City and District Council

St Edmundsbury Borough Council

St Helens Metropolitan Borough Council

Staffordshire County Council

Staffordshire Moorlands District Council

Staffordshire Parish Councils' Association

Standards Board for England

Stockport Metropolitan Borough Council

Stockton on Tees Borough Council

Stoke-on-Trent Labour Local Government Committee

Stoke-on-Trent District Council

Stowmarket Town Council

Strategic Planning Advice

Strategic Services

Stratford-on-Avon District Council

Suffolk Association of Local Councils

Suffolk Coastal District Council

Sunderland City Council

Surrey Chamber of Commerce

Surrey County Council

Surrey Tax Action Group (STAG)

Sussex Beach Leaseholders Association

Sussex Enterprise

Sustainable Development Commission

Swanley Chamber of Commerce Network

Transport & General Workers Union

Tabitha Trust

Tandridge District Council

Taunton Deane Borough Council

Technical Advisors Group Transport Committee

Teesdale District Council

Teinbridge Constituency Labour Party

Tendring District Council

Tesco Plc

Tewkesbury Borough Council

Thames Valley Chamber of Commerce Group

Thanet District Council

The Church in Wales

The Liberal Institute

Torbay Council

Tourism Alliance

Tourism and Conservation Partnership

Tourism Management Institute

Tourism West Midlands

TRAC – The Road Adoption Campaign

Transport For London

Travelodge

Tyne & Wear Fire & Civil Defence Authority

Tynedale District Council

UK Public Health Association

UNISON

Unitary Special Interest Group

University of Gloucester (Derounian)

University of Liverpool (Rowe)

University of Newcastle (Alvanides)

University of Warwick (Orton)

Uplyme Parish Council

Urban Futures

Urban Policy and Sustainable Communities

URBED: Urban & Economic Development Group

Vale of White Horse District Council

Vale Royal Borough Council

Valuation Office Agency

Visit Exmoor Ltd

Vocational Centres UK

Voice of our Age – Alnwick & District Older Persons' Forum

Wakefield Metropolitan District Council

Walsall Metropolian Borough Council

Warrington Borough Council

Warwick Institute for Employment Research

Warwickshire & West Midlands Association of Local Councils

Warwickshire County Council

Watford Borough Council

Waveney District Council

Waverley Borough Council

Wear Valley District Council

Wellington Town Council

West Lancashire District Council

West Lindsay District Council

West Mercia Police Authority

West Midlands Local Government Association

West Midlands Regional Assembly

West Midlands Shire Councils

West Sussex – Voluntary Organisations Liaison Group

West Sussex County Council

West Wiltshire District Council

West Yorkshire Fire Authority

West Yorkshire Police Authority

Westminster City Council

Weston-Super-Mare Senior Citizens Forum

Wigan Metropolitan Borough Council

Wiltshire County Council

Winchester City Residents' Association

Winchester City Council

Winchester Council Tax Action Group

Wolverhampton City Council

Worcestershire County Association of Local Councils

Worthing Borough Council

Wychavon District Council

Wycombe District Council

Wyre Forest District Council

Yealmpton Parish Council

Yorkshire & Humber Association of Local Authorities

Young Foundation

MEMBERS OF THE PUBLIC

Mr & Mrs K Aburrow

Mr F D Adam

Ms S Adams

Mr R Agier

Mr T Alberici

Miss M Allan

Mr J Allcroft

Mr & Mrs B Allen

Mrs M T Amphlett

Mr A H Andrews

Mr C Andrews

Mr A Applebee

Mr T Appleyard

Revd W Armstrong

Mr R Ashby

Mr M Astor

Mr Steve Atkinson

Mr & Mrs D Atkinson

Mrs B Attwood

Mr S G Auld

Mr R Axell

Mr B Axon

Mr & Mrs M Bachmann

Mr J H Bagley

Mr W H Bailey

Mr C Baird

Mr A E Baker

Mr & Mrs T Baker

Mrs S P Ball

Mr J Ballinger

Mrs J Balquin

Mrs C Barker

E Barker

Mr R Barrow

Mr M Bartlett

Mrs G M Bartlett

Mr D S Barton

I H Bass

W Bazley

M M Beaumec

Mr J W Beaumont

Mr & Mrs D Beever

Mr D Bell

Ms C Benfield

Mr D Bennett

Mr J Bennett

Mr N Bennett

Mr V L Benson

Mr R J Berrieman

Mr M Beville

Mr F J Bewlay

Mrs M Bielby

Mr J Biggs

Mr P Bignall

Mr P Birchall

Mrs E S Bird

Mrs A Birrell

Mr V B H Birtles

Ms J Blake

Mr C Boden

Mr M Boon

Mr J Bord

Mr J Borley

S E Boucher

Mr K Bowes

Mr H Bradford

Mrs P K Bray

Miss G Brewster

Ms J E Bridges

Mr I B Bright

Mr D Brock

Mrs T Brock

Mr L Brophy

Mr C Brown

Mrs S Brown

Mr J Brown

Mr P Browning

Mr J H Bulivant

Mr M I R Bull

Mr D Bunting

Mr A Burchmore

Mr G Burke

Ms E D Burnett

Mr M Burningham

Mr T Burton

Mr O Burton

Ms S Burton

Mrs A Bushell

Mr D H Bustard

Mr S Byrne

Mrs R Byron

Mr C Caffin

Mr P Calderley

Mr A Campbell

Mrs C Canning

Mr D Carter

Mr G A Casson

Mr B Catallo

Mr D Cawthorne

Mr & Mrs A Cayley

Mr N Chadwick

Mr & Mrs J Chalk

Mr D Chamberlain

Mrs D J Chaplin

Ms M Chapman

Mr GC Charge

Mrs C Chesters

Mrs G E Choreton

Mr R Clark

Mr M Clasper

Mr F Clements

Mrs K Clinch

Mr W Clovis

Mr W Cobbett

Mr & Mrs D Cogger

B D Coke

Mr G B Colbridge

Mr H Collier

Mr & Mrs Condick

Mr T Constable

Mr D Cooke

Mrs D L Coombe

Ms C Cooper

Mr J S Cooper

Mr D Cope

Mr R Corfield

Mr A C Costin

Mr P Cotterill

Mrs S Cottle

Mr A Coulthurst

P F Crabtree

Mr A W Cracknell

Mr R K Crick

Mrs P Crisford

Mrs B J Crockett

Ms J Crowley

Mrs D A Cummings

Mrs D Currell

Ms S Curzon

Mrs A M Daniels

Mr R Darbar

Mrs D Davies

Mr G L Davis

P H Davis

Mr J Davis

P A Davison

Mr S Davison

Ms H De Meyer

Mr F Deeks

Mr M Deloughery

Mr J Derounian

Mr C H Dewsnap

Mr C Dilloway

Mrs M Dimery

Mr P J Dowler

Mr W N Drysdale-Gordon

Mr D W Dukes

Mr J Dunn

Mr J R Dyson

Dr G D Eades-Willis

Mr W Edgar

Mr B Edmondson

Miss M Egan

Mr R Ellams

Mr D J Elliott

Ms J Ellwood

Mr R Emery

Mr R Etherington

Mr D I Evans

Mrs J Evans

Mr G Ewing

Mr M Faccini

Mr P Falshaw

Miss J E Fenn

Mr H Ferguson

Mrs P Field

Mr J A Fielden

Mr N Fisher

Mrs E Fitch

Mr R Fitzgerald

Mr E Flatman

Mr P Fleckeny

Mrs L M Fleming

Mr B W Fletton

Mr R Forde

Mr R Forrest

E H Forrest

Mr D M Forrester

Mr A Forster

Mr M Forward

Mr J Francis

Mr T Franklin

Mr R Friend

Mr D Frost

Mr T Fryer

Mr J A Fuge

Miss P Furihata

Cllr T Gandy

Mr M Garcia

Mrs J Garwood

Mr J Gater

Ms A M Gatward

Mr R Gee

S A Gefher

Mr R Gent

Mr M Gill

Mr B Gillingham

Mr A Glaister

Mr M Glass

Mr A Godfrey

K B Gold

Mr A Goodenough

Mr B Goodwin

Mr F R Gordon

Mr G Grace

R C Grant

Mr R Grant

Mrs M Grantham

Mr A Graves

Mr B J Gray

C Green

Ms L V Green

Mr L M Greene

Mr A Griffin

Mr K S Grindel

Mr N Grossman

Mr D Groves

Mr C W Gunnee

Mr D Haigham

Mr A C Hall

Mr J Hall

Ms B Hallett

Dr E C Hamlyn

Mr N Hardiman

Mr G Hardwell

Mr & Mrs G Harker

Ms A Harland-Halperin

Mr D Harradine

Mr M Harrington

Mr C Harris

Mr I Harris

Mrs G B Harris

Mrs J F Harris

Mr D Harrison

Mr C Harrison

Mr C Harrison

Mrs C Harvey

Mrs S I Hatton

Mr J Haw

Mr P Hawes

Mrs A Hay

Mr I Hazlewood

Mr K Hearnden

Mr D Heath

Mr M Heath

Mr T Heaton

Mrs M S Henderson

Ms M Henderson

Mr P E Henshaw

Mr D J Heren

Mrs R A Hernandez

Mr K Hewitson

Ms L Hewson

Mr C Heyworth

Mrs H Hiam

Mr A Hillman

Mr & Mrs K Hinchliffe

Mr J Hirsh

S A Hodge

Mrs C Hodgson

Mr G B Hogg

Ms H Holdsworth

Mr R P Hollick

Mr G Holliday

Mr N Hood

Ms H D Hook

Mr R Hooper

Ms H Howard

Mr M Howe

Mr J Howell

D Hughes

Mr D Hughes

Mrs D Hughes

Mr D J Hughes

Mrs P Hughes

Mr M Hulme

Mr J B Hunt

Mr P D Hunt

D J Hunter

Mr D I Ings

Mr D H Ireland

Mr A Ironside Brown

Mr D Irvine

Mr I Irvine

Mr F Irwin

Mr K Isaac

Mr & Mrs J Isaacson

Ms D Issitt

Mr J F Jackson

Mr K Jackson

M G Jackson

Mr W James

Mr M Jeffries

C J Jenkins

Mrs D Jobling

Mr D John

Mr D Johnson

Mr J Johnson

Ms J Johnson

Mr R Johnson

Mr & Mrs J G Johnson

W G Johnson

Mr B J Jones

Brig J M Jones

Mr K Jones

Mr S Jones

Mr J Joseph

Mr T Judge

Mr D Jukes

Mr K Kassam

Mr & Mrs T Keegan

Mr J Keep

Ms J A Kelly

Ms C Kempster

Mr & Mrs J Kent

Mr B Kenyon

Mr F Kerr

C J Kerridge

Mrs E M King

Mr R King

Miss P M Kinghorn

Mr G R Kirby

Father R Kirinich

Mr L Kirkup

Mr R W Knight

Mr D Kwiatek

Mr A Laing

Ms P B Lamm

Mrs A Langton

Mr M Lanyon

Mr R Lascelles

Mr B W Lawrance

Mr R Lawrence

Mr Dave Lea

Mr S G Lee

Mrs M Lee

Mr W K Lee

Ms M Legon

I R Leitch

Mrs S A Lever

Mr H Levy

Mrs M Lewin

Mr C R Lewis

Mr S Lewis

Mr R Lewis

Mr and Mrs E Levi

Mr E Liddell

Mr D Litherland

Ms E Lockton

Mrs B Lockwood

Ms B Long

Mr B Looker

J Lupton

Mr C Luther

Mr T Lyden

Mr G P Lyon

Mrs F Lyons

Mr G MacKay

Mr J MacKenzie

Mr T MacLean

Mr P Madigan

Mr D Magnus

Mr G Maguire

Mr P H Malan

Mrs D Mallett

Mr P Mallinder

Mr B V Marchant

Mr F Marsden

Mr D Martin

Mr P Martin

Mr M J Martin

Mr M Massey

Mr K Matthews

Mr A G Matthews

R W Max

Mr J May

Mr B Maycock

Mr D McConaghty

C G McCormack

Mr W G McDonald

Mr & Mrs T R McEwan

Mr R McFarland

Mr J McPherson

Mr J Merrett-Bloom

Cllr B Metcalfe

Mr S Michael

Mr A Miller

S A Mills

Mr M Mitchell

C T Monk

Sir R Moon

Mr N G Moore

Mrs P M Moore

Mr & Mrs R Morgan

Mr J Morley

Mr & Mrs D Morley

Mr D Morris

Mr R V Morris

Mr W Morris

Mr C L Morriss

Mr C Morrison

Mrs E M Moses

Mr B Moss

Mr R W Moss

Mr T Mullaney

Mr J G Mulroy

Mr G Munro

Mr A Murphy

Mr N D J Murton

Staff Capt. N Nash

Mr M Napier

Mr P Neale

Ms B Needham

Mr D Neesham

Mr D Nettleton

Ms C Neville

Mrs A D Nicholls

Sqd Ldr Retd H Norcross

Mrs E M Norman

Mr H Northcross

Mr T Oakley

Mr B O'Brien

Ms L O'Darian

Mrs V O'Halloran

Mr P O'Keeffe

Ms K Oliver

Mr D Osborne

Mr J Osborne

Mr I Owen

A R Page

Ms J Palmer

Mr D Papworth

Mr G F Papworth

Dr D Parker

Mr D B V Parker

Mr T Parkinson

Wing Co. rtd A W Parr

Mrs K Parr

Mr K Parr

Mr M J Passmore

Mr & Mrs M Payne

Mr E Pearsall

Mr & Mrs Pearson

Mr C S Pearton

Mr P E M Peggie

Mrs T Pering

Mr A D Perry

J Pester

Mr I Pettit

Sir D Pettitt

R V Philips

Mr J Pincham

Mr M Polglase

Mr J Polkinghorn

Mr A Porritt

Mrs M Porteous

Mr D Porter

Mrs J Pratt

Mr N Preston

Mr J C H Prior

Mr I Probert

Mr S Procter

Miss H A Prowse

S D G Pryce

Mr N Psirides

Mr Peter Pym

Mr John Randall

Mr Raven

Mr D J Read

Ms J Reddaway

Mr R Reddey

Mr Rr Redman

Mr D Reed

DBC Reed

D A Reeve

Mrs M Reeves

R G Richards

Mr J K Richards

Mrs A Richards

Mr A Richardson

Mr & Mrs B Richardson

Mr D Richardson

Mr G W Riddel

Mrs U Ridley

Ms M Riley

Mr J Ritson

Mr B Roberts

Mr D Roberts

Mr L J Robjohns

Mr J Roche

Mr D Rockett

Mr M Rogers

Mrs M E Rogers

Mr A Rogers

Mr M Rose

Mr R Rose

Mr D J Rose

Mr T Ross

Mrs P Round

Ms C Rowlands

Mr W F Rowlands

Mr D Rowley

P W Rowsell-Dobson

Ms P Royston

Mr R I Rundle

S J Rushton

Mr & Mrs J B Russell

Mr A Ryde

Mr M Sabin

Ms I M Safah

Mrs M Salt

Mr J Samuels

Mr T Sanchez

Ms P Saunders

J P Saxby

Mr A Scaife

Mr M Schofield

Mr N Scholes

Mr A Scholes

Mrs A Scott

Mr C Scriven

Mr J Seaman

Mr R Searle

Mr K Senior

Mr N C Shannon

Ms C L Shapley

Mr R E Shapley

Mr & Mrs N Sharkey

Mr G Sharpe

Mrs E J Sharpe

Mr S Sheinwald

Mr A Shelton

Ms S Sheppard

Mrs E Sherwood-Stares

Mr G Shompton

Mr P Simonini

Mr T Singh

Mr & Mrs B Skilton

Mr C Skinner

Mr J Slade

Mrs J Sleep

Mr A J Smith

Ms B P Smith

C G Smith

Mr G Smith

G C Smith

Ms J Smith

Mr K A Smith

Mrs M Smith

Mr M Smith

Mr N Smith

Mr R Smith

Mr B Smyth

K Sorensen

Ms C Spratt

Ms J Staal

Mr I Standing

Mr I Steedman

Ms B Steele

L Steven

Mrs G Stephens

W R Stevenson

Prof John Stewart

Ms B Stiff

Ms S Stockley

Mr P Stokoe

Mr K Stone

P H Stones

Mr D R Stowell

Mr & Mrs Sturgess

Mr P G Sugden

Mr & Mrs R J Sullivan

Mr B Sumpter

Mrs S Sykes

Mr M Tapp

B Tarbuck

Mr C J Taylor

Mr J Taylor

Miss E N Taylor

Mrs E Y Taylor

Mr R Taylor

Mr & Mrs L Taylor

Mr R Tettenborn

Mr P Thomas

Mr D Thompson

Mr G Thompson

Mr A Thompson

A Thorne

Mr H G Thorne

Ms J Thornley

Mr S Threadgold

Mr K Tindill

Mr H Tinworth

Mr D J Tolley

Mr A Toms

Ms S Tottman

Mr F Touse

Ms S Towes

Mr C I Travis

Mr B J Trevelyan

T R Troughton

Mr J Tucker

Mrs E Tupling

Mr D Turner

Mrs C P Turnham

Ms M Tye

Mr S Tyler

Mr P Upton

Mrs R VanDenBergh

Mr S Vaughan

Ms C Veal

Mr T Vickers

B Virdee

Mr M Wadsworth

Mr D Wagner

Mr G Walker

Mr P Walker

Mr J Walter

Mr M G Ward

Mr E Ward

Mrs D A Ward

Mr & Mrs T Wareing

Mr Warner

Mr D J Wathen

Mr R D Watkins

Mr A Watson

Mr N Watson

Mr C Wattam

Ms S Wearden

Mr J Webb

Mr P Webb

Mr A Welcome

Mr A C Wells

Ms T Wenn

Mr A West

Mr & Mrs Wheal

Mr A Wheatley

Mr A Wheeler

Mr G Wheldon

Mr S White

Mr J Whiteing

Mr J Whitney

Mr R J Wickham

Mrs B E Wilkinson

Mr & Mrs C Wilkinson

Mr D Williams

Dr R Williamson

Ms H Wilson

Cllor M Wilson

Mr P Winter

Miss J Witty

Mr N Witty

Mr S Wombwell

Mr J Wood

Mr J C Wood

Mr W J Woodman

Mr B Woods

Mr J Woodward

H Wooldridge

Mr R Wootten

Mr J Worthington

DEM Wright

Ms A Wright

Mr V F Wroth

Mr P Wyllie

Mrs J Young

Implications for Scotland, Wales and Northern Ireland

INTRODUCTION

1   Most aspects of policy connected with local government and local government funding are devolved to the administrations in Scotland, Wales and Northern Ireland. However, there are a number of areas of the funding remit where there are potential implications for the devolved administrations, and I was explicitly asked to consider them in my original terms of reference. Reflecting this, I consulted with ministers, officials and other experts in all three countries, including through a constructive dialogue with Sir Peter Burt's independent Local Government Finance Review Committee in Scotland.

2   The most obvious issue that needs to be considered is whether any of my recommendations have consequences for the block grants of the devolved administrations because of the way in which that funding is calculated. In addition, it is also necessary to consider whether the devolved administrations already have the power to introduce similar reforms themselves, or whether the Government will need to consider their views and situations during the preparation of legislation.

BLOCK GRANT

3   My recommendations would not lead to significant changes in the short term in the source of local government revenues, and I do not suggest the creation of major new local taxes to replace government grant. Local authorities in England would continue to be funded through government grants (including redistributed business rates) and council tax, as they are now.

4   The lack of a major change to the balance of funding in England means that there will not be any substantial consequential change in the grant allocations for the devolved administrations calculated by the Barnett formula. In the future, possible decisions on more radical reforms to council tax, such as the introduction of a local income tax, might change this situation. A change in the balance of funding, with new local tax sources being offset by cuts in government grant, would lead to consequential reductions in block grants to the devolved administrations.

5   There are some more complex potential implications arising from my recommendations on business rates reliefs. My suggestions will make the system of reliefs in England somewhat less generous than they are at present. Any additional resources paid by English taxpayers through reductions in reliefs might be used either for reducing the tax rate, increasing spending, or reducing Revenue Support Grant to local authorities, and the Government will need to consider how those changes might feed through into the block grants of the devolved administrations.

BENEFIT SPENDING

6   Policy and spending on benefits is managed on a Great Britain-wide basis, so the changes to council tax benefit that I recommend will therefore affect individuals in Scotland and Wales, and the level of benefit spending in those countries. However, they will not affect the budgets of their devolved administrations. Council tax does not operate in Northern Ireland, but consideration may need to be given if there are any consequential implications for its benefits system.

LOCAL TAXATION

7   My recommendations will have no impact on council tax and rating policy in the devolved administrations for the time being. Decisions on council tax banding and revaluation are devolved matters on which Scotland and Wales have their own policies, and Northern Ireland has an entirely different system of local rates, which is currently undergoing substantial reform.

8   In the longer term, the Government might wish to consider more substantial changes to local domestic property taxation such as a point value property tax or a local income tax. Since I am not recommending that a local income tax be implemented in England in the short or medium term, it would be speculative to go any further into the possible implications for the devolved countries of a future local income tax. If the Government was attracted to a local income tax in future, it would need to consult the devolved administrations on any consequences for them of such a change. The Scottish Parliament has primary legislative power over local taxation issues. The National Assembly for Wales does not have the same powers. Under the current system, substantial changes to council tax or to local taxation more generally would therefore need to be dealt with on an England and Wales basis for the purposes of primary legislation.

9   The Scottish Executive manages Scottish business rates, revenues and reliefs, and the Scottish Parliament has the power to amend its legislation on business rates as part of its powers over local taxation. My recommendations for reforms to business rates will therefore not affect Scotland. Similarly, my recommendations have no direct read across to Northern Ireland because business rates are also devolved there.

10   In Wales, however, business rates are currently administered by the Welsh Assembly Government on the basis of joint England and Wales primary legislation, though the National Assembly for Wales has discretion over some of the reliefs as these are provided for in secondary legislation. The Government will therefore need to work with the Welsh Assembly on any legislation used to implement reform to business rates in England, and the possible implications for Wales, both in respect of changes to reliefs and to the ability of local authorities to set a local supplement on business rates.

ROLE AND FUNCTION

11   My recommendations on the structure and functions of local government relate only to England. However any primary legislation in this area would also potentially impact on Wales, and the Government will therefore need to discuss these issues further with the Welsh Assembly Government.

Glossary

Allocative efficiency	Targeting resources at the things that matter most in different places to increase the overall level of satisfaction and welfare that can be produced from the resources available.
Assignment	Describes a method by which revenues from nationally controlled taxation could be allocated specifically to certain bodies or sevices, in this case – local government.
Balance of funding	The proportion of local authority revenue expenditure financed centrally as against the proportion financed locally. Except where stated otherwise, this report uses a definition based on "local authority income" which includes **specific grants** and income from sales, fees and charges, as well as the core revenue streams of council tax, business rates and revenue support grant. Under this definition council tax represents 16 per cent of local income, with a further 11 per cent from charges for services (including rents).
Billing authority	A local authority that is responsible for collecting the council taxes and business rates for its area. In practice, they are metropolitan districts, shire districts, unitary authorities, London boroughs and the City of London.
Budget requirement	A measure of local authority expenditure. In broad terms, it is the total amount of an authority's expenditure that is financed from **Formula Grant** and council tax.
Business Improvment Districts (BIDs)	Public/private sector partnership schemes in which property and business owners of a defined area elect to make a collective contribution to the maintenance, development and marketing/promotion of their commercial area for set purposes and within set timescales.
Capping	When central government limits a local authority's **budget requirement** and hence the amount by which it can increase its council tax.
Co-production	Where service providers (such as local authorities) work with service users, through active engagement, to improve service delivery outcomes and efficiency.
Collection Rate	The proportion of a tax owed that is actually collected.
Comprehensive Spending Review (CSR)	Spending Reviews set firm and fixed three-year Departmental Expenditure Limits and, through Public Service Agreements (PSAs) define the key improvements that the public can expect from these resources. The comprehensive Spending Review (CSR) reporting in 2007 will represent a long-term and fundamental review of government expenditure. It will cover departmental allocations for 2008-09, 2009-10 and 2010-11.
Convening	A role carried out by local authorities in seeking to influence and bring together the efforts and/or views of the public, private and voluntary sectors to secure the well-being of local citizens.
Council tax burden	The percentage of **net household income** that is paid as council tax.
Council tax requirement	The total amount of council tax that an authority assumes – when setting its budget – it will receive for the financial year. It is dependent upon an assumed **collection rate** and an assumed **tax base**.

Dedicated Schools Grant (DSG)	The grant by which schools funding is provided by the Department for Education and Skills. This money is ring-fenced and cannot be spent on other things. The DSG is paid to local authorities and it is then for each local authority to distribute funding using its locally agreed formula. It is for schools' governing bodies and other providers to decide how to spend their available resources.
Duty to cooperate	A legal term used in the 2004 Children's Act, and the Local Government & Involvement in Health Bill, placing a duty on local authorities to require co-operation between local authorities and other locally determined partners.
Employment and Skills Boards (ESBs)	Employer-led groups proposed in the Leitch review to monitor local skills, productivity and employment, and articulate these needs to the proposed integrated employment and skills service within a locality.
Equalisation	The local government finance system intending to even out the differences between local authorities' **tax bases**, needs and costs.
Fiscal	Relating to government revenue, mainly in relation to taxes.
Floor damping	Involves adjusting the grant allocations calculated for each authority in order to guarantee a minimum year-on-year percentage increase for each class of authority. More details are given in Annex A.
Formula Grant	The collective term for **Revenue Support Grant**, redistributed business rates and Principal Formula Police Grant. From 2006-07, Formula Grant is distributed using the four-block model. Further details are given in Annex A.
Gearing	A measure of the impact on council taxes of increasing budgets. This varies widely between local authorities. An authority that meets 25 per cent of its budget through council tax is said to have a gearing ratio of 4.0. This means a one per cent increase in budget would have a four per cent increase in council tax. See also the box in Chapter 3.
Goverment Offices	Represent central government regionally, and are the primary means by which a wide range of government policies are delivered within these English regions. Government offices play a key role in the negotiation of Local Area Agreements.
Government Office Regions	Nine English regions that are routinely referred to as administrative units by central government, (namely: *North East, North West, Yorkshire & the Humber, East Midlands, West Midlands, East of England, South East, South West and London*).
Learning and Skills Council (LSC)	A non-departmental public body responsible for planning, funding and improving the quality of post-16 education and training (excluding higher education) in England, consisting of a National Council and a number of local LSCs.
Local Area Agreements (LAAs)	Three-year agreements between central government, local authorities and their partners agreed though the **Local Strategic Partnership.**
Local Authority Business Growth Incentive scheme (LABGI)	A financial incentive scheme, encouraging economic growth by allowing local authorities to retain a share of business rates for spending on their own local priorities.
Local Strategic Partnership (LSP)	A single non-statutory, multi-agency body, which matches local authority boundaries, and aims to bring together at a local level the different parts of the public, private, community and voluntary sectors to secure the well-being of their communities.
Net household income	Usually defined as the income received by a household after taking account of taxes and benefits but before accounting for housing costs.

National non-domestic rate (NNDR)	A property tax paid by businesses and other non-domestic bodies – another name for business rates.
Passenger Transport Authorities	Local government bodies which are responsible for public transport within large urban areas, set up as a result of the abolition of metropolitan county councils in the 1985 Local Government Act.
Passporting	A government requirement for local authorities to pass on annual education funding increases to education departments and schools. This was replaced by the **Dedicated Schools Grant** for 2006-07.
Place-shaping	The creative use of powers and influence to promote the general well-being of a community and its citizens. A fuller explanation is found in Chapter 2.
Planning-gain Supplement (PGS)	A proposed levy on the land value uplift resulting from detailed planning consent. It is intended to provide revenues to invest in community development, be collected centrally but be recycled back to the community with the 'overwhelming majority' returning to the 'region' from which they derive.
Postcode lottery	A common term used to intimate how services vary from one locality to another.
Precept	The amount of money (council tax) a local or major **precepting authority** has instructed the **billing authority** to collect and pay over to it in order to finance its net expenditure.
Precepting authorities	Are county councils, police and fire authorities, the Greater London Authority, parishes and some other bodies, which instruct the **billing authority** to collect council tax on their behalf in order to finance their expenditure. Parish councils are classed as local precepting authorities whilst county councils, police and fire authorities along with the GLA are major precepting authorities.
Revenue Support Grant	A general grant which replaced rate support grant in 1990-91. Now distributed as part of **Formula Grant.**
Ring-fenced grants	Grants which fund particular services or initiatives considered a national priority, which must be spent on the service specified.
Section 106 contributions	Payments from the construction of residential and commercial developments whereby the developer is expected to make a contribution to local government's infrastructure costs around the development. Usage set to be scaled back with the introduction of **Planning-gain Supplement.**
Social cohesion	The existence of mutual trust and relationships between individuals and communities of different backgrounds and characteristics.
Specific grants	Grants paid by various government departments outside the main **Formula Grant.** They include **ring-fenced grants** (which have to be spent on a particular service) and specific **formula grants** (which do not, such as the Neighbourhood Renewal Fund).
Tax base	General term for taxable capacity of a local authority. More precisely, the council tax base is the number of band D-equivalent domestic properties within an authority's area and the effective taxbase for business rates is the total rateable value of non-domestic properties within an authority's area.
Third sector	Includes voluntary and community organisations, charities, faith groups, social enterprises, cooperatives and mutuals. The Government's Office for the Third Sector describes the sector as comprising: non-governmental; 'value-driven' organisations primarily motivated by the desire to further social, environmental or cultural objectives rather than to make a profit per se; and to principally reinvest surpluses to further their social, environmental or cultural objectives.
Yield	General term for the amount that is due to be raised from a local or national tax.

Published by TSO (The Stationery Office) and available from:

Online
www.tsoshop.co.uk

Mail, Telephone, Fax & E-mail
TSO
PO Box 29, Norwich NR3 1GN
Telephone orders/General enquiries 0870 600 5522
Order through the Parliamentary Hotline *Lo-call* 0845 7 023474
Fax orders 0870 600 5533
Email book.orders@tso.co.uk
Textphone 0870 240 3701

TSO Shops
123 Kingsway, London WC2B 6PQ
020 7242 6393 Fax 020 7242 6394
16 Arthur Street, Belfast BT1 4GD
028 9023 8451 Fax 028 9023 5401
71 Lothian Road, Edinburgh EH3 9AZ
0870 606 5566 Fax 0870 606 5588

TSO@Blackwell and other Accredited Agents

ISBN 978-0-11-989854-5